CLS 25

Papers from the
25th Annual Regional Meeting of the
Chicago Linguistic Society

Part One:
The General Session

Chicago Linguistic Society
1989

edited by
Caroline Wiltshire
Randolph Graczyk
Bradley Music

First Edition

First printing 1000 copies September, 1989

Library of Congress Catalog Card Number 76-27943

ISSN: 0577-7240
ISBN: 0-914203-32-0

Acknowledgments

The CLS conference and the production of the two volumes of proceedings could not have taken place without sacrifices of time, talent and energy from many people. We would like to thank all of those who have worked diligently to bring this year's conference and proceedings to a successful completion.

Special thanks go to Lynn Nichols, Paul Manning, Manuela Noske, and Eddy Gaytan for organizing the housing arrangements and conference party, and to Diane Brentari, Bill Eilfort, Anne Farley, Karl-Erik McCullough, Barbara Need, Eric Schiller, Elisa Steinberg, Bob Sprott, and David Testen for contributions above and beyond the call of duty.

We also thank Asif Agha, Tista Bagchi, Anna Bosch, Justine Cassell, Stuart Creason, Karen Deaton, Jenny deGroot, Lise Dobrin, Nancy Dray, Zixin Jiang, Kyunghwan Kim, Paul Kroeber, Gretchen Lai, Gary Larson, Jeff Lear, Lynn McCleod, Cynthia Miller, Bert Vaux, James Yoon, and Mike Ziolkowski for their work before the conference reading abstracts, at the conference registering participants and selling books, and after the conference proofreading papers. In addition, the resourceful assistance provided by Mary Pollard and Valerie Jones during the conference in Ida Noyes was greatly appreciated.

We are grateful to the Linguistics Department of the University of Chicago, especially chair Jerrold Sadock; and to Dean Stuart M. Tave, Ena Miller, and the other staff of the Division of the Humanities. Finally, we thank our department secretary Iretha Phillips and CLS coordinator Milan Panic for their ongoing assistance.

The Editors

Caroline Wiltshire
Randy Graczyk
Bradley Music

Contents

---

* indicates that the paper was not presented at the 25th Annual Regional Meeting of the Chicago Linguistic Society.

Grammatical Relations and the Open Season Parameter

Walter Breen
Brown University

0. Introduction

Common to all versions of Government and Binding Theory (which I will hereafter freely abbreviate to GB) is the θ-Criterion, the requirement that each NP (or more accurately, each chain) be assigned exactly one θ-role, and that this uniqueness of θ-role assignment hold at all levels of derivation (i.e., D-Structure, S-Structure, and Logical Form). Also common to all versions of GB is the Case Filter, the requirement that at S-Structure, each NP with a phonological matrix have abstract Case, which may or may not surface morphologically.

Other frequent, if less explicit, assumptions are (1) that Structural Cases are uniquely assigned, i.e., that at most one Nominative Case and at most one Structural Accusative Case will be assigned per clause; related to this is the assumption that at most one θ-role may be assigned externally; and (2) that an argument that has already been assigned Inherent Case will not also be assigned Structural Case.

In this paper, I examine data from a number of languages that raise some doubt as to the universality of these latter assumptions, and propose some modifications in the GB account of lexical representation, lexical derivation and θ- and Case assignment to account for the data.

1. Alternations Introduced by Passive

Some (primarily British) dialects of English permit either the Goal or the Theme to be the subject of a Dative Shifted, Passivized clause, as shown in (1).

(1)   *Dialectal English*
      a. Martha was given a book (by Frederic).
      b. A book was given Martha (by Frederic). (* in SAE)

Examples of similar alternations from Kinyarwanda, a Bantu language, are given in (2) and (3).

(2)   *Kinyarwanda (Bantu)* [Dryer, 1984 (3)]
      a. Íbárúwa   y -oher-er -ej -w -e
         letter   it-send-BEN-ASP-PASS-ASP
            Maríya na Yohaâni.
            Mary   by John
        'The letter was sent (to) Mary by John.'
      b. Maríya y -oher-er -ej -w -e
         Mary   she-send-BEN-ASP-PASS-ASP
         íbárúwa na Yohaâni.
         letter   by John
      'Mary was sent a letter by John.'

1

(3) *With Locative Applicative* [=Dryer (24)]

```
a. Íntebe    y -iicar-i  -w   -é -ho
   chair     it-sit  -BEN-PASS-ASP-on
   umugabo   n -uúmwáana.
   man         by-child
   'The chair is sat on for the man
      by the child.'
b. Umugabo   y -iicar-i  -w   -é -ho
   man        he-sit   -BEN-PASS-ASP-on
   íntebe     n -uúmwáana.
   chair        by-child
   'The man is sat-on-the-chair-for
      by the child.'
```

In (2) and (3), the BEN affix indicates that a Benefactive is a direct argument of the verb, and in (3), the suffix -*ho* 'on' indicates that a Locative is also a direct argument of the verb. Note that as in Dialectal English, the passivization of a clause appears to put subject position up for grabs among the remaining direct arguments of the verb.

Dryer (1984) presents an RG analysis of Applicative-Passive interactions in Kinyarwanda, and Baker (1988a) and Larson (1988) present GB analyses of similar data from other languages. Common to all three approaches is their tendency to introduce violations of the Satellite or Mirror Principle, which states roughly that the ordering of derivational morphemes (from the root outwards) should parallel the application of morphosyntactic rules. Thus, for example, if the morpheme for Passive is closer to the root than the morpheme for an Applicative, then in the unmarked case, Passive is assumed to apply before the Applicative. Crucial to Dryer's RG analysis of passivized clauses in which a Locative is the subject is the assumption that Locative-to-Object must feed Passive; however, the morpheme (an incorporated preposition in Baker's analysis) that reflects the Applicative is further from the root than the Passive morpheme.

In addition, Dryer's analysis of Kinyarwanda subject selection depends crucially on a parametricization of Passive, specifically that in some languages, Passive is not restricted to 2-to-1 Advancement but is more generally an Object-to-1 Advancement, with direct objects, indirect objects and even Benefactives falling under the rubric of Object, depending on the language. Data is presented in the next section which suggests that this kind of alternation is not restricted to passivized clauses, but is part of a more general phenomenon.

As shown in (4), most GB analyses of the Theme/Goal assymetries in SAE conclude that 'give'-type predicates assign Inherent Case to the Theme argument; the passivized verb cannot assign Structural (Accusative) Case, so the Goal argument must move to subject position to receive Nominative Case.

(4) *Standard American English (SAE), GB Analysis*
a. **Mary** was given a book.
    D: was given [$_{xp}$(to) **Mary**] [$_{np}$a book]

    Inh Case

    S: **Mary** $_i$ was given t$_i$ a book

    Struct Case

b.*A book was given Mary .
    D: same as in (a)
    S: A book$_i$ was given Mary t$_i$

    *Caseless

The problem arises in languages with alternations like those seen in (1), (2) and (3). If in (4), the assignment of Inherent Case to the Theme assures that it is the Goal which moves to subject position, how are we to deal with the dialect represented in (1)? One possibility is for the verb to assign Inherent Case at random to either *but not both* of its arguments. This is the solution proposed in Baker (1988b).

Pursuing that analysis and simplifying, the differences between SAE and Dialectal English stem from differences in the constituency of the Goal argument, marked as 'XP' in (4a). In SAE, the Goal is a PP at D-Structure; while the verb θ-marks the entire PP, it does not θ-mark the NP 'Mary' itself and hence it cannot assign it Inherent Case. In Baker's analysis, the abstract preposition 'to' incorporates into the V; its trace cannot assign Structural Case, so 'Mary' must move to subject position to receive Nominative Case.

In contrast, in Dialectal English, the Goal and the Theme are both NPs, and either may receive Inherent Case, leaving the other to move to subject position to receive Structural Case.

Assuming such an analysis for the Kinyarwanda data, the fact that in (2) either the Benefactive argument or the Theme argument may move to subject position to receive Nominative Case implies that either may receive Inherent Case at D-Structure, and hence that they are both NPs at D-Structure. Similarly, the alternation in (3) implies that both the Benefactive and Locative arguments are NPs at D-structure. However, consider (5):

(5) *PASS-LA Interaction* [=Dryer (14)]
    a. Ishuûri   ry-oohere-j -w -é -ho
       school   it-send -ASP-PASS-ASP-to
       igitabo n -úmwáalímu.
       book   by-teacher
    'The school was sent the book by the teacher.'
    b. *Igitabo cy-oohere-j -w -é -ho
       book   it-send -ASP-PASS-ASP-to
       ishuúri n-úmwáalímu.
       school   by-teacher
    'The book was sent-to the school
       by the teacher.'

Again, assuming Baker's analysis, the asymmetry seen in (5) would imply that the Locative argument is a PP at D-Structure, preventing it from receiving Inherent Case and forcing it to move to receive Structural Case. But the conclusion drawn from (3) was that a Locative argument is an NP at D-Structure. A possible way out of this apparent contradiction is to stipulate a rule like (6):

(6)　*Rule (Kinyarwanda): Theme/Locative Interaction*
For those predicates which assign θ-roles of Theme/Patient and Locative, the Locative argument will appear as a PP at D-Structure. For all other predicates that assign a Locative θ-role, the Locative argument will appear as an NP at D-Structure.

This seems at best an odd rule; it implies that the configuration of an argument is dependent not on the argument's own θ-role, but on the presence or absence of another θ-role in the grid. However, even assuming such a rule can be stated without violating any of the constraints of GB theory, it does not work. Consider (7) and (8):

(7)　*DS-PASS-LA Interaction* [=Dryer (18)]
a. Ishuûri　　ry-eerets-w　-é　-mo
　　school　　　it-show　-PASS-ASP-in
　　umukoôbwa　ibíryo　n -úmugabo
　　girl　　　　food　　by-man
　'The school was showed-in (to-the-)girl food by the man.'
b. Umukoóbwa　y -eerets-w　-é　-mo
　　girl　　　　she-show　-PASS-ASP-in
　　ishuûri　ibíryo　n -úmugabo.
　　school　food　　by-man
　'The girl was shown food in the school by the man.'
c. *Ibíryo　by-eerets-w　-é　-mo
　　food　　　it-show　-PASS-ASP-in
　　ishuûri　umukoôbwa　n- úmugabo.
　　school　girl　　　　by-man
　('The food was shown to the girl in the school by the man.')

(8)　θ-role/Constituency Associations for (7), assuming (6)

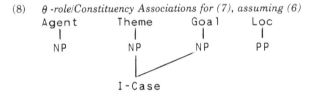

Following (6), given the presence of a Theme argument, the Locative argument appears at D-Structure as a PP. Since all three arguments must be assigned Case at some point and only one can get Structural Case by moving to subject position, I assume that predicates with three arguments must assign two Inherent Cases. Since the Locative argument is a PP at D-Structure, the two

Inherent Cases must be assigned to the Theme and Goal arguments, as indicated in (8). From this it is predicted that after P-Incorporation, the Locative argument must move to subject position to receive Structural Case; if either of the other two arguments moves to subject position, the Locative argument will be left caseless. However, as seen in (7), either the Locative argument or the Benefactive argument may appear in subject position.

My conclusion from all this is that while it is clear that something about the Locative argument's being introduced as a direct argument of the predicate appears to "disqualify" the Theme, it does not appear to be a matter of either argument's constituency.

In the next section I introduce data from several languages that suggests that the kind of variation seen in passivized clauses in Dialectal English and Kinyarwanda is a general phenomenon, not necessarily tied to Passive or any other rule.

2. Alternations Not Introduced by Passive

In Choctaw, NOM case marking is obligatory on any full NP which is the subject of a clause, all other NPs optionally taking OBL case marking:

(9)   *Choctaw* [= Davies, 1986, p. 7 (11)]
```
Hattak-at        alla(-ya)      towa(-ya)
man     -NOM     child-OBL      ball-OBL
   i    -pila -tok
   3DAT-throw-PST
'The man threw the ball to the child.'
```

Example (9) becomes ungrammatical if the NOM suffix is left off *hattak* 'man', or if a NOM suffix is added to either of the other two NPs. Generally, in clauses that contain an Agent, only that argument will have NOM case marking. However, some clauses *lacking* an Agent show an alternation; (10a) and (b) are both acceptable:

(10) *Choctaw Case Alternation* [=Davies, p. 7, (12))]
```
a. Hattak-at       holisso    im  -ihaksi-tok.
   man     -NOM    book       3DAT-forget-PST
b. Hattak-at       holisso-t        im  -ihaksi-tok.
   man     -NOM    book    -NOM     3DAT-forget-PST
'The man forgot the book.'
```

A slightly different alternation occurs in Korean, also with non-agentive (primarily psychological) predicates:

(11) *Korean* [=Gerdts and Youn, 1988, (14)]
```
a. Haksaeng-tîl-eykey ton   -i      philyoha-ta.
   student -pl -DAT    money-NOM    need   -ind
b. Haksaeng-tîl-i     ton-i philyoha-ta.
               -NOM      -NOM
'The students need money.'
```

Korean clauses usually have at most one NP with NOM case marking, but in clauses like (11), the Theme has NOM case, and the Experiencer may have either DAT or NOM case.

What, if any, is the connection between these two alternations and those discussed in the preceding section? In the Dialectal English and Kinyarwanda examples, the Agent has been suppressed, eliminated or demoted to non-argument status by the application of Passive. The Choctaw and Korean examples involve psych predicates which have no Agentive argument to begin with.

As noted above, an RG analysis of the Korean data which tied the observed alternations to a parametricization of the statement of Passive would miss the generalization to be captured, i.e. that the absence of (or elimination of) an Agentive argument appears in some languages to permit an "Open Season" on subjecthood. In RG, grammatical relations exist at all levels of derivation and are the sole primitives, and no reference to thematic roles such as Agent is possible. Recent RG analyses (e.g., Gerdts and Youn (1988) and Davies (1986)) of case alternations in psych verb clauses have attributed the alternations to the advancement or retreat of one or more nominals, case marking to reflect the grammatical relation(s) of a nominal at one or another stratum.

What is needed is an analysis that allows parametric variation in subject selection *only* in cases where an Agent is absent, either inherently or by derivation. The intuitive generalization that we wish to capture is described broadly and informally in (12).

> (12) *Open Season, informal description*
> In the absence of a grammatically available "natural" subject (includes Agent and sometimes Instrument, Source, etc.), some or all remaining arguments (sufficiently high in the thematic hierarchy) may alternate in subject position, or may simultaneously appear in subject position.

3. An Extended Lexical Representation and the OSP

Belletti and Rizzi (1988) propose lexical representations of predicates which include a θ-grid consisting of an unordered list of θ-roles, any of which *may* be marked (via underscoring in B&R) as the external θ-role, the θ-role assigned to subject position. It is assumed that if an Agent is present in the θ-grid, it will be selected as the external θ-role; otherwise, the selection is lexically idiosyncratic, subject to constraints imposed by a set of mapping principles. Also part of the lexical representation is a Case-grid, a specification of the Inherent Cases (if any) idiosyncratically selected by the predicate, each Inherent Case linked to a specific slot in the θ-grid (B&R, p. 343).

> (13) *Lexical Representations, Belletti and Rizzi (1988)*
>
> **temere:** θ-grid [Experiencer, Theme]
>
> Case-grid [–   –]
>
> **preoccupare:** θ-grid [Experiencer, Theme]
> |
>   Case-grid [ACC   –]

Belletti and Rizzi's stipulation that Agents be necessarily selected for the external θ-role and that, by implication, the absence of an Agent opens up the external θ-role selection, seems to come close to capturing the intuitions described informally in (12). I propose that with some modifications and extensions of their model of lexical representation, these intuitions can be captured, and stated more formally in a manner still generally compatible with most versions of GB theory. These modifications and extensions are stated in (14).

(14) *Revised and Enriched Lexical Representation*

        a. θ-roles do not appear unordered in the θ-grid but are ordered according to a Thematic Hierarchy (e.g. Agent > Experiencer > Theme > Ben/Goal, etc.[1])

        b. Rules such as Dative Shift and Passive are lexical rules. In general, lexical rules may disrupt the initial unmarked ordering of the θ-roles in the θ-grid by introducing new θ-roles into the grid, by suppressing an existing θ-role, and/or by stipulating a link between a θ-role and an Inherent Case in the Case Grid. It is the fully inflected predicate with its (possibly) modified θ- and Case grid configuration which is mapped into D-Structure configurations.

        c. Although in the unmarked case, Structural Case is uniquely assigned, some languages may permit multiple assignment of Nominative or Accusative Case.

        d. The selection of the external θ-role is determined not lexically but by rule: The highest (= leftmost) available θ-role (i.e., one that is not suppressed and (generally) not already associated with Inherent Case) will be assigned to external position.

A note is in order as to the nature of Passive, given the revised model outlined in (14). In most GB approaches, Passive suppresses the predicate's ability to assign a θ-role to external position; in the present approach, it is the θ-role itself which is suppressed (* indicates suppression):

(15) *Passive (Universal Characterization)*
θ-grid: $[\theta_1, \theta_2, ...] \longrightarrow [{}^*\theta_1, \theta_2, ...]$
Constraint: θ_2 = Patient or Theme.
Optional.

What does it mean for a θ-role to be suppressed? It means that either the θ-role is not assigned or that if it is assigned to an argument, that argument cannot be assigned Structural Case; thus, an argument associated with a suppressed θ-role receives its θ-role from the predicate, but must be assigned Inherent Case, which may show up at S-Structure either as an oblique case marking or as a case-marking adposition; e.g., the Agent of a passivized clause is marked in English with 'by', in Russian with instrumental case, in French with 'par', etc. Thus, an argument associated with a suppressed θ-role shares with unsuppressed arguments the feature of being θ-marked directly by the verb, and with adjuncts the feature of being optional.

Open Season can now be stated somewhat more formally in terms of the approach just outlined:

(16) *Open Season Parameters*
In the absence of an available Agent (possibly also Instrument, etc.) in the θ-grid, a language may select:
a. *(Alternative Subject Option)* to assign any of the remaining available θ-roles (high enough in the thematic hierarchy) to external position.
b. *(Multiple Subject Option)* to assign more than one θ-role to an equivalent number of distinct external positions.

4. Applications
Returning to the data in the first two sections, we can now account for each of the alternations in turn.
Assuming the rule (17) for Dative Shift in both English Dialects, the lexical derivation of 'give' in (1) and (4) is given in (18)

(17) *English Dative Shift*
θ-grid: $[\theta_1, \theta_2, ...] \longrightarrow [\theta_1, \text{Goal/Ben}, \theta_2, ...]$
Optional.

(18) *Lexical derivation of 'give' in (1) and (4)*
give (Agent, Theme, Goal)
give-Dative Shift (Agent, Goal, Theme)
give-DS-Pass (*Agent, Goal, Theme)

The difference between SAE and Dialectal English is that the latter selects the Alternative Subject Option of (16), so that either Goal or Theme may be assigned to external position. SAE does not have Open Season, so Goal, as the highest available θ-role, must be assigned to external position.
For the Kinyarwanda data, I assume the lexical rules given in (19). The lexical derivation of *eerets* 'show' in (7) is given in (20).

(19) *Lexical Rules for Kinyarwanda*
a. Dative Shift: same as (17), except *obligatory*.
b. Passive: same as (15).
c. Locative Applicative (LA)
θ-grid: $[\theta_1, ... \text{(Theme)} ...] \longrightarrow [\theta_1, \text{Loc}, ... \text{(Theme)}]$
ACC

(20) *Derivation of 'eerets' in (7)*
eerets (Agent, Theme, Ben)
eerets-DS (Agent, Goal, Theme)
eerets-DS-PASS (*Agent, Goal, Theme)
eerets-DS-PASS-LA (*Agent, Loc, Goal, Theme)

ACC

Note that while Dative Shift and Passive are unremarkable in Kinyarwanda, Locative Applicatives both introduce a Locative θ-role into second position in the θ-grid and link Inherent Accusative Case to the Theme, making it unavailable for assignment to external position. Kinyarwanda, like Dialectal

English, adopts the Alternative Subject version of Open Season, and either of the remaining available θ-roles (i.e., Loc or Goal) may be assigned to external position, producing (7a) and (b).

No lexical derivation takes place in the Choctaw example (10). The Multiple Subject version of Open Season that Choctaw adopts can be represented schematically as in (21):

(21) *Choctaw Open Season*
ihaksi θ-grid [Experiencer, Theme]

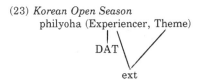

It appears that for 'ihaksi'-type predicates in Choctaw, the Experiencer θ-role is assigned to external position, *and in addition*, the Theme θ-role may also optionally be assigned to a distinct external position. If this is correct, then the Structural Case assignments of (10a) and (b) are as given in (22a) and (b), respectively:

(22) *Structural Case Assignments for (10a) and (b)*
  a. [$_s$ hattak [$_{ip}$ infl [$_{vp}$ holisso [$_v$ ihaksi]]]]
    Nom ⟵⎯⎯⏋   Obl ⟵⎯⎯⏌

  b. [$_s$ hattak holisso [$_{ip}$ infl [$_{vp}$ [$_v$ ihaksi]]]]
    Nom   Nom ⟵⎯⎯⏌

Finally, the Korean alternation in (11) may represent a more divergent version of Open Season. The Experiencer role of *philyoha* 'need' appears to be associated with an Inherent Dative Case; nevertheless, it appears to be available for assignment to external position. Possibly, unlike most languages, only suppression, and not Inherent Case assignment, makes a θ-role unavailable for assignment to external position in Korean. If this is correct, then Korean's version of Open Season for 'philyoha'-type predicates can be represented schematically as in (23):

(23) *Korean Open Season*
  philyoha (Experiencer, Theme)
       │ \   /
     DAT \ /
         ext

Assuming the structure (24) for (11a) and (b), it would appear that if a Korean argument receives two Cases, one Inherent and one Structural, either may appear morphologically.

(24) *S-Structure and Case Assignment for (11)*
  [$_s$haeksaeng-tîl ton [$_{ip}$infl [$_{vp}$philyoha-ta]]]
    Dat (Inh)
    Nom (Str)   Nom (Str)

My assumption that the Experiencer is in external position even though it is assigned Inherent Dative Case may gain some support from a dialect of Korean reported by Gerdts and Youn (1988) which allows a third variant of (11) in which both Inherent Case and Structural Case appear morphologically:

(25) *Dialectal Korean (cf. (11))*
    Haksaeng-tîl-eyKey-ka   ton -i philyoha-ta.
    student -pl -DAT -NOM money-NOM need -ind

5. Multiple Assignment of Structural Accusative Case

In the foregoing, I have claimed that some languages have predicates that assign θ-roles, and therefore Structural Case, to two (or possibly more) external positions. The question arises as to whether any language permits the assignment of Structural *Accusative* Case to more than one argument. Clearly, if my assumptions regarding the relative rarity of Inherent Case assignment are accepted, then multiple assignment of Structural Accusative Case is necessary. Consider (26), the non-passivized version of the English clauses in (1) and (4):

(26) Frederic gave Martha a book.

Since I do not assume any assignment of Inherent Case by 'give'-type predicates, it follows that both the Ben/Goal and the Theme must be assigned Structural Accusative Case. How, then, to explain (27), in which Dative Shift has not applied?

(27) Frederic gave a book to Martha.

One solution would be to amend (17) slightly as (28):

(28) *English Dative Shift, revised*
    θ-grid: $[\theta_1, \theta_2, ..., \text{Goal/Ben}, ...] \longrightarrow [\theta_1, \text{Goal/Ben}, \theta_2, ...]$
                                    |
                                  DAT

In a clause in which Dative Shift has not applied, the Goal/Ben would retain its Inherent Dative Case, which surfaces as the preposition 'to' in English. The revised version of English Dative Shift both moves Ben/Goal to second position in the θ-grid and eliminates its association with Inherent Dative Case.

Similarly, in Kinyarwanda clauses in which both Dative Shift and a Locative Applicative have applied, two arguments are assumed to receive Structural Accusative Case:

(29) *Kinyarwanda (cf. (7))*
    Umugabo   y -eerets-é -mo ishuûri
    man   he-show -ASP-in school
        umukoóbwa ibíryo
        girl   food
    'The man showed the girl food in the school.'

(30) *Lexical Derivation of 'eerets' in (29)*
eerets (Agent, Theme, Goal)
eerets-DS (Agent, Goal, Theme)
eerets-DS-LA (Agent, Loc, Goal, Theme)

ACC

At the end of the derivation in (30), the Agent θ-role is assigned to external position, and both Theme and Goal arguments are assigned Structural Accusative Case.

More evidence for multiple assignment of Structural Accusative Case comes again from Dialectal Korean, which permits the following alternation:

(31) *Case Alternation, Dialectal Korean* [= G&Y (38)]
```
    a. Chelsu-ka    Suni-eykey    chaek-îl
       Chelsu-NOM   Suni-DAT      book -ACC
          cu  -et -ta.
          give-pst-ind
    b. Chelsu-ka    Suni-eykey-lîl   chaek-îl
       Chelsu-NOM   Suni-DAT  -ACC   book -ACC
          cu  -et -ta.
          give-pst-ind
   'Chelsu gave Suni the book.'
```

To account for the fact that in addition to Dative, Accusative morphological case may appear on the Goal argument, I propose that Korean Dative Shift is essentially the same as the revised version of English Dative Shift in (28), except that the Inherent Dative Case is retained:

(32) *Korean Dative Shift*
θ-grid: $[\theta_1, \theta_2, ..., \text{Goal/Ben}, ...] \longrightarrow [\theta_1, \text{Goal/Ben}, \theta_2, ...]$

DAT   DAT

As discussed above with respect to psych predicates, this dialect of Korean permits assignment of Structural Case to an argument that already has Inherent Case, with either showing up morphologically:

(33) *Case Assignment in Dialectal Korean*
[_s Chelsu   [_ip infl [_vp Suni   chaek [_v cu]]]]
                                 DAT (Inh)
    NOM (Str)   ACC (Str) ACC (Str)

6. Summary

In this paper, I have proposed some modifications in θ- and Case Theory to account for some data that challenge some common GB assumptions. These modifications are:

(1) Previous to any lexical derivation, θ-roles are arranged in the θ-grid according to a Thematic Hierarchy.

(2) Relation-changing rules like Passive and Dative Shift are lexical rules.

A Lexical rule may have any or all of the following effects: (a) it may change the ordering of the θ-roles in the grid; (b) it may associate a θ-role with an Inherent Case, or eliminate such an association; (c) it may suppress a θ-role.

(3) Assignment of a θ-role to external position is not lexically idiosyncratic but rather predictable from the order of θ-roles in the grid, assignment to external position generally going to the first available θ-role.

(4) In most languages, the assignment of the external θ-role is fixed (i.e., the choice as to which θ-role is assigned to external position is fully determined by the ordering within the θ-grid) and unique (i.e., only one θ-role may be assigned to external position). However, some languages, given a predicate with a θ-grid lacking an available Agent, will permit an Open Season on θ-role assignment to external position, i.e., will allow any one of several available θ-roles to be assigned to external position, or in some cases, will allow two or more θ-roles to be assigned to an equivalent number of distinct external positions.

(5) Since I claim that some languages allow more than one argument to be θ-marked in external position, and by the Case Filter, all phonologically realized NPs must receive Case, it follows that Structural Case assignment must not be unique in those languages. Thus, Nominative Case is assigned by INFL to *any* θ-marked external argument, and likewise, Structural Accusative Case is assigned by the verb to any θ-marked VP-internal argument.

(6) While availability for assignment to external position is generally restricted to θ-roles which (a) are not *suppressed* (as defined above) and (b) are not associated with any Inherent Case, in some languages the latter requirement is relaxed, leading in some cases to quirky case marking on subjects.

Finally, I am aware that some of my proposals in this paper may represent substantial challenges to the accepted organization of some of the modules of Government and Binding Theory. Given the constantly evolving nature of GB theory, the proposed modifications may well be found to be untenable by some future researcher. If so, my hope is that they will have at least led to a more thorough examination of the languages and phenomena examined herein.

NOTES

[1] Although there is nothing inherently wrong with variations in the ordering of thematic roles within the hierarchy, some of the roles in (14a) are particularly variable, notably Experiencer and Goal/Ben, both of which can appear either before or after Theme/Patient in the hierarchies of different languages. There is evidence that even within one language there may be several distinct hierarchies for different purposes. An even greater departure from (14a) has been proposed by Randall (1988) for nominalizations, in which Theme has the highest position in the hierarchy.

REFERENCES

Baker, Mark C., 1988a. *Incorporation: A Theory of Grammatical Function Changing.* University of Chicago Press.

———, 1988b. Theta Theory and the syntax of Applicatives in Chichewa. *NLLT* 6-3, 353-390.

Belletti, Adriana and Luigi Rizzi, 1988. Psych-verbs and θ-Theory. *NLLT* 6-3, 291-352.

Davies, William D., 1987. *Choctaw Verb Agreement and Universal Grammar.*

Dordrecht: Reidel.

Dryer, Matthew S., 1983. Indirect objects in Kinyarwanda revisited. In *Studies in Relational Grammar 1*, David M. Perlmutter, ed. Chicago: The University of Chicago Press.

Gerdts, Donna and Cheon Youn, 1988. Korean Psych Constructions: Advancement or Retreat? *CLS-24*.

Larson, Richard K., 1988. On the double object construction. *Linguistic Inquiry* 19, 335-392.

Randall, Janet H., 1988. Inheritance. In Wilkins, ed., 1988.

On the Principle of Similarity in Consonantal Assimilation

Young-mee Yu Cho
Stanford University

1 Introduction

This paper examines the so-called 'principle of similarity' that has been assumed to operate in consonantal assimilations in both synchronic and diachronic phonology (Hutcheson 1973, Lee 1975, 1976, Kiparsky 1988). This principle is based on a generalization that assimilation takes place first between segments which are already most similar in their feature composition. It has also been believed to be related to the common prohibition on sequences of minimally distinct consonants (Trnka 1936, Trubetzkoy 1939, Greenberg 1978, McCalla 1980). The crucial assumption linking the principle of similarity to the prohibition on sequences of 'similar' consonants can be stated as follows: since many languages do not allow consonant sequences that are 'too similar', assimilation rules, if they are operative in a particular language, would apply first to these sequences and then extend further along the similarity hierarchy.

I will argue that recent developments within autosegmental theory–in particular, the spreading account of assimilation rules and the theory of Feature Geometry–call into question the existence of such a principle. I will show that all of the cases presented in the literature can be reanalyzed as cases of selecting for the domain of the rule one of the lower class nodes in the Feature Hierarchy, such as the coronal node, thus giving the surface effect of similarity.

I will show that such a principle is not only empirically questionable but also makes a wrong prediction concerning the typology of assimilation rules. Specifically, the principle entails that a more natural rule is one that compares the feature make-up of the consonants involved in the rule. It also allows numerous cases of improbable rules. For instance, a language could have a laryngeal assimilation rule that applies only between two homorganic consonants, to the exclusion of hetero-organic clusters. In the absence of such cases, we can conclude that a simpler rule is one that spreads features without regard to the features specified either in the target or the trigger. I assume that rules could refer to certain features in the target or the trigger but that determining the similarity between the target and the trigger, if allowed, would be a lot more costly and thus cannot be a common principle working in natural languages. In addition to examining some of the crucial cases presented in the literature, I will provide two more examples that appear to argue for the similarity principle, but in fact do not; I will conclude that such a principle is neither desirable on formal grounds nor needed on empirical grounds.

2 Theoretical Background

My reanalyses of the data hinge on the two recent proposals in autosegmental phonology. First, the theory of Feature Geometry groups the phonological features that usually behave as a functional unit into class nodes (Clements 1985, Sagey 1986, McCarthy 1988). In this theory, each class node (such as coronal, dorsal, place, laryngeal, etc.) can be chosen as the site of a particular rule. I will assume the following version of Feature Geometry.

(1)

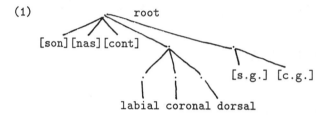

Second, Underspecification Theory requires marked values to be specified and unmarked values unspecified(Kiparsky 1982, Archangeli and Pulleyblank 1986), which enables one to capture the generalization that assimilation tends to spread marked feature specifications to segments (Schachter 1969, Poser 1982, Harris 1984, Kiparsky 1985, Hayes 1986, Mascaró 1987).

With the particular theoretical assumptions set down by these theories, I argue that parameters employed in consonantal assimilation include specifying the site of spreading and the nature of a target, but never the presence or absence of similarity between the target and the trigger. All assimilation rules can be schematized as in (2).

(2)

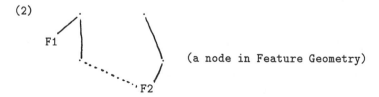

(a node in Feature Geometry)

3   Review of some putative cases

First, I will examine several representative cases from the data presented in the literature and argue that the principle of similarity is not a real principle of grammar, but a mere surface effect. The data presented in this section include English alveolar assimilation, Yakut plural inflection and Finnish gradation. The conclusion to be drawn from the reanalyses is that, given well-motivated assumptions regarding feature representations together with independent principles (such as Structure Preservation and the Obligatory Contour Principle), none of these cases confirms the principle of similarity. I will also discuss Sanskrit sandhi to show that a language with pervasive consonant assimilation does not require such a principle.

3.1   English Assimilation

The data on English assimilation in (3) have been presented to argue for the fact that complete assimilation takes place only when the two segments are already similar.[1]

```
(3) right poor--> righp poor
    good  bye--> goob bye
    right corner--> righk corner
    bad guess--> bag guess
    keep track-->*keet track
    back track-->*bat track
    right bill--> righp bill
    bad police-->bab police
        Bailey (1970), Hutcheson (1974),  Gimson (1960, 1970)
```

There is complete assimilation as in *right poor* and *bad guess* only when the voicing of the target and the trigger agree. When the two segments do not agree in voicing as in *right bill* and *bad police*, there is only partial assimilation. I maintain that this kind of claim proves nothing about the nature of assimilation. Rather, it illustrates that the rule of place assimilation does not care whether or not the consonants involved share other features. Complete assimilation obtains when the segments already happen to share all features other than the propagating ones. In other words, the data argue against a principle of similarity in that assimilation applies whether or not there is a similarity between the relevant segments. A genuine argument would be a case where assimilation is blocked when the features are not shared. Japanese /t/ assimilation will be given as one such case and will be analyzed without recourse to the notion of similarity.

Another example in the literature is the palatalization of /s/ in fast speech, as in such phrases as *horse shoe, is sure, this church, this year*. The fact is that /s/ assimilates only to a palatal consonant and not to a following labial or velar. This restriction has been attributed to the fact that any change in the position of the sibilants would require changing more than just the position of articulation.

I propose, instead, that the reason why the alveolar /s/ assimilates to the palatal articulation but not to the other places is due to the fact that the site of assimilation is the coronal node. In this account, labials and velars do not spread their features because they are not involved in the formulation of the rule. On the contrary, the fact that /s/ assimilates to any palatal, be it a fricative, an affricate, or a glide, demonstrates that there is no principle of similarity at work here: there need be no mention of similarity in the rule other than the restriction that both the target and the trigger have to be coronal, which is ensured by selecting the coronal node as the domain of the rule application.

3.2   Yakut plural inflection

The next example is the alternations of the Yakut plural suffix /-lar/. The initial consonant *l* does not change when following a stem that ends in a vowel, a diphthong, or *l* itself. When following other stems, the *l* regularly changes in the following way.

```
(4)   a. l->t/ voiceless C
         at-lar-->attar 'horses'
         muos-lar-->muostar 'horns'
      b. l->d/voiced C
         ubay-lar-->ubaydar 'elder brothers'
         attir-lar-->attirdar 'stallions'
      c. l-->n/ nasal
         suorvan-lar-->suorvannar 'blankets'
         olom-lar--> olomnor 'fords'
```

This example is supposed to show that /l/ assimilates to /n/ completely because both are sonorants, whereas it does not assimilate completely to non-sonorants. I propose, however, that since /l/ changing to /t/, /n/ or /d/ is not a natural assimilation process, deletion of laterality must be involved. First, /l/ deletes when it is preceded by a consonant. Then there is spreading of features such as voicing and nasality, followed by a default specification of alveolar place. When a voiceless consonant precedes, there is no assimilation and the specification of the empty slot results in /t/. The relevant rules are formulated in (5).

(5) Yakut plural inflection

1)Deletion   2) Assimilation   3)Default specification

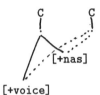

3.3 Finnish gradation

The fourth example is a subclass of Finnish gradation in which a more sonorous
segment affects the following stop as shown in (6).[2]

```
(6) mp--> mm    ampu-mme-->ammumme  'we shoot'
    nt--> nn    ranta-lla-->rannalla  'on the shore'
    nk--> ŋŋ    kenkä-n-->keŋŋän     'of the shoe'

    lt-->ll     kulta-n-->kullan   'of the gold'
    rt-->rr     parta-ssa-->parrassa  'in the beard'

    lp-->lv     halpa-->halvan    'cheap'
    lk-->l      velka-->velan     'debt'
    rp-->rv     arpa-->arvan      'lot'
    rk-->r      virka-->viran     'office (held)'
```

The assimilations involving nasals are complete because all examples of
clusters with nasals involve a nasal and a homorganic stop. When the cluster
involves a liquid plus a stop, the claim made by Hutcheson is that only the
homorganic clusters assimilate precisely because they share place features.

I propose an account involving selective feature spreading. Gradation consists of several rules that spread certain specified features.[3] On my account,
the rule that assimilates /rt/ to [rr] is the same as one that is responsible for
the change of /rp/ to [rv], in contrast to Hutcheson's claim that the former, but
not the latter, is the result of a rule of complete assimilation operating between
two similar consonants. Though morphologically conditioned, the phonological part of the rule spreads the relevant features such as [+nas], [+son] and
[+cont]. Spreading of [+son] or [+nas] results in complete assimilation due
to the fortuitous fact that all the features other than the propagating one are
already the same, and in the case of /t/ there is an empty C slot whose place
specifications are assigned by default, as shown in the first two sets of examples

in (6). However, in formulating the rule there is no need to say that certain features are shared. As for such forms as *lk* and *rk*, the reason that *k* neither assimilates nor surfaces is due to a violation of Structure Preservation. If we assume that the relevant speading feature is [+cont], as in the case of *lp*, /k/ would change into a velar fricative. Since the language does not have a velar fricative independent of this process, I assume that, if one ever arises in the course of a derivation, it cannot surface.[4]

3.4 Sanskrit assimilation

Sanskrit provides a rather clear example of how a case of surface similarity can be accounted for by a language particular choice of assimilation sites. In Sanskrit, the site of obstruent assimilation is the coronal node, with the result that /t/ and /s/ assimilate only to retroflex and palatal obstruents, but not to labials and velars. This case appears to support the principle of similarity, since the target and the trigger are both coronals and therefore similar. Nasal assimilation, on the other hand, selects the place node, which comprises the coronal, the labial and the dorsal nodes. As a result, /n/ assimilates not only to the more similar coronals but to all places of articulation.

Relevant examples are shown below.

```
(7) Coronal Assimilation
        t--->t./ _____t., n., s.
        s--->s./_____s., t., n.
        n--->n./_____n., t.
        t--->c/_____c, s'
        s--->s'/_____c, s'
        n--->n~/_____c, j, s'
        t/s/n---> t./s./n./_____r
    (C. represents a retroflex consonant, /s'/ a palatal
      fricative, /n~/ a palatal nasal.)
    tat jayate-->taj jayate
    etat t.hakkurah-->etat. t.hakkurah
    tat labdham--> tal labdham
    tan labhasva-->tal labhasva
    arn+n.a-->arn.n.a
    jyotis+s.u-->jyotis.s.u
    tat  d.yate-->tad. d.yate
    mahan+kavih-->mahankavih
    mahan+bhagah-->mahambhaghah
    tan+janan-->tan~jamam
    tan+d.imbhan-->tan.d.imbhan
```

Just as in English *s*-palatalization, the reason that only coronals participate in certain cases of assimilations falls out naturally from the fact that the
coronal node has been selected as the site of spreading in obstruents. Thus,
the following parameters apply to Sanskrit sandhi:

```
(8)Sanskrit assimilation
   a. site of assimilation: the coronal node (for obstruents)
                            the place node (for nasals)
   b. target specifications: target should be unspecified and
                             in the coda position.
```

4 Japanese assimilation: a case of apparent similarity

None of the examples shown above constitutes a real argument for the principle
of similarity. Rather, they weigh against such a principle in that all of the rules
can be, and, in fact, should be formulated without access to information on
other tiers. In this section, I present a case that is more challenging, because
similarity between the target and the trigger does appear be a necessary part
of the structural description of the rules.

Japanese /t/ assimilation appears to be a case in which the rule has to
stipulate that the target and the trigger should agree in voicing. In Japanese,
one observes that nasals and coronal stops assimilate to the place features of
a following stop, as shown in (9).

```
(9) hoN+mono-->hommono  'real thing'
    hoN+gen-->hoŋgen 'original field'
    hoN+ki-'-> hoŋki 'seriousness'
    hoN+to--> honto 'really'

    bet-taku-->bettaku  'detached villa'
    bet-kaku-->bekkaku 'different style'
    bet-puu-->beppuu 'separate cover'
    bet-situ-->bessitu 'separate room'
```

Non-coronal stops, however, do not participate in assimilation. Instead, due
to the syllable structure condition that allows only geminates or homorganic
nasal stop clusters, an epenthesis applies to split up clusters that consist of
noncoronal stop and non-homorganic consonant:

```
(10)gak+ko-->gakko    'school''
    gak+see-->*gasse gakusee    'student',
    gak+cyoo-->*gacycyoo gakucyoo 'school president'
    gak+mon-->*gammon *gapmon gakumon 'learning'
```

What is relevant to our discussion is the fact that /t/ does not assimilate to the following voiced consonant (whether oral or nasal), as illustrated in (11).

(11)   it-nen-->itinen (*innen) 'one year'
       it-bai-->itibai (*ipbai, *ibbai, *imbai) 'once'

Should this fact be recognized as a case where the phonological rule has to refer to the fact that both the trigger and the target share the feature [-voice]? Furthermore, whereas the voiceless /t/ does not assimilate to the following voiced consonant, the voiced /n/ undergoes assimilation to whatever consonant follows it. This asymmetry could be interpreted as showing how far each rule has been extended along the similarity hierarchy: the /t/ assimilation rule is confined to more similar segments, but the nasal rule is extended to include other consonants. One could then propose the following rules to account for the data presented above.

(12) a. Homorganic Nasal Assimilation

     b. /t/ Assimilation

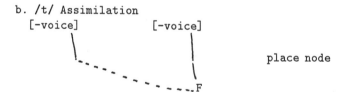

Although the above rules are perfectly legitimate formal expressions in autosegmental phonology, there is something disturbing about the second formulation. It states that a place assimilation takes place only when a feature in the laryngeal tier agrees. If a phonological rule is given power to compare features in the target and the trigger, all sorts of unnatural rules can be just as easily written. Assimilation could, for instance, apply when the laryngeal nodes do not agree in voicing.

Instead, I present a different analysis. I argue that the data in (9) can be accounted for by one simple rule that spreads the feature [+cont] and any features of the place node. (13) summarizes the factors involved in this account of Japanese assimilation.

(13)

Japanese Assimilation: a. site of spreading: Place, [cont]
b. target specifications: target should
be unspecified (only coronals) and
should be in the syllable coda.

There are independent reasons why /t/ fails to assimilate to a following voiced consonant. In the case of /t/ followed by a nasal, because there is no rule spreading Nasality in the langauge, /it-nen/ does not result in [innen] but in the epenthesized form [itinen]. As for /t/ followed by an oral voiced consonant, assimilation is blocked by independently motivated syllable structure constraints of Japanese.[5]

(14) a.

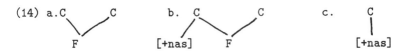

Since the language allows only geminates as in (14a) and Nasal+homorganic C as in (14b), assimilation to a voiced segment yields an ill-formed sequence, as shown below.

(15)   it+bai-->*ipbai (Assimilation)
        --> it i bai (general epenthesis)

Since Japanese lacks a rule of regressive voicing assimilation, [ipbai] cannot be changed into [ibbai] which could then be changed to [imbai].[6] Instead, a general rule of epenthesis applies. This reanalysis thus shows that a condition of similarity is not needed to account for Japanese assimilation, despite first appearances.

5   Conclusion

I have shown in the above discussion that the surface similarity effect is due to two factors. The first is the choice of some class node in Feature Hierarchy which delimits the domain of spreading. The second comprises cases in which some independent constraints such as Structure Preservation and syllable structure constraints are violated, so that the result of spreading does not surface. In no cases have we seen that the principle of similarity is needed.

However, the question of prohibiting a phonological rule from comparing features between the target and the trigger needs to be investigated further. If one ever finds real cases in which place assimilation is limited to fricatives, stops or nasals, or voicing assimilation applies only within homorganic clusters, then a weakened version of the similarity principle might still turn out to be necessary.

It can be also pointed out that there is no reason to classify complete assimilation and partial assimilation as two different processes. In spite of surface differences, I claim that they result from the same rule. Complete assimilation arises fortuitously if two consonants happen to share the same features except for the propagating feature. It can also arise by an independent rule of deleting all features from a root, thus rendering the target empty, with the result of complete assimilation.

Finally, I will briefly touch on the issue of the prohibition on sequences of 'similar' segments. I argue that it can be derived in a principled manner by fine-tuning the Obligatory Contour Principle (McCarthy 1986) and that it does not have a direct bearing on the similarity issue, contrary to the claims made in the literature. Many languages have constraints on tautosyllabic sequences of 'similar' segments, which cannot be attributed to some other principle. If a language does not allow sequences like [pf], [yi], [wu], [pw], or [tl], this must be the result of either underlying syllable structure constraints or output conditions. The following are some examples of language particular OCP conditions.

(16) a. * [+labial][+labial] (English, Korean, etc.)

b. $*\begin{bmatrix} \text{+high} \\ \text{-back} \end{bmatrix}\begin{bmatrix} \text{+high} \\ \text{-back} \end{bmatrix}$ (Korean)

c. * [-back] [-back] (Japanese)

d. $*\begin{bmatrix} \text{+cor} \\ \text{-cont} \\ \text{+voice} \end{bmatrix}\begin{bmatrix} \text{+cor} \\ \text{-cont} \\ \text{+voice} \end{bmatrix}$ (Spanish (Harris 1983))

However, I propose that assimilation is an independent process from the OCP, even though the output of any assimilation rule is subject to it.

6   Notes

[1]It should be pointed out that the similarity argument relies on separatig a rule of complete assimilation from the other cases of partial assimilation.

However, it will be shown throughout this paper. that such a distinction is unwarranted.

[2]Gradation affects syllable-initial stops in closed syllables, as demonstrated in Keyser and Kiparsky(1984).

[3]I will assume that the features involved in spreading are [+nas], [+son] and [+cont]. These features are grouped together under the manner node in Clements (1985) because they concern the degree and manner of constriction. I do not know whether Finnish gradation provides an argument for the controversial manner node. A possible argument against grouping these features as a natural class is found in another kind of gradation in which [+voice] seems to be involved as in *katu→kadun*.

[4]There is another case in which /k/ does not surface (as in *katu→kadun*, *tupa→tuvan* and *haka→haan*). Whether or not what is involved in this type of gradation is [+voice] or [+cont] or both, either voiced [g] or continuant [ɣ] cannot surface since the language does not have either phoneme in the native inventory.

[5]Ito (1986) proposes the following negative coda condition.

$$ * \quad \overset{\displaystyle C]_{\sigma}}{\underset{\displaystyle [-nas]}{|}} $$

Although this negative condition is simpler than my conditions, it makes the incorrect claim that any linked consonant is a well-formed coda. In particular, it allows homorganic clusters such as [pb] as well as voiced geminates. There is evidence, however, that voiced geminates are not allowed as can be found in such derivations as *sid-ta→sidda* (progressive assimilation)→*sinda* (nasalization of coda consonant). Voiced geminates must always be changed into a nasal and obstruent sequence. This dipthongization of voiced geminates is a violation of geminate integrity, which needs to be solved somehow.

[6]Tateishi (1988) proposes the following constraint for sino-Japanese morphemes.

$$ * \quad C \diagdown \diagup C $$
$$ [+voice] $$

7 References

Archangeli, D. and D. Pulleyblank. 1986. <u>The Content and the Structure of Phonological Representations</u>. Ms.

Bailey, C. -J. 1969. "A possible explanation for an assimilation curiosity" <u>Working papers in Linguistics</u> 5, University of

Hawaii.

---- 1970. "Toward specifying constraints on Phonological metathesis." Linguistic Inquiry 1.3: 348-50.

Cho, Y.-M. 1988. '' Korean Assimilation'' In the Proceedings of West Coast Conference on Formal Linguistics 7: 41-52.

---- 1989. "Comments on Mohanan's 'On the Bases of Underspecification'." Paper presented at the Foundations of Phonology Workshop at CSLI, Stanford University.

Clements, G. N. 1985. "The Geometry of Phonological Features" Phonology Year Book 2: 223-50.

Gimson, A. C. 1970. An Introduction to the Pronunciation of English. London: Edward Arnold.

Greenberg, J. H. 1978. "Some Generalizations concerning initial and final consonant clusters". In J. H. Greenberg ed. Universals of Human Language. Stanford University Press.

Harris, James. 1984. "Autosegmental Phonology, Lexical Phonology and Spanish Nasals." In M. Aronoff and R. T. Oehrle eds. Language Sound structure. Cambridge, MA: MIT press.

Hayes, B. 1986. "Assimilation as Spreading in Toba Batak" Lingusitic Inquiry 17: 467-99.

Hutcheson, J. 1973 "Remarks on the nature of complete consonantal assimilation". CLS 9:215-22.

Ito, J. 1986. Syllable Theory in Prosodic Phonology. Doctoral Dissertation. University of Massachussettes.

Karlsson, Fred. 1983. Finnish Grammar. Werner Soderstrom Osakeyntio.

Keyser, S. J. and P. Kiparsky. 1984. ''Syllable Structure in Finnish Phonology.'' In M. Aronoff and R. T. Oehrle eds. Language Sound Structure. Cambridge. MA: MIT Press.

Kiparsky, P. 1982. ''Lexical Morphology and Phonology.'' In Yang,I. ed. Linguistics in the Morning Calm. Seoul: Hanshin.

----- 1985. ''Some Consequences of Lexical Phonology.'' Phonology Year Book 2: 85-138.

----- 1988. ''PhonologicaL Change.'' Linguistics: the Cambridge Survey. vol. 1.

Lee, G. 1975. "Natural Phonological Descriptions 1" Working Papers in Lingusitics, University of Hawaii 7: 85-125.

----- 1976. "Natural Phonological Descriptions 2" Working Papers in Lingusitics, University of Hawaii 8: 25-61.

Mascaro, J. 1984. "Continuant Spreading in Basque, Catalan, and

26

Spanish.'' In M. Aronoff and R. T. Oehrle eds. <u>Language Sound Structure</u>. Cambridge, MA: MIT press.

----- 1987. "A Reduction and Spreading Theory of Voicing and Other Sound Effects." Ms.

McCalla, K. I. 1980. "Phonological and Morphological Forces in Syntagmatic Change." <u>Lingua</u> 51: 1-16.

McCarthy, J. 1986.'' OCP effects: Gemination and Antigemination.'' <u>Linguistic Inquiry</u> 17: 207-63.

----- 1988. ''Feature Geometry and Dependency''. To appear in O. Fujimura, ed., <u>Articulatory Organization</u>. S.Karger, Basil.

Poser, W. 1982. "Phonological Representations and Action-at-a-distance.'' In H. van der Hulst and N. Smith eds. <u>The Structure of Phonological Representations</u> 2. Dordrecht: Foris.

Sagey, E. C. 1986. <u>The Structure of the Melody</u>. Doctoral dissertation. MIT.

Schachter, P. 1969. "Nasal Assimilation Rules in Akan." <u>International Journal of Applied Linguistics</u> 35: 342-55.

Tateishi, Koichi. 1988. "Phonology of Sino-Japanese Morphemes'' To appear in <u>University of Massachusetts Occasional Papers in Linguistics</u> 13.

Trnka, B. 1936. "General Laws of Phonemic Combinations." <u>Travaux du cercle linguistique de Prague</u> 6: 57-62.

Trubetzkoy, N. S. 1939. <u>Principles of Phonology</u>. English translation by C. Baltaxe, Univ. of California Press.

Whitney, W. D. 1889. <u>Sanskrit Grammar</u>. Cambridge, Mass: Harvard Univ. Press.

Illicit Acceptability in picture NPs[1]

Wayne Cowart[2]
The Ohio State University

The empirical generalization addressed by Chomsky's subjacency principle seems to apply to sentences such as (1) (see Chomsky, 1973, 1981, 1986; also Riemsdijk & Williams, 1986, Lasnik & Uriagereka, 1988).

(1)   Who did the Duchess sell a portrait of?

Nevertheless sentences such as this seem fully acceptable and intelligible to many speakers. In consequence, such cases have been regarded as fully grammatical in the linguistic literature.

Broadly speaking, there are two approaches by which a grammatical theory that incorporates some form of the subjacency constraint might accommodate these facts. First, the components of the grammatical theory that capture the subjacency constraint might be formulated in such a way that they do not apply to cases such as (1). Second, the grammar might incorporate principles that have the effect of shielding cases like (1) from the subjacency mechanism(s).

This study takes a different tack, looking more closely at the intuitions about (1) that underlie the assumption that it is grammatical. The study begins from the tentative suggestion that the acceptability of (1) might be spurious, that (1) is in fact ungrammatical, despite its apparent high acceptability. This requires a more systematic approach to assessing intuitions about (1) and close consideration of various alternative cognitive mechanisms that might account for the acceptability of the cases in the face of possible ungrammaticality.

The work reported below assumes that, all other things being equal, it is reasonable to hold the grammar accountable for patterns of judged acceptability. Where observed patterns do not coincide with those predicted by some grammar, it is appropriate to seek an account of the discrepancy in the larger ensemble of mental resources that speaker/hearers bring to language comprehension, in the cognitive processes that realize specifically grammatical knowledge, in the grammar itself, or in some combination of these. These issues are discussed further at the end of the paper.

Experiment 1: Possible Subjacency Effects

The first experiment was designed to determine whether the patterns of judged acceptability obtained with sentences similar to (1) are in reasonable accord with the patterns of grammaticality commonly assumed in the formulation of grammatical theory.

Materials: The target cases are presented in Table I. The Control cases are taken to be uncontroversially acceptable and grammatical. The Specified Subject cases are equally uncontroversially unacceptable and ungrammatical. The status of the other two cases is unclear. The definite cases have sometimes been taken to be acceptable and sometimes

Table I: Materials for Experiment 1

Control:	Why did the Duchess sell Turner's portrait of her father?
Indefinite:	Who did the Duchess sell a portrait of?
Definite:	Who did the Duchess sell the portrait of?
Specified Subject:	Who did the Duchess sell Turner's portrait of?

unacceptable, with corresponding assumptions about grammaticality. The Indefinite cases are patterned on (1), discussed above. Prevailing assumptions about grammaticality in these cases predict that the Indefinite cases will pattern with the Controls, that the Specified Subject cases will be distinctly less acceptable, and that the Definite cases will pattern with either the first set or the second, depending upon whether they are in fact grammatical and acceptable.

There were 24 sets of materials modeled on those in Table I. There were also 96 filler sentences of diverse kinds. Four presentation lists of sentences were constructed so that only one member of each set appeared in each list and so that six items of each of the four types shown in Table I appeared in each list. Thus each subject saw equal numbers of items of each type distributed throughout a much larger list of fillers and no subject saw more than one member of any set.

Methods: For this and all subsequent experiments, the materials were presented to subjects as printed lists. Subjects were asked to read each sentences and to

"...indicate whether the item seems like a fully normal, understandable sentence to you. If it does, please check the box on the far right. If, on the other hand, the sentence seems very odd, awkward or difficult to understand, please check the box on the far left. If your feelings about the sentence are somewhere between these extremes, check one of the middle boxes. THERE ARE NO 'RIGHT' OR

'WRONG' ANSWERS. Please base your responses solely
on your personal judgments, not on rules you may have
learned about what is 'proper' or 'correct' English."
(emphasis in original)

For some experiments a separate machine-scored answer sheet was used.
Subjects responded by way of a four point scale whose extremes were
marked "Odd" and "OK". Subjects were encouraged to respond rapidly
and typically finished the list of 120 sentences, plus additional
background questions, in less than 15 minutes.

Subjects were undergraduate students at The Ohio State University.

Results and Discussion: The results of two separate runs of Experiment
1 with a total of 228 subjects are combined and summarized in Figure 1.
The most important result is that the pairwise difference in acceptability
between the Indefinite and Control cases is highly significant,
$F(1,227)=459.27$, $p<.001$, and indeed is the single largest difference

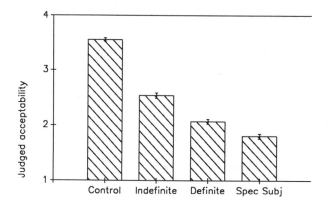

Figure 1: Mean judged acceptability for the four
materials conditions of Experiment 1

observed. The pairwise differences between the Indefinite and Definite
cases and between the Definite and Specified Subject cases, though
numerically smaller, are also highly robust, $p<.001$. The overall decline
in acceptability across the four cases is significant, $F(3,681)=619.69$,
$p<.001$, as is the decline across the Indefinite, Definite and Specified
Subject cases, $p<.001$.

The pattern of results seen in Figure 1 does not fit well with
typical assumptions about the relative acceptability of these kinds of
cases. The Indefinite cases are worse than expected and the difference

between them and the Definite and Specified Subject cases is smaller than expected. One possible view of the pattern in Figure 1 posits that the Indefinite cases are ungrammatical in virtue of being covered by the subjacency generalization and that the decline in acceptability across the Indefinite, Definite and Specified Subject cases reflects increasing specificity in the determiners of the **picture** NPs (Fiengo & Higgenbotham, 1981, Fiengo, 1987). Two alternative hypotheses must be considered. First, the reduced acceptability of the three most impaired cases might result simply from the presence of a preposition at the end of the sentence, regardless of other aspects of the structure of the sentence. Perhaps the common prescriptivist ban on sentences ending in prepositions exerted some influence (despite the instructions to subjects to ignore such considerations). Second, somewhat similarly, it might be that the apparent effect of specificity is not sensitive to the structure in which the determiner occurs but is somehow induced by mere surface variation in the form of the determiner. Neither hypothesis is especially interesting from a linguistic point of view, but they cannot be dismissed out of hand. The second experiment addresses these issues.

Experiment 2: **of** vs. **to**

The strategy of Experiment 2 is to compare cases similar to those used above to others where the prepositional phrase containing the extraction site has **to** as its head and is a sister of the NP to its left, rather than embedded within it. Such cases test the claim about sentence-final prepositions and provide an alternative control case against which to compare the Indefinite cases of Experiment 1.

Materials: A sample set of materials is displayed in Table II. The Control and Indefinite/of cases are drawn from Experiment 1. The Indefinite/to case should be identical to the Indefinite/of case if the

Table II: Materials for Experiment 2

Control:	Why did the Duchess sell Turner's portrait of her father?
Indefinite/of:	Who did the Duchess sell a portrait of?
Indefinite/to:	Who did the Duchess sell a portrait to?
Specified Subject/to:	Who did the Duchess sell Turner's portrait to?

depressed results in the former case result merely from the presence of a preposition at the end of the sentence. The contrast between the Indefinite/to and Specified Subject/to cases likewise tests whether the apparent effect of specificity in Experiment 1 is sensitive to the structural relation of the NP and PP.

Results and Discussion: The most critical result of Experiment 2 is that there is a statistically robust difference between the acceptability of the Indefinite/of and Indefinite/to cases, $F(1,40)=12.93$, $p<.001$. Furthermore, the decline in acceptability from the Control case to the Indefinite/of case is reliably larger than the decline from the Control to the Indefinite/to

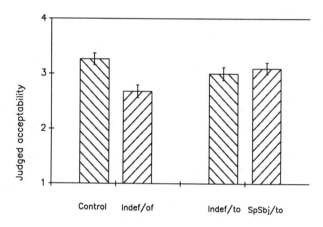

Figure 2: Mean judged acceptability for the four cases of Experiment 2

case, $F(1,40)=12.93$, $p<.001$. This suggests that the unacceptability of the Indefinite/of cases is not to be explained solely by the presence of some preposition at the end of the sentence. This picture is somewhat clouded, however, by the finding that the Indefinite/to cases are also significantly less acceptable than the Control, $F(1,40)=10.20$, $p<.005$. This fact is not explained by either the subjacency or specificity proposals discussed above.

Some support for the specificity proposal is evident in the fact that the Specified Subject/to cases are more, rather than less, acceptable than the Indefinite/to cases. This is opposite to the pattern found in Experiment 1, though the difference here is not robust, $F(1,40)=1.04$, NS. When the PP is outside of the NP, increasing specificity does not compromise acceptability.

The difference between the Control and Indefinite/of cases is robust, $F(1,40)=35.23$, $p<.001$, which replicates Experiment 1. The observed acceptability of the Control cases in Experiment 2 is somewhat lower than that obtained in Experiment 1. Such interexperiment differences and, in general, the absolute numerical values of the acceptability means will not be considered here. There were small differences in the filler sentences used in different experiments, and other minor differences of technique, that may account for any such differences.

In sum, these results are consistent with the claim that the Indefinite cases of Experiment 1 are affected by subjacency and that the acceptability of similar extraction cases is sensitive to the specificity of the NP within which the PP is embedded.

Experiment 3: Depth of Embedding

Another possible confound relevant to the results of Experiment 1 is depth of embedding. Though there is no very clear and generally accepted metric of depth of embedding, nevertheless, it seems clear that the Indefinite/of cases involve extraction from a site that is more deeply embedded in the hierarchical structure of the sentence than is the

Table III: Depth of embedding, bracketing only relevant NPs and Ss.

Why did [the Duchess sell [Turner's portrait of her father] *t*]
Who did [the Duchess sell [a portrait of *t*]]
Who did [the Duchess sell [a portrait] to *t*]
Who did [the Duchess say [Max likes *t*]]

comparable site in the Control sentences or the Indefinite/to cases. Counting only S and NP boundaries, the **of** cases involve extraction from two levels down, while the others require extraction from no more than one level down, as illustrated in Table III.

As a partial control for the possible influence of depth of embedding, Experiment 3 compared the Control/Indefinite contrast of Experiment 1 with pairs contrasting two degrees of embedding where the more deeply embedded case is uncontroversially regarded as acceptable in the linguistic literature, as in the last example in Table III.

Materials: One complete set of materials is illustrated in Table IV. The Subjacency Cases are drawn from Experiment 1. The Shallow Depth Cases involve extraction from the subject of the higher clause, while the

Table IV: Materials for Experiment 3

Subjacency Cases

Shallow: When did the Duchess sell Max's portrait of Bill?
Deep: Who did the Duchess sell a portrait of?

Depth Cases

Shallow: Who said Max likes George?
Deep: Who did the Duchess say Max likes?

Deep cases involve extraction of the object of the lower clause.

Results and Discussion: The results of Experiment 3 are displayed in Figure 3. Most importantly, there is a significant interaction between Depth (Deep vs. Shallow) and Sentence Type (Subjacency Cases vs. Depth Cases), $F(1,27)=5.69$, $p<.05$. This indicates that the difference between the two Subjacency cases is reliably larger than that between the

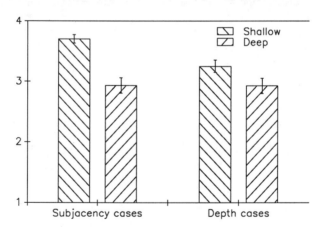

Figure 3: Mean judged acceptability for the four cases of Experiment 3

two Depth cases. There was also a reliable main effect of Depth, $F(1,27)=46.69$, $p<.001$.

This pattern of results is not consistent with the claim that the Control vs. Indefinite contrast of Experiment 1 arose because of a depth of embedding difference between the two extraction sites.

Two notable features of these results are that the Shallow Depth cases are significantly less acceptable than the Shallow Subjacency cases (i.e., the Control cases of Experiment 1), $F(1,27)=27.94$, $p<.001$, and that there is no appreciable difference in acceptability between the two Deep cases. These observations suggest a partial alternative account of the pattern obtained in the first experiment. This account draws a sharp distinction between adjunct extractions (questions with **why, when,** or **where**) and those from argument positions (questions with **who, what,** or **which**), with the latter associated with reduced acceptability and, presumably, greater difficulty. On this account, it was inappropriate in Experiment 1 to use non-argument extractions as controls against which to assess the acceptability of the three cases involving extraction from an argument position. It is, in other words, the distinction between argument and adjunct extraction that best explains the difference between the Control and Indefinite cases of Experiment 1, not the engagement of any effect related to subjacency. This, of course, does not explain the differences among the three cases of argument extraction, nor why the scale of those differences was less than that between the Control and Indefinite conditions.

Further experimental work that will help determine the source of the Control/Indefinite difference in Experiment 1, and which will control for extraction-type, is planned.

Illicit acceptability and its analysis

There are two puzzles implicit in the various findings discussed above. One is why some cases that are regarded as acceptable in the linguistic literature get such poor acceptability ratings with the methods used here.

Another puzzle is that, on either analysis of why the Indefinite cases of Experiment 1 are rated so poorly, some sentence types seem much better than might be expected from one or another point of view. If the results of Experiment 1 are interpreted as evidence that the Indefinite cases are covered by the subjacency generalization, it is surprising that these sentences have been seen as entirely acceptable in the literature. On the other hand, the low ratings of the Indefinites may be due simply to the fact that they involve extraction from an argument position, not to ungrammaticality. On this view, it seems surprising that the Definite and Specified Subject cases were not judged more negatively in Experiment 1. A proponent of this extraction-type analysis must somehow explain why there should be greater differences in judged acceptability when grammatical sentence types are compared to other grammatical types than when grammatical types are compared to ungrammatical types. Thus, from either point of view there seem to be sentences that enjoy a degree of illicit acceptability, i.e., surprisingly high degrees of acceptability associated with ungrammaticality.

Findings such as these suggest as yet undescribed complexities in the relation between strictly grammatical phenomena and the judgments of acceptability on which this study is based. Experiment 4 constitutes a preliminary attempt to identify one potential source of that complexity.

There is a widely held view of the relation between performance phenomena, such as acceptability judgments, and matters of competence, as represented by some grammatical theory. On this view, the standard approach to accounting for many apparent discrepancies between the two is to advert to features of the psychological mechanisms that implement and deploy grammatical knowledge in support of speech behavior and language comprehension. A classic example of this approach appears in the account of doubly center-embedded sentences in Chomsky and Miller, 1963. Here it is maintained that the sentences are grammatical despite their manifest unacceptability on the grounds that their unacceptability arises from characteristic limitations of the memory structures used by the parser. Any discrepancy that can be analyzed in these terms is properly seen as of little or no relevance to grammatical theory. For example, in so far as there might be evidence of informal heuristic mechanisms playing some role in sentence comprehension, this is seen as arising in some way within the mechanisms that implement the grammar.

Another much less widely discussed view situates the linguistic system as but one of several cognitive resources that might be engaged in the course of language comprehension. On this view, the presentation of an utterance will typically engage several discriminable mental competencies and the utterance's effect on the listener might best be viewed as a negotiated result that integrates effects arising from two or more of the participating systems. On this view there are several competing and collaborating kinds of competence and an associated performance theory for each. For example, there are clearly extralinguistic phenomena of deixis. If the competence theory of general deixis turns out to subsume the theory of deixis in language, then the deictic system could be seen as another competency, closely linked to, but also partly independent of, the linguistic system. A similar account might be given of a mechanism that exploits pragmatic knowledge to infer what roles a given set of nouns might play relative to some verb. In that humans clearly have some ability to discern possible sentential interpretations where lexical material is presented with few or no syntactic cues, this too might be seen as another associated but independent competency.

Part of the importance of this second view is that it can lead to a quite different treatment of apparent discrepancies between observed performance and grammatical theory. It becomes possible in this context to ask whether an utterance that is, say, ruled ungrammatical by the grammar-based linguistic component, might nevertheless become acceptable through the intervention of some extralinguistic mechanism (see Bever, 1974, for a discussion of some possible instances where ungrammatical forms may nevertheless be acceptable). On this view the grammatical implications of acceptability are more difficult to discern. The grammar ought to be held accountable only for those utterances whose acceptability does not arise through extra-grammatical means. Thus studies of performance interpreted in this frame have a potential to bear on linguistic theory somewhat more directly than can results interpreted in terms of the more common frame. Experimental observations of performance that argue that a given sentence type comes to be acceptable by way of the involvement of some extragrammatical competency allow grammatical theory to set aside certain sentence types that it would otherwise have to cope with.

Experiment 4: **Which**-effects

The role of Experiment 4 is to examine one suggestion as to how an extragrammatical mechanism might be involved in some cases similar to those in Experiment 1. If the Indefinite cases of Experiment 1 are ungrammatical, this is presumably because grammatically based mechanisms for linking the wh-element and the gap are somehow impaired by the hierarchical configuration of the sentence. If such sentences were to have their interpretability and thus acceptability restored by some extragrammatical mechanism, it is apparently the filler-gap relation that this other mechanism must address. It does not seem far-fetched to suggest that a relevant mechanism could be defined along the following lines: it would maintain only a flat (i.e., non-hierarchical) lexical representation of the utterance and would simply look for overt cues to fillers and gaps. On finding a filler and a gap, it would associate them in some way that would facilitate recovery of an analysis for the entire utterance. If this mechanism were to operate in an informal and heuristic fashion, its performance would likely improve with surface features that somehow made the elements of the filler-gap more salient or conspicuous. Thus, the essential idea of Experiment 4 is simply to manipulate the saliency of the wh-element in sentences like those used in

Experiment 1 to determine whether more salient wh-elements are associated with higher acceptability.

Materials: The materials for Experiment 4 were in part similar to those of Experiment 1. Pairs of sentences of the Indefinite and Specified Subject types of Experiment 1 were matched to other pairs that were identical in every respect except that in the second pair the **who** or **what** was replaced by a **which** phrase. The **which** phrase was identical for the two members of the pair. A sample set of items appears in Table V. The expectation is that if the **which** phrase makes the filler more conspicuous, acceptability will improve in the cases including this structure.

Table V: Sample Materials for Experiment 4

What Cases

What did Sue resent a comment about?
What did Sue resent Tom's comment about?

Which Cases

Which of the new pledges did Sue resent a comment about?
Which of the new pledges did Sue resent Tom's comment about?

Results and Discussion: The results of Experiment 4 are displayed in Figure 4. The most important result is that there is no significant improvement in acceptability in the presence of the **which** phrases,

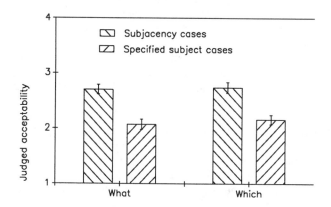

Figure 4: Mean judged acceptability for the four cases of Experiment 4

F(1,66)=2.18, NS, though the experiment did replicate the difference between the Indefinite and Specified Subject cases of Experiment 1, F(1,66)=140.90, p<.001.

These results of course do not support the suggestion that more salient wh-elements are associated with improved acceptability. Close informal examination of the by-sentence results of Experiment 4 suggests, however, a somewhat different picture. Though further experimentation will be required to assess the generality of these effects, it appears that there were numbers of specific materials sets within which the sentences with **which** were more acceptable. The aim of further investigation will be to identify factors that distinguish such sentences from others that did not show a **which** effect.

A multimodal view of language comprehension

The theoretical frame of this study is somewhat different than that conventionally assumed in linguistic and psycholinguistic work that touches on these issues. In the standard view, linguistic competence is imperfectly represented in language behavior due to a variety of phenomena that arise in the psychological and neurological mechanisms that implement the speaker/hearer's knowledge of language. Usually, such phenomena do not motivate changes in the theory of competence any more than the observation that people often make mathematical errors, even systematic ones, would motivate a change in the principles of mathematics. The underlying model of language comprehension might be termed unimodal; it assumes that all utterances are interpreted via the grammar and that all departures from grammatically defined norms must be accounted for by reference to the character and limitations of the mechanisms that apply the grammar.

There is, however, another potential source of discrepancies between the form of language behavior and the principles underlying that behavior, as captured by linguistic theory. It seems quite plausible, especially in language comprehension, that there may be more than one cognitive system that can participate. Thus, while there surely is a parser that implements a grammar, there may also be one or more other cognitive systems that can be involved in comprehension, either in collaboration with the parser/grammar or more independently in cases where the parser/grammar fails to provide an analysis. The availability of such a mechanism is suggested by the seeming facility with which humans can sometimes cope with ill-formed utterances in the speech of immigrants, very young children, and individuals with anatomical or neurological impairments of speech.

Thus, an alternative view is available whenever some discrepancy between grammar and behavior is apparent. On this view, the discrepancy may arise because of some interaction between the core linguistic system and some other system, viewed as an alternative kind of competence, i.e., not as some manifestation of the mechanisms that implement grammatical knowledge. This might be termed a multimodal account of comprehension.

For any given problem, the matter can be put as a question: What is it about this particular discrepancy between grammar and behavior that shows that it is best attributed to implementational aspects of the linguistic system rather than to some interaction between the linguistic system and some other component of the cognitive system?

Where there is no compelling reason to take the implementational view, it seems necessary to consider whether the result in question may bear on linguistic theory, in particular, competence theory. That is, where discrepancies can be attributed to some other mechanism, then they need not be addressed by the theory of grammar. But where there are persistent conflicts between observed performance and what a grammar implies, and no convincing basis for attributing the difference to some other cognitive mechanism, it may be reasonable to hold the grammar responsible for those discrepancies and to consider whether it might be appropriate to modify the grammar to account for the obtained results.

As noted above, one of the arguments for a multimodal account of comprehension is that it offers some hope of accounting for the apparent resiliency of the language comprehension system. It seems plausible to suggest that a collaborating ensemble of mechanisms, each exploiting a different aspect of the information available in the utterance and its context, should, in general, be able to cope with anomalies in the input better than a more unified system. It is worth emphasizing, however, that any resiliency gained in this fashion is available only where the several mechanisms enjoy a high degree of autonomy. The more tightly the work of a given module is linked to that of another, the more vulnerable it will be to anomalies in the input that disrupt the work of the module on which it depends. It is just in so far as each module can make a useful contribution to the analysis of an utterance in the face of failures elsewhere that the multimodal model of language comprehension offers a better account of resiliency.

40

Notes

1.   The work reported in this paper was supported in part by a grant
from the National Institutes of Health (1 R01 NS22606-01).   I am
grateful to Tom Bever, Helen Cairns, Bob Fiengo, Bob Levine, Dana
McDaniels, Craige Roberts, and Michael Studdert-Kennedy for much wise
counsel relevant to these matters.   All responsibility for errors of fact or
judgment that may be found here of course remains entirely with the
author.   Diana Smetters, Ken Williams, Rick Neighbarger, Andy Gudgel,
and Grace Kuo have provided invaluable assistance with various aspects
of the experimental work reported here.

2.   Mailing address: Rm 204 Cunz Hall, Columbus, OH, 43210.   E-
mail: COWART-W@OSU-20.IRCC.OHIO-STATE.EDU.   After September
1, 1989: University of Southern Maine, Portland, ME 04103.

References

Bever, T. (1974) The ascent of the specious, or, There's a lot we don't
        know about mirrors. In Cohen, D. (Ed.) Explaining Linguistic
        Phenomena. Washington, D.C.: Hemisphere Publishing. Pp. 173-
        200.
Chomsky, N. (1973) Conditions on transformations. In S.R. Anderson
        and P. Kiparsky (Eds.) A Festschrift for Morris Halle. New York:
        Holt, Rinehart and Winston. Pp. 232-286.
Chomsky, N. (1981) Lectures on government and binding. Dordrecht:
        Foris.
Chomsky, N. (1986) Barriers. Cambridge: MIT Press.
Chomsky, N. and Miller, G. (1963) Introduction to the formal analysis of
        natural languages. In Luce, Bush and Galanter (Eds.), Handbook
        of Mathematical Psychology, Vol. 2, Ch. 11. New York: John
        Wiley & sons.
Fiengo, R. (1987) Definiteness, specificity, and familiarity. Linguistic
        Inquiry, 18, 163-166.
Fiengo, R. and Higgenbotham, J. (1981) Opacity in NP. Linguistic
        Analysis, 7, 395-421.
Lasnik, H. and Uriagereka, J. (1988) A Course in GB Syntax.
        Cambridge, MA: MIT Press.
Riemsdijk, H. & Williams, E. (1986) Introduction to the Theory of
        Grammar. Cambridge, MA: MIT Press.

The Russian Palatalizations and The Nature of Morphophonological Rules

Bill J. Darden
University of Chicago

One of the earliest changes that took place after the differentiation of the Slavic languages from the rest of Indo-European was the so-called first palatalization of velars. In this change, velars changed to alveopalatals before front vowels and *j* . Despite its age, this change survives as a productive alternation in word formation in all the modern Slavic languages. Examples from Russian, which will be the focus of this talk, are:

znak 'sign'	značit' 'mean'
drug 'friend'	družit' 'be friends with'
grex 'sin'	grešit' 'to sin'

Because *k* under certain conditions became *c,* there is a similar alternation between *c* and *č.*

nemec 'German'   o-nemečit' 'germanicize'

To say that an alternation is productive, however, is not to say that it is phonological. In the history of linguistic theory, the treatment of this alternation has been a central issue in defining the boundaries between what is phonological and what is not.

Theories that differentiate between pure phonology and morphophonology treat the velar palatalizations as morphophonological for the simple reason that the relevant phonological environment was eliminated many centuries ago. Certain suffixes productively condition the change, but it is not because of their surface phonological content. The nonphonological interpretation goes at least as far back as Baudouin de Courtenay (1895). Baudouin called such alternations 'correlations,' which he contrasted to 'divergences,' which we would call phonological rules. He says (in Stankiewicz' 1972 translation), "A correlation is an alternation in which the phonetic difference is connected (associated) with some psychological difference between forms and words, that is, with some morphological or semasiological difference." Divergence "is independent of psychological (morphological or semasiological) factors."

41

The notion that morphophonology is part of the sign system of language, rather than part of the phonology, was greatly expanded by the followers of Roman Jakobson (cf. Stankiewicz 1979).

The versions of generative phonology which arose in the 1960's denied the significance of the distinction between morphophonology and phonology. Theodore Lightner's 1965 dissertation attempted to show that the velar palatalizations, as well as the simple palatalization of dentals and labials, are still conditioned by underlying front vowels.

In the theory of lexical phonology, there is a distinction between cyclic and post-cyclic rules which is close to the traditional notion of morphophonological versus phonological rules. The cyclic rules, however, are still treated as phonological in nature, and abstract phonology is used to make them much more phonological in appearance than would be possible otherwise. Within this theory, David Pesetsky (1979) proposed rules to account for the palatalizations in Russian which are essentially identical to those of Lightner.

In this talk I hope to show that it is unreasonable and uninsightful, if not impossible, to treat the change of velars to alveopalatals as a phonologically conditioned alternation in Russian. I will also attempt to clarify what we mean or should mean when we say that morphophonological rules are part of the morphology of a language, rather than part of the phonology.

The first part of the paper will be devoted to arguing that the velar change is not phonologically conditioned. We will see that:

(1) Surface front vowels do not trigger the change of velars to alveopalatals.

(2) Suffixes which begin with putative front vowels cannot be arranged within the theory of level-ordered morphology so that those which are added at one level trigger the change, while those which are added later do not.

(3) The putative correlation between the velar change and the simple palatalization of dentals and labials, which was used by Lightner to justify abstract underlying forms with front vowels, does not hold.

(4) The abstract vowels which are used by Lightner and Pesetsky to account for both vowel/zero alternations and velar palatalizations are best treated as vowel insertion in the modern language. Where they are not inserted, there is really nothing there to condition the change of the consonant.

Turning to the first point, we find it immediately necessary to resort to abstract phonology to claim that the velar palatalizations in Russian are synchronically conditioned by front vowels. Russian has five surface vocalic phonemes: /a e i o u/. The change is found before suffixes which begin with all five vowels, as well as before suffixes which in the surface begin with consonants, e.g.:

jug 'south'	južak 'south wind'
lgat' 'lie'	lžec 'liar'
drug 'friend'	družit' 'be friends with'
lgat' 'to lie'	lžëš 'you lie'
reka 'river'	rečuška 'river' [affectionate diminutive]
sapog 'boot'	sapožnik 'bootmaker'

In the standard Jakobsonian treatment, the feature front/back is not even a distinctive feature in the system. In the system advocated by Lightner and Pesetsky, all /e/ and any /i/ which palatalizes a preceding dental or labial is considered to be an underlying front vowel. Even if we consider these vowels to be front, we find that they do not consistently trigger the velar palatalization.

Suffixes which palatalize dentals and labials, but fail to change velars to palatals include both native and borrowed affixes. examples are:

Loc. sing -e	durak 'fool'	durake /durak'é/
	sud 'court'	sude /sud'é/
	bob 'bean'	bobe /bob'é/

Imperative -i	peku 'I bake'	peki /p'ik'í/
	vedu 'I lead'	vedi /v'id'í/
	grebu 'I row'	grebi /gr'ib'í/

Possessive adjective formant -in

	Ol'ga	Ol'gin /ól'g'in/
	sestra 'sister'	sestrin /s'éstr'in/
	baba 'woman'	babin /báb'in/

The suffix -in-sk- (a variant of -sk-) which forms adjectives from place names:

	Baku	bakinskij /bak'ínsk'ij/
	Istra	istrinskij /ístr'insk'ij/

The suffix -*(e)c* which forms nouns for inhabitants of places (cf. Darden 1988):

Place	Adjective	Inhabitant
Don (river)	donskoj	donec /dan'éc/
Kačug	kačugskij	kačugec /kačúg'ic/
Ključi	ključevskij	kliučevec /kl'učév'ic/

The suffix -*ič* which forms patronymics

Foma	Fomič /fom'íč/ 'Foma's son'
Luka	Lukič /luk'íč/ 'Luka's son'

The borrowed suffix -*ist*

značok 'badge, pin'	značkist 'one who merits a badge'
štab 'staff'	štabist /štab'íst'/ 'staff officer'
topeda 'torpedo'	torpedist /tarp'id'íst/ 'torpedoman'

Suffixes with this behavior which begin with other vowels are:

The adverbial participle ending -*a*

grebu 'I row'	grebja /gr'ib'á/ 'rowing'
vedu 'I lead'	vedja /v'id'á/ 'leading'
žgu 'I burn'	žgja /žg'á/ 'burning'

The suffix -*or* (French -*eur*)

panika 'panic'	panikër /pan'ik'ór/ 'panic monger'
rutina 'routine'	rutinër /rut'in'ór/ 'rigid person'
stereotip 'pattern	stereotipër 'pattern maker'

It seems obvious that we cannot claim that all suffixes which begin with front vowels condition the change of velars to palatals. Within the theory of level-ordered morphology and lexical phonology, we could save the situation if we could claim that the suffixes which do trigger the change belong to a different level from that of the suffixes which merely palatalize velars. I.e. we could add level one suffixes, change the velars to alveopalatals, then add the suffixes which fail to change the velars. This involves a claim that the suffixes which trigger the alveopalatal transformation will be closer to the root than those that fail to do so.

To check this possibility, we can take formations which combine the above suffixes with suffixes which do trigger the change to alveopalatals. The suffixes which we will use are the suffix -*(o)k-a*, which forms diminutives from feminine nouns and female counterparts to masculine nouns, the suffixes -*(o)k* and -*ik-*, which form diminutives and lexical derivatives from masculine nouns. The (o) in *-(o)k-a* indicates that there is a vowel/zero alternation before the *k*, a phenomenon that we will return to later. Examples which show the alternation are:

reka 'river'　　　　rečka [diminutive]
noga 'leg'　　　　nožka [dim]
siberjak 'siberian' sibirjačka [f] 'siberian'
talnaxec 'person from Talnax'
　　　　　　　　talnaška [f] 'female from Talnax'

drug 'friend'　　　družok [dim.]
znak 'sign'　　　　značok 'badge'

bank 'bank'　　　　bančik [affectionate dim.]
zvuk 'sound'　　　zvučik [aff. dim.]
kuznec 'smith'　　kuznečik [dim.]

These suffixes can be combined with the first set in a variety of orders. From *znak* we get *značok*, then, adding *-ist*, *značkist* 'badge earner', then we can add feminizing *-(o)k-* and diminutive *-(o)k-*, in the locative case we get *značkistočke*, morphologically:

znak-(o)k-ist-(o)k-(o)k-e

which yields:

znač-k-ist-oč-k-e

The first, third, and fourth suffixes change the velars, while the second and fifth do not.

Similarly we can get *bakinskij* from Baku, the masculine and feminine nouns for inhabitants are *bakinec* and *bakinka*. The respective diminutives are *bakinčik* and *bakinočka*. The locatives are:

bak-in-(e)c-ik-e > bak-in-č-ik-e
bak-in-(o)k-(o)k-e > bak-in-oč-k-e

For *bakinčike*, the first, second and fourth suffixes fail to change velars, while the third does. For *bakinočke*, the first and fourth fail to change velars, while the second and third do.

It would seem that level-ordered morphology does not help.

At this point it would be fair to conclude that it is illegitimate to claim that at any level of analysis, all suffixes with front vowels trigger the change of velars to alveopalatals. It might still be the case, however, that there is a correlation between the velar change and front vowels. A weaker claim might be that all suffixes which trigger the change have underlying front vowels or *j*.

I have already mentioned that on the surface this is not true. One justification for the use of abstract phonological forms with underlying front vowels has been the correlation between the velar change and the palatalization of dentals and labials. Historically, front vowels did trigger both changes, so there are indeed a substantial number of suffixes with both behaviors. There are also a substantial number of affixes which fail to trigger either change (the suffixes which began with original back vowels). One could claim that we are missing a generalization if we fail to postulate phonological similarities to account for this correlation.

However, we have already seen that there are suffixes which palatalize dentals and labials, but fail to change velars to alveopalatals. There is also a small class of suffixes which change velars, but fail to palatalize dentals and labials. This means that all four logical combinations are attested. There are suffixes which have both behaviors, suffixes which have neither, and suffixes which have each behavior in the absence of the other.

Suffixes which trigger velar change without palatalizing anterior consonants are:

The suffix *-ušk-a*, which forms affectionate diminutives.

reka 'river'	rečuška
ded 'grandfather'	deduška
baba 'grandmother	babuška
knjaz' 'prince'	knjazjuška
djadja 'uncle'	djadjuška

Various suffixes of the shape *-(o)k-*. This is either one suffix with a variety of functions or several homophonous morphemes. We have already seen several examples. Those which are productive are:

Masculine diminutives and lexical derivatives:

byk 'bull'	byčok [dim]
bog 'god'	božok [dim]
gost' 'guest'	gostëk [dim]
zjat' 'son-in-law'	zjatëk [dim]
kub 'boiler'	kubok 'beaker'
sad 'orchard'	sadok [dim]

Neuter diminutives:

oblako 'cloud'	oblačko [dim]
uxo 'ear'	uško [dim]
pivo 'beer'	pivko [dim]
zoloto 'gold'	zolotko [dim]

vedro 'bucket'   vedërko, [gen. pl.] vedërok [dim]

Diminutives and lexical derivatives in -(o)k-a from feminine nouns and masculine second declension nouns. This suffix preserves the underlying palatalization of second declension nouns, but dispalatalizes palatalized dentals and labials at the end of third declension stems. In new formations palatalized /l'/ and /n'/ are preserved.

djadja 'uncle'   djad'ka [dim]
batja 'father'   bat'ka 'father'
zemlja 'land'   zemel'ka [dim]
berëza 'birch'   berëzka [dim]
izgorod' 'fence'   izgorodka [dim]
cerkov' 'church'   cerkovka [dim]
korob 'basket'   korobka 'box'
ruka 'hand'   ručka [dim]
noga 'leg'   nožka [dim]
postel' 'bed'   postel'ka [dim]
šinel' 'overcoat'   šinelka/šinel'ka [dim]
pristan' 'dock'   pristan'ka [coll. dim]
portfel' [m]'briefcase'   portfel'ka [dim]

Feminine counterparts in -(o)k-a from masculine nouns. This suffix at least dispalatalizes the palatalized /r'/ in the suffix -ar'- , and the final /b'/ of golub' 'pigeon'. /l'/ is not dispalatalized.

golub' 'pigeon'   golubka
pastux 'shepherd'   pastuška
sibirjak 'siberian'   sibirjačka
artist 'performer'   artistka
kuxar' 'cook'   kuxarka
kosar' 'mower'   kosarka
učitel' 'teacher'   učitel'ka [substandard]
prijatel' 'friend'   prijatel'ka [colloquial]

Deverbal derivatives in -(o)k-a.
These derivatives have unpalatalized labials and dentals, but show the change of velars to alveopalatals. Here we may consider the dentals and labials to be actively dispalatalized.

seku 'I cut'   sečka 'cutting'
strigu 'I shear'   strižka 'shearing'
pereorientirovat'   pereorientirovka 'reorientation'
rubit' /rub'it'/   rubka 'cutting'

vygruzit' /vigruz'it'/   vygruzka 'unloading'

Combined with the suffixes which palatalize dentals and labials but fail to change velars to alveopalatals, these suffixes force us to consider the velar palatalizations to be a phenomenon independent of the palatalization of dentals and labials. We should not want to attribute the two alternations to a common abstract phonological environment.

We can now turn to the treatment of vowel/zero alternations in Russian. Pesetsky (1979, 1985), following Lightner, uses abstract vowels to account for the alternations. He uses two vowels, one which palatalizes preceding anterior consonants and turns velars into alveopalatals, one which does nothing to the preceding consonant. I would like to argue that the proper underlying representation of a vowel/zero alternation is literally zero, i.e. nothing. If that is the case, there is no vowel there to trigger the velar change, and it must be morphologically conditioned.

It is impossible to adequately discuss vowel/zero alternations in a brief talk. An entire Harvard dissertation was devoted to them (Klagstad 1954). The best published description is in Townsend (1968; 60-80). Townsend, like most Prague-School linguists, uses an arbitrary mark to indicate the locus of a vowel/zero alternation. Once he has that mark, however, he can predict with reasonable accuracy when it will be a vowel or zero, what vowel it will be, and whether, when the vowel is inserted, the preceding consonant will be palatalized.

I would go one step further, and say that for all reasonably productive cases, we can predict the locus of the alternation as well. Quite simply, stems have vowel insertion between the final two consonants of the stem, and prefixes have vowel insertion after their final consonant. In noun stems the vowel is inserted before a zero ending or before a consonant-initial suffix. This means that for stems, all we need to know is whether the morpheme in question allows vowel insertion. This can be considered part of its lexical behavior, rather than part of its phonological make up. There is an important difference between treating the marking for the alternation as a morphemic feature and treating it as an underlying phonological (or morphophonological) entity.

We can even go a long way toward predicting which stems will have vowel insertion.

(1) Stems with no vowel will allow V insertion.

(2) Stems which end in a consonant plus sonorant will regularly have vowel insertion,

(3) Feminine stems with a k-final cluster will regularly have vowel insertion.

(4) Nominal and denominal-adjectival derivational affixes which consist of a single consonant will have vowel insertion before the consonant.

(5) When a cluster of dental or labial plus dental sonorant is broken up, the initial consonant will be palatalized.

(6) The inserted vowel will be /e/ before /c/ and between palatalized consonants, otherwise it will be /o/.

The few exceptions to (5) are all morphophonological archaisms which have preserved the behavior of actual jers. They include *son*, gen. *sna* 'sleep', *dno*, pl. *don'ja* 'bottom', *posol, posla* 'emissary', *pës, psa* 'dog', and the adjective *zol, zla* 'evil'.

On the other hand, these rules account for historically innovative vowel insertions like :

sestra	gen. pl.	sest'or
vedro	gen. pl.	ved'or
ogon'	gen sing.	ogn'a
doska	gen pl.	dosok
maska	gen. pl..	masok
freska	gen. pl.	fresok

A word like *ogonëček* 'fire [dim]' is morphophonemically:
  ogn'-k-k-Ø
Marking the loci of vowel insertion with * (This is not a step in the derivation):
  og*n'-*k-*k-Ø
Vowel insertion:
  ogon'-ok-ok
Velar palatalization:
  ogon'-oč-ok
Unstressed *o* after *č* merges with *e*, both in spelling (as *e*) and in pronunciation (as /i/), yielding: ogon'óček

Words like *metr* 'meter' and *igra* (gen. pl. *igr*) are simply exceptions. Exceptions are most often found in the nom. sing., which are learned rather than generated by rule. The gen. pl. is much more regular. Exceptions in the gen. pl. are mostly like *igr*, where it is difficult to distinguish between an unstressed vowel after the velar (igor [igər]) and no vowel at all.

Verbs, as is usual in Russian, are more complex. Stems with no vowel insert a vowel before zero endings. The past tense *-l-*, unlike nominal affixes, neither conditions vowel insertion in a root nor has vowel insertion to its left. After a consonant and before a zero ending, where, if it were a noun, we would expect V insertion, the -*l*- simply drops, as in:

p'ok-l-Ø > p'ok 'he baked'

Verbal prefixes which end in a consonant allow vowel insertion to the right of the consonant. The vowel is always *o*. The vowel is regularly inserted before stems which have no vowel or stems which are of the shape CC{e/a}(j)-.

If the initial cluster of the verbal root is broken up by vowel insertion, then the vowel is not inserted after the prefix. Thus we get from:

	pod-žg-l-Ø	pod-žg-l-a
V insertion in root:	pod-žog-l	-------
V insertion in prefix	-------	podo-žg-l-a
l drop / C_ Ø	pod žog	podožgla

This may make it necessary to treat V insertion as cyclic, or as working out from the root in both directions. However, the V-insertion in prefixes is just idiosyncratic enough that we might consider it a separate rule, ordered after the other insertions.

In addition to the above conditions, the prefix *s*- has vowel insertion before clusters which begin with /s/ or /z/, as in *soskočit'* 'jump off'. Any additional deviations from the above rules are probably best considered lexical idiosyncrasies that are to be left for the dictionary.

If this analysis is justifiable, then in formations like:

bereg 'bank'	berež-n-yj [adj]
ruka 'hand'	ruč-k-a [dim]
sapog 'book'	sapož-nik 'bootmaker'

the suffixes are -*n*-, -*k*-, and -*n'ik*-. There are no suffix-initial vowels, and the velar palatalization must be conditioned morphologically.

The Nature of Morphophonological Rules

If morphophonological rules are not phonologically motivated, even in the restricted sense of Lexical Phonology, then we should ask what their grammatical function is. In my opinion, too much is made of the semiotic function of morphophonology in the rhetoric of Prague School linguistics. I agree that morphophonological rules are morphological in nature, but morphology is both form and function. Morphophonology is much more formal than functional.

It certainly makes no sense to claim that the various suffixes which trigger the velar palatalization in Russian share some semiotic function. They do not. What they share is a formal property. The diminutive suffix -*k*- has two formal properties. It contains the segment *k* and it conditions velar palatalization. It makes about as much sense to talk about the semiotic function of the palatalization as to talk about the general function of the segment *k*. The morphophonological behavior and the segment are formal constituents of the morpheme, but it is the morpheme which has semiotic content.

This does not mean that morphophonological rules have no sign value. It is just that they derive their sign value from the fact that they are consituents of signs, as do segments.[1] It is instructive here to look at a derivative like *sapožnik*, 'bootmaker', from *sapog*, boot'. Here we might say that the derivational process involves the addition of the suffix -*n'ik*- and the velar palatalization. In discussing the sign value of the various components, however, it would be wrong to equate the morphophonological change with the formant -*n'ik*. It is more on a par with one of the three segments *n'*, *i*, or *k*. In this particular case, it is probably even less important. If we eliminate one of the segments, we lose the meaning. If we eliminate the rule, we get **sapognik*, which, while grammatically ill-formed, is possibly comprehensible. In other cases, however, we find otherwise homonymous affixes which differ only in their morphophonological behavior. The affectionate diminutive suffix -*uška*, mentioned above, takes presuffixal accent, while the pejorative -*úška* takes suffixal accent, creating the mininal pair *réčuška/rečúška*.

When we say that rules are closer to segments than to morphemes in sign value, we are not saying that they are incapable of directly conveying meaning. As formative elements, rules can create alternations which independently mark grammatical oppositions. This is the case with Germanic umlaut, when it is the sole indicator of a singular-plural opposition. However, segments can also function in this way. Morphemes are often one segment in length. It is umlaut in a particular construction that differentiates plural from singular stems in German. There is no generalizable function that links this to other instances of umlaut, such as the comparative of adjectives or the second and third singular of verbs.

The analogy between the function of rules and the function of segments is particularly apt for word formation. Dennis Ward, in fact, proposed that we could symbolize the various palatalizing behaviors of Russian morphemes by writing either one or two *j*'s at the beginning of the morpheme. This is similar to the gymnastics that Lightner went through to create shared phonological content for affixes which trigger palatalization. I object to this on esthetic grounds, but it would be acceptable as long as one clearly understands that what he is doing is formal morphology and not phonology. Ward, I think, understands this.

There is at least one way, however, that rules differ from segments. This shows up primarily in inflection, although it may play a role in derivation as well. When the rule in question creates two or more allomorphs of the inflectional stem, the rule implements an alternation, and the two allomorphs constitute a mini paradigm. Because of their paradigmatic aspect, rules can get firmly attached to paradigms. In this sense, they are not just constituent parts of words or morphemes; they are constituent parts of paradigms. I have argued (Darden 1981) that in Greenlandic noun inflection, the distinctions in declensional classes are distinctions in complexes of rules rather than differences in complexes of endings. In Slavic as well, paradigms are often complexes of rules and endings.

It is in this interplay with paradigmatic structure that rules seem to have more than just a formal role in the formation of words. We have seen that vowel/zero alternations work differently in nouns and verbs in Russian. It is often the case that rules can be limited to specific kinds of paradigms, or may be eliminated from specific kinds.

This aspect of the Slavic palatalizations is brought out very clearly in Stankiewicz (1966). Slavic had two historically distinct regressive palatalizations of velars before front vowels. We have already seen data from the first. After the first palatalization, new sequences of velars plus front vowel were created when diphthongs in **ai* became *æ* (generally in transliteration written *ě*). Under poorly understood conditions, **ai* could yield *i* in word-final position. These newly derived sequences of velar plus front vowel, as well as borrowed items, underwent the second regressive palatalization.

In Old Russian the second palatalization resulted in alternations between velars and palatalized dentals, as in:

Nom.	Locative
ruka 'hand'	rucě

noga 'leg'   nozě
soxa 'plough'   sosě

The change of the diphthong was a synchronically nonrecoverable change, so the choice of which palatalization rule to apply in a given circumstance was grammatically conditioned.

Stankiewicz points out that in inflection, the first palatalization was characteristic of verbal paradigms (*pomogu,* 'I help,' *pomožeši* 'you help') while the second palatalization was characteristic of nominal declension (see above). This relationship was reversed in the verbal imperative, which had the second palatalization (*pomozi* 'help') and the vocative (*bože* 'god!'), which had the first. This pattern was due to historical accident, but there are some subsequent changes which indicate that it was integrated into the grammar. The possessive adjectives with the suffix -*in-* should have reflected the first palatalization, but this was eliminated in prehistoric times in favor of the second. E.g. *Vol'zin"* from *Vol'ga, (=Ol'ga),* found in the Primary Chronicle (Stender-Petersen 1954: 19, note 61). Since the possessive adjective acted semantically and to some extent syntactically as an inflected form of the noun (it functioned like a genitive and could be conjoined with one), this could be seen as a spread of the second declension from the noun inflection. Russian later eliminated the second palatalization everywhere, but Ukrainian, which kept the second palatalization in the noun, has replaced it by the first palatalization in the imperative of the verb.

The classic case of a morphophonological rule taking over a major role in an inflectional paradigm is of course Germanic umlaut. In Germanic, the merger of vowels in final syllables removed all traces of phonological conditioning for umlaut in the noun inflection. This left only morphological conditioning, and the rule was reorganized to reflect the singular vs. plural opposition.

It is interesting to note that the morphological function of German umlaut and the Slavic velar palatalizations would be expressed in a formal grammar. The rule for umlaut must mention the plural of nouns, and a proper description of the second velar palatalization in Old Russian would say that it takes place before front vowels in noun inflection and in the imperative of verbs.

When morphological categories appear in the environments of rules, those rules obviously serve as subsidiary signs of the categories. This does not mean, however, that it will profit us to look for direct semiotic function in every nonautomatic alternation that we find.[2] Particulary in word-formational systems, we will probably profit more from the study of morphophonology if we look at it as part of a formal system,

If morphophonology is primarily formal, rather than functional, we might well ask why we have it at all. In part, the answer is that we have it by accident. Phonology becomes morphophonology as the result of historical change. Languages do undergo morphologically motivated repair, and that repair may include simplifying or eliminating some of the morphophonology. It may also make the morphological conditioning for rules more rational, as was the case with umlaut. Basically, however, languages are learned as they are, and are pretty stable.

At any given point in its history, the morphophonology of a language serves to help define what is and is not a well formed utterence **from a morphological point of view.** If I had to characterize in one sentence the difference between morphophonology and phonology, I would say that phonology makes things pronounceable, or, in the case of casual speech, more easily pronounceable, while morphophonology makes words grammatical.

Footnotes

1) There is an excellent discussion of this aspect of the sign value of morphophonological rules in Dressler (1985, Chapter 10).
2) An extreme case of this practice is found in Shapiro(1983).

Bibliography

Baudouin de Courtenay, J. 1895. Versuch einer Theorie phonetischer Alternationen. Strassburg-Cracow. translated as: An Attempt at a Theory of Phonetic Alternations, in Stankiewicz 1972, 144-212.

Darden, Bill J. 1988. Truncation and/or Transderivational Constraints in Russian Word-formation. CLS 24.

_____ 1981. On Arguments for Abstract Vowels in Greenlandic. CLS 17. 110-121.

Dressler, Wolfgang U. 1985. Morphonology: The Dynamics of Derivation. Ann Arbor: Karoma.

Lightner, Theodore. 1965. Segmental Phonology of Modern Standard Russian. Unpublished MIT dissertation.

_____ 1972. Problems in the Theory of Phonology, Volume 1. Champaign: Linguistic Research Inc.

_____ 1973. On Vowel-Zero Alternations in Russian. M.S. Flier, ed. Slavic Forum: Esays in Linguistics and Literature. The Hague: Mouton.

Pesetsky, David. 1979. Russian Morphology and Lexical Theory. Unpublished MIT ms.

_____ 1985. Morphology and Logical Form. LI. 16. 2. 193-246.

Shapiro, Michael. 1983. The Sense of Grammar. Bloomington: Indiana University Press.

Stankiewicz, Edward. 1967. Opposition and Hierachy in Morphophonemic Alternations. For Roman Jakobson. 1895-1905. Reprinted in Stankiewicz 1979. 1-13.

_____ 1966.Slavic Morphophonemics in its Typological and Diachronic Aspects. Current Trends in Linguistics 3. 495-520. Revised and reprinted in Stankiewicz 1979. 42-72.

_____ 1972. A Baudouin de Courtenay Anthology. Bloomington: Indiana University Press.

_____ 1979. Studies in Slavic Morphophonemics and Accentology. Ann Arbor: Michigan Slavic Publications.

Stender-Petersen, Ad. 1954. Anthology of Old Russian Literature. New York: Columbia University Press.

Ward, Dennis. 1972. Softening in the Morphophonemics of Russian. D.S. Worth, ed. The Slavic Word. The Hague: Mouton. 215-31.

Morphological Change and Internal Syntax in Eskimo.[1]

Willem J. de Reuse

University of Iowa

1. Introduction.

In this paper, I will assume that the rich affixal morphology of Eskimo can be divided into three types: (1) derivational morphology, (2) a type I will call 'internal syntax', and (3) inflectional morphology. Then, I will argue that there is a historical tendency for affixes of the 'internal syntax' to evolve into either derivational or inflectional affixes, and I will provide a possible explanation for these tendencies. The examples given are from the literature and my own fieldwork on the Central Siberian Yupik Eskimo language (henceforth CSY), spoken on Chukotka peninsula, in the Soviet Far East, and on St. Lawrence Island, Alaska, but the facts discussed here are valid for all Eskimo languages.

Before focusing on the main arguments of this paper, it will be helpful to give a brief overview of Eskimo morphology. As seen in the formula in (1), the Eskimo word contains: one <u>base</u> (or stem); zero, one or several suffixes called <u>postbases</u> in the literature on Eskimo, an obligatory inflectional <u>ending</u>, marking, for nouns, case, number, and sometimes person and number of the possessor, and marking, for verbs, mood and person and number of the subject, as well as person and number of the direct object if the verb is transitive; and finally zero, one, or several <u>enclitics,</u> which are suffixes phonologically bound to the preceding word, but that are functioning as independent discourse marking or conjunctional particles.

(1)   base + postbases^n + ending + enclitics^m
              0   0

With rare exceptions, the ordering of the <u>postbases</u> is based on the semantic principle that a postbase occurring on the right has scope over everything to the left of it. In example (2), the base is the verb *yughagh-* 'to pray', which is followed by a postbase deriving a noun from the verb 'to pray', *-vig-* 'place to V', resulting in *yughaghvig-* 'church'. This is followed by a postbase *-ghllag-* 'big N', deriving a noun from another noun; *yughaghvigllag-* is thus 'big church'. This is followed by a postbase deriving a verb from a noun *-nge-* 'to acquire N', resulting in *yughaghvigllange-* 'to acquire a big church'. Then the verbal postbase *-yug-* 'to want to V' follows, resulting in *yughaghvigllangyug-* 'to want to acquire a big church'. Then follows a verb inflectional ending, which can be segmented into *-tugh-* , marking Indicative mood, and *-t*, marking third person plural subject. The word ends with the enclitic particle *=llu* 'also, and, too'.

(2) yughaghvigllangyugtutlu
     yughagh-vig-ghllag-nge-yug-tugh-t=llu
     pray-place.to.V-big.N-acquire.N-want.to.V-IND-3p-also[2]
     'also, they want to acquire a big church'

This paper will concentrate on the postbases, which constitute by far the richest and most complicated area of Eskimo morphology. Indeed, there are about 400 postbases in Eskimo, and these can occur in relatively long strings after the same stem. For the sake of simplicity, the data in this paper will illustrate postbases that derive verbs from other verbs, such as *-yug-* in (2) (called VV postbases).

2. 'Internal syntax' and 'real' derivational morphology.

In the literature on Eskimo, the postbases have generally been considered derivational suffixes, and indeed they appear to have at least the positional characteristics of derivational suffixes, since they occur between the base and the inflectional ending (Muysken 1986). However, the large majority of these postbases actually have syntactic, semantic, and morphological ordering properties more reminiscent of full words in less synthetic languages, than of the derivational morphology of such languages, and this morphology forms a system more appropriately called 'internal syntax', (Swadesh 1939, 1946). For Eskimo, it will thus be necessary to distinguish between what I would like to call 'real' derivational morphology, (henceforth RD), and this 'internal syntax' (henceforth IS). (3) is a chart of the properties differentiating 'real' derivational morphology and 'internal syntax':

(3)		'Internal Syntax':	'Real' Derivation:
(1)	**Fully productive?**	yes	no
(2)	**Lexicalist hypothesis applies?**	no	yes
(3)	**Recursive?**	yes	no
(4)	**Affixal only?**	yes	no

Property (1), **Productivity**, means that the number of sequences and combinations an element of 'internal syntax' can occur in is so high that native speakers cannot store the resulting sequences in the lexicon. On the other hand, an element of 'real' derivation is not productive in this manner and therefore combinations must be stored in the native speaker's lexicon. Examples of the productivity of IS postbases can be found in the literature on postbase morphology (Smith 1978, Fortescue 1980, de Reuse 1988a).

Property (2), distinguishes between IS and RD regarding the application of the **Lexicalist hypothesis**. The claim of the 'lexicalist hypothesis' (Chomsky 1970) is that derivational word-formation is carried out in the lexicon, and that therefore the syntax cannot have access to and manipulate derived words. It appears that this claim is valid for RD, but not for IS. Examples and further discussion are given in Sadock (1980, 1981), and de Reuse (1988a).

Property (3), **Recursion**, means that the same IS postbase can be used several times within the same word; RD postbases can never be used in this way. Examples are given in de Reuse (1988:115-16).

Property (4), **Affixal**, means that IS postbases cannot be nonconcatenative morphology, such as morpheme internal change or reduplication. This property is actually a corollary of recursion, (property (3)), since it is hard to imagine how nonconcatenative morphology could be fully recursive.

Let us now consider (4), a word containing RD suffixes. By convention, I am using a + boundary to indicate that the two elements joined by it form a nonproductive combination of a base and an RD suffix, or of two RD suffixes. Such combinations must therefore be listed in the lexicon. Expectedly, their meanings are usually not fully predictable from the sum of their parts, and the resulting combination is more conveniently translatable as a unit.

(4)   igamsiqayugviksugapung
       igamsiqa+yug+vig+ke-yug-agh-pung
       feel.thankful.towards-want.to.V-IND-1d>3p
       'we wish to thank them'   (Fieldnotes:6-58)

In (4), the form -*yug*- occurs twice, and both forms are etymologically the same. However, from a synchronic point of view, they are only formally identical, since the first -*yug*- is an RD suffix, translatable as 'to feel (like) V', and is used only with a class of verbs of emotion such as 'to be thankful'. On the other hand, the second -*yug*- is a fully productive element of IS, and means, as seen in (2), 'to want to V'. Before the second -*yug*- , there are two other RD suffixes: the postbase -*vig*- 'place to V', that derives nouns from verbs, and the postbase -*ke*- 'to have as one's N', that derives verbs from nouns.

Now, since I have differentiated between derivation and inflection, it is also necessary to point out the differences between IS and inflection. As shown by Anderson (1982, 1988), inflection is fully productive, and interacts with the syntax. I have shown that this also is true for IS. The difference between the two is that, whereas inflectional morphology is determined by properties assigned to it in the syntax (agreement morphology or case morphology), IS morphology is not determined by syntactic properties. Inflection is also different from IS in that it is not recursive, but rather its forms can be easily listed in a paradigm. Finally, unlike IS, inflection is not necessarily affixal.

I will now argue that IS has a special status as a marked type of morphology and I will support this view by providing historical evidence that IS has a tendency to evolve into a type of morphology that is not marked, such as inflectional or ('real') derivational morphology. The reason why IS is marked is that it is formally morphology, but at the same time it has a number of characteristics of 'external' syntax. Furthermore, it does not occur in most languages of the world, and no language appears to have an IS to the extent that Eskimo has.

Another property of IS that might contribute to its marked status, is that its elements are not psychologically salient, which is somewhat unexpected, since affixes of the IS function very much like independent words in more analytic languages. In other words, the linguistically unsophisticated native speaker of Eskimo is totally unable to recognize the IS elements of an Eskimo word, even though these elements might be as semantically concrete as 'to go to', 'to buy', 'to want to', or 'to eat'; rather, the word is seen as an unanalyzable meaningful whole. I would expect a system like Eskimo, containing both salient words (i.e. elements of the 'external' syntax), and nonsalient IS postbases (i.e. elements of the 'internal syntax') to be more marked than a system simply containing the salient words of 'external' syntax.

3. A case of morphological loss in Central Siberian Yupik.

In CSY, there is a type of morphological reduction which results in the reanalysis of an element of IS into an element of inflectional morphology.

Almost all Eskimo languages possess two VV IS postbases that can be reconstructed as Proto-Eskimo *-yukə- 'to think or believe that oneself or another is V-ing', and *-na+yukə- 'to think that oneself or another might V' (a lexicalized combination of *-na-, marking irrealis or future, and *-yukə-) (Fortescue 1983, Fortescue 1985:217, Jacobson 1984:506, 599, Leer 1985:126, de Reuse 1988a:672-77).

The striking fact is that the CSY cognates do not have the expected morphological and semantic properties; indeed, CSY -yuke- and -na+yuke- do not to mean 'to think', but have become inflectional mood markers. How did such a morphological change come about? The cognates of -yuke- and -na+yuke- in other Yupik languages can occur in several positions between a word, one of which is right in front of the inflection. Furthermore, when these postbases occur in that preinflectional position, this inflection consists of a combination of Indicative mood and person endings that is often homonymous with person endings that would be appropriate after types of moods used only in subordinate clauses, often called subordinate moods. What happened in CSY is that the -yuke- and -na+yuke- that were not in the preinflectional position where lost, but the postbases in preinflectional position were reinterpreted as inflectional mood markers of the subordinate type, and the original mood plus person ending was reinterpreted as being just a person ending. The resulting mood markers have changed semantically, and can be translated as 'for fear that V', 'lest V', and, like the other subordinate verb moods of Eskimo, occur only in subordinate clauses. I have called this new mood, unique to CSY, the Volitive of Fear (VFO); examples are (5) and (6). In (5), it is still possible to see how the change in meaning from 'to think that V' to 'fearing that V' could have come about, since on the surface, (5) could still be semantically interpreted as 'I was afraid, thinking that I might die' as well as 'I was afraid, fearing that I might die'. On the other hand, in (6), the element of fear is conveyed by -na+yuke- only, and not by the main verb *simighaqluki*.

(5)   alingumaanga   tuqunayukama
        alinge-uma-agh-nga   tuqu-na+yuke-ama
        be.afraid-PST-IND-1s   die-VFO-1s
        'I was afraid that I might die'   (Fieldnotes:6-12)

(6)   simighaqluki   naavumanayukata
        simigh-aqe-lu-ki   naave-uma-na+yuke-ata
        replace-PROG-APO-3p›3p   get.ruined-PST-VFO-3p
        'they would replace them (the cartridges on whaling bomb
        guns), for fear that they might have gone bad'
                                      (Apassingok et al. 1985:134)

I have described above the mechanism by which *-yuke-* and *-na+yuke-* became inflectional mood markers. It is not obvious <u>why</u> the original postbases should have been lost, especially since they form the main productive way of expressing the concept 'to think' in other Eskimo languages. The explanation can be given in terms of language contact. For several centuries, speakers of CSY have been in contact with economically and numerically dominant speakers of Chukchi, a Paleo-Siberian language native to a large area of the Soviet Far East. There has been widespread Chukchi-Eskimo bilingualism among the Eskimos, which apparently resulted into the adoption of many Chukchi loanwords into Eskimo, including more than one hundred sentence adverbial and conjunctional particles. These particles are often synonymous to postbases of IS, and in a few cases seem to have caused the disappearance of these postbases. In particular, it is no coincidence that CSY has borrowed many particles from Chukchi that could be loosely translated as 'I think', 'you think', 'he thinks', or 'it is thought'. Some of these particles of Chukchi origin are: *agnepa* 'I think', *gaymaangi* 'maybe, come to think of it', *enekiitek* 'maybe', *entaqun* 'I think', *iitegqun* 'perhaps', *langetaq* 'I think', *luuraq* , *miiwen* , *qemall* , and *wiisam* 'maybe' (de Reuse 1988a). My thesis, then, is that these borrowed Chukchi particles either (1) caused the loss of the semantically corresponding IS postbases, or (2) caused the semantically corresponding preinflectional IS postbases to be reinterpreted as mood endings.

In fact, there is philological evidence that the forms *-yuke-* and *-na+yuke-* existed at one time in CSY as productive IS postbases, and that their reinterpretation as inflectional endings is a fairly recent phenomenon. In the dialogue lines of several versions of the same CSY *ungipaghaan* or traditional story, I have found examples of *-yuke-* and *-na+yuke-* used as IS postbases. Their survival there is due to the fact that folklore texts, in particular dialogues by mythical beings or animals are memorized from generation to generation, and therefore contain forms that are obsolete in the everyday language. The examples below come from several versions of the same *ungipaghaan*, which is the story of a girl held captive by a giant. The girl asks various animals that happen to pass by to help untie her. But the animals all respond in one stereotyped line: 'I think I will free you later!' (and end up not doing it). (7) is a version of this line with *-yuke-*, and (8) is a version of this line with *-na+yuke-*. This line is not part of a subordinate clause, and Indicative mood endings and the personal endings appropriate for the Indicative mood are present. Therefore, a VFO interpretation is not possible, and *-yuke-* and *-na+yuke-* must be postbases of the IS.

(7)   itemuteqaghhnaaghyukamsi
      iteme+ute-qaghte-naagh-yuke-agh-msi
      untie.TR-please.V-V.eventually-think.that.V-IND-1s›2p
      'I think I will untie you (pl.) eventually'
                (Slwooko 1979:7-13, Seppilu [1985], Fieldnotes:52-9)

(8)   itemuteqaghhnayukamsi
      iteme+ute-qaghte-na+yuke-agh-msi
      untie.TR-please.V-think.that.might.V-IND-1s›2p
      'I think I might untie you (pl.)'   (Rookok, [n.d.]:1)

As is to be expected, since this use of the postbase is now obsolete, the storyteller has trouble giving the precise meaning of words containing such forms, and seems to rely on the context to translate them.

4. Conclusions.

In the preceding section, I have reviewed the evidence showing that the IS postbases -*yuke*- and -*na+yuke*- became elements of inflectional morphology, and I assumed that this morphological change was facilitated by the fact the IS is a marked type of morphology. The same argument can be extended to cases in which there is an etymological connection between an RD affix and an IS affix. An example of a form that can be either an RD affix or an IS affix is -*yug*-, already discussed in example (4). Presumably, one could historically consider one type of postbase as original and the other as derived. If the assumption that IS morphology is more marked is correct, one can conclude that, parallel to a tendency for IS elements to be reinterpreted as inflectional endings, there is also a tendency for IS elements to be reinterpreted as RD elements. Conversely, there will be no tendency for either inflectional or RD elements to become elements of the IS. Thus, I postulate that there was a morphological split of an original IS element *-*yug*- into the present-day IS postbase -*yug*- 'to want to V', and the RD postbase -*yug*- 'to feel (like) V', rather than a morphological split of an original RD element -*yug*-.

If there is such a gradual erosion of the IS to benefit either inflection or derivation, one might ask how the IS system has apparently maintained its complexity and relative stability for centuries. Indeed, all Eskimo languages have retained IS postbase systems of comparable complexity, since they all have approximately the same number (circa 300) of IS postbases, and since all use them for marking roughly the same semantic distinctions. Clearly, there is a need for Eskimo to preserve its IS system. However, if the IS system appears to be stable from a purely synchronic perspective, it is not so from a diachronic perspective. Whereas many Proto-Eskimo stems and most elements of the inflectional morphology have cognates in the various Eskimo languages and are thus easy to reconstruct, it appears that of the IS system, only about 122 postbases can be traced back to a Proto-Eskimo form (Fortescue 1985:217-219).[3] This lack of reconstructable cognates must be due to a high rate of postbase replacement, and the problem that needs to be addressed is the origin of these new IS postbases. It appears that the erosion of the IS system is constantly undone by the creation of lexicalized combinations of two IS postbases, which then function like new IS postbases; an example of such a lexicalized combination is -*na+yuke*-

in (8). Nothing prevents such combinations from ultimately moving out of the IS system, and this is of course what happened to the VFO combination -*na+yuke*- in sentences (5) and (6). The argument that most of these lexicalized combinations are not old is supported by the fact that very few can be reconstructed for earlier stages of Eskimo. This means that every Eskimo language has been independently creating its own combinations for a long time.

To conclude, there are tendencies of morphological change within the Eskimo word resulting in elements of the IS moving from their central position in the word in two opposite directions: either towards the stem or towards the inflectional system. If they move towards the stem, they tend to become elements of the 'real' derivational system, and if they move towards the inflection, they are ultimately integrated into it. Furthermore, IS postbases might become frozen lexical units that are themselves new IS postbases.[4]

From the point of view of comparative Eskimo, one can also conclude that both 'real' derivational morphology (RD) as well as inflectional morphology are potentially useful in the internal reconstruction of the 'internal syntax' of polysynthetic languages. Indeed, a lost element of IS might survive either in the inflectional morphology (cf. -*yuke*- and -*na+yuke*- as VFO mood markers), by a process of morphological change that one might call 'inflectionalization'. Alternatively, a lost element of IS might survive in the derivational morphology, by a process of morphological change one might call 'derivationalization'. I have not yet found a clear-cut case of this, but it is easy to conceive of a situation where, for some reason, the IS postbase -*yug*- 'to want to V' is lost, and where the RD postbase -*yug*- 'to feel (like) V' would be retained. If IS is as special and marked as I claim in this paper, one could even claim that the processes of morphological change I have called 'inflectionalization' and 'derivationalization' are nothing but types of 'morphologization', in that the 'internal syntax' has evolved into the two more conventional and unmarked types of morphology, without ever leaving the bounds of the word.

Notes

[1] I wish to thank Linda Badten, Tim Gologergen, Gordon Irrigoo, Vera Metcalf, Jim Toolie, Mary-Ann Wongittilin, and Nick Wongittilin for providing tape-recorded texts and native speaker judgments, Mary

Alexander, Michael Krauss, Elinor Oozeva, Eva Tungiyan, and Willis Walunga for help with written textual data. I am grateful to the University of Iowa Linguistics Department, and to Shobhana Chelliah for comments on earlier versions of this paper, and to Jerry Sadock and Anthony Woodbury for valuable discussions related to the topic of this paper. Financial support for this research was provided by National Science Foundation Grant BNS-8418256 to the University of Texas at Austin.

[2]Abbreviations used in morpheme analyses are:

APO	Appositional verb mood inflection
IND	Indicative verb mood inflection
N	Noun
PROG	Progressive Aspect VV postbase
PST	Past Tense VV postbase
TM	Terminalis case nominal inflection
TR	Transitivizing VV postbase
V	Verb
VFO	Volitive of fear mood inflection
1s	1st person singular subject inflection
1d>3p	1st person dual subject, 3rd person plural object infl.
1s>2p	1st person singular subject, 2nd person plural object infl.
3s	3rd person singular subject infl.
3p	3rd person plural subject infl.
3s>3p	3rd person singular subject, 3rd person plural object infl.

[3]This amount of polysynthesis is, however, a typically Eskimo phenomenon, and can not be traced back to the Proto-Eskimo-Aleut stage, since Aleut has much less IS than any Eskimo language; Fortescue (1985:219-220) gives a list of only 39 Common Eskimo-Aleut postbases.

[4]In all Eskimo languages, there are a few cases of inflectional endings occurring within the IS postbase system, and these could be considered counterexamples to the postulated tendency that inflectional endings never become postbases. A CSY example is:

ilutmiightuq
ilu-tmun-ighte-ugh-ø
inside-TM-go.N.ward-IND-3s
'he/she went inward'   (Badten et al. 1987:76)

66

It should be noted that the only postbase that can follow the Terminalis ending *-tmun* is *-ighte-*, and that *-ighte-* can only occur preceded by *-tmun*. This is evidence that the inflectional ending became a lexicalized combination with the postbase, and that the resulting sequence *-tmiighte-* should be interpreted as a single denominal verbalizing postbase, rather than as a productive sequence of an inflectional ending and a postbase. Therefore, such sequences are not evidence that an inflectional ending has become a postbase, but rather that certain postbases can contain lexicalized inflectional material.

References

Anderson, Stephen. 1982. Where's Morphology? Linguistic Inquiry 13(4).471-612.

Anderson, Stephen. 1988. Inflection. Theoretical Morphology, ed. by Michael Hammond and Michael Noonan, 23-43. San Diego: Academic Press.

Apassingok, Anders, et al. 1985. Sivuqam Nangaghnegha. Siivanllemta Ungipaqellghat. Lore of St. Lawrence Island. Echos of our Eskimo Elders. Volume I: Gambell. Unalakleet, Alaska: Bering Strait School District.

Badten, Linda W., et al. 1987. A Dictionary of the St. Lawrence Island / Siberian Yupik Eskimo Language. Fairbanks: Alaska Native Language Center, University of Alaska.

Chomsky, Noam A. 1970. Remarks on Nominalization. Readings in English Transformational Grammar, ed. by R. A. Jacobs and P. S. Rosenbaum, 184-221. Waltham, Mass.: Ginn and Co.

Fortescue, Michael D. 1980. Affix Ordering in West Greenlandic Derivational Processes. International Journal of American Linguistics 46.259-278.

Fortescue, Michael D. 1983. A comparative manual of affixes for the Inuit dialects of Greenland, Canada, and Alaska. Meddelelser om Grønland, Man and Society 4.

Fortescue, Michael D. 1985. The Degree of Interrelatedness between Dialects as Reflected by Percentages of Shared Affixes. International Journal of American Linguistics 51.188-221.

Jacobson, Steven A. 1984. Yup'ik Eskimo Dictionary. Fairbanks: Alaska Native Language Center, University of Alaska.

Leer, Jeff. 1985. Prosody in Alutiiq. Yupik Eskimo Prosodic Systems: Descriptive and Comparative Studies, ed. by M. E. Krauss. Alaska Native Language Center Research Papers 7.77-133. Fairbanks: Alaska Native Language Center, University of Alaska.

Muysken, Pieter. 1986. Approaches to affix order. Linguistics 24.629-643.

de Reuse, Willem J. 1988. The Morphology/Semantics Interface: An Autolexical Treatment of Eskimo Verbal Affix Order. Chicago Linguistic Society 24.112-25.

de Reuse, Willem J. 1988a. Studies in Siberian Yupik Eskimo Morphology and Syntax. Unpublished University of Texas, Austin dissertation.

Rookok, Ruby. [n.d.] Panekellemaa. Ayumiim Ungipaghaatangi V. Stories of Long Ago V. Unpublished ms. draft, 4 p. Fairbanks: Alaska Native Language Center, University of Alaska.

Sadock, Jerrold M. 1980. Noun incorporation in Greenlandic: a case of syntactic word formation. Language 56.300-319.

Sadock, Jerrold M. 1985. Autolexical Syntax: A Proposal for the Treatment of Noun Incorporation and Similar Phenomena. Natural Language and Linguistic Theory 3.379-439.

Seppilu, Myra. [1985]. *Ungipaghaan* entitled Yuuggaaqa, recorded for the Eskimo Heritage Program, in Savoonga. Ms. nr. SV/HP-85-36-T1 in the Eskimo Heritage Program files, Bering Strait Native Corporation, Nome, Alaska.

Slwooko, Grace. 1979. Sivuqam Ungipaghaatangi II. St Lawrence Island Legends II. Anchorage: National Bilingual Materials Development Center, Rural Education Affairs, University of Alaska.

Smith, Lawrence R. 1978. Some properties of Labrador Inuttut verbal derivation. Études Inuit/Inuit/Studies 2(2).37-48.

Swadesh, Morris 1939. Nootka Internal Syntax. International Journal of American Linguistics 9.77-102.

Swadesh, Morris 1946. South Greenlandic (Eskimo). Linguistic Structures of Native America. (Viking Fund Publications in Anthropology 6), ed. by Harry Hoijer et al., 30-54. New York: Viking Fund.

A temporal analysis of quantifying adverbials

Henriëtte de Swart
University of Groningen

0. Outline*

In this paper I want to discuss the analysis of
quantifying adverbials in French. Frequency adverbs have
been studied in temporal semantics and in quantifier theory.
Both approaches can only present a partial solution to the
problems which arise in the interpretation of temporal
quantifiers. I will argue that a combination of ideas from
temporal semantics and Generalized Quantifier Theory in a
broader perspective results in a more natural and coherent
analysis of temporal quantification.

1. Relational interpretations and frequency readings

Adverbs of quantification do not constitute a
homogeneous group, but come in different subclasses. We can
globally distinguish between iterative adverbs (1),
frequency adverbs (2) and adverbs expressing some kind of
'generic' quantification (3):

(1) L'année dernière Anne est allée au cinéma à
plusieurs reprises
'Last year Anne went to the cinema several times'
(2) L'année dernière Anne est rarement allée au
cinéma
'Last year Anne seldom went to the cinema'
(3) Le samedi Anne va généralement au cinéma
'On Saturday Anne generally goes to the cinema'

Frequency adverbs and iterative adverbs do not quantify
over time in the same way. Iterative adverbs such as **deux
fois** ('twice'), **à plusieurs reprises** ('several times') are
used to count events; they refer to the cardinality of a set
of situations in a certain context (e.g. last year). In
sentence (2) however, we are not interested in the total
number of times that Anne went to the cinema, but we
consider the frequency of this type of event with respect to
a given stretch of time, namely last year. This induces a
more or less regular distribution over time: for instance
Anne went to the cinema less than once a month. Frequency
adverbs such as **souvent** ('often'), **toujours** ('always') thus
denote some kind of relative quantity.

---

* I wish to thank the participants in the Quantification
seminar (Amherst, spring 1989) for helpful discussion. Part
of this research was carried out during my stay in Amherst,
which was made possible by a grant of the Netherlands
Organization for Scientific Research (NWO).

'Generic' adverbials such as **habituellement,**
('habitually'), **généralement** ('generally') differ from
frequency adverbs in that they are not purely quantitative.
Their interpretation always involves some kind of 'nomic'
aspect. In this paper I will mainly concentrate on frequency
adverbs.

Lewis (1975) already observed that there is a lot of
contextual variation in the interpretation of the adverbs of
quantification. A main distinction has to be made between
what can be called 'temporal' and 'atemporal' readings. The
Q-adverb (= quantifying adverb) in (4) seems to quantify
over something temporal, times, situations or whatever:

(4) Pierre se lève toujours de bonne heure
'Pierre always gets up early'

In sentences like (5) however, the adverb does not have a
clear temporal meaning. It seems to quantify over
individuals or 'cases':

(5) Les chats ont le plus souvent les yeux verts
'Cats mostly have green eyes'

In the last few years, the analysis of Q-adverbs has
been worked out by Lewis (1975), Heim (1982), Kratzer (1988)
and others. Most of these recent proposals are particularly
concerned with the interaction of generic NPs and Q-adverbs,
as in (5). On the other hand, traditional grammars such as
Grevisse and Mauger, or studies in temporal semantics like
Vet (1980), Vlach (1981), Van Eynde (1987), focus on the
temporal readings. They consider iterative and frequency
adverbs as a kind of temporal adverbials, along with other
subclasses, such as frame adverbials, adverbs of duration,
etc. In view of the integration of quantificational
expressions in modern temporal semantics the analysis of Q-
adverbs in sentences like (4) thus has an independent
interest. I think that the model I will develop for the
temporal readings can be extended in order to account for
the sentences in (5), maybe along the lines of the proposals
made by Berman (1987) or Chierchia (1988). Still, in this
paper I will not discuss the interaction between Q-adverbs
and generics.

Even if we restrict ourselves to examples of temporal
quantification, different meaning effects can arise. Some
uses of the Q-adverbs give rise to relational
interpretations, others create frequency readings. The
relational interpretation comes in two types. The major
difference between the two resides in the selection of the
arguments, in other words what shows up in the antecedent
and the consequent part of the relation. The first type is a
relation such that:

(i) the first argument gives a temporal frame with respect to which a type of event, given by the second argument, is interpreted

(6a) Quand il se lève tard, Marc a parfois mal à la tête
'When he gets up late, Marc sometimes has a head ache'
(6b) Le samedi Anne va le plus souvent au cinéma
'On Saturday Anne mostly goes to the cinema'
(6c) Après sa promenade avec le chien Pierre fume toujours une cigarette
'After his walk with the dog Pierre always smokes a cigarette'

The normal paraphrase of these sentences is something like the following: "Under such and such circumstances it happens sometimes/ often/ always/ ... that an event of type E occurs." In general, the set of occasions is given by a sentence adverb or an adverbial clause, while the type of event is expressed by the main clause. Since the event referred to in the consequent is considered with respect to the frame introduced by the antecedent, we need to specify the temporal relation between the two clauses. Some kind of existential quantification over events and reference times seems to be necessary. Although this is an important problem, I will abstract away from it in this paper (cf. Partee, 1984 for discussion).

The second type of relational interpretation can be described as a relation where:

(ii) the first argument introduces a type of event and the second argument focusses on a specific aspect of that event

(7a) Anne se promène le plus souvent au Luxembourg
'Anne mostly takes a walk in the Luxembourg garden'
(7b) Georges écrit souvent avec un stylo rouge
'Georges often writes with a red pencil'
(7c) Jeanne tricote toujours des chandails norvégiens   (Nef 1986)
'Jeanne always knits Norwegian sweaters'

This type of relation can generally be paraphrased in the following way: "When (s)he V's (s)he sometimes/ mostly/ always/ ... V's that/ there/ in such a way/..." While in the first type of relational interpretation the main verb is analysed in the consequent of the relation, it comes up in the antecedent part here. This means that we have the same temporal reference in both arguments, so there is no problem of specifying the temporal relation between the two clauses, as in (6). The most obvious instantiation of this type of

relation is given by verbs, modified by an adverbial as in
(7a and b). The semantic character of the modifier must be
such that the combination of the verb and the modifier
denotes a subset of the main verb. In other words these
modifiers have the property of 'introspection' as Van
Benthem (1986: 62, 68) calls it. The relation is then
between the verb and a subset of the VP.

Other sentences are not so strictly introspective, for
instance when a direct object plays a role in the relation.
Some of these examples allow more than one decomposition and
are ambiguous between several readings (e.g. 7c). In these
cases focus can help us disambiguating the sentence (cf.
Schubert and Pelletier, 1987 and Rooth, 1986 for
discussion).

The two types of relational readings are obviously
instances of restricted quantification. The quantifier does
not range over the whole universe of discourse, but only
over a restricted subset of it.

Not all occurrences of quantifying adverbs correspond
to relational readings, though. When we compare sentences
(8a and b), examples inspired by Stump (1986), we see that
they do not give rise to the same meaning effects:

(8a) Jane often uses a calculator
(8b) Jane often uses a calculator when figuring
her taxes

If there are few occasions where Jane has to figure her
taxes, and those are the only situations where she uses a
calculator, (8b) might be true, while (8a) will be false.
When we replace **often** by **seldom** in the same situation, we
obtain the opposite result: the frequency of Jane using a
calculator may be very low, but still she might do it often
or even always when figuring her taxes. Clearly these
differences are related to the normative interpretation of
often/ seldom. In sentence (8a) the pure frequency of Jane's
use of a calculator is compared to a certain norm, maybe the
average use people make of a calculator. This frequency can
be described by adverbials such as **daily, twice a week** which
Stump (1986: 173, 174) calls "fixed" frequency adverbs,
because they specify frequencies whose periods are of a
fixed length. In sentence (8b) on the other hand, it is the
proportion of these situations with respect to the set of
occasions where Jane has to figure her taxes which is
compared to some average proportion. Fixed frequency adverbs
cannot be used in this interpretation. So the meaning of the
Q-adverb in a sentence like (8a) is not constructed in the
same way as in (8b).

We can capture this insight in distinguishing a third
interpretation type, where the Q-adverb does not get a
relational meaning, but expresses a mere frequency:

(iii) frequency

(9a) Fido aboie rarement
'Fido seldom barks'
(9b) Marie joue parfois du piano
'Marie sometimes plays the piano'
(9c) Le bébé pleurait souvent
'The baby often cried'

In general, sentences such as (9) describe the repetition of a type of event with a certain frequency and a more or less regular distribution over time. This means that we can paraphrase these sentences as: "It happens quite seldom that Fido barks", "Once in a while Marie is engaged in the event of playing the piano", etc. This shows that the frequency reading of Q-adverbials somehow describes the relative quantity of a set of events with respect to (a part of) the time axis. This involves a partition of the temporal domain in appropriate time units. Because of the direct import of the real time axis on the interpretation, this frequency reading can be characterized as much more temporal in nature than the relational interpretations. If a relation is established between sets of situations, the real time axis is only indirectly involved through the temporal order in which the events present themselves.

2. A temporal version of Generalized Quantifier theory

The informal distinction between three types of interpretation implies that our theory has to account for the meaning effects showing up with different uses of the Q-adverbs, and has to be sufficiently general to capture quantification over times, events, occasions, etc. The tools we need to construe our model are to be found in analyses developed in temporal semantics and Quantifier theory. As far as the interpretation of temporal quantification goes, these frameworks are more or less complementary. Studies in temporal semantics (such as Vet 1980, Vlach 1981, Van Eynde 1987, Kleiber 1987) concentrate on frequency readings, because of the direct import of the real time axis on the interpretation. The standard first-order models of predication over time are unable to give an adequate description of the relational readings, for these require a real second order interpretation in terms of Generalized Quantifiers. On the other hand, analyses developed in the framework of Quantifier theory (such as Lewis 1975, Stump 1986, Schwarzschild 1989) interpret the adverbs as binary operators. In this paper I propose to unify these approaches by means of the construction of a temporal version of Generalized Quantifier theory (= GQ-theory). That is, I will use a temporal structure which allows second order entities, and a more dynamic perspective on Generalized Quantifiers, which accounts for the cyclic effects of quantification over a temporally ordered set.

If frequency adverbs are to be interpreted as
Generalized Quantifiers over the temporal domain, we may
wonder what exactly they are quantifying over. Since Lewis
(1975) this is a much debated question. I will not really
enter this debate, but simply assume that we are quantifying
over a temporal 'something'. Notions as occasion, event or
eventuality may play a role here. In this paper I will take
over the temporal semantics proposed by Ter Meulen (1983).
She introduces a set of 'processes', chunks of the temporal
domain, from which VP-interpretations, intervals and moments
are constructed. The set of processes P is partially ordered
by the relations of precedence and overlap. Quantifying
adverbials can now be interpreted as binary relations
between sets of processes.

Barwise and Cooper (1981) introduce a careful
distinction between Determiners and Generalized Quantifiers.
NPs correspond to Generalized Quantifiers, that is sets of
sets of individuals. A simple sentence NP VP is true if the
denotation of VP is a member of the set of sets the
determiner lives on. In the temporal domain this view of
Generalized Quantifiers is not particularly useful, for
there is no syntactic evidence for something like an NP:
there is no constituent of the sentence, which intuitively
corresponds to a set of sets. Therefore I propose to take a
somewhat different, but equivalent approach to Generalized
Quantifiers, which has been advocated by Zwarts (1983), and
Van Benthem (1986): in this perspective, a determiner is
defined as a functor Q, which assigns to each universe E a
binary relation Q_E between subsets A and B of E. The
relational interpretation of quantified NPs can be pictured
as follows:

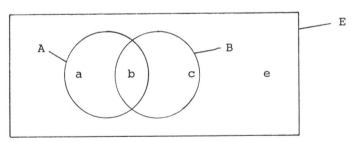

In this picture $a = |A - B|$, $b = |A \cap B|$, $c = |B - A|$, $e = |E - (A \cup B)|$.

Not every such binary relation between sets counts as a
possible determiner denotation, however. A number of
principles have been formulated to restrict the range of
admissible interpretations of natural language determiners.
The most important of these principles are Extension,
Conservativity and Quantity, defined as follows:

Extension: if Q_E AB and E $\subseteq$ E', then $Q_{E'}$ AB

Conservativity: Q_E AB <=> Q_E A (A ∩ B)

Quantity: for every permutation f of E: Q_E AB <=> Q_E f[A]f[B]

Extension guarantees that the determiner has the same structure in every model. Conservativity is the same principle as the 'live on' property defined by Barwise and Cooper (1981). It restricts the universe to the left-hand argument: individuals in B - A are irrelevant to the evaluation of the determiner relation. Quantity states that determiners respect only the size of A and B, not the identity of their elements. The combination of these three properties makes the interpretation of natural language quantifiers only dependent on the cardinality of A and A ∩ B, that is a and b.

Now, if we want to interpret adverbs of quantification as Generalized Quantifiers, we should know how to transpose this relational model in the temporal domain. This means that we should answer at least the following three questions:

(i) What is the universe of discourse, or the domain of quantification of the Q-adverb?
(ii) How do we find the two arguments A and B?
(iii) Do the standard properties of Extension, Conservativity and Quantity carry over in a straightforward way?

It will soon be clear that Conservativity is crucial to my analysis and although I will not prove here that Q-adverbs are conservative, it can safely be assumed. We will see that as far as Extension and Quantity are concerned the definitions are to be refined in view of the ordering on the temporal domain and the more dynamic approach of Generalized Quantifiers in terms of semantic automata. I will concentrate here on the first two questions.

3. The interpretation of relational interpretations

Examples of the first type of relational interpretation have been given under (6):

(6a) Quand il se lève tard, Marc a parfois mal à la tête
'When he gets up late, Marc sometimes has a head ache'
(6b) Le samedi Anne va le plus souvent au cinéma
'On Saturday, Anne mostly goes to the cinema'
(6c) Après sa promenade avec le chien, Pierre fume toujours une cigarette

'After his walk with the dog Pierre always smokes
a cigarette'

In these examples, the temporal clause introduced by a
connective (**quand, avant, après**) or the generic adverbial
determines the first argument (the antecedent) of the
relation, while the main clause gives the second argument
(the consequent). Since the Q-adverb has scope over the
temporal clause, respectively the sentence adverb, it has to
function as a sentence operator. Tense and frame adverbials
such as **l'année dernière, dans sa jeunesse** function as
restrictors on the universe of discourse. Tense selects a
subset of the set of processes P for the quantifier to
operate on. In (6) the present tense gives us a kind of
"extended present" with vague boundaries.
The interpretation of the sentences (6) is given under
(10):

(10a) Quand il se lève tard, Marc a parfois mal à
la tete
SOMETIMES$_{PR}$ (MARC GETS UP LATE, MARC HAS A HEAD
ACHE)

Here the upper case indicates the set-theoretic denotation
of the linguistic expressions: MARC GETS UP LATE is the set
of processes which denotes **Marc se lève tard**, etc. The
subscript PR gives the domain of quantification of the
adverb: the relation expressed by **parfois** is evaluated in
the extended present, a subset of P.

(10b) Le samedi Anne va le plus souvent au cinéma
MOSTLY$_{PR}$ (SATURDAY, ANNE GOES TO THE CINEMA)

(10c) Après sa promenade avec le chien Pierre fume
toujours une cigarette
ALWAYS$_{PR}$ (AFTER HIS WALK WITH THE DOG, PIERRE
SMOKES A CIGARETTE)

The truth conditions of these sentences are essentially
proportional:

$$(11a) \frac{|\text{MARC GETS UP LATE} \cap \text{MARC HAS A HEADACHE}|}{|\text{MARC GETS UP LATE}|} > 0/1$$

$$(11b) \frac{|\text{SATURDAY} \cap \text{ANNE GOES TO THE CINEMA}|}{|\text{SATURDAY}|} > 1/2$$

(11c) AFTER HIS WALK WITH THE DOG $\subseteq$ PIERRE
SMOKES A CIGARETTE

So sentence (10a) is true if the proportion of sentences in
which Marc gets up late and has a headache with respect to

the set of situations in which he gets up late is more than 0/1.

The second type of relational interpretation was exemplified in (7):

(7a) Anne se promène le plus souvent au Luxembourg
'Anne mostly takes a walk in the Luxembourg garden'
(7b) Georges écrit souvent avec un stylo rouge
'Georges often writes with a red pencil'
(7c) Jeanne tricote toujours des chandails norvégiens
'Jeanne always knits Norwegian sweaters'

Intuitively the relation established by the adverb is between the verb and the modified verb phrase: **se promener/ se promener au Luxembourg, écrire/ écrire avec un stylo rouge**. Thanks to Conservativity the analysis of this type of sentences is straightforward. We need not construe a relation between the verb and the modifier, but we can establish a relation between the verb (with an explicit or implicit existentially quantified variable in place of the focussed modifier) and the modified VP, denoting a subset of the verb. The domain of quantification is again restricted by tense and time adverbials. The interpretation of the sentences (7) is given under (12):

(12a) Anne se promène le plus souvent au Luxembourg
MOSTLY$_{PR}$ (ANNE TAKES A WALK (SOMEWHERE), ANNE TAKES A WALK IN THE LUXEMBOURG GARDEN)

(12b) Georges écrit souvent avec un stylo rouge
OFTEN$_{PR}$ (GEORGES WRITES, GEORGES WRITES WITH A RED PENCIL)

(12c) Jeanne tricote toujours des chandails norvégiens
This example allows two decompositions:
ALWAYS$_{PR}$ (JEANNE KNITS (SOMETHING), JEANNE KNITS NORWEGIAN SWEATERS)

ALWAYS$_{PR}$ (JEANNE KNITS SWEATERS, JEANNE KNITS NORWEGIAN SWEATERS)

Since the selection of the arguments by the Q-adverb is not bound to particular syntactic positions, certain examples show a multiplication of readings.
    The truth conditions here are quite similar to those given in (11), again the interpretation is essentially proportional:

(13a) |ANNE TAKES A WALK IN THE LUX GARDEN|
       -- > 1/2
       |ANNE TAKES A WALK|

(13b) |GEORGES WRITES WITH A RED PENCIL|
       ------------------------------------ > m/n
       |GEORGES WRITES|

(13c) JEANNE KNITS (SOMETHING) $\subseteq$ JEANNE KNITS
NORWEGIAN SWEATERS

JEANNE KNITS SWEATERS $\subseteq$ JEANNE KNITS NORWEGIAN
SWEATERS

m/n in (13b) is a certain norm, recovered from context and
situation: we compare the frequency of Georges' writing with
a red pencil in the set of his writing situations with some
prototypical proportion. The standard can be provided by
some average person, or by Georges' behaviour in the past.
This vagueness implies that we cannot fix the exact value of
the proportion.

As far as truth conditions are concerned, these
interpretations are not crucially different from those
proposed for determiners in standard GQ-theory. The
differences come in when we evaluate the Generalized
Quantifiers in our model in order to calculate the truth
value of the sentence. The dynamic nature of time blocks the
standard evaluation in terms of static sets.
In De Swart (1988) I argued that a more dynamic
interpretation of quantification over a temporally ordered
set can be given if we use semantic automata, following Van
Benthem (1987). In this perspective, iterative adverbs (**deux
fois**, ...) correspond to first-order quantifiers, computable
by means of finite state automata. Frequency adverbs
(**souvent, toujours**, ...) are essentially proportional and
require the use of push down automata. These machines have a
memory in the form of a stack, to which the element read is
compared.
The semantic difference between iteration and frequency
is parallelled by a distinction in domains, reflected in the
tenses the adverbs can combine with. The cardinality
expressed by iterative adverbs is interpreted in bounded
domains; they can occur with the Passé Simple or the Passé
Composé, but not normally with the Imparfait or the Présent
(unless the sentence gets a habitual meaning), cf. (14a and
b):

(14a) Marie joua/ a joué deux fois du piano
'Marie played/ has played the piano twice'
(14b) ?Marie jouait/ joue deux fois du piano
'Marie played/ plays the piano twice'

This corresponds to the fact that the truth value of an iterative sentence is calculated after a finite number of steps, when the whole domain of quantification has been considered.

Frequency adverbs on the other hand are not subject to such restrictions. They combine freely with all tenses and can thus be interpreted in bounded as well as unbounded domains. In order to account for quantification over temporally ordered, open classes, we cannot delay the verification until the end of the procedure. We have to evaluate the frequency 'gradually', as we go along in time. This can be effectuated by means of a restriction on the number of positions in the memory stack. In this way we obtain a cyclic meaning effect: the stack must be regularly emptied and the evaluation depends on the order of presentation.

In the examples of restricted quantification we quantify over the set of processes denoted by the antecedent, so the structure of the memory stack is provided by the reference set of the proportion. In a sentence such as (6a) this means that we consider the set of situations in which Marc gets up late, and note a 1 when, in such a situation Marc has a headache, and a 0 when he does not. Since the memory stack is to be regularly emptied, it is not enough to have a positive instantiation once in order to verify **parfois**. The constant evaluation procedure requires the proportion to remain more than 0/1 as we go on in time, so we must read a 1 once in a while. This mechanism induces a more or less regular distribution of positive and negative instantiations over the reference set. The proportional relation is only indirectly related to the time axis, through the temporal order on the reference set. This means that, if the events of getting up late occur irregularly in Marc's life, there need not be a regular distribution in time of situations in which he has a headache. In this respect relational interpretations are less temporal in nature than pure frequency readings. Both interpretations, however, can be essentially characterized by the constant evaluation procedure in terms of push down automata with a limited stack.

In this proposal, Q-adverbs do not obey Quantity and Extension as defined in section 2.2. Van Benthem (1986) points out that the intrinsic order in the temporal domain requires a principle of Quality rather than mere Quantity. That is to say, permutations are allowed, but only insofar as the temporal order on the permuted structure is respected. Extension assumes a certain independence of the universe of discourse, as long as the sets A and B remain untouched. In the case of temporal quantification, this property is too static in its standard formulation. When the universe of discourse is extended, the sets of processes involved in the quantificational relation will generally grow too, because of the intrinsic order on the temporal domain. Moreover, proportions in unbounded domains require a mechanism of constant evaluation rather than the restriction to fixed, closed universes. The cyclic interpretation procedure defined here is compatible with a principle of Graduality (Van Benthem 1986: 32). That is to say, if adding elements to A results in a change of the truth value of QAB, we can restore the original truth value by enlarging A - B or A ∩ B.

4. The interpretation of frequency readings

Examples of this use of Q-adverbs have been given under (8):

(8a) Fido aboie rarement
'Fido seldom barks'
(8b) Marie joue parfois du piano
'Marie sometimes plays the piano'
(8c) Le bébé pleurait souvent
'The baby often cried'

These sentences express a mere frequency, which can be specified by adverbs such as **deux fois par semaine**. This meaning effect is not obtained in the relational interpretations of (6) and (7), where the Q-adverb establishes a binary relation between sets of situations. The interpretation of the frequency adverbs in (8) is constructed in a different way and the proportional truth conditions given in (11) and (13) are inappropriate for this case.1
This observation requires a revision of the analysis outlined in the previous section, because there I claimed that the difference between iteration and frequency is captured by the distinction between cardinal and proportional quantifiers. The distinction is parallelled by the ability of frequency adverbs to be interpreted with respect to unbounded domains, while iterative adverbs are always evaluated in a bounded domain. These characteristics are reflected in the semantics proposed and lead to the interpretation of iterative adverbs as finite state automata and the evaluation of frequency adverbs by means of push down automata with a limited stack. If we cannot maintain the proportional truth conditions for the Q-adverbs in (8), and have to interpret them instead as cardinal quantifiers, it seems that we reduce the frequency adverbs to iteratives. However, the sentences in (8) are partially in the Imparfait, partially in the Présent, which are exactly the contexts where standard iterative adverbs are blocked. So although the Q-adverbs here are not proportional in nature, they can be interpreted with respect to unbounded domains. The conclusion must be that the two criteria of cardinal/ proportional quantifiers and interpretations with respect to bounded/ unbounded domains are relatively independent. I claim that a unified analysis of frequency adverbs in

---

1 Thanks to Barbara Partee for pointing this out to me.

different readings cannot ultimately be formulated at the
level of truth conditions, but depends crucially on the
automata associated with the different temporal quantifiers.

I assume that Q-adverbials in pure frequency readings
do not denote proportional relations, but are in some sense
cardinal in nature. Still, this cardinality is not used to
simply count a number of event in a bounded domain. The Q-
adverbs in (8) are sensitive to the recurrence of a type of
events after a certain time. The cardinality they describe
corresponds to the quantity of a set of situations relative
to (part of) the time axis. Because of the intrinsic
temporal order in a potentially unbounded domain this leads
to the interpretation of pure frequency readings as
iteratives in a cyclic perspective. They are thus conceived
as similar in meaning to fixed frequency adverbs such as
deux fois par semaine, mensuellement. The main difference is
that these adverbs specify frequencies whose periods are of
a fixed length, while **souvent, rarement, ...** are vague and
context-dependent.

I take the cyclic meaning aspect to be an important
characteristic of the frequency readings. Since it cannot be
captured by a finite state automaton, we need a constant
evaluation procedure in terms of a push down automaton with
a limited stack. In the absence of a proportional
interpretation, the structure of the memory stack cannot be
provided by the reference set. Instead, it is given by a
certain partition of the domain of quantification, which
divides the time axis in appropriate units, such as days,
weeks, ... The constant evaluation procedure then induces a
more or less regular distribution of positive and negative
instances over the temporal domain.

In this interpretation of pure frequency readings,
adverbs such as **parfois, souvent, rarement** correspond to
expressions of cyclic iteration. Their semantics cannot be
captured by ordinary cardinality truth conditions, because
these would underdetermine the meaning of the Q-adverb. The
dynamic interpretation of Generalized Quantifiers, based on
semantic automata, has a greater explanatory value, for it
turns out that only in this perspective we can give a
unified semantics of Q-adverbs in relational interpretations
and frequency readings.

5. Concluding remarks

In this paper I have developed a temporal analysis of
quantifying adverbials. Even if the discussion has
concentrated on French, many meaning effects also show up in
other languages. The integration of ideas from temporal
semantics and GQ-theory yields some interesting results.
'Classical' GQ-concepts have been shown to carry over to
the temporal domain, although the dynamic nature of time
requires several modifications of the framework. The
constant evaluation procedure in terms of automata theory
explains characteristic properties of temporal quantifiers

in cases where truth conditions alone are insufficient.
Although other GQ properties such as monotonicity,
persistence, etc. remain to be investigated in this
perspective, the view on Generalized Quantifiers as automata
seems to be a fruitful approach to the phenomenon of
temporal quantification in natural languages.

It may be interesting to relate these observations back
to nontemporal cases which show unbounded effects, such as
generics and generic-like quantifiers in examples like:

(15) La plupart des enfants aiment recevoir des
cadeaux à Noël
'Most children like to get presents at Christmas'

If we take this to be a general statement about children, we
need some mechanism to give the sentence a truth value even
if we are unable to go through the whole set of children,
because this is an open, potentially changing domain. Since
the domain of individuals is not intrinsically ordered,
however, the constant evaluation procedure of a proportion
does not give rise to the same cyclic meaning effects as in
the temporal case.

References

Barwise, J. and R. Cooper (1981). 'Generalized Quantifiers
and natural language', Linguistics and Philosophy 4, p. 159-
219.

Benthem, J. van (1986). Essays in logical semantics,
Dordrecht: Reidel.

Benthem, J. van (1987). 'Semantic automata', in: J.
Groenendijk, D. de Jongh, and M. Stokhof (eds.) Studies in
Discourse Representation Theory and the theory of
Generalized Quantifiers, Dordrecht: Foris, p. 1-25.

Berman, S. (1987). 'Situation-based semantics for adverbs of
quantification', UMOP 12: Issues in Semantics, p. 45-68.

Chierchia, G. (1988). 'Dynamic Generalized Quantifiers and
donkey anaphora', in: M. Krifka (ed.). Genericity in natural
language, Tübingen: SNS, p. 53-84.

Eynde, F. van (1987). 'Iteration and quantification', in: J.
Groenendijk, M. Stokhof and F. Veltman (eds.). Proceedings
of the sixth Amsterdam Colloquium, Amsterdam: ITLI,
University of Amsterdam, p. 43-64.

Heim, I. (1982). The semantics of definite and indefinite
noun phrases, PhD dissertation, UMass, Amherst.

Kratzer, A. (1988). 'Stage-level and individual level
predicates', manuscript, UMass, Amherst,

Lewis, D. (1975). 'Adverbs of quantification', in: E. Keenan (ed.). Formal semantics of natural language, Cambridge: Cambridge University Press, p. 3-15.

Meulen, A. ter (1983). 'The representation of time in natural language in: A. ter Meulen (ed.) Studies in modeltheoretic semantics, Dordrecht: Foris, p. 177-191.

Nef, F. (1986). Sémantique de la reference temporelle en francais moderne, Bern: Peter Lang.

Partee, B. (1984). 'Nominal and temporal anaphora', Linguistics and Philosophy 7, p. 243-287.

Partee, B. (1988). 'Many quantifiers', to appear in the Proceedings of ESCOL 1988.

Rooth, M. (1986). Association with focus, dissertation, UMass, Amherst.

Schubert, L. and F. Pelletier (1987). 'Problems in the interpretation of the logical form of generics, bare plurals and mass terms', in: LePore (ed.) New directions in semantics, London: Academic Press.

Schwarzschild, R. (1989). 'Adverbs of quantification as generalized quantifiers', to appear in The proceedings of NELS 19.

Stump, G. (1986). The semantic variability of absolute constructions, Dordrecht: Reidel.

Swart, H.E. de (1988). '**Quelques fois** and **quelquefois:** about iteration and frequency in French', in: P. Coopmans and A. Hulk (eds.). Linguistics in the Netherlands 1988, p. 149-158.

Vet, C. (1980). Temps, aspects et adverbes de temps en francais moderne, Geneve: Droz.

Vlach, F. (1981). 'La sémantique du temps et de l'aspect en anglais', Langages 64, p. 65-80.

Zwarts, F. (1983). 'Determiners: a relational perspective', in: A. ter Meulen (ed.). Studies in modeltheoretic semantics, Dordrecht: Foris, p. 37-62.

Article-Noun Order

Matthew S. Dryer
University of Alberta

It is almost accepted wisdom (cf. Greenberg 1963, Vennemann 1976, Hawkins 1983) that OV languages tend to place modifiers before nouns while VO languages tend to place modifiers after nouns. But discussions in word order typology rarely consider the order of article and noun. If one adopts the traditional view that articles are modifiers of nouns, then the accepted wisdom regarding word order correlations would predict that articles should tend to follow the noun in VO languages and to precede the noun in OV languages. Based on a sample of 125 languages, I argue in this paper that both of these predictions turn out to be false and that there is in fact a correlation in the opposite direction. In section 1 I discuss my criteria for identifying articles cross-linguistically; in section 2 I present the evidence regarding the correlations with the order of article and noun; in section 3 I discuss the theoretical implications of these correlations; and in section 4, the conclusion, I briefly discuss differences between articles and demonstratives with respect to their word order behaviour.

1. Identifying articles

While there is little difficulty identifying some categories, like nouns, cross-linguistically, it is less obvious what criteria count for identifying a word as an article. I use here two criteria to identify articles: (1) the word indicates definiteness or indefiniteness, or some related discourse notion; (2) the word serves as a noun phrase marker in the sense that noun phrases in the language (other than pronouns) typically occur with one of the words in question. Articles in English, as in many languages, satisfy both of these criteria: except for proper nouns, bare plurals (as in *Dogs bite*), and bare mass nouns (as in *Snow is white*), English noun phrases containing a noun occur with an article (or some other determiner). But I also treat a word as an article if it satisfies either one of these two criteria. Vietnamese has a word *cái*, illustrated in (1), which Binh (1971: 117) describes as an identifier and whose function is something like that of a definite article.

(1) cái   nhà   tôi   bán   hôm   qua
     the   house I   sell   day   past
     the house I sold yesterday (Binh 1971: 118)

But *cái* does not appear to serve as a noun phrase marker like *the* in English in that it is normal for noun phrases in the language not to contain *cái* or any other word that contrasts with it. It appears to be the case from Binh's description that *cái* is only used when the noun is followed by some other modifier. In other words, while *the* in English belongs to a class of words that is obligatory in certain syntactic environments, *cái* in Vietnamese appears to be simply an optional modifier of the noun.

On the other hand, there are languages which employ words that serve as noun phrase markers but which do not code discourse notions like definiteness or indefiniteness. Many Austronesian languages, for example, have words that occur obligatorily in noun phrases (except for certain syntactic environments) and which vary according to whether the noun is a proper noun or a common noun as well as various other grammatical features of the noun phrase. Fijian, for example, employs two such words: *a* (with common nouns) and *o* (with proper nouns), illustrated in (2).

(2) sa   tau-ra   a   drano   o   Boumaa
     asp   hold   com   lake   prop   Boumaa
     Boumaa held the lake.   (Dixon 1988: 243)

Dixon (1988: 114) says that although these words are called *articles* within the Fijian grammatical tradition, the term *article* is used in a somewhat unusual sense, apparently because they are unlike articles in many other languages in that they do not code notions like definiteness and indefiniteness. But they are like articles in English and many other languages in being noun phrase markers. It is presumably on the basis of this second characteristic that they are called articles within the Fijian grammatical tradition.

For many languages there is some difficulty deciding whether a word is to be considered a definite article or a demonstrative. In languages like English there is little difficulty: the definite article is distinct from the demonstratives and the demonstratives usually carry clearly deictic meaning. But in many languages, the distal demonstrative is used in a way that "comes between" the use of *the* and *that* in English: it is used much more than *that* is used in English, so that many instances of its use seem more like *the* than *that*. The distal demonstratives in Mandarin Chinese are often used in contexts in which English would simply use the definite article. And in Western Tarahumara there is a word that Burgess (1984) glosses as "that" but which in the sample text (pp. 145-149) occurs in most noun phrases referring to the main participants in the text. The existence of such languages should not be surprising, since as both Greenberg (1978: 61) and Givón (1984: 418-419) have noted, distal demonstratives are a common diachronic source for definite articles. What apparently happens is that a word which at one time was used primarily as a true deictic demonstrative is used increasingly in contexts where the spatial meaning is absent, so that eventually its use converges on that of a definite article. If a demonstrative is frequently used in this way, I treat it here as a definite article. In section 2, however, I compare the word order properties of different kinds of definite articles: those which are also demonstratives, those which resemble demonstratives (and which therefore may have developed recently from demonstratives), and those which are quite distinct in form from true demonstratives in the language.

Analogous to the problems in distinguishing definite articles from demonstratives are problems in distinguishing indefinite articles from a numeral meaning "one". In some languages, like French, the indefinite article also functions as a numeral meaning "one". In other languages, the word meaning "one" is used in a subset of the contexts in which the indefinite article is used in English, but still much more widely than the numeral *one* is used in English, its use apparently occurring typically in contexts where the noun phrase is highly pragmatically referential in the sense of Givón (1984: 423-427). Both Mandarin Chinese and Western Tarahumara, discussed above as examples of languages in which the demonstrative is often used as a definite article, are also examples of languages in which the numeral for "one" is often used where English would use an indefinite article. Where this usage appears to be common in a language, I treat the word as an indefinite article. In section 2, however, I provide a breakdown of the data on the basis of whether the indefinite article is identical to the numeral meaning "one", similar to it, or clearly distinct from it. It should be stressed that even if the indefinite article and the numeral for "one" are identical in form, they may be distinguishable syntactically. For example, Lewis (1967: 54) reports that the word *bir* in Turkish functions as an indefinite article when it occurs between an adjective and the noun, as in *büyük bir tarla* "a large field", but as a numeral meaning "one" when it occurs before an adjective, as in *bir büyük tarla* "one large field".

I should note that I use the terms *definite* and *indefinite article* somewhat loosely in this paper. The actual use of these articles often varies from that of the articles in English, not only in the kinds of cases just discussed where only a subset of definites or indefinites occur with the relevant article, but also in that the relevant distinction in some cases is apparently really specific vs. nonspecific (e.g. West Futuna-Aniwa, Dougherty 1983: 22-23).

Unless otherwise specified, I exclude from consideration inflectional affixes that code the kind of meanings coded by article words, as in the following example from Somali.

(3) nink-i ad áraktei
     man-def you saw
     the man that you saw (Kirk 1905: 19)

The data I present in this paper does not include such affixes, since including them might obscure the fact that the correlation to be demonstrated is one that holds for article words. On the other hand, I treat bound morphemes as article words rather than as affixes if they are demonstrably clitics in the sense of phrasal affixes. For example in Ngizim the definite article is a clitic that attaches either to the noun or to the last element of the noun phrase, as in (4).

(4) agwai waařa aarawii-gu
     eggs rel white-def
     the eggs which were white (Schuh 1972: 168)

I should note that I do not have data on all the relevant characteristics for all the languages in my sample. To the contrary, for many languages I lack relevant data, either because I am unable to determine the characteristics from my source or because some of the data was collected at an earlier time from sources which I have been unable to obtain access to in order to obtain further data. The data presented here comes from a larger project on word order universals for which data has been collected for over 600 languages (cf. Dryer 1986, 1988a, 1988b). The total number of languages with article words in my data base is 125. It is difficult to determine from this what proportion of the languages of the world employ articles, since some of the languages in my data base for which I have limited data may have articles even though I do not have a record of such. But we can get an idea of how many languages employ articles by comparing the number for which I have data on articles with the number of languages for which I have data on demonstratives, since, except for the relatively few languages in which demonstrative meanings are expressed by affixes, all languages employ demonstratives. Since I have data on demonstratives for 399 languages and on articles for 125 languages, it appears that about a third of the languages of the world employ articles. Table 1 lists the number of languages in my sample with articles of each of the different types I will discuss.

Table 1: Number of languages with different types of articles

Definite	74	
Indefinite	51	
Noun phrase marker	16	

Def=Dem	11	Indef=One	15
DefLikeDem	21	IndefLikeOne	8
DefNotDem	20	IndefNotOne	11

Def=Dem indicates definite articles which are identical to a demonstrative; DefLikeDem indicates definite articles which are similar in form to the demonstrative, but distinct (like *the* and *that* in English); and DefNotDem indicates definite articles which are quite distinct from the demonstrative. The categories for indefinite articles are analogous, except the form is compared to the numeral meaning "one".

It should be noted that there are many languages with either a definite article or an indefinite article but not both. For example, Kobon (Davies 1981: 60) employs an indefinite article but definites are unmarked. In fact, only 31 languages of those listed in Table 1 have both a definite and an indefinite article. Nor if a language has both types of articles need they belong to the same word class. In two languages in my sample (Hausa and Chaha), there is an indefinite article which precedes the noun and a definite article which follows. There are also languages in which an indefinite article can co-occur with a noun phrase marker article, as in the following example from Jacaltec.

(5) hune'   no'   txitam
    a   class pig
    a pig (Craig 1977: 137)

The word *no'* belongs to a class which Craig (1977: 133) calls noun classifiers; these count as noun phrase marker articles in the sense of this paper since it is normal for a noun phrase to contain a word from this class. Hence both *hune'* and *no'* count as articles in this paper.

2. The word order patterns

For the purposes of testing hypotheses, the data is presented here in a manner that is explained and justified in greater detail in Dryer (to appear a). Briefly, the languages in my data base are first grouped into genetic groups I call *genera* which are roughly comparable in time-depth to the subfamilies of Indo-European. These genera are then further grouped into six large geographical areas (Africa, Eurasia (excluding southeast Asia), Southeast Asia & Oceania, Australia & New Guinea, North America, and South America). In order to test whether a given language type is significantly more common than another language type, the number of genera containing languages of each type in each of the six geographical areas is determined. If one of the two types is more common in each of the six areas, then it is concluded that there is a significant linguistic preference for that type over the other. The statistical test is a simple sign test: the chance of all six areas containing more of a given type under the null hypothesis is 1 in 64. Hence if all six areas do contain more of a given type, the result is statistically significant at a level better than.02.

For example, Table 2 gives the data for prepositions and postpositions in OV languages.

Table 2: Postpositions vs. prepositions in OV languages

	Africa	Eurasia	SEAsia&Oc	Aus-NewGui	NAmer	SAmer	Total
OV&Postp	[15]	[23]	[5]	[16]	[24]	[17]	100
OV&Prep	3	2	0	1	0	0	6

The square brackets indicate the more frequent type within each of the six areas. It can be seen from Table 2 that OV&Postpositional languages are more common than OV&Prepositional languages in each of the six areas. We can therefore conclude that there is a statistically significant preference for OV languages to be postpositional rather than prepositional.

Table 3 give comparable data for article-noun order as opposed to noun-article order in OV languages.

Table 3: Order of article and noun in OV languages

	Africa	Eurasia	SEAsia&Oc	Aus-NewGui	NAmer	SAmer	Total
OV&ArtN	1	2	0	1	4	[3]	11
OV&NArt	[5]	2	[2]	[4]	4	1	18

The data in Table 3 does not provide clear evidence of any pattern for the order of article and noun among OV languages. Although NArt order is slightly more common overall, it is more common in only 3 of the 6 areas. We cannot conclude that there is any tendency for OV languages to be NArt. The examples in (6) illustrate these two orders of article and noun in OV languages.

(6) a. Nevome (OV&ArtN)
macco occi an'-t'-igui abamabua
a/one woman 1sg-perf-irr fondle
I fondled a woman (Shaul 1982: 66)
b. Lakota (OV&NArt)
Mathó ki wa-kté.
bear the 1sg-kill
I killed the bear. (Van Valin 1987: 376)

Table 4 gives comparable data for VO languages.

Table 4: Order of article and noun in VO languages

	Africa	Eurasia	SEAsia&Oc	Aus-NewGui	NAmer	SAmer	Total
VO&ArtN	2	[6]	[6]	[1]	[14]	[4]	33
VO&NArt	[9]	0	3	0	2	0	14

A clearer pattern emerges from Table 4 than emerged from Table 3: in 5 of the 6 areas there are more genera containing VO&ArtN languages than there are genera containing VO&NArt languages. One area, Africa, exhibits a preference in the opposite direction. Because VO&ArtN is more common in only 5 of the 6 areas, an overall preference for ArtN order among VO languages falls short of statistical significance. But since 5 of the areas do exhibit such a preference, and since the total number of VO&NArt genera outside Africa is considerably lower than the total number of VO&ArtN genera (5 vs. 31), we can say that there is a trend toward VO languages being ArtN that falls short of statistical significance. The examples in (1) and (2) above from Vietnamese and Fijian (as well as the articles in English) exemplify the typical ArtN order; (7) from Fulani illustrates the NArt order that is less typical in a VO language.

(7)   Bello hokkii   Mamman   sheede   ɗen.
         gave   money   the
      Bello gave Mamman the money. (Arnott 1970: 28)

   Given the fact that there is no statistically significant preference for one order of article and noun among either OV languages or VO languages, we might conclude that there is no evidence of any correlation between the order of article and noun and the order of object and verb. However, if we compare the proportions of genera containing ArtN languages (as opposed to NArt languages) in OV as opposed to VO languages, a statistically significant pattern emerges. The data is given in Table 5.[1]

Table 5: Proportions of genera containing ArtN languages

	Africa	Eurasia	SEAsia&Oc	Aus-NewGui	NAmer	SAmer	Average
OV	.17	.50	.00	.20	.50	.75	.35
VO	[.18]	[1.00]	[.67]	[1.00]	[.88]	[1.00]	.79

Although the difference in proportions in Africa is marginal, it is still the case that the proportion of genera containing ArtN languages is higher among VO languages in all six areas. We can therefore conclude that VO languages exhibit a statistically significantly greater tendency to   place articles before the noun than OV languages do. Because of that we can say that there is a statistically significant correlation between the order of article and noun and the order of object and verb.

   The direction of this correlation, however, is the opposite of what traditional assumptions might lead us to expect. If one adopts the traditional assumption that articles are modifiers of nouns and the common view that modifiers tend to precede the noun in OV languages and to follow in VO languages, then we would expect articles to precede the noun more often in OV languages than they do in VO languages. But the correlation shown in Table 4 is in the opposite direction. I will return to the question of how to reconcile these results with traditional assumptions in section 3.

   One question that arises, however, is that of how much the correlation demonstrated in Table 5 is due to one subtype of article and whether the various kinds of words I have treated as articles all exhibit this correlation. These questions are difficult to answer in a rigourous statistical fashion because the small numbers of languages of each sort make it difficult to obtain statistically significant results. For this reason, much of my discussion will be in terms of trends.

   Consider first definite articles. Table 6 gives the number of genera containing each of the four possible language types for the different orderings of object and verb and of definite article and noun.

Table 6: Order of definite article and noun

	Africa	Eurasia	SEAsia&Oc	Aus-NewGui	NAmer	SAmer	Total
OV&DefN	1	0	0	1	3	[2]	7
OV&NDef	[4]	[1]	0	1	[4]	0	10
VO&DefN	1	[5]	[4]	0	[11]	[4]	25
VO&NDef	[8]	0	2	0	2	0	12

The general pattern in Table 6 is the same as the pattern that we saw for articles in general: NDef order is slightly more common among OV languages while DefN order is considerably more common among VO languages, though the trend falls short of statistical significance, primarily because VO&NDef order is much more common in Africa.

Table 7 gives the data on proportions for definite articles, comparable to the data for articles in general given in Table 5.

Table 7: Proportions of genera containing DefN languages

	Africa	Eurasia	SEAsia&Oc	Aus-NewGui	NAmer	SAmer	Average
OV	[.20]	.00	--	.50	.43	1.00	.43
VO	.11	[1.00]	.67	--	[.85]	1.00	.73

The two entries in Table 7 of the form "--" are cases where the proportion cannot be determined since there are no genera containing languages of the given sort in my sample: e.g. there are no OV languages in my sample from Southeast Asia & Oceania with definite articles, so that the proportion would be 0/0. Because of this, we cannot compare proportions for two areas. But in only two of the remaining four areas is the proportion of DefN order higher among VO languages, considerably short of statistical significance. We therefore have no clear evidence that definite articles tend to precede the noun more often in VO languages than in OV languages.

On the other hand, the data in Table 7 includes definite articles which are also demonstratives. If we exclude such words and include only definite articles which are distinct from demonstratives, clearer evidence of a correlation emerges. The relevant data is given in Table 8.

Table 8: Order of definite article and noun for definite articles distinct from demonstratives

	Africa	Eurasia	SEAsia&Oc	Aus-NewGui	NAmer	SAmer	Total
OV&DefN	1	0	0	0	0	0	1
OV&NDef	1	[1]	0	[1]	[2]	0	5
VO&DefN	1	[4]	[2]	0	[6]	[3]	16
VO&NDef	[5]	0	1	0	2	0	8

While the numbers in Table 8 fall short of statistical significance, the direction of the trend is more striking than that for definite articles in general given in Table 6: the righthand column of Table 8 shows that if we exclude definite articles which are also demonstratives NDef order is overall more common among OV languages by 5 to 1, while DefN is more common among VO languages by 16 to 8. In no area is DefN more common among OV languages and in only one area (Africa) is NDef more common among VO languages.

Table 9 shows further that the more distinct the definite article is from demonstratives, the more likely its position relative to the noun will correlate with the order of verb and object. Because the numbers are rather small, I have not given the breakdown by area but have simply used the total number of genera, though I do give the average proportion of DefN genera within each area.

Table 9: Definite articles by subtype

		Def=Dem	DefLikeDem	DefNotDem
OV	DefN	4	1	0
	NDef	1	3	2
	Aver. proportion DefN	.67	.17	.00
VO	DefN	3	7	10
	NDef	1	6	2
	Aver. proportion DefN	.75	.67	.83
Difference in proportions between VO and OV		.08	.50	.83

We can see from the first column of Table 9 that there is no apparent difference between OV and VO languages in the position of definite articles which are identical to demonstratives. On the other hand, the third column of Table 9 shows that there is the greatest difference between OV and VO languages in the position of definite articles which are quite unlike demonstratives. In fact, out of the 16 languages in my sample of this sort, only two languages, Lelemi and Huave, fail to conform to the correlation. Hence we can conclude that there is a correlation in the case of definite articles and that it increases with the degree to which the definite article is distinct from demonstratives.

One reasonable conclusion one might draw is that it is mistaken to treat demonstratives which often function like definite articles as articles. After all, the evidence here suggests that they do not exhibit the word order properties that "true" definite articles do. Nevertheless, there is evidence that even when such definite articles are identical to demonstratives, they are still subject to different word order "pressures". There are two languages in my sample in which the definite article is identical to the demonstrative in form but in which the two occur on opposite sides of the noun. Or to put it differently, in these two languages, there is a word whose function depends on which side of the noun it occurs. In Swahili, the demonstrative *yule* (or more accurately the demonstrative *-le*, which takes different prefixes depending on the noun class of the noun it is accompanying) either precedes or follows the noun, but when it precedes the noun, "its function corresponds to that of the definite article in English" (Ashton 1947: 59). Hence *mtu yule* means "that man" while *yule mtu* means "the man". The opposite situation holds in Ute (Givón 1984: 419), in which the demonstrative has demonstrative meaning when it precedes the noun, but functions as a definite article when it follows. Significantly the fact that Swahili and Ute are opposite in this respect can be understood in terms of the correlations discussed in this paper. Namely, since articles precede the noun more often in VO languages than they do in OV languages, we might expect that if two languages differed in this respect, the one in which the demonstrative functions as an article when it precedes the noun is more likely than the other language to be VO. And in fact Swahili *is* a VO language while Ute is an OV language. This suggests not only that the position of definite articles cannot be explained (at least not in all cases) in terms of the position of the demonstratives from which they arose, but also that words with the meaning of definite articles are subject to word order "pressures" that demonstratives are not subject to. As I point out in the conclusion, demonstratives do not exhibit the correlation with the order of verb and object that I have shown articles exhibit.

Consider now indefinite articles. Table 10 gives the data comparable to the data given in Table 6 for definite articles.

Table 10: Order of indefinite article and noun

	Africa	Eurasia	SEAsia&Oc	Aus-NewGui	NAmer	SAmer	Total
OV&IndefN	1	1	0	0	2	1	5
OV&NIndef	[2]	[2]	0	[3]	2	1	10
VO&IndefN	2	[4]	[3]	0	[4]	[1]	14
VO&NIndef	[3]	0	1	0	0	0	4

The general pattern for indefinite articles in Table 10 is generally similar to that in Table 6 for definite articles: NIndef order is somewhat more common among OV languages, while IndefN order is more common among VO languages, except in Africa, but in both cases we fall short of statistical significance. The data for proportions is given in Table 11.

Table 11: Proportions of genera containing IndefN languages

	Africa	Eurasia	SEAsia&Oc	Aus-NewGui	NAmer	SAmer	Average
OV	.33	.33	--	.00	.50	.50	.33
VO	[.40]	[1.00]	.75	--	[1.00]	[1.00]	.83

Again, because of the absence of certain language types in certain areas in my sample, we cannot compare proportions for all six areas. However, in the four areas for which we can compare proportions, the proportion of genera containing IndefN languages rather than NIndef languages is higher among VO languages. Furthermore, if we treat the instances of "--" in Table 11 as .50 (i.e. treat 0/0 as .50, mathematically inaccurate but with some justification in the present instance), then the proportion would be higher in all six areas. In addition, there is a large difference in the average proportions: .33 for OV languages and .83 for VO languages. For these reasons we can conclude that there is a statistically significant correlation between the order of indefinite article and noun and the order of object and verb.

Again it is worthwhile distinguishing three subtypes of indefinite articles: those which are identical to the numeral meaning "one" (Indef=One), those which are similar to "one" though distinct, like the Dutch indefinite article *een* [ən] (cf. *één* [en] "one") (IndefLikeOne), and those which are quite distinct from the numeral meaning "one" (IndefNotOne). Table 12 gives data on such subtypes, analogous to that given in Table 8 above for definite articles.

Table 12: Indefinite articles by subtype

		Indef=One	IndefLikeOne	IndefNotOne
OV	IndefN	5	0	0
	NIndef	2	0	3
	Aver. proportion IndefN	.70	--	.00
VO	IndefN	5	3	5
	NIndef	0	2	1
	Aver. proportion IndefN	1.00	.63	.92
Difference in proportions between VO and OV		.30	--	.92

Although the trend in Table 12 is less clear than it was for definite articles, it appears to be the case that there is the greatest difference between OV and VO languages among indefinite articles which are quite distinct from the numeral "one". This suggests that the correlation between the order of article and noun and that of verb and object may be strongest for articles which are categorially more distinct from other words.

The third class of articles is that of noun phrase markers, illustrated by the Fijian example in (2) above. The number of these is considerably smaller than for definite and indefinite articles: only 16 languages in my sample employ such articles, occurring in a total of 8 genera, and 9 of these languages are Austronesian. But despite the small numbers, two clear patterns emerge: first, all such markers precede the noun; and second, with one exception, all of the noun phrase marker articles occur in VO languages.

3. Explanations

As noted above, the general correlation documented in the previous section between the order of article and noun and the order of object and verb runs counter to what we might expect, at least given two traditional assumptions: that articles are modifiers of nouns, and that modifiers tend to precede the noun in OV languages and to follow in VO languages. The evidence from the previous section is evidence that at least one of these two assumptions must be false. It is not my intention here to argue that one of these assumptions but not the other is false. In fact, I believe that there are good reasons to question both of these assumptions. What I will do in this section is summarize reasons for questioning each of them.

The belief that OV languages tend to place modifiers before nouns while VO languages tend to place them after nouns partly stems from a widespread belief that adjectives tend to precede nouns in OV languages and to follow them in VO languages. I have shown elsewhere (Dryer 1988a), however, that there is no evidence of any correlation between the order of adjective and noun and the order of object and verb, that it is actually more common for OV languages to place the adjective after the noun, and that adjectives precede the noun in VO languages as often as they do in OV languages. I have also shown (Dryer 1986) that there is no evidence that OV languages place demonstratives or numerals before the noun more often than VO languages do. And I have shown (Dryer, to appear b) that plural words, separate words in noun phrases indicating grammatical plural, exhibit a strong tendency to precede the noun in VO languages and to follow the noun in OV languages, the opposite of what one might expect if plural words are modifiers of nouns. In fact, the only modifiers of nouns that exhibit a correlation are genitives and relative clauses (Dryer 1986). Hence there is no evidence of a general tendency for modifiers to precede nouns in OV languages and to follow in VO languages. Thus, even if one maintains the traditional assumption that articles are modifiers of nouns, there would be no reason to expect them to precede the noun more often in OV languages than in VO languages.

But that leaves unexplained why we in fact find the opposite correlation in the case of articles. I have proposed elsewhere (Dryer 1988a, 1988b) that the word order correlations in general reflect a tendency to consistently order phrasal constituents with respect to nonphrasal ones, that consistent OV languages are consistently left-branching (placing phrasal constituents before nonphrasal ones) while consistent VO languages are consistently right-branching. If one accepts the common assumption in generative grammar that determiners in English combine with an N' constituent, then the correlation documented here for article-noun order is explained: in a noun phrase like *the tall man* the article *the* is a nonphrasal category combining with the phrasal N' *tall man*. In other words, by placing the article at the beginning of the noun phrase in English, the result is a right-branching structure, consistent with the general right-branching nature of the language. On the other hand, if English were to place articles after the noun, then the structure of noun phrases would be left-branching. Such a structure, though it might conform to noun-modifier order, would actually produce inconsistency in the language since English is generally right-branching.

An alternative approach to explaining the correlation discussed in section 2 would be to question the traditional assumption that the article is a modifier of the noun. In fact, a number of linguists (cf. Vennemann & Harlow 1977, Hudson 1984: 90-91, Abney 1987) have questioned this assumption, arguing instead for an analysis under which the article is the head, the N' some sort of dependent of the article. While the arguments are often somewhat theory-dependent and/or English-specific, there are a number of typological facts that lend credence to the idea that articles are the real heads of noun phrases. Under such an approach, the difference between articles and pronouns is rather akin to the difference between transitive and intransitive verbs. In other words, articles and pronouns belong to a single category, which we can arbitrarily call articles, the difference being that articles like *the* are transitive articles, while pronouns are just intransitive articles. There are a number of languages in which, unlike English, a single word functions both as an article and as a personal pronoun. For example, in Jicaltepec Mixtec, it is common for noun phrases to consist of a pronoun followed by a noun in a structure which Bradley (1970: 63) describes as consisting of a pronoun as "center" with the noun as "attribute", illustrated by the word *rá* in (8).

(8) číká̠   ča?a ña sa?ma či̠?i̠ rá ahili
    thing-that give she clothes to he angel
    That's why she gave the clothes to the angel. (Bradley 1970: 79)

As indicated by Bradley's gloss, *rá* otherwise functions as a pronoun in the language. But except for this fact, *rá* accompanied by a noun is very much like articles in other languages, at least as a kind of noun phrase marker. I therefore treat it as an article in this study. But in doing so, it is not my intention to deny the appropriateness of Bradley's analysis. If one takes the position that articles are simply pronouns modified by nouns, then these words *are* articles, even on Bradley's analysis.

Another phenomenon found in a number of languages that provides further support for treating articles as heads of noun phrases is the following. In some languages, noun phrases that occur as arguments of the verb always occur with an article, but when they occur in predicate position they do not. Thus in the Cebuano examples in (9), the predicate (which is initial) is an N' and does not occur with an article while the subject occurs with an article.

(9) a. babaye ang duktur.
      woman art doctor
      The doctor is a woman.
    b. duktur ang babaye
      doctor art woman
      The woman is a doctor.

It is in general not normal for nonmaximal projections of a head to occur where they are not a constituent in a maximal projection. If we treat articles as modifiers of nouns, combining with an N', then the occurrence of an N' in predicate position would be an exception to this generalization. On the other hand, if we treat the article as the head of the so-called noun phrase, then the N' would be the maximal projection.

Articles change the category of an N' in a way that modifiers generally do not. While we can say, loosely speaking, that an N' is semantically a predicate, a so-called NP is a referring expression. Hence the semantic category of the article is that of a word that changes a predicate into a referring expression. The Cebuano facts illustrated in (9) are thus not surprising: an NP in argument position is semantically a referring expression while an N' in predicate position is semantically a predicate.

If articles are the heads of NPs, then the correlation demonstrated in section 2 is partly explained: it reflects a tendency for heads to precede dependents in VO languages more often than in OV languages. However, as noted above, there is no general tendency of this sort: the order of adjective and noun does not correlate with the order of object and verb. On the other hand, it turns out that in those cases where we do find a correlation, the dependent is always a phrasal category. If articles are heads, then the N' that the article combines with is a phrasal category. Hence the correlation demonstrated in section 2 may reflect a tendency for *phrasal* dependents to follow their heads more often in VO languages than in OV languages.

4. Conclusion

I have demonstrated in this paper that the order of article and noun correlates with that of verb and object, that the article precedes the noun significantly more often in VO languages than it does in OV languages. But the functional similarity between demonstratives and articles (especially definite articles), the fact that distal demonstratives are a very common diachronic source for definite articles, and the kinds of explanations discussed in the preceding section would all lead us to expect that the order of demonstrative and noun would exhibit the same correlation. But it does not. Table 13 gives the basic data.

Table 13: Order of demonstrative and noun

	Africa	Eurasia	SEAsia&Oc	Aus-NewGui	NAmer	SAmer	Total
OV&DemN	10	[17]	[4]	8	[21]	[11]	71
OV&NDem	10	1	2	[9]	5	4	31
VO&DemN	4	[8]	7	[5]	[17]	[9]	50
VO&NDem	[24]	1	[11]	0	6	1	43

No pattern emerges from Table 13: there is a trend towards DemN order in OV languages, though the number of OV&DemN genera is larger in only four areas. The totals figures in the righthand column might suggest that the proportion of NDem is higher in VO languages than it is in OV languages, but the majority of VO&NDem genera are in Africa, so the total figure is somewhat skewed by this one area. As before, it is necessary to compare proportions, as in Table 14.

Table 14: Proportions of genera containing DemN languages

	Africa	Eurasia	SEAsia&Oc	Aus-NewGui	NAmer	SAmer	Average
OV	[.50]	[.94]	[.67]	.47	[.81]	.73	.69
VO	.14	.89	.39	[1.00]	.74	[.90]	.68

Table 14 shows no evidence of a correlation: DemN order is more common among OV languages in four areas but more common among VO languages in the other two areas. In addition, the average proportion (shown in the righthand column) is almost the same for OV as it is for VO languages. And even if we were to interpret the evidence as showing a weak trend, the direction of the trend is the opposite from that shown in this paper for articles.

There is clear evidence, then, that demonstratives exhibit very different word order properties from articles. Unfortunately it is beyond the scope of this paper to discuss the possible reasons for this. But this issue is clearly one that warrants attention if we are to understand the causes of word order correlations.

Acknowledgement

I am indebted to the Social Sciences and Humanities Research Council of Canada for Research Grants 410-810949, 410-830354, and 410-850540, which supported the research for this paper.

Notes

[1] To see how the figures in Table 5 are computed, consider the figure .17 for OV languages in Africa given in the upper left hand corner of the table. This figure can be obtained from Table 3, which shows that there is one genus in Africa containing OV&ArtN languages and 5 genera containing OV&NArt languages. The proportion of genera containing OV&ArtN languages is thus 1 out of 6 genera (1+5), or .17.

The characterization given here for the proportion of genera is misleading in one respect. Namely, it ignores the possibility that some genus may contain languages of both sorts. In general, this does not happen, since languages within a genus are typically similar in their word order characteristics. However, it turns out that the example discussed provides an instance of this situation. The sole genus in

Africa containing an OV&ArtN language in my sample is Semitic, the language in question being Tigre. But Semitic is also one of the genera containing an OV&NArt language, namely Chaha. Thus, strictly speaking, there are only 5 genera containing OV&ArtN or OV&NArt languages. The figures in Table 5 can be more accurately characterized as giving the proportion of *subgenera* , where a subgenus is a subset of languages in a genus that are identical with respect to the set of word order characteristics being examined. In general, each genus will contain exactly one subgenus. But in the case of Semitic, there are two subgenera with respect to the order of article and noun among OV languages. Thus Table 5 does give accurate figures for the proportions of *subgenera* containing ArtN languages.

Bibliography

Abney, Stephen Paul. 1987. *The English Noun Phrase in its Sentential Aspect.* Unpublished MIT dissertation.

Arnott, D. W. 1970. *The Nominal and Verbal Systems of Fula.* Oxford: Clavendon Press.

Ashton, E. O. 1947. *Swahili Grammar.* Second Edition. London: Longmans, Green & Co.

Binh, Duong Thanh. 1971. *A Tagmemic Comparison of the Structure of English and Vietnamese Sentences.* The Hague: Mouton.

Bradley, C. Henry. 1970. *A Linguistic Sketch of Jicaltepec Mixtec.* Summer Institute of Linguistics.

Burgess, Don. 1984. Western Tarahumara. In Ronald W. Langacker ed., *Studies in Uto-Aztecan Grammar*, Volume 4. The Summer Institute of Linguistics and the University of Texas at Arlington.

Craig, Collette. 1977. *The Structure of Jacaltec.* Austin: University of Texas Press.

Davies, John. 1981. *Kobon.* Lingua Descriptive Studies 3. Amsterdam: North-Holland.

Dixon, Robert M. W. 1988. *A Grammar of Boumaa Fijian.* Chicago: University of Chicago Press.

Dougherty, Janet W. D. 1983. *West Futuna-Aniwa: An Introduction to a Polynesian Outlier Language.* University of California Publications in Linguistics, Volume 102. Berkeley: University of California Press.

Dryer, Matthew S. 1986. Word order consistency and English. In S. Delancey and R. Tomlin, eds., *Proceedings of the Second Annual Pacific Linguistics Conference.* Eugene, Oregon.

Dryer, Matthew S. 1988a. Object-verb order and adjective-noun order: dispelling a myth. *Lingua* 74: 77-109.

Dryer, Matthew S. 1988b. Universals of negative position. In M. Hammond, E. Moravcsik and J. Wirth, eds., *Studies in Syntactic Typology*, pp. 93-124. Amsterdam: John Benjamins.

Dryer, Matthew S. To appear a. Large linguistic areas and language sampling. To appear in *Studies in Language.*

Dryer, Matthew S. To appear b. Plural words. To appear in *Linguistics.*

Givón, Talmy. 1984. *Syntax: A Functional-Typological Introduction, Volume 1.* Amsterdam: John Benjamins.

Greenberg, Joseph H. 1957. Order of affixing: a study in general linguistics. In *Essays in Linguistics.* Chicago: University of Chicago Press.

Greenberg, Joseph H. 1963. Some universals of grammar with particular reference to the order of meaningful elements. In J. Greenberg, ed., *Universals of Language*. Cambridge, Mass.: MIT Press.

Greenberg, Joseph. 1978. How does a language acquire gender markers? In J. Greenberg, ed., *Universals of Human Language, Volume 3: Word Structure*, pp. 47-82. Stanford: Stanford University Press.

Hawkins, John A. 1983. *Word Order Universals*. New York: Academic Press.

Hudson, Richard. 1984. *Word Grammar*. Oxford: Basil Blackwell.

Kirk, J. W. C. 1905. *A Grammar of the Somali Language*. Farnsborough, Hants.: Gregg International Publishers Ltd.

Lewis, G. L. 1967. *Turkish Grammar*. Oxford University Press.

Schuh, Russell G. 1972. *Aspects of Ngizim Syntax*. University of California, Los Angeles, Ph.D. Dissertation. Ann Arbor: University Microfilms.

Shaul, David Leedom. 1982. *A Grammar of Nevome*. University of California, Berkeley, Ph.D. Dissertation. Ann Arbor: University Microfilms.

Van Valin, Robert D., Jr. 1987. The role of government in the grammar of head-marking languages. *International Journal of American Linguistics* 53: 371-397.

Vennemann, Theo. 1976. Categorial grammar and the order of meaningful elements. In A. Juilland, ed., *Linguistic Studies Offered to Joseph Greenberg on the Occasion of His Sixtieth Birthday*. Saratoga, California: Anma Libri.

Vennemann, Theo, and Ray Harlow. 1977. Categorial grammar and consistent basic VX serialization. *Theoretical Linguistics* 4: 227-254.

Compound *suru* Verbs and Evidence for Unaccusativity in Japanese[1]

Stanley Dubinsky
University of California at Santa Cruz

There is a class of Japanese verbs, here called NP-*suru* verbs, that are formed from the combination of what Martin (1975) calls *verbal nouns* and the verb *suru* 'do'. These verbal nouns are predicates and select arguments, but cannot by themselves be inflected. As a consequence, they regularly combine with the generic verb *suru* 'do' to form a tensed clause. For example, the verbal noun *benkyoo* 'study' combines with *suru* to form the verb *benkyoo-suru* 'study'.

The focus of this paper is a set of syntactic anomalies observed within the class of intransitive verbal nouns. I will argue that these differences may be explained by appeal to the Unaccusative Hypothesis, under which certain intransitive verbs select an initial subject, while others select an initial direct object. Section 1 examines the case marking of verbal nouns by *suru* and its distribution. Section 2 presents an analysis of the types of constructions in which a verbal noun may appear. Section 3 shows how the proposed analysis and the assumption of initial unaccusativity correctly predicts the behavior of certain intransitive verbal nouns, and goes on to provide additional evidence for the account.

1. *o* marking within NP-*suru* verbs

The verbal noun in an NP-*suru* verb may, subject to certain conditions, appear with the accusative postposition *o*. Observe the alternation between *benkyoo-suru* and *benkyoo o suru* in (1).

(1) Ziroo wa   benkyoo (o)   siteiru.
        TOP study   (ACC) do.PRG.IMP

    'Ziro is studying.'

The following discussion examines the apparently irregular distribution of this *o* marker and demonstrates that its distribution can be accounted for by reference to the initial unaccusativity of certain predicates.

Before proceeding, it is first necessary to show that another condition, the Double *o* Constraint, is operative in accounting for some of the constraints on its distribution. In (2), we note that *o* marking of *benkyoo* is no longer possible when the predicate *benkyoo-suru* takes an accusatively marked direct object.

(2) Ziroo wa suugaku o   benkyoo (*o)   siteiru.
    TOP math   ACC study   (ACC) do.PRG.IMP
    'Ziro is studying math.'

The ill-formedness of the doubly *o* marked variant of (2) has been attributed to a surface case filter called, appropriately, the Double *o* Constraint and proposed by Harada (1973:135-39).[2]

(3) The Double *o* Constraint

A derivation is marked ill-formed if it terminates in a surface structure
which contains two occurrences of NPs marked with *o*
both of which are dominated by the same VP node.

It is clear from further data is that Harada's constraint does not account for all those instances in which NP *o suru* is impossible. There are optionally transitive NP-*suru* verbs which do not permit *o* marking of their verbal noun even when intransitive. These verbs are similar to the English verb *break* in that they are either transitive or inchoative. The verb *hunsitu-suru* 'lose' is one such predicate. It can occur with either two nominal arguments (i.e. 'someone loses something') or only one (i.e. 'something is lost').

(4) Taroo wa   konyaku-yubiwa o   hunsitu (*o)   sita.
    TOP engagement-ring ACC lose   (ACC) do.PRF
    'Taro lost the engagement ring.'

(5) Konyaku-yubiwa ga   hunsitu (*o)   sita.
    engagement-ring NOM lose   (ACC) do.PRF
    'The engagement ring disappeared.'

The Double *o* Constraint, or whatever is operative in ruling out the *o* marked variant in (2) would lead us to expect, correctly, that *hunsitu* may not be *o* marked in (4). However, nothing we have noted thus far would seem to rule out the *o* marking of *hunsitu* in (5), analogous to that of *benkyoo* in (1). Contrary to expectations, the *o* marked variant of (5) is ill-formed.

We also find that intransitive NP-*suru* verbs split into two classes with respect to the grammaticality of NP *o suru*. Some can appear with the verbal noun *o* marked, while others cannot.

(6) Tanaka ga   kikoku   (o)   sita.
    NOM return.home (ACC) do.PRF
    'Tanaka returned to his homeland.'

(7) Hanako ga   kakeoti (o)   sita.
      NOM elope   (ACC) do.PRF

   'Hanako eloped.'

(8) Tanaka ga   zikosuisen   (o)   sita.
      NOM self.recommend (ACC) do.PRF

   'Tanaka recommended himself.'

(9) Mary ga   sissin   (*o)   sita.
      NOM pass.out (ACC) do.PRF

   'Mary lost consciousness.'

(10) Ondo   wa zyoosyoo (*o)   sita.
      temperature TOP rise   (ACC) do.PRF

   'The temperature went up.'

(11) Yane ga   amamori (*o)   sita.
     roof NOM leak   (ACC) do.PRF

   'The roof leaked.'

(12) Watasi wa   munasawagi (*o)   suru.[3]
    I   TOP unease   (ACC) do.IMP

   'I am uneasy.'

I will claim in section 3 that *o* marking is ruled out in (5) and (9)-(12) because each of the clauses is initially unaccusative. In order to articulate this claim however, it is first necessary to elucidate the different types of NP *o suru* and NP-*suru* constructions.

2. NP-*suru* vs. NP *o suru*

      The verbal noun in construction with *suru*, where the NP is not *o* marked, is discussed in the literature in Inoue(1976), and Kageyama(1976-77)and(1982), among others. Most recently, the NP *o suru* construction has received a detailed treatment in Grimshaw and Mester(1988)[4].It is clear from the aforementioned work that the verb *suru* appears in three different types of constructions: one in which it is the main verb of a clause, and both selects and case marks its own arguments; another in which it case marks the verbal noun, but it is the verbal noun which selects arguments; and, finally, one in which *suru* affixes directly to the verbal noun, neither assigning case nor selecting arguments. I will briefly mention the first of these before turning to the second and third, which are of concern to us here.

The first construction, which we will not examine here, is one in which the verb *suru* is a transitive main verb selecting a subject and direct object. It is similar to the non-auxiliary use of the English verb *do* or *make* as in: *John did what we asked him*, or *Jim made a salad*. Like its English equivalents, *suru* as a main verb requires an agentive subject. This is not the case with the other two constructions.

Following terminology developed by Jesperson (1954) and Cattell (1984), Grimshaw and Mester refer to this construction as *heavy suru*, while *suru* in construction with a verbal noun is called *light*. In English, the term 'light' verb refers to the thematically empty use of verbs such as the English *give, make,* and *have* in constructions in which "the action is spelt out in the nominal that follows" [Cattell 1984, p.2]. Combinations of 'light' verb plus a nominal generally alternate with a verbal cognate of that nominal which carries much the same meaning. Some pairs are: *dash, make a dash; kiss, give a kiss; rest, have a rest; move, make a move;* and so on. Notice that in an English 'light' verb construction, the nominal determines the argument structure. Thus, while the predicate *make* in (13) does not take a goal marked by the preposition *to*, both *offer* and *make an offer* do so.

(13) a. Jim made a salad for/*to the guests.
    b. Jim offered money to/*for the hospital.
    c. Jim made an offer of money to/*for the hospital.

The Japanese 'light' verb construction has these same properties: *suru* assigns case and carries inflection, but does not directly assign any thematic roles. While *suru* is the surface verbal element and the verbal noun can sometimes be its direct object, it is the verbal noun which determines the argument structure and selectional restrictions. Thus, when *suru* is in construct with a verbal noun in this way, nominals bearing initial relations other than and in addition to 1 and 2 can occur, in accordance with the requirements of that verbal noun.

(14) Taroo ga   tenisubu   ni   nyuukai o   sita.
       NOM tennis.club DAT join   ACC do.PRF

    'Taro joined a tennis club.'

(15) Taroo wa   tenisubu   ni   nyuukai-sita.
       TOP tennis.club DAT join-do.PRF

    'Taro joined a tennis club.'

Further, the subject in this construction need not be agentive (as (14) and (15) also demonstrate), indicating, inasmuch as it does not impose selectional restrictions on it, that *suru* in each case has not selected the subject (see also (5) and (9)-(12) above).

If a verbal noun assigns thematic roles to arguments (inside or outside of its nominal boundaries), we may assume that it determines initial GRs and heads an initial P-arc. On the other hand, since it does not have the capacity to carry inflectional morphology, we might reasonably propose that one of the properties of the verbal noun is the inability to head a final P-arc in a tensed (main) clause. This being the case, a clause consisting of a verbal noun and its arguments can escape ungrammaticality only by forming a union construction with a 'light' verb such as *suru*.

(16)

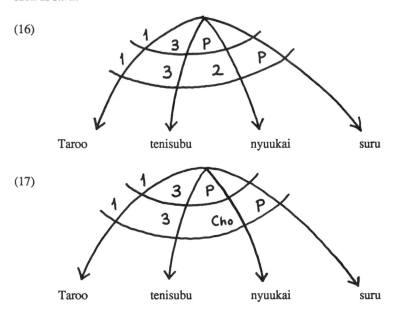

| Taroo | tenisubu | nyuukai | suru |

(17)

Union constructions (or multipredicate clauses) have been proposed for a range of constructions across a great number of languages. The most familiar and ubiquitous type of union construction is Causative Union. Following Davies and Rosen's (1988) monoclausal representation of union, the causative predicate heads a non-initial P-arc and introduces its own subject, while the embedded 1 is generally revalued to an object relation (2 or 3). The embedded predicate is put en chomage.[5]

Contrasting Causative Union with the union RN proposed above, we note that the union predicate *suru* introduces no extra arguments of its own (recall that 'light' verbs are thematically empty). Accordingly, *suru* simply inherits the arguments initialized by the embedded verbal noun *nyuukai*. The salient difference between the two 'light' constructions, (14) and (15), is that in the first the verbal noun is marked with accusative case. To account for this, I have proposed that the P revalue to 2. This revaluation will have the effect of putting en chomage any initial direct object of the verbal noun that might be present. This is of little consequence in these examples, but will be crucial to the account of intransitive verbal nouns.[6]

3. Unaccusativity

Having presented an account of the verbal noun constructions, this section returns to the original question; namely, what are the distributional constraints that preclude certain intransitive verbal nouns from appearing in constructions in which the verbal noun is *o* marked? Specifically, we want to account for the following contrast.[7]

(18) Ziroo wa   benkyoo (o)   siteiru.
        TOP study   (ACC) do.PRG.IMP

       'Ziro is studying.'

(19) Konyaku-yubiwa ga   hunsitu (*o)   sita.
        engagement-ring NOM lose   (ACC) do.PRF

       'The engagement ring disappeared.'

I propose that the syntactic differences between (18) and (19) can best be captured by appeal to the Unaccusative Hypothesis, which roughly stated says that the superficial subject of some intransitive clauses is a direct object "in a more abstract subjectless structure".[8] In other words, where the subject of (18), *Ziroo*, heads a 1-arc initially and finally, the single nominal in (19), *konyaku-yubiwa*, is an initial 2 that advances to 1 in the final stratum of the clause.

3.1 Analysis of unaccusative verbal nouns

According to the analysis of verbal noun constructions just presented, the *o* marked and non *o* marked variants of (18) have, respectively, the two RNs in (20).

(20) (without *o*)   (with *o*)

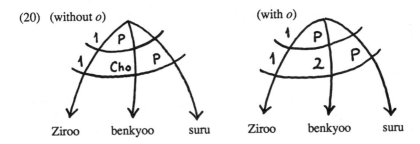

If we were to assume, as proposed here, that *hunsitu* in (19) is unaccusative and that its surface subject, *yubiwa*, is an initial 2, what RNs would be available to the two variants? The RN for the acceptable non *o* marked variant is straightforward.

(21)   (without *o*)

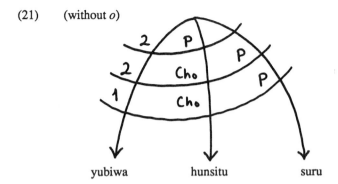

yubiwa   hunsitu   suru

In (21), the verbal noun *hunsitu* initializes *yubiwa* as a 2, is itself put en chomage in the union stratum by *suru*, and the 2 advances to 1 to satisfy the Final 1 Law.

In the case of the *o* marked variant, initial unaccusativity provides an explanation for why it is ill-formed, as RN (22) demonstrates.

(22)   (with *o*)

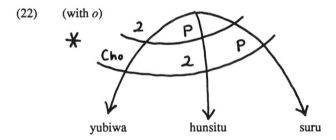

yubiwa   hunsitu   suru

If, as in (22), *yubiwa* is initialized as a 2 and *hunsitu* is revalued to 2 in the subsequent stratum, the initial 2 is put en chomage and cannot then advance to 1, as precluded by the Chomeur Advancement Ban, which states that if a dependent heads a Cho arc in some stratum, then it heads Cho arc in the final stratum [cf. Perlmutter and Postal 1984b, p.117]. (22), as it stands, violates the Final 1 Law and is ill-formed.

3.2 Supporting evidence

There are two phenomena which corroborate the analysis of intransitive *hunsitu-suru* as an unaccusative verb. Miyagawa (1989) has noted that direct objects and subjects of transitive active clauses exhibit certain differences with regard to their ability to float numeral quantifiers. He further observes that the subjects of certain intransitive verbs, specifically those identified here as initially unaccusative, exhibit object-like behavior in this regard.

Miyagawa demonstrates that a numeral quantifier phrase (NQP) that is construed with a direct object may be separated from it by another constituent. In (23), the direct object is scrambled away from the NQP.

(23) =(6a) [Miyagawa 1989]
     Hon o   Hanako ga   ni-satu katta.
     book ACC   NOM 2-CNT buy.PRF

     'Books, Hanako bought two.'

Such is not possible with the subjects of transitive clauses as (24) and (25) demonstrate.

(24) =(7) [Miyagawa 1989]
     *Gakusei ga   hon o   san-nin katta.
     student NOM book ACC 3-CNT buy.PRF

     ('Students, three bought books.')

(25) =(11) [Miyagawa 1989]
     ?*Kodomo ga   kono kagi de san-nin doa o   aketa.
     child   NOM this key INS 3-CNT door ACC open-PRF

     ('Children, three opened the door with this key.')

In (25), an instrumental phrase separates the subject *kodomo* and the NQP *san-nin*, and the sentence is ill-formed.

Turning our attention to the optionally transitive verbal nouns *benkyoo* and *hunsitu*, we observe that the subject of *benkyoo* exhibits subject-like behavior with respect to NQP floating in both transitive and intransitive clauses.

(26) a. ??Tomodati ga   watasi to   san-nin nihongo o   benkyoo-siteiru.
        friend   NOM I   with 3-CNT Japanese ACC study-do.PRG

        ('Friends, three are studying Japanese with me.')

     b. ??Tomodati ga   watasi to   san-nin benkyoo-siteiru.
        friend   NOM I   with 3-CNT study-do.PRG

        ('Friends, three are studying with me.')

Here, the infelicity of both (26a) and (26b) indicates that *tomodati* is equally a subject in both cases. On the other hand, for the verbal noun *hunsitu*, the ability of the subject to be construed with a non-adjacent NQP is dependent on whether the clause is transitive.

(27) a. ??Keisatukan ga   hutyuuide   san-nin okane o   hunsitu-sita.
        policeman NOM inadvertently 3-CNT money ACC lose-do.PRF

        ('Policemen, three inadvertently lost money.')

b. Yubiwa ga   keisatukan no   hutyuui   kara   hutatu hunsitu-sita.
   ring   NOM policeman GEN inattention because 2.CNT lose-do.PRF

'Rings, because of the policeman's inattention two got lost.'

In (27b), the subject allows construal with a non-adjacent NQP. The manifestation of this direct object-like property by the subject of intransitive *hunsitu-suru* is readily explainable if the verb determines an unaccusative initial stratum. The ability to host non-adjacent numeral quantifiers can then be attributed to initial 2s.

As in section 1, which examined case marking anomalies, we would also expect that intransitive NP-*suru* verbs should split into two classes with regard to Miyagawa's NQP floating phenomenon. The judgements here are delicate and the differences are expressed in terms of relative felicity rather than out and out grammaticality. Nevertheless, the final subjects of unaccusatives do exhibit a greater propensity to allow non-adjacent NQPs than do the subjects of unergatives.

(28) Jyogakusei   ga   watasi ga   matteiru aidani san-nin sissin-sita.
    female.students NOM I   NOM wait.PRG while 3-CNT faint-do.PRF

'Female students, while I was waiting three fainted.'

(29) ??Ryuugakusei   ga   hikooki de   san-nin kikoku-sita.
    exchange.student NOM plane   INS 3-CNT return.home

('Exchange students, by plane three returned home.')

In (29), the non-adjacent NQP *san-nin* is deemed less acceptable because the final 1 heads no 2-arc.

Another property that distinguishes initially unaccusative clauses is the inability to appear in the construction known variously as 'indirect passive' or 'adversative passive'. Indirect passive is possible for both transitive and intransitive verbs.

(30) a. Sensei wa   kodomo o   sikatta.
     teacher TOP child   ACC scold.PRF

'The teacher scolded the child.'

b. Watasi wa sensei ni   kodomo o   sikar-(r)areta.
   I   TOP teacher DAT child   ACC scold-PSS.PRF

'The teacher scolded my child on me.'
(Lit: 'I was scolded my child by the teacher.')

(31) a. Hisyo wa hayaku kaetta.
   secretary TOP early go.home.PRF

   'The secretary went home early.'

  b. Watasi wa hisyo ni hayaku kaer-(r)areta.
    I TOP secretary DAT early go.home-PSS.PRF

   'The secretary went home early on me.'
   (Lit: 'I was gone home early by the secretary.')

In each of the (b) examples above, the embedded verb is suffixed with the morpheme *-rare*. This is accompanied by the addition of an argument whose thematic role is that of 'affectee'. An analysis of these sentences will not be articulated at this point, but suffice it to say that *-rare* is claimed to be a union predicate analogous to the causative *-sase*, and that in each of the (b) examples above, *watasi* is an argument of that predicate.

  Turning to NP-*suru* verbs, we find that any such transitive verb may form an indirect passive. This is seen to be so for the verbal nouns *ziman* 'boast' and *hunsitu* 'lose'.

(32) a. Tonari no hito ga kuruma o ziman-sita.
   next GEN person NOM car ACC boast-do.PRF

   'A next door neighbor boasted about his car.'

  b. Tanaka ga tonari no hito ni kuruma o ziman-sareta.
    NOM next GEN person DAT car ACC boast-do.PSS.PRF

   'Tanaka suffered a neighbor boasting about his car.'

(33) a. Taroo ga konyaku-yubiwa o hunsitu-sita.
    NOM engagement-ring ACC lose-do.PRF

   'Taro lost the engagement ring.'

  b. Hanako ga Taroo ni konyaku-yubiwa o hunsitu-sareta.
    NOM DAT engagement-ring ACC lose-do.PSS.PRF

   'Hanako suffered Taro's losing the engagement ring.'

It is further the case that intransitive NP-*suru* predicates, like other intransitive verbs, may form an indirect passive. In (34), an intransitive sentence formed with *ziman* is shown to occur in an indirect passive construction.

(34) a. Tonari no hito wa ziman-sita.
   next GEN person TOP boast-do.PRF

   'The neighbor boasted.'

b. Tanaka wa   tonari no   hito   ni   ziman-sareta.
    TOP next   GEN person DAT boast-do.PSS.PRF

'Tanaka suffered his neighbor's boasting.'

When one attempts to embed an intransitive sentence formed with the verbal noun *hunsitu* in an indirect passive, the construction is ill-formed even though there is nothing about the meaning of *hunsitu* per se that prevents it from combining with *sareta* (cf. (33b) above).

(35) a. Konyaku-yubiwa wa   hunsitu-sita.
      engagement-ring TOP lose-do.PRF

    'The engagement ring disappeared.'

b. *Hanako ga   konyaku-yubiwa ni   hunsitu-sareta.
    NOM engagement-ring DAT lose-do.PSS.PRF

('Hanako was disappeared by the engagement ring.')

Turning once again to intransitive NP-*suru* verbs, we find that they divide into the same two classes as they did with case marking of the verbal noun and NQP floating. The grammaticality judgements are much more clear-cut with the interaction of intransitive verbs and indirect passive than they were with NQP floating. Here, indirect passives formed with initially unaccusative verbs are decidedly ill-formed.

(36) a. Tanaka no   tuma ga   kikoku-sita.
      GEN wife NOM return.home-do.PRF

    'Tanaka's wife went back (to Japan).'

b. Tanaka ga   tuma ni   kikoku-sareta.
    NOM wife DAT return.home-do.PSS.PRF

    'Tanaka's wife went back (to Japan) on him.'

(37) a. Tanaka no   musume ga   kakeoti-sita.
      GEN daughter NOM elope-do.PRF

    'Tanaka's daughter eloped.'

b. Tanaka ga   musume ni   kakeoti-sareta.
    NOM daughter DAT elope-do.PSS.PRF

    'Tanaka's daughter eloped on him.'

(38) a. Mary ga   munasawagi-sita.
      NOM presentment-do.PRF

     'Mary was uneasy.'

b. *Taroo ga   Mary ni   munasawagi-sareta.
     NOM   DAT presentment-do.PSS.PRF

('Taro suffered Mary being uneasy.')

(39) a. Kion   ga   jyoosyoo-sita.
     temperature NOM rise-do.PRF

     'The temperature went up.'

b. *Ziroo ga   kion   ni   jyoosyoo-sareta.
     NOM temperature DAT rise-do.PSS.PRF

('The temperature went up on Ziro.')

    In all the examples seen thus far, an indirect passive involves the addition of an argument and the marking of the embedded subject with the postposition *ni*. The grammaticality of indirect passive constructions is predictable if we maintain that the nominal that is ultimately *ni* marked must be an initial 1 in the embedded clause.

    Thus, the proposed unaccusativity of certain intransitive verbal nouns is found to correlate with three distinct syntactic phenomena: (1) the inability of such verbal nouns to be *o* marked, (2) the ability of their surface subjects to be construed with a non-adjacent numeral quantifier, and (3) their ill-formedness in indirect passive constructions.

Notes

[1] I wish to thank the following individuals for their helpful comments and discussion of the issues: Judith Aissen, Sandra Chung, William Davies, Shoko Hamano, Junko Ito, William Ladusaw, Armin Mester, Geoffrey Pullum, and Carol Rosen. I am indebted to the Board of Linguistics and the Syntax Research Center at UCSC for the hospitality and logistical support given me during the preparation of this manuscript. I bear responsibility for all errors and omissions.

[2] That this is a surface constraint is supported by the fact that *benkyoo o suru* in (2) is grammatical if *suugaku* is topicalized:
(a) Suugaku wa   Ziroo ga   benkyoo o   siteiru.
    math   TOP   NOM study   ACC do.PRG.IMP
     'As for math, Ziro is studying (it),'

[3] Kageyama (1982:245) points out that 'NP *ga suru*' marking is possible for certain NP-*suru* verbs.
(a) =(56a) [Kageyama (1982:245)]
    Kono yane wa   amamori ga   suru. (amamori-suru)
    this   roof TOP rain-leak NOM do-IMP
    'This roof has a bad leak.'

(b) =(56b) [Kageyama (1982:245)]

Watasi wa   munasawagi ga   suru. (munasawagi-suru)

I   TOP unease   NOM do-IMP

'I have an uneasy feeling.'

Although these NP *ga suru* verbs behave like the other verbal nouns that do not allow NP *o suru* forms, it appears that optional *ga* marking is attributable to other factors. Aside from these two examples, the verbal nouns that do not permit *o* marking, do not permit *ga* marking either.

[4] I am grateful to Armin Mester for discussing some aspects of their paper with me.

[5] The P-Chomeur may be seen as analogous to an embedded P's heading a U-arc in the main clause in a biclausal account of union.

[6] The general approach to the analysis of these constructions was developed in concert with Judith Aissen (cf. Aissen and Dubinsky (1989)).

[7] The inadmissability of the *o* marking of the verbal noun in transitive sentences will henceforth be ignored, since it has already been shown to be attributable to a surface constraint and is not relevant to the discussion at hand.

[8] For an enlightening commentary on the provenance of this idea, see Pullum (1988).

References

Aissen, Judith, and Stanley Dubinsky: 1989, 'Nominal Predicates and 'Light' Verbs in Japanese: A Union Analysis', unpublished ms., UCSC.

Aissen, Judith, and David Perlmutter: 1976, 'Clause Reduction in Spanish', *BLS* 2, 1-30. Revised version in Perlmutter (ed.).

Cattell, Ray: 1984, *Composite Predicates in English*. Academic Press Australia, North Ryde, New South Wales.

Davies, William, and Carol Rosen: 1988, 'Unions as Multi-Predicate Clauses', *Language* 64, 52-88.

Dubinsky, Stanley: 1985, *Union Constructions in Japanese: A Unified Analysis of -sase and -rare*, Ph.D. dissertation, Cornell University.

_____: (forthcoming) *Complex Predicates in Japanese: Causative and Affective Union*, D. Reidel, Dordrecht.

Grimshaw, Jane, and Armin Mester: 1988, 'Light Verbs and θ-Marking', *Linguistic Inquiry* 19, 205-32.

Hamano, Shoko: 1989, 'On the Two Verbs 'Stop' in Japanese -- With Apology to David Perlmutter', unpublished ms., UCSC.

Harada, S.I.: 1973, 'Counter Equi-NP Deletion', *Bulletin of the Research Institute of Logopedics and Phoniatrics* 7, 113-48. University of Tokyo.

Inoue, Kazoku: 1976, *Henkei bunpoo to nihongo*. Taisyuukan Syoten, Tokyo.

Jesperson, Otto: 1954, *A Modern English Grammar on Historical Principles*, George Allen & Unwin, London.

Johnson, David, and Paul Postal: 1980, *Arc Pair Grammar*, Princeton University Press, Princeton.

Kageyama, Taro: 1976-7, 'Incorporation and Sino-Japanese Verbs', *Papers in Japanese Linguistics* 5, 117-55.

_____: 1982, 'Word Formation in Japanese', *Lingua* 57, 215-58.

Kuno, Susumu: 1973, *The Structure of the Japanese Language*, MIT Press, Cambridge.

Martin, Samuel: 1975, *A Reference Grammar of Japanese*, Yale University Press, New Haven.

Miyagawa, Shigeru: 1989: 'Light Verbs and the Ergative Hypothesis', *Linguistic Inquiry* 20.2.

Permutter, David, ed.: 1983, *Studies in Relational Grammar 1*, University of Chicago Press, Chicago.

Perlmutter, David, and Paul Postal: 1983, 'Some Proposed Laws of Basic Clause Structure', in Perlmutter (ed.).

Pullum, Geoffrey: 1988, 'Citation Etiquette beyond Thunderdome', *Natural Language and Linguistic Theory* 6, 579-88.

Rosen, Carol: 1983, 'Universals of Causative Union: A Co- Proposal to the Gibson-Raposo Typology', *CLS* 19, 338-52. Revised version: 'Chomeur Causees and the Universals of Causative Union', *Cornell Working Papers in Linguistics* 5, 179-98.

THE GRAMMAR OF ENGLISH HOW ABOUT CONSTRUCTIONS

William H. Eilfort
The University of Chicago

The group of constructions in English beginning with how about are both an interesting and little-studied group. Although these constructions are quite common in everyday usage, they tend to be heard as somewhat colloquial, a fact which may account for the lack of scholarly treatments of them. The how about collocation cooccurs grammatically with a variety of syntactic complements, yielding constructions with a variety of meanings and uses. The task of this paper will be to connect the syntactic frames of the how about constructions with both semantic and other grammatical frames and suggest how these different constructions may be related. In attempting this task, I will also try to show that it is necessary to posit a level of grammatical structure (i.e., that is non-pragmatic) to help account for some of the constructional idiosyncrasies that will be uncovered.

The most sustained discussion of these constructions to be found in the literature is that in Sadock (1974), where he submits for our approval the following dialogue between a waiter and a customer (118, f n. 2):

(1)   X: How about a beer?
        Y: O.K., How about a beer?

Sadock notes that this dialogue is only plausible where X is the waiter and Y is the customer; i.e., where X's utterance is an offer or suggestion, while Y's reply is a request. Sadock treats both utterances as semantic suggestions and posits different underlying verbs taking a beer as the object to account for the difference between the two. Sadock's underlying verb for X's utterance is something semantically like have; therefore, the putative underlying form for X's utterance would be something like (2):

(2)   I suggest to you that you have a beer.

Notice that (2) could not be the underlying form for Y's response, since Y (if making a suggestion at all) is suggesting that X bring a beer. So far, we have the basis of a combined semantic/pragmatic account of the data, since on Sadock's analysis, we could have regular syntactico-semantic transformations deleting the performative higher clause (see Sadock 1974) and the you of the lower clause (presumably using something like Equi-NP deletion or some other deletion-under-identity rule), while the have would be deletable under conditions of pragmatic recoverability.

Matters, of course, do not turn out to be as simple as this account might suggest. To begin with, this account treats how about as a sort of idiom for the performative clause I suggest to you that, optionally inserted late in a derivation. On this account, how about is closely related to other grammaticized indirect speech acts, some of which I will discuss later in the paper. It is not true, however, that how about can always be substituted for I suggest (to you) that, as (3) will illustrate:

(3)   a. It is with trepidation that I suggest that you have a beer.
        b.*It is with trepidation (that) how about a beer.

As Sadock states (1974, 118), "This leaves a great deal of syntactic adjustment to be done by the syntactic component in an apparently ad hoc manner." Our problems are also compounded by the fact that, even if offers and requests can both be assimilated to underlying suggestions, there are how about + NP constructions that cannot be so assimilated. The first use is illustrated in (4), where X is a waiter bringing a drink order to a table where Y is sitting. Y has already ordered a beer, but the waiter has not brought it with the other drinks.

(4)   X: I have a scotch, a bourbon, a pernod, and an ouzo.
        Y: How about a beer?

In (4), Y is asking how a beer fits in to the situation. This use of a how about construction is truly interrogative, unlike the uses in (1), a point which I will argue for later. This use, however, is the same one Bolinger (1957) ascribes to what about, a fact which will come into greater play further in the analysis.
        The third use of the how about + NP construction is illustrated in (5):

(5)   a. How about them/those Cubbies!
        b. How about that Dan Quayle!
        c. How about *a/that jerk who ran into me this morning on the freeway!

In these uses, the how about construction is exclamative. As an exclamative, it is unlikely to be passing new information along to a hearer; therefore, the referent of the NP should be known to all participants in the conversation. Once again, however, it would be complicated to simply come up with an underlying verb of exclaiming to account for (5a), since exclamations can normally be embedded under I can't believe but how about + NP constructions cannot, as (6) illustrates:

(6)   a. What a great team the Cubbies are!
        a'. I can't believe what a great team the Cubbies are!
        b. How big your teeth are, Grandma!
        b'. I can't believe how big your teeth are, Grandma!
        c. How about that maniac who jumped off the Sears Tower!
        c'. *I can't believe how about that maniac who jumped off the Sears Tower!

On the other hand, (5a) can be used with such prototypically exclamative prefaces as boy, wow, gee, etc. I should also note here that yes/no exclamatives such as Is Orel Hershiser (ever) a great pitcher! and alternative question exclamatives such as Is goulash great, or what! also cannot be embedded under I can't believe, but that a how about exclamative should pattern with other wh-exclamatives, since a how about question is, as (4) shows, a wh-question.
        To sum up so far, a syntactico-semantic account of the data such as was presented partially in Sadock (1974) would have to posit three separate homophonous idioms each of which is transformationally substituted for various performative formulae (I suggest, I ask/request that you tell me, I exclaim) under somewhat complicated and messy conditions. A further possible complaint against this account is that it establishes no clear links between the three constructions, although these links intuitively exist. One alternative to this type of treatment would

be to establish one of these constructions as basic and generate the others pragmatically, possibly using such principles as Gordon and Lakoff (1975) used in their treatment of certain grammaticized indirect speech acts. The question now becomes, which construction is the basic one? For several reasons, it seems clear that it is, in fact, the interrogative use as in (5) that is most basic.

Although it is difficult to find any mention of the how about construction in older grammars of English, one occasionally finds mention of the related what about construction. It is not far-fetched to claim that the how about construction began to be used in analogy to the what about construction. As (6) illustrates, there are other constructions where how and what show a close relationship of this kind. Any discussions of the what about construction to be found regard it as a somehow elliptical question. As opposed to the underlying verb posited by Sadock taking the NP as its object, these analyses posit an elliptical verb between the what and the about, yielding a non-elliptical what do you think/say about NP as the underlying form. This account does seem plausible as an historical account of the origin of the construction. The how about interrogative construction could then be seen as constructed directly on analogy to what about with the elliptical verb perhaps being something like feel, as in (7):

(7)   X: How do you feel about (having) a beer?
        Y: O.K.
           Fine.
           Wonderful.
           Horrible.
           Lousy.
           *No, thanks.

Notice here that Y's first three responses are equally applicable to X's utterances in (1) and (7), while the next two are applicable in (7) but would not be in (1) while the last response is applicable in (1) but not in (7). Another argument against the synchronic existence of an underlying feel is illustrated in the paradigm in (8)

(8)   a. I would like to know how you feel about (having) a beer.
        b.*I would like to know how about (having) a beer.
        c. How about you and me go for a little drive in the country?
        d.*How do you feel about you and me go for a little drive in the country?

The difference in acceptability between (8c) and (8d) points to an especially interesting fact, in that (8d) is acceptable where the complement of how about is a gerund with possessive subject (i.e., a syntactic NP as opposed to clause). Therefore, the unacceptability of (8d) really comes as no surprise, since about, as a preposition, typically takes an object NP. What is surprising is that (8c) is acceptable, since here about takes a clausal complement, an unusual syntactic behavior. We can draw two conclusions from these facts: first, the conclusion that how about, although probably historically derived from a construction with a verb in between how and about, cannot be synchronically described as having that verb there underlyingly; second, the conclusion that how about is therefore an idiomatic collocation with its own grammar, not referable to the grammar of how or of about.

Abandoning an account of how about in terms of the grammar of how and of about, however, does not prevent us from attempting to analyze all three of the constructions discussed so far as synchronically syntactico-semantically unified, leaving pragmatics to account for the differences between these constructions when uttered. This possibility leads us inevitably to a discussion of direct versus indirect speech acts. Intuitively, a direct speech act consists of a construction whose form and force have what may be considered a default correlation, a notion referred to by Sadock and Zwicky (1985) as "sentence type". For example, the declarative sentence type is prototypically used to make assertions, while the interrogative type is prototypically used to ask questions. An indirect speech act, on the other hand, is one that requires pragmatic reasoning to understand. Gordon and Lakoff (1975) give a number of rules for successfully generating indirect speech acts having to do with the conditions of use of the direct speech acts upon which they are based. For example, if a speaker wants a hearer to feed the cat, she could make a direct request to that effect in the imperative form, or she could use a number of strategies for indirectly accomplishing the same goal requiring inferencing on the part of the hearer. As Gordon and Lakoff (1975) point out, she can question a hearer-based condition for the request or state a speaker-based condition for the request, as illustrated in (9):

(9) a. Are you able to feed the cat?
     b. Can you feed the cat?
     c. Would you feed the cat?
     d. Are you willing to feed the cat?
     e. I would like you to feed the cat.
     f. I want you to feed the cat.
     g. I need (for) you to feed the cat.
     h. The cat is hungry.
     i. The cat has been gnawing on my hand again.

Notice that (9h) and (9i) here are not statements of speaker-based conditions on requesting, but nonetheless may amount to a request in the proper context. Sadock has named the class of utterances that use an interrogative form in an imperative way "whimperatives". How about, where it is used to make a suggestion, can be seen as a whimperative, since it uses an interrogative form in an imperative way. The important question to be answered is that of directness or grammaticization. Morgan (1975) has pointed out convincing examples of conventions of language use that end up being grammaticized; that is, of pragmatic strategies such as those proposed by Gordon and Lakoff turning into grammatical constructions.

For example, notice the difference between (9a) and (9b). Semantically and syntactically, they are very much parallel, and, as such, should be able to trigger the same pragmatic inferences leading to the same indirect speech acts: requests to feed the cat. These two examples, however, are grammatically different in a number of ways. For instance, the grammatical marker of requests for English, please, may be uttered with (b), but not with (a)(and with (c) but not (d), (h), or (i)). Since please may freely occur with any direct request, but not with any direct question or assertion, this fact would indicate that (a), (d), (h), and (i), at least, are not direct requests. That is, these four can be seen as direct speech acts of the type suggested by their form, with pragmatic inferencing determining their use in specific contexts. (b) and (c), at least, can be read as ambiguous without regard to context between requests and questions. That there is a difference in the amount of inferencing required to get from the utterance of either (9b) or (9i) to a request to feed the cat is undeniable, as is the fact that there are grammatical consequences of this difference. The pragmatic theorist, consequently, would be forced to the conclusion that indirectness is only a matter of degree. In other words, there is context-sensitive pragmatic inferencing involved even in the use of a declarative sentence to assert, though less than that required to get a request from the same sentence. Against this view is the notion of sentence-type itself, since, if the difference between an assertion and a request, for example were completely recoverable from the context and the combinatoric semantics of the utterance, the difference in form between the two would be completely redundant; however, we find sentence types correlated to the English declarative, imperative, and interrogative in language after language (see Sadock and Zwicky 1985).

Another grammatical test of directness for whimperatives is what Sadock calls (1974) "fracturing", i.e., the parentheticalization of a portion of the sentence that is not part of the direct speech act, as (10) illustrates:

(10)   a. *Feed the cat, are you able (to)?
       b. Feed the cat, can you?
       c. Feed the cat, would you?
       d.*Feed the cat, are you willing to?

Notice in the grammatical examples in (10) that what is left over when the interrogative material is parentheticalized is imperative in form and that these utterances can only be interpreted as requests. If the fracturing construction were a syntactic transformation sensitive to the semantics and illocutionary force of the utterance, then there is no reason for the ungrammaticality of (10a) and (10d). The claim being made here, then, is that (9b) and (9c) are grammatically ambiguous between a direct question and a direct request while (9a) and (9d) are grammatically direct questions and only indirect requests in the proper contexts.

At this point, I need to introduce two constructions related to the ones under discussion here: the aforementioned what about construction and the highly colloquial howsabout construction. What I will show from here on is that the how about construction is ambiguous in the same way as the other grammatical whimperatives and that this ambiguity can be brought out by substitution of what about for the interrogative uses of these constructions and of howsabout for the imperative/suggestive uses. The exclamative uses will not be discussed again until the end. To begin with, the offer of or request for an NP (both of which can be seen as suggestions for the hearer to undertake a certain course of actions) and a question about an NP can both be expressed by how about + NP or what about + NP, as illustrated in (11):

(11)   a. How about a beer?
       b. What about a beer?
       c. Howsabout a beer?

Notice that (11c) cannot be a question about how a beer fits in to the situation, as will become clearer with more examples. The claim being made here is that the use of (11b) as an offer or request is indirect while it is direct for (11c) and one reading of (11a).

To further establish the correspondences noted here, I will use grammatical tests designed to pick out either interrogatives or imperatives, comparing these constructions with the prototypical whimperative, could you. First of all, notice that please can combine with how about and howsabout, but not with what about, as (12) illustrates:

(12)   a. How about a beer, please? (= request only)
       b. Howsabout a beer, please?
       c.*What about a beer, please?
       d. Could you bring me a beer, please? (= request only)

Next, we can use Bolinger's (1968) test of adding an indefinite vocative to pick out a request, as (13) illustrates:

(13)   a. How about a beer, someone? (= offer or request, but not question)
       b. Howsabout a beer, someone?
       c.*What about a beer, someone?
       d. Could you bring me a beer, someone? (= request only)

A third test for a request is its ability to take a parenthetical if-clause stating a felicity condition on making the request, as in (14):

(14)   a. How about a beer, if there are any left? (= request only)
       b. Howsabout a beer, if there are any left?
       c.*What about a beer, if there are any left?
       d. Could you bring me a beer, if there are any left? (= request only)

A test for a question, on the other hand, is its ability to take a parenthetical stating a felicity condition on asking, such as in (15):

(15)   a. How about a beer, I'd like to know? (= question only)
       b.*Howsabout a beer, I'd like to know?
       c. What about a beer, I'd like to know?
       d. Could you bring me a beer, I'd like to know? (= question only)

The pragmatic theorist would have to give a Gordon and Lakoff-style condition for the use of these constructions to make a request, if we regard their interrogative uses as direct. The story might go as follows: in asking about how the NP referent fits in the situation at hand, the speaker brings it to the attention of the hearer, who then infers the proper suggestion relating to the referent, depending on his contextual knowledge of whether the speaker is in a position to offer it or is requesting it. While this is a plausible pragmatic story for the use of what about constructions as indirect suggestions, and also diachronically for the use of how about constructions to make indirect suggestions, the distributional facts with respect to howsabout and the ability of how about to combine with markers of direct requests militate against regarding how about as strictly interrogative and requiring its use in suggestions to be pragmatically inferred (i.e., indirect).

I will now turn to some constructions where how about combines with units larger than a simple NP. In the most minimal of these, the complement is a subjectless gerund, as in (16):

(16)   a. How about bringing me a beer?
       b. What about bringing me a beer?
       c. Howsabout bringing me a beer?
       d.*Could you bringing me a beer?

Notice that, in the cases where these can be requests, the gerund is controlled by the hearer, as (17) shows:

(17)   a. How about bringing *you/yourself a beer? (as a request)
       b. What about bringing you/yourself a beer? (as a question)
       c. Howsabout bringing *you/yourself a beer?
       d. I'd like to know about bringing you/yourself a beer? (as a question)

This restriction on the controller of the gerund for the request cases is just like that in direct requests in the imperative form where no subject is present. Furthermore, gerunds share with infinitives the property that they may semantically refer to courses of action rather than realized situations, making them useful in the reporting of, although not the making of, imperative requests (see Hamblin 1987 and Huntley 1984). Also, the <u>yourself</u> in (b) and (d) may be replaced by <u>oneself</u>. The fracturability facts reinforce this correlation, especially since the non-fractured portion of the sentence can no longer be a gerund, but must be in the same form as a direct request, bringing this construction in line with other whimperatives, as (18) illustrates:

(18)   a. Bring me a beer, how about?
       b. Bring me a beer, howsabout?
       c.*Bring me a beer, what about?
       d. Bring me a beer, could you?

These facts combine to indicate that <u>how about</u> (in one of its uses) and <u>howsabout</u>, but not <u>what about</u> may be used to mark direct requests instantiated as subjectless gerunds.

When we look at the gerund with a possessive specifier, we find a different set of results that accord with our expectations based on semantic knowledge. These gerunds may refer to realized situations (although perhaps in possible worlds other than the real world) as in <u>Jerry's buying a round of beers was/would be an act of unparalleled generosity</u>. For this reason, these gerunds make poor expressions for courses of events, unlike the subjectless gerunds in (17), as (19) illustrates:

(19)   a. How about Jerry's supplying all the beer at CLS?
       b.*Howsabout Jerry's supplying all the beer at CLS? (as a request)
       c. What about Jerry's supplying all the beer at CLS?

Here, (a) and (c) could be used in response to, for instance, a CLS officer's listing of generous acts during the conference while leaving out Jerry's contribution. Notice that if one were to want to suggest that a course of action be undertaken wherein Jerry were to supply all the beer at CLS, a non-possessive specifier would have to be used (i.e., <u>Jerry</u> instead of <u>Jerry's</u>). The non-possessive specifier used with a gerund in this way tends to sound contrastive, and if one wants to suggest one's own course of actions in this type of construction, one must use a contrastively-stressed <u>me</u> rather than <u>I</u>. Not surprisingly, these utterances could be used in the same contexts as direct requests with overt subjects (except that, of course, in adult speech at least, one cannot utter contrastively stressed <u>me</u> as the subject of an imperative sentence: *<u>Me paint the house!</u>).

Although we have been shifting semantic and pragmatic factors around to yield different results, we have not, as yet (depending on one's syntactic analysis of subjectless gerunds) changed syntactic frames in this construction, since up to now, we have only been discussing how about + NP, to the extent that these gerunds are NPs. We can find, however, examples of the syntactic extension of how about to unambiguously clausal constructions, a recent extension if the grammaticality judgments of my subjects is any indication. These constructions are exhibited in (20):

(20) a. How about you bring me a beer? (= request only)
      b. Howsabout you bring me a beer?
      c.*What about you bring me a beer?
      d.*How about you bring me a beer, I'd like to know?
      e. How about you bring me a beer, if there are any left?

These sentences can only function as requests or suggestions, and this result is forced on us by the semantics of the clausal complement, which must refer to an unrealized state of affairs (see Huntley 1984) and thus is suited to use as a suggestion (see Hamblin 1987). Notice the important point that, although clauses of this form (referring semantically to courses of action) are well-suited to use as suggestions, they need not be so used. The indication of this use is, however, grammatical and not pragmatic. For example, the same clause with the same semantics is found in the utterance Jerry demanded that you bring me a beer. In this case, however, although the clause refers to an unrealized situation as a course of action, it does not and cannot have the direct force of a request for you to undertake that course of actions (although it could have that indirect effect). The same clause in (20), on the other hand, must constitute a suggestion (i.e., count as an attempt to get the addressee to undertake the course of action specified). Clearly, then, these facts are non-syntactic, non-semantic, yet still grammatical facts (i.e. also non-pragmatic, since they are about direct, non-inferenced force) of English.

Finally, we come to the construction how about + if-clause, as illustrated in (21):

(21) a. How about if you bring me a beer?
      b. Howsabout if you bring me a beer?
      c. What about if you bring me a beer?
      d. How about if you brought me a beer? (= question only)
      e.*Howsabout if you brought me a beer?
      f. What about if you brought me a beer?
      g. How about if you bring me a beer, I'd like to know? (= question only)
      h. How about if you bring me a beer, if there are any left? (= suggestion
         only)
      i. How about if you brought me a beer, I'd like to know? (= question only)
      j.*How about if you brought me a beer, if there are any left?

What is important in these examples is the difference between the unmarked hypothetical clauses and the subjunctively marked hypothetical clauses. According to Huntley's account (1984), any mood-marking forces a clause to semantically refer to a realized state of affairs, even where that state of affairs is realized in a different possible world. Therefore, since English only uses clauses referring to unrealized states of affairs (functioning as courses of action) in direct requests, the constructions in (21) with subjunctive complements can only be questions about non-real states of affairs. On the other hand, where there is no overt mood-marking on the hypothetical clauses, they are free to refer either to unrealized states of affairs (and therefore function as courses of action suitable to requests) or to states of affairs that are realized in the hypothetical world being set up (since indicative mood in English is not morphologically marked). Since the normal use of an if-clause in English is to set up a hypothetical possible world, the reading of (21a) as a question should be foremost and (21b) should sound a bit odd. I believe that the facts here speak for themselves.

I have now shown that a purely pragmatic account of the variety of how about constructions is impossible synchronically, although I have suggested that pragmatic regularities of the sort proposed by Gordon and Lakoff (1975) have diachronically influenced these constructions by grammaticizing conventions of use into conventions of language, in the sense of Morgan (1975). The same sort of diachronic pragmatic-to-grammatical account, by the way, can be given for the exclamative use of this construction. It is rather obvious, upon perusal of garden-variety exclamatives, such as were illustrated in (6), that many of them have a quasi-interrogative form. For example, wh-exclamatives look like wh-questions, except that they are not in inverted form and there is no wh-question corresponding to (6a). Yes/no exclamatives look like yes/no questions, and, in fact, differ only in intonation. Alternative exclamatives also resemble alternative questions with the exception that the alternative must be no real alternative. All of these correspondences can be explained diachronically if we regard these exclamatives as the result of the grammaticization of rhetorical questions. Since the point of a rhetorical question is not to elicit information, but instead is to suggest that the answer to the question is quite obvious, there is a further suggestion, when referring to situations mutually familiar, that the conveyed assertion is not only true, but true to a surprising degree. Thus, this pragmatic effect gets grammaticized as an exclamative. Such, I would claim, is the case of the how about construction in (6).

Nevertheless, I have not yet ruled out an analysis of the facts in which we have how about standing idiomatically for three different performative clauses, although I have indicated that it would force complicated syntactico-semantic accounts on us. If we follow this analysis in spite of these complications, however, we are forced into an analysis, like the Performative Hypothesis (PH) (see Sadock 1974), in which the force of an utterance is represented semantically. Where there is no overt force indicator, a PH adherent must posit an underlying one that gets deleted during a derivation. The charm of the PH is that these underlying force markers are verbs of English, the same as we find in overt performative utterances and in reports of these utterances, as in (22):

(22) a. Feed the cat.
      b. I suggest that you feed the cat.
      c. Karen suggested that I feed the cat.

Here, what is important is that (22a) and (22b) are roughly equivalent, while (22c) can be a report of either (22a) or (22b). The verb suggest, found overtly expressed in (22b) and (22c) and covertly expressed in (22a), is semantically the same verb in each case. Unfortunately, while this account does explain why (22c) can be a report of an utterance such as (22b), it does not explain why (22b) isn't also a report of a concurrent action, in which case it would be a true report just in case the speaker was in fact making that suggestion. If this were the case, one could claim that (22b) was in fact a report and its force as a suggestion was indirect (i.e., pragmatically determined). This move, however, fails to explain why (22c) fails to have these possibilities for use as a suggestion. Furthermore, since this account still claims that a covert <u>suggest</u> is present in (22a), we are left with the conclusion that (22a) is only indirectly a suggestion, a position I argued against earlier, combining the principle of sufficient reason in grammar with the notion of sentence type. In other words, if we have the same semantics for <u>suggest</u> in all of the sentences in (22), then it is difficult to see why the ordinary truth conditions hold for (22c) but not for (22a) or (22b), both of which are neither true nor false. If, following Sadock (1985a), we posit two notions of truth, one applying to the entire underlying sentence and one only to the complement of the performative clause, it is still difficult to see why the clause <u>that I feed the cat</u> in (22c) should have a different truth value from the equivalent clause in (22b) for the pragmatic notion of truth (the second one mentioned). That is, Sadock fails to tell us how we know which part of the sentence will be the part for pragmatic truth-evaluation, except that it is embedded somewhere in the larger sentence.

What we need, then, is an analysis which treats all three uses of <u>how about</u> separately, as Sadock's account would, but also correlates these constructions with their proper forces. In other words, <u>how about</u> must be able to combine with certain syntactic and semantic entities without itself being semantically evaluated along with its complement in the cases where it functions as strictly a force-indicating device. A suitable framework for such an analysis is Sadock's (1985b) Autolexical Syntax, where pieces of information from various levels of grammar can be correlated through the mediation of the lexicon to yield strings with different combinatoric properties on different levels. Notice that this type of framework has no need of derivations, since those strings are licensed that obey the combinatoric rules on each level. The failure of both pragmatic and semantic analyses to account for the data presented in this paper leads me to suggest an additional level of grammatical structure (see Eilfort, to appear), which I have called the Illocutionary Module, but which might just as well be called the Rhetoric Module or something of that sort.

In any case, we could now account for all the facts pertaining to the <u>how about</u> constructions in three lexical entries with reference to the syntactic, semantic, and rhetoric levels of structure. The first entry, for the interrogative <u>how about</u>, would contain the syntactic information that <u>how about</u> is of a syntactic type that combines with NPs or clauses to yield sentences. Unlike other interrogative sentences, these sentences would lack the syntactic default feature [+ Inverted]. Semantically, <u>how about</u> might be null or it might have the same semantics as <u>where-fit-in</u>, and could combine semantically with entity expressions or situation expressions, as long as they were not marked as [- Realized]. Rhetorically, <u>how about</u> would be marked as [+ Information Passing, + Addressee Directed] (i.e., the illocutionary type "question").The second entry, for the suggestion <u>how about</u>, would contain the same syntactic information as the first entry. Semantically, however, the entry would be null but combine only with entity expressions or situation expressions not marked [+ Realized]. Rhetorically, it would be a speaker attitude marker indicating lack of strength and would be marked as combining with an expression that was [- Information Passing] (and either + or - with respect to the feature [Addressee Directed]) to yield an expression of the same type. Whether this expression (Sadock's "suggestion") turned out to be an offer or request would be determined pragmatically in the case of simple NP complements. Finally, with regard to the exclamative <u>how about</u>, the syntactic information would indicate that it combines with only an NP to form a sentence, the semantic information would allow it to combine with only a [+ Definite] entity or [+ Realized] situation to form an entity of the same type, while the rhetorical information would make it a speaker attitude marker of amazement or something of that sort which would yield an expression of the type [+ Information Passing, - Addressee Directed], or an assertion. What about would have lexical information matching only the first of the three how about entries, while howsabout would have two entries, corresponding to the second two how about entries.

As with any suggestions regarding any lexical entries in Autolexical Syntax, the correctness of the information contained therein can only be substantiated by correct combination with all other possible lexical entries at all levels. Despairing of this, I can only claim that these are possible directions for the lexical entries to take. What I have argued, roughly, is that there are three separate, though historically related, types of how about construction, one (the original) interrogative, one imperative (or suggestive, if you will), and one exclamative, and that the combinatoric facts regarding these constructions can only be stated with reference to a heretofore unstudied level of grammar, the illocutionary or rhetorical level.

How about Jerry Sadock, Jim McCawley, Sandy Caskey, Eric Hamp, Randy Graczyk, Caroline Wiltshire, Karl-Erik McCullough, Karen Deaton, and anyone else who helped me with judgments reflected herein! Aren't they great? Howsabout I apologize for any errors or unclarities in the paper? What about the footnotes?

References

Bolinger, Dwight. 1957. Interrogative structures of American English: the direct question. American Dialect Society 28. Huntsville: University of Alabama Press.

_____ 1968. The imperative in English. In To honor Roman Jakobson: essays on the occasion of his seventieth birthday, vol. 1. The Hague: Mouton.

Eilfort, William H. To appear. The illocutionary module in an automodular grammar. Unpublished doctoral dissertation, University of Chicago.

Gordon, D. and G. Lakoff. 1975. Conversational postulates. In P. Cole and J. Morgan, eds., Syntax and semantics 3: speech acts. New York: Academic Press.

Hamblin, C. L. 1987. Imperatives. Oxford: Basil Blackwell.

Huntley, Martin. 1984. The semantics of English imperatives. Linguistics and Philosophy 7:2, 103-134.

Morgan, Jerry L. 1975. Two types of convention in indirect speech acts. In Peter Cole, ed., Syntax and semantics 9: pragmatics. New York: Academic Press.

Sadock, Jerrold. 1974. Toward a linguistic theory of speech acts. New York: Academic Press.

_____ 1985a. On the performadox, or a semantic defense of the performative hypothesis. In R. Chametzky et. al., eds., University of Chicago Working Papers in Linguistics 1, 160-169.

_____ 1985b. Autolexical syntax: a proposal for the treatment of noun incorporation and similar phenomena. Natural Language and Linguistic Theory 3:4, 329-440.

_____ and Arnold Zwicky. 1985. Speech act distinctions in syntax. In Timothy Shopen, ed., Language typology and syntactic description: clause structure. Cambridge: Cambridge University Press.

On the "Reflexive Middle" in English

Christiane Fellbaum
Princeton University

In this paper I examine the properties of the so-called "reflexive middle" construction, exemplified by (1) and (2):

(1) The gears on my new bike shift THEMSELVES
(2) Honda--the car that sells ITSELF

The reflexive pronoun in these constructions receives sentence stress (indicated by capitalization), in contrast to an ordinary reflexive, which is normally unstressed:

(3) John CUT himself

A subject/Theme usually cannot occur in a reflexive sentence with the intonation pattern of a "regular" reflexive that has a prototypical Agent subject:

(4) *This car DRIVES itself
(5) *These novels SELL themselves

The constructions in (1) and (2) have been compared to, and equated with, the (non-reflexive) middle exemplified in (6) and (7) (see, for example, Lakoff (1977), Fiengo (1980), and Hale & Keyser (1987)):

(6) This car drives easily
(7) Rushdie's novels no longer sell like hotcakes

The principal similarities between the constructions in (1)-(2) and (6)-(7) are the active morphology on the verb and the externalized Theme. The requirement that the external argument in reflexive middles really be the semantic Theme is much stricter than it is for plain middles. Thus, apparent middles, such as (8) below, with an Instrument subject

(8) This saw cuts easily

do not have a reflexive counterpart:

(9) *This saw cuts ITSELF

The Agent that the verb selects for is unexpressed in both kinds of middles. We will see that despite the similarity between the two sentence types, the reflexive middle is not a middle syntactically, although semantically the two kinds of middles are closely related. Formation of the reflexive middle is more tightly constrained by the semantics of the verb. Besides contrasting middles and reflexive middles, we will establish the relationship of these two constructions to the unaccusative.

The class of verbs that form (nonreflexive) middles falls into two subgroups. The verbs in both classes assign two arguments, one of which is a Theme, which is externalized. In addition to the Theme, verbs entering the middle select for either an Agent or a Cause, which is suppressed. Verbs of the first subgroup, such as *sell*, *drive*, *type*, etc., always assign as their second argument an Agent when they are used transitively. Verbs of the second group usually can assign, in addition to the Theme, either an Agent or a Cause in transitive constructions; they tend to form both middles (with a suppressed Agent) and unaccusatives (with an unexpressed Cause.) This class includes *break, crumble,* and *move*[1]. While not all verbs whose argument structure conforms to that of the first group (let's call it the *sell* group) can undergo middle formation, it turns out that the verbs that form reflexive middles form an even smaller and more constrained group that partially overlaps with that of the verbs forming "plain" middles. Thus, *eat* forms neither a plain middle nor a reflexive middle; *sell* forms both a middle and a reflexive middle; *shave* forms only a plain middle but not a reflexive middle, while a small number of verbs, like *suggest*, form reflexive, but not plain middles:

(10)a *This bread eats well
   b *This bread eats ITSELF
(11)a This car sells well
   b This car sells ITSELF
(12)a Heavy beards don't shave easily
   b *Heavy beards don't shave THEMSELVES
(13)a *This solution suggests easily
   b This solution suggests ITSELF

The second group of verbs--let's call it the *break* group--(those that either select an Agent or a Cause in addition to the Theme and can form both middles and unaccusatives) is much larger than the *sell* class, whose verbs select always for a Theme and an Agent argument. Within the *break* class, the verbs that can form reflexive middles again form a more constrained subset. Thus, for example, *open* and *shut* form both plain and reflexive middles but *bleed, crumble,* and *spill* form only nonreflexive middles:

(14)a This gate opens/shuts easily
   b This gate opens/shuts ITSELF
(15)a These patients bleed easily
   b *These patients bleed THEMSELVES
(16)a This material crumbles easily
   b *This material crumbles ITSELF
(17)a Oil spills easily
   b *Oil spills ITSELF

We will see below that the same constraint operates on both the *sell* and the *break* class with respect to reflexive middle formation.

Fiengo (1980) asserts the similarity of middle adverbs such as *easily* and the stressed reflexives in sentences like (1) and (2), which he claims function syntactically as adverbs, and to which he attributes the meaning of, roughly, *without help*, as in (18):

(18) John did it HIMSELF

Fiengo bases his equation of *easily* and the reflexive in sentences like (1) on the following distributional evidence: English generally prohibits the cooccurence of two manner adverbs in the same sentence:

(19) *John did it carefully easily (Fiengo's (97a))

The same appears to be true, Fiengo notes, for active sentences like (20) with both the manner adverb *easily* and the stressed reflexive, indicating that the latter is indeed an adverb[2]:

(20) *John did it HIMSELF easily

Similarly, a middle with *easily* is incompatible with the presence of the stressed reflexive:

(21) *These problems solve THEMSELVES easily

The reason for the ungrammaticality of (21), however, is not the one suggested by Fiengo (i.e., a restriction on the coocurrence of two manner adverbs.) Rather, we will see below that sentences with a stressed reflexive are not middles at all, and that *easily* in sentences like (21) functions not as a manner adverb, but as a middle adverb; therefore, it is not compatible with the reflexive construction.

It turns out that when *easily* is moved either into preverbal position or into the position between a modal and the main verb, sentences with both an *easily*-type adverb and a stressed reflexive are good:

(22) These problems could easily solve THEMSELVES
(23) This condo (may) easily pay(s) for ITSELF

The explanation for these data lies in the properties of the different adverbs. Based on an analysis by Vendler (1984), I have shown elsewhere (Fellbaum, 1985) that adverbs like *easily* and *quickly* are polysemous, and their interpretation can vary with their position in the sentence. Thus, the prototypical middle adverb *easily* (as in (6)) can only occur postverbally; it is a "facility" adverb referring to the ease with which *any* agent can carry out the action denoted by the verb. It is similar to the *easy (to V)* of Tough-movement sentences, where it also refers to a property of the subject/Theme. In (19) and (20), as well as in (24) below, on the other hand, *easily* is a manner adverb that can be paraphrased as, roughly, *with ease*; here, the adverb refers specifically to John's way of doing something, rather than to a property of the Theme that makes the action easy to carry out for a non-specific agent.

(24) John did it easily

The same use of *easily* occurs in such pseudo-middles as (25) with an Instrument subject:

(25) This saw cuts easily

where *easily* is not a facility, but a manner adverb, as (26) shows:

(26) *This saw is easy to cut

Another *easily* occurs preverbally; this is an adverb referring to the probability of the event taking place; this adverb does not imply an Agent and is compatible with unaccusatives. In fact, this *easily* can serve to distinguish unaccusatives from middles[3]:

(27)a This car drives easily (middle reading only)

   b *This car easily drives (*sell*-type verb: cannot form unaccusative)

(28)a This fabric tears easily (middle)

   b This fabric easily tears (unaccusative)

The adverbs in (22) and (23) above appear to be of the latter kind: the fact that *easily* in the reflexive middle can occur only preverbally indicates that it is not a middle adverb but rather a "probability" adverb referring to the chance with which the event referred to will occur. Note especially that sentences like (22)-(23) tend to be best with an epistemic modal: this seems to confirm the "probability" sense. The adverb in (21) then, is not, as Fiengo assumes, a manner adverb; rather, from its position we can infer that it is a middle (facility) adverb. The fact that it cannot occur in this middle position in a sentence like (21) leads us to suggest that such sentences are not middles at all.

It turns out that just as there are several different adverbs with the same surface form *easily, quickly*, etc., there are at least two functionally distinct reflexives. The stressed reflexive with the interpretation suggested by Fiengo can only occur in active transitive constructions like (1) and (2), but it is barred from unergatives (29), unaccusatives (30), and passives (31):

(29) *John danced/sang/swam HIMSELF

(30) *The ambassador arrived HIMSELF

(31) *The washing machine was sold ITSELF

In other words, the reflexive does not behave like a manner adverb, whose distribution is ordinarily unrestricted, but rather like a reflexive anaphor. Note that sentences (29)-(31) become acceptable when the reflexive is replaced by a true adverbial like *by him/herself* or *without help*. This argues against the equivalence of the reflexive and such an adverbial.

However, in sentences like (29)-(31), a stressed reflexive can appear as a kind of emphatic adjunct to the subject, meaning roughly *...and nobody else*; see (32)-(34)[4]:

(32) John HIMSELF danced/sang (instead of the professional he had hired)

(33) The ambassador HIMSELF arrived (and not his deputy)

(34) The washing machine ITSELF was sold (but not the service contract)

In the reflexive middle, on the other hand, the reflexive cannot occur in this adjunct position, but only postverbally:

(35)a *This solution ITSELF suggests

   b This solution suggests ITSELF

(36)a *These problems THEMSELVES will solve

   b These problems will solve THEMSELVES

The position of the reflexive in the good sentences, then, argues against its interpretation as an emphatic adjunct, which appears to be restricted to a position immediately adjoining the NP[5]. On the other hand, we saw that the stressed reflexive in postverbal position can only occur in active transitive sentences, but that it is excluded from passives, unaccusatives, and unergatives. In these sentences, the stressed reflexive is barred from occupying an argument position: the empty position left by an internal argument that has been raised to subject position ((30) and (31)) or from the site of a (optional) cognate object (29). Given this, one would expect reflexive middle sentences like (1) and (2) to be ruled out as well, since the reflexive here, too, would have to occupy the site left by the internal argument that has been externalized by middle formation[6]. But since sentences like (1) and (2) are perfectly fine, we can conclude that no movement has taken place, and that the subjects of reflexive middles are not derived subjects at all. The fact that the object position filled by the reflexive indicates that the constructions are transitive, rather than being detransitivized middles. Therefore, the reflexive middles must be standard reflexives. They differ only in so far as both the reflexive and its antecedent are linked to the semantic Theme, while the Agent role that the verb normally selects for is not expressed; we will see, though, that just like in plain middles, the Theme has not replaced the Agent semantically, and that the distinction between the two theta roles is maintained.[7]

How can we formulate the lexico-semantic condition(s) on the class of verbs that can form reflexive middles[8] ? As we saw earlier, the class of reflexive middle verbs is not co-extensive with the class verbs that can form "plain", nonreflexive middles; rather, it is a smaller and more constrained set (contrary to Hale & Keyser's (1987:17) statement that verbs that form middles for the most part also form reflexive middles.) Eligible verbs must select not only for a Theme but also for an (optional) Agent argument, since in reflexive middles agenthood is transferred to the Theme. Thus, unaccusative verbs like *rot, mold, corrode*, (which in a transitive construction can assign only a Cause but not an Agent argument) cannot form reflexive middles:

    (37)a *His mother/All that sugar rotted Johnnie's teeth
      b Johnnie's teeth rotted
      c *Johnnie's teeth rotted THEMSELVES

Like in middles, the Theme selected for by the verb has taken the place of the Agent that is ususally associated with the verb, but that is not assigned in reflexive middles. On the other hand, unlike in middles, the verb is transitive, so two theta roles must have been assigned. However, even though Agenthood has been transferred onto the Theme, it does not satisfy the semantic specifications for an Agent as required by the verb. The external argument is still understood as the semantic Theme selected for by the verb, distinct from an Agent. In the (b) sentences below, the external arguments have animate/human referents which are naturally interpreted as Agents, rather than as Themes selected for by verbs like *bribe, photograph*, and *kill*, because they satisfy the semantic conditions for agenthood. These sentences can only be read as standard (emphatic) reflexives, without the "middle" interpretation of sentences like (1) and (2), where an Agent distinct form the surface subject is understood. By contrast, the (a) sentences, where one argument position has not been filled, and where an Agent (not coreferent with the externalized Theme) is implied, are good middles[9] :

(38)a Bureaucrats bribe easily
    b Bureaucrats bribe THEMSELVES
(39)a Attractive people photograph easily
    b Attractive people photograph THEMSELVES
(40)a Chickens kill easily
    b ??Chickens kill THEMSELVES

The sentences in (40) are particularly good examples: The (b) sentence is odd precisely because the chickens are interpreted as the (suicidal) Agent; the middle in the (40a), where they are the Theme, is fine. The same pattern obtains for the few psych verbs that allow middle formation:

(41)a Sue frightens/scares easily
    b Sue frightens/scares HERSELF

Unlike the (a) sentence, which is read as a regular middle, the (b) does not receive the reflexive middle interpretation. Only very few psych verbs form good middles; middles with verbs like *depress, shame, frustrate, vex, cheer up, humiliate, enrage, enfuriate,* seem bad. This may be related to their thematic structure, which, according to Belletti and Rizzi (1988) lacks an Agent, and is made up of Theme and Experiencer. Verbs like *scare* and *frighten* can be said to have two different readings: One where the cause of the fright is a (passive) Theme, such as a thunderstorm, and one where it is an Agent that actively, volitionally, and intentionally does something to scare/frighten the Experiencer. It appears that both kinds of middle are possible only with the reading implying an Agent.

Relatively few verbs from the *sell* class, which always select for an Agent and a Theme, can form reflexive middles; among them are *sell, buy, solve, resolve, suggest, pay for.* Verbs of affect, which tend to form good middles, are generally excluded from the reflexive middle, as (42)-(44) show:

(42) Soft wood saws easily/*ITSELF
(43) These rolls slice well/*THEMSELVES
(44) Smooth surfaces paint over quickly/*THEMSELVES

Similarly, *crush, pierce, shave*, and other similar verbs can occur only in regular middles. These verbs all refer to a change in the surface, consistency, or integrity of the affected Theme. They also imply a strong Agent involvement in the action as well as an instrument (either a tool or a hand) employed by the Agent. In this respect, they differ crucially from verbs like *sell* and *solve* that can form reflexive middles.

We saw that reflexive middles are, syntactically, no different from regular reflexives, except that it is the Theme, rather than the Agent selected for by the verb, that is the subject and that is interpreted, in a metaphorical sense, as an Agent[10]. In this respect, reflexive middles differ crucially from regular middles, which imply an agent whose referent is disjoint from the theme. The violation of the semantic structure of verbs like *sell* and *solve* that occurs in reflexive middle formation is permissible in so far as the Theme can be interpreted metaphorically as an Agent, but it is constrained by the degree to which an Agent's involvement is required for the action to be carried out. Thus, verbs like *saw* or *slice*, where the Theme is physically acted upon, have a stronger Agent requirement than verbs like *solve* and *sell*; in addition, the former imply an instrument, and instruments necessarily presuppose an Agent. Similarly, verbs of ingestion, which strongly require an Agent/Consumer, are excluded from reflexive middles. Note that some of these verbs form good plain middles, where a distinct Agent/Consumer is implied. Formation of the middle, which refers to some property of the subject/Theme and is subject to different constraints, is not contingent on the strength of the Agent requirement by the verb.

(45) This bean curd digests {easily/*ITSELF}
(46) This pipe smokes {easily/*ITSELF}

Among the verbs in the *break* class, which select in addition to the Theme either an Agent or a Cause and can form either middles or unaccusatives, some can occur in the reflexive middle construction:

(47)a John/The draft closed the door
   b The door closes easily
   c The door closed
   d This door closes ITSELF

The difference between the middle and the unaccusative is that the middle implies an Agent whereas the unaccusative does not; the force closing the door is implicitly attributed to a Cause. The reflexive middle, on the other hand, precludes an interpretation with either an Agent or a Cause, stating instead that the Theme acted upon itself without external influence. In this respect, this construction differs from the others.

Hale & Keyser (1987) propose the following LCS for the *break* class:

(48) [x cause [y undergo change], (by...)]

This LCS, however, is only a necessary, but not a sufficient condition on the formation of both plain and reflexive middles. Many verbs like *split* and *shatter* can form regular middles, but they cannot occur in a reflexive middle:

(49)a Maple wood splits easily
   b *Maple wood splits ITSELF
(50)a These glasses shatter quickly
   b *These glasses shatter THEMSELVES

Similarly, *crumble, tear, rip, crush*, etc. do not form reflexive middles. Just as in the case of the *sell* class, the verbs that are excluded from reflexive middle formation are those that strongly require an Agent or Cause with a physical impact upon the Theme. Note that, again, *close, shut* and *open* are exceptions to this generalization. These verbs, like *sell* and *resolve*, but unlike *split, crumble,* and *shatter*, do not refer to a change in the physical integrity of their Themes, and therefore they have a much weaker agent requirement than *crush* and *split*.

Verbs of creation as a class tend to be excluded from reflexive middle formation, as the sentences below show:

(51) *Twelve tone music composes ITSELF
(52) *These clay pots threw THEMSELVES
(53) *My new sweater crocheted ITSELF

Creation verbs by their nature have a very strong Agent (i.e., creator) requirement. It is difficult to interpret the created object as its own creator; therefore, the reflexive middle tends to be imcompatible with these verbs.

In sum, while there are many verbs that enter into middles, reflexive middles, and unaccusatives, the three constructions can be clearly distinguished. Middles have an unrealized, but implicit, Agent, while unaccusatives similarly imply a Cause. In reflexive middles, by contrast, both arguments subcategorized for by the verb are realized on the surface. However, there are limits to the degree to which the Theme can assume the semantic features of an Agent (such as ingestion, employing instruments, and creation), and reflexive middle formation is constrained by the degree to which such agenthood is required by the verb.

Notes

This work was supported in part by a grant form the James S. McDonnell Foundation and by contract N00014 86 K 0492 between the Office of Naval Research and Princeton University. I thank Derek Gross for valuable discussions.

1. A third group of verbs, which does not interest us here, assigns only a Cause argument in addition to the Theme, and can only form unaccusatives, but not middles; these verbs include *corrode, rot, deteriorate, disintegrate*. These verbs never form "reflexive middles" because this construction, as we shall see, is conditional upon the selection of an Agent argument by the verb.

2. Lakoff (1977) also notes the inacceptability of such sentences but draws a different conclusion.

3. Moreover, the stress patterns for unaccusatives and middles differ: In middles, where the potential action itself is generally presupposed, the adverb is asserted and consequently receives heavy stress; in unaccusatives, the event is asserted and thus the verb is the focus of the sentence.

4. Fiengo notes this meaning as well, but asserts--falsely, I argue--that it can be identical to the meaning of the reflexive in sentences like (1) and (2).

5. Derek Gross has pointed out to me that the stressed reflexives in the (b) sentences can marginally receive the emphatic interpretation if they are interpreted in a way such that the reflexive has been moved out of its postnominal into sentence final position; the

disclocated reflexive must be preceded by an intonation break, and the verb is stressed:

(i) ?This car will SELL, ITSELF

6. The standard accounts in the literature on middle formation agree that the verb is detransitivized, i.e., the subject role is not realized, which forces the internal argument to be externalized, in a operation akin to that of Passive formation.

7. Note that this emphatic reflexive can occur with regular middles, which have a derived subject, just like the sentence types in (17)-(19):

(ii) This problem ITSELF solves easily (it's just those small details...)

Sentences like

(iii) The car ITSELF drives

seem to pose a counterexample to (20) and (21) because they appear to be reflexive middles with the emphatic adjunct. However, these sentences are regular middles. Even though most middles have an adverb like *easily*, it is not required if the middle expresses some contrast; cf.:

(iv) This seat belt adjusts

We can see that (ii) is a regular, rather than a reflexive middle, by the fact that a verb like *solve*, and *suggest* which form only reflexive, but not regular middles, cannot occur in a structure like (ii) above:

(v) *The solution ITSELF suggested

8. Grammaticality judgments for reflexive middles tend to improve in the presence of a hedging adverb like *virtually* or *practically*. I will disregard such sentences here because these hedges obscure the conditions for reflexive middles formation.

9. The presence of an implied Agent in middles is disputed, but there is strong evidence for it, such as an analysis of middle adverbs. In any case, we are concerned here with the presence or absence of an argument that satisfies the semantic structure of the verb.

10. Lakoff (1977) expresses a similar intuition in saying that reflexive middles state that little effort was needed on the part of the Agent, who, in these sentences, is not the principal source of energy for the action. However, Lakoff views reflexive middles as implying that certain properties of the Theme obviate the Agent's "responsibility" for the action; my analysis, on the other hand, is based on the semantics of the verb and assumes that properties of the Theme play a role only in regular middles.

References
Belletti, A. and L. Rizzi (1988). Psych verbs and Theta-Theory. Natural Language and Linguistic Theory. 6.3.291-352.

132

Fellbaum, C. 1985. Adverbs in agentless actives and passives. In: *Papers From the Parasession on Causatives and Agentivity*, eds. W. Eilfort et al. Chicago: Chicago Linguistic Society. 21-31.

Fiengo, R. 1980. *Surface Structure and The Interface of Autonomous Components*. Cambridge, MA: Harvard University Press.

Hale, K. and J. Keyser. 1987. A View From the Middle. Cambrige, MA: MIT Lexicon Working Papers no.10.

Lakoff, G. 1977. Linguistic Gestalts. In: *Papers From the Thirteenth Regional Meeting*, eds. W. Beach et al. Chicago: Chicago Linguistic Society. 236-301.

Vendler, Z. 1984. Adverbs of Action. In: *Papers From the Parasession of Lexical Semantics*, eds. D. Testen et al. Chicago: Chicago Linguistic Society. 297-305.

Nominal Hydras
A GPSG Approach to Agreement in the German NP*

Klaus Fenchel
University of California, Santa Cruz

1. In GPSG the notion 'head of a phrase' is a technical one. A head is an underspecified category, a kind of variable in a phrase structure rule. The exact feature composition of any node in a tree which corresponds to this head variable is determined by a universal principle of the theory, the Head Feature Convention (HFC) which states roughly that the features on the mother and the head daughter have to be identical. This oversimplified characterisation will be stated more precisely below. As a direct result of its technical nature, the notion 'head' is deceptively contentless when compared to more traditional intuitions (see Zwicky 1985 for a good overview).

The way 'head' is defined in GPSG allows for multi-headed constructions which play an important role in the analysis of coordination (Sag et al. 1985). However, nothing in the theory restricts the use of multiple heads to this kind of construction. In fact, it is tempting to analyze a construction as multi-headed when a considerable number of features of its constituents have to covary. The German NP is a good example since all its main components (determiner, adjective, and noun) have to agree in the features gender, number, and case. In the present paper I want to explore the idea that the German NP might be a multi-headed construction. I will show that, even though the idea seems to be counterintuitive at first, it is possible to set up a rather simple grammar that covers a considerable fragment of NP constructions.

However, as soon as the scope of the investigation is extended beyond the simple NP, namely to coordination, problems arise which are not easily accommodated. This suggests that there should be more content to the notion 'head' which rules out in principle analyses of this kind.

2. Heads in GPSG are introduced in ID-rules[1] as the symbol H, which stands for an underspecified syntactic category. In Gazdar et al. (1985, p.51) H is introduced as follows:

(1)   In a rule of the form $C \rightarrow ...H...$
        H is a *head*.

The HFC in its simplest instantiation requires that a local tree which is admitted by a certain phrase structure rule have the same HEAD features on the mother and on the head daughter. The set of HEAD features is defined in the grammar. For English the major category features N and V, are HEAD features while e.g. CASE is not.

A rule of the form (2a) together with the HFC will admit a tree like (2b), with the features fleshed out in (2b).

(2) a. $V^2 \to H^0$, NP   b.   [+V,-N,BAR 2]

                                   [+V,-N,BAR 0]   [-V,+N,BAR 2]

     The requirement of complete identity of HEAD features on a mother and head daughters is too strong. The actual formulation of the HFC in GPSG allows for two principled exceptions to this: First, the head feature specifications of the mother must be identical to the intersection of the head feature specifications of the head daughters. Hence if there is a feature specification conflict between two head daughters, the HFC can be satisfied by leaving the mother node unspecified. Thus given the rule in (3a) the tree in (3b) meets the HFC in this respect:

(3) a. $X \to H, H$ b.   [+N,BAR 2]

                                 [+V,+N,BAR 2]   [-V,+N,BAR 2]

This is relevant for examples like 'Pat is either stupid or a liar' where an AP and an NP are coordinated[2].

     Second, the HFC can only force identity of HEAD features that are freely instantiated. HEAD feature specifications that are fixed by an ID-rule or by other principles of the grammar, such as Feature Cooccurrence Restrictions (FCR), are not free. Hence the HFC is overridden when rules require disagreement of HEAD features between the mother and the head daughter. In rule (2a) the feature BAR, which is a HEAD feature for English, cannot be instantiated freely on the head daughter since it is mentioned in the ID rule; therefore it is not subject to the HFC, as can be seen in the tree in (2b)[3].

3. We turn now to consider   the analysis of a simple German NP, consisting of a determiner, an adjective, and a noun as given in (4). The components of the NP are annotated with the relevant syntactic features[4].

(4)

	der	alte	Mann	(the old man)
N:		+	+	
V:		+	-	
GEND:	m	m	m	
NUM:	sg	sg	sg	
CASE:	nom	nom	nom	
Determiner type:	II			
DECLCLASS:		wk		

     The agreement in gender, number, and case is obvious from (4). The feature GEND can take on three different values: m(asculine), f(eminine), and n(euter). There are two values for NUM: sg (singular), and pl(ural), and four for CASE: nom(inative), gen(itive), dat(ive), and acc(usative).Violation of gender, number, or case agreement yields ungrammatical NPs, as shown in some examples in (5):

(5) a. $der_{[m,sg,nom]}$ $alte_{[m,sg,nom]}$ $Mann_{[m,sg,nom]}$
    b. $^*der_{[m]}$ $alte_{[m]}$ $Frau_{[f]}$ (gender)
    c. $^*der_{[sg]}$ $alte_{[sg]}$ $Männer_{[pl]}$ (number)
    d. $^*der_{[nom]}$ $alte_{[nom]}$ $Mannes_{[gen]}$ (case)

The type of determiner and the feature DECLCLASS show a more complex interaction. Determiner type governs the value of DECLCLASS on the adjective. There are three values for the feature DECLCLASS which, following tradition, will be called wk (weak), mx (mixed), and str(ong). Determiners are distinguished on purely syntactic grounds, depending on which adjective declension they trigger. The classification of the determiners into three determiner types cuts right across the semantic definite/indefinite distinction. Strong declension on adjectives occurs with determiners of type I (e.g. *manch* 'some', *solch* 'such'), and in the absence of a determiner. Determiners of type I are uninflected. Weak declension is required by determiners of type II (e.g *der* 'the', *dieser* 'this', *mancher* 'some'), and mixed declension by determiners of type III (e.g. *ein* 'a', *kein* 'no', *mein* 'my'). Determiners of type II and III inflect for gender, number, and case. Some contrasts between NPs containing the different determiners are shown in (6).

(6) a. $der_{[II]}$ $alte_{[wk]}$ Mann $ein_{[III]}$ $alter_{[mx]}$ Mann
    b. $die_{[II]}$ $alten_{[wk]}$ Männer $manch_{[I]}$ $alte_{[str]}$ Männer
    c. (mit) $einem_{[III]}$ $alten_{[mx]}$ Mann   (mit) $manch_{[I]}$ $altem_{[str]}$Mann

Mismatching determiner type and DECLCLASS yields ungrammatical NPs, as exemplified in (7).

(7) a. $manch_{[I]}$ $alter_{[str]}$ Mann $^*manch_{[I]}$ $alte_{[wk]}$ Mann
    b. $der_{[II]}$ $alte_{[wk]}$ Mann $^*der_{[II]}$ $alter_{[mx]}$ Mann
    c. $ein_{[III]}$ $alter_{[mx]}$ Mann $^*ein_{[III]}$ $alte_{[wk]}$ Mann

Thus there are two different things that a grammar for the NP has to accomplish. First of all, it has to account for the agreement of determiner, noun, and adjective in the features GEND, NUM, and CASE. Second, it has to capture the fact that the declension class of the adjective is determined by the type of determiner present.

4. The central idea to the solution of the agreement problem is that the features NUM, GEND and CASE must covary. This immediately raises two more questions: How can covariation of features be formalized, and how can it be restricted to the relevant subtree? Features can be restricted to a certain domain by means of Feature Cooccurrence Restrictions (FCRs), as will be shown at the end of this section. In this paper, covariation is implemented by assuming that all constituents that share the specifications for the features GEND, NUM, and CASE are heads. The HFC will then account for the agreement of these constituents. This requires that GEND,

NUM, and CASE are HEAD features[5]. The set of features I assume to be in HEAD for this analysis is given in (8).

(8)   HEAD = {DECLCLASS, GEND, NUM, CASE, V, N, BAR}

In addition, DECLCLASS is assigned to the adjective via subcategorization[6] between the determiner and the N^1.

Now consider the following NP rules in (9) and the corresponding lexical entries for some determiners in (10).

(9)   a. $N^2 \rightarrow H[27], H^1[wk]$

       b. $N^2 \rightarrow H[28], H^1[mx]$

       c. $N^2 \rightarrow (\{[SUBCAT\ 29]\}), H^1$

(10)   a.   <*der*, [[SUBCAT 27], [NUM sg],[GEND m],[CASE nom]], **der'**>
       b.   <*ein*, [[SUBCAT 28],[NUM sg],[GEND m],[CASE nom]], **ein'**>
       c.   <*manch*, [SUBCAT 29], **manch'**>

Rule (9a) states that an NP can consist of a lexical head that has the feature [SUBCAT 27], and of a phrasal head of BAR level 1 that has the feature [DECLCLASS wk]. The corresponding lexical entry (10a) for the determiner also has the feature [SUBCAT 27]. This is GPSG's way of ensuring that *der* can only be inserted in the tree projected from rule (9a). The ID-rule contains the information about subcategorization. Every determiner has one of three values (27, 28, or 29) for the feature SUBCAT. [SUBCAT 27] corresponds to what was earlier determiner type II, [SUBCAT 28] is determiner type III, and [SUBCAT 29] is determiner type I. ID-rule (9a) admits the following local tree (the lexical items are inserted for expository purpose only).

(11)

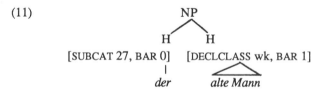

Rule (9b) introduces determiners of type III, and the corresponding mixed declension class, Rule (9c) takes care of determinerless NPs and NPs that contain a determiner of type I. Note that no value for DECLCLASS is specified. Strong adjective declension is the default case since it is not restricted to the two cases mentioned above (lack of determiner or presence of a determiner of type I), but appears also in possessive constructions or with numerals. A Feature Specification Default (FSD) is the tool in GPSG to formalize this generalization.

(12)   FSD: [+N] $\supset$ [DECLCLASS str]

This default has the effect of instantiating [DECLCLASS str] on any category that is [+N] if no other rule or principle of the grammar determines the value for this feature.

The N^1-rule that introduces the AP is more complicated. Remember that all constituents which covary in the features GEND, NUM, and CASE have to be heads. Thus the AP has to be a head of N^1. The crucial question is how an AP can be a (phrasal) head of N^1, and still keep its categorial integrity. In GPSG all major syntactic categories are decomposed into sets of syntactic features. Syntactic rules can be underspecified and may refer explicitly to specific features. This is a very powerful tool which can be used to determine the value of the major category feature V of the [BAR 2] head in the ID-rule (13a).

(13) a. $N^1 \rightarrow H^2[+V], (H)$ b.   [+N, -V, BAR 1]

H   H
[+N, +V, BAR 2]   [+N, -V, BAR 1]
| |
alte   *Mann*

This example shows very clearly how it is possible to exploit in a non-trivial way the fact that the HFC does not force complete identity of HEAD features on the mother and head daughter: The features [+V] and [BAR 2] on the left hand daughter are specified in the ID-rule. Therefore the HFC cannot instantiate the features [-V] and [BAR 1] on this head. However, all the HEAD features of the mother can be instantiated on the second head. I will have more to say about the peculiarities of this N^1 rule towards the end of this paper. The remaining ID-rules and corresponding lexical entries for nouns and adjectives are given in (14) and (15).

(14) a. $N^1 \rightarrow H[22]$

   b. $A^2 \rightarrow (Adv), H^1$

   c. $A^1 \rightarrow H[40]$

(15) a. *<alte*, [[SUBCAT 40], [+N], [+V],
          [DECLCLASS wk], [NUM sg],[GEND m],[CASE nom]], **alt'>**

   b. *<alter*, [[[SUBCAT 40], [+N], [+V],
          [DECLCLASS mx], [NUM sg],[GEND m],[CASE nom]], **alt'>**

   c. *<alter*, [[SUBCAT 40], [+N], [+V],
          [DECLCLASS str], [NUM sg],[GEND m],[CASE nom]], **alt'>**

   d. *<Mann*, [[SUBCAT 22], [+N], [-V],
          [NUM sg],[GEND m],[CASE nom]], **mann'>**

There are still two problems with the feature distribution in the NP. First, consider the tree in (11) again. The HFC would require the node directly dominating the determiner to have the feature DECLCLASS. However, it is not needed there since it does not do any work. The domain to which this feature should be restricted is N^1. This can be achieved by a FCR (16). As a consequence of (16), the feature DECLCLASS will be specified in all head paths in N^1, but not on the NP or the determiner. I will argue below that this is indeed a desired result.

(16)   FCR1:   NP $\supset \neg$[DECLCLASS]

Second, the grammar defined so far would still admit trees for the ungrammatical *$alte$ [nom]$Mannes$[gen] as shown in (17).

(17)

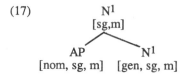

The clash of the CASE features on the two heads does not rule out (17) because the HFC allows the head mother to be unspecified for those HEAD features which have differing specifications on the head daughters. It is therefore necessary to cancel out this property of the HFC in this case by enforcing the specification of the features GEND, NUM, and CASE on each node that has the feature [+N]. FCR2 does exactly this. It rules out trees like (17) and the corresponding ungrammatical constituents.

(18) FCR2:   [+N] $\supset$ [GEND, NUM, CASE]

I will discuss this FCR more extensively in the last section of this paper where I try to point out some of the problems of this approach.

5. In this section I want to show a consequence of the fact that the feature DECLCLASS has N^1 as its domain. The difference between NPs consisting of a determiner and an adjective such as *der alte* 'the old one', and NPs consisting of a determiner and a deadjectival noun such as *der Alte* 'the old one/man' is accounted for immediately if it is assumed that *Alte* in the latter NP is actually a noun, even though it still shows adjectival inflection. Below I will try to establish some evidence for the claim that deadjectival nouns are really nouns.

The constructions covered by the grammar are given in (19). The two NPs mentioned above are included as (19c ii) and (19d).

(19) a.   **det-adj⁺-n** (adj⁺ means one or more adjectives):
            der (lustige) alte Mann   'the (funny) old man'

     b.   **adj⁺-n** (if the noun is a mass noun or the NP is plural):
            kalter Schnee   'cold snow'
            (lustige) alte Männer   '(funny) old men'

c. **det-n:**
   i. der Mann   'the man'
   ii. der Alte   'the old one'

d. **det-adj⁺:**
   der alte   'the old one'
   as in: Ich habe zwei Füller. Der alte macht Klekse.
   'I have two fountain pens. The old one produces only ink stains.'

e. **n** (plural or sg mass):
   i. Schnee   'snow'
   ii. Alter   'old man'

f. **adj⁺** (sg: understood as modifying a missing mass noun; plural)
   alter   'old (one)'
   as in: Frischer Kaffee schmeckt besser als alter.
   'Fresh coffee tastes better than old (coffee)'

I want to argue that the form *alte* in *der alte* (19d) is an adjective while *Alte* in *der Alte* (19c ii) is a noun. It is difficult to find arguments which, beyond any doubt, support this claim since the categorial flexibility of German words often causes considerable insecurity in judgements with respect to their semantic and syntactic properties. However, the following four facts are suggestive:

(i) *der alte* can only be used anaphorically. It is infelicitous if used sentence initially and no context is given from which the missing noun could be recovered (20a). Given an appropriate context the sentence is acceptable (20b). *Der Alte* in (20c) on the other hand is not anaphoric. Thus there is a clear difference between (20a) and (20c).

(20) a. ??Das alte ist zu klein.   'The old one is too small.'
     b. A: Warum kaufst Du ein neues Sofa? 'Why do you buy a new sofa?'
        B: Das alte ist zu klein.   'The old one is too small.'
     c. Der Alte ist zu klein.   'The old one/guy is too short.'

(ii) It is possible to modify a noun by both a prenominal participle phrase and an adjective. The two possible orderings of the two adjuncts with respect to each other are both grammatical (21a). Given the right context this is also true for the anaphoric NP (21b). However, it is not possible for the NP in (21c).

(21) a. Das [pres.part im Flur stehende] [A alte] Sofa ist zu klein.
        Das [A alte] [pres.part im Flur stehende] Sofa ist zu klein.
        'The old sofa that is standing in the hallway is too small'
     b. A: Warum kaufst Du ein neues Sofa? 'Why do you buy a new sofa?'
        B: Das [pres.part im Flur stehende] [A alte] ist zu klein.
        C: Das [A alte] [pres.part im Flur stehende] Sofa ist zu klein.
        'The old one that is standing in the hallway is too small'
     c. Der [pres.part im Flur stehende] [Alte] liest die Zeitung.
        *Der [Alte] [pres.part im Flur stehende] liest die Zeitung.
        'The old guy who is standing in the hallway is reading the paper'

This suggests very strongly that *Alte* in (21c) is a noun that is dominated by N^0, and not an adjective like *alte* in (21a) and (21b).

(iii) There seems to be a small but consistent difference in meaning between adjectives and the derived deadjectival nouns. Consider the following examples.

(22) a. der$_{[m]}$/die$_{[f]}$/??das$_{[n]}$ Alte kam zur Tür herein
'the old one came through the door'
b. Das Alte muß erhalten werden.
'The Ancient has to be saved.'
c. der$_{[m]}$/die$_{[f]}$/??das$_{[n]}$ Schöne verbrachte die Nächte mit betrunkenen Matrosen.
'the beautiful one spent the nights with drunken sailors'
d. Das Schöne$_{[n]}$ erfreut die Seele
'Beauty pleases the soul'

There is a very strong tendency to interpret der$_{[m]}$/die$_{[f]}$ *Alte* as referring only to human beings. This is excluded for das$_{[n]}$ *Alte*, which has to refer to some kind of abstract entity[7]. This is rendered in (22b) by 'Ancient'. The same phenomenon can be seen again in (22c) and (22d). *Das Schöne*$_{[n]}$ is definitely an abstract category, and cannot refer to an animate or human entity as der$_{[m]}$/die$_{[f]}$ *Schöne*. On the other hand, der$_{[m]}$/die$_{[f]}$/das$_{[n]}$ *schöne* is completely undetermined with respect to animacy and concreteness. To sum up this point, there is a subtle but definite and regular change in meaning which lends support to the assumption of a categorial change of the adjective.

(iv) There is a clear orthographic distinction between nouns and adjectives: nouns are always capitalized while adjectives are not. There are some marginal exceptions to this rule, but they do not invalidate it. It seems to me that the orthographic distinction reflects a grammatical difference. However, this is only an indirect argument supporting the general claim that deadjectival nouns are real nouns.

I have given some arguments for the claim that deadjectival nouns are really nouns. They may be derived by a lexical category changing rule that yields for every lexical entry of category [+N,+V] a new lexical entry of category [+N,-V], and an appropriate change of meaning. Yet, these deadjectival nouns still have one important adjectival property: they are sensitive to the type of determiner present. This is shown in (23) where the two columns represent the opposition between nouns and adjectives, and the two rows the opposition between weak and mixed declension.

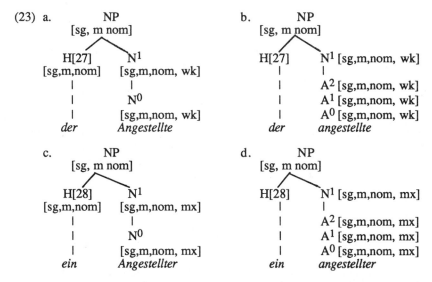

(23) a.

NP
[sg, m nom]

H[27]	N¹
[sg,m,nom]	[sg,m,nom, wk]
	N⁰
	[sg,m,nom, wk]
der	*Angestellte*

b.

NP
[sg, m nom]

H[27]	N¹ [sg,m,nom, wk]
	A² [sg,m,nom, wk]
	A¹ [sg,m,nom, wk]
	A⁰ [sg,m,nom, wk]
der	*angestellte*

c.

NP
[sg, m nom]

H[28]	N¹
[sg,m,nom]	[sg,m,nom, mx]
	N⁰
	[sg,m,nom, mx]
ein	*Angestellter*

d.

NP
[sg, m nom]

H[28]	N¹ [sg,m,nom, mx]
	A² [sg,m,nom, mx]
	A¹ [sg,m,nom, mx]
	A⁰ [sg,m,nom, mx]
ein	*angestellter*

We get the following result: The feature DECLCLASS is put via subcategorization onto N¹. The HFC requires that it appears on all heads of N¹. Thus, unless some further steps are taken to prevent this, DECLCLASS will not only appear on the AP but also on N. This predicts that there be Ns which are sensitive to the type of determiner present. I argued that this prediction is indeed correct.

6. Let me turn now to some problematic aspects of this analysis. First of all consider again FCR2 from (18) above: [+N] ⊃ [GEND, NUM, CASE]. It forces agreement of the features GEND, NUM, and CASE in all categories that are [+N]. However, NP coordination in GPSG is analysed as having two or more nominal heads conjoined under an NP mother. It is a well-known fact about NP coordination that the conjuncts can disagree in gender and number.

(24) a. NP → H, H

b.

N²[nom]

N²[sg,m,nom]	N²[pl,fem,nom]
der Alte	*und seine Töchter*

'the old (man) and his daughters'

Thus an NP like that in (24b) is grammatical but it would be ruled out by FCR2. And it is for structures like (24) that the HFC was formulated in a permissive way. It is possible to augment the grammar to get around this problem. But this would involve stating a whole set of specific and unintuitive FCRs, which would result in a considerable loss of simplicity of the analysis.

Second, the rule: N¹ → H²[+V], (H), which introduces the AP as a head of N¹, does not obey a condition on X-bar grammars that was termed Succession in

Pullum (1985). Informally, Succession means that the bar level of a head daughter is one less than the bar level of the mother. This constraint in its strong form is, as Pullum observes, not obeyed by most current syntactic theories that make use of 'some version of X-bar theory'. However, a weak version of it, requiring only that the bar level of the head daughter is equal to, or one less than the bar level of the head mother, seems to be obeyed widely. But even this weaker condition is violated by the rule above, since the bar level of a daughter is actually one more than that of the mother. Succession could be weakened further by requiring that there is at least one head daughter that has a bar level equal to or lower than the head mother which would then be the 'real' head of the phrase. At this point it seems obvious that the notion 'head', as used in this paper, is too weak to distinguish between mere feature copying and headedness.

7. Let me distinguish two levels of the analysis given in this paper. First, the constituents of the NP covary in the feature specifications for GEND, NUM, and CASE, while the value for DECLCLASS is assigned by the determiner to N^1. As a result of this, both N and A must have the feature DECLCLASS. I argued that this is indeed a correct prediction. In addition, that principle which accounts for covariation of the features GEND, NUM, and CASE will also account for the specification of the feature DECLCLASS in N^1.

Second, there is the attempt to formalize these two facts by assuming that the constituents which show agreement are heads, and use the HFC to account for the covariation of GEND, NUM, and CASE, and the specification of DECLCLASS within N^1. The problems described in the previous section affect the second point, not the first.

The first problem is theory internal. The analysis runs into empirical problems as soon as it is extended to coordination, because a property of the HFC that is crucial for the analysis of coordinate NPs has to be turned off in order to account for the agreement within the simple NP. Thus, the grammar as presented cannot account for coordination. An extension of the grammar would complicate it by adding ad hoc rules and principles.

The second problem emerges on a more general level: one of the ID-rules violates any intuitions one might have about the notion 'head'. One part of this intuition that underlies almost all work in X-bar syntax is made precise in Pullum's definition of Succession.

Both problems point to a general weakness in the notion 'head' in GPSG: although it is not apparent at first sight, heads in GPSG serve essentially as feature copying mechanisms (in cooperation with the HFC). I demonstrated this with the hydra analysis of the German NP. Adding the constraint of Weak Succession as an obligatory part of GPSG (instead of just stating that most analyses obey it) would be a step towards a stronger notion of 'head'.

Notes:

* Part of this research was funded by a fellowship from the DAAD (German Academic Exchange Service). Support was also received from the Syntax Research Center of the University of California, Santa Cruz. I want to thank Chris Barker, Sandy Chung, Thomas Hukari, Bill Ladusaw, Jim McCloskey, Louise McNally, and Geoff Pullum for their critical and supportive comments on earlier drafts of this paper. None of them should be blamed for remaining errors or shortcomings.

1 In GPSG the information contained in traditional phrase structure rules is divided up in two different rule types: immediate dominance rules (ID-rules), written as e.g. S → NP, VP, implying no particular order between the two daughters, and linear precedence rules, e.g. NP<VP.

2 X symbolizes a maximally underspecified category which matches almost any categorial description. The actual coordination rule used in GPSG is more complex than rule (3a) which is a simplified version to illustrate the particular point I want to make.

3 In GPSG the assignment of [BAR 0] to the lexical head is more complicated than it appears from the simplified example above. Rule (2a) would actually have the form V2 → H[SUBCAT 11], NP. The feature SUBCAT determines which lexical entries can be inserted under this head. A Feature Cooccurrence Restriction forces [BAR 0] on all categories that have the feature SUBCAT which in turn prevents the HFC from matching the BAR features of the mother and the head daughter.

4 A complete set of paradigms for nouns, determiners, and adjectives is given in the appendix. It is not the goal of this paper to propose a solution to the problem of the massive syncretism. Interested readers may consult Zwicky (1986b).

5 Another approach would be to define a set of features, call it SPREAD, and a corresponding 'Spread Feature Convention' that forces SPREAD features to covary. This solution would require a considerable extension of the theory.

6 Zwicky (1986) argues against this approach. His own solution, involving government, requires the introduction of some new theoretical machinery which seems exclusively designed to account for this single problem.

7 There are some complications with respect to animals: *das Alte, das Junge* can be used to refer to old/young animals respectively that stand in a parent-child relationship. This may be a lexicalization, however.

References:

Eisenberg, Peter. 1986. Grundriß der deutschen Grammatik. Stuttgart: Metzler.

Gazdar, Gerald, Ewan Klein, Geoffrey Pullum and Ivan Sag. 1985. Generalized phrase structure grammar. Cambridge, Mass.: Harvard University Press.

Grundzüge einer deutschen Grammatik. 1981. Von einem Autorenkollektiv unter der Leitung von Karl Erich Heidolph, Walter Flämig und Wolfgang Motsch. Berlin: Akademie-Verlag.

Pullum, Geoffrey. 1985. Assuming some version of X-bar theory. CLS 21: Papers from the 21st Regional Meeting.

Sag, Ivan, Gerald Gazdar, Thomas Wasow and Steven Weisler. 1985. Coordination and how to distinguish categories. Natural Language and Linguistic Theory, 3, 117-171.

Zwicky, Arnold. 1985. Heads. Journal of Linguistics, 21, 1-29.

Zwicky, Arnold. 1986a. German adjective agreement in GPSG. Linguistics, 24, 957-990.

Appendix: Paradigms

NOUNS

	Tisch (M) (table) sg	pl	Katze (F) (cat) sg	pl	Haus (N) (house) sg	pl
CASE:						
nom	Tisch	Tische	Katze	Katzen	Haus	Häuser
acc	Tisch	Tische	Katze	Katzen	Haus	Häuser
gen	Tisches	Tische	Katze	Katzen	Hauses	Häuser
dat	Tisch	Tischen	Katze	Katzen	Haus	Häusern

ADJECTIVES

klein- (small) (the paradigm contains only the adjectival suffixes)

DECL-CLASS:	wk						mx						str					
NUM:	sg			pl			sg			pl			sg			pl		
GENDER:	m	f	n	m	f	n	m	f	n	m	f	n	m	f	n	m	f	n
CASE:																		
nom	e	e	e	en	en	en	er	e	es	en	en	en	er	e	es	e	e	e
acc	e	e	e	en	en	en	en	e	es	en	en	en	en	e	es	e	e	e
gen	en	en	en	en	en	en	en	en	en	en	en	en	es	er	es	er	er	er
dat	en	en	en	en	en	en	en	en	en	en	en	en	em	er	em	en	en	en

DETERMINERS

	der (type II) sg m	f	n	pl m/f/n	kein (type III) sg m	f	n	pl m/f/n	manch (type I) pl m/f/n
CASE:									
nom	der	die	das	die	kein	keine	kein	keine	
acc	den	die	das	die	keinen	keine	kein	keine	
gen	des	der	des	der	keines	keiner	keines	keiner	
dat	dem	der	dem	den	keinem	keiner	keinem	keinen	

Licensing, Inalterability,
and Harmonic Rule Application

John Goldsmith
The University of Chicago

0. Introduction

The purpose of this paper is to describe and
discuss an extention of the notion of the phonological
syllable, which I call autosegmental licensing.[1] In
order to accomplish this task, I will, first, suggest a
way of stepping back from our present view of the
syllable, and offer a summary of what is central to
that view, and then discuss the notion of coda
weakening, from both a static and a processual point of
view. This traditional notion will then serve to
motivate the idea of the syllable coda as a weak
licenser of distinctive features or autosegments. I
will then illustrate how this notion of coda licensing
naturally accounts for a range of possible syllable
types, including especially the range of languages
which permit geminates and nasal clusters
intervocalically but little else in the way of coda
material, and show how this notion of licensing, when
combined with what we may call a harmonic theory of
rule application, provides a deep and satisfying
account of inalterability phenomena. Finally, I will
point out that the notion of quantity-sensitivity is
simply a special case of coda-licensing.

1. The Syllable

The syllable is, indeed, at present a mainstream
concept in phonological theory in a way that it never
was before on this side of the Atlantic. In the 1940s,
Kenneth Pike encouraged the extension and application
of the developing notion of constituent structure
(immediate constituent analysis) to phonology in the
guise of the syllable, and in the 1950s, Einar Haugen's
voice was added to his; but by and large, reference to
the syllable as a unit in post-Bloomfieldian phonology
was heterodoxy. In the quite reasonable rush to
integrate the insights of syllable-related analysis
into phonological theory, we must not be overly hasty
in uncritically accepting the particular style of
analysis of the syllable, based as it explicitly was on
the transfer to phonology of a particular mode of
syntactic analysis. Current work on the syllable has
largely focused on the usefulness of the syllable in
two respects: first, major simplifications emerge for

the study of accent systems when viewed from a syllabic perspective, and second, rules of epenthesis and vowel-deletion are typically governed by the extent to which their input or outputs satisfy syllabification requirements of the language in question.

Both of these uses of the syllable focus on what Pike (1947) called the phonological syllable, in contrast to a phonetic syllable. The difference between these two is quite important to the view which we shall develop here, because we focus on a characteristic of the syllable which is found only at what is metaphorically called a deep level: that is, we will only be concerned here with representations of contrastive (or distinctive) phonological information, as in (1).

I would like to present a simple model in which the phonological syllable serves as a level of organization of phonological information, a level at which no more than one occurrence of a distinctive feature may be found per syllable. The syllable is not primarily a set of ordered (syntagmatic) slots; it is a unit of information organization, within which each distinctive feature may be specified no more than once. In fact, we may think of there being a symbiotic relation between the syllable, on the one hand, and the distinctive features in [that is, autosegments associated with] the syllable: the syllable is composed of those features, and the features are <u>licensed</u> by that syllable node. Each feature must be autosegmentally licensed by a licenser such as the syllable node, and each such licenser can license only one occurence of a given feature.

(1)

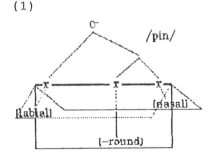

/pin/

2. Coda weakening

Now, this may sound too restrictive as it stands: how could such a view ever be true in view of the two contrasts in voicing found in the four words <u>pad</u>, <u>pat</u>, <u>bad</u>, and <u>bat</u>? If we take voicing to be a privative feature, with the unmarked value being that which is found in a voiceless consonant, we find the four-way contrast in (2). So voicing is surely specified twice per syllable, is it not?

(2)

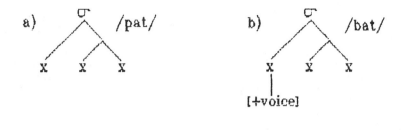

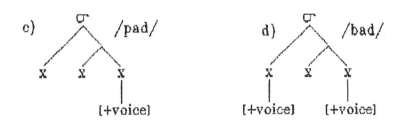

Indeed, to be sure, it is -- in English, where all four
words just mentioned are possible. But the fact is
that not just any CVC string of segments can be strung
together to form a possible syllable in a given
language; there are generally serious restrictions on
what can appear in the coda position -- that is, the
syllable-final position.

Firthian prosodic theory provides good terminological
resources for describing this; Firthians refer to the
(paradigmatic) range of possible segments in a given
position in a syllable structure as a system; this
allows them to make the observation simply that the
coda system is typically a subset of the onset system.
For various reasons that I will not pursue here, I
would prefer to focus not on the set of segments as
such that may appear in the coda, but rather on the set
of distinctive features that may appear in the coda
position, as opposed to those that may appear in the
onset position. Focusing on features rather than
segment inventories, though, clearly allows us to go
beyond the irrelevant problems that might arise due to
observations of the sort that angma appears in the coda
of an English syllable, though not in the onset.

The coda is an organizational constituent that allows
(or licenses) just a reduced set of features, and we
shall indicate that subset licensed by the coda in
braces, as in (3). The range of features licensed by
the coda is a subset of the entire range of features of
the language, which is the range of features licensed
by the syllable node.[2] We may think about the coda, if
you will, as a mini-syllable, or a degenerate syllable,
that is tacked on to the right-edge of the basic CV
syllable, linearly speaking, but which allows within it
only a part of the information that a true syllable
will.

We may summarize the point as follows: the set of
features that may be specified [contrastively] in the
coda is typically a subset of the entire set of
distinctive features in a language. If we represent
features autosegmentally, placing each on a separate
tier, then we will be able to express this
generalization in the following way:[3]

(3)

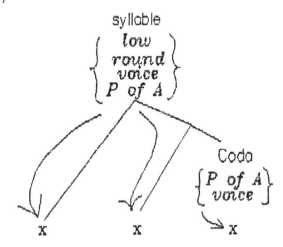

(4) Licensing Criterion
      Each distinctive feature in a representation must
      be licensed by its closest licenser, as in (3).
      Each licenser may license no more than one
      occurrence of each feature.

The licensing criterion in (4), then, allows us to
summarize in a direct manner, for each language, the

static or distributional notion of coda weakening. We shall return below to the dynamic, or processual, notion of coda-weakening.

Thus the English examples in (2a-d) are possible and well-formed only because in English, the coda position licenses the feature voicing. In a language such as German, where the coda does not license voicing, the feature voicing may not appear in the coda, and only (2a,b) are well-formed in conformity with the Licensing Criterion.

It is important to bear in mind that autosegmental licensing is distinct from association: a given autosegment may associate to a position without being licensed by that position, just in case that autosegment is licensed by some other licenser. This is sketched in (5).

(5)

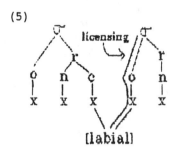

3. Weak Coda Licensers

The picture in (5) suggests immediately an analysis, or interpretation, of a phenomenon that has received a certain amount of discussion in the phonological literature since our attention was drawn to it by Prince (1984), who observed that there is a wide range of unrelated languages which share a restriction on the possibilities of what can appear intervocalically. In these "Prince languages", as we may call them, we find any single consonant of the language appearing intervocalically in the interlude, as in (6a), or a geminate version, as in (6b), or a homorganic nasal-consonant cluster, as in (6c).

(6) a) a p a   b) a p p a   c) a m p a
       a t a   a t t a   a n t a
       a k a   a k k a   a ŋ k a

In such languages, no consonant may appear in a coda that has a distinctive point of articulation that is not itself shared with the following onset.

It is our good fortune now to be able to observe that this precise state of affairs is predicted by the

system centered around the Licensing Criterion as
stated in (4). This result has been adumbrated already
in (5), where we see that the point of articulation
feature -- represented here as [labial] -- is
associated with both the coda and the onset positions,
even though it is licensed only by the onset position.
Just as the examples of the interludes in (6b) are
represented as in (5), so the interludes in (6c) are
represented as in (7). What makes a Prince-type
language a Prince-language, then, is precisely this:
its coda licenses only the feature {nasal}; in every
other respect, what associates to the coda position
must also be associated with something else, which is
better equipped to license it -- that is, the following
onset.

In (8), I briefly summarize some facts regarding
Selayarese, a Prince-language discussed and analyzed in
Mithun and Basri (1986), as well as in Goldsmith (1989,
to appear).

(7)

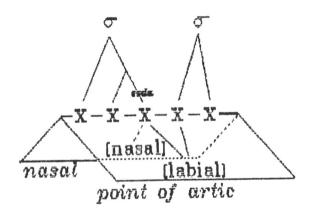

In Selayarese, we find word-medially only the syllabic
possibilities of a Prince language, though at the end
of the phonological word at a deep level (the W-level,
as discussed in Goldsmith (1989)), the word may end in
an s,l, or r, permitted -- that is, licensed by -- the
third kind of licenser, a word-peripheral appendix Ω).

On the surface, however, the appendix is not permitted, and this appendix s, l, or r becomes the onset of a final syllable whose nuclear vowel is a vowel that echoes the quality of the immediately preceding lexical vowel. It is quite noteworthy that the licensing possibilities of a syllable, a coda, and an appendix can all three be quite distinct.

(8) Selayarese (Indonesia; Austronesian)

  Word-medially, permits intervocalically only

single consonant	[sá:po]	'house'
geminates	[sáppo]	'missing front teeth'
nasal clusters	[sóm:po]	'carry over shoulder'
? + voiced C	[ta?gáraŋ]	'get stained'

  Word-initially, no clusters

  Word-finally, only:

light open syllable	[sássa]	'wash'
velar nasal	[pó:?oŋ]	'tree'
glottal stop	[sássa?]	'lizard'

o Word-level: <u>Coda</u> licenses {nasal};
                  <u>Ω (appendix)</u> licenses {continuant, liquid, lateral, consonantal}, i.e., s,r,l.

o Phrase-level: coda licenses {nasal}

4. Inalterability

We have now arrived at a point where we can see that Prince-languages such as Selayarese fit into a natural place in a formal typology of syllable types. A Prince-language, with interludes as (6), is a language where the coda licenses just the feature {nasal}. A language whose coda licenses no features at all (i.e., licenses the null set {∅}) can have geminates or long vowels in its coda, which is, we see, a smaller range of possibilities than in a Prince-language. The larger the set of features licensed by the coda, the larger the range of possible codas, and the entire typology then forms not a hierarchy, but what is technically a lattice. From a working phonologist's point of view, it is of interest to note that we find a number of what we might call impure Prince-languages, in the sense that (1) geminates and nasal clusters are allowed, (2) true stop clusters are not permitted, but (3) certain other clusters are permitted, showing us that a single continuant (typically /s/) and/or sonorants are permitted in the coda. Hausa is a well-known example of this sort, for a range of possible features can be licensed by the coda; point of articulation, however, cannot be, and so we find no distinctive point of articulation there.

This is illustrated in (9).

(9) (capital letter marks glottalization)
continuant
    [cont]   kaskoo 'bowl'   kasàakee 'bowls'
sonorant
    [rhotic]   turmii 'mortar'   turàamee 'pl.'
    [lateral] gulbii 'stream'   gulàabee 'pl.'
    [trill]   kuřfoo 'whip'   kuřàafee 'pl.'
glides   Kaymii 'spur'   Kayàamee 'pl.'
            Kyawree'door'   Kyawàaree 'pl.'
homorganic nasal
    [nasal]   dumBuu 'whip'   dumBàayee 'pl.'
            kundii 'paper wad' kundàayee 'pl.'
            zankoo 'crest'   zankàayee 'pl.'

An active diachronic change was involved in the loss of distinctive point of articulation in coda position, noted first by Klingenheben, as in (10), and remains active in synchronic alternations (Schuh (1972) disputes this, though largely on grounds that are weak within the present framework).

(10) Klingenheben's Law: labials, velars > w/ --$
                          coronals   > ř/ --$
talawcii 'poverty'   cf.   talaka 'poor person'
zuwciyaa 'heart'   zukaataa 'hearts'
juwjii   'rubbish heap'   jibaajee 'pl.'
zuwciyaa 'heart'   zukaataa 'hearts'
Bawnaa   'buffalo'   Bakaanee 'pl.'
gwauroo 'bachelor'   gwagwaaree 'pl.'
taushii 'drum'   tafaashee 'pl.'
kyauroo 'arrow-shaft'   kyamaaree 'pl.'

The synchronic effects of Klingenheben's Law, as illustrated in (10), do not extend to geminates, as has been noted on a number of occasions (see, for example, Hayes (1986)); this effect is a paradigmatic example of what Kenstowicz and Pyle referred to as the inalterability of geminates. Hayes (1986) and Schein and Steriade (1986) have offered formal explanations of the failure of a weakening rule such as Klingenheben's Law to apply to geminates, as in (11). Our present framework allows us a deeper and more compelling account, however, we would suggest.[1]

(11) Geminates give rise to labials and velars in codas, which do not undergo Klingenheben's Law:
    garukkàa   'pens'   kakkaRànta   'reread'
    babbabbaku 'be well roasted' etc.

A large range of rules apply in a manner that I have
referred to elsewhere as "harmonic" in application,
meaning that they apply just in case their output
actively creates a representation that satisfies
phonotactic conditions in a superior fashion to their
input.[5] Such rules apply not on the condition that
their structural description is satisfied, as in the
production-rules of a generative grammar, but on a
goal-oriented condition of the sort I have just
described. Such a general theory of architecture and
of rule-application in phonology requires a well-
articulated theory of phonotactic conditions, to be
sure, to specify in a principled way what may count as
a tactic or target structure, and coda licensing should
be understood as a contribution to this task.

This point can be restated in the following way. The
clearest general examples of inalterability effects of
geminate consonants all involve coda-weakening
processes to which the geminate is somehow
invulnerable. This is no coincidence; it is, rather,
evidence that the theoretical perspective pursued by
the field has been misguided. The question up to now
has always been why a rule should not apply to a
segment if, after all, the structural description of
the rule has been met by the segment in its environment
(e.g., an obstruent in the Hausa coda). But the right
way to formulate the rule is one which leads to rule
application not solely on the basis of satisfaction of
a structural description, but rather when the rule
serves the purpose of creating a representation that
satisfies the Licensing Criterion (4) above. Geminates
satisfy the Criterion, as we have argued; hence
Klingenheben's Law does not apply to them. Nothing
more need be said.

5. Quantity-Sensitivity

One final point to discuss involves the relation of
syllable licensing to the metrical grid. It has been
argued (Halle and Vergnaud 1988) that the relation of
the bottom or mora row (Row 0) of the metrical grid to
the skeleton is essentially one of autosegmental
association. If that is correct, then the Licensing
Criterion has certain consequences for the account of
stress systems. Let us consider them.

In any given language with a stress system, the
association to the mora row will be licensed by the
syllable node, since that licenser licenses all
possible associations. Let us refer to this

154

particular association as "association to moras". When
we consider the possibilities of coda licensing, we see
that there are, of course, two possibilities: either
the coda can license association to moras also, or it
cannot. If it cannot, then only one mora can be
associated per syllable. This is a quantity-
insensitive system. If the coda can license
association to moras, then it follows that a syllable
with a coda will be able to associate to two moras, and
a syllable with no coda will be able to associate to
only one mora. In short, if the coda licenses mora-
association, then it is what we have up to now known as
quantity-sensitivity, as in (12a). If the coda does
not license mora-association, the system is quantity-
insensitive, as in (12b).

(12)a.   b.

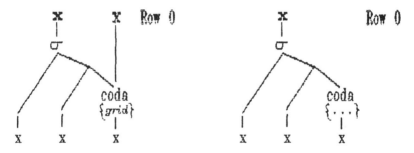

Thus   quantity-sensitivity reduces in the simplest
possible manner to coda licensing, a notion introduced
for quite separate reasons.

6. Conclusion

To conclude: I have in this paper only sketched a few
of the central reasons motivating the notion of
licensing as a fundamental well-formedness condition on
word-level phonological structure. In fact, I have not
discussed its word-level character, nor the importance
and relevance of word-level appendices, and how that is
treated in parallel fashion. This brief discussion
illustrates, however, how a number of issues treated
separately if at all till present can be capture in one
single, elementary, and straightforward fashion.
Looking ahead, however, I suggest in work in progress,
cited above, that the notions of licensing units, which
refine the traditional notions of syllable, coda, and
appendix, can be shown to arise in a natural fashion
out of a connectionist architecture that involves very

few specifically structural -- i.e., "wired in" --
assumptions. We thus begin to see a serious
possibility of convergence between phonological theory,
in the strict sense, and an implementation of phonology
within a larger cognitive context.

Notes

(1) This notion is discussed also in Goldsmith (1989)
and Goldsmith (in preparation), as well as in Brentari
(1988), Bosch (1989), and Wiltshire (1988).

(2) I ignore here, for expository reasons, the
stress/unstressed distinction, being explored by A.
Bosch in work in progress. This is extremely
important, however; the possibilities of both vowel and
consonant contrasts in unstressed syllables is
typically far reduced from the range of possible
contrasts in stressed syllables.

(3) Pursued further, the present analysis strongly
supports a reanalysis of fundamental syllable structure
as in (i), a position which develops towards both the
demisyllable of Fujimura (1979) and Clements (1989),
and the moraic account of Hyman (1985). This notion is
developed further in Goldsmith (in press); I retain the
structure as in (2) because of its familiarity.
(i)

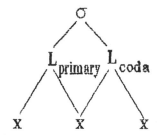

(Demisyllables: Fujimura)

(4) Ito (1986) similarly proposes to link the existence
of Prince languages and the inalterability of
geminates, though her account uses, rather than
explains, the inalterability effects of Hayes and
Schein and Steriade.

(5) This is discussed in Goldsmith (1989, Chapter 6),

156

and Goldsmith (in preparation).

References

Bosch, Anna. 1988. Syllable Structure in Scottish
Gaelic. Unpublished paper, University of Chicago.
Brentari, Diane. 1988. Licensing in ASL Handshape
Change. To appear in the proceedings of the 1988
Gallaudet University Conference on Theoretical Issues
in Sign Language.
Clements, G.N. 1989. The Sonority Cycle and Syllable
Organization. Ms.
Fujimura, Osamu. 1979. English Syllables as core and
affixes. Zeitschrift für Phonetik,
Sprachwissenschaft und Kommunikationsforschung
32:471-76.
Goldsmith, John. 1989. Autosegmental and Metrical
Oxford and New York: Basil Blackwell.
Goldsmith, John. In preparation. Harmonic Phonology:
Phonology as an Intelligent System.
Halle, Morris and Jean-Roger Vergnaud. 1988. An Essay
on Stress. Cambridge: MIT Press.
Hayes, Bruce. 1986. Inalterability in CV Phonology.
Language 62: 321-51.
Hyman, Larry M. 1985. A Theory of Phonological Weight.
Dordrecht: Foris Publications.
Ito, Junko. 1986. Syllable Structure in Prosodic
Phonology, PhD dissertation, UMass Amherst.
Kenstowicz, Michael and Charles Pyle. 1973. On the
phonological integrity of geminate clusters. In
Kenstowicz and Kisseberth, eds., Issues in
phonological theory. 27-43. The Hague:Mouton.
Marianne Mithun and Hasan Basri. 1986. The Phonology of
Selayarese. Oceanic Linguistics. 25:210-54 (1986).
P.Newman and B.A. Salim. 1981. Hausa Diphthongs Lingua
55:101-21.
Pike, Kenneth. 1947. Phonemics. Ann Arbor: University
of Michigan Press.
Prince, Alan S. 1984. Phonology with Tiers. Language
Sound Structures, ed. Mark Aronoff and Richard
Oehrle. Cambridge, Mass: MIT Press.
Schein, Barry and Donca Steriade. 1986. On Geminates.
LI 17: 691-744.
Schuh, Russell. 1972. Rule Inversion in Chadic. Studies
in African Linguistics 3: 379-97.
Wiltshire, Caroline. 1988. Syllable Structure in IRula.
Unpublished paper, University of Chicago.

On Stress Placement and Metrical Structure

Morris Halle [1]
MIT

1. Stress as a Reflex of Metrical Constituency

Research conducted in the last fifteen years has led to a major reconceptualization of the nature of stress. As a result many problems connected with stress now appear in a radically different light from that in which they have been traditionally viewed. In what follows I describe the new conception of stress, sketch a formal framework for dealing with stress and then illustrate how this framework illuminates certain accentual phenomena that have been discussed in the Indo-European literature.

The change in views on the nature of stress arose from the recognition of the fact that sequences of linguistic units of all kinds are not just simple concatenations of entities like beads on a string. Rather, in sequences of linguistic units we find that one unit is promoted to play a more prominent role than the rest, that of <u>head</u>, while the rest of the units -- those not so promoted --constitute its (the head's) domain. We find this type of organization in syntax, where a sentence such as

(1)   many arrows hit the explorers

is composed of the noun phrase <u>many</u> <u>arrows</u>, whose head is the noun <u>arrows</u>, and of the verb phrase <u>hit</u> <u>the</u> <u>explorers</u>, whose head is the verb <u>hit</u>. It is worth noting that what the two constituents have in common is that their heads are next to the constituent boundary: the noun phrase in the sentence above is right-headed, whereas the verb phrase is left-headed. We owe to Mark Liberman (1975) the suggestion that stresses be viewed as heads of metrical constituents. Under this proposal an English word such as <u>autobiographic</u> would be composed of the three left-headed metrical constituents shown in (2).

157

```
                 \      \      /
(2)        (auto)(bio)(graphic)
```

On this account, stress is no longer viewed as a phonetic feature
on a par with such other phonetic features as lip rounding,
nasalization or tenseness. Rather stress is a phonetic reflex of
the organization of a word or phrase into metrical constituents,
and languages may differ from one another in how they implement
this.
    Stress characteristically is assigned only to certain sounds
(phonemes) in a string. In the most familiar cases only heads of
syllables can be stress-bearing -- all other phonemes in a
sequences never bear stress -- but there are languages where
phonemes other than syllable heads can be stress-bearing.[2] Since
languages differ as to what units in the sequence are potential
stress-bearers, we must have a formal means to reflect this fact.
In the theoretical framework that is utilized below -- that of
Halle and Vergnaud 1987 -- the computation of stress is carried
out on a separate (metrical) plane and the sounds that are
potential stress-bearers are marked on this plane in a linear
sequence. As illustrated in (3) it is on this line of marks --
designated as <u>line 0</u> -- that metrical constituents or <u>feet</u> are
constructed. The examples in (3b) are from Winnebago, a Siouan
language, and those in (3a) are, of course, English. Following
Liberman's idea I have represented each stressed unit as the head
of a metrical constituent.[3]

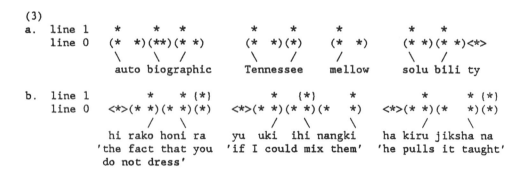

(3)
a. line 1   *   *   *   *   *   *   *   *
    line 0   (* *)(**)(* *)   (* *)(*)   (* *)   (* *)(* *)<*>
              \   \   /   \   /   /   \   /
             auto biographic   Tennessee mellow   solu bili ty

b. line 1   *   * (*)   *   (*)   *   *   * (*)
    line 0   <*>(* *)(* *)(*)   <*>(* *)(* *)(*   *)   <*>(* *)(*   *)(*)
                /   \   /   \   \   /   \
             hi rako honi ra   yu uki ihi nangki   ha kiru jiksha na
             'the fact that you 'if I could mix them' 'he pulls it taught'
             do not dress'
```
```

As noted, in a metrical constituent not all elements are equal. Rather, one is selected as head to which the rest are subordinated. Constituent heads are marked by placing an asterisk on the line immediately above it. There are severe constraints on the location of the head. In the unmarked cases -- the only ones to be discussed here -- the head must be next to the constituent boundary, and the only choice that the language can make is whether the constituent is left-headed or right-headed. In English -- i.e., in (3a) -- the constituents are all left-headed, whereas in Winnebago -- see (3b) -- they are right-headed. These constituent assignments reflect the differing types of stress patterns of English and Winnebago.

It is readily seen that if right-headed binary constituents are constructed from left to right, this procedure results in every even-numbered element being a head and therefore also being stressed. As illustrated in (3b), however, in Winnebago stress falls not on even-numbered moras, but on odd-numbered moras except for the first. This distribution of stresses would result if constituent construction began with the second, rather than with the first mora. We therefore need a device that allows us to skip the first element we encounter and to begin constituent construction with the second element. This skipping device has been named extra-metricality and we reflect it in the representations by enclosing the element in question in angled brackets. Thus, in Winnebago the left-most stress-bearing element in a word is marked extra-metrical, and right-headed constituents are then constructed from left to right.

In English words like solubility the situation is the mirror-image of that in Winnebago, stresses fall on alternating syllables beginning with the third syllable from the end of the word. We therefore postulate that in English the constituents are left-headed, that they are constructed from right to left, rather than from left to right, and that construction begins with the penultimate syllable rather than with the ultima. In English therefore the last syllable is marked extra-metrical, whereas in Winnebago it was the first mora that was extra-metrical. Moreover, in English extra-metricality is somewhat idiosyncratic -- suffixes such as -ic, -id, -ish are never extra-metrical -- whereas in Winnebago initial extra-metricality admits of no exceptions to my knowledge.

In addition to constraints on stress placement within constituents there are also severe restrictions on constituent size. In the examples discussed to this point we have encountered only bounded -- i.e., binary -- constituents. In rare instances ternary constituents are found, but I shall have nothing to say

about these here. By contrast, metrical constituents that are
unbounded as to length are quite common. We meet up with
unbounded constituents as soon as we try to answer the question as
to how to capture formally the fact that in English and Winnebago
not all stresses in a word are equal, rather one of the stresses
is more prominent than the rest. In English it is the last stress
in the word, whereas in Winnebago it is the first stress that is
the most prominent. An obvious way of expressing this in the
notation   used here is by organizing the stressed elements --
those projected onto line 1 in (3) -- into an unbounded
constituent. As shown in (4) this unbounded constituent is
right-headed in English (4a) and left-headed in Winnebago (4b).

(4)
a. line 2   *   *   *   *
    line 1   (*   *   *)   (*   *)   (*)   (*   *)
    line 0   (* *)(**)(*   *)   (* *)(*)   (* *) (* *)(* *)<*>
              auto biographic   Tennessee   mellow solu bili ty

b. line 2   *   *   *
    line 1   (*   * (*))   (*   (*)   *)   (*   * (*))
    line 0   <*>(* *)(* *)(*)   <*>(* *)(* *)(*   *) <*>(* *)(*   *)(*)
              hi rako honi ra   yu uki ihi nangki   ha kiru jiksha na

It is not the case that line 0 constituents are invariably binary
and line 1 constituents are unbounded. Unbounded constituents on
line 0 are found in languages such as Koya, Komi, Huasteco and
Eastern Cheremis, but because of limitations on time I can do no
more here than refer to the discussion of these stress systems in
Halle and Vergnaud 1987.
        Consider next the stress pattern in a language such as
Macedonian, where in the great majority of words stress is
assigned to the antepenultimate syllable as illustrated in (5a).
(Data from Lunt 1952.)

(5)   /   v   /v   v/
    vodenicar 'miller'   vodenicari 'millers'   vodenicarite 'the millers'

Formally this is captured by the rules in (6).

(6) i. Mark the last syllable extrametrical.

   ii. On line 0 construct left-headed binary constituents from right to left and mark the heads on line 1.

   iii. On line 1 construct a right-headed unbounded constituent and mark its head on line 2.

We illustrate the operation of these rules in (7).

(7)
```
     line 2        *                    *                       *
     line 1     (*  *)              (*     *)                (*  *    *)
     line 0     (*)(* *)<*>         (* *)(* *)<*>            (*)(* *)(* *)<*>
                 /    v              /                       /
                              / v                           v/
             vo deni car        vode nica ri            vo deni cari te
```

Although the rules developed to this point assign the main stress correctly they also generate a number of subsidiary stresses. Macedonian however differs from English and Winnebago in that the word does not have subsidiary stresses. In languages like Macedonian we therefore assume that subsidiary stresses are removed by the operation of a special rule which we shall term the rule of <u>Conflation</u>.

2. Stress in the Indo-European Proto-language

Consider next the stress patterns of modern Russian. As is well known, stress is one of the most difficult things to master in learning Russian. To the beginner it almost seems that every form of every word can take stress on any arbitrary syllable. In reality things are not quite as bad as this but they are of fair complexity, as illustrated in (8) with two of the half a dozen stress paradigms found in the Russian nominal declension.

(8)

	'horror'	'town'	'swamp'	'cloud'
nom. sg.	užas	gorod	bolot-o	oblak-o
dat. sg.	užas-u	gorod-u	bolot-u	oblak-u
nom. pl.	užas-y	gorod-a	bolot-a	oblak-a

dat. pl.   úžas-am   gorod-ám   bolót-am   oblak-ám

In each of the two declensions illustrated in (8) we have two
patterns: one where the stress is fixed on a particular syllable
in the stem, and one where the stress alternates between the case
ending and the initial syllable of the word. In the latter two
paradigms -- those of <u>gorod</u> and <u>oblak</u> some desinences
(case-suffixes) are always stressed -- i.e., the nom. pl. /a/
and the dat. pl. /am/ -- whereas the rest -- i.e., the nom.
sg. /o/, the dative sg. /u/ and nom. pl. /y/ -- are never
stressed.
     The stress patterns of the Russian declension were studied
by Kiparsky and Halle 1978, and we concluded that in Russian,
stress is a distinctive property of each morpheme; i.e. that in
committing a morpheme to memory the speaker not only has to learn
its phoneme composition but also whether or not it is stressed.
In our examples (8) the stems /užas/ 'horror' and /bolot/ 'swamp'
as well as the desinences nom. pl. /a/ and dat. pl. /am/ are
stressed, whereas the nom. sg. /o/, the dat. sg. /u/ and nom.
pl. /y/ as well as the noun stems /gorod/ 'town' and /oblak/
'cloud' are without lexical stress.
     Since stress is distinctive for every Russian morpheme, a
Russian word can in principle have as many lexically assigned
stresses as it has constituent morphemes, or as few as none. On
the surface, however, the word invariably appears with a single
stressed syllable. To account for this fact Kiparsky and Halle
1978 proposed the Basic Accentuation Principle, which locates the
surface stress on the left-most stressed syllable, or, in the
absence of a stressed syllable, on the word-initial syllable.
Formally this stress distribution -- left-most stressed, or
left-most -- is implemented by the rule (9a). I have illustrated
the effects of this rule in (9b).

(9)   a.   Construct a left-headed unbounded constituent on line 1 and
           mark its head on line 2.

      b.   * .   .   . * .   . . *   * .   .   line 2
             (# . #)   (. # .)   (. . #) (. .   .)   line 1
              * * *   * * *   * * *   * *   *   line 0
              /   /   /   /
             úžas-am   bolot-u   gorod-am   oblak-o

In (9b) I have indicated lexical stresses by means of the

cross-hatch, whereas stresses assigned by rule (9a) are
represented by an asterisk; syllables not projected upward are
marked by dots.

Like Macedonian Russian has no secondary stresses. In order
to eliminate the secondary stresses that our rules would generate,
e.g., on the desinence of the dat. pl. /užasám/ we shall assume
that Russian like Macedonian is subject to the rule of Conflation,
which eliminates all but the main stress of the word. The correct
stress patterns are generated now in all cases except for forms
that have no lexically supplied stresses like, e.g., oblak-o cited
last in (10b). As pointed out in Halle and Vergnaud 1987, forms
of this type require a special convention to deal with the case
where a constituent is constructed on an empty line in the
metrical grid. This special convention stipulates that if there
is no asterisk on a line in the metrical grid, the constituent is
constructed over the asterisks on the next lowest line in the
grid. In the case of oblako this means that we construct a
left-headed constituent over the asterisks of line 0. It is
obvious that this procedure results in the correct assignment of
stress to the word initial sylable.

Russian has a number of additional stress patterns of which
the so-called oxytone pattern, where stress invariably falls on
the post-stem syllable, has attracted considerable interest in the
last thirty years because of important discoveries due to Stang,
Illic-Svityc and Dybo, which unfortunately can only be mentioned,
but not discussed here.

In (10) and (11) I have illustrated the stress patterns in
the declensional paradigms of Lithuanian and **Sanskrit**
respectively. These are essentially similar to that of Russian
(8) in that they are generated by distinctively stressed morphemes
subject to the Basic Accentuation Principle of IE, i.e. rule
(9a).

(10)	I	III	II	IV
d. sg.	vaasar-ai	doovan-ai	masin-ai	zin,-ai
n. pl.	vaasar-oos	doovan-oos	masin-oos	zin,-oos
l. sg.	vaasar-ooje	doovan-ooje	masin-ooje	zin,-ooje
i. pl.	vaasar-oomis	doovan-oomis	masin-oomis	zin,-oomis
	'summer'	'gift'	'machine'	'news, report'

Just like Russian Lithuanian has two major classes of stems: I,
II, which are inherently stressed, vs. III, IV, which are
inherently unstressed. And just like in Russian, there are in
Lithuanian two classes of suffixes: d. sg. and n. pl. which
are inherently stressless, vs. loc. sg. and instr. pl., which
are inherently inherently stressed. The same rule as in Russian
-- i.e., (9a) -- assigns the correct surface stress in the cases
under discussion.

There are two basic differences between Lithuanian and
Russian. In Russian only syllable heads can bear stress, in
Lithuanian there is a special class of long syllables where
nonheads, rather than heads, are stress-bearing -- these are
called circumflex in the literature and are marked by a special
diacritic. In all other syllables of the language the syllable
head is stress bearing. This distinction is exemplified in the
stem stress of the words vaásarai vs. dóovan-ai in (10).

This prosodic distinction between syllables lies at the base
of de Saussure's Law, which accounts for the different stress
paradigms between classes I and II, on the one hand, and III and
IV, on the other (Saussure 1896). In classes II and IV the last or
only stem syllable is either short or circumflex. When by the
basic Indo-European stress rule (9a) stress would be assigned to
this syllable -- i.e., to a stem final syllable that is circumflex
or short -- and the following syllable is long but not circumflex,
the stress is advanced to the latter syllable by de Saussure's
Law.

Once we abstract away these special Lithuanian developments
-- i.e., the distinction between circumflex and other syllables
and the effects of de Saussure's Law -- the Lithuanian stress
pattern is literally identical with that of Russian.

The Sanskrit nominal accentuation parallels that of Russian
and Lithuanian, as illustrated in (11).

(11)

		/	//	# # #	/	/	# #
loc. sg.		marut-i	asv-e < asv-a-i		duhitr-i	dev-e < dev-a-i	
		/	//		/	/	
acc. sg.		marut-am	asv-a-m		duhitar-am	dev-a-m	
		/	//		/	/	
voc. sg.		marut	asv-a		duhitar	dev-a	
		'wind'	'horse'		'daughter'	'god'	

Here again we find the familiar contrast between stressed and

stressless stems -- <u>marut, a͟s͟v͟a͟</u> vs. <u>duhitar, deva</u> -- and between
stressed and stressless suffixes. The special features of
Sanskrit are the following. In the Sanskrit noun declension,
stressless case suffixes assign stress to the preceding syllable:
we therefore get <u>duhita'ram</u> in place of the expected <u>du'hitaram</u>.
Secondly, in the vocative, noun stems lose their inherent stress;
as a consequence we find initial stress in all four examples cited
in (11).

In Russian, Lithuanian, and Sanskrit stress is thus assigned
by the same means, i.e. by rule (9a) operating on sequences of
morphemes with lexically supplied stresses. The same is true of
several other IE languages -- e.g., Pashto, Serbo-Croatian,
Slovenian. Moreover, when cognate morphemes in these languages
are compared, a significant proportion also agree in the presence
or absence of lexically assigned stress. These facts provide the
basic evidence for the proposition that in the IE proto-language,
stress was governed by rule (9a) and that morphemes were lexically
marked for stress.

We now inquire what happens if a language subject to the
Indo-European stress rule (9a) suppresses all stress indications
in its lexical representation of morphemes. It is obvious that
when no stresses are supplied in the lexicon there will also be no
stressed syllables in underlying representations; all words will
have metrical grids like the Russian word <u>oblako</u> in (9b).
Moreover, as pointed out to me by Donca Steriade, if the
Indo-European stress rule (9a) were still operative at this point,
stress would invariably be assigned to the initial syllable of the
word. In view of this it is worth noting that in many
Indo-European languages that have lost the historical contrast
between stressed and **stressless morphemes**, initial **stress is the**
rule. This is true of Germanic, it is true of Czech and Slovak,
and was at one time also true of Polish, it is true of Latvian as
well as of the Žemaitian dialects of Lithuanian (see Lačjute
1979). Initial stress was also the rule in Old Irish and
supposedly also in early Latin.

While initial stress is, of course, not the only direction
in which Indo-European stress has evolved, initial stress is the
one that the greatest number of daughter language have opted for.
What is especially interesting is that initial stress developed in
Indo-European languages that are widely separated both
geographically and temporarily. Thus, this development could not
plausibly be attributed to a single source; rather what we have
here is several independent developments each of which has
resulted in initial stress. In the light of the theory that has
been presented here this is perfectly plausible. We are

witnessing here the loss of lexically supplied stress in a number
of languages where stress is governed by the Indo-European stress
rule (9a). This loss happened at different times in the different
languages. The theory we have developed here predicts that if
nothing else changes at this point the result will be initial
stress on all words. And this prediction is well supported by the
evidence.

3. Stress and Cyclic Rule Application

Unlike in Macedonian words, stress in English words does not
invariably fall on the antepenult. Instead in a large fraction of
the English vocabulary stress falls on the penult when this is
"heavy"; i.e., has a branching rime; and only when the penult is
not "heavy", does stress fall on the antepenult. Examples are
given in (12).


```
         /          /          /
(12) javelin   American   original
         /          /          /            \    /      /    \    /
       agenda    utensil    parental        Arizona museum  anecdotal
```

In order to capture formally both the similarities and the
differences between English and Macedonian we can assume as a
first approximation that English has the same stress rules as
Macedonian -- i.e., those in (6) -- but that these are
supplemented by the addition of the rule (13).

(13) Assign stress -- line asterisks -- to syllables with "heavy" rimes"

This rule is ordered between rules (6-i) and (6-ii). Hence at the
point where (6-ii) applies the representations are of the form
illustrated in (14a), and the effects of applying the stress rules
(6-ii, iii) to the representations (14a) are shown in (14b).


```
(14)
a.  line 1                        #            #
    line 0    * * *<*>        * * <*>      * * *<*>
              America          utensil      Arizona
```

b. line 2   *   *   *
   line 1   (* *)   (* #)   (* #)
   line 0   (*)(* *)<*> (*)(*)<*> (* *)(*)<*>
           A meri ca   u tensil   Ari zo na

This procedure places main stress correctly. Additional rules
eliminate the extra secondary stresses generated by this
procedure. Significant for the present discussion is the manner
in which constituents were constructed by rule (6-ii) in the words
utensil, Arizona. Although rule (6-ii) ordinarily constructs
binary left-headed constituents, in these cases the first -- i.e.,
the right-most -- constituent constructed is unary. The reason
for this is that all rules of constituent construction respect
previously assigned stresses and metrical structure. (See the
Faithfulness Condition in Halle and Vergnaud 1987). Because of
this convention, rule (6-ii) had to construct a constituent so
that its head would be the stressed penultimate syllable of the
word. Since the construction proceeds from right to left and
since the last syllable is excluded because it is marked
extra-metrical, rule (6-ii) has no alternative but to construct a
unary constituent. Once such a constituent has been constructed,
rule (6-ii) moves to the rest of the string and constructs
constituents there. Since in the case of utensil the rest of the
string consists of a single syllable, a second unary constituent
is constructed. In the word Arizona the rest of the string is
bi-syllabic; hence a bi-syllabic constituent is constructed by
rule (6-ii).
    Consider next the different locations of main stress in the words
in (15a) and (15b).

             /   /   /
(15) a. origin-al-ity   univers-al-ity   organ-iz-at-ion-al

               /   /   /
   b. un-reason-able-ness   mean-ing-less-ness   express-ion-less-ness

In (15a) placement of the main stress is determined by outermost
suffix; whereas in (15b) stress falls on the innermost stem. It
is generally accepted that the basis for this difference are the
suffixes. Suffixes such as -ness, -able, -ul are said to be
"stress-neutral",whereas suffixes such -al, -ity, -ion are
"stress-sensitive". Our next task is to spell out how these
classes of suffixes generate the different placements of main
stress illustrated in (15). The account presented below is a
somewhat modified version of the one given in Halle and Vergnaud

1987.
    It is proposed there that the rules of the word phonology
are organized into two blocks or <u>strata</u>. In English the stress
rule of interest here -- i.e., those of (6) -- are assigned to
Stratum 1 exclusively, and no stress rules figure in Stratum 2. It
is moreover postulated that

(16)   a. The rules of Stratum 1 apply in cyclic fashion beginning with
            the innermost morphological constituent and ending with the
            entire word.

        b. The application of the (cyclic) rules of Stratum 1 is subject
            to special constraints of which the most important here is
            that they are <u>not</u> triggered by "stress-neutral" suffixes.

        c. On each pass through the rules of Stratum 1 all previously
            assigned metrical structure and stresses are erased.

These principles insure that the outermost "stress-sensitive"
suffix will determine where the main stress is placed, because by
virtue of (16c) all metrical structure and stresses assigned will
be erased at the beginning of the last pass through the rules of
Stratum 1.
    After the rules of Stratum 1 have thus applied to each
constituent of the word, the entire word is subjected <u>once</u> to the
rules of Stratum 2. Since the stress erasure convention (16c) is
not applicable in Stratum 2, "stress-neutral" suffixes have no
effect on the placement of main stress: the metrical constituent
structure assigned by the rules of Stratum 1 remains intact.
    An important result of studies of phonological rules
organized into strata is that a given rule may be assigned to more
than one stratum. In particular, it was shown by Halle and
Mohanan 1985 that it is necessary to assign the IE stress rule
(8a) to both the cyclic Stratum 1 and noncyclic Stratum 2 in order
to account properly for the different stress effects of "dominant"
and "recessive" suffixes in Sanskrit that had been noted by
Kiparsky 1982.
    As the Sanskrit facts have been discussed by Halle and
Mohanan 1985 I shall not discuss them here, instead I want to
inquire at this point as to how stress is assigned in a language
that differs from English in that its stress rules figure not only
in Stratum 1, but are assigned to both Stratum 1 and 2.
Specifically I shall assume the stratum assignment of the rules in
(17).

(17)   Stratum 1 (cyclic)   Stratum 2 (noncyclic)

    i. Extrametricality (6-i)   i. Extrametricality (6-i)

   ii. "Heavy" syllable stress (13)   ii. "Heavy" syllable stress (13)

  iii. Line 0 stress (6-ii)   iii. Line 0 stress (6-ii)

                                        iv. Line 1 stress (6-iii)

I shall assume that the hypothetical language has both
"stress-sensitive" class I suffixes -- the counterparts of the
English -ity, -al, -ion -- and stress-neutral" class II suffixes
-- the counterparts of -ness, -ing, -ful. We now investigate how
the rule system (17) assigns stress to the hypothetical words in
(18).

(18)   a. Stem + I + I + I   b. Stem + I + I + I + II

To simplify matters I shall assume that the words are composed
exclusively of light monosyllabic morphemes. As a consequence,
there is no occasion to apply the "heavy" syllable rule (13).
Since, as noted, class I suffixes are cyclic and therefore erase
all stresses and metrical structure erected on earlier cycles, the
rules of Stratum 1 will generate the metrical structure in (19a).
Since none of this structure is erased in Stratum 2, the only
effect of applying the rules of Stratum 2 is to construct the line
1 constituent which determines the location of the main stress in
the word, as shown in (19b).

(19) a.   line 2   b.   *
              line 1   *   *   (*   *)
              line 0   (*) (*   *) <*>   (*) (*   *) <*>
                  Stem + I + I + I   Stem + I + I + I

In the derivatin of the example (18b) the input to the rules of
Stratum II will be as shown in (20a).

```
(20) a. line 2                            b.                    *
        line 1    *    *                      (*    *      *)
        line 0   (*)  (*  *)  *   *           (*)  (*  *)  (*)  <*>
                 Stem + I + I + I + II        Stem + I + I + I + II
```

The presence of the Class II suffix removes extra-metricality assigned on the first cycle, but the stresses and metrical structure generated by the rules of Stratum 1 will remain intact. The rules of Stratum 2 will now apply: first, the extra-metricality rule renders the word final syllable invisible to the stress rules. As noted, there will be no occasion for the "heavy" syllable rule (13) to apply. Next in order is the line 0 stress rule (6-ii). Since rules constructing metrical constituents must respect metrical structure already in place, the only element in (19a) to which (6-ii) can apply is the asterisk above the last class I suffix. Rule (6-ii) therefore constructs a unary constituent on that single asterisk. Rule (6-iii) then assigns main stress to this syllable. The answer to the question raised above is therefore that in a language where stress rules of type (6) are assigned to both Stratum 1 and 2, words ending with a class II suffix will have main stress on the prefinal syllable, because this syllable was extra-metrical at the point where the rules of Stratum 1 applied.

A language that has stress behavior very much like that just discussed is classic Latin. As illustrated in (21), in Latin words without enclitics, stress falls on the antepenult if the penult is "light", and on the penult, if it is "heavy".

```
        /              /              /                /
(21)  opprimit     opprimunt      opprimitur       opprimuntur
        /              /              /                /
      oppo:nit      oppo:nunt      oppo:nitur       oppo:nuntur
```

Stress in Latin is therefore assigned by rule (6-ii) interacting with the extra-metricality rule (6-i) and the "heavy" syllable rule (13). The patterns illustrated in (21) do not exhaust all attested cases of Latin stress. Steriade 1988 has drawn attention to the fact reported by the Latin grammarians that before enclitics stress falls on the last syllable of the orthotonic (uncliticized) word. She quotes the Latin grammarian Servius, who wrote:"For the moria -- i.e., the small particles such as que, ve, ne, ce -- whenever they are joined to other forms, place the

accent before them (on) whatever syllable may precede them,
whether short or long." Some of the examples given by Steriade
are reproduced in (22).

(22)   lí:mina   'thresholds'   lí:mina-que 'and thresholds .. .'

       Mú:sa   'the muse'   Mú:sa-ne   'whether the muse . . .'

       álter   'other'   álter-uter   'one of two'

       úbi   'where'   úbi-libet   'wherever'

In the examples (22) stress is assigned in exactly in the same way
as in the hypothetical example (20). We conclude therefore that
the Latin **stress** rules are essentially identical with those in
(17); i.e., that in Latin the stress rules are assigned both to
Stratum 1 and Stratum 2.

    Latin is by no means the only language that exhibits this
type of alternation between orthotonic and enclitic stress. In
Halle (in press) I have shown that Manam, an Austronesian
language, exhibits essentially the same stress behavior as Latin.
Moreover, Steriade 1988 shows that enclitic stress in Greek also
involves stress assignment to previously extra-metrical
syllables.

    The reality of the enclitic stresses in (22) has been
questioned by some scholars. Allen 1973, e.g., characterized the
rule of the classical grammarians as "simply another example of
the grammarians' copying of Greek models" and suggested that the
type of clitic stress exemplified in (22) did not exist in Latin.
As I have analyzed Allen's argumentation in Halle (in press) I
shall not discuss it here except to remark that Allen's skepticism
about the enclitic stresses reported by the Latin grammarians is
not based on any factual evidence. He finds the statements of the
Latin grammarians incredible because of his a priori assumptions
about what possible stress systems are like. In the light of what
has been learned in the last fifteen years about stress -- a
fraction of which I have attempted to sketch here -- the facts
reported by the Latin grammarians are not at all outlandish, but
are actually to be expected for reasons that have been outlined
above. There are therefore no cogent reasons for doubting the
statements of the Latin grammarians of classical antiquity anymore
than there are grounds for doubting the facts reported about
Sanskrit in Panini.

172

Notes

1. Because of prior publishing commitments the text of my
presentation at the 25th meeting of the CLS cannot be printed
here. In its stead I am offering the text of a lecture given at
the Eighth East Coast Indo-European Conference at Harvard
University on June 16, 1989, which dealt with many of the same
issues as my Chicago talk. I am grateful to Donca Steriade for
advice in the preparation of this lecture.

2. For example, in Winnebago long vowels consist of two
stress-bearing units. Winnebago thus is, in Trubetzkoy's
terminology mora-counting, whereas the majority of languages are
syllable-counting. Even more interesting is the situation in the
Baltic languages -- Latvian and Lithuanian -- where a given
syllable can have only one stress bearing element, but this
element need not be the head: in the so-called circumflex
syllables it is the non-head rather than the head that is
stress-bearing. Some brief remarks about Lithuanian are to be
found in sec. 2 below.

3. In the Winnebago examples stress on certain syllables is
removed by rules not discussed here, these nonsurfacing stresses
are enclosed in braces. The Winnebago data are from Hale and
White Eagle (1980) and from K. Hale p.c.

Bibliography

Allen, W. Sidney: 1973, Accent and Rhythm Cambridge : Cambridge University Press.

Dybo, Vladimir A.: 1981, Slavjanskaja akcentologija Moscow : Nauka.

Hale, Kenneth and J. White Eagle: 1980, "A Preliminary Account of Winnebago Accent," International Journal of American Linguistics 46, 117-132.

Halle, Morris : in press "Respecting Metrical Structure," Natural Language and Linguistic Theory.

Halle, Morris and K. P. Mohanan : 1985 "Segmental Phonology of Modern English," Linguistic Inquiry 16, 57-116.

Halle, Morris and Jean-Roger Vergnaud: 1987, An Essay on Stress Cambridge : MIT Press.

Illich-Svitich, Vladislav M. : 1979 Nominal Accentuation in Baltic and Slavic Cambridge : MIT Press.

Kiparsky, Paul : 1982 "The Lexical Phonology of Vedic Accent," ms. MIT, Cambridge, Massachusetts.

Kiparsky, Paul and Morris Halle : 1978 "Towards a Reconstruction of the Indo-European Accent," Southern California Occasional Papers in Linguistics 4, 209-238.

Lacjute, IU. A. : 1979 "Akcentuacionnye osobennosti imen suščestvitel'nyx v žemajtskom dialekte litovskogo jazyka," in S. D. Kacnel'son, ed., Issledovanija v oblasti sravnitel'noj akcentologii indo-evropejskix jazykov Leningrad : Nauka, pp. 143-191.

Liberman, Mark Y. : 1975 The Intonational System of English PhD dissertation, Cambridge : MIT.

Lunt, Horace G. : 1952 A Grammar of the Macedonian Language Skopje.

Saussure, Ferdinand de : 1896 "L'accentuation lituannienne" Indogermanische Forschungen 6 Anzeiger, 157-165.

Stang, C. : 1957 Slavonic Accentuation Oslo.

Steriade, Donca : 1988 "Greek Accent: A Case for Preserving Structure" Linguistic Inquiry 19, 271-314.

The Licensing and Identification of <u>pro</u> and the Typology of AGR

Gabriella Hermon and James Yoon
University of Delaware and University of Chicago

1. Introduction

In this paper we outline a theory of licensing and identification for the empty pronominal category <u>pro</u>. Although we concentrate on the issue of the licensing and identification of <u>pro</u> in so-called 'cool' languages, i.e., languages like Chinese which lack overt agreement morphology, we also take up crosslinguistic issues in some detail. The approach to identification presented here is embedded in a general theory of agreement, utilizing the notion of feature unification (Gazdar et. al., 1985; Pollard and Sag 1987).

As opposed to approaches which claim that in 'cool' languages AGR is missing altogether (Huang 1984 and 1989) or that AGR in these languages may not have phi-features (Rizzi 1986), we claim that 'cool' languages like Chinese have AGR nodes with full-fledged phi-features. We claim that the Chinese-type languages have an AGR node with an underspecified phi-feature matrix, the values for which are filled in from discourse. We present several pieces of independent evidence showing that AGR does indeed play a role in the grammar of these languages.

2 Approaches to licensing and Identification

The question of what determines whether or not a language allows null pronouns (the so called <u>pro-drop parameter)</u> has been one of the central topics of GB research. Although some researchers mainly deal with the question of the distribution of **referential** null pronouns (see Huang 1984 and Borer 1989, among others), most current approaches to the problem distinguish between **licensing** (which holds of all null pronouns: argumental, quasi-argumental and expletive) and **identification** (which only holds of referential pronouns).

As discussed in Rizzi (1986) and Jaeggli and Safir (1989), given the distinction in distribution between referential and expletive <u>pro</u>, it seems desirable to separate the licensing requirement from the identification requirement. Licensing then boils down to the question of whether the language allows null pronouns of any type (referential or expletive), while identification addresses the issue of how the referential content of <u>pro</u> is determined once it is licensed.

2.1 A typology of expletive and referential pro-drop

Gilligan (1987) contains a survey of 100 languages representing about twenty different major language families. On the basis of his discussion, we can distinguish the following types of languages with respect to whether the language allows expletive and referential null pronouns:
1. **Core null-subject languages (NSL):** These languages have

obligatory null expletives and optional null referential pronouns. Examples include languages with 'rich' AGR like Italian and Spanish (Huang's 'hot' languages) and languages with no overt AGR, like Chinese and Korean (Huang's 'cool' languages).

2. **Core non-NSL:** These languages allow neither expletive nor referential null pronouns. Languages of this type (far less frequent than core NSLs) include English and French (which have 'weak' AGR) and also Mainland Scandinavian languages (Swedish, Norwegian and Danish) and Dutch A.

3. **Restricted NSL:** This group consists mainly of V-2 languages which allow null expletives in certain environments (such as in non-initial positions in main clauses and in embedded clauses). In addition, these languages allow optional null referential pronouns in certain restrictive environments. For example in Old French and in Bavarian referential pro is permitted in main clauses (which have V-raising) but not in embedded clauses in which no V-raising takes place.

4. **Expletive NSL:** These languages permit null expletives (sometimes in restricted environments if the language is V-2) but never allow null referential pronouns. This group includes V-2 languages like Icelandic and German, and also languages with no overt verbal morphology at all like Papiamentu, Duka, Guaymi and Tagalog.

We turn next to a comparison of how various approaches to licensing account for the crosslingusitc distribution of pro.

2.2 Previous approaches to licensing

2.2.1 Agreement based licensing

There are a number of versions of this approach, but the insight (introduced into the Extended Standard Theory by Taraldsen 1978) is that there is some inherent connection between the richness of agreement and pro-drop. It claims that 'rich AGR' (AGR with person and number specifications) found in some core NSLs (like Italian) is required to license a null pronominal.

A modified version of this approach due to Huang (1984) claims that both a rich AGR and a null AGR found in languages like Chinese license pro-drop, and that it is only 'mixed' languages like English and French (with 'degenerate' AGR) that do not allow pro-drop.

It is quite clear from the examples cited in the literature that no version of licensing based exclusively on agreement can account for all the data. The rich AGR based theory does not work for languages like Chinese and Korean. On the other hand, Huang's approach, which was designed to account for the possibility of pro-drop in 'cool' languages like Chinese, fails to account for three types of languages:

a. languages with rich AGR but no referential pro-drop (like Icelandic and German);

b. languages with no AGR and with no referential pro-drop (expletive NSLs like Papiamentu and Tagalog);

c. languages with mixed/weak AGR but which allow pro-drop (Irish).

Irish verbal paradigms have mixed synthetic (with agreement) and

analytic forms (without agreement) and yet allow pro-drop (see
McCloskey and Hale 1984). For example, the present indicative
paradigm for the verb <u>cuir</u> 'put' in Irish looks quite similar to
mixed present tense paradigm for this verb in English in that only
one form is inflected distinctly for person, a fact which would seem
to indicate that the AGR is weak:

(1) Irish 'mixed' paradigm:
    S1: cuirim
    All other persons: cuireann

    English 'mixed' paradigm:
    S3: puts
    All other persons: put

Irish, however, has referential pro-drop with its synthetic forms and
expletive pro-drop with analytic forms, while English allows neither
expletive nor referential null pronouns. We conclude therefore that
a licensing approach based on overt morphological agreement is doomed
to failure, since there does not seem to be a direct correlation
between morphological agreement and the licensing of null pronouns in
some languages. This is not to say that there is no correlation
between AGR and the identification process which is required of
referential pronouns. All we are suggesting is that the link between
syntactic AGR and morphological agreement is less direct than
previously thought.

2.2.2 The morphological uniformity principle (MUP)

Jaeggli and Safir (1989) argue that null pronouns should be
licensed by morphological uniformity. Morphological uniformity has no
direct correlation to richness of AGR, or to any other inherent
property of INFL or AGR (such as tense or Case). A paradigm is
uniform if all its forms are either derived or underived. For
example, Italian is uniform since all forms in the verbal paradigm
are inflected and so is Korean and Japanese, languages in which all
forms of a paradigm are inflected for tense. Chinese is also uniform,
since none of the forms are derived. English and French on the other
hand have mixed derived and underived forms in their verbal
paradigms. Hence these languages do not license <u>pro</u>.
    Morphological uniformity does not require that the derived forms
contain an AGR specification. Thus, Irish paradigms count as uniform,
even though only some forms are inflected for person. This is because
none of the forms are base forms. Thus, it is correctly predicted
that Irish will be a NSL.
    Since the uniformity hypothesis does not make any connection
between the nature of AGR and pro-drop, it avoids some of the
problems faced by the agreement based approaches. However, it
predicts that core non-NSLs like Swedish and Danish should allow pro-
drop. This is because in Swedish verbs are marked with a tense
suffix, and in some paradigms also number and gender (Anward 1988).
Swedish (and presumably all other Mainland Scandinavian languages)

is quite uniform, but does not allow any kind of pro-drop, as
discussed in Platzack (1987) and Holmberg (1988). Hence,
morphological uniformity cannot be sufficient to license pro-drop.

More seriously, it is unclear whether the notion of uniformity is
a paradigmatic notion or whether it is determined language by
language. Jaeggli and Safir define uniformity only in relation to a
certain paradigm, and indeed this is the only way to make sense of
this notion. Note, however, that as far as licensing is concerned,
it is uniformity of a language as a whole rather than uniformity of a
paradigm which determines whether the language allows null pronouns.
For example, French has to be non-uniform for them since French does
not license null pronouns. Indeed, French is non-uniform in the
present tense since it contains four base forms (the example is for
the verb placer base form: plas):

(2) plas, plas, plas, plas-õ̃, plas-e, plas

In most other paradigms, however, all forms are derived. The example
below is for the verb aimer 'love' in the future tense:

(3) aem-re, aem-ra, aem-ra, aem-rṍ, aem-re, aem-rõ̃

According the the MUP, it is irrelevant that some of the verbal
endings are nondistinct. The paradigm in (3) contains no base forms
(base form: aem) and hence should count as uniform. The same is true
for the past tense inflection in English: none of the form are base
forms. Jaeggli & Safir then would need to add the following condition
on uniformity:

(4) Uniformity is determined for a language as a whole. If a certain
    paradigm in the language is non-uniform, the whole language
    counts as non-uniform.

Such a principle then can guide the learner in deciding whether a
certain language obeys uniformity. If children, as suggested in
Hyams and Jaeggli (1987), start out with a positive setting for the
MUP, learning a single non-uniform paradigm will allow them to reset
the parameter which licenses null pronouns. Again, something more
will have to be said about languages like Swedish, which are uniform
but nevertheless do not license pro. Assuming that there is an
independent reason why the Scandanavian languages do not allow pro-
drop, the MUP is capable of making fairly accurate predictions about
the distribution of null pronouns, even though it is far from clear
conceptually why there should be a connection between the ability of
licensing null pronouns and having all inflected or uninflected forms
in a paradigm.

In conclusion, it is hard to judge how successful the MUP is in
predicting the distribution of pro crosslinguistically. In Gilligan's
sample, only four (out of 100) languages are non NSLs. These include
French and English which the MUP correctly predicts to be non NSLs,
but also Swedish as well as Dutch A (which like English and unlike
Swedish is non-uniform). Given these non-NSLs, the MUP correctly

handles French and English (and perhaps Dutch A), although Dutch B, which is non-uniform and allows null expletives, and Swedish are problematic for the MUP. It seems then that the MUP is based on the common properties of French and English (namely, the non-uniformity of some paradigms in these languages) and fails when confronted with a larger body of data.

2.2.3 Directionality of government

Adams (1985) proposes a rather different view of licensing. Based mainly on data from Old French (a verb-second, SVO language which allows pro-drop), Adams claims that there is no need for a special pro-drop parameter, but that the availability of null pronouns follows from the interaction of two independent parameters: directionality of government and the head parameter. Licensing is then simply the requirement that pro's position be licensed, and empty categories are in general licensed by a governing head (INFL for subject pronouns). Government, for Adams, includes directionality. In addition she requires the content of the empty category to be identified by coindexation with the proper features. In order for INFL to license pro it must then be able to govern it in the proper direction (government to the right in a head first language and to the left in a head final language).

One thing that is clear from her identification requirement is that she does not take expletive pro-drop to be subject to the same principles, since presumably null expletives need not be licensed. In an SVO language (such as Italian) the subject may be VP final (inversion in Italian), allowing INFL to canonically govern it. In Old French, inversion is not an option, but the V-INFL complex is raised to C (in main clauses), allowing INFL to canonically govern the subject position. Since English allows neither free inversion nor V to C raising, it cannot license pro. Moreover, in SOV languages, even after V to C raising, INFL cannot canonically govern the subject position. This, according to Adams, is why German and Dutch are not pro-drop.[1]

This approach appears to be plagued by a number of theoretical and descriptive problems. Theoretically, as argued in Rizzi (1982), it may not be advisable to collapse licensing of the empty pronominal category with licensing of the position in general. As far as the distribution of pro across languages is concerned, the account seems to incorrectly predict that all SVO languages which allow V-2 should be pro-drop. While Old French behaves in the predicted way, Icelandic (another SVO verb-second language) does not, since Icelandic does not allow referential pro-drop (Platzack 1987 and Holmberg 1988). It seems then, that Adams' account is too language specific and that it fails to generalize to crosslinguistic data.

2.2.4 Licensing as an independent parameter

Rizzi (1986) suggests that the distribution of pro cannot be accounted for by connecting it to a rich AGR. He proposes the following licensing schema:

(5) <u>pro</u> is governed by a Case marking licensing head X⁰,

What is implied in (5) above is the claim that the class of licensing heads can vary from language to language. In other words, Rizzi is suggesting that one should not look for a connection between licensing and other properties in NSLs.

The notion that Case marking by the licensing head is crucial is supported by languages like Portuguese. According to Raposo (1989), in the inflected infinitival construction in this language, <u>pro</u> can occur if AGR can assign Case to the empty position. Since AGR can only be a Case assigner in this construction if it itself happens to get Case marked from a higher verb, the distribution of <u>pro</u> in this construction is rather limited.

Rizzi's account is not open to the same criticisms as the agreement based account or the MUP, simply because it allows languages to arbitrarily choose whether they license pro-drop or not. Thus English, French and mainland Scandinavian languages simply do not instantiate the option for a licensing head, while other languages do. Clearly, this account then is very powerful and adopting it amounts to admitting that there is no principled way to distinguish between NSLs and non-NSLs.

2.2.5 Conclusions about licensing

Most of the accounts surveyed in this section run into problems with at least the mainland Scandinavian languages (Swedish, Norwegian and Danish). This would seem to reinforce Rizzi's point that the choice of licensing heads is arbitrary. On the other hand, it may very well be that an account similar to the one proposed by Jaeggli and Safir (the MUP) can ultimately be made to work for all V-2 languages if the additional conditions that effect pro-drop are worked out. After all, Insular and Mainland Scandinavian have been shown to differ in many ways, as discussed in Holmberg (1988).[2] However, as a working hypothesis, we will adopt Rizzi's ideas.

Adopting it makes licensing a rather uninteresting question from a theoretical point of view. Therefore, in the remainder of the paper, we concentrate on the question of identification.[3]

2.3 Various approaches to identification

In this section we will review various approaches to identification. Most researchers agree that identification is a requirement imposed on referential <u>pro</u> only, and that expletives need not be identified. What we have to say then concerns only referential <u>pro</u>.[4]

Let us make clear that we mean by identification the identification of grammatical phi-features and not of reference. Researchers vary with respect to what the crucial features are which enable identification of referential <u>pro</u> to take place, but in general it is agreed that identification of at least subject null pronouns is intimately connected to the nature of the AGR node, with PERSON being a crucial feature. In what follows we review some major approaches suggested in the literature and then propose a new approach to identification based on a new typology of AGR.

2.3.1 Identification and the Generalized Control Rule

In Huang (1986/9) it is proposed that pronominal null subjects (and objects) are subject to a control principle (Generalized Control Rule, GCR hereafter) which states that null pronominals must find a controller in their Control Domain (CD).

The definition of CD is based on the notion of Accessible Subject. Hence, in languages which have AGR (Italian) the CD for a null proniminal is the tensed clause in which it appears. A 'rich' AGR in this domain will identify pro. If AGR is too meager (English), identification cannot take place and the GCR is violated. In languages like Chinese, AGR is absent, and the GCR forces identification from a higher domain (the next clause up or perhaps the discourse, which is represented via a null topic in Chinese).

Huang's account does not extend to Quechua, however. In Imbabura Quechua (IQ), null subjects can be referential in embedded clauses without any overt agreement marker. In general, these null pronouns behave like null pronouns in Chinese: they can be identified by either a c-commanding NP or from discourse. However, IQ has AGR, even though AGR is missing in most embedded clauses (see examples 15-16 in section 4). The account of what counts as an AGR-less language will then have to be complicated to exclude cases like IQ embedded clauses. Moreover, in languages like Hebrew, only third person past and future tenses allow identification from outside the clause, while first and second person in these tenses require identification by local AGR (examples 19-20 of section 4). Huang's account must then be made more explicit to encompass such cases.

A problem arises from the way in which Huang makes the identification from discourse and discourse orientation. He draws this connection by positing an empty topic node (in spec of CP) for the relevant languages and correlating this with other signs of topic orientation, such as the ability to have multiple gap topics. As discussed in section 4, this correlation cannot be maintained. For example, IQ is not topic oriented (see Cole 1987) but allows identification from discourse. Neither does Hebrew possess the necessary diagnostics for discourse-orientation. Vietnamese allows null discourse identified pronouns, but does not exhibit evidence of a null topic (E. Platt, personal communication). Hence, we need to assume that the ability to have multiple gap topics is not directly connected to the ability to have discourse identification.

Finally, the languages which pose the biggest problem for a Huang-type approach are the expletive NSLs. Dutch B could be explained as a failure of identification, since verbal morphology for person is indeed weak: there are only three distinct person markers for the six distinct person/number combinations in the present paradigm (illustrated with the verb werken 'to work'):

(6) werk (1s), werkt (2s), werkt (3s) , werken (1p), werken (2p), werken (3p)

Icelandic, however, has fully specified phi-features for each person and German has pretty 'rich' agreement morphology. The Icelandic case is illustrated below:

(7) hef (1s), hefur (2s), hefur (3s), hofum (1p), hafi
    (2p), hafa (3p)

Why does Icelandic fail to identify pro? Some additional conditions (in addition to richness of AGR) must be at work here. At the other extreme are languages like Papiamentu, which lack any agreement morphology, and hence should behave like Chinese in Huang's system. Yet these languages do not allow null referential pronouns, according to Gilligan (1987).

(8)1s *(mi) ta bini
               PROG come
   2s *(bo) ...
   3s *(e)   ...
   1p *(nos) ...
   2p *(boso)...
   3p *(nan) ...

Not all languages which lack overt AGR morphology then behave the same way, pointing to the need for a more sophisticated theory of identification.[5]

2.3.2 Borer's theory of anaphoric AGR

In Borer (1989) it is proposed that identification of the empty pronominal (which for Borer includes both PRO and pro) is due to the requirement that all ecs be I-identified - i.e. be coindexed with an I-identifier, which is a coindexed antecedent with a set of sufficiently rich i-(nflectional) features.
    Borer suggests that there is a direct connection between richness of AGR and referential pro-drop. This is encoded in the feature [+IDENT] which allows an AGR to identify pro. However, in certain languages which have no overt agreement (like Chinese), AGR can be marked [+ANAPHORIC]. An AGR so marked inherits its phi-feature specification from a preceding (c-commanding) NP. A pro that is coindexed with such AGR can be identified. In sum, there are two ways in Borer's system to identify pro: a [-ANAPH, +IDENT] type AGR (the rich AGR of Italian tensed clauses) or a [+ANAPH, -IDENT] type AGR (in Chinese). With these two features, Borer takes care of core NSLs covered by Huang's GCR.
    However, Borer is able to extend her account to languages like Hebrew which we noted were problematic for the GCR. She does so by marking the AGR in 3rd future/past tenses as [+anaphoric], while other persons are [-anaphoric], as shown in examples (19-20) in section 4. Being [+anaphoric], the AGR will pick up its phi-features from a matrix argument, in turn passing it on to the pro it governs.
    A problem with Borer's otherwise very interesting proposal is that it seems to be impossible in her framework to predict which

languages and which paradigms in which languages have AGR marked with the [ANAPH] or [IDENT] feature. Borer remarks that the anaphoricity of AGR in, say, English can only be tested by the presence of pro: if pro is i-identified by an AGR which receives its features from the clause above, we have anaphoric AGR. But this seems circular. What we want is an indication independent of pro-drop that would allow one to predict the anaphoricity of AGR.

The only correlation with other features of the grammar is the connection between anaphoric AGR and empty COMPs since she assumes that AGR has to move to the empty COMP position in order to be bound by a matrix argument. If COMP is filled, AGR cannot move, with the result that AGR can only be bound by its own I-subject. However, empty COMPs provide only part of the story, since English allows null COMPs and yet does not allow pro-drop, meaning that it lacks an anaphoric AGR.

In what follows we propose a theory of identification which embeds it within a general theory of agreement. In a sense, our approach is similar to Borer's idea of I-subjects and i-identification. We will attempt, however, to specify the morphological and syntactic correlates of the various types of AGR nodes proposed.

3.0 A theory of subject-predicate agreement

It is our belief that the question how pro is identified in various languages is best understood when it is situated within the broader context of subject-predicate agreement phenomena in natural languages.

Let us take the subject NP as the controller of agreement and the predicate/AGR/INFL complex as the control target. The intuition behind this approach is that the reference of a nominal argument can be determined independently of the interpretation of any functor expression which depends on the nominal, while the converse is not true (Keenan and Faltz 1984; Gazdar et. al. 1985). Based on this idea we can state the following principle:

(9) Agreement Principle: The unification of feature structures of controller and control target must yield a fully specified set of phi-features, which include at least person (with number and gender being optional, depending on the language).

Having spelt out the outlines of a theory of agreement, we would like to turn next to a closer examination of the nature of AGR, which we take to be the agreement target.

3.1. Feature matrices associated with AGR

In this section, we develop a theory of AGR-types across languages which is based on the phi-feature make-up of AGR. We propose that the content of AGR may vary from language to language, and that the variation lies in the nature of the feature matrix associated with AGR. The matrices range from those with a full specification of phi-features to those lacking matrices for certain key phi-features.

Unlike Borer, we seek to ground our typology of AGR on independently observable morphosyntactic features of a given language or paradigm. We propose then that UG contains the following options for the instantiation of AGR:

1. **Fully specified AGR:** If a certain verbal inflection unambiguously is marked for person (and number and gender), the AGR matrix associated with it is assumed to be fully specified. This is the case with Italian, Spanish and all other core NSLs which identify <u>pro</u> via AGR. An example of such a matrix is given below:

$$
(10) \quad \begin{bmatrix} \text{PERS:} & 3 \\ \text{NUM:} & \text{SG} \\ \text{GEN:} & \text{M} \end{bmatrix}
$$

Following Rizzi (1986), we take PERSON to be the crucial phi-feature in referential pro-drop. Thus, we will refer to an inflectional form as "fully specified" when it is distinctively marked for person even when the specification of other phi-features is not distinctive.

In addition, unlike Kornfilt (1988) who proposes that a full paradigmatic alternation for each member in a paradigm is a precondition for identification by AGR, we simply count any form which has distinct person marking as fully specified. This has the advantage that even when a single form in a paradigm is marked distinctively for relevant phi-features (i.e., synthetic forms in Irish), the AGR specification of that form will count as fully specified, allowing identification of <u>pro</u>. We defer the discussion of analytic forms till section 4.[6]

2. **Underspecified/[+pronominal] AGR:** Languages/paradigms with an underspecified AGR are those in which all inflectional forms lack overt morphological marking for PERSON. Such forms typically also lack specification for other phi-features as well, leading us to believe that there is a hierarchy of features involved.[7] A typical feature of underspecified AGR is that it may be deictic or [+pronominal], much in the manner of a pronoun, which means that it candirectly refer to a salient entity in discourse or superordinate linguistic context. For a language to have underspecified AGR rather than no AGR (i.e. no specification at all), it must possess evidence for AGR (as discussed in section 4.2). A sample matrix associated with an underspecified AGR is given below:

$$
(11) \quad \begin{bmatrix} \text{PERS:} & 0 \\ \text{NUM:} & 0 \\ \text{GEN:} & 0 \end{bmatrix}
$$

3. **Partially underspecified/[+anaphoric] AGR:** is a matrix associated with an inflectional form that lacks a person specification while all other members of the paradigm are fully specified for PERSON. We take such AGR to be [+anaphoric], essentially following Borer. Such AGR can pick up the missing phi-feature from a matrix antecedent

(presumably after moving to C as suggested by Borer). A sample
feature matrix associated with such AGR is given below:

$$(12) \begin{bmatrix} \text{PERS:} & 0 \\ \text{NUM:} & \text{SG} \\ \text{GEN:} & \text{M} \end{bmatrix}$$

AGR cannot be anaphoric if ALL the forms in the paradigm lack
PERSON specification, or where more than one form lacks it. We base
this claim on Hebrew and on the fact that Papiamentu does not allow
referential pro-drop and lacks phi-feature specification throughout
the paradigm. In addition, in Sao Tome Creole, where all but the
first person form are unmarked for person, only first person allows
pro-drop.

4. **AGR matrix lacking PERSON:** We propose that a paradigm as a whole
or some of its members may have an AGR matrix associated which lacks
a slot for PERSON altogether. The absence of PERSON implies that no
identification will be possible at all. Below are some examples of
paradigms/inflectional forms that we take to lack PERSON in its AGR
matrix:

    a. the analytic forms in Irish verbal paradigm;
    b. the entire verbal paradigm in Papiamentu;
    c. the "weak" paradigm in Turkish with a morphological agreement
marker that is non-alternating throughout the paradigm.
    d. the present tense paradigm in Hebrew;
    e. "Equatives" in Arabic (Mohammed 1988)

As one can observe from the above list, the question of what the
correlates are of PERSON-less AGR is not simple. For example, certain
languages/paradigms (such as Hebrew present tense marked for number
and gender but not person, Papiamentu which probably has bare stems)
lack overt morphological marking for person. On the surface, these
are indistinguishable from Chinese or Chamorro discussed earlier.

The Irish analytic forms are similarly unmarked for phi-features
altogether, although the forms are morphologically complex. The weak
paradigm with non-alternating unspecified AGR in Turkish has an
invariant morpheme taking up the slot allotted to agreement
morphemes, though we do not count it as AGR. At present, we do not
have a generalization that cuts across all these cases, although we
will suggest some reasons for the lack of AGR matrix in section 4. A
sample matrix lacking PERSON is given below.

$$(13) \begin{bmatrix} \text{NUM:} & \text{SG} \\ \text{GEN:} & \text{M} \end{bmatrix}$$

In sum, we posit four types of AGR matrices. In the next section,
we return to the theory of subject-predicate agreement and show how
lexical and empty NPs put different demands on AGR. We follow this
with a detailed demonstration of how the proposed typology of AGR
manifests itself in empty NP-predicate agreement.

4. Agreement and the identification of empty NPs

4.0 A difference between lexical and empty NPs

Given the theory of agreement and the typology of AGR, a question
arises as to how lexical NPs are possible as subjects in ALL
languages regardless of the type of AGR involved. The answer is quite
simple for R-expressions and pronouns. Since they are capable of
deictic use, they will always be fully specified with respect to the
phi-features a language demands of an agreement pair. Even when the
AGR has a radically underspecified matrix, a partially underspecified
one, or one lacking PERSON altogether, the unification of the feature
structures of the AGR and a lexical NP will always yield a fully
specified matrix because the lexical NP is always fully specified.
This makes the AGR-typology essentially irrelevant to these NPs.

As for anaphors, we have to consider two cases: those that are
specified for phi-features (e.g. English himself, Chinese taziji)
pose no problem for the agreement principle since they already have
phi-features. In case an anaphor lacks phi-feature specification
(e.g. Chinese ziji, Korean casin), we assume that they will inherit
the relevant set of phi-features necessary for agreement from their
antecedent that is assigned to them by other modules of grammar.

With respect to empty categories, however, there is a difference.
The difference is this: unlike lexical NPs which are inherently
specified for phi-features, empty NPs are inherently underspecified
for phi-features. That is, they are associated with a matrix like
that of type 2 AGR. Taking the specification of phi-features to be a
prerequisite for reference assignment (cf. Huang and Tang 1988), an
immediate consequence is that null pronouns cannot refer by
themselves, and they need to "pick up" phi-features in order to be
referential. This process of picking up phi-features is the process
of agreement described above. Let us propose that null pronouns may
pick up phi-features only from a governing INFL (with AGR node) via
the process of feature unification. This then is the so-called
identification requirement.

This view of the relation between the controller (the null
subject) and the control target (AGR) entails that since the null
pronoun is featureless, the licensing head must be specified with
respect to the relevant phi-features. Since the AGR node itself varies
in terms of feature make-up, this difference shows up with the empty
categories they identify.

Let us then examine what types of AGR feature matrices can combine
with null subjects if the agreement principle is to be satisfied,
giving examples from a number of languages discussed in the
literature.

4.1 Identification of null subjects

4.1.1 Null subjects and fully specified AGR

The classical case of pro-drop involves a fully specified AGR.
This is the AGR found in some core NSLs like Italian or Spanish, the

synthetic forms in Irish, first and second person in Hebrew future
and past, and first person in Sao Tome creole (Gilligan 1987). The
unification of such a feature matrix with the underspecified matrix
of the empty NP subject obeys the agreement principle since the
necessary phi-features are fully specified in the resulting feature
structure.

Certain V-second languages with full-fledged AGR appear
problematic for our account. Since we claim that fully specified AGR
can always identify pro as long as a language licenses empty
pronouns, there is no explanation for why a language like Icelandic
does not allow referential pro but only null expletives. We cannot
blame this on a lack of phi-features, for Icelandic has rich agreement
morphology, distinguishing all persons and numbers, as seen in the
following present indicative paradigm of the verb 'take' (Holmberg
1988):

(14) 1s   tek   1p   tokum
     2s   tekur   2p   taki
     3s   tekur   3p   taka

This must then be due to some additional constraints on
identification which are not connected to agreement. Perhaps, as
suggested in Jaeggli and Safir (1989), in verb second languages Case
is assigned by tense from COMP, and not from AGR. One could then add
a requirement that AGR also assign Case to pro, following Raposo
(1989). This is also similar to Borer's requirement that [+IDENT] AGR
also be [+NOM] (a Case assigner in her system). This raises other
problems though: in Old French (which was verb-second and SVO, like
Icelandic) referential pronouns were allowed. Moreover, standard
German does not allow referential pro, but Bavarian and Franconian
German do, according to Gilligan (1987). The issue of why certain
verb-second languages do not permit referential pro needs further
investigation, but it is doubtful that the answer is connected to the
nature of AGR in these languages.

4.1.2 Null subjects and deictic AGR

Another way for pro to fix its phi-feature specification is when its
empty matrix is unified with that of an erstwhile underspecified
[+deictic] AGR (AGR with null values) which has picked up phi-
features from discourse or from a preceding NP. Since the AGR is
fully specified, the null subject will be licensed and the agreement
relation be licit. We claimed that pro-drop in Chinese-type languages
work in this manner.

We turn here to a question raised earlier. Since a language that
lacks morphological specification for phi-features could be either
type 2 ([+deictic] AGR) or type 4 (PERSON-less AGR), is there a way
to determine whether a language will be type 2 instead of type 4?

As is obvious, the complete lack of morphological agreement
throughout the language cannot be a reliable diagnostic, as languages
like Papiamentu fit this description and yet have type 4 AGR.
Imbabura Quechua, a Highland Ecuadorian Quechua language which has

lost agreement in embedded nominalized clauses and does not have agreement in adjoined adverbial clauses nevertheless allows referential <u>pro</u> in them. Imbabura then is a language in which only certain paradigms lack AGR specification which would make it a 'mixed' AGR language like English. However, it seems to have type 2 AGR in these clauses since identification is either from a matrix NP or from discourse, as discussed in Hermon (1985):

(15) Juan-ga$_i$ [pro$_i$,$_j$ llugshi-na-ta]   ni-rka
     Juan-top   leave-Nom-acc   say-3s/pst
     'Juan$_i$ said that he$_i$,$_j$ will leave.'
(16) pro$_i$ Kitupi ka-jpi,   Maria-ka   riku-wa$_i$-rka
          Quito-in   be-DS Maria-top see-1OM-3s/pst
     'While (I) was in Quito, Maria saw me.'

The question that remains to be answered is why only certain languages (such as Chinese, Vietnamese, Korean, Japanese, Thai and Imbabura nominalized clauses) but not others (Papiamentu) exercise the option of having deictic AGR.

Huang (1984) tried to answer a similar question by positing a null topic operator which could license null subjects in these languages. However, there is an obvious difficulty in adopting his ideas because not all the languages cited here provide evidence for a null operator in topic position. According to Cole (1987), Imbabura Quechua does not exhibit any of the criteria which Huang cites as indicative of null-topic languages: it has no non-gap topics, it has no null topics and it has strong subject-object asymmetries with regard to the ECP. As we suggested earlier, Vietnamese may not allow null or multiple topics either.

It is striking, however, that even though the non-gap topic feature may not correlate with deictic AGR, all the languages in this group exhibit some other forms of discourse oriented behavior which can be explained by recourse to deictic AGR. For example, all the languages in this group (with the exception of Quechua) have reflexive forms which are not marked inherently for phi-features. These are typically long-distance bound and can even be discourse-bound.

We suggested earlier that specification of phi-features is necessary prior to reference assignment. Since the discourse-bound anaphors are also those that lack phi-feature specification, they have to "pick up" phi-features. We suggested that anaphors can do so from their antecedent. But when they are discourse bound, they lack a sentence-internal antecedent. They cannot refer directly to the discourse antecedent since they are referentially dependent (this is what it means for something to be an anaphor) and lack the capacity to be used deictically. We suggest then that they pick up phi-features from their governing INFL/AGR which itself is deictic. The deictic AGR picks up its phi-features from discourse and shares them with the anaphor via agreement.

(17) <u>Korean</u>
John$_i$-i Mary-lul ponayss-ni?
  NOM   ACC send-Q

Ani, caki$_i$-ka   AGR   wass-e
No. self-NOM $\begin{bmatrix} P:3 \\ N:sg \\ G:m \end{bmatrix}_i$ came

    There are other indications of the existence of AGR in these
languages. Even though a language like Korean has no subject verb
agreement, Korean has optional 'honorific' subject-predicate
agreement   we can take to be a realization of AGR (cf. Choe 1988).
This is seen in the following sentence where the honorific form of
nominative marker triggers the choice of honorific suffix on the
verb.

(18) <u>Korean</u>
   Apeci-**kkeyse**   tokse-lul   ha-si-nta
   father-NOM(HON) reading-ACC do-HON-DECL

    We noted that languages with deictic AGR also allow long-
distance reflexives. At least one current analysis of these
reflexives (Cole et al, 1988) assumes that reflexives are adjoined to
INFL and that they undergo some sort of person agreement with the
INFL/AGR they adjoin to, explaining the so-called 'blocking effects'
in these languages. This may then be another case where AGR plays a
role in the grammar of these languages.[8]
    To summarize, we claim that null pronouns are identified by
deictic AGR rather than by a null topic in languages like Chinese,
Korean, Vietnamese and Quechua.[9] However, languages which look
superficially like Chinese where we find no evidence for deictic AGR,
such as Papiamentu or Tagalog, instead have an AGR matrix lacking the
PERSON slot altogether.

4.1.3 Null subject and partially underspecified AGR

Modern Hebrew presents us with an example of partially underspecified
AGR. Hebrew allows pro-drop in the past and future tenses in main
clauses, with the exception of the third person:

(19) <u>Modern Hebrew</u>:
axal-ti	axal-ta	*axal
ate-1s	ate-2s/m	ate-3s/m
noxal	toxlu	*yoxlu
ate-1pl	ate-2pl	ate-3pl

As discussed in Borer (1989) among others, third person can have a
null referential pronoun if the pronoun is identified by an NP from
the matrix clause:

(20) Rina   biksha me-david$_i$ she-igmor pro$_i$ le'exol
     Rina   asked   of-David   that-finish   eating
     'Rina asked David$_i$ that (he$_i$) finish eating.'

Borer argued that AGR in these instances is [+anaphoric], forcing
movement of AGR to a COMP to allow binding of AGR from the clause
above. We will adopt a modified version of this analysis and say
that if a single form in a given paradigm is lacking PERSON
specification, its AGR is underspecified with respect to the value
for that feature. AGR will then fill in the value for its person·phi-
feature from a preceding NP antecedent. We thus impose a much more
stringent restriction on "anaphoric" AGR than Borer.

4.1.4 Null subjects and AGR lacking PERSON

Recall that we distinguish between underspecified AGR and an AGR
matrix with no PERSON slot. Such paradigms will not allow
referential pro-drop at all, for reasons stated earlier.
    For example, the present tense in Hebrew never allows pro-drop,
not even when embedded under a matrix clause with a potential
antecedent NP. The same is true for so-called equatives in Arabic
(Mohammad 1988) and adjectival and nominal predicative sentences in
Hebrew:

(21) *oxel   bananot
      eat-m/s   bananas
     *baxur   nexmad
      fellow nice-m/s

The present tense in Hebrew crucially does not contain a person
feature even though it has number and gender which may be due to its
adjectival status. Hence when the radically underspecified AGR matrix
of the null subject is unified with this person-less matrix, it will
still fail to satisfy the requirement for a full phi-feature
specification, since the value for PERSON is still null. The same is
true of equatives in Arabic.
    Since the paradigm as a whole is missing the person feature, AGR
cannot be marked [+anaphoric] as this is only possible in paradigms
which lack at most one person marker. Hence, even if pro in the
present tense has an antecedent, pro cannot be used:

(22) *amarti   le-david she-mekabel   pras
      say-1/s to-David that-get-m/s prize
     'I told David$_i$ that (he$_i$) is getting a prize.'

    The so-called weak inflection in Turkish is another example of
PERSON-less AGR. According to Kornfilt (1988), Turkish has rich AGR,
agreeing in number and person with the subject. Pro-drop is an
option, since phi-features on AGR are fully specified. Turkish,
however, has an alternate verbal form with a 'dummy' (non-agreeing)
3/sg AGR, which does not allow pro-drop:

(23) *Asker-ler$_i$ [pro$_i$ ol-eceg-in]-e   inan-iyor-lar
     soldier-pl   die-Fut-3/s-dat believe-prog- 3/pl
   'The soldiers$_i$ believed that pro$_i$ were going to die'

Crucially, as shown in (23), AGR cannot be deictic or anaphoric
in these instances, i.e. pro-drop fails even when the weak form is
embedded under an NP which could identify pro. We claim that deictic
AGR is not available in Turkish since the language has equivalent
forms with fully specified AGR, and anaphoric AGR is not possible
since in the weak inflection persons are unspecified in all verbal
forms of the weak paradigm. Turkish weak inflection may lack all
phi-features. The fact that on the surface we have a third person
'dummy' marker in AGR is probably due to the fact that Turkish
morphological template structure demands that the AGR slot be
obligatorily filled.
   There are also languages which   lack AGR throughout the
language rather than in certain paradigms. We suggested that
Papiamentu has unspecified AGR, since there is never any person
marking in Papiamentu. As discussed in Gilligan (1987), pro in this
language cannot appear even when it is coindexed with an NP in the
matrix clause.

(24) Maria$_i$ sa   ku   *(e$_i$)   ta sabi
     Maria$_i$ know that (she$_i$) be smart
   'Maria knows that she is smart'

5.0 Conclusion

We have claimed that identification of referential pro is part of a
general process of agreement. We furthermore suggested that Huang's
'cool languages' have an AGR node, and that
languages/paradigms/inflectional forms may differ in their choice of
AGR. We have attempted to find morphological and syntactic
correlations for the various types of AGR nodes proposed in this
work. Clearly, the ideas need to be tested against a larger corpus,
but we believe this to be a first step in the right direction.

Notes

1. German allows expletive pro-drop, but as pointed out in the
previous paragraph, Adams' proposals are not intended to cover
expletives.

2. This is the topic of Holmberg (1988). He suggests that mainland
Scandanavian languages differ from languages like Icelandic and
German in having V rather than I as the head of S. Only those
languages in which I is the head of S and which also allow V to C
movement are pro-drop languages in his system. Holmberg's approach
may provide a reason as to why Swedish does not allow expletive pro-
drop. Note, however, that his approach may not work for French, which
a la Pollock (1987), has an S headed by I and also allows V-raising.

3. The theory of identification in Jaeggli and Safir is simply a restatement of Huang's ideas. They distinguish among identification by local AGR, by an argument of a higher clause, and by a discourse topic. Since they do not adopt the GCR, they have to assume that local identification has precedence over other forms of identification.

4. This view entails that the third person singular form in English is associated with a fully specified AGR matrix, and could potentially identify pro, if English were a pro-drop language. On our view, English fails to license null pronouns in the first place, making questions of identification irrelevant.

5. Chamorro (Chung 1984) has been cited as a language which has number but not person agreement, in which pro is identified by discourse. This indicates that the complete lack of all phi-features typical in East Asian languages is not a prerequisite for this kind of AGR. Cf. also footnote 7.

6. Quechua does not have long-distance/discourse-bound reflexives. However, it exhibits other signs of discourse orientation. It has a large number of validators which mark verbs and NPs for discourse functions. It is interesting that Korean, Thai, and Japanese also have such markers (the so-called sentence-final particles. See Kendall and Yoon 1986 for discussion).

7. This leads us to conclude that the availability of non-gap topics is not an integral part of discourse orientation. Non-gap and multiple topics also require Case to be assigned to them. Therefore, while only discourse oriented languages allow an obligatory topic position in all clauses, the languages must also have the resources to assign Case to such topics. It is well-known that Korean, Japanese and Chinese allow "double/multiple nominative" constructions, indicating that they have such resources.

References

Adams, M. (1985) Old French, Null Subjects, and Verb Second Phenomena, Doctoral dissertation, UCLA, Los Angeles, California

Anward, J. (1988) "Verb Agreement in Swedish", McGill Working Papers in Linguistics, Department of Linguistics, McGill University, Montreal

Borer, H. (1989) "Anaphoric AGR", in Jaeggli, O. and K. Safir, eds. The Null Subject Parameter, Kluwer Academic Publishers, Dordrecht

Choe, H.S. (1988) Restructuring Parameters and Complex Predicates - A Transformational Approach, Doctoral dissertation, MIT, Cambridge, MA

Chung, S. (1984) "Identifiability and Null Objects in Chamorro", BLS-10

Cole, P. (1987) "Null Objects in Universal Grammar", in Linguistic
    Inquiry 18, 597-612
Cole, P., G. Hermon and L. Sung (1988) "Long Distance Reflexives in
    Chinese", ms., University of Delaware, Newark, Delaware
Gazdar, G., Klein E., Pullum G. and I. Sag (1985) Generalized
    Phrase Structure Grammar, Harvard University Press, Cambridge,
    Mass
Gilligan, G.M. (1987) A Cross-Linguistic Approach to the Pro-Drop
    Parameter, Doctoral Dissertation, USC, Los Angeles,
    California.
Hermon, G. (1985) Syntactic Modularity, Foris, Dordrecht.
Holmberg, A. (1988) "The Head of S in Scandinavian and English",
    McGill Working Papers in Linguistics, Department of
    Linguistics, McGill University, Montreal
Huang, C.T.-J. (1984) "On the Distribution and Reference of Empty
    Pronouns", Linguistic Inquiry, 15, 531-574.
Huang, C.T.-J. (1986/9) "Pro-drop in Chinese: A Generalized
    Control Approach", in Jaeggli and Safir eds.
Huang, C.T.-J. and J. Tang (1988) "Local and long-distance
    reflexives in Chinese", paper presented at NELS-19
Hyams, N. and O. Jaeggli (1987) "Morphological Uniformity and the
    Setting of the Null Subject Parameter," NELS-18
Jaeggli, O. and K. Safir (1989) "The Null Subject Parameter and
    Parametric Theory," in Jaeggli, O. and K. Safir eds.
Jaeggli O. and K. Safir eds. (1989) The Null Subject Parameter,
    Kluwer Academic Publishers, Dordrecht
Kendall, S.A. and J. Yoon (1986) "Sentence-final particles as
    evidence for morphosyntactic interaction", CLS-22
Kornfilt J. (1987) "A Typology of Morphological Agreement and its
    Syntactic Consequences," CLS-24
McCloskey J. and K. Hale (1984) "On the Syntax of Person-Number
    Inflection in Modern Irish," Natural Language and Linguistic
    Theory, 1, 442-487.
Mohammad, M.A. (1987) "Nominative Case, I-Subjects, and Subject-
    verb agreement," CLS-24
Pollard, C. and I. Sag (1987) Information-Based Syntax and Semantics,
    vol. 1, CSLI Lecture Notes, University of Chicago Press
Platzack, C. (1989) "The Scandinavian Languages and the Null
    Subject Parameter," Natural Language and Linguistic Theory, 5,
    377-401.
Raposo, E. (1989) "Prepositional Infinitival Constructions in
    European Portuguese", in Jaeggli and Safir eds.
Rizzi, L. (1982) Issues in Italian Syntax. Foris, Dordrecht
Rizzi, L. (1986) "Null Objects in Italian and the Theory of pro," LI
    17, 501-557.
Taraldsen, T. (1978) "On the Nominative Island Constraint,
    Vacuous Application, and the That-Trace Filter", in S. Keyser ed.
    Recent Transformational Studies in European Languages, MIT Press,
    Cambridge, Mass
Travis, L. (1984) Parameters and Effects of Word Order Variation,
    Doctoral Dissertation, MIT, Cambridge, Mass

Flipped out: AUX in German

Erhard W. Hinrichs and Tsuneko Nakazawa
University of Illinois

1. Introduction

Contrary to den Besten/Edmondson (1983) and Uszkoreit (1987a, 1987b), this paper argues that auxiliaries in German have to be treated as sisters of main verbs, rather than as sisters of VP or S. Thus, German differs from English in that in German main verbs combine with auxiliaries before they combine with NP complements, while in English NP complements and main verbs form constituents before any auxiliaries are added. Strong evidence against the analyses of Uszkoreit and den Besten/Edmondson and in favor of aux/main verb constituents can be derived from the phenomenon of auxiliary flip. Auxiliary flip refers to a word order in which certain auxiliaries which normally appear in final position in the verbal complex appear, instead, in initial position.

We will show that the auxiliary flip construction merely involves constituent reordering, if auxiliaries and main verbs are assumed to form constituents. At the same time we will argue that auxiliary flip poses serious problems for any analyses such as Uszkoreit's and den Besten/Edmondson's in which main verbs first combine with their NP arguments, before such constituents in turn combine with any auxiliaries. Under their analyses the auxiliary flip construction would produce discontinuous constituents of NP complements and main verbs which are broken up by fronted auxiliaries.

Before we will discuss the actual syntatctic evidence that favors our account over its rivals, let us briefly contrast the constituent structures assumed in the two types of analyses. Uszkoreit's analyses of German VP structure can be exemplified by analysis trees such as (1). The tree in (1) is taken from Uszkoreit (1987a).

(1)

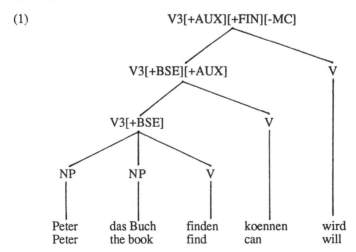

Uszkoreit assumes that main verbs such as *finden* first combine with their NP complements (including the subject) before any auxiliary verbs are added. As a result, auxiliaries are treated as sisters of V3 constituents. For all practical purposes we can equate V3 nodes with sentence nodes. In other words, Uszkoreit treats auxiliaries as sisters of S. The auxiliary hierarchy is determined by the use of features such as [+ FIN] (for finite) and [+ BASE] for (bare infinitive). Word order of auxiliaries relative to other constituents in the sentence is determined by the feature MC (for main clause). The feature MC is used to distinguish between main and subordinate clauses and their attendant differences in word order. Since (1) shows the structure of a subordinate clause as embedded in (2), the highest V3 node carries the feature [- MC].

(2) Hans bezweifelt dass Peter das Buch finden koennen wird.
     Hans doubts   that Peter the book find   can   will
     "Hans doubts that Peter will be able to find the book."

However, the topic of word order differences between different clause types would take us too far afield in this paper. For details on that aspect of German syntax, see Uszkoreit (1987a , 1987b) and Hinrichs & Nakazawa (1989).

In contrast to Uszkoreit's analysis, we want defend an account that can be exemplified by the tree in (3).

(3)

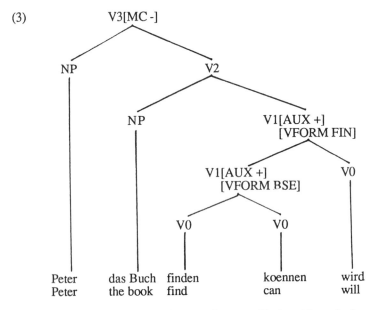

There are two main differences between Uszkoreit's analysis and our account: 1. in our analysis main verbs such as *finden* first combine with all auxiliaries, before NP complements are added. 2. In Uszkoreit's analysis NP complements form a flat structure with their main verb sister, whereas in our analysis NP complements are added one at a time. In the following section, we will concentrate on the first of these two differences, namely the constituent structures that main verbs form vis-a-vis their NP complements and vis-a-vis auxiliary verbs.

2. Auxiliary Flip

The auxiliary flip construction which is exemplified by the sentences in (4) provides crucial data for the constituenthood of auxiliaries and main verbs.

(4) a. Ich wusste, dass er das Examen hat   bestehen koennen.
         I   knew   that he the exam   has[FIN] pass[INF] can[INF]
        "I knew that he has been able to pass the exam."

      b. Ich wusste, dass er das Examen wuerde   bestehen koennen.
         I   knew   that he the exam   would[FIN] pass[INF] can[INF]
        "I knew that he would be able to pass the exam."

Notice that the *dass*-clauses in (4) do not follow the normal word order characteristic of German subordinate clauses. Namely, in subordinate clauses the finite verb occurs in sentence final position, as in the case in (5).

(5) Ich glaube, dass Hans das Haus bauen wird.
     I   believe that Hans the   house build   will
    "I believe that Hans will build the house."

The finite auxiliary *wird* appears as the final element of the VP. However, this is not the case in the examples in (4). In (4a) the finite auxiliary *hat* and in (4b) the finite auxiliary *wuerde* do not appear in sentence-final position. Instead, they occur in initial position within the aux/main verb complex and are followed by infinitival verb forms of main verb and auxiliary. Hence, the construction is also called double-infinitive. As Heidolph et al. document in their 1981 grammar of German, this construction is occasioned by a small set of triggering verbs given in (6) which govern the bare infinitive as its complement and whose morphological paradigm does not include regular forms for the past participle.

(6)   Double Infinitive Triggering Verbs

      modal verbs: koennen "can", wollen "will", duerfen "be allowed to",
                    sollen "shall", moegen "may", muessen "must"

      lassen "let", sehen "see", hoeren "hear", fuehlen "feel", helfen "help"

If these infinitive governing verbs appear embedded under a form of perfective *haben* , then the auxiliary form of *haben*, as the head of the construction, has to appear in initial position within the verbal complex. The triggering verbs themselves appear in the infinitive, thereby compensating for the lack of the past participle forms that *haben* ordinarily subcategorizes for. The example in (7), which are taken from Heidolph et al. (1981), show that past participle forms such as *gemusst* or *gekonnt* are unavailable for the verbs in (6).

(7)   a.* (Nach allem), was sie bei dem Vormarsch durchmachen
gemusst/muessen hatten.
b.* Sie wogten, wie sie kein Filmregisseur wogen lassen gekonnt/koennen
haette.
c.* Sie wogten, wie sie keiner wogen gelassen/lassen hat.

The examples in (8) show that fronting of the finite form of *haben* is obligatory in each case.

(8)   a.   (Nach   allem),   was sie   bei dem Vormarsch
after   everything that they on   the   attack
"after everything that they had to overcome during the attack, ..."

hatten durchmachen muessen...
have   overcome   must

b.   Sie   wogten, wie sie   kein Filmregisseur
they   rolled   how them no   director
"They rolled how no director would have been able to make them roll."

haette   wogen lassen koennen.
would have roll   make   can

c.   Sie   wogten, wie sie   keiner   hat   wogen   lassen.
they   rolled   how them nobody has roll   make
"They rolled how nobody has made them roll."

In the above examples of the auxiliary flip construction, auxiliary fronting is obligatory. The example (9), on the other hand, show that in some cases fronting is merely optional.

(9)   a.   Ich glaube nicht, dass Peter   das   Buch finden koennen wird.
I   believe not   that Peter the   book find   can   will
"I don't believe that Peter will be able to find the book."

b.   Ich glaube nicht, dass Peter das Buch wird finden koennen.

Notice that in (9) *koennen* is not embedded under *haben*. Thus, koennen is not used as a substitute infinitive form in lieu of a past participle, but rather as a regular infinitive. The auxiliary flip construction is, therefore, not restricted to those instances of infinitives that substitute for past participles, but is triggered by infinitives of the verbs listed in (6) in general. The only difference between the two cases is that in the case of substitute infinitives auxiliary flip is obligatory, whereas for regular infinitives auxiliary flip is merely optional. Therefore (9a) is grammatical, whereas the sentences in (7) are not.

      Consider next the kind of constituent structures that make it possible to account for the phenomenon in the first place. As Johnson (1986) has quite correctly pointed out, the auxiliary flip construction is completely consistent with the view that auxiliaries and main verbs form constituents. Under such an analysis, the auxiliary flip construction merely involves constituent reordering. This point can be easily demonstrated if we compare the tree in (10a) for the subordinate clause in (9a) with the tree in (10b) for the flipped auxiliary order in (9b).

(10) a.

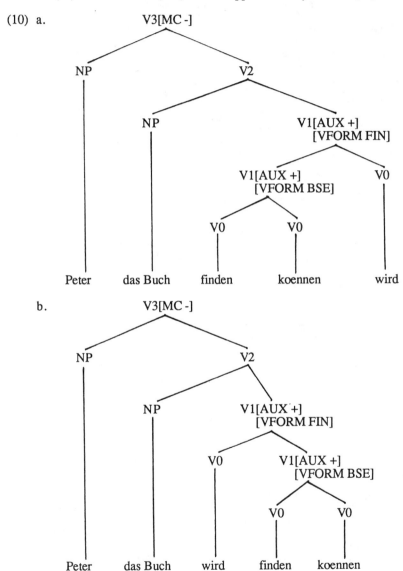

b.

The difference between the two trees merely involves the constituent order of the finite auxiliary *wird* relative to its V1 complement.

However, the auxiliary flip construction poses serious problems for analyses such as Uszkoreit's in which main verbs first combine with their NP arguments, before such constituents in turn combine with any auxiliaries. Notice that under such an analysis the auxiliary flip construction would produce discontinuous constituents of NP complements and main verbs which are broken up by the fronted finite auxiliary. Moreover, the putative rule of auxiliary fronting would have highly idiosyncratic properties not shared by any other widely accepted movement or extraction rules. Ordinary extraction rules such as Wh-movement or topicalization always move phrasal material over potentially unbounded syntactic domain, while the auxiliary fronting rule (as indicated by the arrow in 11) would move lexical, non-phrasal material within the boundary of a single S-node.

(11)

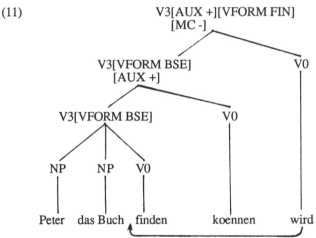

To make matters worse, the auxiliary flip construction may require more than a single auxiliary to appear in initial position within the VP. In (12b) the non-finite auxiliary *haben* has been fronted together with the finite auxiliary *wird*.

(12) a.* Ich glaube nicht, dass er die Lieder singen wird koennen haben.
        I believe not that he the songs sing will can have
        "I don't believe that he will have been able to sing the songs."

    b. Ich glaube nicht, dass er die Lieder wird haben singen keonnen.

Incidentally, examples such as (12b) clearly show that the widespread belief that auxiliary flip affects only finite auxiliaries is mistaken. Instead, a more accurate characterization of the phenomenon is that it affects all auxiliaries that take one of the verbs listed in (6) as its complement.

Given our assumptions about German VP constituent structure, such multiple frontings have a straightforward explanation. They are simply cases of multiple constituent reorderings. The relevant trees for (12b) is given in (13).

(13)

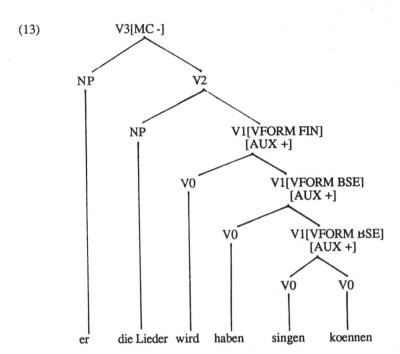

Notice, however, that in Uszkoreit's analysis of VP structures, one would have to assume multiple applications of the same extraction rule within the same clause. To complicate matters further, these multiple extractions have to be interdependent in order to generate the correct word order among fronted elements, which is a mirror image of its clause final counterpart.

3. Additional Syntactic Evidence: Single Constituent Fronting

Additional evidence against the analyses of Uszkoreit and den Besten/Edmondson and in favor of aux/main verb constituents can be derived from the well-known phenomenon of constituent fronting in assertion main clauses of German.

Assertion main clauses obey what von Stechow(1978) has called Drach's Law, named after the German linguist Erich Drach. Drach (1963) was the first to point out that in main assertion clauses of German, a finite verb in second position can be preceded by any major constituent in sentence initial position. In (14a) the subject NP is fronted. In (14b) and (14c) non-subject NPs appear in sentence initial position. In (14b) it is the main verb alone, and in (14e) it is the adverbial *heute*.

(14) a. Peter hat   dem   Jungen das Buch   heute   gegeben.
      Peter has   the   boy   the   book   today   given
      "Peter gave the boy the book today."

  b. Das Buch hat Peter dem Jungen heute gegeben.
  c. Dem Jungen hat Peter das Buch heute gegeben.
  d. Gegeben hat Peter dem Jungen das Buch heute.
  e. Heute hat Peter dem Jungen das Buch gegeben.

Moreover, fronting is unbounded, since the fronted constituent can be the filler of a gap in a lower S as in (15).

(15) Ueber dieses Thema hatte Fritz Peter gebeten, einen Vortrag _ zu halten.
      on   this   topic   had   Fritz Peter asked   a   lecture   to give
      "Fritz had asked Peter to give a lecture on this topic."

However, there are two restrictions on what type of syntactic material can be fronted. Even though the fronted constituent need not be phrasal (as 14d shows), not every syntactic constituent can be fronted. Determiners without accompanying nouns, as in (16), cannot appear in sentence initial position.

(16) * Dieses hat Peter dem Jungen Buch heute gegeben.
      the   had Peter the   boy   book today given

One restriction that has to be placed on fronting, therefore, seems to be that only major syntactic constituents can be fronted. The notion of a major syntactic constituent is, of course, to some extent a fuzzy one, whose exact denotation will not need to concern us here. However, the second limitation on fronting will be of great importance for our analysis of VP structure. It is the restriction that exactly one constituent, but not more than one constituent, is fronted. Thus (17), in which two object NPs appear before the finite verb is ungrammatical.

(17) * Dem Jungen das Buch hat   Peter heute gegeben.
      the   boy   the book had   Peter today given

In fact, the constraint that only a single constituent be fronted, in turn, provides one of the most reliable tests for constituenthood in German. As Nerbonne (1985, 1986) has correctly pointed out, sentences as in (18) argue for a hierarchical, i.e. non-flat structure, of main verbs and non-subject NP complements.

(18) a. Das Buch gegeben hat Peter heute dem Jungen.
  b. Dem Jungen gegeben hat Peter heute das Buch.

Recall that one of the differences between the trees in (1) and (3) that contrasts Uszkoreit's analysis with our account of VP constituent structure involves the way in which NP arguments are added. In Uszkoreit's analysis a flat structure is assumed, whereas in our account of NPs a hierarchical structure is assumed in which NPs are added one at a time. The data in (18) provide evidence against Uszkoreit's flat structures and evidence in support of the hierarchical structures that we are assuming. Only if *das Buch* and *dem Jungen* are added one at a time, can each one alone be fronted with the main verb. A flat structure analysis would make the wrong prediction that (18a) and (18b) should be ungrammatical, when, in fact, they are perfectly grammatical.

Given the lithmus-test character of German fronting for determining constituenthood, now consider the sentences in (19) in which a main verb has been fronted together with one or more auxiliaires.

(19) a. Verkauft haben muessen wird Peter das Auto
       sold   have   must   will Peter the car
       "Peter will have had to sell the car."

     b. Verkauft haben wird Peter das Auto.
        sold   have will Peter the car
        "Peter will have sold the car."

The fact that main verbs can be fronted in conjunction with any number of auxiliaries strongly suggests that main verbs and auxiliaries have to be treated as constituents. This finding again contradicts Uszkoreit's analysis of German VP structures in which main verbs are taken to first combine with their NP complements, before they combine with any auxiliaries.

4. Conclusion

We therefore conclude that there is strong evidence that suggests that in German auxiliary verbs first combine with main verbs, before any NP complements are added. This finding in turn points to an interesting difference between two West Germanic languages. While in German auxiliaries and main verbs form constituents, this is not the case in English, for which it is widely assumed in the current syntactic literature that main verbs first combine with non-subject NP complements before any auxiliaries are added. German and English therefore part ways not only with respect to word order of verb and nominal elements, but also with respect to the internal constituent structure formed by these elements.

References

Besten, H. den, and J. Edmondson (1983). 'The verbal complex in Continental West Germanic'. Abraham, Werner ed. *On the Formal Syntax of the West Germania.* Amsterdam: Benjamins.

Drach, Erich (1963). *Grundgedanken der deutschen Satzlehre* Darmstadt: Wissenschaftliche Buchgesellschaft.

Heidolph et al. (1981) *Grundzuege einer deutschen Grammatik* Akademie Verlag, Berlin.

Hinrichs, Erhard and Tsuneko Nakazawa (1988) 'German word order and constituent structures'. Linguistic Society of America Annual Meeting. New Orleans.

Hinrichs, Erhard and Tsuneko Nakazawa (1989) 'Word order and constituent structure in German.' Review of Uszkoreit (1987a). *Language* Vol. 65, No. 1.

Johnson, Mark (1986). 'A GPSG account of VP structure in German'. *Linguistics*, Vol. 24-5, pp.871-882.

Nerbonne, John (1985). *German Temporal Semantics: Three-dimensional Tense Logic and a GPSG Fragment*. New York: Garland.

Nerbonne, John (1986). `"Phantoms" and German fronting: poltergeist constituents'. *Linguistics*, Vol. 24-5, pp. 857-870.

Pollard Carl, and Ivan A. Sag (1987) *Information-Based Syntax and Semantics* Vol.1 Fundamentals. Stanford: CSLI Lecture Notes No. 13.

Uszkoreit, Hans (1987a). *Word Order and Constituent Structure in German*. Stanford: CSLI Lecture Notes No.8.

Uszkoreit, Hans (1987b). 'Linear precedence in discontinuous constituents: complex fronting in German'. Huck, Geoffrey J. and Almerindo E. Ojeda eds. *Syntax and Semantics*, Vol. 20, pp.405-425.

Von Stechow, A. (1987) *Deutsche Wortstellung und Montague-Grammatik*. Sonderforschungsbereich 99 Linguistik, Univ. Konstanz.

Determining Thresholds for the Emergence of Perfective Aspect
in Indo-Aryan Languages

Peter Edwin Hook
University of Michigan and Cornell University

ABSTRACT: While a great deal of attention has been devoted
to properly characterizing the perfective aspect in individual (usually Slavic) languages and a few contrastive studies have been made, very little work has been done on its
genesis and emergence, its development over time. The Indo-
Aryan language family in which the expression of perfective
aspect as a regular grammatical category is a recent innovation (and one which has yet to occur in certain members
of the family) provides us access to spatial and temporal
sequences of successive stages for comparative study. Using
diagnostic tests and statistics, I identify the presence or
absence of perfective aspect at different points in the
history of Hindi-Urdu and Marathi and show that a text frequency of about 10% is required for it to emerge as a regular category of the verb. END OF ABSTRACT.

This paper is part of an ongoing attempt to give an accurate description of aspect in Indic and part of a broader
effort in linguistics to develop typologies for functional
categories like "perfective aspect" that are independent of
the morphological peculiarities of given languages. In particular it is an attempt to direct productive enquiry to a
rarely-explored area: the diachrony of aspectual systems.
How do aspectual contrasts emerge in language? How do they
develop into general paradigmatic categories? What are the
precursor categories from which they evolve?

With the exceptions of the northern dialects of Shina
and some languages spoken in southern Rajasthan <1> every
form of contemporary Indo-Aryan has a set of auxiliary (or
"vector") verbs homophonous with members of its inventory
of basic lexical verbs. As full lexical verbs these express
change in location or posture or action that entails such a
change: GO, GIVE, TAKE, POUR, LET GO, GET UP, STRIKE, FALL,
COME, SIT, etc. A compound verb (CV) comprises a non-finite
or stem form of a main or primary verb followed by a finite
(or non-finite) form of one of these. In 1h and 2h kah and
guzar are non-finite forms of primary verbs, while dUUgaa &
jaate are (respectively) finite and non-finite forms of the
vectors de GIVE and jaa GO (h = from Hindi-Urdu):

1h jaa-ne se   pahale ... kah dUUgaa "phir milEge"   <2>
    go-INF from before   say GIVE-1sg-FUT   <3>
    'Before going I will say, "See you later!"' Vaid 1966:14
2h sab prahaar paanii kii-tarah guzar jaa-te rahe the
    all blows   water like   pass GO-ing stayed had
    'All threats had kept passing by harmlessly.' Vaid 1966:9

For every CV there is almost always a corresponding non-
compound or simple verb (SV) in which the auxiliary is absent and the primary verb bears the desinential affixes:

```
1h' jaa-ne se    pahale ... kah-UU-gaa "phir milEge"
    go-INF from before      say-1sg-FUT
    'Before going I will say, "See you later!"'
2h' sab prahaar paanii kii-tarah guzar-te rahe    the
    all blows   water  like      pass-ing stayed had
    'All threats had kept passing by harmlessly.'
```

In Indo-Aryan, CV auxiliaries or vector verbs exhibit a
greater or lesser degree of semantic bleaching. The difference in meaning which stems from their presence as opposed
to their absence also varies from one language to another.
For some languages it can be shown that the CV/SV opposition has become part of a system of regular semantic contrasts, a part of the verb paradigm, functioning to express
perfective (versus aspectually unspecified) conceptualiza-
tion of actions and events. For others (Marathi, Kashmiri)
it can be shown that this has not (yet) happened (Hook 1988
and to appear). The problem I address here is how to determine when an evolving CV/SV system assumes aspectual value.
    Slavic-speaking Indologists (as well as the occasional
Indic-speaking Slavicist) are among those who identify the
Hindi-Urdu CV as being a perfective <4>. To buttress their
intuitive judgements with explicit procedures I have developed independent diagnostic tests. For instance, in aspect-
ological studies of Russian it has been observed (Forsyth
1970: 258-61 & 297) that clauses which are dependent on expressions of fear and anxiety show a preference for perfective forms which borders on being categorical:

```
3r mat'   bojalas' kak-by eё syn ne zabolel
   mother feared   lest    her son NEG took-sick-PFV
   'The mother was afraid that her son might get sick.'
```

Rassudova (1984:174) reports a similar preference.
    There is a similar (if not quite so strong) preference
for perfective forms in clauses introduced by expressions
which mean 'until' (4r from Forsyth 1970:133):

```
4r ona budet ubajukivat' rebёnka poka on ne zasnёt
   she will  rock        child   while he NEG sleeps-PFV
   'She will rock the baby till it goes to sleep.'
```

There are also environments which strongly disfavor the
perfective. For example, the complements of phasal verbs in
Russian bar the occurrence of perfective aspect:

```
5r on načinaet čitat' predloženie    (*načinaet pročitat')
   he begin-3s read-IMPFV sentence    begin-3s read-PFV
   'He begins to read the sentence.'
```

These asymmetries <5> in the distribution of perfective forms in Russian are closely paralleled by Hindi-Urdu CV's:

3h mujhe Dar thaa ki kahII tum use ciTThii na <u>de   do</u>
    to-me fear was that lest you him letter NEG <u>give GIVE</u>
    'I was afraid that you might give him the letter.'
4h tum yahAA Thaharo jab-tak vo tumhE ciTThii na <u>de   de</u>
    you here stay   until   he you letter NEG <u>give GIVE</u>
    'Wait here until he gives you the letter.'   <6>
5h vo khaanaa <u>paros-ne</u> lagii   (*<u>paros   le-ne</u> lagii)
    she food   serve-INF began   serve TAKE-INF began
    'She began to dish out the food.'

But in Marathi, a closely related Indic language where the text frequency of CV's is from four to five times less, these diagnostic environments do not show the favoring (or disfavoring) effects they have in Hindi-Urdu or Russian:

3m ma-laa kaaLji hoti ki tu tyaa-laa patr <u>de-Sil</u>
    me-to anxiety was that you him-to   letter give-FUT
    'I was afraid that you might give him the letter.'   <7>
4m to tu-laa patr <u>de-i</u>   paryant itha thaamb
    he you-to letter give-INF until   here wait
    'Wait here until he gives you the letter.'
5m ti ann <u>vaaDh-un   ghe-u</u>   laagli
    she food dish-out-CP TAKE-INF began
    'She began to dish out the food.'   Chirmule 1967:60

These data show there is a difference in the functions of the CV/SV opposition for these two Indo-Aryan languages and that that difference is statable in terms of the semantics of perfective aspect.

     Hook (1988) and Hook (to appear) are attempts to treat these differences as successive phases in a diachronic progression: The compound verb is an innovation in Indo-Aryan. Assuming that CV-rich languages were at one time similar to languages that are still CV-poor, it is possible to study the development of the CV system through apparent time as a first step toward a general account of aspectogenesis. With counts of CV-frequency carried out on texts from different periods, it is possible now to show that the assumption of a common direction of development in the evolution of Indo-Aryan CV systems was a correct one. For example, Marwari of the seventeenth century had a CV whose text frequency was the same as Marathi's is today, while the frequency of the CV in modern Marwari resembles contemporary Hindi's. If the slope for this diachronic change is the same for Marathi as it has been for Marwari, we may expect the CV/SV system in Marathi to closely resemble that of contemporary Hindi-Urdu sometime in the twenty-third century:

Figure 1. Ratio of CV to total verb forms in Marwari and
Marathi from 1670 until the present.

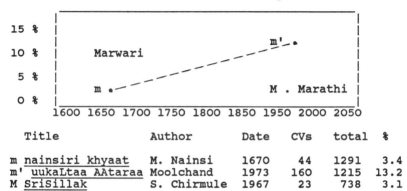

Title	Author	Date	CVs	total	%
m	nainsiri khyaat	M. Nainsi	1670	44	1291	3.4
m'	uukaLtaa AAtaraa	Moolchand	1973	160	1215	13.2
M	SriSillak	S. Chirmule	1967	23	738	3.1

Since prose publication in Hindi goes back only slightly more than a century, and published works in Urdu prose,
no more than two <8>, it is more difficult to establish the
slope of change in Hindi-Urdu CV frequency. Counting from a
wide sample of texts, we find a regression line which is
quite similar to that shown for Marwari in Figure 1:

Figure 2. Ratios of CV to total verb forms in Hindi-Urdu
of the nineteenth and twentieth centuries.

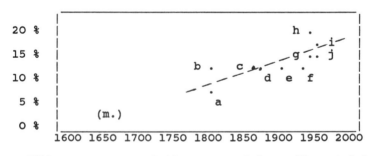

	Title	Author	Date	CVs	total	%
a	baagh-o-bahaar	Mir Amman	1802	103	1333	7.7
b	raanii ketkii	I.K. Insha	1818	112	830	13.5
c	bhaagyavatii	Phillauri	1877	158	1193	13.2
d	pariikSaa-guru	L.S.N. Das	1884	121	1000	12.1
e	narendra-mohinii	D.N. Khattri	1910?	143	1150	12.4
f	Sekhar	Vatsyayan	1940	149	1232	12.1
g	SaiDoz	K.B. Vaid	1966	194	1204	16.1
h	ajanabii	K.B. Vaid	1966	230	1159	19.8
i	duusre kinaare se	K.B. Vaid	1970	227	1263	18.0
j	Adhere band kamre	M. Rakesh	1967	208	1247	16.7

One of the findings of the contrastive study of modern Hindi-Urdu and Marathi is that as the frequency of the CV increases overall, there is a proportionately much greater growth in its use with certain classes of primary verbs, in particular verbs expressing articulate communicative acts: say, tell, ask, answer, etc. As a class such verbs are over fifteen times more likely to occur in compound form in Hindi-Urdu than they are in Marathi even though the overall frequency of the CV in Hindi-Urdu is only some four to five times greater than in Marathi. A preliminary count of four different texts in Hindi-Urdu shows a similar suddenness in growth of CV manifestation for this group of main verbs:

Table 1. Ratio of CVs to total: verbs of communication.

Title	Date	CVs	total	%
baagh-o-bahaar	(1802)	3	135	2.2 %
bhaagyavatii	(1877)	12	140	8.6 %
narendra-mohinii	(1910)	9	95	9.5 %
ajanabii	(1966)	21	88	23.9 %

A theory of aspectogenesis must account for this.

The difference can be understood if we recognize that perfective aspect has a more redundant semantic value for verbs of communication than it has in other categories. For instance, if we apply the Aristotelian taxonomy of inherent aspectual properties (as extended and refined by Z. Vendler and David Dowty) to broad classes of verbs:

6

	-culmination:	+culmination:
-activity:	State	Achievement
+activity:	Activity	Accomplishment

we observe that most verbs of communication in context are successful Accomplishments (with extremely short periods of activity leading up to their culminations or completions):

7m "saaDe caar" ti na SAAgitla '"4:30," she said.'
   half four she ERG said   (Chirmule 65)
8m mAI xaamoS rah saktii thii lekin mAI ne kah diyaa "hAA"
   I silent stay be-able was but I ERG say GAVE yes
'I could have kept quiet but I said, "Yes."' (Vaid 1970:29)

If we assume that innovations enter linguistic systems in order to resolve communicative problems (Traugott 1988: 414), it follows that they would take root first in domains where they are maximally informative. Since most verbs of

articulate communication express activities that are either
inherently short or clearly delimited in temporal extent we
should expect a system which formally marks completeness to
be extended to them rather later than it would be to other
classes of verbs whose aspectual values are inherently less
determined. For example, we find that predicates expressing
a change in psychic or emotional state (a semantic field in
which thresholds or culminations are neither given nor even
always directly observable) show a more moderate variation
in frequency of CV occurrence:

9   Change of psychic state: CV's total   %

          Marathi   (Chirmule)   4   59   6.8 %
          Hindi-Urdu (Vaid 1970)   6   52   11.6 %

Such predicates are among the earliest to appear in CV form.
     Over time as the frequency of explicit marking of com-
pleteness grows, predicates expressing actions and events
which are complete by their very nature are drawn into the
domain of the compound verb. We see this in the CV manifestation in Hindi-Urdu of prototypical Achievements such as
'find', 'catch', 'arrive', and 'begin' which in Marathi are
always SV:

10h ek aadmii ne apnii patnii ko ain mauqe par pakaR liyaa
    one man ERG his   wife DAT right moment at catch TOOK
    'A man caught his wife red-handed...' (Vaid 1970:16)
10m ekaa maaNsaa na baayko laa ain   veLe-s pakaDla
    one man   ERG wife DAT right time-at caught
    'A man caught his wife red-handed...'
    (*ekaa maaNsaa na baayko laa ain   veLe-s pakaDun ghetla
    one man   ERG wife DAT right time-at catch TOOK)
11h mAI ne uske hoThO ko...TaTol-naa...Suruu kar diyaa
    I ERG her lips DAT feel-INF   start do GAVE
    'I began to feel her lips.' (Vaid 1970:13)
11m mi titse oTh tsaatsap-na suru kela   (*kar-un dila)
    I-ERG her lips touch-INF start did   do-NF GAVE
    'I began to feel her lips.'

     Somewhat paradoxically verbs of inarticulate communica-
tion (cry, laugh, whine, etc.) also show a marked increase
in CV manifestation as one moves from a CV-poor language
like Marathi to a CV-rich one like Hindi-Urdu. These verbs
express Activities that rarely lead to culminations:

12h to mAI Saayad khisiyaa-kar hAs detaa (Vaid 1970:12)
    then I maybe embarrassed-CP laugh GAVE-CTF
    'Then maybe I would have laughed in frustration.'

Here the presence of a vector delimits the inception of the
Activity or State denoted by the primary, not its culmination <9>. The Marathi counterpart of 12h cannot have a CV:

12m mag mi kadaacit laadz-un   hasto   (*has-un deto)
     then I perhaps embarrassed-CP laughed-CTF laugh GAVE-CTF
     'Then maybe I would have laughed in frustration.'

Thus, as CV frequency in Indo-Aryan increases overall,
it shows proportionately greater increases in semantic domains where the processes leading to culmination of action
or event are very short or non-existent ones and in others
where there is no culmination at all. It is the emergence
of these secondary classes of CV that universalizes the CV-
construction to the extent necessary for it to evolve from
a system of Aktionsarten <10> to one of abstract aspectual
contrasts regularly expressed as a morphological dimension
of the verbal paradigm. This change in the domain of the CV
can be schematized as in 13:

13 Pre-perfective phase   Perfective phase

     Accomplishment CV's ──── Accomplishment CV's
     Change of state CV's   Change of state CV's
                               Inceptive CV's (Procedurals)

Achievement CV's
Isochronic CV's (say, etc.)

                         Endnotes

<1> The languages of south Rajasthan are exceptions only in
that they form their compound verbs by adding adverbs (ur-
'toward' and par- 'away') rather than vectors. Although the
resulting opposition differs in form, it is no different in
its functions from the compound:non-compound system that is
found in Marwari, Mewari, Braj, Hindi-Urdu, and other Indic
languages of the surrounding area: Hook and Chauhan 1988.
Tessitori (1916, para 147) suggests an historical source.
<2>. The transcription system used in this paper for Hindi-
Urdu, Marwari, Marathi, and other NIA languages is the one
generally found in the Indo-Aryan linguistics literature
with the following exceptions: Contrastive length in vowels
is indicated by doubling the symbol (not by a macron or
colon); nasality in vowels, by capitalization (not by tilda
or a following capital N); retroflexion of apical stops and
flaps, by upper case letters (not by sublinear dots); and
palatal fricatives, by capitalization of the symbol for the
corresponding alveolar fricatives.
<3>. Abbreviations used in this paper are:
     CP...............conjunctive participle marker
     CTF....................counter-factual mood
     DAT...............dative case or postposition
     ERG.............ergative case or postposition
     FUT...............................future tense
     IM................................imperfect stem
     IMP................................imperative
     IMPV..............................imperfective

```
INF.........................infinitival form
m...........................masculine gender
NEG.........................negative particle
P...........................perfect stem
PFV.........................perfective form
sg..........................singular number
```

<4> Pořízka (1967) and the Barannikovs (1956) inter alia. A recent (1988) study by R. Chatterjee makes the same case.

<5> Parallels exist in secondary aspectual functions, too. In both Russian and Hindi-Urdu, non-perfective forms in the imperative are felt to be more polite than the perfective:

```
A   teacher:  vojdite    v klass      klaas mE aa jaa-iye
              enter-PFV  in class     class in come GO-IMP
              'Come into the classroom!'

B   host:     vxodite                 andar aa-iye
              enter-IMPFV             inside come-IMP
              '(Please) come in!'
```

Russian data from Isačenko (1954) cited in Babby (1964:10).

<6> The procedure used to obtain the data in 3h and 4h was to ask several dozen English knowing speakers of Hindi-Urdu to translate from English into their native tongue. In over 95% of the translations CV's appeared as indicated in 3-4h.

<7> Of course, a CV in 3m or 4m would not be ungrammatical. Rather when asked to translate from English into Marathi, speakers of Marathi did not use CV's any more frequently in these environments than in others.

<8> I gratefully acknowledge the help rendered by Professor R. N. Srivastava (Delhi University), Professor C. M. Naim (University of Chicago) and Dr. Omar Afzal (Cornell University) in suggesting titles and authors of prose works from earlier periods of Hindi-Urdu literature.

<9> Comparison may be made with the category of "procedurals" (sposob dejstvija) in Slavic aspectology.

<10> Most primary verbs in Hindi-Urdu as well as in Marathi can be made into CV's with a choice of CV auxiliaries. This allows secondary semantic contrasts to obscure the general distinction between perfective and non-perfective aspect:

```
a) darvaazaa khol do        b) darvaazaa khol lo
   door      open GIVE         door      open TAKE
   'Open the door (for us).'   'Open the door (for yourself)'
   '(Push) open the door.'     '(Pull) open the door.'
   'Open the door (dammit)!'   'Open the door (and then...)'
```

These secondary distinctions have led some analysts to propose Aktionsart as the main function of the CV/SV system in all of the Indo-Aryan family (including Hindi-Urdu) and to ascribe perfective aspectual function to the morphological opposition of perfect versus imperfect stem:

```
c) aaj   vo aa-y-aa    hai    d) roz    vo aa-t-aa    hai
   today he come-P-msg is        daily  he come-IM-msg is
   'He has come today.'          'He comes every day.'
```

Since the perfect stem only occurs in past tenses (never in futures or imperatives), it is not properly characterizable as a perfective form: see discussion in Hook 1978:90ff.

Bibliography

Amman of Dihli, Mir. See Mir Amman of Delhi.

Babby, Leonard H. 1964. Aspect Selection in the Negated Imperative Compared to the Affirmative in Modern Russian. Unpublished MA thesis, Harvard University.

Bahl, K. C. 1972. On the Present State of Modern Rajasthani Grammar. Jodhpur: Rajasthani Shodh Sansthan.

Barannikov, A. P., and P. A. Barannikov. 1956. Khindustani: Khindi i Urdu. Moscow: Foreign Literature Pub. House.

Borodic, V. V. 1953. 'K voprosu o formirovanii soversennogo i nesoversennogo vida v slavjanskix jazykax'. Voprosy Jazykoznanija 6:68-86.

Brecht, Richard. 1985. 'The Form and Function of Aspect in Russian'. In Flier and Brecht, Eds. Pp. 9-34.

Chatterjee, Ranjit. 1988. Aspect and Meaning in Slavic and Indic. Amsterdam: John Benjamins.

Chirmule, S.V. 1967. SriSillak. Bombay: Mauz Prakshan Grih.

Comrie, B. 1976. Aspect. Cambridge University Press.

Das, L. S. 1974. pariikSaa-guru. Delhi: Rishabh Charan Jain evam Santati (reprint of 1884 edition).

Dowty, David. 1972. Studies in the Logic of Verb Aspect and Time Reference in English. Austin.

Flier, M. S. and R. D. Brecht, Eds. 1985. Issues in Russian Morphosyntax. Columbus, OH: Slavica.

Forsyth, J. 1970. A Grammar of Aspect: Usage and Meaning in the Russian Verb. Cambridge University Press

Grierson, G. A. 1919. Linguistic Survey of India. Calcutta: Govt. of India. (1968 reprint by Motilal Banarsidass).

Hendriksen, Hans. 1944. Syntax of the Infinite Verb Forms of Pali. Copenhagen: Einar Munksgaard.

Hook, P. E. To appear. 'The Emergence of Perfective Aspect in Indo-Aryan Languages'. In Grammaticalization, edited by B. Heine and E. Traugott. Amsterdam: J. Benjamins.

_____. 1988. 'Paradigmaticization: a Case Study from South Asia'. In Proceedings of the Fourteenth Annual Meeting of the Berkeley Linguistics Society. Pp. 293-303.

_____. 1978. 'Perfecting a Test for the Perfective: Aspectual Parallels in Russian, Lithuanian, Modern Greek, Hindi and Pashto'. In University of Michigan Papers in Linguistics, 2:89-104.

_____. 1974. The Compound Verb in Hindi. Ann Arbor: Center for South & Southeast Asian Studies, Univ. of Michigan.

Hook, P.E., and M.M. Chauhan. 1988. 'The Perfective Adverb in Bhitrauti'. WORD 39:177-186.

Insha, I.Kh. 1974. raanii ketkii kii kahaanii, edited by A. S. Dalvi. Bombay: M. Gandhi Memorial Research Center.

Isačenko, A.V. 1954. 'O imperative v ruštine a slovenštine - Využitie vidovych odtienkov v imperative'. Sovetska jazykoveda 4.

Kapp, Dieter B. 1972. Das Verbum paraba in seiner Funktion als Simplex und Explikativum in Jayasis Padumavati. Wiesbaden: Verlag Otto Harrassowitz.

Khattri. D. N. 1966. Narendra-Mohini. Thirteenth edition. Varanasi: Lahari Book Depot. (First printed in 1910?)

Masica, Colin P. 1976. Defining a Linguistic Area: South Asia. Chicago: University of Chicago Press.

Maslov, IU. S. 1984. Očerki po Aspektologii. Leningrad: Izdatel'stvo Leningradskogo Universiteta.

Mir Amman of Delhi. 1861. Bagh o Bahar, 6th edition. London Sampson Low, Marston & Company. (First printed in 1802)

Moolchand "Pranesh". 1973. uukaLtaa AAtaraa, siiLaa sAAs. Bikaner: Rajasthani Bhasa Prachar Prakashan.

Nainsi, M. 1960. naiNasiirii khyaat, edited by B.P. Sakaria Jodhpur: Rajasthan Prachavidya Pratishthan.

Nespital, Helmut. 1981. Das Futursystem im Hindi und Urdu. Wiesbaden: Franz Steiner Verlag.

Phillauri, S.R. 1973. bhaagyavatii. New Delhi: Sharda Prakashan (reprint of 1877 edition).

Porízka, Vincenc. 1967-69. 'On the Perfective Verbal Aspect in Hindi (Some features of parallelism between New Indo Aryan and Slavonic languages)'. Archív Orientální 35: 64-88, 208-231; 36:233-251; 37:19-47, 345-364.

Rakesh, Mohan. 1967. Adhere band kamre (Dark Closed Rooms). Delhi: Rajkamal Prakashan.

Rassudova, O. P. 1984. Aspectual Usage in Modern Russian. Moscow: Russky Yazyk.

Regnell, C.G. 1944. Über den Ursprung des slavischen Verbal Aspektes. Lund: H. Ohlssons Boktryckeri.

Sweetser, E. 1984. 'Grammaticalization and Semantic Bleaching'. In S. Axmaker, A. Jaisser and H. Singmaster, Eds. Proceedings of the Fourteenth Annual Meeting of the Berkeley Linguistics Society. Pp. 389-405.

Tessitori, L. P. 1914-16. 'Notes on the Grammar of the Old Western Rajasthani'. Indian Antiquary. Passim.

Tikkanen, Bertil. 1987. The Sanskrit Gerund: a Synchronic, Diachronic and Typological Analysis. Studia Orientalia, Vol. 62. Helsinki: Finnish Oriental Society.

Timberlake, Alan. 1985. 'The Temporal Schemata of Russian Predicates'. In Flier and Brecht, Eds. Pp. 35-57.

Traugott, E.C. 1988. 'Pragmatic Strengthening and Grammaticalization'. In S. Axmaker, A. Jaisser & H. Singmaster, Eds Proceedings of the Fourteenth Annual Meeting of the Berkeley Linguistics Society. Pp. 406-416.

Trenckner, V. 1879. Pali Miscellany. London: Wms & Norgate.

Vaid, K.B. 1966. meraa duSman (My Enemy). Delhi: Rajkamal.

_____. 1970. duusre kinaare se... (From the other shore). Delhi: Radhakrishna Prakashan.

Vatsyayan, S.H. 1958. Sekhar: ek Jiivanii. Varanasi: Saraswati Press. (First published in 1940).

Vendler, Zeno. 1967. 'Verbs and Times'. In Linguistics and Philosophy. Ithaca. Pp. 97-121.

Zbavitel, Dušan. 1970. Non-finite Verbal Forms in Bengali. Prague: Czechoslovak Academy of Sciences.

The Closed Licensing Domain[*]

Hunter Huckabay
University of Washington

Syntactic licensing has been a central concern of generative grammar since Chomsky (1986b) advanced the principle of Full Interpretation (FI), which says that in language every element must be licensed for interpretation. For conditions such as the ECP, binding, subjacency, Visibility, the Chain Condition, and so on, licensing for FI is often effected under the auspices of a syntactic chain. As the theory of chains stands, all of these conditions have parallel, non-intersecting domains of application that are not necessarily related to one another.

I will propose that the broadest domain of application for a licensing condition is the universal principle of the Closed Licensing Domain, which can replace subjacency as a necessary but not sufficient condition on chain formation. As a necessary but not sufficient condition, the Closed Licensing Domain is in some syntactic contexts overridden by narrower conditions on licensing. In the case to be considered here, a parameterized condition relevant in Romance languages, the Romance AGR Parameter, applies in conjunction with the Closed Licensing Domain to account for some otherwise mysterious discrepancies between parasitic gaps in English and parasitic gaps in Romance languages. Thus, the theory of chains is grounded in a principles and parameters explication.

Parasitic gaps and resumptive clitics are in complementary distribution when submerged in adjunct clauses as in (1) and (2).

(1) a.   ¿Qué articulos archivaste antes de   leer?
            what articles you-filed   before   to read
            "what articles did you file before reading?"
      b.   *¿Qué articulos archivaste antes de que leiste?
            what articles you-filed   before   you-read
            "what articles did you file before you read?"

(2) a.   *¿Qué articulos archivaste antes de   leerlos?
            what articles you-filed   before   to-read-them
            "what articles did you read before reading them?"
      b.   ¿Qué articulos archivaste antes de que los   leiste?
            what articles you-file   before   them   you-read
            "what articles did you file before you read   them?"

As pointed out by Bordelois (1986) and demonstrated by (1), parasitic gaps are licensed only when the adjunct they appear in is untensed. As such, the parasitic gap in the untensed clause in (1a), *antes de leer*, is acceptable, while the same gap cannot be licensed and is therefore unacceptable in the tensed clause *antes de que leiste* in (1b). Clitics, on the other hand, as demonstrated by (2) have the opposite property of appearing only in tensed adjuncts that are A'-bound.

The ungrammaticality of (1b), whose S-structure is given in (3)[1], is troublesome for accounts of parasitic gaps such as that proposed in Aoun and Clark (1984) which focuses on the binding relation between the null operator that binds the trace and the overt operator.

(3) *¿[CP Qué articulos$_i$ [VP t'$_i$[VP [VP archivaste t$_i$] [PP antes de[CP Op$_i$ que leiste e$_i$]]]]]?

Aoun and Clark (1984) argue that the null operator in (3) is an A'-anaphor which must be bound in its governing category, with the governing category for an anaphor in SPEC(CP) being a superordinate CP. By this analysis, the governing category for Op in (3) is the matrix CP, and so the null operator is bound in its governing category just as it is in (1a). Thus, Aoun and Clark's binding analysis cannot distinguish between (1a) and (2a).

Browning (1986), arguing that the null operator in a parasitic gap construction must be 1-subjacent[2] to its local antecedent, would also find the contrast between (1a) and (1b) puzzling. As shown by (3), only the barrier PP separates the null operator from its binder, the VP-adjoined trace, exactly as is the case in (1a), and in compliance with the 1-subjacency condition. So, according to Browning's account, (1b) should parallel (1a) in grammaticality just as they parallel each other in subjacent relations between the null and overt operators.

Bordelois (1986) dispenses with the null operator analysis of parasitic gaps and posits a +anaphor specification for parasitic gaps and a +pronominal specification for clitics, making parasitic gaps sensitive to principle A of the binding theory and clitics sensitive to principle B. Moreover, Bordelois argues that a governing category extends when a matrix verb is adjacent to an infinitive verb. So, according to Bordelois, the sentences of (1) and (2) will have the S-structures shown in (4) and (5) respectively, where the governing categories are bracketed.

(4) a. ¿[gov cat Qué articulos$_i$ archivaste t$_i$ antes de leer e$_i$]?
    b. *¿[gov cat Qué articulos$_i$ archivaste t$_i$] [gov cat antes de que leiste e$_i$]?
(5) a. *¿[gov cat Qué articulos$_i$ archivaste t$_i$ antes de leerlos$_i$]?
    b. ¿[gov cat Qué articulos$_i$ archivaste t$_i$] [gov cat antes de que los$_i$ leiste]?

In (4a), the preposition *sin* , . being monosyllabic, is not substantial enough to offset adjacency between the matrix and the embedded verb so that the matrix verb *archivaste* incorporates the embedded verb *leer* so that the governing category of the parasitic gap *e* extends to include the entire sentence. Being anaphoric, the parasitic gap, under aegis of the restructured governing category, is properly bound to its A'-antecedent through the mediation of the A-position trace in accordance with principle A. In (4b), the tensed embedded verb *leiste* disallows extension of the governing category so that the anaphoric parasitic gap has no antecedent in its governing category and (4b) is therefore unacceptable as a principle A violation.

In (5a) and (5b), the clitic *los* has the same respective governing category as the parasitic gap does in those untensed and tensed contexts, and so where the anaphoric parasitic gap is properly bound in (4a), in (5a) the pronominal clitic is a principle B violation. The situation reverses in (5b) where the clitic is correctly isolated by tense from its antecedent in the embedded governing category. Thus, by exploiting the binding theory Bordelois accounts for the fine contrast highlighted in (1) and (2).

However, contrary to Bordelois' claims, verbs separated by more than a monosyllabic preposition permit the appearance of parasitic gaps. For instance, as Contreras (to appear) points out, *para* patterns with *sin* in allowing a parasitic gap in an untensed clause.

(6) ¿Qué libros$_i$ compraste t$_i$ para leer e$_i$?
     "which books did you buy in order to read?"

According to Bordelois, since *para* is disyllabic rather than monosyllabic, the adjacency of the verbs is offset and so the governing category for the parasitic gap *e* cannot restructure so that the antecedent for *e* is included in its governing category. Thus, virtual adjacency of the matrix and embedded verbs does not seem to be a key to the licensing of parasitic gaps.

Furthermore, Bordelois' account is subverted by the obliviousness of English parasitic gaps to tense. That is, as shown by (7) where the governing categories for the parasitic gaps are marked, contrary to the predictions made by Bordelois, in English parasitic gaps can appear in untensed clauses as in (7a) or in tensed clauses as in (7b).

(7) a. [$_{gov\ cat}$ Which articles$_i$ did you file t$_i$ before reading e$_i$]?
     b. Which articles$_i$ did you file t$_i$ [$_{gov\ cat}$ before you had read e$_i$]?

By Bordelois' analysis, (7b) should parallel its Spanish counterpart (1b) in its ungrammaticality since in both sentences the anaphoric parasitic gap is unbound in its governing category, the adjunct clause, in violation of principle A of the binding theory.

By the same token, if Bordelois (1986) were correct, (8a) would be as unacceptable as (2a) since (8a) would allow the same extension of the governing category that resulted in the principle B violation in (2a).

(8) a. [$_{gov\ cat}$ Which articles$_i$ did you file t$_i$ before reading them$_i$]?
     b. Which articles$_i$ did you file t$_i$ [$_{gov\ cat}$ before you read them$_i$]?

However, as was the case with parasitic gaps, English pronouns are oblivious to tense. In other words, as it stands, Bordelois' binding account for the parasitic gap/clitic asymmetry in Spanish leads to the wrong predictions in English.

An explanation that captures the distinction between Spanish and English will obviously have to allow parametric differentiation. Since the only mechanisms at work in Bordelois' account of the contrasts shown in (1) and (2) derive from binding theory, her analysis can only be maintained in the face of (7) and (8) if we allow for parametric variation in the binding theory so that perhaps English and Spanish have different governing categories.   Since binding theory is a linchpin of universal grammar, we should reject any analysis such as Bordelois' that forces a parametric approach to binding.

Thus, based on (7), I assume the governing category for parasitic gaps to be the same in tensed and untensed clauses in all languages, and since therefore the parasitic gap is properly bound in (7b), it is properly bound in (1b) as well and so the ungrammaticality of that sentence cannot be attributed to binding.   If, in consideration of the Θ-criterion concerns raised by Contreras (1984), a parasitic gap is A'-bound as a variable by a null operator, as in (3), repeated here as (9), then the $[Op, e]$ chain does not disrupt grammaticality in (9) since (10) shows the same sort of wh-chain can exist in a tensed embedded clause in Spanish.

(9)   *¿[CP Qué articulos$_i$ [VP t'$_i$[VP [VP archivaste t$_i$] [PP antes de[CP Op$_i$ que leiste e$_i$]]]]]?

(10)   a.   Juan se pregunta [CP que articulos$_i$ leiste t$_i$]
"John wonders what articles you read"

b.   Archivé los articulos después de saber [CP cuales$_i$ había leido t$_i$]
"I filed the articles after realizing which ones you had read"

In both (10a) and (10b), a $[wh, e]$ chain forms in a tensed embedding, showing that the ungrammaticality of (9) is not related somehow to the $[Op, e]$ chain.   Obviously, the chain formed by the overt movement of *qué articulos* in (9) is well-formed since that sort of movement generates simple questions.   Therefore, in (9), the only chain link unaccounted for and therefore responsible for the deviation of the structure is the chain link $[t', Op]$ so that licensing of the null operator is blocked in this context.   Based on (7b) the English counterpart to (9), we have rejected a binding account of the illicitness of this chain. Because, (9) has the same structure as (1a), given here as (11), we know the deviation in this chain link cannot be attributed to subjacency as Browning (1986) would have it.

(11)   ¿[CP Qué articulos$_i$ [VP t'$_i$ [VP archivaste t$_i$] [PP sin [CP Op$_i$ leer e$_i$]]]]

In (9) and in (11), Op and t' are separated by only one barrier, the PP, in accordance with the condition of subjacency, yet Op can be licensed in (11) but not in (9).   That is, subjacency has nothing to do with the licensing of the null operator in these structures.   Clearly, as suggested in the introduction, there is some domain that subsumes subjacency as a necessary but not sufficient environment for all licensing processes. In (9), this licensing domain contains the null operator but not its chain link t' , and so Op is denied licensing.

Because this licensing domain will subsume subjacency, it should explain all the subjacency cases plus those cases where subjacency is inadequate.   In this regard, bounding theory is not capable of making fine distinctions concerning long-distance movement such as in (12) and (13).

(12)   Which fish$_i$ do you know [CP how$_j$ to scale t$_i$ t$_j$]?
(13)   *Which fish$_i$ do you know [CP how$_j$ the alaskan scaled t$_i$ t$_j$]?

According to Chomsky's (1986a) version of subjacency sketched in note 2, the judgements of both (12) and (13) are suprising since in both sentences *which fish* is separated from its trace by a barrier at the embedded CP, with the result being a supposed weak subjacency violation. However, (12) is no more marginal than a typical case of Comp-to-Comp movement, such as (14) where no barriers are crossed, while (13) is as unacceptable as a clear-cut subjacency violation such as that entailed in (15) where the Complex NP Constraint is violated when two barriers are crossed.

(14)   Which fish$_i$ did you say [t'$_i$ that you would scale t$_i$]?
(15)   *Which fish$_i$ did you know [the boy$_j$ [Op$_j$ that t$_j$ caught t$_i$]]?

Besides correlating (12) and (13) with each other rather than with (14) and (15) respectively as would be proper, bounding theory also does not distinguish between the relatively acceptable (16a) and the unacceptable (16b).

(16) a. the sweaters$_i$ [Op$_i$ that John likes [NP music$_j$ [CP Op$_j$ PRO to knit t$_i$ by t$_j$]]]
     b. *the sweaters$_i$ [Op$_i$ that John likes [NP music$_j$ [CP Op$_j$ that Tom knits t$_i$ by t$_j$]]]

In both (16a) and (16b), Op_i must cross barriers at the marked CP and the NP so that, by bounding theory, both of these sentences should be ruled out as subjacency violations. However, (16a) is clearly more acceptable than (16b), again suggesting that in (16a) the domain which allows licensing contains the chain $[Op_i, t_i]$ while in (16b) this licensing domain breaks up the $[Op_i, t]$ chain and so the trace cannot be licensed by its operator. Hence, (16b) does not comply with FI since it contains an unlicensed trace.

Contrasting (12) with (13) and (16a) with (16b) indicates that the bounds of this licensing domain are affected by the presence of tense. That is, in the grammatical (12) and (16a) all traces and their binders are dominated by the same CP that is tensed. On the other hand, in the ungrammatical (13) and (16b), the trace is dominated by one tensed CP while the operator that binds it is dominated by another tensed CP. In recognition of this observation, we can posit a preliminary version of the Closed Licensing Domain with a schematic representation in (17) and its corollary principle of proper licensing, which is actually a specific application of the principle of FI.

(17) **Closed Licensing Domain (CLD)**
      The licensing domain for an element α is the nearest CP that

dominates a finite I that locally c-commands α.[3]

(18) CLD:

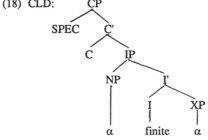

(19) **Proper Licensing**
An element must be licensed in its licensing domain.

The CLD would analyze (12) and (13) as (20) and (21) respectively with the licensing domains bracketed.

(20) [CLD Which fish$_i$ do you +finite know how$_j$ to scale t$_i$ t$_j$]?

(21) *Which fish$_i$ do you know [CLD how$_j$ the alaskan +finite scaled t$_i$ t$_j$]?

In the grammatical (20), the matrix CP contains both the finite I which c-commands the trace of *which fish* and the binder of that trace, and so *which fish* can license its trace within the CLD; whereas in the deviant (21), the embedded CP forms a CLD as it contains a finite I which c-commands the trace of *which fish*, but that embedded CP does not contain the binder of the errant trace. Thus, in the bad example under consideration, a trace is blocked off from licensing within the its CLD, the tensed embedded CP, and the structure is rejected by (19).

Notice however, the CLD does permit movement out of a tensed embedding in cases like (14), the example of Comp-to-Comp movement. (14) must insure that two different traces are bound in their own licensing domains. Thus, the relevant Closed Licensing Domains for (14) are given in (22), where (22a) marks the licensing domain for the most embedded trace and (22b) marks the licensing domain for the intermediate trace.

(22) a. CLD (t$_i$): Which fish$_i$ do you say [CLD t'$_i$ that you +finite would scale t$_i$]

b. CLD (t'$_i$): [CLD Which fish$_i$ do you +finite say t'$_i$ that you would scale t$_i$]

From (22a), we see that the CLD for t_i is the embedded CP, since t_i is locally c-commanded by the finite I dominated by that embedded CP. As the CLD for t_i contains both the trace and its binder, the intermediate trace, the most embedded trace can be licensed under (19).

In (22b), the intermediate trace is c-commanded by the matrix I, and so the matrix CP is its CLD. As was the case for the lower trace, the CLD for the intermediate trace contains both the pertinent gap and its binder, *which fish*, so that licensing of the intermediate trace is confined to the CLD of that trace in accordance with (19). Thus, the locality restrictions on licensing as proscribed by the CLD correctly permit the long-distance movement in (12) and **(14)** while prohibiting a similar movement in (13) and (15).

The terms of the CLD as given in (17) can be refined in light of Chomsky's (1988) expansion of the inflection structure schematically situated between the preverbal subject and the VP. According to the developments presented in this work and represented in (23), IP is headed by a node AGR-S responsible for effecting predicate agreement with the subject. AGR-S takes as its complement a maximal projection FP whose head marks the clause as ±finite. Finally, FP dominates another agreement node AGR-OP that selects VP as its complement and insures verbal agreement with the object.

(23)

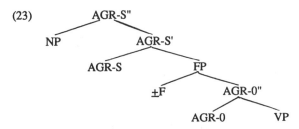

Within this configuration, the node that reflects tense and so therefore by (17) triggers the formation of a CLD for an element is the F head of FP. As we can see from (23), however, ±F, that is, the tense node, does not c-command the subject NP. As such, a characterization of closed licensing domains that refers directly to tensing, by the innovations given in (23), incorrectly identifies the subject NP as an escape hatch from a tensed CP since ±F has no structural relationship with the subject. Thus, if c-command by +F triggers the formation of a CLD, then the embedded subject trace in (24), being locally c-commanded by the matrix tense, will have the matrix CP as its CLD and would therefore be predicted to be acceptable.

(24) *[CLD Which Alaskan$_i$ do you +F know how t$_i$ scaled the fish]

Suppose then that AGR is crucial to CLD formation. The subject is c-commanded by the AGR-S node, and if c-command by AGR triggers the formation of a CLD, then only the SPEC(CP) would stand as a clausal escape hatch. As such, the AGR nodes in a tensed structure must be affected in some way that enables them to mark a CP as a CLD for an element. In fact, Chomsky (1988) points out that a tensed or +F head of FP does affect the AGR nodes in a way that -F does not. Though he is somewhat ambiguous about it[4], Chomsky says that an FP headed by +F results in AGR nodes that are "strong" in the sense that a strong AGR imposes on the phrase marker an inflection structure that strongly influences other segments of the structure. Therefore, in a tensed sentence, every element, including of course the subject, is c-commanded by a strong AGR except the SPEC(CP) escape hatch and the head of CP, which is not a possible extraction site by the Head Movement Constraint. Based on this innovation, the CLD as described in (17) can be redefined as in (25).

(25) **The Closed Licensing Domain**
The licensing domain for an element α is the nearest CP that dominates a strong AGR that locally c-commands α.

The principle of proper licensing given in (19) applies as before, and illicit subject traces such as the one in (24) are ruled out just as the illicit object trace was in (21). Thus, the CLD explains the necessity of Comp-to-Comp movement in tensed clauses such as (21) and (22) and the exemption from such movement in untensed clauses such as (20) far more accurately than bounding theory does.

Applying the CLD analysis to parasitic gaps, we must insure that the null operator and its local antecedent are situated in the same CLD[5]. To see that this is so, consider (1a), (1b), and (7b), given here as (26a-c) with the CLD for the null operator marked[6].

(26) a. [$_{CLD}$ Qué articulos$_i$ AGR t'$_i$ archivaste t$_i$ sin Op$_i$ leer e$_i$]
   b. *[$_{CLD}$ Qué articulos$_i$ AGR t'$_i$ archivaste t$_i$ antes de Op$_i$ que leiste e$_i$]
   c. [$_{CLD}$ Which articles$_i$ did you AGR t'$_i$ file t$_i$ before Op$_i$ you had read e$_i$]

In these parasitic gap structures, the null operator is locally c-commanded by the strong AGR in the matrix CP, and so the CLD for the null operator will be that matrix CP which dominates the relevant strong AGR. Further, the null operators in (26a-c) are all locally bound and licensed by the VP-adjoined trace, which also is dominated by the matrix CP, and so in all cases of parasitic gaps, as demonstrated by (26), the null operator can be licensed in its CLD. However, in (26b) the null operator is not licensed, and so the notion of the CLD will have to be altered or supplemented.

Notice, however, the CLD is misguided only where the languages under consideration don't pattern together as in the case of parasitic gaps. When languages do pattern together, the CLD, more than any other grammatical principle that might apply, makes the correct predictions. For example, in English, Spanish and French, as shown by (27) and (28) where the English sentence is followed by its Spanish and French counterpart, non-subjacent movement is possible only out of untensed clauses, exactly as the CLD predicts.

(27) a. [$_{CLD}$ Which fish$_i$ do you wonder how to eat t$_i$]
   b. [$_{CLD}$ Qué pescado$_i$ te preguntas cómo comer t$_i$]
   c. [$_{CLD}$ Quel poisson te demandes-tu comment manger t$_i$]

(28) a. *Which fish$_i$ do you wonder [CLD how the boy ate t$_i$]
    b. *Qué pescado$_i$ te preguntas [CLD cómo el chico comía t$_i$]
    c. *Quel poisson te demandes-tu [CLD comment le garcon a mangé t$_i$]

In other words, even in light of the inaccurate prediction it makes for (26b), the CLD still looks to be a universally necessary context for licensing, and in the case of (27) and (28) it is sufficient as well. In (26b), the necessary condition for licensing is met within the CLD, but some sufficient condition is not met. If then we retain the CLD as a principle of universal grammar, we are left to rule out (26b) and its French counterpart, (29b), through some parameter that will explain the exceptional lack in Romance languages of parasitic gaps in tensed clauses.

(29) a. Quel livre$_i$ as-tu perdu t$_i$ avant Op$_i$ de lire e$_i$?
      "What book did you lose before reading?"
    b. *Quel livre$_i$ as-tu perdu t$_i$ avant Op$_i$ que Sprout a lu e$_i$?
      "What book did you lose before Sprout read?"

To define the operative parameter that prevents the occurrence in French-type languages of parasitic gaps such as (26b) and (29b), we might start by acknowledging that in Romance languages, as Chomsky (1988) suggests, the AGR node is endowed with some syntactic character that the English AGR node lacks. For example, the French AGR can support overt raising of a verb so that *mange* in (30b) can raise from its D-structure position to the left of the adverb *souvent* while the English AGR cannot support a raised verb so that the English verb *eats* in (30a) remains in its base position at S-structure.

(30) a. Sprout often eats the salad.
    b. Sprout mange souvent la salade.

As such, the AGR node in Romance languages exerts a more influential impact on a structure, and it is not unreasonable to hypothesize that when it is marked as +strong by a +F head of FP, the Romance AGR will so affect the structure that contains it as to heighten opacity. Tentatively, then we could posit (31) as the relevant parameter.

(31) **Romance AGR Parameter**
    A CP that dominates a +strong, Romance AGR is a barrier to licensing.

For convenience of terminology, I will call a CP that is a barrier to licensing a "closed" CP.
    (31) would prevent the null operator in (26b) and (29b) from being licensed as that null operator is contained in a closed CP which would require the null operator to be licensed within the embedded CP. However, (31) would also prevent Comp-to-Comp movement out of a

tensed clause, as in (32), and (31) also predicts that tensed relative clauses such as (33) are impossible in Romance languages.

(32) Qué chica$_i$ [$_{VP}$ t"$_i$ [$_{VP}$ dijiste [$_{CP}$ t'$_i$ que Juan AGR   vio t$_i$]]]
                                                                    Romance
     "What girl did you say that John saw?"

(33) [$_{NP}$ la chica$_i$ [$_{CP}$ O$_i$ que Juan AGR   vio t$_i$]]
                                                    Romance
     "the girl that John saw"

In (32), the VP-adjoined trace t'' licenses the trace t' in the SPEC of the embedded CP even though that embedded CP dominates a +strong, Romance AGR and so by (31) it is closed to outside licensing. In (33), the NP *la chica* licenses the null operator even though this null operator also is a constituent of a closed CP that by (31) permits only CP-internal licensing. Clearly then, (31) is too powerful as a result of being aimed directly at (26b) and (29b), and it must be modified.

If we compare the parasitic gap structure we wish to rule out with (32) and (33), which the theory must accept, then the correct form of the Romance parameter on licensing emerges. The offending structure, with the relevant bracketing, is given in (34).

(34) *Qué articulos$_i$ [$_{VP}$ t'$_i$ [$_{VP}$ archivaste t$_i$] [$_{PP}$ antes de [$_{CP}$ Op$_i$ que AGR
                                                                              Romance

     leiste e$_i$]]]

In (34), the embedded CP dominates a +strong AGR since the CP is tensed and that AGR is also marked as +Romance which allows it to support a raised verb as in (30b). Because this CP dominates a +strong, Romance AGR, the licensing possibilities for its constituents are limited, but by (32) and (33) we know that a closed CP is receptive to external licensing from a measured distance.

Contrasting (32) and (33) with (34), it appears that a null operator dominated by a closed CP can be licensed only if the maximal projection that immediately dominates the closed CP does not exclude the potential licenser. That is, in (32), the VP-adjoined trace can license the trace in the SPEC of the closed CP because VP, the maximal projection that immediately dominates the closed CP, does not exclude the VP-adjoined trace. Likewise, the NP *la chica* in (33) can license the null operator in the closed CP because the licensing NP is not excluded by the maximal projection, the NP, that immediately dominates the closed CP. On the other hand, in (34), the closed CP containing the null operator is immediately dominated by the PP which excludes any potential licenser for the null operator. These observations are codified in (35).

(35) **Romance AGR Parameter**
     An element contained in a CP that dominates a +strong, Romance AGR can only be licensed within the maximal projection that

immediately dominates the CP in question. (where "within"= "not excluded by")

Applying (35) in combination with the CLD we correctly rule out parasitic gaps in tensed adjuncts such as in (26b) while allowing all other instances of parasitic gaps or movement that meet the necessary condition for licensing within the CLD.

Now only the ungrammaticality of (2a), repeated here as (36), remains to be accounted for.

(36) *¿Qué articulos$_i$ archivaste t$_i$ antes de leerlos$_i$?
      "What articles did you file after reading them?"

Taking clitics to be self-licensing pronominals, the ungrammaticality of (36) is suprising since the clitic *los* is at a far enough remove from its binder *qué articulos* that neither Aoun's (1981, 1985) generalized binding conditions on A'-bound pronominals nor Contreras' (1987) anti-subjacency condition on A'-bound pronominals would be violated. Furthermore, as (2b), given again as (37), shows, a clitic can appear in the same embedded context that *los* in (36) appears in.

(37) Archivé los articulos$_i$ antes de leerlos$_i$.
      "I filed the articles without reading them."

(36) contrasts minimally with (37) in that in the ungrammatical sentence the clitic is A-bound, giving rise to the possibility that clitics operate under some sort of A' anti-c-command condition. This possibility appears confirmed by the discrepancy between (38a) and (38b)[7].

(38) a.   Juan le dio el libro$_i$ a los niños para leerlo$_i$.
           "John gave the book to the kids in order to read it."
      b. *¿Qué libro$_i$ le dio t$_i$ Juan a los niños para leerlo$_i$?
           "What book did John give to the kids in order to read it?"

However, as proved by (2b), which is repeated as (39), the aversion of clitics to A'-binding does not hold when the clitic is contained in a tensed adjunct.

(39) ¿Qué articulos$_i$ archivaste t$_i$ antes de que los$_i$ leiste?
      "What articles did you file after you read them?"

In other words, a clitic can be A'-bound as in (39) only where a null operator in the embedded SPEC(CP) could not be licensed. By the same token, a clitic cannot be A'-bound as in (36) if it is located in an embedded CP that would allow a null operator to be licensed. If, therefore, we posit a null operator associated with the clitic at D-structure, as demonstrated by (40), then the interaction of the Romance AGR Parameter with Contreras' (1987) anti-subjacency condition on A'-

bound pronominals given in (41) accurately predicts a clitic can only be A'-bound when it is contained in an untensed clause.

(40)   a. *¿Qué articulos$_i$ archivaste t$_i$ antes de[Op leerlos$_i$]?

      b. ¿Qué articulos$_i$ archivaste t$_i$ antes de[Op que los$_i$ leiste]?

(41) **Contreras' Anti-Subjacency Condition**

     An A'-bound pronominal must be nonsubjacent to its A'-binder.

Following Browning (1986), I assume a null operator has no index until it is licensed by Chomsky's (1986b) strong binding at S-structure by its antecedent. If it is strongly bound, the null operator assumes its binder's index, and if it is not strongly bound, the null operator deletes. As the licensing possibilities for the null operators in (40) are the same as they were for the corresponding parasitic gap structures where only the null operator in the untensed clause can be licensed, the respective S-structures for (40) are given in (42).

(42)   a. *¿Qué articulos$_i$ archivaste t$_i$ antes de[Op$_i$ leerlos$_i$]?

      b. ¿Qué articulos$_i$ archivaste t$_i$ antes de[e que los$_i$ leiste]?[8]

In (42a), because the clitic and its associated null operator appear in a CLD that includes a licenser for the null operator, the null operator is strongly bound and therefore adopts an index rather than deleting. As *Op* is subjacent to *los* , the pronominal it binds, (42a) is a violation of Contreras' anti-subjacency condition. On the other hand, in (42b) the null operator associated with the clitic cannot be licensed as the Romance AGR Parameter blocks strong binding, and the null operator deletes. As such, the pronominal clitic is anti-subjacent to its nearest A'-binder, *qué articulos* , and so (42b) results in an acceptable structure.

    So it is that a universally necessary domain for licensing, the CLD, predicts the length of structure in which an element must be licensed in fulfillment of the principle of FI. In addition, a parameterized restriction on licensing, the Romance AGR Parameter, explains the absence of parasitic gaps in tensed adjunct clauses in Romance languages without precluding the possibility of that sort of parasitic gap appearing in other languages where permitted by the CLD. As such, we have a theory of chain licensing that begins to root out certain narrow theoretic formulations such as subjacency to lead grammatical theory to a stricter adherence to the principles and parameters approach to the language faculty.

---

* I would like to thank Heles Contreras, Carlos Otero, and Pascual Masullo for their advice, encouragement, and most of all, their easygoing attitude towards having their native Spanish hacked apart by a Southern accent. Also, I am supremely grateful to and for my wife Bridget who makes even the gray life of graduate study sparkle. Of course, even with the surpassing quality of the afore mentioned help, I made all errors contained herein by myself.

[1] I follow the standard practice of denoting with "*t* " the "real" gap created by overt *wh*-movement, while I represent the parasitic gap with "*e* ".

[2] Browning (1986) uses Chomsky's (1986a) definition of subjacency, which is as in (i):

(i) β is *n*-subjacent to α if there are fewer than *n* + 1 barriers for β which exclude α .

A barrier is any maximal projection except IP that is not Θ−marked or any maximal projection, including IP, that immediately dominates a barrier or an IP. α is excluded by a maximal projection only if every segment of that maximal projection dominates α. Thus, in (ii), A excludes α, but B does not, and both A and B exclude β.

(ii) ...β...[$_B$...α...[$_B$...[$_A$...]...]...]

[3] By c-command, I take basically the m-command definition from Chomsky (1986a) given in (i).

(i) α c-commands β iff α does not dominate β and every maximal projection that dominates α dominates β.

[4] Initially, Chomsky claims that only French type languages have strong AGR and that English type languages always have weak AGR. Later however, he plainly states that a finite clause has a strong AGR. Either way, whether labelled "strong" and "weak" or whether identified by some other terminology (cf. Pollock (1988)), a finite clause will clearly distinguish its AGR nodes in a way a nonfinite clause will not. Also, in setting the parameter that accounts for the occurrence of parasitic gaps in tensed clauses in English but not in the French type languages (cf. the contrast between (1a) and (2a)), I attribute to the AGR in Romance languages a special qualitity which can be exploited to explain the fact that V raises in Romance languages but not in English type languages.

[5] Recall that besides the chain [t', Op] , all the other chain links involved in an parasitic gap structure such as (i) are formed by intra-clausal *wh*-movement. So, the other chains in (i), [wh , t' , t] and [Op , e] , are formed by the same action that yields (ii) and (iii) respectively, and thus the CLD involved for these chains in the containing CP.

(i)   Which book$_i$ did you [t'$_i$ [file t$_i$ before [Op$_i$ you had read e$_i$]]]?

(ii)   Which book$_i$ did you [t'$_i$ [file t$_i$]]?

(iii)   Which book$_i$ had you read t$_i$?

[6]Because (7a), the case of the English parasitic gap in an infinitival adjunct, has the same structure and analysis as its Spanish counterpart (24a), I have omitted it in this paradigm.

[7]Spanish judgements involving embedded clitics are treacherously slippery, and many speakers consider both sentences of (36) to be unacceptable. Even so, the crucial point is that some dialects do accept (36a) (the River Plate dialect of Argentina in particular), but no dialect (one shudders to speak with such finality on matters of Spanish judgements) accepts (36b).

[8]If the null operator in a parasitic gap construction should delete the way it does in (39b), then the sentence errs in not licensing e , the parasitic gap itself.

REFERENCES

Aoun, J. (1981) *The Formal Nature of Anaphoric Relations* . Ph.D. Thesis, MIT.

Aoun, J. (1985) *A Grammar of Anaphora* . Cambridge: MIT Press.

Aoun, J. & R. Clark (1984) On Non-overt Operators. ms. USC.

Bordelois, I. (1986) Parasitic Gaps: Extensions of Restructuring. In I. Bordelois, H. Contreras, K. Zagona (eds.), *Generative Studies in Spanish Syntax.* Dordrecht: Foris.

Browning, M. (1986) Null Operators and Their Antecedents. NELS 17, vol. 1., 59-78.

Chomsky, N. (1986a) *Barriers* . Cambridge: MIT Press.

Chomsky, N. (1986b) *Knowledge of Language* . New York: Praeger.

Chomsky, N. (1988) Some Notes on Economy of Derivation and Representation. ms., MIT.

Contreras, H. (1984) A Note on Parasitic Gaps. *Linguistic Inquiry* , 15, 698-701.

Contreras, H. (to appear) *Operators , Binding , and Subjacency.* ms., University of Washington, Seattle. (To be published by Reidel.)

A New Typology of Complement Clauses

Zixin Jiang
University of Chicago

Introduction

A distinction commonly made between complement clause types is the distinction between finite and non-finite clauses. Chomsky (1981,1982) among others has made this distinction. McCawley (1988) also recognizes such a distinction. In some theories, explanation for a number of linguistic phenomena impinges on this finite/nonfinite dichotomy. For instance, in GB (cf. Chomsky (1982)), this dichotomy is used to explain empty category phenomena among others. The questions are whether this finite/nonfinite dichotomy is universal and whether there are syntactic typologies of clauses other than this which have not yet been recognized.

To the first question, Huang's (1982) answer seems to be implicitly positive, because he thinks that even in a language like Chinese, in which no morphological evidence can be found to sustain this finite/nonfinite dichotomy, this dichotomy still exists, which is used to explain some empty category phenomena in Chinese. We will discuss this question in this paper.

To answer the second question is the major task of this paper. In this paper, we propose that the evidence for the existence of the finite/nonfinite dichotomy in Chinese is insufficient while a new syntactic typology of Chinese complement clauses should be recognized. Because the new typology of Chinese clauses concerns the syntactic notions of topic and subject in Chinese, we will, first of all, have a brief discussion of topic and subject in Chinese and make clear our assumptions. Secondly, we will try to show that the evidence to sustain the finite/nonfinite dichotomy in Chinese is insufficient. Then, we will propose the new typology of Chinese complement clauses, which will be followed by some concluding remarks.

Topic and subject in Chinese

Li and Thompson (1976) have pointed out that for an adequate description of Chinese syntax there should be, in addition to the notion of subject, also the notion of topic. In contrast to subjects, topics in Chinese are not subcategorized for by the main verb and their semantic roles are not determined by the main verb (or VP). The function of topics is only to express what the rest of the sentence is about.

The syntactic reflection of the notion of topic in clear cases is an additional NP (or, according to Xu and Langendoen (1985), any maximal projection) to the left of the subject. For instance,

> (1) Zhe chang huo xiaofangdui lai   de hen   zhao.
>   this UNIT fire fire-brigade come DE very early
>   (As for) this fire, the fire-brigade came very early.

In (1), *zhe chang huo* (this fire) is a topic, which is not subcategorized for by the main verb[1] *lai* (come) and its semantic role is not determined by the verb either, and *xiaofangdui* (fire-brigade) is the subject because it is subcategorized for by the verb and its semantic role is determined by the verb. In some cases, things are not as clear. For instance,

(2) a. Lisi kanjian guo Zhangsan.
        see   ASP
     Lisi has seen Zhangsan before.
     b. Zhangsan Lisi kanjian guo.
                    see   ASP
     Lisi has seen Zhangsan.
     c. Zai zhongguo Zhangsan you hen duo   pengyou.
        in China   have very many friend
        In China Zhangsan has many friends.
     d. Chi fan Zhangsan zhi chi yi   wan.
        eat rice   only eat one bowl
        Zhangsan only eats one bowl of rice.

(2a) is ambiguous in that *Lisi* can be a topic with an empty subject in front of the verb or simply a subject. In (2b), *Zhangsan* is also considered as a topic, even though, in the semantic interpretation of this sentence, it seems to be subcategorized for by the verb *kanjian* (see) and have its semantic role determined by the verb. This is because the position which *Zhangsan* takes in (2b) is a topic position and the normal position for an object is behind the verb. We will treat sentences like (2b) as having an empty object following the verb and the topic gets interpreted as if it were an object of the verb through semantic interpretation. In (2c) and (2d), the PP *zai zhongguo* (in China) and the VP *chi fan* (eat rice) are also topics according to Xu and Langendoen (1985). We don't want to take a stand as to whether they are also topics. However, as will be shown later, they stand in the same structural relation with the rest of the sentence as those NP topics. Topics can also appear in embedded clauses, for instance, in (3),

(3) Zhangsan zhidao Lisi Wangwu meiyou kanjian.
         know   NEG   see
    Zhangsan knows that Wangwu didn't see Lisi.

Lisi is a topic in the complement clause of the verb *zhidao* (know). Quite a number of linguists have studied topics in Chinese. Interested readers are referred to Li & Thompson (1981 pp. 85-102), Huang (1982) and Xu and Langendoen (1985) among others.
    We will assume here without showing too much evidence that, in terms of constituency structure, a topic (as well as the other maximal projections in the same position, if they are not topics) is a sister node of an S node dominated by another S, namely, (4), as Xu and Langendoen (1985) have proposed

(4)   ╭─S─╮
        XP^2 S

There is some evidence for it. In McCawley (1988), tests for constituency structure have been proposed. One   such test can very well be applied to test the structure in (4). In such sentences as (5)

(5) a. Lisi Zhangsan meiyou kanjian danshi Wangwu   kanjian le .
                      NEG   see   but   see   ASP
        Zhangsan didn't see Lisi but Wangwu saw (Lisi).

b. Zai zhongguo Zhangsan you hen duo pengyou danshi Lisi you
   in China   have very many friend but   have
   hen duo zhouren.
   very many enemy
   In China, Zhangsan has many friends and Lisi has many enemies.

the topic *Lisi* and the PP *zai zhongguo* (in China) are followed by two S's
connected by the conjunction *danshi* (but). (4) provides an explanation for the well-
formedness of (5).

For subjects, we will assume that they are sisters of VP's dominated by an
S, namely,

(6)

$$\text{NP} \diagup \text{S} \diagdown \text{VP}$$

It is more difficult to show that subjects are really sisters of VP's because, in most
cases, 'subjects' are ambiguously subjects or topics. However, as Li & Thompson
(1981) have pointed out, topics in Chinese are always at least specific and in most
cases definite.[3] Thus, when a subject is non-specific, it will not have a chance of
being a topic. In Chinese, the word *youren* is ambiguous in that it can either mean
some people/a certain person or there-are-people/there-is-a-person. When it carries
the latter sense, it cannot be a topic. Thus, in (7),

(7) Youren   meiyou lai.
    there-are-people NEG   come
    There are people who didn't come.

youren (there-are-people) cannot be a topic but only a subject. In such cases, the
string of *meiyou lai* (didn't come) can only be conjoined with other VP's but not
S's, e.g.,

(8) a. Youren   meiyou lai   yie meiyou tongzhi Zhangsan.
        there-are-people NEG   come also NEG   notify
        There are people who didn't come and didn't notify Zhangsan
        either.
     b. *Youren   meiyou lai   danshi Zhangsan qu baifang le.
        there-are-people NEG   come but   go visit ASP
        There are people who didn't come but Zhangsan went to visit.[4]

We will also assume that the top nodes in (4) and (6) are both S's because a
clause in the form of (4) can conjoin with a clause in the form of (6), as in

(9) Lisi wo bu   zhidao huibuhui   lai danshi youren   hui lai.
      I NEG know will-not-will come but there-are-people will come
    I don't know whether Lisi will come but there are people who will
    come.

In sum, we will assume here that topics (as well as the other maximal
projections in this position) are sisters of S's dominated by another S node while
subjects are sisters of VP's dominated by an S node. It seems that there are reasons

to claim (4) and (6) are two types of clauses in Chinese, to which we will return. However, before getting into the discussion of these two types of clauses, we will first discuss briefly the existence of the finite/nonfinite dichotomy in Chinese.

The finite/nonfinite dichotomy in Chinese

In languages such as English and French, where there are tense and person inflections, it seems to be well-grounded to claim that there is a distinction between finite and non-finite clauses. Moreover, in some languages, such as English and German, there are morphemes marking the non-finiteness, for instance, *to* and *ing* in English and *zu* in German. In contrast to these languages, Chinese doesn't have any tense inflections for the verbs or morphemes marking the non-finiteness. For such a language as Chinese, cautions must be taken before any conclusion can be drawn as to whether the finite/nonfinite dichotomy exists.

To account for such a contrast as between (10a) and (10b),

> (10) a. *Lisi Zhangsan yao *e* qu meiguo.
>   want   go   US
>   Zhangsan wants Lisi to go to the States.
> b. Lisi Zhangsan zhidao *e* meiyou qu meiguo.
>   know   NEG go US
>   Zhangsan knows that Lisi has not gone to the States.

Huang (1982) has evoked the finite/nonfinite dichotomy. His explanation is that in (10a) the *e* is not governed, the string of *e qu meiguo* (*e* go to the States) being a non-finite clause while in (10b) the *e* is governed, the string of *e meiyou qu meiguo* (*e* hasn't gone to the States) being a finite clause. He provides mainly one piece of evidence to support his claim that the finite/nonfinite dichotomy does exist in Chinese, which is that verbs in non-finite clauses cannot take aspect markers such as *le* (perfective) and *guo* (experiential) while verbs in finite clauses can, for instance,

> (11) a. *Zhangsan yao qu le   meiguo.
>   want go ASP US
>   Zhangsan wants that (Zhangsan) has gone to the States.
> b. Zhangsan zhidao Lisi qu le   meiguo.
>   know   go ASP US
>   Zhangsan knows that Lisi has gone to the States.

However, if the ability of the verb to take an aspect marker is taken as the diagnostic test for the finiteness/nonfiniteness of a clause, then there can be found cases where an empty subject in a finite clause cannot be bound by a variable (topic) either , for instance,

> (12) a. *Lisi Zhangsan houhui *e* qu le   meiguo.
>   regret   qo ASP US
>   Zhangsan regrets that Lisi has gone to the States.
> b. *Lisi Zhangsan fouren qu guo meiguo.
>   deny go ASP US
>   Zhangsan denies that Lisi has been to the States.

In (12a), the verb *qu* (go) has the perfective aspect marker *le* and thus according to

Huang (1982) the string of *e qu le meiguo* (*e* has gone to the States) should be a finite clause, in which the *e* should be governed and should be able to be bound by the topic *Lisi* . The case with (12b) is similar except that the aspect marker is the experiential *guo* .

Y. Li (1985) and A. Li (1985) have both come up with more arguments for the finite/non-finite dichotomy in Chinese. However, Xu (1986) has shown that the evidence they provided for their claim is insufficient, and suggested that the ability for the verb in the complement clause to take aspect markers is determined by the semantics of the matrix verb.

Thus, the evidence for the existence of finite/nonfinite dichotomy in Chinese is far from conclusive. For a language like Chinese, where there are found no overt marking for the finiteness or nonfiniteness of a clause, far more evidence is needed before one can claim with confidence that such a dichotomy exists.

On the other hand, if we put Chinese under a new perspective, a new typology of Chinese clauses will emerge, which is surely better-grounded than the finite/nonfinite dichotomy. This is the focus of discussion of the next section.

A new typology of clauses

As we have noted in an earlier section, we will assume that (4) (repeated here)

(4)
$$S \atop XP \quad S$$

is the constituent structure for a clause with a topic or some other maximal projection in this position. We will also assume here that the constituent structure of a clause with a verb and both its internal and external arguments but without any constituent in the topic position is like (6) (repeated here).

(6)
$$S \atop NP \quad VP$$

We will call clauses in the form of (4) <u>Saturated Clause</u> (SC) and clauses in the form of (6) <u>Non-saturated clause</u> (NSC). It will be shown below that certain verbs take only NSC's as complements while others take either type. Of course, before we can do this, we need to show first that certain verbs do take clausal complements. In the following, we will take *xiangxin* (believe), *xihuan* (like) and *qiangpo* (force) as representative of verbs taking clausal complements. We will show first that both *xiangxin* (believe) and *xihuan* (like) take clausal complements while *qiangpo* (force) takes as complements a NP and a VP/S.[5] Then, it will be shown that *xihuan* (like) can only take as complements NSC's but not SC's while *xiangxin* (believe) can take either SC's or NSC's.

Look at the following sentences:

(13) a. Zhangsan xiangxin Lisi qu kan le Wangwu.
           believe   go   see   ASP
    Zhangsan believes that Lisi has gone to see Wangwu.
  b. Zhangsan xihuan Lisi qu kan Wangwu.
          like   go   see
    Zhangsan likes that Lisi goes to see Wangwu.

232

   c. Zhangsan qiangpo Lisi qu kan   Wangwu.
       force   go   see
    Zhangsan forced Lisi to go to see Wangwu.

If no constituency structure is given, all the sentences in (13) look linearly the same, namely, they are all

    (14) NP V   **NP**   **VP**

However, when they are scrutinized, using tests developed in McCawley (1988) or developed following the spirit of McCawley (1988), it is revealed that they are structurally different. We want to propose here that the constituency structures of (13a, b and c) are respectively

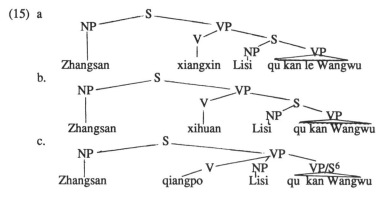

As is set up in (15), it can be seen that the complements of both the verbs *xiangxin* (believe) and *xihuan* (like) are S's while the verb *qiangpo* (force) takes a NP in addition to a VP/S complement. There are quite a few pieces of evidence supporting this view.

The first piece of evidence has to do with existential sentences (cf. Li (1972)) and meteorological sentences. By existential sentences, I am referring to such sentences as

    (16) you ren   qu   kan   Wangwu.
       have people go   see
    There are people going to see Wangwu.

(16) can be analyzed in either of the following two ways. One of them is that it is just like *there* -sentences in English without the existential *there* . The other way is to treat *you ren* (have people) as a NP with an indefinite meaning. If it is considered as a NP, it cannot function as the object of a verb. For instance,

    (17) *Zhangsan da   le   you   ren.
           hit ASP have people
    Zhangsan hit somebody.

Under either of the two analyses of (16), it can be predicted that an ungrammatical sentence will result when (16) is embedded under the verb *qiangpo* (force). This is because, as (15c) shows, the verb *qiangpo* (force) takes a NP and a VP/S, and, if (16) is an existential sentence like the English counterpart , then the verb *qiangpo* (force) lacks a NP, or, if *you ren* (have people) is a NP, it cannot function as the object NP of the verb *qiangpo* (force). The prediction is borne out:

(18) *Zhangsan qiangpo you ren   qu kan Wangwu.
          force   have people go see

On the other hand, since both the verbs *xiangxin* (believe) and *xihuan* (like) take clausal complements, as is shown in (15a,b), grammatical sentences should result when (16) is embedded under either *xiangxin* (believe) or *xihuan* (like). This prediction is also borne out:

(19) a. Zhangsan xiangxin you ren   qu kan Wangwu.
             believe   have people go see
        Zhangsan believes that there are people going to see Wangwu.
     b. Zhangsan xihuan you ren   qu kan Wangwu.
             like   have people go see
        Zhangsan likes that there are people going to see Wangwu.

By meteorological sentences, I am referring to sentences talking about weather such as:

(20) Xia   yu.
      fall   rain
      It is raining.

Unlike meteorological sentences in English, in which a meteorological *it* is needed to function as the subject, Chinese meteorological sentences usually don't have any NP in front of the verb. When sentences like (20) are embedded under the verb *qiangpo* (force), the result should be ungrammatical since the verb will be lacking an object NP:

(21) *Zhangsan qiangpo xia yu.
          force   fall rain
       Zhangsan forced it to rain.

When (20) is embedded under either the verb *xiangxin* (believe) or the verb *xihuan* (like), the results are grammatical since both these verbs take only sentential complements:

(22) a. Zhangsan xiangxin xia yu le.
              believe   fall rain ASP
        Zhangsan believes that it is raining.
     b. Zhangsan xihuan xia yu.
              like   fall rain
        Zhangsan likes it to be raining.

To sum up, the fact that existential and meteorological sentences cannot be embedded under the verb *qiangpo* (force) but they can under the verbs *xiangxin* (believe) and *xihuan* (like) supports the structures set up for the complements of these verbs in (15).

The second piece of evidence has to do with topics. As Xu and Langendoen (1985) point out, a topic should be one maximal projection. The relevant facts we can find out about the verbs *xiangxin* (believe), *xihuan* (like) and *qiangpo* (force) are that the complements of the former two can be topics[7] while the NP and the VP/S after the verb *qiangpo* (force) cannot be a topic.

(23) a. Lisi qu kan le Wangwu Zhangsan xiangxin.
        go see ASP   believe
      (As for) Lisi has gone to see Wangwu, Zhangsan believes (it).
   b. Lisi qu kan Wangwu Zhangsan xihuan.
        go see   like
      (As for) Lisi goes to see Wangwu, Zhangsan likes (it).
   c.*Lisi qu kan Wangwu Zhangsan qiangpo.
        go see   force
      (As for) Lisi goes to see Wangwu, Zhangsan forced (him to).

The grammaticality of (23) is predicted by the structures of the complements set up in (15) for the three verbs.

Linguists have studied cleft and pseudo-cleft sentences. Teng (1979) has studied what he calls cleft sentences in Chinese. I know of nobody who has suggested that there are also pseudo-cleft sentences in Chinese and studied them. However, there are, in Chinese, such sentences as:

(24) Zhangsan chi de shi yu.
           eat DE be fish
    What Zhangsan eats is fish.

The function of sentences like (24) is similar to English pseudo-cleft sentences, namely, focusing one constituent in the sentence. Here in (24), the object NP *yu* (fish) of the verb *chi* (eat) is focused. The syntactic device used in sentences like (24) is also similar to that used in English pseudo-cleft sentences, namely, nominalization/relativization. I will call such Chinese sentences as (24) pseudo-cleft sentences. For Chinese pseudo-cleft sentences, just like their English counterparts, only one constituent can be focused. Thus, the following sentences are both bad

(25) a. *What John gave is Mary a book.
   b. *Zhangsan gei de shi Lisi yi ben shu.
             give DE be   one UNIT book
    What Zhangsan gave is Lisi a book.

because two constituents are in the focus position. This can be used as a test for the constituency structure of the complements of those verbs in Chinese I have been discussing.

The complements of both the verbs *xiangxin* (believe) and *xihuan* (like) can appear in the focus position in pseudo-cleft sentences while the complements of the verb *qiangpo* (force) cannot.

(26) a. Zhangsan xiangxin de   shi Lisi qu kan le   Wangwu.
            believe DE   be   go see   ASP
            What Zhangsan believes is that Lisi has gone to see Wangwu.
     b. Zhangsan xihuan   de   shi Lisi   qu kan Wangwu.
            like   DE   be   go see
            What Zhangsan likes is for Lisi to go to see Wangwu.
     c. *Zhangsan qiangpo de   shi Lisi   qu kan Wangwu.
            force   DE   be   go see
            What Zhangsan forced is for Lisi to go to see Wangwu.

If the structures in (15) are accepted as the respective structures of the complements of the verbs, then we have an explanation for the contrast in grammaticality in (26).

More revealing is that the VP/S complement of the verb *qiangpo* (force) can appear in the focus position of a pseudo-cleft sentence while the same thing cannot be done with the complements of the other two verbs. For example,

(27) a. *Zhangsan xiangxin Lisi de   shi qu kan   le Wangwu.
            believe   DE   be go see   ASP
            What Zhangsan believes Lisi is that (he) has gone to see Wangwu.
     b. *Zhangsan xihuan   Lisi de   shi qu   kan Wangwu.
            like   DE   shi qu   kan Wangwu.
            What Zhangsan likes Lisi is to go to see Wangwu.
     c. Zhangsan qiangpo Lisi de   shi qu   kan Wangwu.
            force   DE   be go   see
            What Zhangsan forced Lisi is to go to see Wangwu.

It seems that the Chinese pseudo-cleft examples given above support the structures set up in (15) for the complements of those three verbs.

The conjoining phenomenon also provides support to the structures in (15). McCawley (1988) has pointed out that, in conjoining, one single constituent should conjoin with another. It will be ungrammatical if two or more constituents conjoin with other constituents. With regard to the complements of the three Chinese verbs we have been discussing, the complements of the verbs *xiangxin* (believe) and *xihuan* (like) can conjoin with another sentence while the complements of the verb *qiangpo* (force) cannot.

(28) a. Zhangsan xiangxin Lisi qu kan le Wangwu Zhaoliu qu kan le
            believe   go see ASP   go see ASP
            Qianqi.
            Zhangsan believes that Lisi has gone to see Wangwu and Zhaoliu
            has gone to see Qianqi.
     b. Zhangsan xihuan Lisi qu kan Wangwu Zhaoliu qu kan Qianqi.
            like   go see   go see
            Zhangsan likes that Lisi goes to see Wangwu and Zhaoliu goes to
            see Qianqi.
     c. *Zhangsan qiangpo Lisi qu kan Wangwu Zhaoliu qu kan Qianqi.
            force   go see   go see
            Zhangsan forced Lisi to go to see Wangwu and Zhaoliu to go to
            see Qianqi.

If the complements of the verb *qiangpo* (force) consist of a NP and a VP/S, then the ill-formedness of (28c) is predicted.

One further piece of evidence is related to the omission of constituents. It is usually the case that, if the subject of a complement clause is retained, then, at least, the main verb of that clause will have to be retained as well. Let's first have a look at a clear-case complement clause.

> (29) Zhangsan gaosu Lisi Wangwu qu   kan le   Zhaoliu.
>   tell   go   see ASP
>   Zhangsan told Lisi that Wangwu has gone to see Zhaoliu.

In (29), it is beyond any doubt that *Wangwu qu kan le Zhaoliu* (Wangwu has gone to see Zhaoliu) is a complement sentence, and in the complement clause of the second sentence in the following example,

> (30) Zhangsan gaosu Lisi Wangwu qu kan le Zhaoliu. Lisi gaosu
>   tell   go see ASP   tell
>   Zhangsan Qianqi yie qu (kan) le.
>   too go see ASP
>   Zhangsan told Lisi that Wangwu has gone to see Zhaoliu. Lisi told
>   Zhangsan that Qianqi has too.

the subject *Qianqi* as well as the main verb *qu* (go) is present and (30) is grammatical. However, in (31):

> (31) *Zhangsan gaosu Lisi Wangwu qu kan le Zhaoliu. Lisi gaosu
>   tell   go see ASP   tell
>   Zhangsan Qianqi (yie).
>   too
>   Zhangsan told Lisi that Wangwu has gone to see Zhaoliu. Lisi told
>   Zhangsan Qianqi has (too).

the subject of the complement clause in the second sentence is present but the main verb has been deleted together with the other constituents of the VP and (31) is ruled out.

The possibility of omission in the complements of the three verbs *xiangxin* (believe), *xihuan* (like) and *qiangpo* (force) seems also to support the structures in (15). For the first two verbs, the situation is just like that in (31).

> (32) a. *Zhangsan xiangxin Lisi qu kan le Wangwu. Zhaoliu xiangxin
>   believe   go see ASP   believe
>   Qianqi.
>   Zhangsan believes that Lisi has gone to see Wangwu. Zhaoliu
>   believes that Qianqi (has gone to see Wangwu).
>   b. *Zhangsan xihuan Lisi qu kan Wangwu. Zhaoliu xihuan Qianqi.
>   like   go see   like
>   Zhangsan like Lisi to go to see Wangwu. Zhaoliu likes Qianqi (to
>   go to see Wangwu).

That (32) are both bad can be explained by the structures in (15), namely, the verbs *xiangxin* (believe) and *xihuan* (like) both take clausal complements. On the other hand, the verb *qiangpo* (force) behaves differently.

(33) Zhangsan qiangpo Lisi qu kan Wangwu. Zhaoliu qiangpo Qianqi.
        force   go see   force
    Zhangsan forced Lisi to go to see Wangwu. Zhaoliu forced Qianqi
    (to go to see Wangwu).

(33) is good though the VP/S is left out. This supports the claim that the NP and the VP/S complements of the verb *qiangpo* (force) don't form one clause.

    To sum up, it seems that the evidence supporting (15) is quite overwhelming. No sign of RAISING can be found either in the complements of the verbs of *xiangxin* (believe) and *xihuan* (like). If the structures in (15) are correct, then the complements of both *xiangxin* (believe) and *xihuan* (like) are a single S.

    The complements of both the verbs *xiangxin* (believe) and *xihuan* (like) are S's. However, these two verbs take as complements different types of clauses, namely, *xihuan* (like) can only take NSC's while *xiangxin* (believe) takes SC's, which will look sometimes like NSC's when the XP position is empty.

(34) a. Zhangsan xiangxin Wangwu Lisi qu kan le.
              believe   go see   ASP
      Zhangsan believes that (as for) Wangwu, Lisi has gone to see
      (Wangwu).
    b. *Zhangsan xihuan Wangwu Lisi qu kan.
           like   go see
      Zhangsan likes (as for) Wangwu Lisi goes to see (Wangwu).

In (34), the complements of both the verbs are SC's. However, (34b) is bad while (34a) is perfect. Verbs which, like *xihuan* (like), can only take NSC's as complements include: *xiangyao* (want), *fouren* (deny), *yingchi* (cause), *zhaochen* (result in), *houhui* (regret) among others.

    A question might be raised, namely, is the ill-formedness of (34b) due to the restriction that the verb *xihuan* (like) cannot take NSC's as complements or due to the restriction that there can only be one preverbal NP in the complement? The answer seems to be that it is due to the former restriction.

    If there is only one preverbal NP but it is a topic rather than a subject in the complement, it is still ungrammatical.

(35) *Zhangsan xihuan Lisi zhuazou.
            like   arrest
    Zhangsan likes Lisi to be arrested.

In (35), the NP *Lisi* is a topic in the complement clause and the subject (the person who arrested Lisi) is left out unexpressed. There is only one pre-verbal NP in it but it is still bad. However, when *bei* shows up in the complement clause, the sentence immediately becomes grammatical, because *Lisi* can be the subject in such a passive clause.

(36) Zhangsan xihuan Lisi bei zhuazou.
           like   BEI   arrest
    Zhangsan likes Lisi to be arrested.

With the object of *bei* present, the sentence is also grammatical.

(37) Zhangsan xihuan Lisi bei   jingcha zhuazou.
              like   BEI   police   arrest
              Zhangsan likes Lisi to be arrested by police.

The reader may recall that SC's have an XP as the sister of an S and in the above we have only shown that verbs like *xihuan* (like) cannot take clauses in the form of (38),

(38)

$$\text{NP} \underset{\diagup}{\overset{\diagup \text{S} \diagdown}{}} \text{S}$$

Can those verbs take SC's as complements with other maximal projections instead of the NP in (38)? In Chinese, time and place PP's can also appear in that position, as in (39) and (40).

(39)   (Zai) chufangli Zhangsan zenzai   ku.
         in kitchen   ASP   weep
         In the kitchen Zhangsan is weeping.

(40)   (Zai) xingqiyi Lisi qu kan le Wangwu.
         on Monday   go see ASP
         On Monday Lisi went to see Wangwu.

We will call the PP's in (39) and (40) sentence-initial PP's.
    Verbs like *xiangxin* (believe) can take clausal complements with sentence-initial PP's, as in (41).

(41) a. Zhangsan xiangxin (zai) chufangli Lisi zenzai   ku.
           believe   in kitchen   ASP   weep
           Zhangsan believes that (in) the kitchen Lisi is weeping.
      b. Zhangsan xiangxin (zai) xingqiyi Lisi qu kan le Wangwu.
           believe   on Monday   go see ASP
           Zhangsan believes that (on) Monday Lisi went to see Wangwu.

However, verbs like *xihuan* (like) cannot take clausal complements with sentence-initial PP's but only with PP's after the subject, as shown in (42).

(42) a. Zhangsan xihuan Lisi zai chufangli kan shu.
           like   in kitchen   read book
           Zhangsan likes Lisi to read in the kitchen.
      b. Zhangsan xihuan Lisi (zai) xingqiyi   qu kan Wangwu.
           like   on Monday go see
           Zhangsan likes Lisi to go to see Wangwu on Monday.
      c. *Zhangsan xihuan (zai) chufangli Lisi kan shu.
           like   in kitchen   read book
           Zhangsan likes Lisi to read in the kitchen.
      d. *Zhangsan xihuan (zai) xingqiyi Lisi qu kan Wangwu.
           like   on Monday   go see
           Zhangsan likes Lisi to go to see Wangwu on Monday.

The contrast between (41) and (42) seems to show that the difference between the clause types verbs like *xiangxin* (believe) and verbs like *xihuan* (like) can take is not merely whether the clauses can accommodate a NP topic or not, but really the difference between (4) and (6), namely, between SC's and NSC's.

As a matter of fact, not only time and place PP's are relevant here but also some other PP's. In matrix sentences, some PP's can appear in front of the subject. In the following sentences,

(43) a. Guanyu zhe jian   shi Lisi mei   fabiao   yijian.
       about this UNIT matter   NEG publish opinion
       About this matter, Lisi didn't voice (his) opinion.
     b. Weile Zhaoliu Lisi qu   kan le Wangwu.
        for   go   see ASP
        For Zhaoliu, Lisi went to see Wangwu.

the PP's *guanyu zhe jian shi* (about this matter) and *weile Zhaoliu* (for Zhaoliu) are in front of the subject. As complements of verbs like *xiangxin* (believe), such sentences are fine.

(44) a. Zhangsan xiangxin guanyu zhe jian shi Lisi mei   fabiao   yijian.
                 believe about   this UNIT matter NEG publish opinion
        Zhangsan believes that about this matter Lisi didn't voice (his) opinion.
     b. Zhangsan xiangxin weile Zhaoliu Lisi qu kan le Wangwu.
                 believe   for   go see ASP
        Zhangsan believes that for Zhaoliu Lisi went to see Wangwu.

However, they are ruled out as complements of verbs like *xihuan* (like).

(45) a. *Zhangsan xihuan guanyu zhe jian   shi Lisi bu   fabiao yijian.
                  like   about this UNIT matter NEG publish opinion
        Zhangsan like about this matter Lisi not to voice (his) opinion.
     b. *Zhangsan xihuan weile Zhaoliu Lisi qu kan Wangwu.
                  like   for   go see
        Zhangsan likes for Zhaoliu Lisi goes to see Wangwu.

The other types of maximal projections, for instance, VP's (see (2d)), behave the same way as sentence-initial PP's when they appear in the XP position in (4).

From the above, it can be seen that certain verbs which take clausal complements can only take NSC's as their complements while others take SC's. Thus, it will be well-grounded if Chinese complement clauses are typologically divided into NSC's and SC's.

In English it seems that the ability of taking a sentence-initial constituent coincides with the finiteness of the clauses, for instance,

(46) a. We know that in New York people walk at a fast pace.
     b. *John would like frequently for Mary to exercise.

In Chinese, if the finite/non-finite distinction existed and the ability of the verb to take an aspect marker were the sign of finiteness, then the ability of taking a sentence-initial constituent and the finiteness of the clause don't coincide, for example,

(47) *Zhe jian shi   zhaochen Lisi Zhangsan meiyou qu kan.
    this UNIT matter result-in   NEG go see
    This incident resulted in Zhangsan not having gone to see Lisi.

in which the verb in the complement clause of the verb *zhaochen* (result in) takes *meiyou* (NEG), which, according to Wang (1965), is the negative counterpart of *le* (perfective aspect marker), and the complement clause should be a finite clause. However, such a complement clause still doesn't allow a sentence-initial constituent. Thus, the distinction between NSC's and SC's is an independent distinction and cannot be subsumed under the finite/non-finite dichotomy.

Conclusion

In the previous section, evidence is shown to support the claim that both the verbs *xiangxin* (believe) and *xihuan* (like) take clausal complements with no RAISING having taken place while the verb *qiangpo* (force) takes as complements a NP and a VP/S, and it is also shown that even though the former two verbs both take clausal complements, their complement clauses belong to different types. The verb *xiangxin* (believe) takes as a complement either a SC or a NSC while the verb *xihuan* (like) takes only a NSC. The difference between a SC and a NSC is that a SC expands into XP S while a NSC only into NP VP.

In a way the difference between SC and NSC seems to be related to the topic phenomenon in matrix sentences. A matrix topic in a sentence with *xiangxin* (believe) as the main verb can be interpreted as the subject of the complement S (a SC) while it cannot in a sentence with *xihuan* (like) as the main verb as the subject of its complement S (a NSC).

(48) a. Lisi Zhangsan xiangxin qu   kan le Wangwu.
                      believe   go see ASP
      (As for) Lisi, Zhangsan believes that (Lisi) has gone to see
      Wangwu.
      b. *Lisi Zhangsan xihuan qu kan Wangwu.
                  like   go see
      (As for) Lisi, Zhangsan likes (Lisi) to go to see Wangwu.

This contrast between (48a,b) cannot be explained by utilizing the difference between a SC and a NSC and stipulating that the matrix topic is interpreted as the topic of the complement S first and then the subject. This is because there is subject-object asymmetry (cf. Huang (1982)).[8] A matrix topic can be interpreted as the subject of the complement S of *xiangxin* (believe) but cannot in case of *xihuan* (like). However, a matrix topic can be interpreted as the object in the complement S in both cases.

(49) a. Wangwu Zhangsan xiangxin Lisi qu kan le.
                     believe   go see ASP
      (As for) Wangwu, Zhangsan believes that Lisi has gone to see
      (Wangwu).
      b. Wangwu Zhangsan xihuan Lisi qu kan.
                  like   go see
      (As for) Wangwu, Zhangsan likes Lisi to go to see (Wangwu).

If the above-mentioned line of explanation is taken, then why (49b) is grammatical will remain a problem because the complement S is a NSC and the NP *Wangwu* cannot be interpreted as the topic of the complement S first and then as the object. This will have to wait for further research.

Another phenomenon that is still a puzzle is that SC's can be cleft sentences (cf. Teng (1979)) while NSC's cannot.

(50) a. Zhangsan xiangxin Lisi shi qu kan le Wangwu.
               believe   be go see ASP
       Zhangsan believes that it is Wangwu that Lisi has gone to see.
     b. *Zhangsan xihuan Lisi shi qu kan Wangwu.
             like   be go see
       Zhangsan likes it to be Wangwu that Lisi goes to see.

The fact that NSC's don't allow cleft sentences cannot be attributed to semantic reasons because NSC's allow pseudo-cleft sentences.

(51) Zhangsan xihuan Lisi qu kan de   shi Wangwu.
           like   go see DE   be
     Zhangsan likes (the person) Lisi is going to see to be Wangwu.

A possible direction to go is to see whether in cleft sentences the constituents in front of *shi* (be) are topics. If they are topics, then we have an explanation, that is, NSC's don't have a position for topics. However, much further research is needed before anything certain can be said.

Footnote

[1] We are neutral as to whether there should be a distinction between verbs and adjectives.

[2] According to Xu & Langendoen (1985), all maximal projections can be topics, and consequently, XP is used here instead of NP.

[3] By being specific, we mean that the reference is known at least to the speaker, and, by being definite, we mean that the reference is known both to the speaker and addressee.

[4] This sentence is good if it means that certain people didn't come but Zhangsan went to visit (them).

[5] Here, due to spatial limitations, only an outline of arguments can be given. For more details, readers are referred to Jiang (1989).

[6] Whether this node is a S with a controlled subject or simply a VP doesn't concern us here for the purpose of this paper.

[7] I am not assuming that topics are results of movement. When I say the complements of these verbs can be topics, what I mean is that the topics are interpreted as the complement clauses of the verbs.

[8] Here the asymmetry I am talking about is different from what Huang (1982) is talking about. Huang's (1982) asymmetry is that an empty subject can be coreferential with a higher subject while an empty object cannot. The asymmetry I am talking about is that a matrix topic can be interpreted as the object in the complement clause but may not as its subject.

Bibliography

Chao, Yuenren. 1968. A Grammar of Spoken Chinese. Berkeley, CA: Univ. of California Press.

Chomsky, Noam. 1982. Some Concepts and Consequences of the Theory of Government and Binding. Cambridge, Mass: MIT Press.

_____. 1981. Lectures on Government and Binding. Foris: Dordrecht.

Huang, James. 1982. Logical relations in Chinese and the theory of grammar. MIT PhD Dissertation.

Jiang, Zixin. 1989. A constraint on topic in Chinese. In University of Chicago Linguistics Working Papers: Vol. 5.

Keenan, Edward. 1976. Toward a universal definition of 'subject'. In Charles Li (ed.), Subject and Topic. pp. 314-345. New York: Academic Press.

Li, Andrey. 1985. Abstract case in Chinese. USC PhD Dissertation.

Li, Charles and Sandra Thompson. 1981. Mandarin Chinese: A Functional Reference Grammar of Contemporary Chinese. Berkeley CA: Univ. of California Press.

_____. 1976. Subject and topic: a new typology of language. In Charles Li (ed.), Subject and Topic. New York: Academic Press. 457-490.

Li, Yingche. 1972. Sentences with be, exist and have in Chinese. Lg. 48.573-83.

Li, Y. F. 1985. Pronominal EC's and control theory. MA thesis, Shandong Univ. Jinan, China.

McCawley, James. 1988. The Syntactic Phenomena of English. Chicago: Univ. of Chicago Press.

Teng, Shouhsin. 1979. Remarks on cleft sentences in Chinese. JCL 7.1.111-126.

Wang, William S-Y. 1965. Two aspect markers in Mandarin. Lg 41.457-470.

Xu, Liejiong. 1986. Towards a lexical-thematic theory of control. The Linguistic Review, Vol. 5, pp. 345-376.

Xu, Liejiong and D. T. Langendoen. 1985. Topic structure in Chinese. Lg 61.1.1-28.

The autonomy of consonant and vowel planes*

Hyunsook Kang
University of Texas, Austin

1. Introduction

In recent years many questions have been asked about why some phonological rules such as assimilation and some constraints such as the OCP apply to certain sets of features as often as they apply to single features. This issue has led researchers to investigate the way a segment is represented. Currently, a segment is understood as having hierarchical structure: features which behave as a set for certain well-defined phonological rules are represented under a shared node.

In the course of this investigation, another issue has arisen: can the hierarchical structure, feature geometry, explain V/C metathesis in languages such as Yawelmani and Miwok? McCarthy (1989) argues that feature geometry cannot properly account for V/C metathesis in these languages and thus, the bi-planar representation is necessary for these languages although separate planes are not motivated by morphological evidence. McCarthy (1989) notes that these languages with V/C metathesis are templatic languages.

McCarthy (1989) also argues that morphemes with the rigid canonical structure can be represented with the bi-planar representation such as (1) which does not show the direct linear ordering of the consonants and the vowels with respect to each other. Therefore, the underlying representation of /pat/ with a rigid template would be {pt, a, CVC} with no direct ordering relation of the consonants and the vowels with each other. They will be ordered with each other only by association to the skeleton.

(1)

```
p   t
|   |
C V C
  |
  a
```

In this paper, we will assume these proposals made in McCarthy (1989) and look into the details of Miwok morphology and phonology. We will show two phonological manifestations of the autonomous consonant and vowel planes: first, what the autosegmental representation is when a stem is concatenated with a suffix and second that the OCP suggested in McCarthy (1986) is not active in Miwok.

2. Miwok Morphology

According to Smith (1985), there are two kinds of suffixes in Miwok: (most) inflectional suffixes which do not provide templates for stems, but follow basic templates; and derivational suffixes which provide the various derived templates for the stems. The form of the template is determined by the suffix.

The underlying basic stem types are CVV-, CVCC-, CVCVV-CVCCV-, CVCVVC-, etc. These are designated as Stem 1 in (2). Some templates which result upon suffixation are shown as Stems 2, 3, and 4 in (2) (Broadbent (1964, p38)). Stem 2 has CVCVC template; Stem 3 has CVCCVC[1] template; and Stem 4 has CVCCV template. If there are not sufficient consonants or vowels in basic templates to fill the derived templates, the default vowel /y/[2] or default consonants /h/ or /?/ are supplied (eg. /?ynn-/, /hyyja-/, etc. in (2)).

(2)

Stem 1	Stem 2	Stem 3	Stem 4	Gloss
loot-	lot[3]-	lottu̲?[4]-	lot?u	to catch
?ynn-	?ynyh-	?ynny?-	?yn?y-	to come
lak-h-	lakyh-	lakkyh-	lakhy-	to appear
mussa-	musah-	mussa?-	mus?a-	to be ashamed
kowta-	kowat-	kowwat-	kowta-	to bump into

As noted by Broadbent (1964) and Smith (1985), if the stem and the suffix together are short enough to be interpreted as one of the basic templates, it can undergo new template suppletion provided by another template-supplying suffix. For example:

(3)
a. syyk-   'to mark'
b. syk-wa   'to mark up, to write all over'
c. sykkaw-hii-me   'it is all marked up'
   cf. d. tela-   'paint, dye'
       tella?-hii-me- 'it is painted, dyed'

In (3a) /syyk-/ represents the basic template [CVVC]. The suffix /-wa-/, meaning 'iterative', provides a [CVC] template for the preceding stem, thus forming /syk-wa-/ in (3b). The combination of stem and suffix also happens to correspond to a basic template [CVCCV]. If /syk-wa-/ is followed by another template-supplying suffix like /-hii-me-/ which provides a [CVCCVC] template, it surfaces as /sykkaw-hii-me/. /-hii-me-/ is a predicative suffix which can be followed by an additional inflectional past tense suffix /-hhy-/.

3. The representation of root and suffix

Consider what is taking place in (3c): the consonant and vowel of the suffix /-wa-/ is metathesized before the suffix /-hii-me-/. As Prince (1987) notes for Yawelmani, however, to posit a rule of metathesis for this kind of case would be missing a generalization about desired output, since this metathesis applies only if it produces the desirable target. In (3d), insertion of the default consonant /?/ for the stem /tela-/ occurs, rather than metathesis, before the same suffix /-hii-me-/.

What would the autosegmental representation of (3b) be in which a root with V and C planes is concatenated with a suffix? Suppose that it is represented as (4) with three separate planes: one vocalic and one consonantal plane for the root, and one plane for the suffix. Two planes for the root is suggested following McCarthy (1989).

(4)
```
s   k
|   |   w a
|   |   | |
C V C + C V
    |
    y
```

Consider what must be done to this representation to accomplish the desirable output /sykkaw-/ when the template [CVCCVC-] is provided by /-hii-me-/. If nothing happens to (4), the following derivation will occur.

(5)
```
s   k                       s   k
|   |   w a                     w a
|   |   | |
C V C + C V -----------------> C V CC V C   + /-hii-me-/
    |            [CVCCVC] selection
    y                           y
```

At this point, the Universal Association Convention does not specify how to associate melody elements with skeletal slots since the two sets of consonants, {s,k} and {w}, are not ordered with regard to each other. Even if the consonant melodies are associated with the template properly, vowel melody [a] still cannot be associated with V$_2$ in (6b) without crossing an association line.

(6)

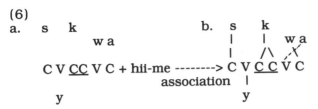

a.
```
   s    k                b.  s    k
        w a              |    |  w a
                         |   /\  ,´X
C V CC V C + hii-me --------> C V CC V C
            association    |
   y                         y
```

We can conclude that multi-planar representation in (6) is not the right representation at this stage.

Thus, in order not to violate the crossing constraint shown in (6), the consonant melody and the vowel melody of the suffix must be bi-planar as in (7b). If a new template is supplied to (7b), no violation of the crossing constraint occurs as is shown in (7d).

(7)

```
a.   s   k                 b.
     |   |  w a                s   k   w
     |   |  | |                |   |   |
     C V C + C V ------------> C V C + C V --------------->
     |            separate PC  |         | [CVCCVC] selection
     y                         y         a


c.   s   k   w             d.   s   k   w
                               |   |\  |
     C V C C V C + hii-me ----------------> C V C C V C + hii-me
               association        |     |
     y     a                      y     a
```

This provides some empirical motivation for preservation of vocalic and consonantal planes after a suffix is concatenated to the root.

In what fashion is a plane of suffix concatenated to the planes of roots? Note that the suffixes which can combine into the canonical form of Stem 1 all have the structure of CV or C. Following the spirit of McCarthy (1989), suppose that morphemes whose syllabic/prosodic structure are rigid are underspecified with regard to information concerning linear ordering of consonants and vowels with each other. Then the suffix /-wa-/ in (3b) will be represented as {CV, w, a} in (8a), with two melody elements whose linear order is not specified. Only by association to the skeleton in (8b) will {w, a} come to be ordered. The V/C metathesis does not cause any problem as is shown in (8b).

(8)

```
a.  s    k                    b.  s    k
            w                      |    |   w
                                   |   /\  |
       C V C + C V  ------------>  CVCCVC + hii-me
                                   |    |
            a                      |    a
       y                           y
```

However, it seems that the representation in (8) does not directly provide the ordering relationship of the two sets of consonants {s, k} and {w} and likewise two sets of vowels {y} and {a}. Therefore, we suggest that these suffixes like /-wa-/ do not provide their own planes[5]: Rather they are concatenated directly with the planes of the roots. Then the ordering relations of the two sets of consonants and likewise two sets of the vowels will be directly provided. Thus, when they are suffixed to the stem, the representation would be (9). No violation of the crossing constraint in V/C metathesis occurs, either.

(9)

```
    s    k    w                    s     k     w
                                   |    /\     |
    C V CC V C  + hii-me --------> C V  CC  V C
                                   |          |
    y    a                         y          a
```

Thus, we suggest that Miwok provides the evidence not only for autonomous planes for consonants and vowels but also no autonomous plane for some suffixes.

4. The OCP and vowel melodies in Miwok

Since it is clear that a vowel plane exists in stems as well as some suffixes in Miwok, we expect that the segmental OCP proposed by McCarthy (1986) is active. First, we will examine the relationship of the OCP and melodies of skeletally adjacent segments in Miwok.

In (10a) /kuhta-/ has changed its shape to /kuhat-/ when a CVCVC template is provided. However, as is shown by Broadbent (1964) and Smith (1985), when a morpheme does not have sufficient melodies to fill the templates as in (10b, c), a default consonant and vowel are supplied by rule (11). ([?] for a consonant, [y] for a vowel for these cases). Default consonants and vowels are underlined in (10).

(10)
a. kuhta- 'to hit, to punch'

```
        kuhat-kuu-      : nt. (it) has been obviously hit
b. ?ynn-    'to come'
        ?yny?-kuu-      : nt. one who obviously came
c. wemm-  'to dig a hole'
        wemy?-kuu       : nt. obviously dug
d. hyyja-   'to arrive'
        hyjah-
```

(11)
a.

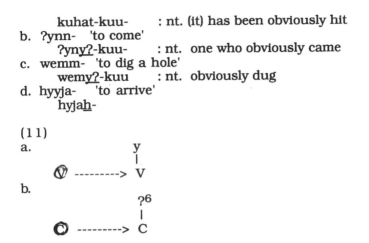

b.

Thus, we see that there is no spreading of melodies in Miwok when melodies are associated with a template.

What should the underlying representation of morphemes with the geminate structures be? If the UR of (10c) is (12a), a default consonant will be supplied to C3 by (11), resulting in a correct surface form. If the UR of (10c) is (12b) with three consonants, we expect that the third consonant [m] will be associated with the last C slot of CVCVC template. However, as shown in (12b) this will give us an incorrect surface form. We can ascribe this representation in (12a,b) to the OCP (McCarthy 1986) in (13), which will prohibit roots with adjacent identical consonants. (cf. A similar OCP effect is disucssed in Smith (1985) where a root final consonant is concatenated with an identical consonant initial suffix.)

(12)
a. UR: /wm, e, CVCC/: /wemm-/

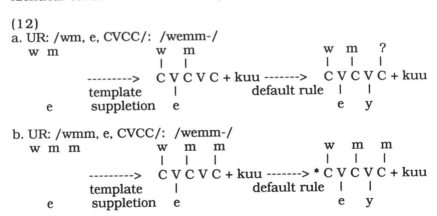

b. UR: /wmm, e, CVCC/: /wemm-/

(13) Obligatory Contour Principle
At the melodic level, adjacent identical elements are prohibited.

What about the UR of (10d) with a long vowel? Presumably it also cannot have two /y/ vowels underlyingly for two reasons: /yya-/ violates the OCP; also it does not give the right output when a new template is supplied. For example, if a CVCVC template is supplied to /yya-/ as in (14b), a second [y] will be associated with the second vowel slot, resulting in an incorrect surface form. Thus, the vowel melody of /hyyja-/ in (10d) should be represented as /ya-/.

(14) UR: /hj, yya, CVVCV-/: to arrive, /hyyja-/
a. y y a   b. y y a
  | | | | |
 CVVCV --------------> *CVCVC
          template suppletion

However, when the /ya-/ vowel melody is associated with the original template CVVCV as in (15), we expect it surface as /hyaja-/ by the left to right association convention. However, this is not the case. That is, a VV sequence in the same syllable does not appear with two different vowel melodies. We will assume the constraint (16), suggested by Smith (1985).

(15)   (16)
 y a   y a   A B
          | ⌐ | |
CVVCV --------->* CVVCV   *VV]$_\sigma$

The melodies of the second V slot in VV sequence will be filled in by the local spreading (17). The derivation is in (18).

(17)
A   A
| /\
VV] σ --------> VV

(18)
 y   a   y a   y a
            | | /\ |
CVVCV ------------> CVVCV -----------------> CVVCV
      association   (17)

Thus, the OCP appears to be active for skeletally adjacent segments in Miwok.

Now, let us discuss the relationship of the skeletally non-adjacent vowel melodies of Miwok and the OCP. We rewrite the OCP as (19) which McCarthy (1986) proposes as a universal constraint on phonological representation.

(19) Obligatory Contour Principle
At the melodic level, adjacent identical elements are prohibited.

If the OCP is a universal constraint as is proposed, we expect that in non-concatenative languages, where V/C melodies exist autonomously, that identical vowel sequences in CV_1CCV_1, CV_1CV_1C, etc. should be represented with a single vowel melody as in (20). (20b) is derived by the association convention. In (20c), [y] is inserted by a default feature insertion rule (11). However, an incorrect surface form appears. Rather we should allow the spreading of /i/ melody from V_1 to a non-adjacent V_2 as in (20d).

(20) /stl, i, CVCCV; to sprinkle/ [sitli-]
```
a. s t l       b.  s t l         c.    s  t l
                   |  |  |              |  | |
   CVCCV ------> CVCCV ------->* CVCCV
      association  |         default   |   |
   i               i         insertion i   y

                               d.  s  t l
                                   |  | |
                        --------> CVCCV
                        spreading  \  /
                                     i
```

Now, we have two different feature-supplying rules in Miwok: the default feature insertion rule in (11) and the feature spreading rule as is shown in (20). The difference seems to lie in the fact that in (12a), melody elements are associated with the derived template and in (20), melody elements are associated with the underlying template.

Therefore, to maintain the OCP as a principle of underlying grammar, we have to hypothesize that in Miwok there are two distinct melody supplying rules as in (21).

(21)   a. The long- distance spreading of vowels as in (20) is allowed only if melodies are associated with the original template.
       b. Otherwise, a default feature insertion rule (11) applies as in (12).

The consequence for the OCP becomes more serious if we consider the derived templatic structures of Stem 1 with identical vowel sequences. Let us consider (22).

(22) /lpt, o, CVCVVC/; st1. to form a lump ---> [lopoot-]

```
l  p   t
|  |   |
CVCVVC
 \ //
   o
```

When a CVCCV template is supplied to (22) by the suffix -jee-nY-, meaning discontinuity in space, we predict the incorrect derivation (23).

(23)

```
a.  l  pt        b.  l  pt              c.  l  pt
                     |  ||                  |  ||
    CVCCV --------> CVCCV ------------->*CVCCV -jee-nY
         association   |     default rule   |  |
       o               ʋ     (21b)        o    y
                                             *[lopty-jee-nY-]
```

A desired surface form: /lopto-jee-nY-/; to have goose bumps

In (23b) the melody [o] is associated with V1. In (23c), [y] is inserted by rule (21b) since the melody elements are being associated with a new template. However, an incorrect surface form results: V2 should surface as [o]. Some other forms involving identical vowels are given in (24).

(24)
a. ma?<u>aat</u>-   st1. to fall apart, to fork (intr.)
   ma?<u>ta</u>-la-   nt. forked, fork of tree
b. ha?<u>ta</u>-   st1. to throw down
   ha?<u>aat</u>-nY-   vb. to throw to (repeatedly?), to throw to
c. kaw<u>aa</u>jo-   nt. horse
   kaw<u>ja</u>-meH-   (he) has lots of horses

As is shown in (24), basic stems with identical vowel sequences show the same vowel sequences even when they change their prosodic structure upon suffixation. This contradicts (21b).

How can we resolve this contradiction? One way would be to relax the OCP constraint for lexical items such as (22) so that the representation of (22) is (25) which has two /o/ melodies underlyingly. Then as is shown in (25), the problem of the association of the melodies with the template disappears.

(25) /lpt, oo, CVCVVC/; stl. to form a lump ---> [lopoot-]
a. with the underlying template

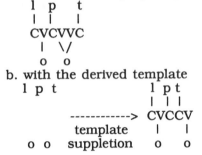

b. with the derived template

```
l p t                    l p t
                         | | |
        ------------> CVCCV
        template     |   |
  o o   suppletion   o   o
```

If there are only a few cases like (24), we might consider them as lexical exceptions to the OCP. However, a search in the dictionary (Broadbent 1964) shows that the identical vowel sequences appear as frequently as any other vowel sequences. Some of these examples are given in (26).

(26)
ha?ta: to throw down
heleep: to disagree with someone
hutuul: to roll
killim: to freeze
limiij: to ripple, of water

Thus, marking the items in (26) as exceptions to the OCP is not an alternative. However, giving up the OCP is equally unattractive. The OCP has been shown to be a universal constraint (Leben 1979, McCarthy 1986, etc.) especially in the non-concatenative languages and Miwok is a language in which a non-concatenative system is well motivated. Let us consider the possibilities for salvaging the OCP. Two suggestions will be discussed briefly below.

My first suggestion is like this. Suppose that the OCP is active in Miwok. Then the sequences of identical vowel melodies should be represented as (27) and the vowel spreading rule (28) is motivated.

(27)

```
  l  p   t                    l  p   t                    l  p   t
                              |  |   |                    |  |   |
  CVCVVC  ------------>  CVCVVC  ------------>  CVCVVC
        association       |      spreading(28)      \ //
     o                         o                        o
```

(28)

```
  aF                        aF
  |                         / \
  V   V  --------->      V   V
```

Suppose a new template is supplied to (27) as a parafix in the fashion similar to that suggested by Clements (1985) for reduplication. As is shown in (29), moras of the supplied templates are linked to moras of the underlying templates by the left-to-right association. The melodies are transferred from the underlying templates to the supplied templates. Thus, in (29a) /lopoot-/ appears as /lopto-/.

However, as is shown in (29b), when a supplied template with two syllables are linked to the underlyingly one syllable template, only the first mora of the supplied template is linked to the mora of the underlying template. Note that in (29b) V$_2$ of the supplied template is not linked to the V$_2$ of the original template since they belong to two different syllables. We suggest that this is due the the constraint suggested in Clements (1985), written here as (30). Thus, a default vowel is supplied to the empty vowel slot of the supplied template in (29b). However, unlike the reduplication, we have to delete the original template.

(29) (m) represents a mora within a syllable)

```
a.  o                        b.   o
   / \\                          /\
  m mm   /lopoot-/           mm]  /loot-/
   |   \                      |
  m   m]  /lopto-/          m] m]
   \  /                      |   |
     o                        o    y (default vowel)
```

(30) Association
a. link Vs to Vs pairwise in the direction of mapping, skipping no eligible V.
Condition: if VV is a syllable nucleus, its image under the mapping is also a nucleus.

With this transfer function, we can now express the fact that both vowel slots in (29a) are supplied with melodies whereas in (29b) only the V_1 is supplied with the melodies.

However, this suggestion does not solve the OCP violation in consonants where a prosodic constituent, a mora, cannot be motivated. Let us consider some cases in Miwok where the OCP violation occurs in consonant melody elements.

(31)
hohiil-	: to tangle
hohiim-	: to hoot like an owl
hysaas-	: to hatch
jooj-	: to praise
kook-	: to graze
momaak	: to kiss

Thus, to explain the OCP violation in vowel melodies as well as in consonant melodies, we would like to suggest another solution for the OCP violation in Miwok. Suppose that the OCP behaves differently depending on the languages. Suppose that in Miwok, the OCP operates only for two strictly adjacent segments. Consider (32).

(32)
a. i   i   b. i   i
                             | |
    CVCCV ----------> CVCCV

(32b) does not violate the OCP in this sense since two /i/ melodies are associated with Vs not adjacent to each other. However, adjacent VV sequences cannot be associated with two identical melodies since it violates the OCP between adjacent segments (cf. (14)).

Why doesn't Miwok show the same OCP effects manifested in other non-concatenative languages, like Arabic? It seems that there is an interesting relationship between the OCP and the vowel spreading rule. In Arabic languages, the OCP is active and at the same time, the spreading of the root node is allowed. Thus, /sm/ appears as /smm/ when a triconsonantal template is provided. Whereas in Miwok, the OCP is not active and at the same time, spreading of the root node is not allowed except in certain morphologically conditioned cases.

There are some other non-concatenative languages in which the OCP seems to be violated. Odden (1988) shows that there is an OCP violation in Yawelmani such as /do:lul-hun/, etc[7]. Also note that in Yawelmani, there is no spreading of the consonant root node (Archangeli, 1984). Broselow (1984) also argues that in Amharic, there are no spreading of root nodes of consonants and no OCP; if she is right, it supports our hypothesis shown in (33).

(33) Hypothesis
Languages allow the (skeletally-nonadjacent) OCP violation if they do not permit the root node spreading.

Imaginably, as is shown in (34), different URs (34a) /clk, a, CVCC/ and (34b) /clk, a, CVCCV/ would show the same surface forms with the derived CVCVC template if the OCP were active and no feature spreading were allowed. This opacity makes a functional explanation possible such that in unmarked cases, languages do not take this combination of options: no feature spreading and the OCP.

(34) imaginable cases (do not exist)

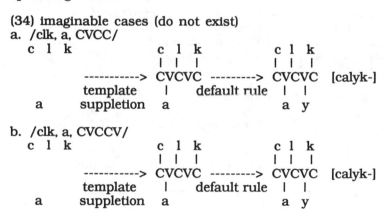

a. /clk, a, CVCC/

```
   c  l  k              c  l  k              c  l  k
                        |  |  |              |  |  |
        -----------> CVCVC ---------> CVCVC   [calyk-]
        template     |     default rule |  |
   a    suppletion   a                  a  y
```

b. /clk, a, CVCCV/

```
   c  l  k              c  l  k              c  l  k
                        |  |  |              |  |  |
        -----------> CVCVC ---------> CVCVC   [calyk-]
        template     |     default rule |  |
   a    suppletion   a                  a  y
```

In any case, it seems that the OCP as is proposed by McCarthy (1986) seems to be too strong for Miwok, one of the well motivated non-concatenative languages.

5. Conclusion
In this paper, we have discussed two phonological consequences of the autonomous consonant and vowel planes of Miwok, with the assumption that separate melody planes exist although they are not motivated by morphological evidence. First, we have shown that the V/C metathesis can be applied even to the combination of a root and some suffixes. This provides some evidence for the preservation of the bi-planar representation when a suffix is concatenated to a root.

Also we have discussed another consequence of separate planes, namely, the OCP in segmental melodies. We have shown that the OCP in its most general form suggested by McCarthy

(1986) is not active in Miwok similar to the claim made for Amharic by Broselow (1984) and Yawelmani by Odden (1988): Miwok, Yawelmani and Amharic do not seem to allow spreading of the root node in umarked cases and the skeletally non-adjacent OCP at the same time. We hypothesize that languages might allow the skeletally non-adjacent OCP violation if they do not permit the spreading of the root node.

Notes

* I would like to thank Juliette Levin, Armin Mester, and Tony Woodbury for the helpful comments for an earlier version of this paper. Needless to say, I alone am responsible for any errors or oversights.

1. In this template, two Cs underlined must constitute a geminate. This kind of idiosyncracy of the template should be encoded as a rule (Smith 1985). In this paper, we will underline two adjacent consonantal slots if they must be filled by a single melody element.

2. [y] represents a high unrounded back vowel [ɨ].

3. If Stem 1 has CVVC- template, Stem 2 has CVC- template instead of CVCVC.

4. An inserted vowel [y] became [u] by rounding harmony.

5. A similar suggestion was made for a mediopassive suffix /-n-/ in Yawelmani by Archangeli (1984).

6. Or [h]. The specific features of the default consonant depends on the following suffix.

7. J. Goldsmith has pointed this out to me.

References

Archangeli, D (1983) "The Root CV-Template as a Property of the Affix: Evidence from Yawelmani," Natural Language and Linguistic Theory 1, 348-384.

Archangeli, D (1984) Underspecification in Yawelmani Phonology and Morphology, Doctoral dissertation, MIT, Cambridge, Massachusetts.

Broadbent, S. (1964) The Southern Sierra Miwok Language, University of California publications in linguistics v.38.

Broselow, E. (1984) "Default Consonants in Amharic Morphology," MIT Working Papers in Linguistics 7, p19-31.

Campbell, L. (1974) "Phonological Features: Problems and Proposals," Language 50, 52-65.

Clements, G. N. (1985) "The Geometry of Phonological Features," Phonology Yearbook 2, 225-252.

Clements, G. N. (1985) "The problem of transfer in non-linear morphology," ms, Cornell University.

McCarthy, J. (1981) "A Prosodic Theory of Nonconcatenative Morphology," Linguistic Inquiry 12, 373-418.

McCarthy, J. (1986) "OCP Effects: Gemination and Antigemination," Linguistic Inquiry 17, 207-263.

McCarthy, J. (1989) "Linear Order in Phonological Representation," Linguistic Inquiry 20, 71-99.

McCarthy, J. and A. Prince (1986) "Prosodic Morphology," ms., University of Massachusetts, Amherst, and Brandeis University.

Odden, D (1988) "Anti Antigemination and the OCP," Linguistic Inquiry 19, 451-475.

Prince, A. (1987) "Planes and Copying," Linguistic Inquiry 18, 491-510.

Sagey, E. (1986) The Representation of Features and Relations in Nonlinear Phonology, Doctoral dissertation, MIT, Cambridge, Massachusetts.

Smith, N (1985) "Spreading, Reduplication, and the Default Option in Miwok Nonconcatenative Morphology," in H. van der Hulst and N. Smith, eds., Advances in Nonlinear Phonology, Forist Dordrecht.

Steriade, D. (1986) "Yokuts and the Vowel Plane," Linguistic Inquiry 17, 129-146.

Steriade, D. (1987a) "Locality Conditions and Feature Geometry," in J. McDonough and B. Plunkett, eds., Proceedings of the 17th Annual Meeting of NELS, GLSA, Department of Linguistics, University of Massachusetts, Amherst.

Yip, M. (1987) "Feature Geometry and Co-occurrence Restrictions," ms., Brandeis University, Waltham, Massachusetts.

Yip, M. (1988) "The OCP and Phonological Rules: A Loss of Identity," Linguistic Inquiry 19, 65-100.

Inverse Voice and Head-Marking in Tanoan Languages*

M.H. Klaiman
California State University - Fullerton

Tanoan languages belong to a subfamily of the Kiowa-Tanoan languages spoken in the Rio Grande valley of New Mexico and on the Hopi mesa in northern Arizona. The present work concerns whether a certain grammatical voice behavior common to these languages comprises passivization or inverse voice. Inverse systems or systems of direct/inverse voice alternations occur in several language groups; they are said to include Wakashan languages of the Pacific northwest (Whistler 1985) and Chukotko-Kamchatkan languages of Siberia (Comrie 1980), while better-known instances include Apachean languages such as Navajo (Jelinek 1985:172) and, of course, all members of the great Algonquian family of languages.

There is not a language in which the status of direct/inverse voice alternations has been uncontroversial, except perhaps Tanoan languages, whose voice patterning seems to have been interpreted by all previous writers as a kind of passivization. The label passive has also been applied to the relevant behaviors in many other languages, including Algonquian languages. However, the present discussion is based on a premise that direct/inverse and active/passive are distinct behaviors. This assumption arises from the observation that direct and inverse alternates, such as (1a,b) in the Algonquian language Plains Cree, generally have distinct content. (These examples are from Wolfart 1973:25.)

(1) a. ni- sēkih -ā   -nān atim
         1p scare theme DIRECT 1pl   dog
         'We scare the dog'

     b. ni- sēkih -iko   -nān atim
         1p scare theme INVERSE 1pl   dog
         'The dog scares us'

Generally in active/passive alternates, given that the content of subject and nonsubject grammatical positions in the sentence are reversed, the information content which is expressed is the same; and in particular, the assignments of argument referents to logical statuses of subject and object is the same in an active and in its corresponding passive. However, in an alternation of direct and inverse forms as in (1a,b), there is a reversal of argument-logical status

258

relations. Each of (1a,b) includes two arguments, one
referring to a first person referent and the other to a
third person singular referent 'dog'. In each alternate
the former is indexed on the verbal complex by a
person-marking prefix ni- and a plurality suffix
-nān, while the latter is not indexed by an overt
marker on the verb and is represented by the nominal
atim. The sole signal of the reversal of argument-
logical status relations in (1a,b) is the alternation of
direct[1] and inverse markers, or theme signs, in the
verbal complex.

Generally in alternations of direct and inverse
sentence forms, this non-equivalence of argument-logical
status relations is characteristic. In Algonquian
languages, like Plains Cree, the only exceptions to this
I know of are cases of transitive animate predicates
each of whose arguments belong to a subclass of the
third person category called obviative (this term is to
be explained below). In Cree, alternates such as (2a,b)
(from Dahlstrom 1986:54) are essentially equivalent in
content (although it does not necessarily follow that
they are interchangeable in use within a discourse).

(2) a. wāpam-ē-yi-wa
         see-direct-obviative-sg obv
         'He (obv) sees him (obv)'

     b. wāpam-iko-yi-wa
         see-inverse-obviative-sg obv
         'He (obv) sees him (obv)'

Examples such as (2a,b) are, however, rare, and the
non-equivalence of information content and argument
structure illustrated in (1a,b) is the prevailing
pattern in inverse systems. In light of this essential
difference between direct/inverse type and
active/passive type systems, grounds exist for treating
inverse behavior as a manifestation of a distinctive
voice type. This is the assumption made in the present
work. Before examining voice typology in Tanoan
languages it will be useful to mention a few additional
characteristics of inverse systems.

First, languages with inverse voice generally
belong to the head-marking type (as described by Nichols
1986). Among other things, this entails that these
languages do not have systems of case markers rich
enough to disambiguate logical status assignments of
core arguments in transitive predications--a fact which
is obvious in (1a,b) and (2a,b). To be sure, head-
marking (and its converse, dependent-marking) are
matters of degree rather than of absolute
classification, and some inverse systems conform more

faithfully to a strict pattern of head-marking than do others (as will be discussed below).

Second, all inverse systems presuppose a hierarchy of ontological saliency of core argument referents such that, in a transitive predication, one argument generally can be ranked above the other in terms of its status in the situation of discourse and/or in the situation denoted by the predication. In all inverse systems the relative ranking of nominals for ontological saliency is interrelated with a ranking of nominals for grammatical person in such a way that arguments with third person reference never have the same saliency as speech act participant (SAP) arguments (first and second persons), or to show it schematically:

(3)   SAP > non-SAP   (SAP=Speech Act Participant)

Correspondingly, in all inverse systems, local transitive predications, or predications involving no third person referents (but only SAP referents), fail to participate in the alternation of direct and inverse marking. Furthermore, in any transitive predication exactly one of whose arguments is SAP, there is no alternation; the shape of the predicate is either direct or inverse depending respectively on whether the action proceeds in the ontologically expected direction, i.e. with the SAP argument depicted as acting on the non-SAP (third person) argument, or in a manner inverse to the ontologically expected direction of action, i.e. with the non-SAP argument depicted as acting on the SAP argument. Each of these possibilities is illustrated in the following Plains Cree examples (4a,b), (5a,b) (from Wolfart and Carroll 1978:72).

(4)   a.   ni-wāpam-āw   -ak
          1   see   dir sg 3pl
          'I see them'

      b.   ni-wāpam-ikw-ak
          1   see   inv 3pl
          'They see me'

(5)   a.   ki-wāpam-āw   -ak
          2   see   dir sg 3pl
          'You (sg) see them'

      b.   ki-wāpam-ikw-ak
          2   see   inv 3pl
          'They see you (sg)'

Inverse systems differ according to the treatment of transitive predications both of whose core arguments are third person or non-SAP. It is well known that in Algonquian languages there is a constraint requiring at least one of the two arguments to be marked as ontologically nonsalient. In the literature on Algonquian the standard term for this is obviation (also sometimes called fourth person marking). Non-obviative or proximate third persons are ranked ontologically above obviative third persons, as indicated by the pattern of direct vs. inverse theme marking in (6a,b) below (from Dunnigan, O'Malley and Schwartz 1978:9-10).

(6) a. wākoss̓́ o- wāpam-ān   pis̓iw-an
         fox   3p see direct + obviative lynx obv
         'The fox (proximate) sees the lynx'

     b. pis̓iw-an   o- wāpam-ikōn   wakoss̓́
         lynx obv 3p see   inverse + obviative fox
         'The lynx (obviative) sees the fox'

In Algonquian, assignment of proximate and obviative statuses to third person nominals usually is correlated with their relative significance at particular points in the unfolding of a discourse.[2] Outside of Algonquian, however, other criteria may apply. For instance, the relative ranking or saliency of two third-person core arguments in a transitive predication may depend on an assessment of the degree of control each exercises in the denoted real-world situation (as is well-discussed in the literature on Apachean; see, inter alia, Witherspoon 1977, 1980 and Shayne 1982). Alternatively, it is said that in certain inverse systems (not illustrated in the present work) third person singular arguments rank above third person plurals (Comrie 1980, Whistler 1985:262). Another logical possibility is that there may be no morphological differentiation of subclasses of third person arguments; it is this situation that, I will argue, characterizes inverse patterning in Tanoan languages.

Tanoan voice behavior will be illustrated in the first instance using data from Kroskrity 1985 on the language Arizona Tewa. In Arizona Tewa, as in Tanoan languages generally, there is an elaborate system of paradigms of core argument-crossreferencing bound pronominals. These pronominals occur obligatorily within the verbal complex, with a minimum of two distinct paradigms of these pronominals occurring in each Tanoan language. Kroskrity states that in Arizona Tewa one prefix set encodes only logical subjects of transitive predicates (accordingly, its forms are labeled in glosses to examples below as 'subjective'). However, the forms in this set only occur when an argument with

first, second or third person reference comprises
logical subject acting on a distinct argument with third
person reference as logical object. This prefix
paradigm contrasts with a distinct set of prefixes to be
glossed in examples below as 'objective'. (Kroskrity's
respective terms for the two prefix paradigms are
'active' and 'passive'.)

Assuming that both logical subject and logical
object of a transitive predicate have non-SAP (third
person) referents and are of equivalent definiteness,
then the predicate may alternatively select prefixes of
either paradigm. The alternation of the two is shown
below in (7) (from Kroskrity, p. 309). However,
transitive predications cannot be encoded in alternate
voices if one or both core arguments are SAP.
Predicates construe with subjective ('active') prefixes
and not with objective ('passive') prefixes just if the
logical object is third person, hence outranked
ontologically by the logical subject.

In the remaining class of possibilities, such as
when a transitive predicate assigns a non-third person
logical object outranking the logical subject, the
predicate selects a prefix of the objective ('passive')
set. The paradigm for this set is reproduced in (8)
(from Kroskrity, p. 308). The elements of this paradigm
index the following possibilities: (a) second person
logical subject acting on first person logical object;
(b) first person logical subject acting on second person
logical object; (c) any situation which amounts to what
would be inverse ontological directionality of action,
i.e. any combination of an argument comprising logical
subject whose referent is non-SAP with an argument
comprising logical object whose referent is SAP; (d)
logical object and logical subject both non-SAP (as in
ex. 7b).

(7) a. hę'i sen nÉ'i 'enú mán-   k^{hw}Édi
         that man this boy 3sgsubj hit
         'That man hit this boy'

     b. nÉ'i 'enú hę'i sen -di   'ó:-   k^{hw}Édi
         this boy that man oblique 3sgobj hit
         'This boy was hit by that man'

(8)

	person of agent			
	1	-1	(2 or 3)	3
person of patient				
1				dí-
2	wí-			
2sg				wó:-
2du				wó:bén-
2pl				wó:bé-
3sg				'ó:-
3du				'ó:bén-
3pl				'ó:bé-

Objective ('passive') prefix series in
Arizona Tewa

At first appraisal it might seem as though the morphology of the Arizona Tewa verb is greatly different from that of an inverse system, given the absence in the Tanoan language of a specific inverse morpheme. Nonetheless the pattern of allowable and nonallowable predications is very similar: when a predicate is local, i.e. takes only SAP arguments, it does not participate in a voice alternation; when the transitive verb has just one SAP argument it becomes the formal subject of the predication, and the verbal morphology is determined according to the above (3), with no actual alternation of voices. But in the remaining class of cases, when both arguments of a transitive verb are non-SAP, alternate voices of a predication are grammatically possible. This holds whether one speaks of Arizona Tewa or of an Algonquian-type inverse system. The majority of writers on Tanoan languages do not, however, see this patterning as evidence of an inverse voice system. They are by and large committed, rather, to an active/passive paradigm of analysis.

For instance, Zaharlick 1982:45, writing on the related Tanoan language Picuris, refers to what are glossed above as subjective and objective verbal forms respectively as active and passive, and offers the following generalization as to the distribution of the two voices (where the terms 'subject' and 'object' refer strictly to logical statuses):

(9) (a) When subject and ... direct object are both third person, either active or passive sentences will occur, i.e. passive is optional.

(b) When subject and ... direct object are both non-third person ... [or] ... when subject is non-third person and ... direct object is third person, active sentences will occur and passive is not possible.

(c) When subject is third person ... and direct object is non-third person, passive is required.

Conditions on alternations of prefixal paradigms in Picuris

Nearly the same statement will also adequately characterize the distribution of the two bound pronominal sets in Arizona Tewa.[3] A characterization like (9) commits one to a position that passivization behaves peculiarly in Tanoan languages in that it can be alternately suppressed or made obligatory, and that these possibilities arise from Tanoan voice being sensitive to the same hierarchy of ontological saliency which characterizes inverse systems. In fact, in (9) one could as well replace the terms 'active' and 'passive' with the respective terms 'direct' and 'inverse', without invoking optional vs. required alternates, with the result that one would be describing an Algonquian-type inverse system. Given the proposed rewording, for instance, (a) of (9) would simply say that if both core arguments of a transitive verb are non-SAP, both direct and inverse forms of the verb are grammatical possibilities; (b) would state that under the conditions noted only direct forms occur; and (c) would state that under the conditions noted only inverse forms occur.

We are suggesting that in Arizona Tewa the opposition of prefix paradigms is isofunctional to a system of direct vs. inverse marking. The principal difference between an Algonquian inverse system and that of Arizona Tewa is the absence in the latter of a specific morpheme within the verbal complex for marking inverse directionality of denoted action. Nonetheless, such a morpheme does occur in other Tanoan languages. For instance, a suffix -mia, illustrated in the b-examples of (10) and (11), fulfills this function in Picuris. Note of the Picuris examples in (10)-(11) (these examples are from Zaharlick 1982) that either the so-called 'passive' (or inverse) voice form or the so-called 'active' (or direct) voice form are respectively unavailable--because, in the former, the predication involves an ontologically superior or SAP argument as logical subject combined with an ontologically inferior or non-SAP argument as logical object; and because, in the latter, the directionality of the action is inverse to the ontologically expected pattern.

(12) (also from Zaharlick 1982) illustrates the instance in which both voices of a predicate truly alternate, i.e. where both core arguments of a transitive verb are non-SAP. (Note that in Picuris, unlike Arizona Tewa, the third person singular prefixes of so called 'active' and 'passive' alternates converge in shape--both are ∅--so that apart from the absence or presence of the morpheme -mia there is no way to tell the two forms apart.) (13a,b) are examples from another Tanoan language, Southern Tiwa (spoken in the pueblos of Sandia and Isleta, New Mexico). (13a,b) are respectively very parallel to (12a,b) (except for the matter of noun incorporation, which we overlook for present purposes). Again, these examples illustrate that in transitive forms with two singular third person arguments the absence or presence of a special morpheme of voice (here, -che) is crucial, since bound pronominals of 3sg/3sg predications have the same (zero) shape in both direct and inverse counterparts.[4]

```
(10)   a.   'ACTIVE'   sənene ti-   /'a-    mǫn
                       man    1sgII /2sgII  see

                       -'ąn
                        verbal suffix
                        'I/you saw the man'

       b.  'PASSIVE'   *sənene ∅-   mǫn -mia -'ąn
                        man    3sgI  see -mia  verbal suffix

                       ną -pa/  'ę -pa
                       I  -obl/ you -obl
                       'The man was seen by me / by you'

(11)   a.   'ACTIVE'   *sənene ∅-       mǫn -'ąn
                        man    3sgII     see  verbal suffix
                        'The man saw me/you'

       b.  'PASSIVE'   ta-/   'a-    mǫn  -mia -'ąn
                       1sgI  / 2sgI  see  -mia  verbal suffix

                       sənene-pa
                       man    -obl
                       'I was/you were seen by the man'
```

(12) a. 'ACTIVE' (sənene) ∅-   mǫn -'ạn
                    (man)   3sgII see   verbal suffix
                    'He (the man) saw him'

      b. 'PASSIVE' ∅-   mǫn -mia -'ạn
                     3sgI see -<u>mia</u>   verbal suffix

                     (sənene-pa)
                     (man   -obl)
                     'He was seen (by the man)'

(13) a. seuanide ∅-   hliara- mu -ban
          man   3sg/3sg   lady   see past
          'The man saw the lady'

      b. hliarade ∅-   mu -che -ban
          lady   3sg   see -<u>che</u> past

          seuanide-ba
          man   instrumental
          'The lady was seen by the man'

As earlier noted, the analysis of Tanoan languages
has previously been uncontroversial in that prior
writers on these languages seem to agree that the voice
patterning is active/passive. An obvious problem with
this view for Tanoan is the same problem mentioned at
the outset of this work in regard to Algonquian, namely,
that in transitive predications involving exactly one
SAP argument there never are 'active' grammatical forms
from which the supposed 'passive' variants can be
derived. Nevertheless all writers simply stop with
assuming that the voice patterning of Tanoan languages
represents some sort of passivization, with one
exception: Kroskrity 1985:319 seriously weighs the
feasibility of an alternative inverse analysis for
Arizona Tewa. His grounds for rejecting the alternative
are significant, because they are the only explicit
grounds published, and so we quote them here in their
entirety.

     (14)   First, Tewa has no 'direct/inverse'
     contrast in its verbal morphology. Second,
     the pronominal prefix in Algonkian remains the
     same in both inverse and direct constructions;
     it simply indexes the participant which is
     higher in animacy. Finally, and perhaps most
     important, Algonkian languages like Fox never
     have a transitive construction in which agent
     and patient are equal in animacy, and thus
     capable of the stylistic alternation available

in A[rizona] T[ewa] 3/3 constructions. These significant differences show that the inverse pattern hardly provides a suitable framework for understanding the data.

In responding to these three allegedly crucial hallmarks of Tanoan-style systems, I will take points one and two together since they are, it will be argued, related.

While it is clear that Arizona Tewa does not have a specific morpheme of inverse voice, a comparison of other Tanoan languages makes it equally plain that there is some degree of trade-off between the existence of an overt, specifically inverse morpheme as part of the verbal complex and the character of paradigmatic oppositions in argument-encoding bound pronominals. A Tanoan language whose bound pronominals do not exhaustively index distinctions in argument status assignments (see e.g. the Picuris examples 12a,b and Southern Tiwa examples 13a,b) does and must have some morpheme in the verbal complex specific to signaling inverse voice. The same function is equally achieved, though differently marked, in Arizona Tewa thanks to its exhaustively explicit opposition in shapes of pronominals of two sets <u>sans</u> an explicit inverse morpheme. If this plausibly accounts for certain Tanoan languages having an explicit inverse morpheme, there is no reason why the same argument cannot account as well for the presence of explicit inverse morphology in Algonquian systems, which demonstrate no opposition whatever in shapes of bound pronominals. Aside from this, Arizona Tewa hardly seems to represent a paradigm case or exemplary model for Tanoan languages as a class, several of which have specific inverse morphology. Hence Arizona Tewa doesn't appear to comprise an adequate basis for distinguishing a Tanoan voice type from the inverse type represented by Algonquian.

This concludes the discussion of the first two points raised in passage (14) from Kroskrity 1985. The other ground mentioned there for distinguishing Algonquian and Tanoan voice types is the purported fact that Algonquian languages do not permit transitive 3/3 constructions with two core arguments of equivalent 'animacy' (i.e., what the present work has termed ontological saliency). This claim, however, is false, as illustrated by the alternation of 3obviative/3obviative transitive direct and inverse forms earlier illustrated for Cree in (2a,b). Note that such alternates do not violate the Algonquian constraint against two third person core arguments of a predication each being marked positively for ontological saliency-- as would occur if both were non-obviative, or proximate.

As (2a,b) show, when both the ontological subject
and nonsubject of a Cree predicate are obviative, there
is no finer category of ontological saliency available
to differentiate them; in Algonquian the available
categories of nominal status are limited to first
person, second person, proximate, and obviative.
Consequently, in an instance like (2a,b) either the
direct or inverse form of the predication is
grammatically possible (again, it is not claimed that
the two are necessarily interchangeable in discourse).
Each form does equate to the other in informational
content (i.e. as regards propositional content and
tense/modality).

Tanoan languages behave otherwise only in the
respect that, lacking as they do a subcategorization of
the third person into proximate and obviative, they have
direct and inverse forms of 3/3 predications which
comprise grammatical alternates (although again, this
is not necessarily to claim that both alternates are
isofunctional in discourse). Thus between Algonquian
and Tanoan systems the only essential difference seems
to be the existence in the former vs. absence in the
latter of specific morphological devices for signaling
obviative vs. proximate status within the third person.
The way obviation is signaled in Tanoan is by extending
the function of something that ordinarily serves as an
adpositional particle, i.e. -di in Arizona Tewa (see ex.
7b) or -pa in Picuris (see ex. 12b) (the corresponding
Southern Tiwa marker is -ba in 13b). As glosses in
these examples indicate, each of these morphemes
ordinarily marks certain noncore nominal statuses; each,
for instance, includes instrumental marking among its
functions. Given their other functions, it might be
appropriate to refer to the relevant Tanoan morphemes as
'quasi-obviative' markers, reserving the label
'obviative' for markers in other systems (e.g.
Algonquian) which lack case functions and are used in
transitive predications for signaling low relative
ontological saliency of a third person argument. It
also seems reasonable to conclude that the difference
between a system with true obviative markers and one
with only a quasi-obviative is the difference between a
system which conforms more closely as against a system
which conforms less closely to the head-marking type.
As was just remarked, quasi-obviatives arise from case
particles. Moreover, as shown in the present work, their
presence typifies those inverse systems which have
caselike alternations of pronominal paradigms--as
contrasted with systems having true obviative markers,
like Algonquian languages, which are simultaneously
languages without morphological case or caselike devices
to mark the statuses of core arguments.

In sum, the difference between Algonquian type and Tanoan type voice patterning is not based on an opposition in their voice typology, i.e., active/passive type vs. direct/inverse type. Rather, both groups of systems are of one and the same voice type, direct/inverse,[5] the essential differences between them being based on a distinction between close conformity to the head-marking type with the concomitant presence of morphology specific to obviation, as against looser conformity to the head-marking type and absence of the obviative as a specific morphological category.

Footnotes

*I am indebted for clerical assistance to R. Bauman, for a copy of Rosen 1989 to Carol Rosen, and for content comments to Bernard Comrie. Errors are solely the author's responsibility. Glosses to examples include the following abbreviations: I = paradigm I; II = paradigm II; dir = direct; inv = inverse; p = person; pl = plural; obl = oblique; obv = obviative; sg = singular.

[1]In the Cree example (1a) the direct voice morpheme has phonetic content. However, in some direct/inverse voice systems some or all instances of the direct category, in contrast with the inverse, receive zero marking. According to the position taken in the present work, all Tanoan language data below illustrate zero-marking of the direct voice.

[2]Because of its importance in the organization of and maintenance of coherence in discourse, some writers treat the proximate/obviative subclassification of third person arguments in inverse systems as a form of reference tracking or as akin to switch-reference marking. Since the present work does not allow for a full discussion of obviation and its functions, the reader is invited to consult one of the best published concise treatments, that of Goddard 1984.

[3]There is one point on which Picuris and Arizona Tewa differ in regard to distribution of elements of bound pronominal paradigms. In both languages alternations of verbal paradigms are not possible in the case of local verbal forms, or transitive predications in which both logical subject and object are SAP. While Picuris handles the situation by treating all such forms morphologically as direct forms, in Arizona Tewa such forms are inverse or, in Kroskrity's parlance, 'passive'. Note, however, that it is just on the grounds that Arizona Tewa's local prefixes wi- and di- appear in (8) (cited from Kroskrity 1985) among other inverse ('passive') prefixes that they are treated here as not belonging to the direct prefix paradigm.

[4](13a,b) are cited from Allen and Gardiner 1981:293. It should be noted that there is a complex body of factors which determine conditions of permissible and obligatory incorporation of nominals on verbal bases in Southern Tiwa. Details of these conditions are given in Allen, Gardiner and Frantz 1984, in Frantz 1985, and in Rosen 1989. For present purposes all that need be said is that incorporation or its failure is not a sufficient criterion for assigning logical roles to arguments of 3sg/3sg transitive predications in this language; the presence or absence of the -che morpheme discussed in the main text is indeed crucial as stated.

[5]A detailed survey of the typology of major classes of voice behaviors, including the direct/inverse type, is in progress (Klaiman to appear). The present work is based on a portion of one chapter of this work, which remains in preparation at the time of this writing.

References

Allen, B. and D. Gardiner. 1981. Passive in Southern Tiwa. In C. Elerick (ed.), Proceedings of the Ninth Southwestern Areal Language and Linguistics Workshop, 291-302. El Paso: University of Texas.

Allen, B., J. Gardiner, and D. Frantz. 1984. Noun incorporation in Southern Tiwa. Intl J. of American Linguistics 50.3:292-311.

Comrie, B. 1980. Inverse verb forms in Siberia: Evidence from Chukchee, Koryak, and Kamchadal. Folia linguistica historica 1:61-74.

Dahlstrom, A. 1986. Plains Cree morphosyntax. Ph.D. diss., University of California-Berkeley.

Dunnigan, T., P. O'Malley, and L. Schwartz. 1978. A functional analysis of the Algonquian obviative. Minnesota papers in linguistics and the philosophy of language 5, 7-21.

Frantz, D. 1985. Syntactic constraints on noun incorporation in Southern Tiwa. In BLS 11, 107-116. Berkeley: Berkeley Linguistics Society.

Goddard, I. 1984. The obviative in Fox narrative discourse. In W. Cowan (ed.), Papers of the 15th Algonquian Conference, 273-286. Ottawa: Carleton University.

Jelinek, E. 1985. Ergativity and the argument type parameter. In S. DeLancey and R. Tomlin (eds.), Proceedings of the First Pacific Linguistics Conference, 168-182. Eugene, OR: Department of Linguistics, University of Oregon.

Klaiman, M.H. Grammatical voice. Cambridge: Cambridge University Press. In preparation.

Kroskrity, P. 1985. A holistic understanding of

Arizona Tewa passives. Language 61.2:306-328.

Nichols, J. 1986. Head-marking and dependent-marking grammar. Language 62.1:56-119.

Rosen, C. 1989. Southern Tiwa: Another view of its morphosyntax. Ms.

Shayne, J. 1982. Some semantic aspects of yi- and bi-in San Carlos Apache. In P. Hopper and S. Thompson (eds.), Syntax and semantics 15: The grammar of transitivity, 379-407. NY: Academic.

Whistler, K. 1985. Focus, perspective, and inverse person marking in Nootkan. In J. Nichols and A. Woodbury (eds.), Grammar inside and outside the clause, 227-265. Cambridge: Cambridge University Press.

Witherspoon, G. 1977. Language and art in the Navajo universe. Ann Arbor: University of Michigan.

Witherspoon, G. 1980. Language in culture and culture in language. Intl J. of American Linguistics 46.1:1-13.

Wolfart, H.C. 1973. Plains Cree: A grammatical study. Transactions of the American Philosophical Soc. n.s. 63, pt. 5.

Wolfart, H.C., and J. Carroll. 1973. Meet Cree: A practical guide to the Cree language. Edmonton: University of Alberta.

Zaharlick, A. 1982. Tanoan studies: Passive sentences in Picuris. Ohio State University Working Papers in Linguistics 26, 34-48.

ASPECT-MARKING IN Gĩgbe PREPOSITIONS:
A COGNITIVE APPROACH TO MULTI-CATEGORIALITY

Marshall Lewis
Indiana University

0. Introduction*

Cross-categorial affinities between verbs and prepositions have attracted the attention of researchers with a wide range of orientations. Jackendoff [1977], for example, proposes to express the commonalities between Vs and PREPs in English through shared lexical-category features. Practitioners of generative semantics, e.g. Becker & Arms [1969], go further, deriving English PREPs and Vs from a common underlying category to account for shared formal properties. A similar derivational relationship is posited within the Case Grammar framework of Chafe [1970] to account for shared semantic characteristics, with PREPs treated as underlying Vs.

Languages whose prepositions are homophonous with verbs, as is routinely the case in languages with serial verb constructions, present the strongest kind of *prima facie* motivation for analyses which relate these categories. Linguists describing such languages sometimes conclude that the grammar does not recognize a separate lexical category of PREP, as the words that fulfill the functions allocated to PREPs in European languages are found to display the morphological behavior the author takes as criterial for verbhood. The usual situation in serializing languages, though, is that such items exhibit some but not all of the characteristics of verbs, so that their categorial status becomes a point of controversy. Even where a distinct category of PREPs is assumed, a relationship is inevitably postulated on the diachronic plane: the claim of Lord [1973] and Givón [1975] that present-day PREPs in the serializing languages of Africa have developed from erstwhile verbs enjoys a very widespread (if almost wholly uncritical) acceptance.

The present paper takes a different approach, exploring the cognitive basis for the V-PREP connection, whether considered from a synchronic or a diachronic standpoint. Attention will be focused on a pattern of aspectual marking in Gĩgbe,[1] whereby some--but not all--PREPs may bear the suffix which marks Habitual Aspect. The occurrence and selective applicability of this characteristically verbal property within the category of PREPs in Gĩgbe is shown to be semantically motivated, and to follow from a localistic model of functional clause structure in the language. This model is in fact claimed to embody a skeletal definition of the concept EVENT which exerts a pervasive organizational influence on Gĩgbe syntax, serving to shape and constrain a number of central constructions.

This paper is conceived as an ecumenical contribution toward the development of cognitively-oriented perspectives on linguistic phenomena. In presenting the analysis, though, I will draw freely on some useful concepts enunciated within the specific framework of Cognitive Grammar (CG), as set forth e.g. in Langacker [1983].[2] While CG provides a vocabulary which is particularly favorable to the natural expression of the ideas presented here, the essentials of the account should be compatible with a variety of approaches.

1. PREPs and Vs in Gɛ̃gbe

Like many other serializing languages, Gɛ̃gbe deploys a small lexical class of PREPs, most of which are homophonous with verbs. PREPs are defined here as morphemes which: (a) introduce NPs into clauses, composing with them to form phrasal constituents; and (b) contribute to the identification of the semantic role assigned to the following NP; but (c) cannot function as the main predicate in a clause. The first two properties are common to Vs and PREPs; the third distinguishes the two categories. Gɛ̃gbe forms which function in both categories are shown in Table 1 along with (approximations to) their basic meanings:

	[só]	[tó]	[Dó]	[dó]	[ná]
PREP	from	via	to	against	for
VERB	start from	pass by	place	set	give

Table 1: Gɛ̃gbe forms with both V and PREP guises[3]

While there is clearly some kind of semantic affinity between each PREP in Table 1 and its verbal homophone, the PREP guise must be distinguished from the corresponding verb. For example, when ná occurs in a minimal clause, i.e. in the frame [NP __ NP NP], it is necessarily interpreted as meaning "give". When it follows another VP, in contrast, ná may introduce Benefactive NPs (and some other kinds of abstractly affected human participants). More generally, the actual meaning assigned to a given token of a word in Table 1 correlates directly with the syntactic context in which it occurs.

This functional difference is manifested in many disparities in morphosyntactic behavior between PREPs and Vs. For example, Vs can be fronted for Focus in the Copy-Cleft construction, whereas PREPs cannot. Similarly, Vs but not PREPs may serve as bases for the various types of derived nominalization. In addition, VPs but not PPs can be combined to form a Consecutive construction by the insertion of a Connective morpheme sɔ́ before the non-initial Vs. Finally, and most directly relevant to the concerns of this paper, PREPs do not in general attract morphological exponents of verbal operator categories (e.g. Tense, Modality, Status, etc.). Thus, ná in [1] is necessarily interpreted as a PREP; if a separate Future marker were to precede it, ná could only be attributed its verbal sense "give", which would render the sentence unacceptable:

```
1. wó lá tó   nya sugbɔ̌ (*lá) ná  Ayí
   33 FUT emit word many   FUT PREP A.
   "They will say many things to Ayi."
```

2. Habitual-Aspect marking on Gɛ̃gbe PREPs

There is, however, one notable exception to the general lack of congruity between the morphological behavior of PREPs and Vs: the phenomenon of Habitual Aspect-marking on certain PREPs. Gɛ̃gbe clauses are marked as Habitual through affixation to the verb of a lexically toneless postclitic -na (HAB). HAB obligatorily appears on the main verb, but in some cases it may optionally recur on a subsequent PREP, as in [2]:

2. a) wó tó-ná   nya sugbɔ̌ ná (-ná) Ayí
    33 emit-HAB word many PREP -HAB A.
    "They say many things to Ayi."
  b) Ayí da-na   kpé Dó (-ná) si-me
    A. throw-HAB stone PREP -HAB water-interior
    "Ayi throws stones into the water."

This morphological capacity to recapitulate the HAB-marking on the
verb is not, however, a property of all PREPs, as seen in [3]:

3. a) wó vá-ná   Lome tó (*-ná) France
    33 come-HAB L.   PREP -HAB F.
    "They come to Lome via France."
  b) wó De-na   kpé só (*-ná) si-me
    33 remove-HAB stone PREP -HAB water-interior
    "They remove stones from the water."

Thus we cannot account for the distribution of HAB in terms of any
simple mechanism which would assign this morphology on the basis
of lexical category or shared categorial feature.

    On the other hand, it would miss a significant generalization
if susceptibility to HAB-marking were stipulated in the lexicon as
an arbitrary fact about certain PREPs, as this property partitions
the class on a principled semantic basis: <u>PREPs whose object NPs
represent Goals may bear HAB, while PREPs which introduce other
sorts of roles may not.</u>[4] This is further illustrated in [4a-c] for
the most concrete type of case, i.e. PPs that specify the spatial
Goal in events involving displacement of a Theme:

4. a) wó gɛ́-ná   Dó (-ná) kpá-me
    33 fall-HAB PREP -HAB courtyard-interior
    "They fall into the courtyard."
  b) wó gɛ́-ná   só (*-ná) atí-jí
    33 fall-HAB PREP -HAB tree-top
    "They fall from the treetop."
  c) wó gɛ́-ná   tó (*-ná) xɔta-jí
    33 fall-HAB PREP -HAB roof-top
    "They fall through the roof."

As shown, HAB optionally marks the PREP <u>Dó</u> which codes Locative
Goal, but not the Source-coding PREP <u>só</u> or the Route-coding <u>tó</u>.
    The ability of Goal-coding PREPs to bear HAB is not limited
to literal motion scenes, but also holds for PREPs that introduce
Goals of a more abstract type, as in [2a] above and [5b-c]:

5. a) wó sã́-na   bó Dó (-ná) gli-a ŋútí
    33 tie-HAB charm PREP -HAB wall-DEF surface
    "They attach amulets to the wall."
  b) wó sã́-na   gbe dó (-ná) mí
    33 tie-HAB voice PREP -HAB 11
    "They cast spells on us."
  c) wó sã́-na   kɔ̃́ ná (-ná) mí
    33 tie-HAB knot PREP -HAB 11
    "They tie knots for us."

Each of the sentences in [5] depicts an event in which the gesture designated by the verb sã is directed toward the final NP. These three event-types differ, however, in the relative abstractness of the path. [5a] reports a typical spatial displacement event, with a concrete Theme relocated in familiar space. In [5b] the Theme is less concrete, but the expression continues to exploit the image of a transmitted object set on a course to its terminus; this path is, however, situated not in three-dimensional space but rather in the abstract domain of the Agent's intentionality. Similar remarks apply to [5c], in which the Benefactive object of the PREP ná is the participant targeted by the subject to be ultimately affected by the energy expended. More will be said about the relationship between concrete spatial and abstract Goals in Section (7).

To sum up, the ability to bear HAB-marking is a morphological property exhibited by all verbs and a subset of PREPs in Gĩgbe; it is in fact the only such property which PREPs display. In the rest of this paper, I shall develop an account of this phenomenon which seeks to explain why: (a) verb-morphology may be found with PREPs; (b) the only such marker is HAB; (c) the only PREPs that can bear HAB are those which introduce Goals; (d) this capacity extends to PREPs which introduce various types of abstract Goals; (e) HAB is never obligatory on PREPs--if it can occur at all, it is optional.

3. CG preliminaries: Vs and PREPs compared and contrasted

Part of the similarity between Vs and PREPs is rooted in the fact that--in CG terms--words in both classes designate Relations, i.e. they express "interconnections among participating entities" (Langacker [1983:230]). More specifically, those Gĩgbe PREPs which have verbal homophones (i.e. the forms in Table 1) are those PREPs which, like verbs, denote Complex Relations: that is, the semantic representation of each item depicts a changing configuration. This is obvious for the Verbs, which denote change-of-position events; similarly, the locative PREPs só, tó, and Dó (introducing spatial Source, Route, and Goal, respectively) encode path sub-components of such events, which track these changes in relation to specific coordinates. As noted above, the distribution of HAB suggests that the PREPs ná and dó, which introduce sentient Targets of directed action, are likewise modeled semantically as dynamic paths. Thus, abstract paths to non-spatial Goals are treated in the same way as concrete paths bounded by spatial Goals: as series of points which represent a developing relationship to some reference participant.

It is no surprise, of course, to find that those PREPs which have verbal homophones--as well as those which may bear the Aspect marker HAB--all have the dynamic semantic character prototypically associated with verbs. The common semantic content shared by these Verbs and PREPs will be referred to henceforth by saying that both represent VECTORS, i.e. progressive paths in three-dimensional or teleological space. Whereas the semantic content of a V suffices to project an entire clausal predication, however, a PREP can only specify a component Relation within this projected scene. A basic factor distinguishing Vs and PREPs is thus the function of coding INDEPENDENT vs. DEPENDENT VECTORS. This difference, in turn, can be understood as part of a considerably more pervasive network of Figure-Ground contrasts, a topic explicated in the next section.

4. Aspect-marking and Figure-Ground contrast

A central tenet of CG is that all grammatical constructions have inherent semantic value, in that they represent conventional patterns for the expression of conceptual structure. The syntactic unit clause, for instance, serves as a theatre for the linearized representation of a complex conceptual unit which we may call an EVENT. The grammar of any language consists in large measure of a set of resources--morphological, syntactic, intonational, etc.-- for imposing multiple levels of figure-ground organization on the semantic components of an Event. At the highest level of clausal organization, the division into subject and predicate constitutes a conventional format for casting some participant as the primary figure, i.e. the starting-point for Event-tracking in the clause.

Of more crucial relevance to this paper are the ways in which smaller constituent units in the clausal infrastructure likewise embody figure-ground contrasts. Within the predicate, for example, a verbal object (if present) is similarly endowed with the status of (secondary clausal) figure in relation to any remaining NPs, in virtue of its prototypical role as the participant most directly affected by the process the verb designates. In parallel fashion, the verb enjoys a pre-eminence among the various Relation-coding elements composing the predicate, in its capacity as the primary semantic determinant of the Event-type represented in the clause. The inherent prominence which accrues to the principal grammatical relations thus derives from their function of expressing the core arguments of the verb, i.e. the entities involved in the featured or Profiled Relation that serves as the centerpiece of the clause.

As noted above, figure-ground contrasts may be signaled by a variety of devices. One of the most common resources of this sort involves aspectual morphology, which imposes a particular Temporal Profile on a conceived Event by specifying its internal temporal contour. As observed in Bybee [1985], the strong cross-linguistic tendency of such morphemes to be attracted to verbs has an obvious motivation: as the verb typically denotes the most dynamic aspect of a situation, it is the element most affected semantically by these markers, and is thus a natural locus for their realization. By this means, those words which do most to define the nature of the Event are directly imbued with prominence by the morphology which supplies them with the added temporal dimensionality. This is exactly the situation in Gĩgbe: the Aspect marker HAB attaches to verb-roots, identifying and highlighting the profiled Relation in the clause, which concomitantly foregrounds those participants most directly engaged in the focal (inter)action.[5]

From this functional perspective, the option of extending HAB to PREPs as well as Vs suggests a certain degree of flexibility in the imposition of figure-ground organization on the components of a scene. This conjecture is corroborated by a consideration of the semantic/pragmatic values associated with exercising this option. Alternative versions of a clause which differ only in the presence vs. absence of HAB on a PREP depict the same objective situation. Typically, however, native speakers consulted would describe the version with HAB as "emphatic" in some sense. Though in some cases the exact nature or target of this emphasis proved difficult to articulate, it was usually said to focus on the object of the PREP.

These intuitions are fully consonant with an analysis of the internal structure of the textual attestations of PREPs bearing HAB found in various published sources. Certain types of context appear to enhance the likelihood that a given PREP will be marked by HAB: in all cases, specific features of the sentence induce or facilitate an increase in the prominence of the Goal NP. There are basically two such types of configuration. In the first of these, the object of the PREP is cast in the pre-clausal Focus position, a construction whose function is to invest the preposed NP with high salience and information value, as shown in [6]:

6. ka   xóxó nǔ   wó gbe-na   yéyé-á Dó-ná
   rope old mouth 33 twist-HAB new-DEF PREP-HAB
   "It's the old rope's end one braids the new strands onto."
   PAZZI [1985:265,#1149]

The second type of context favorable to HAB on a PREP is a clause in which the verbal object is expressed in a way that accords this participant a low measure of "individuation" (in roughly the sense of Hopper & Thompson [1980]) within that clause, as in [7a-b]:

7. a) wó ŋlɔ-na   nú   ná-ná   Anagó-á-wó
      33 write-HAB thing PREP-HAB A.-DEF-PL
      "They wrote things for the Anago people."
      WESTERMANN [1931:30]
   b) ..., éyé b-é   sa-na   ná-ná-m
      and COMP-3 sell-HAB PREP-HAB-1
      "..., and she would sell [it] for me."
      WESTERMANN [1931:35]

Generic NPs like nú "thing" in [7a] represent one kind of poorly individuated object common in the textual examples featuring HAB on a PREP; other types include indefinite and non-referential NPs. The lower limit on individuation for a participant within a clause is zero realization; this is the case with the understood Theme of sa "sell" in [7b], whose overt antecedent serves as direct object in the preceding clause.

Thus, the optimal conditions for marking a PREP with HAB seem to involve circumstances in which the object of the PREP acquires increased prominence, surpassing the direct object (if present) as the affected participant whose role in the event is most in focus. The PREP which defines the nature of this role is included as part of the profiled Relation in the clause by the application of HAB. Not surprisingly, this upgrade is only possible for dynamic PREPs, which resemble (prototypical) verbs semantically in that they code evolving configurations; thus, PREPs such as kú "with" and le "at" which designate static Relations never bear HAB. As we have seen, however, there are other PREPs which apparently possess this same dynamic, path-like quality, yet they never bear HAB: só "from" and tó "via". In the next section, an explanation is given of the fact that only PREPs which introduce Goals can bear HAB in Gɛ̃gbe.

5. Modeling Gɛ̃gbe clause structure: the EVENT TEMPLATE

Canonical Gɛgbe clause structure is organized by a functional
matrix that I will call the EVENT TEMPLATE (ET). The ET is defined
in terms of an ordered array of Thematic macro-roles, which may be
identified with the cardinal localist roles Source, Theme and Goal
(in respective linear order). The most important of these is Goal,
as it serves as terminal bound of the ET. The ET may be thought of
as a semantically-constituted schema mediating between conceptual
representations and linear syntactic organization. It embodies a
skeletal model of the architecture of the conceptual unit EVENT,
which constrains the internal structure of any linguistic unit in
Gɛ̃gbe that functions to represent an Event.

The organizing influence of the ET on grammatical patterns in
Gɛ̃gbe is manifested over a wide range of constructions at various
levels of syntactic complexity. The smallest domain in which it is
operative is the individual lexical verb. Within the lexicon, the
Source:Theme:Goal thematic matrix defines the maximal role-cluster
associated with a monomorphemic verbal entry; thus, no verb may
have a valency above three without recruiting a PREP to introduce
each additional role. Canonical mappings of these arguments into
clausal positions, moreover, are likewise governed by the ET: the
unmarked NPs associated with a ditransitive verb appear in the
linear order Subject, Direct Object and Indirect Object, bearing
the thematic values Source, Theme and Goal, respectively.

Many Gɛ̃gbe clauses depict an Event by some more complicated
structure like the serial verb construction (SVC), a paratactic
sequence of VPs whose linear order must recapitulate the order of
occurrence of the corresponding actions.[6] As established in Lewis
[1988], the ET continues to exert its organizational influence in
this domain, embodying another fundamental semantic constraint on
the serializability of VPs in Gɛ̃gbe: as soon as a NP expressing a
Goal occurs, the ET is terminally bounded and no further VPs may
extend the series. This restriction is illustrated in [8a-d]:

    8. a) Ayí yi (*asime) ple te
          A. go market buy yam
          "Ayi went (to the market) & bought yam."
       b) Ayí tó/*vá   asime gbɔ
          A. pass/come market return
          "Ayi passed by/came to the market & returned home."
       c) wó lé   Ayí wu
          33 seize A. kill
          "They caught & killed Ayi."
       d) wó lé   azé Ayí (*wu)
          33 seize charm A.   kill
          "They cast a spell on Ayi (& killed him)."

In [8a], an object of yi "go" would realize a Goal, which would
terminate the ET and thus block any further (serialized) VPs; a
second VP is fine, however, if yi has no object. The contrast in
[8b] shows that Thematic role is indeed the crucial factor, as the
locative direct object of tó "pass"--specifying a non-final point
that defines the Theme's Route--fails to terminate the ET, while
the corresponding sentence where this locative expresses a Goal of

vá "come" is ungrammatical. Finally, in [8c] where Ayí is a Theme, a second VP may follow; in [8d], on the other hand, Ayí is a Goal (the role of the second unmarked object of any ditransitive Gẽgbe verb, as stated in Note 3) and thus no further VPs may occur.

These Goal-based restrictions on lexical argument structure and serializability can be seen as specific consequences of a more general constraint: constituents that realize material included in the ET must appear in a linear order which recapitulates the flow of energy in the Event in iconic fashion. This constraint likewise serves to explain the patterns of HAB-marking on Gẽgbe PREPs, and affords deeper insight into the relationship between PREPs and Vs. As shown in [3a-b], PREPs--unlike Vs--can introduce thematic terms counter-iconically; however, such PREPs cannot be marked with HAB. This suggests that the profiling function associated with HAB in Section (4) is directly related to the ET, the domain in which the constraints obtain. The ET is thus an integral part of the system for imposing figure-ground organization on the semantic content of the clause. The essentially atemporal character of PREPs follows from their typical exclusion from the ET: as non-featured Vectors, they are not accorded a Temporal Profile, and accordingly are not subject to the continuous tracking that applies to Vectors in the ET. Thus PREPs may introduce terms in counter-iconic order. The application of HAB-marking to a PREP, however, brings it into the ET, where tracking must be iconic; thus HAB only marks PREPs whose objects do not violate this constraint, i.e. those coding Goals.

The ET is thus constituted by a selected VECTOR CHAIN, which, when maximally elaborated, connects Source, Theme, and Goal in that order--an alignment which iconically recapitulates the flow of energy in the Event. This arrangement provides the necessary cohesion for the Vector Chain to be continuously tracked. A Vector which introduces a Thematic term in a counter-iconic position, in contrast, cannot be situated within the ET, as this would result in a processing anomaly (retrograde tracking).

A central claim of this paper, then, is that the possibility of marking PREPs with HAB in Gẽgbe reflects a pragmatic option in the imposition of figure-ground relations on the component Vectors which comprise the Event. The Aspect morphology that furnishes the featured predicate(s) with a Temporal Profile thereby highlights a particular Vector Chain that traces the flow of energy iconically in relation to selected participants in the Event. In appropriate circumstances, this marking may be extended to a PREP that codes a Goal in some domain, thus expanding the ET to accommodate an added Vector. This elasticity of the terminal bound of the ET represents the crucial factor in understanding the ostensibly ambi-categorial behavior of Goal-coding PREPs with respect to HAB.

6. Displacement Events and Subtrajectories

So far attention has been focused on why PREPs should display Aspectual marking at all. The further question arises, however, as to why this marking should be optional. To gain insight into this facet of the problem, it is natural to consider any other kinds of configurations in which HAB is optional on some item. As reported in Lewis [1989], this marking pattern may be observed in two other construction-types: Verb-Particle combinations and certain SVCs.

In this section, the optional nature of HAB-marking in all these contexts will be attributed to a single semantic factor. Central to this analysis is a particular notion of lexical decomposition, which is most readily explicated in connection with motion events.

The semantic subclass of verbs which I will call DISPLACEMENT VERBS designate event-types wherein a Theme participant undergoes a change of location. Displacement verbs in Gẽgbe (as in English) typically subcategorize optional or obligatory PPs which identify the course described by the Theme. Adapting terminology developed within the CG framework, I will distinguish between two components of motion events. The Trajectory is concerned with the onset of an event, i.e. the initial, counter-inertial mode of participation of the subject. The characterization of the Trajectory is the primary semantic contribution of the verb, which identifies the nature of the subject's involvement with the AFFECTEE (Theme in displacement events). The Subtrajectory is that aspect of the lexical semantics of a verb which has to do with the nature of the effect; where the Affectee is a Theme set in motion, the Subtrajectory is equatable with the induced path.[7] This terminology is exemplified in [9]:

9. | AGENT | TRAJ. | THEME | SUBTRAJ. | GOAL |
|-------|-------|-------|----------|------|
| Ayí | da | kpé | (Dó | si-me) |
| A. | throw | stone | PREP | water-interior |

   "Ayi threw a stone (into the water)."

A Subtrajectory is always implicit in the lexical semantic content of verbs such as da "throw", but its overt expression is typically optional. The PP Dó si-me in [9] which specifies the path is said to Elaborate the Subtrajectory; if no constituent were present to elaborate this path, the Subtrajectory would remain Sublexical.

Other kinds of constituents besides PPs can also elaborate a Subtrajectory, and optional HAB-marking is likewise a feature of these constructions. Closely related to PREPs, first of all, are a handful of Particles (PCLs) which collocate with certain verbs to form complex lexical items.[8] While it is difficult to formulate a precise characterization of the semantic content of any PCL which holds consistently across all the expressions it participates in, PCLs all seem to have some kind of directional import in relation to the Theme, and can thus be said to express Subtrajectories. As shown in [10], PCLs may optionally bear HAB:

10. a) wó kplɔ -na   Ayí dó (-ná)
       33 accompany-HAB A. PCL -HAB
       "They follow Ayi."
    b) wó kɔ-na   si   Dέ (-ná)
       33 pour-HAB water PCL -HAB
       "They pour out libations."

Like other serializing languages, Gẽgbe also deploys verbs to elaborate Subtrajectories; the use of this construction specifies that the motion induced by the Agent in the Theme also involved some energy input from the latter.[9] HAB is also optional on verbs which fulfill this function, as illustrated in [11]. Crucially, SVCs of this type contrast morphologically with others in which

the non-initial VPs do not express a Subtrajectory. In the latter
type of combination, HAB is obligatory on both verbs, as in the
examples shown in [12]:

11. a) wó nya-na   Ayí vá (-ná) asime
       33 chase-HAB A. come -HAB market
       "They chase Ayi here to the market."
    b) wó dɔ̃-ná   Ayí yi (-na) Lome
       33 send-HAB A. go -HAB L.
       "They send Ayi to Lome."
12. a) wó je-na   klo fã   -na/*ø kwě
       33 engage-HAB knee intone -HAB   prayer
       "They kneel & pray."
    b) aŋwízṹ mú nɔ-na   aŋwízũ-jí yi -na/*ø o
       ebb   NEG stay-HAB ebb-top   go -HAB   NEG
       "The ebb cannot stay at its maximum depth
                    & also flow on."   PAZZI [1985:281]

Thus, HAB is optional on any item expressing a Subtrajectory,
regardless of its categorial affiliation (assuming the Vector that
it realizes satisfies the ET-based continuous-tracking constraint,
and is accordingly eligible to bear HAB in the first place). What
matters is the status of the non-initial Vector in relation to the
lexical semantics of the preceding main verb: HAB is optional on
elements that code Vectors which are semantically dependent on the
main verb, obligatory on items that are independent in this sense.
    This conclusion is re-enforced by a consideration of the fact
that PCLs, PREPs, and Vs do not exhibit equal propensities toward
HAB-marking. When a Subtrajectory is expressed by a V, the normal
tendency is for HAB to occur, whereas a PREP serving this function
usually remains unmarked, and HAB on PCLs is very uncommon. These
three types of morpheme that express Subtrajectories thus form a
cline in terms of amenability to HAB-marking. This property can,
moreover, be correlated with the extent to which the Subtrajectory
is represented as a distinct Vector, conceptually independent of
the sub-event expressed by the preceding verb (the Trajectory). A
PCL-coded Subtrajectory is highly deficient in this regard: with
no object to identify its terminus, such a path is specified only
in terms of its starting-point. As this point is defined relative
to the participants involved in the Trajectory sub-event, such a
Subtrajectory is minimally dissociable from the verb. A PREP, on
the other hand, has an object NP of its own, which furnishes the
principal specification of the Subtrajectory (its terminus) in
terms of a participant not involved in the Trajectory sub-event.
Even so, though, the sub-event of the Theme following this path is
entirely dependent causally on the initial sub-event in which the
Agent acts upon the Theme. When a verb realizes the Subtrajectory,
in contrast, the displacement is partially dependent on an energy
contribution by the Theme, as noted above. Subtrajectories coded
by verbs are thus more distinct from the Trajectory sub-event than
those coded by PREPs (and, *a fortiori*, those coded by PCLs).

7. <u>Extending the analysis: Subtrajectories and Intentional Goals</u>
    The above account attributes the occurrence of HAB on certain
PREPs to the Goal role their objects bear, and the optionality of
HAB on such PREPs to their function of expressing a Subtrajectory.
This term has so far been defined as a path that is: (a) traversed
by the Theme argument of the preceding verb, and (b) semantically
implicit in the lexical meaning of that verb. This section will be
concerned with cases of optional HAB on PREPs which the account as
developed so far fails to cover, and will modify it accordingly.
    First of all, it was noted earlier that the option of marking
Goal-coding PREPs with HAB extends to the PREP <u>ná</u> which introduces
Benefactive NPs, as in [13]:

    13. é po-na   abi ná-ná-m
        3 strike-HAB sore PREP-HAB-1
        "She tended my wounds."   WESTERMANN [1931:4]

In this usage, <u>ná</u> does not elaborate a Subtrajectory as this term
is defined above. While Benefactive <u>ná</u> can plausibly be claimed to
express a conceived path, it is not a path along which a Theme NP
is displaced, but rather a path in an abstract domain toward the
target of the Agent's intentionality. Moreover, it is generally
assumed that Benefactive is a peripheral role which is extrinsic
to the lexical-semantic content of the verb. To the extent that
Benefactive <u>ná</u> codes some kind of path, then, it is one that would
seem to satisfy neither of the above criteria for a Subtrajectory.
    These cases can be encompassed within the above analysis by
extending the notion of Subtrajectory. It has already been noted
in Section (2) that this term must be construed broadly enough to
include various kinds of non-spatial path-analogs; let us suppose
that these may include paths in the abstract domain of the Agent's
Intentionality, or INTENTIONAL SUBTRAJECTORIES. (The question of
what it is that follows such paths is addressed below.) As for the
second criterion in the above definition of Subtrajectory, I would
argue that the widespread view of Benefactives as extrinsic to the
lexical meaning of the main verb is simply incorrect: Intentional
Subtrajectories are indeed implicit in the verbal semantics. To
clarify the sense in which this is so, however, it is necessary to
articulate a richer conception of lexical decomposition than has
been presented up to this point.
    The basic notion here is a factoring of the semantic content
of a verb into the INTENTIONAL LEVEL and the EFFECTUAL LEVEL. The
former is an abstract domain in which causal energy originates and
its teleology is determined, while the latter involves the domain
in which this energy impinges on an Affectee and its consequences
are realized. This dichotomy cross-cuts the distinction between a
Trajectory and a Subtrajectory, which is pertinent to both levels.
The relationships among the resulting semantic "quadrants" can be
most easily explicated in regard to a specific example, like [14]:

    14. Ayí da   kpé   (Dó   si-me)   (ná   mí)
        A.   throw stone PREP water-interior PREP   11
        "Ayí threw a stone (into the water)   (for us)."

As stated above, Trajectories involve the onset of an event,
i.e. the character of the subject's involvement with the Affectee.
This component of the verbal semantics can now be further analyzed
into an Intentional Trajectory, which specifies volitionality (or
the lack thereof), and the Effectual Trajectory, which identifies
the manner in which the subject behaves so as to impinge on the
Affectee. The semantic Trajectory components of both levels may
provide for the expression of a Subtrajectory. Thus, the PREP Dó
in [14]--which expresses the displacement of the Affectee on the
Effectual level--realizes a path implicit in the Manner semantics
of da "throw", since the nature of the Agent's physical activity
necessarily imparts motion to the Theme. The Benefactive PREP in
[14], meanwhile, elaborates an Intentional Subtrajectory--a path
projected from the volitional specification of da, i.e. provided
for in the verb's Intentional Trajectory.

When both types of Subtrajectory co-occur in a Gĩgbe clause,
moreover, the Effectual must precede the Intentional, as in [14].
The constituents which express the Effectual-Level semantics thus
form a continuous sequence preceding any Intentional-Level PPs.[10]
This may be seen as another manifestation of the requirement that
Event sub-units must track the flow of energy in iconic fashion,
assuming that Gĩgbe grammar operates with a model of the internal
structure of (volitional) Events along the following lines: causal
energy originates in the Intentional domain, produces consequences
for an immediate Affectee in the Effectual domain, and this action
serves in turn as the means of affecting some further participant
targeted as ultimate Affectee in the abstract Intentional domain.

The sequence of Effectual-Level Vectors also constitutes an
integral unit of semantic organization in other respects. As noted
above, although Benefactive ná is claimed here to express a path,
there is no individual NP that can be associated with the role of
Theme as is the case in motion events. Instead, what is projected
along the abstract Intentional path is some anticipated advantage
issuing from the deed performed by the Agent. The analog of Theme
with Benefactives, then, is the deed that serves as a teleological
vehicle--i.e. the composite set of Effectual-Level Vectors. Thus
the proposed schema for decomposition makes it possible to follow
through on the localist model for PREPs coding abstract Goals.

In addition to bringing ná within the scope of the analysis,
the proposed bicameral structure for verbal semantics immediately
provides a solution to another potential snag. This involves the
PREP dó, which poses a serious problem as long as it is conceived
as elaborating a Subtrajectory in the original sense of the term,
i.e. a path traversed by the Theme. On this construal, the object
of dó fails to bear a consistent thematic role in relation to the
Theme, as a comparison of [15] (=[5b]) with [16] shows:

```
15.   wó sã-na    gbe   dó  (-ná) mí
      33 tie-HAB voice PREP -HAB  11
      "They cast spells on us."
16.   ...., wó só  wlá-ná   dó-ná    nyɔ́nu
            33 CONN hide-HAB PREP-HAB woman
      "...and so they hide [such matters] from women."
                                           [Radio Snippet]
```

While the object of dó in [15] appears to be a Goal, in [16] this
PREP codes a path that leads away from its object. This apparently
variable directionality of dó damages the account in two respects:
first, it becomes impossible to attribute a uniform semantic value
to this PREP; even more seriously, the possibility of HAB on dó in
[16] would contradict the generalization that the only PREPs which
can bear HAB are those whose objects are Goals. These difficulties
disappear once we identify the path coded by dó as an Intentional
Subtrajectory. The constant factor in the semantics of dó is not
the relationship of its object to the Theme, but the relationship
of its object and the Agent: dó introduces a "Target of contrary
activity by the Agent". This role is a sub-case of the macro-role
Goal--an appropriate label is ANTIGOAL--and may thus bear HAB.
    One possible implication of the distinction between Effectual
and Intentional Levels is that G̃gbe grammar might well tolerate a
particular kind of exception to the constraint that bars more than
one Goal term within the ET. It is clear from [14] that both types
of Subtrajectory can co-occur in a clause; it is thus plausible to
suspect that they might be able to co-occur as profiled Vectors as
well. This hypothesis is in fact borne out by data like [17-18]:

    17. ...éyé wó dó-ná   é-me vo   ná-ná   wó...
        and 33 set-HAB 3-in elsewhere PREP-HAB 33
        "...and they (would) set some of it aside for them..."
                                        SCHROEDER [1936:69]
    18. avṹ mú Du-na   ví-á   yi-na lãjɛ̃-me ná-ná-E   o
        dog NEG bite-HAB child-DEF go-HAB flesh-in PREP-HAB-3 NEG
        "A dog doesn't bite a child down into his flesh."
                                        WESTERMANN [1954:126]

Here, HAB occurs on the PREP ná even though a Goal term is already
expressed, by the indirect object wó in [17] and the direct object
lãjɛ̃me in [18]. Such examples would appear to violate the ET-based
constraint against profiling additional Vectors once the Goal role
has been realized, given the assumption that presence of HAB on a
PREP reflects inclusion of the corresponding Vector within the ET.
These data can be easily explained on the proposed analysis simply
by recognizing that the ET can accommodate both an Effectual Goal
and an Intentional Goal. Hence the constraint is preserved, though
it must be qualified as applying only to Effectual-Level Vectors.
    There is thus considerable motivation for the conception of
lexical decomposition proposed here, as it provides for a unified
analysis of HAB-marking on PREPs, accounts for all of the relevant
data, makes correct predictions, and preserves a number of strong
ET-based constraints by explaining away apparent counter-evidence.
In addition, the recognition of the Effectual-Level action as the
analog of Theme in the Intentional domain establishes the crucial
semantic link between the concrete Displacement Events denoted by
ditransitive verbs like ná "give" and dó "set" and the Intentional
Subtrajectory function of their role-coding PREP counterparts. In
treating Effectual and Intentional Subtrajectories alike, G̃gbe
exploits a widespread linguistic metaphor relating the teleology
of action to the directedness of motion.

8. Conclusion

The occurrence of Habitual-Aspect marking on certain PREPs in Gᶤgbe is a highly structured phenomenon, governed by principles of semantic organization which shape the linguistic representation of events across a wide range of constructional schemas. Of central importance is the functional notion of a thematically constituted Event Template, whose Source:Theme:Goal structure serves as a root metaphor for the grammar--this localistic matrix is projected over a broad spectrum of configurations, from the argument structure of individual lexical verbs on up through progressively more elaborate assemblages. Gᶤgbe syntax thus reflects the ontogeny of events-- and presumably our cognitive experience and processing of events-- in direct iconic fashion.

The optional occurrence of HAB on PREPs in Gᶤgbe, along with the homophony between HAB-markable PREPs and verbs, would suggest to many that this morphological phenomenon represents a vestigial verbal property not yet entirely lost in the ongoing evolution of PREPs from verbs in Gᶤgbe. While this path of grammaticization has been posited by numerous writers for a host of languages, detailed characterizations of such change in progress are extremely scarce. Those who propose such accounts generally have little to say about the actual forces which drive this diachronic process, or what the systems in transition look like, e.g. which verbal properties are most tenacious, which verbal lexemes seem to be most resistant to erosion of their verbal identity, etc. If the consensus diachronic position is indeed correct, the Aspect-marking patterns considered here provide a window on a pivotal stage in the little-understood phenomenon of lexical-category genesis. What is especially notable about this diachronic stage is that the presumed category change is proceeding in a very systematic fashion, and in accordance with the same semantic principles which organize many of the stablest syntactic constructions in the language. In these circumstances, one may even come to question whether the data actually do reflect ongoing re-analysis or rather long-standing ambi-categoriality.

The central goal of this paper is conceived in a way that is neutral between these two possibilities: to elucidate the semantic factors that underlie the well-established dynamic tension between verbs and PREPs, whether on the synchronic or diachronic plane. On the assumption that the integration of these two perspectives must be a basic objective for a unified science of language, an optimal account of patterns such as those examined here should be equally applicable to both dimensions of linguistic analysis. The present study has attempted to advance this syncretic ideal in proposing an analysis whereby the same set of factors which govern tightly constrained grammatical regularities in Gᶤgbe can also be seen to structure the more variable patterns suggestive of ongoing change. In sum, this paper has hopefully shown that significant prospects for holistic convergence in linguistic theory lie in cognitively oriented approaches to natural language phenomena.

NOTES

* I am indebted to Linda Schwartz for valuable comments on earlier drafts, and to Ronald Langacker for helpful discussions of some of the ideas herein. I assume full liability for all remaining flaws.

1. Gᷥgbe is a SVO Kwa language spoken in Togo and southern Bénin.
The transcription used here is a slightly modified version of the
standard orthography. Only lexical tone is reflected (low tonemes
remain unmarked). Ḍ represents the voiced alveo-palatal retroflex
stop. Examples cited from other works have been converted from the
source orthography; morpheme glosses and translations are my own.
2. Technical terms particular to CG will be kept to a minimum, and
will appear underlined with an initial capital letter where first
defined. I will also employ a few idiosyncratic terms which enjoy
no such imprimatur, but which should be fairly transparent; these
appear in upper case where first introduced. Any other underlining
(of English words) is for ordinary emphasis. Many terms denoting
specific categories of Gᷥgbe grammar also bear initial capitals.
3. As PREPs só, tó and Dó take locative NP objects; the first two
also have this complement structure as Vs. As PREPs dó and ná take
objects whose referents are (presented as) human. As verbs, Dó, dó
and ná may occur with two unmarked NP objects, but can also appear
with other valencies. The role-structure in ditransitive frames is
regularly Theme-Goal. Despite tantalizing correspondences between
the V and PREP guises of these items, a host of empirical problems
attend any attempt at a conflationary analysis.
4. This generalization also holds for the three PREPs that have no
verbal homophones (not shown in Table 1): kú "with" and le "at" do
not introduce Goals and cannot bear HAB, while DóDá "toward" which
introduces anticipated spatial Goals can also bear HAB.
5. Since the category Tense also has temporal import, the question
may arise as to why FUT may not extend to PREPs the way HAB does.
This disparity in morphological behavior is directly attributable
to the essential functional difference between these two temporal
categories. Tense situates the Event as a whole in relation to an
external--i.e. deictic--frame, while Aspect is concerned with the
internal temporal extension of an individual lexical predicate. In
Lewis [1989], the clitic HAB was demonstrated to be unique among
the verbal operator exponents in Gᷥgbe in having as its functional
domain the individual Vector (i.e. VP or PP). FUT lá, in contrast,
is a free auxiliary; as such, it precedes all Vectors and has the
entire clause as its scope. Since Tense treats an Event globally,
each FUT marker is associated with a separate Event unit. Aspect,
in contrast, operates within more local a domain, at the level of
Event sub-units (i.e. Vectors), and is thus uniquely suited to the
function of reflecting relative prominence among Event components.
6. There is general agreement among writers on serialization with
the oft-quoted assertion of Lord [1973:269] that the component VPs
of a SVC "refer to subparts or aspects of a single overall event".
Many spontaneous metalinguistic observations by native speakers of
Gᷥgbe in the course of serialization research amply bear out this
dictum as psychologically valid, for this language at least.
7. The values attached to the terms Trajectory and Subtrajectory
in this paper represent a slight departure from the way they are
used in Langacker [1983:279].
8. Of the five PCLs--dó, Dó, DóDá, Dá, Dἑ--the first three have a
homophone among the Goal-coding PREPs; they differ from the latter
in that they do not have objects of their own and do not generally
contribute to the semantics of the clause in a compositional way.

As with PREPs and verbs, an attempt to reduce PCLs to intransitive PREPs meets with several impediments; in any case, an analysis of PCLs as PREPs would have no effect on the proposals in this paper. 9. I know of only one potential exception in Gĩgbe to this claim-- the following data given in Jondoh [1980:81], which involve a type of SVC commonly cited by writers on other languages, suggest that this generalization may not strictly hold for all Gĩgbe speakers:

(a) avũ-á lɔ keké-á gɛ̃   (b) Marie tutu Afí je   anyí
dog-DEF ram bike-DEF fall   M.   push A. engage ground
"The dog toppled the bike."   "Marie pushed Afi down."

Gĩgbe speakers I consulted uniformly rejected (a), along with any SVC alternatives. In contrast, some speakers did half-heartedly accept (b). Interestingly, though, the verb gɛ̃ in (a) carries a lexical specification of Non-Volitional, while je (anyí) in (b) is unspecified for Volitionality. The generalization in question thus appears to cast some sort of shadow even here.
10. This generalization also holds of SVCs, of course, since Verbs never express Intentional-Level Vectors.

REFERENCES

Becker, A.L., and D.G. Arms. 1969. Prepositions as predicates. CLS 5:1-11.

Bybee, Joan L. 1985. Morphology. Amsterdam: John Benjamins.

Chafe, Wallace L. 1970. Meaning and the structure of language. Chicago: University of Chicago Press.

Givón, Talmy. 1975. Serial verbs and syntactic change: Niger-Congo. In Charles N. Li, ed., Word order and word order change, 49-112. Austin: University of Texas Press.

Hopper, Paul J., and Sandra A. Thompson. 1980. Transitivity in grammar and discourse. Language 56.2:251-299.

Jackendoff, Ray. 1977. X-Syntax: a study of phrase structure. Cambridge, MA: MIT Press.

Jondoh, Edina E.A. 1980. Some aspects of the predicate phrase in Gĩgbě. Unpublished Indiana University PhD dissertation.

Langacker, Ronald W. 1983. Foundations of Cognitive Grammar. Bloomington: Indiana University Linguistics Club.

Lewis, Marshall. 1988. Semantic parameters of serializability: switch-trajector SVCs in Gĩgbe. Paper presented at the 19th Conference on African Linguistics, Boston, April 16, 1988.

------. 1989. Morphological subclassification of serial verb constructions in Gĩgbe. Paper presented at the 20th Conference on African Linguistics, Urbana-Champaign, April 19, 1989.

Lord, Carol. 1973. Serial verbs in transition. Studies in African Linguistics 4.3:269-296.

Pazzi, Roberto. 1985. Les proverbes du peuple Gɛn-Mina au littoral Togo-Bénin. Lomé, Togo: Institut National des Sciences de l'Education, Université du Bénin.

Schroeder, Johannes. 1936. Formenlehre des Gɛ̃-dialektes der Ewesprache. Durlach: Christliche Verlagsdruckerei Gebr. Tron.

Westermann, Diedrich. 1931. Kindheitserinnerungen des Togonegers Bonifatius Foli. Mitteilungen des Seminars für Orientalische Sprachen 34.3:1-69.

------. 1954. Texte in der Gɛ̃-Mundart des Ewe. Afrika und Übersee 39:1-5,119-127.

The Plural Word in Chalcatongo Mixtec[1]

Monica Macaulay
Purdue University

1 Introduction

Plural marking in Chalcatongo Mixtec[2] is entirely optional. When the plural is overtly expressed, it is not marked directly; that is, there is no nominal affixation which marks argument plurality. One of the alternative strategies which is employed instead is use of the free morpheme hiná?a, which simply means 'plural', and is illustrated in (1) through (4):

(1) káisiokú=∅ táa=rí hiná?a
    be+here=3 parent=1 plural
    My parents are here
(2) táa=rí hina?a na-šuk^wíi=∅ šiã
    parent=1 plural REP-turn=3 tomorrow
    My parents will return tomorrow
(3) ni-hãã=rí k^wa?à yu?à káni hiná?a
    CP-buy=1 many rope long plural
    I bought many long ropes
(4) Juan híndee=∅ hĩ-ĩĩ=ka ñayĩũ wãã hína?a
    Juan be+located+in=3 with-one=ADD people
       that plural
    Juan is there among those people

(1) contains a postverbal plural subject (táa=rí hiná?a);[3] (2) a topicalized plural subject (táa=rí hiná?a again); (3) a plural object (k^wa?à yu?à káni hiná?a); and (4) a plural oblique argument (ñayĩũ wãã hína?a).

Plural words such as the one just illustrated are the topic of Dryer 1987. Dryer defines "plural word" as follows:

> [The plural word is] a morpheme whose meaning and function is similar to that of plural affixes in other languages, but which is a separate word that functions as a modifier of the noun (Dryer 1987:1).[4]

Dryer surveys 307 languages which contain some kind of overt plural argument marking (this formulation is meant to exclude plural agreement marking on the verb). Of those 307 languages, 259 mark plural through affixation on the noun, and the remaining 48 make use

of a plural word. Dryer discusses a number of characteristics which the plural words in these 48 languages
have in common, as well as typological characteristics
of languages which have plural words. Both of these
topics will be considered below.

2   The Lexical Category of Hiná?a

The lexical category of hiná?a is somewhat unclear. The two most plausible options are pronoun and
quantifier, although we will see below that neither is
entirely satisfactory.
Examples like (5) and (6) illustrate the pronoun-
like behavior of hiná?a:

(5) káisikú=Ø hiná?a nù-mesa
be+located=3 plural face-table
They'll be on the table
(6) ká-hã?ã̃=Ø hiná?a be?e
PL-go=3 plural house
They went to their house

In both examples, one might be tempted to argue
that hiná?a is a subject pronoun in postverbal position. There are several reasons, however, why this
solution cannot be correct.
First, although free pronouns do cooccur with
clitic pronouns in Mixtec, they are normally barred
from postverbal subject position. Free subject pronouns may only appear in topic position.
Second, if hiná?a were a pronoun, it would be a
rather deviant one, since it is neutral with respect to
person. In fact, it can be overtly marked for any
person, through attachment of a pronominal clitic, as
in (7) and (8):

(7) ndɨ?ɨ=rí hiná?á=rí ni-čà-koyo=rí
all=1 plural=1 CP-come-pour=1
Wę all came
(8) kɨ?ɨ=ni hiná?a=ni
go=2RESP plural=2RESP
(You plural) go!

In addition to the fact that this lack of an inherent person category makes hiná?a quite unlike any
true pronoun in Mixtec, we can observe that the true
pronouns never allow attachment of a pronominal clitic
at all, even one of the same person. Yet we see a

variety of clitics attaching to hiná?a -- additional
examples are given in (9) and (10):

(9) ndíto=to hiná?a=to
    be+awake=3RESP plural=3RESP
    They are awake
(10) ro?o híná?á=ro kí?ĩ kóyo=ro
    you plural=2 go pour=2
    You (plural) will go

    Such evidence clearly indicates that hiná?a is not
a pronoun. In examples like (5) and (6), the zero
third person marker is what functions as the pronominal
subject, with hiná?a marking that subject as plural,
just as it may for any overt clitic pronoun (as in, for
example, (8) and (9)).

    With respect to the hypothesis that hiná?a is a
quantifier, however, the evidence is not quite so
clear.   Consider first (11) through (14), which provide examples of four typical Chalcatongo Mixtec quantifiers, and (15), which provides an example with a
numeral:

(11) ñani=rí ni-hà?à=Ø kʷà?à sú?ũ nuu=rí
    brother=1 CP-give=3 much money face=1
    My brother gave me a lot of money
(12) kʷáā=rí hoò lana
    buy=1 a+little wool
    I'm going to buy a little wool
(13) tɨnɨ há?a ká-hitá=rí ini be?e eskʷela
    various time PL-sing=1 stomach house school
    We often [lit: various times] sang in school
(14) ni-s-kéé=rí ndɨ?ɨ sè?è=ri
    CP-CAUS-eat=1 all child=1
    I fed all my children
(15) ni-hìni=rí ùù halúlí
    CP-see=1 two child
    I saw two children

    The semantics of hiná?a would seem to be consis-
tent with analysis as a quantifier, but comparison of
the data in (1) through (4) with the examples just
given shows that hiná?a does not exhibit the same word
order with respect to the head as other words do which
are unarguably quantifiers. The quantifiers (and the
numeral) illustrated in (11) through (15) precede the
head, while, as we saw in (1) through (4), hiná?a
follows the head.

    Dryer, in examining the categorial status of the
plural words in the languages of his sample, employs
strictly grammatical factors (that is, cooccurrence

possibilities and word order) as the primary criteria
for classification. Thus he would conclude from these
data that the Chalcatongo Mixtec plural word is not a
quantifier.

Furthermore, Dryer points out that plural words
are not precisely parallel in their semantics to quantifiers like some and many. Plural words are semantically less complex than quantifiers are. That is, quantifiers tend to code more than just plurality -- as
Dryer points out, they can be restricted to sets larger
than two, they can signal indefiniteness, and so on.
Plural words do not do any of this; they simply code
argument plurality.

Thus syntactic and semantic evidence would seem to
indicate that hiná?a is not a quantifier. The best solution to the problem of its lexical category might be
to assign it to a minor word-class of its own, which
is, in fact, one of the more common options Dryer finds
in his sample.

Despite the arguments that hiná?a is not a quantifier, however, we will see in the next section that it
shows some behavior which is quite similar to that
shown by clear cases of quantifiers in other languages.

3 Syntactic Properties of Hiná?a

Up to this point, hiná?a has been presented in
just two syntactic configurations:[5] first, in a phrase
which also contains the head it marks as plural (as in
(1) through (4)), and second, with a verbal clitic --
overtly expressed or not -- as head (as in (5), (6),
(8), and (9)). In the former case, the linear ordering
of hiná?a with respect to the head and other elements
of the phrase is as shown in (16).

(16) (QP) - N - (Adj) - (Det) - (hiná?a)

That is, hiná?a follows all other material in the
NP. Whether it is a sister to the head, or adjoined as
sister to the NP, however, is an issue to be discussed
further below.

In addition to the structures already presented,
there is another distributional possibility for hiná?a:
it can also be discontinuous with the head, as shown in
(17) through (19):

(17) tó?o wáā kúyaa=∅ nundùa hiná?a
     person that live=3 Oaxaca plural
     Those people will live in Oaxaca

(18) kúyaa=ri núndua hína?a=ri
    live=1 Oaxaca plural=1
    We will live in Oaxaca
(19) ña?à=ní hīī=ná hiná?á=ní
    come=2RESP with=1RESP plural=2RESP
    (You plural) come with me

These examples all contain (among other things) a
subject (topicalized or clitic), an intervening non-
subject argument, and a subject-modifying hiná?a in
sentence-final position.

As pointed out earlier, unmarked word order in
Mixtec is VSO. SVO order is often observed, however,
and seems to be preferred when there is a full NP subject. What is especially interesting about the discontinuous construction is that postposed hiná?a does not
occur when there is a full NP subject in post-verbal
position, as (20) illustrates:

(20) *nì-hitã?ã=∅ čàà wã īī hasì?ɨ hiná?a
    CP-fight=3 man that one woman plural
    *The men fought over/for/about a woman

There are two questions which are relevant at this
point with respect to the syntax of Mixtec: First, what
is the internal constituent structure of an NP which
contains hiná?a? Second, how is extraposition of the
plural word from post-verbal subject position blocked?

With respect to the first question, I would argue
that hiná?a is in an adjunction relationship to the
other material in the NP, since, as (21) illustrates,
it is possible to separate the rest of the NP from the
plural word, and move it to sentence-initial topic
position:

(21) táa=rí čakú=∅ hiná?a Mexico
    parent=1 live=3 plural Mexico
    My parents live in Mexico

This is one of the respects in which hiná?a bears
some resemblance to a quantifier in, for example,
English or French: the structure I am proposing is similar to what Sportiche (1988:426) calls a "partitive
quantifier." These structures are shown in (22):

(22) Partitive Q: [$_{NP}$ Q NP]

    Mixtec plural word: [$_{NP}$ NP hiná?a]

As for the second question posed above, a full
treatment is beyond the scope of this paper. What is

needed is a way to block sentences like (20), while allowing for sentences like (17) through (19). This will be accomplished by allowing extraposition of hiná?a from topic position to CP, while prohibiting such adjunction from postverbal subject position to IP. This is shown schematically in (23):[6]

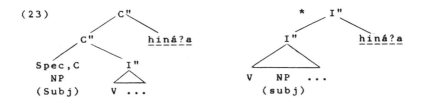

(23)

4 Plural Words in Other Dialects of Mixtec

This brings us now to other dialects of Mixtec, in which we find, unfortunately, not much data available on plural words. Daly (1973) mentions a plural word in Peñoles Mixtec (and in fact, Dryer includes this in his sample), and Alexander (1980) mentions one for Atatlá-huca Mixtec. Aside from these two, I have found no mention of such an element in any of the other dialects of Mixtec.[7]

The data from Peñoles Mixtec are quite dissimilar to those from Chalcatongo Mixtec. The first construction in which Daly mentions the plural word is the quantified NP, as shown in (24) through (27):

(24) kúmí ñáž‡u   'four people'
     four people
(25) bài ñáž‡u   'many people'
     many people
(26) kwee tée   'men'
     plural men
(27) ókó kwee tée   'twenty men'
     twenty plural men
     [Daly 1973:20]

Comparing example (26) with the others in this set, we see that in Peñoles Mixtec the plural word conforms to the usual linear ordering for quantifiers, in that it precedes the head. This is contrary to what is found in Chalcatongo Mixtec, in which the plural word is not ordered with the quantifiers.

Peñoles Mixtec also has a discontinuous plural
construction, as shown in (28):

(28) tǎtà=í ndɨ?ɨ ditó=í kɨ̃-na-ku?ñu-kwè=dé ñu?u
     father=1 with uncle=1 go-REP-irrigate-plural=3M
     ground
     My father and my uncle are going to irrigate the
     field
     [Daly 1973:42]

The difference between this example and the ones
from Chalcatongo Mixtec is that, according to Daly's
analysis, kwe(e) in (28) is not a free word, but is
instead a bound morpheme. If it is obligatorily bound,
it no longer qualifies as a plural word (under Dryer's
definition). However, it is possible that this example
simply shows the result of rapid-speech contraction (a
common phenomenon in Mixtec). In that case, this would
be an example like (21), in which the plural word is in
post-verbal subject position, marking as plural a topicalized NP.[8]
The data from Atatláhuca Mixtec, contrary to those
from Peñoles, are quite comparable to the Chalcatongo
Mixtec data. The first relevant point is that the plural word in the Atatláhuca dialect occurs after the
head, as it does in Chalcatongo Mixtec:[9]

(29) yùkʷǎ ĩ́ĩ loko tɨndàku ácí tó?ò hijnã?ã=de
     there exist many worm say authority plural=3M
     Over there, there are many worms, say the
     authorities
     [Alexander 1980:54]

This dialect also employs the discontinuous plural
construction, as shown in (30):[10,11]

(30) te-ká-sá?a ñã?ã-ũ ayate hijnã?ã=ña
     and-PL-make woman-the ayate plural=3F
     And the women make ayates [cloth made of maguey
     fiber]
     [Alexander 1980:55]

One point of difference here is that apparently
the Atatláhuca dialect does permit a full postverbal
subject NP with a postposed plural word.
     (31) summarizes the data from the three dialects:

(31)

DIALECT	FORM	PRE/POST HEAD	DISCONTINUOUS
Chalcatongo	hiná?a	post	yes
Atatláhuca	hijnã?ã	post	yes
Peñoles	kwee	pre	yes

The plural words in Chalcatongo and Atatláhuca
Mixtec are obviously cognate, and exhibit virtually
identical grammatical behavior. The plural word in
Peñoles Mixtec, however, appears not to be related to
the plural word in the other dialects, and is only partially similar in behavior.[12]

5 Typological Considerations

This section presents a few brief observations
about Chalcatongo Mixtec and Dryer's typological findings concerning plural words.
First, (32) presents Dryer's findings with respect
to word order type and the relative order of plural
word and head noun. In this table, the numbers represent linguistic groups comparable, Dryer says, to the
subfamilies of Indo-European, rather than individual
languages. (The reason for this kind of categorization
is that tabulation of these data simply by number of
individual languages per category would likely skew the
results, due to the fact that a large number of the
languages containing plural words in the sample are
closely related. Thus tabulating for larger linguistic
groupings is intended to control for this problem.)

(32) WORD ORDER TYPE AND ORDER OF PLURAL WORD
AND HEAD NOUN

	Plur-N	N-Plur
OV	0	11
VO	10	2

Recall that Peñoles Mixtec is one of the languages
which Dryer includes in his sample. It is counted in
this table as a VO language which positions the plural
word before the noun. However, if we were to add Chalcatongo Mixtec to the table, it would belong to the
small group of VO languages which have the plural word
after the noun.
This poses a problem for the method of categoriz-
ing the languages of the sample: how can we categorize
the languages by subfamily when two related languages

(in fact, dialects of a single language) show different
relative orderings?

Dryer points out that the data in (32) are the inverse of what one would expect, given well-known claims
about word order universals; in particular, the claim
that modifiers tend to precede the noun in OV languages, and tend to follow the noun in VO languages.[13]
He uses such data to argue that the universals are simply incorrect. The full argumentation and range of
data involved in this claim are much too complex to go
into in this paper.[14] Restricting ourselves only to the
present case, however, note first that the Chalcatongo
data support the predicted tendencies, rather than contradict them. Second, it must be noted that Dryer's
claim rests on the tacit assumption that plural words
are modifiers. If my conclusions about the constituent
structure of the NP and the plural word in Chalcatongo
Mixtec are correct, the plural word is not, strictly
speaking, a modifier. Nor does it fit into any of the
categories that e.g. Lehmann (1973) calls "nominal pre-
modifiers." Thus, universals of modifier-noun ordering
may be irrelevant to these data. Before we can compare
such universals with data on the ordering of plural
words and their associated nouns, we first must establish the category and constituency of the plural words
with respect to those nouns.

In a final section, Dryer mentions typological
characteristics that languages with plural words have
in common. These are listed in (33):

(33) TYPOLOGICAL CHARACTERISTICS OF LANGUAGES WITH
     PLURAL WORDS

    1. They tend to have classifiers
    2. They show a tendency towards isolating/
       analytic structure, although:
    3. Some verbal inflection is common
    4. Case marking on nouns is rare
    5. Pronominal possessive marking on nouns
       is found in about half the sample

Chalcatongo Mixtec fits the profile quite well.
While it no longer has productive nominal classification, it has clear relics of such classification, and
many other Mixtec dialects still do make productive use
of classifiers. Chalcatongo Mixtec has some verbal inflection, no case marking, and pronominal possessive
marking on nouns. Because of the verbal inflection, it
cannot be said to have isolating structure, but it is
true that inflection is limited in this language.

Unfortunately, as Dryer points out, there is no ready explanation for the occurrence of plural words in languages with this particular set of characteristics. It is obvious why plural words occur most often in languages with little or no nominal inflection -- clearly, it is an alternative means of marking plurality -- but the rest of the characteristics remain unexplained.

6 Conclusion

This paper has presented a detailed description of an instance of the little-known phenomenon of plural words (a phenomenon which is little-known either in Otomanguean languages, or in the languages of the world, for that matter). The lexical category of this form and aspects of its syntactic behavior have been considered, it has been compared with similar forms in other dialects of Mixtec, and finally, it has been evaluated with respect to the findings of Dryer (1987).

There is one general point which bears repeating: the syntactic findings point up the need for caution in making typological generalizations. Admittedly one of the hazards of doing broad typological studies is the fact that one is at the mercy of one's sources, since the level of detail required is often quite simply not present in the grammars one consults. It is to be hoped that a study like this one will help to provide that level of detail.

Notes

1. I would like to thank Claudia Brugman, Amy Dahlstrom, Matthew Dryer, Charles Jones, and Joe Salmons for their comments on previous versions of this paper. Of course none of them is responsible for the final product.

2. This paper is based on data from the Chalcatongo dialect of Mixtec (an Otomanguean language spoken primarily in the state of Oaxaca, Mexico), collected between 1981 and 1988. Abbreviations which are used in the examples are as follow: 1, 2, 3 - First, second, third person; ADD - Additive; CAUS - Causative; COND - Conditional; CP - Completive; F - Feminine; M - Masculine; NEG - Negative; PL - plural; REP - Repetitive; RESP - Respect.

3. Unmarked word order in Mixtec is VSO.

4. Whether or not the Chalcatongo Mixtec plural word should be considered a modifier is discussed below.

5. I would especially like to thank Charles Jones for his help with this section. The usual disclaimers apply.

6. I am assuming, for the purposes of exposition, an analysis along the lines of Sproat (1985), in which VSO word order is derived from underlyingly configurational SVO word order. Surface SVO word order is considered topicalization, i.e. subsequent movement of the subject to specifier of C position.

7. It is likely that this is an oversight, not a statement about the incidence of plural words in dialects of this language.

8. Daly formulates this as an agreement transformation, and, interestingly, says that it is obligatory. This is noteworthy because marking of plurality is optional in all of the other dialects of Mixtec with which I am familiar.

9. I have adjusted Alexander's orthography to conform more closely to standard Americanist transcription. The only exception is her "jn," which I believe is a voiceless nasal. I have left it as is since I'm not entirely sure what it represents.

10. Note in this example that the third-person feminine clitic, =ña, makes it clear that it is the subject, ñá?ã 'woman', which is pluralized by hiná?a, rather than the object, ayate.

11. One additional point in the comparison between these two dialects is that, according to Alexander, the plural word in the Atatláhuca dialect is restricted to animate entities. In contrast, my data from Chalcatongo Mixtec include repeated examples in which hiná?a is used with inanimates. However, while trying recently to test the grammaticality of various examples containing hiná?a, my consultant spontaneously told me that it was reserved for animate NPs. This is the same consultant who had earlier provided me with the inanimate examples. I leave this an unsolved problem.

12. Relevant topics which deserve further study are: What are the sources of the two plural word types? And, what form do other dialects have (assuming that they do have plural words)?

13. e.g. in Lehmann 1973, Greenberg 1963.

14. For more on this issue, see Dryer 1986 and 1988.

References

Alexander, Ruth Maria. 1980. Gramática Mixteca: Mixteco de Atatláhuca. México, D.F.: Instituto Lingüístico de Verano.

Daly, John P. 1973. A Generative Syntax of Peñoles Mixtec. Norman: Summer Institute of Linguistics.

Dryer, Matthew. 1986. Word Order Consistency and English. In Delancey and Tomlin (eds.): Proceedings of the Second Annual Pacific Linguistics Conference. Eugene, Oregon.

------. 1987. Plural Words. Paper given at LSA, San Francisco, December 1987. (To appear 1989, Linguistics.)

------. 1988. Object-Verb Order and Adjective-Noun Order: Dispelling a Myth. Lingua 74:185-217.

Greenberg, Joseph H. 1963. Some Universals of Grammar with Particular Reference to the Order of Meaningful Elements. In: J. Greenberg (ed.), Universals of Language. Cambridge, MA: MIT Press.

Lehmann, W.P. 1973. A Structural Principle of Language and Its Implications. Language 49:47-66.

Sportiche, Dominique. 1988. A Theory of Floating Quantifiers and Its Corollaries for Constituent Structure. Linguistic Inquiry 19:425-449.

Sproat, Richard. 1985. Welsh Syntax and VSO Structure. Natural Language and Linguistic Theory 3:173-216.

Nominal and Clausal Event Predicates

Friederike Moltmann
Massachusetts Institute of Technology

1. Introduction

Davidson(1967) has proposed that PPs like *in the morning* as in (1)a. and adverbs like *slowly* as in (1)b. are to be analysed as predicates over events. These events are primitive entities and occupy an additional argument place of the verb.

(1)a. John ate in the morning.
   b. John ate slowly.

In this account, (1)a. and (1)b. are analysed as (2)a. and (2)b., respectively.

(2)a. $\exists e$ eat(e, John) & in(e, the morning) & PAST(e)
   b. $\exists e$ eat(e, John) & slowly(e) & PAST(e)

In this paper, I argue that not only PPs and adverbs can act as predicates over the event argument of the verb, but certain NPs and certain clauses can, as well. I will give syntactic and semantic arguments that NPs that are cognate objects and clauses of (at least some) nonbridge verbs are optional predicates over the event argument of the verb. With respect to clauses, I will argue that for independent reasons the meaning of both independent and embedded sentences can be construed as event-properties, namely as properties over intentional events.

2. Cognate Objects as Event Predicates

In the following, I will discuss the properties of 'true' cognate objects, as exemplified in (3). They differ in the relevant properties from the cognate objects as in (4), which behave as arguments of the verb rather than as cognate objects in the narrow sense (cf. Jones 1988).

(3)a. John died a painful death.
   b. John screamed a terrifying scream.
(4)a. Mary danced this dance very often.
   b. Mary said these words.

I claim that the cognate objects in (3) are optional predicates over the event argument of the verb. In this account, (3)a. is semantically represented as in (3').

(3') $\exists e$ die(e, John) & painful death(e) & PAST(e)

Two types of evidence support this analysis. Cognate objects exhibit characteristic properties of adjuncts on the one hand and characteristic properties of predicates on the other hand.

As adjuncts, cognate objects are in general optional, as the correlates of (3) in (5) show.

(5)a. John died.
   b. John screamed.

Furthermore, cognate objects disallow passivization (noted in Jones 1988).

(6)a. *A painful death was died by John.
   b. *A terrifying scream was screamed by John.

Finally, cognate objects do not affect the *have*/*be* alternation in a language such as German. Cognate objects in German bear accusative Case. Direct objects in German require the auxiliary *have*. Therefore if cognate objects were arguments, they would require the auxiliary *have* rather than *be*. But, as (7) shows, the presence of cognate objects allows auxiliary *be* if *be* is the auxiliary selected by the verb, and it is incompatible with auxiliary *have* if *have* is not selected by the verb.

(7)a. Hans ist/*hat gestorben.
     'John is/ has died.'
   b. Hans ist/*hat einen qualvollen Tod gestorben.
     'John is a painful   death died.'
   c. Maria ist/*hat gesprungen.
     'Mary is/ has jumped.'
   d. Maria ist/*hat einen weiten Sprung gesprungen.
     'Mary is/has a wide jump jumped.'
   e. Maria hat/*ist geweint.
     'Mary has/is wept.'
   f. Maria hat/*ist ein paar Traenen geweint.
     'Mary has/is a few tears wept.'

These data are immediately explained if cognate objects are taken as adjuncts rather than arguments of the verb.
   The predicative status of cognate objects is most notably shown by the fact that cognate objects exhibit the indefiniteness effect.

(8)a. *A death occurred today in this clinic. It was John who died that death.
   b. *John screamed this scream/every scream we heard today.

The predicative status of cognate objects might also be related to the impossibility of topicalization. Notice that certain adverbial event predicates such as *slowly* and obligatory controlled clauses cannot be topicalized either (the latter has been noted by Safir(1986), footnote 3, chap.3.).

(9)a. *A painful death, John died t.
   b. *A shrill scream, John screamed t.
   c. This man, John saw t today.
(10)a. *Slowly, John ate the cake.
    b. *Beautifully, Mary sang the song
(11)a. *PRO to go to school, John intends.
    b. *PRO to study Linguistics, John persuaded Mary.

Syntactic predication (Williams 1980) requires that subjects c-command their predicate. The data in   (11) might indicate that in English the predication relation (in the sense of Williams 1980) must hold even after topicalization (though not after wh-movement). Thus, *John* does not c-command PRO *to go to school* in (11)a.

But how can predication explain (9)? What is the subject of an adverbial event predicate or a cognate object? From the point of view of Davidsonian event-semantics the answer is obvious. If adverbial event predicates or cognate objects are predicated over the event argument of the verb, then the verb is the subject in the relevant semantic sense, since the event argument is not expressed syntactically by any other constituent. Therefore in order to satisfy conditions on predication, the verb must c-command an adverbial event predicate and the cognate object. Since *died* in (9)a. does not c-command *a painful death*, (9)a. is ruled out by predication theory.

Note that certain adverbials that have been taken as event predicates do not generally have to obey syntactic conditions of predication. These adverbials can freely be preposed, as shown in (12).

(12)a. In the kitchen, John ate.
    b. When John was tired, he ate.

However, there is evidence that these adverbials are in fact not event predicates, but rather predicates of situations, where situations are described by the entire sentence, whereas events are only designated by the verb. Consider (13).

(13)a. On a stormy day, everybody came to work late.
    b. Everybody came to work late on a stormy day.
    c. When it started raining everybody rushed home.
    d. Everybody rushed home when it started raining.

In (13)a. *on a stormy day* has wider scope than *everybody*, which in turn has wider scope than the event quantifier of *come*. Thus *on a stormy day* cannot be a modifier of the event, but rather of the entire situation in which everybody was involved in an event of coming late. Only in (13)b., *on a stormy day* can be taken as a modifier of the event, and also in this case conditions on predication are satisfied. A similar contrast is found in (13)c. and (13)d.

Notice that predication theory may - for the same reasons - rule out lack of passivization with cognate objects, as well. Passivization is impossible also with predicative NPs.

(14) A man was become/remained by John.

Now it appears that like the event predicates mentioned, certain clauses must stand in the syntactic predication relation to the verb. These types of clauses are the topic of the next section.

3. Clauses as Event Predicates

3.1. Sentence Meanings Construed as Event Properties

Before I discuss the types of clauses that I have in mind, I would like to motivate a construal of sentence meanings as event predicates and elaborate this for simple cases.

The leading idea with this construal is that sentences do not denote absolute propositions (such as sets of possible wolds or situations or functions from contexts into such sets), but rather are in an essential way related to an event, namely either a given event of uttering the sentence or - in the case of embedded sentences - the event described by the matrix verb.[1]

The main empirical motivations for construing sentence meanings as event properties are indexicality and intensionality phenomena. With respect to independent sentences, most indexical aspects (in a broad sense) of a sentence can be taken to involve a relation to the utterance of the sentence in a specific situation. With respect to embedded sentences, indexical aspects are to an extent not dependent on the utterance of the entire sentence, but rather on the event described by the matrix verb. I will illustrate the dependence of indexical aspects on an event (an utterance or a described event) first with independent sentences. Consider (15).

(15) The ghost disappeared.

Suppose u is an utterance of (15). Then in order to find out whether (15) is true or false, we must know the following. First, we must know what the speaker of u refers to with *the ghost*. Second, we must know the time of u. Third, we must know which domain of events (for instance at a specific time interval) the speaker of u considers for there being an event of disappearing of the ghost. Only if these indexical aspects of (15) are fixed that way, can we find out whether (15) is true or false.

If we take these indexical aspects of (15) as properties of utterances, then we can construe the meaning of (15) as a whole as a property of utterances, namely in the following way. If a given utterance u has the utterance property expressed by (15), then (15) is true (with respect to u).

Informally speaking (15) is true of an utterance u if roughly the following conditions hold.

(16) The speaker of u refers with the utterance of *the ghost* to exactly one
    thing x that belongs to the set of discourse referents of u and is a ghost,
    and there is an event e in the set of discourse events of u previous to u
    such that e is an event of disappearing of x.

Let me symbolize the notions that occur in (16) as follows. $ag(u)$ is the speaker of u, $u(K)$ the part of u that is the utterance of K (where K is a constituent)[2]. Ref is the relation of speaker reference such that $Ref(ag(u), u(K), x)$ holds if $ag(u)$ refers with $u(K)$ to x. $UD(u)$ (from 'universe of discourse') is the set of discourse referents relevant at u. Finally $<$ is temporal precedence (a relation that may hold between events).

Now we can symbolize the meaning of (15) as given in (16) in the following way.

(17) $\lambda u[\exists !x\ (Ref(ag(u), u(\textit{the ghost}), x)\ \&\ x \in UD(u)\ \&\ ghost(x))\ \&\ \forall x$
    $(Ref(ag(u), u(\textit{the ghost}), x) \rightarrow \exists e\ (e \in UD(u)\ \&\ disappear(e, x)\ \&\ e < u)]$

(17) is the property which holds of an utterance u iff there is exactly one thing relevant at u that the speaker of u refers to with uttering *the ghost* and for all x the speaker refers to with uttering *the ghost* there is a relevant event e (which is for instance relevant at a given time) previous to u such that e is a disappearing of x.

Now consider (15) as an embedded sentence, namely as the clausal complement of *say* in (18).

(18) John said that the ghost disappeared.

Think of (18) as being uttered in a situation in which John uttered *the ghost died* and believed - contrary to the speaker's belief - that there are ghosts and that a particular ghost had disappeared previous to John's coming to believe this. In this situation (18) is true.

In this reading, apparently the relevant indexical aspects of (15) do not depend on the utterance of the entire sentence (18) , but rather on the utterance of John that is described by (18). John refers by uttering something like *the ghost* (possibly in a language other than English) to exactly one ghost in the set of discourse referents dependent on u, and there is an event of dying of the ghost among the discourse referents dependent on John's utterance, and this event is previous to John's utterance. The set of discourse referents dependent on John's utterance may contain entities only John, but not the speaker uttering (18), has committed himself to (see below).

The dependencies of indexical aspects of the clauses in (18) on the described utterance rather than the utterance of the entire sentence can be accounted for in a rather simple fashion given the analysis in (17). We can take the clause in (18) to have exactly the same meaning as in (17) but now the content of the clause is not related to a potential utterance of (18), but rather to the described utterance of John. Formally, this means the event predicate given in (17) is predicated over an act of saying by John, which is the event argument of *say* .

So abbreviating the event predicate in (17) with P, (18) can schematically be represented as in (19).

(19) λu[$\exists$!x (Ref(ag(u), u(*John*), x) & x $\in$UD(u) & x is called John) & $\forall$x (Ref(ag(u), u(*John*), x) --> $\exists$e (e $\in$UD(u) & say(e, x, P) & e<u))]

In order to get predication of the clause over the described event, we will assume the following lexical postulate for the verb *say*.

(20) Lexical Postulate for *say*
    say(e, x, P) iff e is an utterance by x and P(e)

If we apply P to e, the utterance of John as described in (18), we get the following proposition.

(21) $\exists$!x (Ref(ag(u), u(*the ghost*), x) & x $\in$UD(u) & ghost(u) & $\forall$x (Ref(ag(u), u(*the ghost*), x) --> $\exists$e (e $\in$UD(u) & disappear(e, x) & e < u)

That is, the speaker of u, John, refers with the utterance of something similar in meaning to *the ghost* to exactly one ghost in the set of discourse referents dependent on John's utterance (the event argument of *say*) and there is among the discourse referents of John's utterance an event of dying previous to the utterance involving the ghost John refers to.

We have construed the set of discourse referents involved in (18) as a function of John's utterance. This is a way to account for phenomena of intensionality. The set of discourse referents depending on John's utterance may contain entities that only John conceives of, but not the speaker. So in order for (18) to be true, the speaker need not believe in ghosts. Thus, we may tentatively characterize sets of discourse referents as functions of events in the following way.

(22) UD(u) = the set of (actual or nonactual) entities which ag(u) conceives of and which are relevant for ag(u) at u.

Furthermore, we have to interpret u(K) for a constituent K not strictly as the utterance of K, but as the utterance of something similar in meaning to K. Thus we can give the following characterization of u(K).[3]

(23) u(K) = the part of u that is similar in meaning to K.

This analysis accounts for other propositional attitude verbs, as well. Consider the examples in (24) and suppose *the ghost* is interpreted de dicto, rather than *de re*.

(24) a. John believes that the ghost disappeared.
   b. John imagines that the ghost disappeared.
   c. John sees that the ghost disappeared.

In (24)a. the set of discourse referents depends on a state of believing, in (22)b. on an act of imagining and in (24)c. on a state of seeing. Like *say, believe, imagine* and *see* will denote three-place relations between events, agents and event properties, and the same postulate as for *say* given in (20) will hold of these verbs. We only have to generalize some notions that occur in (17). ag(u) is more generally the agent or intentional subject of the mental state u, u(K) is interpreted as the part of such a state that corresponds in meaning to K. Tense and reference, as well, are related to mental states as described by the verbs in (24).

Not all verbs denote three-place relations between events, agents, and event properties, which express the content of the event. As might be expected from the event-based theory of clauses, verbs may take *that* clauses which do not denote an argument of the verb, but rather act as modifier of the event, specifying that the event has a certain content.

3.2. Clauses as Adjuncts

As has often been noted (e.g. Stowell 1981), certain *that* clauses exhibit the properties of adjuncts, rather than arguments. These clauses include clausal complements of certain manner of speaking verbs such as *sigh* and *scream*.

In the event-based semantics of clauses, the semantics of adjunct clauses is straightforwardly accounted for. For instance, (23) can simply be analysed as in (26) (in the relevant respects).

(26) John sighed that the ghost died.
(27) $\exists e$ (sigh(e, John) & PAST(e) & P(e))

In the following I will list some of the indications for the adjunct status of these clauses.
   First, clausal complements of *sigh* and *scream* do not allow *wh* extraction, as observed in Erteschik-Shir(1977) (where these verbs are therefore labelled 'nonbridge verbs').

(28) a. *What did John sigh that Mary did t?
   b. *What did Mary scream that Bill discovered t?
(29) What did John say/believe/imagine/see that Mary saw t?

Impossibility of extraction from adjunct clauses as in (28) follows from recent generative syntactic theory (Chomsky 1986). Adjunct clauses do not receive a theta role from the verb and thus are not L-marked in the sense of Chomsky (1986). Therefore they create barriers for extraction.

Second, like all adjuncts, adjunct *that* clauses are generally optional.

(30)a. John sighed.
    b. John screamed.
(31)a. *John said.
    b. *Mary believed/imagined/saw.

Third, adjunct *that* clauses disallow passivization.

(32)a. *That the room was too cold was sighed by everybody.
    b. *That Mary was in danger was screamed suddenly by John.
(33)a. That snow is white was believed by everybody.
    b. That snow was edible was imagined by every Eskimo during the hunger period.

Fourth, adjunct clauses disallow topicalization.

(34)a. *That it is raining, John sighed t.
    b. *That Mary is in danger, John screamed t.
(35)a. That snow is white, everybody believes/says t.
    b. That snow was edible was imagined by every starving Eskimo t.

As with cognate objects this can be explained by predication theory. The verb, which acts semantically as the 'subject', must c-command the clause. C-command is not satisfied in sentences with topicalization or passivization.

Safir(1986) gave an explanation of the data in (34) in terms of Case theory. The crucial assumptions in this explanation are that variables (the traces t in (34)) must be assigned Case and that *sigh* and *scream* are not Case-assigning verbs. However, this explanation is weakened by the fact that cognate objects - which bear accusative Case - are possible with *scream* and the fact that other verbs that take clausal arguments do not assign Case as argued in Pesetsky (1982).

Finally, adjunct clauses are not allowed with certain nominalizations, as in (36) and (37).

(36)a. *Mary's sigh that it was always raining.
    b. *the scream that Mary is in danger
(37)a. John's belief that the ghost disappeared
    b. Mary's assertion that snow is white

Notice that the clauses in (37) are appositives, rather than complements, since the nominals in (37) refer not to the events (John's belief state in (34)a. or Mary's assertion in (37)b.), but rather to the content of the events, as expressed by the clause. I will therefore call these nominalizations 'content nominalizations'. That the nominals in (37) refer to the content rather than the event is further confirmed by the fact that they disallow indefinite or quantifying determiners (as observed in Higginbotham 1986, following Montague).

(38) a. *a belief that it is raining
    b. *every belief that it is raining
(39) a. *an assertion that it is raining
    b. *most assertions that it is raining
(40) a. the fact that snow is white
    b. *a fact that snow is white
    c. *every fact that snow is white

This arguably follows from the fact that propositions are uniquely determined by a *that* clause. That is, a *that* clause, for instance *that it is raining*, describes one and only one proposition, in this case the proposition that it is raining (at the relevant location). Apparently a description that determines necessarily a unique referent can only go with the definite article. Compare this to the obligatoriness of the definite article with superlatives, which also necessarily determine a unique object, as seen in (40).

(40) a. the tallest man
    b. *a tallest man
    c. *every tallest man

Given the event-semantic assumptions and the theory of clauses developed so far, (37)a. is to be analysed semantically roughly as in (41), where P is the event predicate given in (17).

(41) $\iota Q \ [\exists e \ \text{believe}(e, \text{John}, Q) \ \& \ Q - P]$

From this analysis of nominalizations with appositives, the unacceptability of (36)a. and (36)b., however, does not yet follow immediately. We must make an additional assumption about the interpretation of clauses in the complement position of deverbal nominalizations. Notice that the nominals in (36)a. and b. without the clauses are fine.

(42) a. the scream
    b. Mary's sigh

scream and *sigh* in (43) refer to events of screaming or sighing. In this interpretation, they also allow for modifiers that are predicates over the events such as *on that night* in (43)a. or *without any pause* in (43)b.

(43) a. The scream on that night worried John for several days.
    b. Mary's long sigh without any pause embarrassed John.

If *that*-clauses are just predicates over events we would expect that the event nominals in (42) should take *that* clauses in the same way as the event modifiers in (43). But, as we can see from (36), this is not the case. The nominals in (36) cannot refer to events. This suggests that *that* clauses which are in the complement position of deverbal nominalizations must obligatorily be interpreted as appositives, thus forcing the nominal to refer to the content, rather than to the event. This observation calls for a syntactic explanation that I am unable to provide in this paper.

Given this generalization about the interpretation of *that* clauses as appositives with deverbal nominalizations, we can explain the unacceptability of (36) as follows. The event predicates expressed by the clauses in (36)a. and b. do not occupy an argument position of the verb. Therefore an interpretation of (36)a. and b. as in (41), the only admissible interpretation, is impossible.

It appears that adjunct *that* clauses are possible with any verb under appropriate semantic conditions. However, the verb must describe events that can be intentional events, i.e. events that can represent a state of affairs. This follows from the way the event properties which constitute the content of *that* clauses are conceived. Event properties as expressed by *that* clauses can only hold of intentional or potentially intentional events. For instance, an event of trembling can never have an intentional content. Therefore *tremble* disallows *that* clauses as adjuncts, as (44)a. illustrates. But notice that *tremble* allows for cognate objects, which do not imply intentionality, as seen in (44)b.

(44)a. *John trembled that Mary suddenly entered the room.
   b. John trembled a small earthquake.

There are two kinds of adverbials, adverbials that are optional,as in (45), and adverbials that are syntactically obligatory, as in (46)

(45)a. Mary sang badly.
   b. Mary sang.
(46)a. John behaved badly.
   b. *John behaved.

Badly in (46)a. is syntactically selected by *behave,* yet it certainly does not denote an argument of the relation designated by *behave.* The semantic function of *badly* in (45)a. is simply that of a predicate of the event argument of *behave.*

The clauses that we have considered in this section have (as event-predicates) syntactically the same status as *badly* in (46)a. In the next section, I argue that there are clauses that have syntactically and semantically the status of *badly* in (46)a., namely clauses that are syntactically selected event predicates and that are semantically not arguments of the verb.

3.3. Selected Clauses without Argument Relation

Clausal complements of *seem* and *appear* are syntactically obligatory.

(47)a. It seems/appears that John is tired.
   b. *It seems/appears.

However, there is some evidence that complement clauses of *seem* and *appear* are not arguments. Nominalizations of *seem* and *appear* do not take clausal appositives.

(48)a. *the appearing   that John is tired
   b. *the seeming that John is tired

Furthermore, topicalization of clausal complements of *seem* or *appear* is disallowed.

(49)a. *That John is here, it seems t.
   b. *That John is here, it appears t.
(50)a. *That John is here seems.
   b. *That John is here appears.

We may take this as an indication (though not conclusive) that clausal complements do not express arguments of *seem* or *appear*. But as lack of topicalization shows, the clausal complements of *seem* or *appear* must nonetheless fullfill the syntactic conditions of predication, namely, they must be c-commanded by the verb. If it is correct that clausal complements of *seem* and *appear* are not arguments, but rather selected modifiers of the verb, then there is a natural explanation at hand why the clausal complements must stand in the syntactic predication relation to the verb. If predication of the clause over the event argument of the verb is not governed by the lexical meaning of the verb such as the condition in (20), then semantic predication over the event argument must be based on the syntactic predication relation, which requires c-command of the clause by the verb. Notice that this explanation holds also for (50) whether the clauses in (50) are taken to be in topic position (Koster 1978) or in subject position.

There is independent evidence that clausal complements of *seem* and *appear* are event predicates. Notice that *seem* and *appear* allow for *as if* clauses, as shown in (51).

(51)a. It seemed as if John was tired.
 b. It appeared as if it would rain all day.

As if clauses are typical event predicates in other contexts. As adverbials, they clearly modify the event argument of the verb. In (52)a. we see a selected *as if* clause and in (52)b. an adjunct *as if* clause.

(52)a. John behaved as if he was tired.
 b. John walked as if he had drunk too much.

Apparently, *as if* clauses are restricted to certain types of events. Propositional attitude verbs generally do not allow for *as if* clauses, and predicates that take sentential subjects such as *is probable* or *is true* disallow *as if* clauses.

(53)a. *John believed as if it was raining.
 b. *It is probable/true/obvious as if it was raining.

It should follow from a semantic analysis of *as if* that only events of a certain type (events of evidence or certain behaviours) are totally correct for *as if*.
 As if clauses can also occur with *seem* and *appear* in a small clause construction, as in (54).

(54)a. *John* seemed/appeared [t as if he was sick].
 b. *John* seemed/appeared [t sick].

In (54)a. the *as if* clause is predicated over John rather than the event argument of *seem*. However, this shows only that *as if* clauses can in certain circumstances be predicates of objects rather than events. Therefore (54) does not weaken the general point that *as if* clauses can be predicates over events. Notice that (51)a. and b. cannot be reanalysed along the lines of (54), namely with *it* being weather *it* or more generally ambient *it* (see Napoli(1988)), as in (55).

(55) *It* seems/appears [t as if John was tired].

It in (51) is clearly expletive it, rather than ambient *it*, since it is unable to control, as (56)a. shows.

(56)a. *It seemed as if it was raining, without seeming as if it was snowing.
   b. It rained without snowing.

Therefore we can conclude that the *as if* clauses in (51) are indeed predicates of the event arguments of *seem* and *appear*.

   I have suggested that both adjunct *that* clause and selected *that* clause complements of *seem* and *appear* must enter a syntactic predication relation with the verb. In neither case do the clauses denote an event property that satisfies an argument position of the verb as occurs with the clausal complements of *say, believe, imagine* and *see*. In the case of verbs like *say*, predication of the clause over the event argument is a matter of the lexical meaning of these verbs, a consequence of a 'meaning postulate' such as (20). Therefore predication over the event argument need not be represented in sentence meaning. Unlike adjunct clauses and clausal complements of *seem* and *appear*, clausal complements do not have to enter syntactic predication relation with respect to the verb, as we have seen.

   We have observed certain correlations with respect to semantic argumenthood and syntactic predication. A clause that is a semantic argument of the verb need not enter a syntactic predication relation with the verb. But a clause that is not an argument of the verb must enter such a syntactic predication relation. So the lack of semantic argumenthood correlates with syntactic predication. A clause that is semantically not an argument of the verb must be represented as a predicate of the event argument of the verb in the sentence meaning. Now it is clear why syntactic predication must hold. In order for the semantic operation of predication to apply, the clause must stand in a specific syntactic relation to the verb, which in this case is syntactic predication. In contrast, a specific syntactic relation is not required if a semantic operation is based on a lexical condition.

Appendix

In this appendix I will outline a small fragment of the event-based semantics that was employed in this paper.

   In this fragment, the basis of semantic operations are not syntactic rules combining constituents, but rather either the syntactic category of a constituent or syntactic relations holding among subconstituents of a constituent. Thus semantic composition essentially consists in the correlation of either a syntactic category C or a syntactic relation R and a semantic operation O. So if a constituent in a sentence belongs to category C or consists of subconstituents $c1$ and $c2$ such that R holds between $c1$ and $c2$, then the semantic operation correlated with C or R applies to the meaning m of c and yields the meaning m' of c with respect to the category C, or the semantic operation applies to the meaning of $c1$ and the meaning of $c2$ and yields the meaning (or part of the meaning) of c.

   Thus we have (roughly) the following principles for semantic composition for a correlation of syntactic categories or syntactic relations and semantic operations <C, O> or <R, O>, where m(c) is the (lexical or structural) meaning of a constituent c.

Principles of Semantic Composition for a Language L:
Let C be correlated with O and R be correlated with O' in L and let c be a constituent of an expression in L, then

(1) if c is a C, then $m(c) = O(c)$ or $m(c) = m(m'(c))$
(2) If c consists of constituents c1 and c2 and $R(c1, c2)$, then $m(c) = O'(m(c1), m(c2))$

The Fragment:

Categories of English:
$Det = \{the, a, every\}$
$N = \{man, ghost, scream\}$
$V = \{seem, scream, disappear\}$

Metalinguistic Symbols:
$l(c)$: the lexical meaning of c (taken as properties or relations)
L_n: variable ranging over lexical meanings that are n-place relations
E: variable ranging over event properties
E_1: variable ranging over 2-place relations between events and objects, ...,
E_n: variable ranging over (n+1)-place relations between events and n objects.

Correlation of Syntactic Categories or Relations and Semantic Operations:
$< L, B>, <L', B'>, <C1, O1>, <C2, O2>, <C3, O3>, ..., <C8, O8>$

Semantic Basic Operation for Lexical Cateories:
L: lexical category (N or V) and not head of a predicative NP,
B: $B(L_n) = \lambda ux_1...x_n [l(c)(x_1, ..., x_n) \& x_1 \in UD(u)]$

Interpretation of Predicates:
L': head of predicative NP or predicative NP
B': $B'(L_n) = L_n$

Referential Conditions for Referential NPs:
$C1$ = NPs of the form *the* N
$C2$ = NPs of the form *a* N (but not predicative) and NPs of the form *every* N

$O1$: $O1(c, E_1) = \lambda u[\exists !x (Ref(ag(u), u(c), x) \& E_1(u, x)]$
$O2$: $O2(c, E_1) = \lambda u[\forall x (Ref(ag(u), u(c), x) <--> E_1(u, x)]$

(=nonspecific reading of indefinite NPs)
Note: As an exception, O1, O2 apply to pairs of constituents and event-object relations
(The constituents are NPs, the event-object relations are the result of applying B to the
head nouns, thus O1, O2, schematically speaking, apply to a pair $<NP, B(N)>$.

Tense Interpretation:
$C3$ = verb form in past tense
$O3$: $O3(E_1) = \lambda ux[\exists e (E_1(e, x) \& e<u)]$

Event Predication:
$C4$ = is event predicate of
$O4$: $O4(E_n, E) = \lambda uex_1...x_n[E_n(e, x_1,...,x_n) \& E(e))]$

Constuction of Propositions:

C5 = is clausal complement of
O5: $O5(E_n, E) = \lambda uex_1...x_{n-1}[E2(e, x_1,..., x_{n-1}, E)]$

C6 = is complement of the form *the* N or *every* N of
O6: $O6(c1, E_1) = \lambda ue[\forall x (Ref(ag(u), u(c1), x) --> E_1(e, x))]$

C7 = is complement of the form *a* N of
O7: $O7(c1, E_1) = \lambda ue[\exists x (Ref(ag(u), u(c1), x) \& E_1(e, x))]$

Conjunction of Referential Conditions and Proposition:
C8 = the relation that holds between c1 and c2 iff c1 is referential complement of the main verb of the clause c2
$O8(E, E') = \lambda u[E(u) \& E'(u)]$

Examples:

(3) *The man screamed a scream*

Syntactic Categories and Relations in (3):
man and *screamed* are lexical expressions, hence Ls;
a scream is predicate, hence an L';
a scream is event predicate to *screamed*, hence <*a scream, screamed*> is in C4;
screamed a scream is VP in the past tense, hence an C3;
a man is definite complement to *screamed a scream*, hence <*the man, screamed a scream*> is in C1;
a man is complement of *scream* of (3), hence <*the man, scream*> is in C6.

Application of Semantic Operations on the Basis of Syntactic Categories or Relations in (3):
$m(\textit{man}) = B(l(\textit{man}) = \lambda ux[man(x) \& x \in UD(u)]$
$m(\textit{screamed}) = B(l(\textit{scream}) = \lambda ux[scream(e, x) \& e \in UD(u)]$
$m(\textit{a scream}) = B'(l(\textit{scream})) = \lambda e[scream(e)]$
$m(\textit{scream a scream}) = O4(m(\textit{screamed}), m(\textit{a scream})) = \lambda uex[scream(e, x) \& e \in UD(u)$
   $\& scream(e)]$
$m(\textit{screamed}+\text{past tense } \textit{a scream}) = O3(m(\textit{scream a scream}) = \lambda ux[\exists e(scream(e) \& e \in$
   $UD(u) \& e<u]$
$m(\textit{the man}) = O1(\textit{the man}, m(\textit{man})) = \lambda u[\exists!x Ref(ag(u), u(\textit{the man}), x) \& man(x) \& x \in$
   $UD(u)]$
   (= the referential condition of (3))
$m(\textit{the man screamed a scream}) = O6(\textit{the man}, m(\textit{screamed}+\text{past tense } \textit{a scream}) =$
   $\lambda ux[\forall x (Ref(ag(u), u(\textit{the man}), x) --> \exists e (scream(e, x) \& e \in UD(u) \& scream(e))]$
   (= the proposition of (3))
$m'(\textit{the man screamed a screamed}) = \lambda u[m(\textit{the man})(u) \& m(\textit{the man screamed a}$
   $\textit{scream}]$

(4) Every man screamed

$m(\textit{Every man screamed})$
$= O8(O2(\textit{every man}, B(l(\textit{man})), O6(\textit{every man}, O3(B(l(\textit{scream})))))$

$= \lambda u[(\forall x \ (\text{Ref}(ag(u), u(\textit{every man}), x) <--> man(x) \ \& \ x \in UD(\textit{man}) \ \& \ \forall x \ (\text{Ref}(ag(u),$
$u(\textit{every man}), x) \ -->\exists e \ (\text{scream}(e, x) \ \& \ e \in UD(\textit{scream}) \ \& \ e<u))]$

(3) A man screamed

$m(\textit{A man screamed})$
$= O8(O2(\textit{a man}, B(I(\textit{man})), O7(\textit{a man}, O3(B(I(\textit{scream})))))$
$= \lambda u[(\forall x \ (\text{Ref}(ag(u, u(\textit{a man}), x) <--> man(x) \ \& \ x \in UD(\textit{man})) \ \& \ \exists x \ (\text{Ref}(ag(u), u(\textit{a man}), x)$
$\& \ \exists e \ (\text{scream}(e, x) \ \& \ e \in UD(\textit{scream}) \ \& \ e<u))]$

(4) It seemed that the ghost disppeared

$m(\textit{It seemed that the ghost disappered})$
$= O3(O4(B(I(\textit{seem})), O8(O1(\textit{the ghost}, B(I(\textit{ghost})), O6(\textit{the ghost},$
$O3(B(I(\textit{disappear}))))))$
$=\lambda u[\exists e \ (\text{seem}(e) \ \& \ e \in UD(\textit{seem}) \ \& \ \lambda u'[\exists !x \ ((\text{Ref}(ag(u), u(\textit{the ghost}), x) \ \& \ ghost(x) \ \& \ x \in$
$UD(\textit{ghost})) \ \& \ \forall x(\text{Ref}(ag(u), u(\textit{the ghost}) \ -->\exists e \ (\text{disappear}(e, x) \ \& \ e \in UD(\textit{disappear})$
$\& \ e < u'] \ (e)]$

Notes

I would like to thank Phil Branigan, Jim Higginbotham, Richard Larson, Robert Stalnaker and especially Barry Schein for help and discussion.

[1] The dependence of sentence meanings on utterances and speakers, rather than on contextual 'indices' has been emphasized by Burge(1974) and has been formalized in a more explicit way in the theory of Lieb(1979, 1983). Both authors employ the notion of speaker reference roughly in the way it is conceived in this paper. What is mainly new in this paper on the background of the proposals by these authors is that the dependencies of sentence meanings on utterance and speaker can be shifted in embedded contexts from the utterance to the event described by the matrix verb.

[2] Concerning the notion u(K) for a constituent K, I will assume for simplification that K is unique in the sentence under consideration. That way we can further below more or less adequately say that the part of u is uniquely determined by similarity in meaning to K. But in order to account for cases in which an expression occurs twice in a sentence or two expressions with the same meaning, we must take into account the position of K in order to get a unique correlate of K in an event u.

[3] The employment of the function u, where u(K) is the part of u similar in meaning to K, is reminiscent of Davidson's(1969) suggestions in his analysis of indirect speech. However, the motivations of this notion for Davidson's analysis and the analysis of embedded clauses in this paper are rather different. In contrast to Davidson's analysis, the similarity relation does not play a crucial role in accounting for intensionality. In the theory of this paper intensionality would rather be traced to the set of discourse referents of an event u, UD(u), than to the similarity relation between constituents and event parts. In order to account for intensionality I conceive UD(u) such that it may contain both nonactual objects and partial objects (as conceived by ag(u)). This then accounts for lack of existential generalization and lack of substitutivity of coextensional terms.

References:

Burge, T. (1974): 'Demonstrative Constructions, Reference, and Truth.' The Journal of

314

Philosophy 71

Chomsky, N. (1986): <u>Barriers</u>. MIT Press, Cambridge (Mass.)

Davidson, D. (1967): 'The Logical Form of Action Sentences.' In N. Rescher(ed.): <u>The Logic of Decision and Action</u>. University of Pittsburgh Press, Pittsburgh, Pennsylvannia

--------- (1969): 'On Saying *that*' In D. Davidson/J.Hintikka (eds.): <u>Words and Objections: Essays on the Work of W.V. Quine</u>. Reidel, Dordrecht, Holland

Erteschik-Shir, N. (1977): <u>On the Nature of Island Constraints</u>. Ph. D. dissertation, MIT, Cambridge (Mass.), reproduced: Indiana Linguistics Club, Bloomington, Indiana

Higginbotham, J.(1986): "Elucidations of Meaning.' <u>Lexicon Project Working Papers</u>, MIT, Cambridge (Mass.)

Jones, J. (1988): 'Cognate Objects and Case Theory.' <u>Journal of Linguistics 28</u>

Koster, J. (1978): 'Why Subject Sentences Don't?.' In S. J. Kayser (ed.): <u>Recent Transformational Studies in European Languages</u>. MIT Press, Cambridge (Mass.)

Lieb, H. (1979): 'Principles of Semantics.' In F.W. Heny/ H. Schnelle (eds.): <u>Syntax and Semantics Vol. 10: Selections from the Third Groningen Round Table</u>. Academic Press, New York

-------- (1986): <u>Integrational Linguistics. Vol.I: General Outline.</u> Benjamins, Amsterdam

Napoli, D.(1988): 'Subjects and External Arguments. Clauses and Non-Clauses.' <u>Linguistics and Philosophy 11</u>

Pesetsky, D. (1982): <u>Paths and Categories</u>. Ph. D. dissertation, MIT, Cambridge (Mass.)

Safir, K. (1986): <u>Syntactic Chains</u>. Cambridge University Press, Cambridge

Stowell, T. (1981): <u>Origins of Phrase Structure</u>, Ph. D. dissertation, MIT, Cambridge (Mass.)

Williams, E. (1980): 'Predication.' <u>Linguistic Inquiry 11</u>

WHAT IS WRONG AND WHAT IS RIGHT WITH I-WITHIN-I

Jack Hoeksema, University of Pennsylvania
and
Donna Jo Napoli, Swarthmore College

1. Introduction.

There is, in the Government and Binding literature, a condition on binding and coindexation which is referred to more often than motivated and which, in spite of frequent invocations, seems to be treated as the stepchild of the binding theory. Clearly, we are not referring to one of the three famous clauses A, B and C of Chomsky's (1981) Binding Theory. While there are many articles and even books devoted to these crown jewels of GB, our target, the i-within-i condition, is usually mentioned only when it can be of service to shed light on something else. We suspect that there is a reason for this. Whenever one takes a hard look at the i-within-i condition, it appears to wither away. While some of the evidence for it is real, it has been forced to carry a greater explanatory burden than it should have and that many of the phenomena which it is supposed to explain are either spurious or better accounted for by other means. Our paper has two main parts: After a brief introduction, we discuss a number of well-known proposals which appeal in one way or another to the i-within-i condition and show that they are incorrect insofar as they assume this condition to apply to anything but circular reference cases; in the second part of the paper we discuss the nature of the condition, arguing that it does not apply to bound anaphora but only to unbound or free pronouns and propose a condition on circular chains, originally suggested by Higginbotham and May, as an alternative to the i-within-i condition.

2. What is i-within-i?

The i-within-i condition is the requirement that no phrase be coindexed with one of its proper constituents, and is commonly stated as in (1):

(1) $*[...@_i...]_i$

A look at the history of the i-within-i condition informs us that it is a generalization of Vergnaud's (1974: 34) Disjunction Condition on Anaphora, which was stated as in (2):

(2) *Disjunction Condition on Anaphora*

If, in a string, two noun phrases NP_1 and NP_2 are anaphorically related, then the string must be analyzable as ...NP_1...NP_2... or as...NP_2...NP_1....

In other words, anaphoric NPs must not be contained in their antecedents or vice versa. The main motivation for this condition was that it correctly characterizes circular anaphoric dependencies such as the ones exemplified in (3) as illegal:

(3) a. *[The son of the woman who killed $him_j]_i$ was a Nazi
   b *[The book by the man who designed its_j cover]$_i$ will be
      coming next week.
   c.*[A proof is its_j existence]$_i$ is not forthcoming.

The modern i-within-i condition is a generalization of Vergnaud's constraint. [1] First, it applies to expressions of all categories, not just NPs and second, it constrains all relationships expressed by coindexation, not just anaphoric dependencies. The second extension crucially changes the nature of the condition. Cases such as the ones in (3) are often viewed as semantically odd, because of the circular way in which reference is established. The more recent extensions of the scope of the condition push it in the direction of a purely syntactic condition on any relation expressed in terms of indices.

3. What i-within-i is not: Three examples.

3.1 For an illustration of the extended scope of the i-within-i condition in modern GB, let us take a look at Chomsky's (1981) account of the grammaticality of picture-noun reflexives in sentences such as (4):

(4) John$_i$ saw that [a picture of himself$_i]_j$ INFL$_j$ was on the wall

The issue here is to find a way to enlarge the domain in which the reflexive can be bound so as to include the antecedent in the matrix clause. Chomsky proposes to do this by defining this domain partly in terms of the notion "accessible SUBJECT". A SUBJECT is INFL just in case INFL contains AGR (the agreement marker) , otherwise it is the structural subject. A SUBJECT is accessible to some phrase just in case that phrase is c-commanded by it and coindexation with the SUBJECT would not lead to an i-within-i violation. Given that the INFL of the embedded clause in (4) is coindexed with the subject NP *picture of himself* by virtue of the agreement relation, it is not accessible to *himself* because coindexation would violate the i-within-i condition. For similar reasons, the structural subject cannot be a SUBJECT accessible to *himself*. So the accessible SUBJECT must be found in the matrix clause and the nonlocal binding of the reflexive follows. Notice what is going on here. The potential violation of i-within-i has nothing to do with coreference or anaphoric dependencies between the reflexive and the container NP. Rather, the violation would stem from the fact that two other relations, viz. subject-predicate agreement and the accessible SUBJECT relation, are expressed in the same way by coindexation. It is useful at this point to recall a point made by Higginbotham (1983), namely that coindexation is just a device, and often not a very appropriate one, to express syntactic relationships. Had we used different notational devices for each syntactic relation, this particular violation of i-within-i would have never arisen. For some, this may be an illustration of the explanatory power of notational conventions. For us, it is somewhat unsatisfactory, because we would like to know why entirely different relationships pattern in the same way, if indeed they do. One might object, at this point, that subject-predicate agreement may not be different from anaphora if we take Chomsky's idea seriously that AGR is a pronominal. Then coindexation of the subject with AGR would be entirely similar to the binding relation between a dislocated topic, say, and the pronominal argument to which it is linked. And so appealing to the i-within-i condition here would be entirely natural. Bresnan and Mchombo (1987) have motivated such an analysis for Chichewa object-agreement, but we do not believe such an analysis is feasible for English subject-verb agreement. The properties which they give of anaphoric agreement, such as discourse or long-distance binding, simply do not characterize English subject-agreement. As a matter of fact, there is good reason to reject Chomsky's account on empirical grounds. For example, Kuno (1987) notes that Chomsky's proposal is still too restrictive in that it rules out examples like (5a) and Keenan (1988) points out examples such as (5b) where the problematic reflexive is located in the object, rather than the subject:

(5) a. They made sure that nothing would prevent each other's pictures from being put on sale.
    b. Mary complained that the teacher gave extra help to everyone but herself.

(See also Johnson 1987 for a critique of the notion "accessible SUBJECT".) In one of Chomsky's more recent works, *Knowledge of Language*, (Chomsky 1986) , he suggests a radically different approach to long-distance anaphora in English, using movement to INFL at the level of Logical Form . As one of the advantages of this new approach he cites that it allows him to eliminate the i-within-i condition, and so to simplify the binding theory. This alternative theory still makes wrong predictions in cases such as (5), but we can't discuss it in detail here because it does not concern our main topic. We just mention it to illustrate the extent to which Chomsky seems to view the i-within-i condition merely as a rider on various clauses of his binding theory, rather than an independently motivated constraint. Whatever one thinks of picture-noun reflexives with nonlocal antecedents, there are still other phenomena which are usually delegated to the i-within-i condition , so an alternative account of long-distance anaphors does not necessarily allow one to drop it. However, in the remainder of this paper we argue that there may be great wisdom in Chomsky's desire to eliminate i-within-i.

3.2 As our next illustration of the extended use of the i-within-i condition we discuss the explanation in Williams (1982) for the ungrammaticality of examples such as (6):

(6) *John's arrival dead
     * Fred's departure drunk

The observation to be explained is that nominalizations do not support the adjectival adjuncts which can be found in the corresponding verbal constructions. Williams proposes an account of this observation which appeals to the i-within-i condition. More precisely, he appeals to a condition ruling out coindexation of two NPs if one is contained in the other. Another constraint, the Strict Opacity Condition, requires that all expressions, including therefore adjectival adjuncts, either be coindexed with a sister NP or else with the node immediately dominating them. In the case of nominalizations such as the ones in (6), this phrase is the N'. This N' in turn is coindexed with its mother node so as to express the head-of relationship. The genitive NP is coindexed with the adjective to express the predication relation. This creates the desired violation of NP-i within NP-i, since the genitive NPs are now coindexed with the container NPs. Notice how this account rests on the use of the notational device of coindexation for three distinct syntactic relations. In particular the use of coindexation to express the head-of relation is surprising, given that X-bar notation is already available to express it. It is also peculiar that Williams explicitly notes that his NP-i within NP-i constraint only applies to referential NPs and is intended to bar circular referential dependencies of the kind discussed by Vergnaud and others. But of course there is absolutely no referential dependency between the phrase *John's arrival nude* and its genitival specifier. There is good reason then to be suspicious of this account. We cannot deal with Williams' proposal in detail here, so we just note some empirical problems. It seems to us that Williams' initial observation must be modified, because certain nonadjectival adjuncts can occur in nominalizations, as we see in (7):

(7) Jones' exposure as a Nazi by Wiesenthal
   Graham's unexpected death at only 64
   Juliana's abdication as Queen of the Netherlands
   Bush's election as president of the US
   Harry's arrival with hardly any clothes on
   Betty's first deed as a doctor

Another set of cases which we consider to be significantly better than the cases in (6) involve either constrastive intonation or heavy adjuncts (the second example is taken from Napoli 1989):

(8) Hunter's explanation sober was no better than his explanation drunk
   Gary's arrival at precisely 8:15 buck naked threw the party into chaos
   his first appearance dressed as a nurse

Given that these adjuncts exhibit the same predication relationship as the adjectives in (6) and assuming that there is no reason to use a different device than coindexation in this case, these examples ought to be equally bad, but they are not. Therefore the i-within-i account fails in our opinion to shed any light on these cases. It seems more likely that the contrast we find between regular adjectival adjuncts on the one hand and *as*-phrases and heavy adjectival phrases on the other is simply due to the general constraint against regular adjectives in postnominal position in English, which does not apply to the latter.

3.3. Our third illustration comes from Hornstein (1984). Hornstein argues that the i-within-i condition applies to all indexing dependencies, including the predication relation. One of his concerns is sentence (9), which does not appear to allow the possessive pronoun *his* to be construed with *John* as its antecedent.

(9) John is his cook

If we indicate the fact that *his cook* is predicated of *John* by coindexation, and also express the antecedency relation in this way, we see that the illegal reading is ruled out by i-within-i. There is reason to believe that predication is involved here, since there is no comparable restriction in (10):

(10) John fired his cook.

However, other examples suggest that the matter is not so simple:

(11) a. Michael is his own cook.
   b. Sam is his father's best friend
   c. She is the last of her tribe.

In order to handle such cases, Hornstein (1984: 113) is led to propose a modification of the i-within-i condition so that "it applies only to a phrase that is both coindexed with a containing phrase and of relatively low embedding in that phrase". In Hornstein's hands, i-within-i comes to resemble another old acquaintance, the A-over-A condition. This move narrows the scope of the condition down too much. For example, Vergnaud's original data now can not be treated anymore, since they involve fairly deep levels of embedding (see the examples in (3)). Furthermore, we have found crosslinguistic variation with examples such as (9) which we did not find for Vergnaud's data. Whatever rules out (9) appears to be a capricious condition that varies by individual languages and calls for more study. While Dutch and German present facts parallel to those found in English, Swedish presents a slightly different picture. This language has both reflexive and nonreflexive possessive pronouns. In predication structures we find that the nonreflexive possessive is ungrammatical, while a reflexive possessive followed by the word for "own" is allowed:

(12) *Sven$_i$ ar [hans$_i$ lakare]$_i$
    Sven is his   doctor
(13) Sven$_i$ ar [sin$_i$ egen lakare]$_i$
    Sven is his own doctor

So far, these data are compatible with Hornstein's theory, provided we assume that the occurrence of *egen* makes the pronoun *sin* occur more deeply embedded. In Norwegian, however, the word for *own* can be omitted:

(14) Per er doktoren sin
    Per is doctor   his
    "Per is his own doctor"

When the nonreflexive pronoun[2] is used, the word for *own* must be present as well:

(15) Per er hennes egen doktor
    Per is his   own doctor

However, before we jump to conclusions here, we note that in a third Scandinavian language, Danish, nonreflexive possessives without *egen* are fine:

(16) Jens er hans laege
Jens is his doctor

This sentence is ambiguous as to whether Jens is his own doctor or someone else's. To make it unambiguous, the reflexive pronoun cannot be used in Danish, in striking contrast to Norwegian and Swedish. We are not sure what causes the variation among these closely related languages. Our main goal here is to establish that the exact counterpart to example (9) is grammatical with internal coreference in a number of languages. Among the languages we identified as differing from English in this regard is Armenian, exemplified in (17) and possibly Finnish (in the case of Finnish we obtained conflicting judgments, so we do not discuss it here):

(17) Janu eer [pujheesk eh]
John is doctor his

On the other hand, Russian, Malaysian, Japanese, Turkish, Amharic, Hebrew, Chinese, Igbo and several Romance languages all disallow the counterpart to our English example (9).

A further complication in this story arises when we distinguish identity statements from predicational statements. It seems to us that as an identity statement (18) is acceptable:

(18) Eddie$_i$ is not his$_i$ boss

Compare this to example (19):

(19) Eddie$_i$ is not his$_i$ own boss

Sentence (18) is only an identity statement, saying that Eddie and his boss are two different individuals. Sentence (19) has a very different reading, which says that Eddie does not work for himself. Similarly, the sentence *John is his own doctor* is interpreted as meaning that John "doctors" himself, so to speak. If these observations are correct, then we have evidence here for distinguishing two kinds of sentences involving the copula *be*, statements of identity and statements of predication. We are aware that this is a matter of some controversy in the literature (cf. Montague (1974) for a defense of a single meaning of *be* (and Partee 1986 for a very interesting elaboration of Montague's theory in terms of type-shifting operations) and Williams (1982) and Doron (1988) , among others, for opposite points of view). It seems to us that differences such as those exemplified in (18) and (19) are important in resolving this debate. We also note that with other predicational structures, where there is no separate identity interpretation, one does not find good counterparts to (18), but plenty of counterparts to (19), compare e.g. (20) and (21):

(20) #Let's make Eddie$_i$ his$_i$ boss

(21) Let's make Eddie$_i$ his$_i$ own boss

Of course, in eliciting informant judgments, one must be careful and we did not in all cases control for the subtle distinction between identity and predicational uses of the copula. It seems to us that genitives function as arguments in cases such as (21), while the identity statements as well as nonpredicative statements in general allow the genitives to act as specifiers. In the latter case the semantic role of the genitive is much freer. Consider for example the possible interpretations of ((22) and (23):

(22) Grace wants to be her own doctor
(23) Grace wants to be her doctor

In (22), Grace is said to want to doctor herself, while (23) says that Grace wants to swap identities with her doctor. In the second case, her doctor does not have to be the person who doctors her at all. It could be any doctor who is in some salient way connected to Grace, maybe the doctor she is dating or the doctor she is working for or the doctor she is painting. The specifier reading is also available for *her own*, but then calls for a contrastive reading of (22). Argument readings depend on the possibility of interpreting the noun as a relational concept. However, the argument reading appears not to be available to regular possessive pronouns in English, presumably due to the same factors which bar personal pronouns from argument positions when their antecedent is a c-commanding clause-mate, if we accept Higginbotham's (1983) suggestion that possessive pronouns modified by *own* can sometimes function as local anaphors. It is this , and not i-within-i, which accounts for the perceived unacceptability in languages such as English of sentences such as (9) with internal coreference.

4. Constraining i-within-i.

In this section we consider the question of what the proper domain of the i-within-i condition is, and how it can be stated in the most general way. First of all, we argue that it is strictly a condition on anaphora, and does not concern coreference in general. This point can be made quickly by considering cases such as:

(24) a. that madman Hitler
     b. my friend the Governor
     c. Ivan the Terrible

In each case there is a noun phrase coreferential with the noun phrase containing it. Analogous examples can be found in many languages, we just cite here some counterparts to (24a):

(25) a. quel matto di Giorgio (Italian)
        "that idiot (of) George"
     b. die oen van een Jaap (Dutch)
        "that idiot (of a) Jaap"
     c. dieser Schwachkopf Schulze (German)
        "this weakhead Schulze"
     d. mon cretin de mari (French)
        "my cretin of a husband"

In other cases, it may take some computation to see that the i-within-i condition is violated:

(26) a. John's father's only son
　　 b. the square of 1
　　 c. the egotist's favorite person

None of these cases involve anaphoric dependencies and we have not found any examples of this type where the i-within-i condition holds . This makes sense if the real reason why the Vergnaud examples in (3) were bad is the circular way in which reference is established there. In a compositional semantics, the interpretation of a complex expression is a function of the interpretations of its parts. When the interpretation of a part in turn depends on the interpretation of the whole, this is viewed as paradoxical. In the cases we just looked at, there is no such circularity. While a part is coreferential to the containing NP, it is dependent on that NP for its interpretation or reference.

Let us now turn to examples where the inner index is attached to a pronominal. The first relevant observation is that pronouns linked to a wh-operator are always exempt from the condition:

(27) a. [the man who $_i$ gave his $_i$ paycheck to his $_i$ wife]$_i$
　　 b. [the rocket $_i$ that$_i$ destroyed itself too soon]$_i$
　　 c. [a manager who$_i$ does not have to prove herself $_i$]$_i$

This makes sense on the assumption that pronouns bound to an operator are sensitive only to that operator and effectively shut off from their environment. It is interesting to note now that other kinds of modifiers seem to behave in much the same way as relative clauses, as is evidenced by the examples in (28):

(28) a. [a cat too tired to lick itself]
　　 b. [a woman looking for her cat]
　　 c. [a professor in love with himself]
　　 d. [people with children of their own]
　　 e. [characters in search of their author]

It seems attractive to us to explain these cases in the same terms as the earlier examples with relative clauses, by appealing to an operator, invisible in this case, which binds the pronouns in question. This analysis may be viewed as an interpretive version of the old whiz-deletion analysis of adjectival modifiers which postulated a wh-operator in underlying form that is deleted together with the verb *to be*. As semantic representations of the modifiers in (29), we propose the formulas in (30), which express the binding relations explicitly in terms of binding by a lambda-operator:

(29) a. a woman cooking for herself
　　 b. a woman cooking for Richard

(30) a. λx: (cooking for x)(x)
    b. λx : (cooking for Richard)(x)

This representation predicts correctly the pattern of reflexive and nonreflexive forms that we find in such modifiers: we find reflexives in the same positions which may contain reflexives in corresponding relative clauses and nonreflexive pronouns elsewhere.[3] In argument phrases, on the other hand, no binding is apparent, which follows naturally from the fact that arguments are not predicative in any way and the observation that lambda-operators formalize the notion of predication.

We may compare this account with the analysis given in Haik (1987), who notes the difference between (31) a and b:

(31) a. a picture of its frame
    b. a man next to his dog

In (31a), *it* must find its antecedent outside the containing NP, whereas (31b) allows *his* to have a man as its antecedent. This modifier-argument asymmetry is given a structural interpretation by Haik. In particular, she proposes the following two trees to indicate the structural differences:

(32)   a.

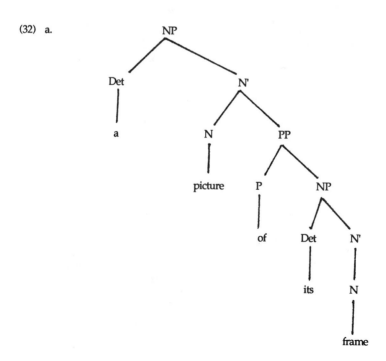

324

b.

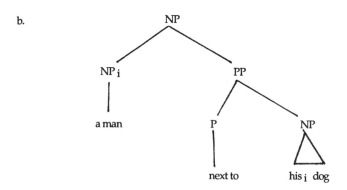

In the first diagram, there is a violation of the i-within-i condition, but the second one is acceptable because the modifier is adjoined to the antecedent of the pronoun *it*, and this makes it unnecessary to use the containing NP as the antecedent.   This account is fairly similar to ours, in that it makes the i-within-i condition sensitive to the presence of local binders which preclude circular anaphoric dependency chains from arising. The main difference from our proposal is that Haik's does not rely on abstract or invisible operators but rather on differences in syntactic constituency.   The tree structure given by Haik is unlikely to be correct however and does not extend to languages such as Dutch or German where modifiers may precede the head noun.   In these languages we find clear evidence that the modifiers which concern us here are not sisters of NP but of N (or N'), because the modifier is placed between the determiner and the head and not, as we would expect, before the entire NP:

(33) a. een op zichzelf verliefde professor (Dutch)
        a   on himself in-love   professor
        "a professor in love with himself"
      b. die mit sichselbst zufriedene Frau (German)
        the with herself content woman
        "the woman content with herself"

Such examples do not pose any problems for our proposal.

Finally, let us consider the proper formulation of the i-within-i condition. First of all, we state it as a condition on the relationship between free pronominals and their antecedents.   In other words, we side with Reinhart (1983) and others who distinguish the binding conditions for free pronouns from those for bound variables (whether personal pronoun or reflexive pronoun).   Second, we agree with Haik (1987) and others (e.g. Higginbotham and May (1981), Brody (1982)) that the i-within-i condition falls under a larger constraint on circular readings, which also includes cases of circularity without containment, such as the example in (34), discussed in Jacobson (1977):

(34) *[His $_i$ wife]$_j$ hates [her$_j$ husband]$_i$.

This example is ungrammatical under the given interpretation provided that the pronouns are not resolved by sentence external antecedents. In context, such examples can be acceptable:

(35) Most men have loving wives but not John. His wife hates her husband.

An interesting observation, due to Jacobson, is that substitution of one of the pronouns by its antecedent leads to violations of i-within-i which are unacceptable:

(36) Her husband's wife hates him.

On the other hand, so-called Bach-Peters sentences show acceptable cases of crossing coreference:

(37) The pilot who shot at it downed the MIG that followed him

And here substitution leads to acceptable results:

(38) The pilot who shot at the MIG that followed him downed it

This suggests very clearly, of course, that the same constraint is at work in Jacobson's crossing coreference cases which we saw at work earlier on in Vergnaud's evidence for the Disjunction Condition on Anaphora.   We cannot give an account of Bach-Peters sentences here, but will adopt a constraint which deals with both Vergnaud's and Jacobson's data. This constraint is the one given in Higginbotham and May (1981), which we formulate thus:

(39) Condition on Circular Chains

Let * stand for either --> (the antecedency relation) or < (the containment relation). A chain $X1* X2*...*Xn$ is circular just in case $Xi = Xj$ for some i,j such that $i = j$ and $1 < i,j < n$. Circular chains are ungrammatical.

As an illustration of this condition, consider example (40):

(40) *[her $_i$ childhood friend's wife] $_i$

The chain corresponding to this example is:

(41) her childhood friend's wife > her --> her childhood friend's wife

which is obviously circular.   A similar chain shows the circularity in (34). Higginbotham and May claim that their condition is not a principle of grammar, but a principle of language use.   To interpret the noun phrase in (40), one must interpret its parts, and to interpret the pronominal part, one must have the antecedent and so we seem to be in an infinite loop -- clearly not something a language user would want to be in. Brody (1982) has taken issue with this claim and notes that cases such as (40) ought serious problems of use such as infinite loops in their interpretation procedure. After all, if it were grammatical, it would just mean "the one who is the wife of her childhood friend", which is not that difficult to process. Note that we predict this paraphrase to be grammatical, because the pronoun is bound to a relative clause operator. We conclude therefore that we are dealing with a grammatical constraint which is sensitive to the structural environment of the pronoun.

Notes.

*We thank Per-Olof Petterson and Gisela Bergau Savage, our Swedish informants, Gudmund Iversen , our Norwegian informant, Inger Fay, our Danish informant, John Kedeshian and his parents , our Armenian informants , Leila Kevorkian, Irja Alho, Riitta Valimaa -Blum and Joel Nevis, our Finnish informants, and for participating in our survey of other languages, the foreign students at Swarthmore College 1988/89.

1. Besides Chomsky's (1981) formulation of the i-within-i condition and Vergnaud's (1974) Disjunction Condition, we also note the existence of variants such as Zwarts' (1976) extension of Vergnaud's condition to all projections of N, and Aoun's (1985) restriction of i-within-i to overt elements with an overt binder. Aoun's restriction is not compatible with the analysis we present of "whiz-deletion" exceptions to i-within-i below.

2. Hellan (1986) argues that the Norwegian reflexive anaphor sig is acceptable only if it is contained in a constituent understood as predicated of the antecedent. If this is correct, then Norwegian reflexives are more than just exceptions to the i-within-i condition as interpreted by Hornstein: They are acceptable only if they violate this constraint.

3. Jullens (1983) draws attention to the interesting case of prepositional phrases introduced by *with* or *without* , or rather, their Dutch counterparts - we use English examples. Here we find nonreflexive forms rather than the expected reflexive forms:

(i)   socks with holes in them/*in themselves
(ii) skies without stars in them/*in themselves

This seems to tally with the pronominal forms found in semantically related clauses with the verb *have* :

(iii) These socks have holes in them

Jullens also makes the crucial observation that anaphora which seem to violate the i-within-i condition (or Vergnaud's Disjunction Condition) are bound variables.

References.

Aoun, Joseph, 1985, *A Grammar of Anaphora.* . MIT-Press, Cambridge,

Massachusetts.

Bresnan, Joan and Sam Mchombo, 1987, "Topic, Pronoun, and Agreement in Chichewa", in: *Language* 63, no. 4, pp. 741-782.

Brody, Michael, 1982, "On Circular Readings", in: N. V. Smith (eds.), *Mutual Knowledge*, Academic Press, New York, pp. 133-46.

Chomsky, Noam, 1981, Lectures on Government and Binding. Foris Publications, Dordrecht.

Chomsky, Noam, 1986, *Knowledge of Language: Its Nature, Origin and Use.* Praeger, New York.

Doron, Edit, 1988, "The Semantics of Predicate Nominals", *Linguistics* 26, pp. 281-301.

Haik, Isabelle, 1987, "Bound VPs that Need to Be", in: *Linguistics and Philosophy* 10-4, pp. 503-530.

Hellan, Lars, 1986, "On Anaphora and Predication in Norwegian", in: Lars Hellan and K. Koch Christensen, eds., Topics in Scandinavian Syntax. D. Reidel, Dordrecht, pp. 103-124.

Higginbotham , James, 1983, "Logical Form, Binding and Nominals", in: Linguistic Inquiry 14, pp. 395-420.

Higginbotham, James and Robert May, 1981, "Crossing, Markedness, Pragmatics", in: A. Belletti, L. Brandi and L. Rizzi, eds.,Theory of Markedness in Generative Grammar, Scuola Normale Superiore di Pisa, Pisa, pp. 423-444.

Hornstein, Norbert, 1984, *Logic as Grammar.* MIT-Press, Cambridge, Mass.

Jacobson, Pauline, 1977, *The Syntax of Crossing Coreference Sentences.* Doctoral dissertation, University of California at Berkeley, distributed by the Indiana University Linguistics Club and published 1979 by Garland Press, New York.

Johnson, Kyle, 1987, "Against the Notion "SUBJECT"", *Linguistic Inquiry* 18, pp. 354- 61.

Jullens, Jan, 1983, "Over het pronominale *er* ", in: TABU 13-1, pp. 26-34.

Keenan, Edward, 1988, "Complex Anaphors and Bind @", in: CLS 24.

Kuno, Susumo, 1987, *Functional Syntax. Anaphora, Discourse and Empathy.* University of Chicago Press, Chicago.

Montague, Richard, 1974, *Formal Philosophy.* Ed. by Richmond H. Thomason, Yale University Press, New Haven.

Napoli, Donna Jo, 1989, *Predication Theory: A Case Study for Indexing Theory.* Cambridge University Press, Cambridge.

Partee, Barbara , 1986, "Noun-Phrase Interpretation and Type-Shifting Principles", in: J. Groenendijk, D. de Jongh and M. Stokhof (eds.), *Studies in Discourse Representation Theory and the Theory of Generalized Quantifiers.* Foris, Dordrecht, pp. 115-143.

Reinhart, Tanya 1983, *Anaphora and Semantic Interpretation.* University of Chicago Press, Chicago.

Vergnaud, Jean-Roger, 1974, *French Relative Clauses.* Doctoral dissertation, MIT.

Williams, Edwin, 1982, "The NP Cycle", *Linguistic Inquiry* 13, pp. 277-95.

Zwarts, Frans, 1976, "Over de Disjunctie Conditie op Anafora", in: *TABU* 6-4, pp. 35-9.

Lambek Calculus and Preposing of Embedded Subjects
Richard T. Oehrle & Shi Zhang
University of Arizona
<u>in memory of Sunseek Oh</u>

0. The following syntactic paradigm in English is well-known:

1) **Kim said that Sandy likes chimichangas.**
2) **Kim said Sandy likes chimichangas.**
3) ***I wonder who Kim said that _ likes chimichangas.**
4) I wonder who Kim said _ likes chimichangas.
5) I wonder what Kim said that Sandy likes _.
6) I wonder what Kim said Sandy likes _.

A variety of accounts of this paradigm have been offered in the literature. We mention Bresnan's (1972) Fixed Subject Constraint and the *that-trace filter of Chomsky & Lasnik (1977) and subsequent work in the GB tradition. These two accounts share the view that the explanation of the oddity of (3) lies in prohibiting an element of a certain sort -- namely, the complementizer **that** -- from preceding a gap of a certain kind. In this paper, we investigate the problem from a somewhat different angle. We assume an analytic framework in which there are no gaps, and hence, no gaps of the sort required by the accounts of either Bresnan or Chomsky & Lasnik.

    We first review the properties of two categorial systems, the Associative Syntactic Calculus **AL** (Lambek, 1958) and the NonAssociative Syntactic Calculus **nAL** (Lambek, 1961), and show how they are adapatable to the analysis of simple sentences. We then show, following Steedman (1985), how categorial systems of this kind can treat discontinuous dependencies of the sort found in English topicalization and wh-movement in simple clauses. It is not altogether obvious how to treat the paradigm above within this framework of assumptions. The remainder of the paper is devoted to showing how this can be done.

1.0 Associative and NonAssociative versions of the Lambek Calculus
In general, categorial grammar is an approach to grammatical analysis in which the linguistic properties of a complex expression are taken to be a function of the corresponding properties of its component parts.[1] In their pure form, the Lambek Calculi exemplify a systematic approach to categorial analysis: that is, allowable principles of type-assignment are assumed to apply to expressions of every type.

    Let a countable set **P** of primitive types be given. The full set **C** of categories is the least set containing **P** and, when it contains x and y, contains (x/y), (y\x), and (x.y). (In what follows, we exhibit types in a way that ignores unnecessary parentheses.) The arrow x -> y means that any expression of type x is also assigned the type y. The following axioms and inference rules characterize the Associative Calculus **AL**. The nonAssociative Calculus **nAL** lacks the associative rules A2 and A2'.

A1.   x -> x

A2.   (x.y).z -> x.(y.z)   A2'.   x.(y.z) -> (x.y).z

R1.   x.y -> z   **R1'.**   x.y -> z

           -------   -------

           x -> z/y   y -> x\z

R2.   x -> z/y   **R2'.**   y -> x\z

           --------   --------

           x.y -> z   x.y -> z

R3.   x -> y   y -> z

                     ----

                          x -> z

Among the theorems common to **AL** and **nAL** are the following:

apply: x/y.y -> x   ;   y.y\x -> x

lift: x -> y/(x\y)   ;   x -> (y/x)\y

There are also derived rules of inference valid in both systems:

R4.   x -> x'   y -> y'

           ----

                 xy -> x'y'

R5.   x -> x'   y -> y'

           ----

              x/y' -> x'/y

If we regard elements of type x/z as functors with domain z and co-domain x, R5 reflects the fact that for any function f: **D** -> **C**, if **D'** is a subset of **D** and **C'** is a superset of **C**, there is a unique function f': **D'** -> **C'** such that f'(d) = f(d) for all **d** in **D'**.

      In addition, a number of other interesting theorems which are not derivable in **nAL** hold in **AL**:

compose: (x/y).(y/z) -> x/z   ;   (z\y).(y\x) -> z\x

divide: x/y -> (x/z).(y/z)   ;   y\x -> (z\y)\(z\x)

swap: (x\y)/z <-> x(y/z)

Curry: (x/y)/z <-> x/(z.y)

      Both **AL** and **nAL** are decidable. In addition, **AL** has the property of <u>structural completeness</u> (Buszkowski, 1988), which means that if there is a proof of the validity of an arrow relative to one bracketing, there are proofs of the arrow for every well-formed bracketing.

2. Linguistic applications.

If we are given a vocabulary **V**, assign each element of **V** to a finite, non-empty set of types, and assume that a sequence $v_1,...,v_k$ of words (on a fixed bracketing if we are working in **nAL**) is assigned to the type z (a fact we represent by the arrow $v_1,...,v_k$ -> z) just in case there are types x_i assigned to each v_i ($1<i<k$) such that $x_1...x_k$ -> z (on the same bracketing, if we are working in **nAL**) is a theorem. For example, relative to following assignments,

Kim -> np
put -> ((np\s)/pp)/np
Nim -> np
near -> pp/np
Zim -> np

the sequence of words **Kim put Nim near Zim** is assigned to the type s, since
the sequence of types **np.(((np\s)/pp)/np).np.(pp/np).np -> s** is a theorem of
AL. Here is a proof, which uses a rule of inference (easily derivable from **R4**)
that allows substitution of a type z for a sequence of types $y_1...y_k$ just in
case $y_1...y_k$ -> z is a theorem. Each step is annotated with the name of the
theorem involved.

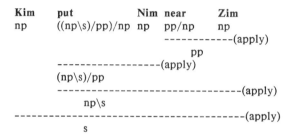

In **nAL**, of course, this proof requires the bracketing (**Kim . ((put.Nim) .**
(near.Kim)). But in **AL**, proofs exist relative to other bracketings:

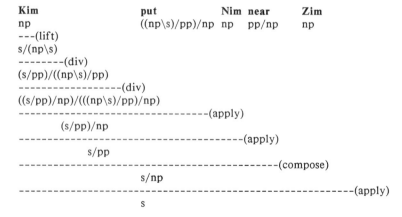

This proof corresponds to one version of a left-to-right incremental parse. In
AL, there are a variety of other proofs as well. The fact that categorial
systems that respect the axioms of **AL** are structurally complete suggests that
they offer an interesting framework in which to investigate such problems as
"non-constituent" conjunction (Steedman, 1985; Dowty, 1988; Oehrle, 1987), the

bracketing paradoxes in morphology (Moortgat, 1988; Hoeksema, 1985), and the relation of syntactic structure and prosodic phrasing (Moortgat, 1989; Oehrle, 1988).

2.1 Wh-movement in AL.

The symmetry of the Lambek operators \ and / suggests a rule which replaces one by the other, a rule we call permutation:

permutation: x/y <-> y\x

The Lambek Calculi as formulated above are permutation-free.[2] That is, none of the axioms or rules of inferences permutes expressions. To account for alternations such as wh-movement or topicalization, an additional rule must be added. Consider first two possible proofs of the sentence **Kim greeted Zim**, assuming that **greeted -> (np\s)/np** and, as above, **Kim -> np** and **Zim -> np**:

```
Kim      greeted        Zim        Kim  greeted        Zim
np       (np\s)/np      np         np   (np\s)/np      np
         ----------------(apply)        ----(swap)     ----(lift)
              np\s                      np\(s/np)      (s/np)\s
-----------------------(apply)         --------------(apply)
          s                                  s/np
                                    ----------------------(apply)
                                                s
```

In the proof on the right, **Zim** is lifted to the category (s/np)\s. Now, to generate structures involving topicalization, we need only add a rule which permutes lifted types whose "co-domain category" is S. (This idea is based on Ades & Steedman (1982) and Steedman (1985).) In the simplest cases, we may formulate the rule as follows:[3]

permutation-lifting into s: **np -> s/(s/np)**

To see how this works, consider:

```
Zim,     Kim  greeted
np       np   (np\s)/np
         -------------(as above)
              s/np
--(permutation-lifting)
s/(s/np)
--------------------(apply)
      s
```

Remarks. First, it is easy to arrange matters so that if we wish to provide an interpretation of such a language (as we should wish to do), the interpretation of simple cases of the kind illustrated here will be equivalent to the interpretations of the two derivations of **Kim greeted Zim** given earlier. Second, there are some wrinkles that have to be attended to. As stated, permutation-lifting allows multiple instances of (nested) topicalization, which seems forced in English. In addition, this formulation only works for right-peripheral "gaps". These points, which are orthogonal to the issues we wish to address here, can be resolved by restating permutation-lifting as **PL** below (where **X** is a variable ranging over the union of the set of types and **0**: if **X** matches **0**, then $y/X = X\backslash y = y$).

8) **PL**: np -> (s[F]/X)/((s/X)/np)

For example, suppose that embedded questions are of the category s[q], which we shall abbreviate as **q**. Let **who** be assigned to the type **(q/X)/((s/X)/np)**. To see the consequences of this type-assignment, we shall examine its application to some of the cases we began with. (We write "inst X" to mark the step which instantiates the variable X in a particular way.)

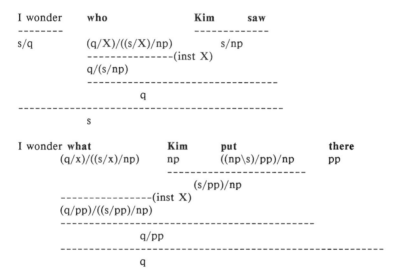

```
I wonder    who                    Kim       saw
--------                           -------------
s/q         (q/X)/((s/X)/np)            s/np
            ---------------(inst X)
            q/(s/np)
            --------------------------------
                        q
------------------------------------------------
            s

I wonder what        Kim      put            there
         (q/x)/((s/x)/np)  np   ((np\s)/pp)/np   pp
                               -----------------------
                                   (s/pp)/np
         ----------------(inst X)
         (q/pp)/((s/pp)/np)
         -------------------------------------------
                      q/pp
         -----------------------------------------------------
                      q
```

Having shown the extension of **AL** to **AL+PL** can account for simple cases of peripheral and non-peripheral "extraction" (without movement rules), we turn to the analysis of the paradigm mentioned at the outset.

3. Assumptions.
We shall suppose that the complementizer **that** is assigned the type c/s and that (1) and (2) are distinguished by lexically assigning **said** two different types: (np\s)/c and (np\s)/s. One proof of **Kim said that Sandy likes chimichangas** is given in (9) below. And a proof of **Kim said Sandy likes chimichangas** which simply removes **that** and replaces the type (np\s)/c with the type (np\s)/s is given in (10).

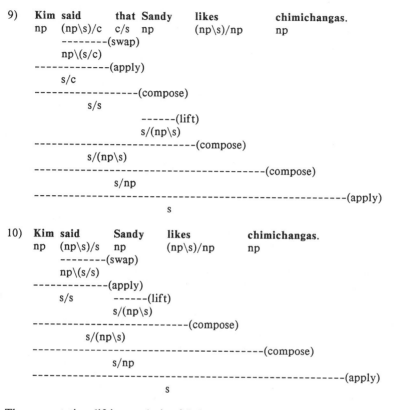

9) Kim   said   that Sandy   likes   chimichangas.
   np   (np\s)/c   c/s np   (np\s)/np   np
           --------(swap)
           np\(s/c)
   -------------(apply)
        s/c
   -----------------(compose)
           s/s
                         ------(lift)
                         s/(np\s)
   --------------------------(compose)
           s/(np\s)
   ---------------------------------------(compose)
                s/np
   --(apply)
                         s

10) Kim said   Sandy   likes   chimichangas.
    np   (np\s)/s   np   (np\s)/np   np
         --------(swap)
         np\(s/s)
    -------------(apply)
         s/s   ------(lift)
                   s/(np\s)
    --------------------------(compose)
            s/(np\s)
    -------------------------------------(compose)
                s/np
    --(apply)
                         s

The permutation-lifting analysis of "wh-movement" discussed above can be
straightforwardly applied to cases of non-subject extraction. Here are proofs of
(5) and (6) above, assuming that **what** is assigned the type (q/X)/((s/X)/np)
and **wonder** is assigned the type (np\s)/q:

I   wonder   what   Kim   said   that Sandy   likes
np   (np\s)/q   (q/X)/((s/X)/np) np   (np\s)/c   c/s np   (np\s)/np
------------   ------------------   --(lift)
     s/q   s/c   s/(np\s)
                                                     -------------(compose)
                                                     c/(np\s)
                                   -----------------------------(compose)
                                           s/(np\s)
                   -----------(inst X)-----------------------------------(comp)
                   q/(s/np)   s/np
                   ---(apply)
                                       q
---(apply)
                         s

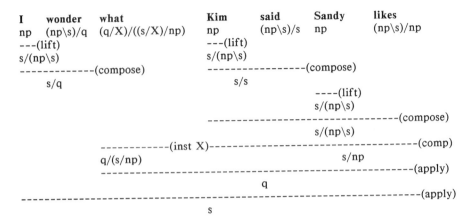

```
I      wonder    what                         Kim      said       Sandy     likes
np     (np\s)/q  (q/X)/((s/X)/np)             np       (np\s)/s   np        (np\s)/np
---(lift)                                     ---(lift)
s/(np\s)                                      s/(np\s)
------------(compose)                         --------------(compose)
      s/q                                              s/s
                                                        ----(lift)
                                                        s/(np\s)
                                              ----------------------------(compose)
                                                              s/(np\s)
          -----------(inst X)---------------------------------(comp)
          q/(s/np)                                     s/np
          ----------------------------------------------------(apply)
                                  q
--------------------------------------------------------------(apply)
                  s
```

4. Subject "extraction" in the complementizerless case.

Consider now the extension of the account developed above to cases involving a "gap" in subject-position. Suppose we apply our strategy of assigning the permuation of a lifted type to the wh-phrase and compiling the material between the wh-phrase and the gap into a single constituent assigned to a type of the form (s/X)/np. This yields:

```
... who                  Kim  said         likes         chimichangas
(q/X)/((s/X)/np)         np   (np\s)/s     (np\s)/np     np
                         --------(as above) --------------(apply)
                              s/s               np\s
```

At this point, no further reduction is possible. To resolve this problem, various nostrums have been suggested. Our discussion here is based on remarks by Steedman (1987, section 3.2.2, pp. 421ff.). One possibility, following a suggestion in GKPS (1985), is to assign to **said** and similar verbs the category (np\s)/(np\s). This still requires that new forms of reduction be countenanced. Although Steedman (1987) is similar to the account we propose below, an early draft took a different approach: assign **said** and similar verbs to the category ((np\s)/np)/(np\s). On this approach, extraction in such cases is assimilated to right-peripheral extraction, which is in itself unproblematic. A drawback here, however, is the prediction that we should allow structures in which the embedded subject is shifted to the right, as in *Kim said likes chimichangas Sandy. We prefer a theory which excludes such cases.

Within the general framework of **AL+PL**, in fact, extraction of the type that we have been discussing is completely unproblematic. We first prove the following lemma, which is simply a special case of the derived rule of inference **R5**, mentioned earlier in section 1:

Lemma 1.   X/s -> X/(np.(np\s))
proof: X -> X   np.(np\s) -> s
           ---R5
                X/s -> X/(np.(np\s))

Now note that the arrow **X/(np.(np\s))** -> **(X/(np\s))/np** is an instance of Currying (theorem (6), so that by the transitivity of the arrow, we have the theorem **X/s** -> **(X/(np\s))/np**. This proves Lemma 2:

Lemma 2. X/s -> (X/(np\s))/np

The proof that **who Kim said likes chimichangas** -> **q** is now completely straightforward:

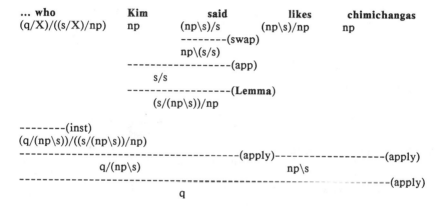

```
... who                Kim          said           likes         chimichangas
(q/X)/((s/X)/np)       np           (np\s)/s        (np\s)/np     np
                                    --------(swap)
                                    np\(s/s)
                                    -----------------(app)
                                      s/s
                                    -----------------(Lemma)
                                      (s/(np\s))/np

--------(inst)
(q/(np\s))/((s/(np\s))/np)
------------------------------------------(apply)-----------------(apply)
              q/(np\s)                             np\s
-----------------------------------------------------------------(apply)
              q
```

5. Subject "extraction" and complementizers.

In the system **AL+PL**, given the syntactic categories thus far assumed, there is a proof of ***I wonder who Kim said that _ likes chimichangas**. Here is the crucial sub-proof that **who Kim said that likes chimichangas** is assigned type q. As in the case just discussed, the proof makes use of Lemma 2, which shows that the arrow c/s -> (c/(np\s))/np is valid.

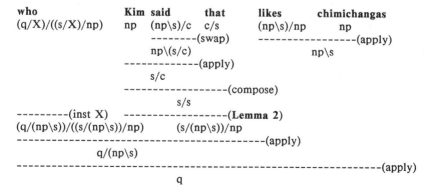

```
who                Kim  said      that    likes          chimichangas
(q/X)/((s/X)/np)   np   (np\s)/c   c/s     (np\s)/np      np
                        --------(swap)     -----------------(apply)
                        np\(s/c)            np\s
                        -------------(apply)
                        s/c
                        -----------------(compose)
                        s/s
--------(inst X)        -----------------(Lemma 2)
(q/(np\s))/((s/(np\s))/np)   (s/(np\s))/np
--------------------------------------------(apply)
              q/(np\s)
-----------------------------------------------------------------(apply)
              q
```

It is just as clear that if it is impossible to assign the phrase **Kim said that** a non-product type of the form (s/X)/np, no proof will be available which detects a "gap" after **that**. Since it is necessary on independent grounds to allow the combination of **Kim said** into a single non-product type, our problem can be solved if we can find a way to solve a related problem: blocking the composition of **said** and **that**. We can achieve this goal by adopting as a framework a Lambek system which is <u>partially-associative</u>.

6. Empirical constraints on partial associativity.

From the present perspective, there are clear empirical constraints on the properties that a partially-associative syntactic calculus of the right kind may have. First, as just noted, we must require that the following inference step never be allowed:

$$x.(that.y)$$
$$\text{----------}$$
$$(x.that).y$$

The strategy we will implement below is to ensure that certain elements, including the complementizer **that**, introduce brackets grouping them with their arguments.

A second point in the case at hand is the nature of the argument type in the lexical type-assignment of **that**. The type assumed above, namely c/s, is not the only possible type that could be lexically assigned to **that**: another possibility is $(c/(np\backslash s))/np$. Since c/s readily accommodates conjoined complements, however, and $(c/(np\backslash s))/np$ does not,[4] we shall assume here that c/s is at least one type available to **that**. (In **AL**, note that $c/s \rightarrow (c/(np\backslash s))/np$ is a theorem, derived by means of **R5** and Currying.) But in order to allow extraction out of the complement clause at all, it is necessary to allow **that** to compose with a proper initial type of **s**. That is, we must countenance the inference:

$$(that.x.y)$$
$$\text{----------}$$
$$(that.x).y$$

7. A partially associative version of the Lambek calculus.

Let **Phon** = $<Syl^+, \{\ .\ \}, (\ .\ )>$ be a structure on which two functions $\{\ .\ \}$ and $(\ .\ )$ are defined. We use underlined letters $\underline{a}$, $\underline{b}$, $\underline{c}$, etc. as members of an infinite set of variables ranging over Syl^+. We write $\{\underline{a}.\underline{b}\}$ and $(\underline{a}.\underline{b})$ to indicate the operation of the functions $\{\ .\ \}$ and $(\ .\ )$ on $\underline{a}$ and $\underline{b}$.[5] The function $\{\ .\ \}$ is associative and thus satisfies:

$$\{\{x.y\}.z\} = \{x.\{y.z\}\}$$

The function $(\ .\ )$ is not associative, but satisfies the two laws:

$$(x.(y.z)) = ((x.y).z)$$
$$(x.\{y.z\}) = \{(x.y).z\}$$

In addition, we impose the following requirement: the closure of the co-domain of $(\ .\ )$ under the operation $\{\ .\ \}$ is contained in Syl^+. This sub-structure of

Syl$^+$ is thus a semigroup.

Relative to a set **P** of primitive categories, the set of grammatical categories is defined inductively as the smallest set **C** such that

1. If x is in **P** and <u>a</u> is a variable ranging over Syl$^+$, then <x,<u>a</u>> is in **C**.

2. If <x,<u>a</u>> and <y,<u>b</u>> are members of **C**, then so are:

$$<<x,\underline{a}> . <y,\underline{b}>, \{\underline{a.b}\}>$$
$$<<x,\underline{a}> . <y,\underline{b}>, (\underline{a.b})>$$
$$<<x,\{\underline{a.b}\}> / <y,\underline{b}>, \underline{a}>$$
$$<<x,(\underline{a.b})> / <y,\underline{b}>, \underline{a}>$$
$$<<y,\underline{b}> \backslash <x,\{\underline{b.a}\}>, \underline{a}>$$
$$<<y,\underline{b}> \backslash <x,(\underline{b.a})>, \underline{a})>$$

Note that there are now six different categorial types, rather than the three forms of types in **AL**: for each type in **AL**, there are now two types, one containing the phonological form {<u>a.b</u>} and one containing the phonological form (<u>a.b</u>). The purpose of this contrast is to allow certain elements to introduce intrinsic bracketings. In the presentation of the axioms and inference rules below, we write <..., [<u>z</u>]> for either <..., {<u>z</u>}> or <..., (<u>z</u>)>. When we choose a given instantiation for one occurrence of square brackets in a rule, we must choose the same instantiation for all occurrence of square brackets within the rule.

We turn now to the formulation of axioms and rules of inference for this system, which we call **partial AL**. We begin with a set of phonological axioms:

P1.   {a.{b.c}} <->$_P$ {{a.b}.c}

P2.   (a.{b.c}) <->$_P$ {(a.b).c}

The first of these is simply the associativity axiom for { . }. The second allows an element <u>a</u> which introduces non-associative bracketing to shrink the bracketing to an initial subsequence of an argument formed by the associative product.[6]

The version of the Lambek system we propose has a single axiom and a number of inference rules. Upper-case letters are used as variables over the left projections of elements of **C**:

A1.   <x, [<u>a</u>]> -> <x, [<u>a</u>]>

R0.   [[<u>x.y</u>].<u>z</u>] ->$_P$ [<u>x.[y.z]</u>]

        <<<X.Y>,[<u>x.y</u>]>.<Z,<u>z</u>>,[[<u>x.y</u>].<u>z</u>]> -> <<<X,<u>x</u>>.<<Y.Z>,[<u>y.z</u>]>,[<u>x.[y.z]</u>]>>

R0'.   [x.{y.z}] ->$_P$ {[x.y].z}

        <<X, <u>x</u>>.<<Y.Z>,{<u>y.z</u>}>,[<u>x.{y.z}</u>]> -> <<<X.Y>, [<u>x.y</u>]>.<Z, <u>z</u>>, {[<u>x.y</u>].<u>z</u>}>

R1. $<<X.Y>, [\underline{x.y}]> \to <Z, [\underline{x.y}]>$ **R1'.** $<<Y.X>, [\underline{y.x}]> \to <Z, [\underline{y.x}]>$
-----------------------------   -----------------------------
$X \to <<Z, [\underline{x.y}]>/Y, \underline{x}>$ $X \to <<Y\backslash<Z, [\underline{y.x}]>, \underline{x}>>$

R2. $X \to <<Z, [\underline{x.y}]>/Y, \underline{x}>$ **R2'.** $X \to <Y\backslash<Z, [\underline{y.x}]>, \underline{x}>$
-----------------------   -----------------------
$<<X.Y>, [\underline{x.y}]> \to <Z, [\underline{x.y}]>$ $<<Y.X>, [\underline{y.x}]> \to <Z, [\underline{y.x}]>$

R3. $<X, \underline{x}> \to <Y, \underline{y}>$ $<Y, \underline{y}> \to <Z, \underline{z}>$

                 $<X, \underline{x}> \to <Z, \underline{z}>$

The proof of rightward functional application then takes the following form:

$$<<Z, [\underline{x.y}]>/Y, \underline{x}> \to <<Z, [\underline{x.y}]>/Y, \underline{x}> \quad \text{(A1)}$$
------------------------------------ **R2**
$$<< <Z, [\underline{x.y}]>/Y, \underline{x}>.Y>, [\underline{x.y}]> \to <Z, [\underline{x.y}]>$$

This is valid whether we construe $[\underline{x.y}]$ as $(\underline{x.y})$ or as $\{x.y\}$. From the conclusion of the above proof, by rule **R1'**, we have:

$$Y \to <<<<Z, [\underline{x.y}]>/Y, \underline{x}> \backslash <Z, [\underline{x.y}]>>, \underline{y}>$$

This analogue of one of the two symmetrical forms of type-lifting is also valid regardless of how we construe $[\underline{x.y}]$.

But composition and the other theorems that depend on it are not valid for all forms of types containing a product compatible with $[\underline{x.y}]$. In particular, we have the following cases of rightward composition:

C1. $<<<Z, [\underline{z.\{y.v\}}]>/<Y, \{\underline{y.v}\}, \underline{z}> \; . \; <<Y, \{\underline{y.v}\}>/<V, \underline{v}>, \underline{y}>, [\underline{z.y}]> \to <<<Z, \{\underline{z.y.v}\}>/<V, \underline{v}>>, [\underline{z.y}]>$

C2. $<<<<Z, \underline{z.(y.v)}>/<Y, (\underline{y.v})>, \underline{z}> \; . \; <<Y, (\underline{y.v})>/<V, \underline{v}>, \underline{y}>>, \underline{z.y}> \to <<<Z, \underline{z.(y.v)}>/<V, \underline{v}>>, \underline{z.y}>$

C1 covers two cases, depending on whether we interpret the expressions $[\underline{z.\{y.v\}}]$ and $[\underline{z.y}]$ as $\{\underline{z.\{y.v\}}\}$ and $\{\underline{z.y}\}$ or as $(\underline{z.(y.v)})$ and $(\underline{z.y})$. Both interpretations are valid (because of the role played in **R0** by the phonological axioms **P1** and **P2**, respectively). But **C2** is underivable in this system.

As a consequence, if we recharacterize the cases discussed earlier in the framework of **partial AL**, and if we assign the complementizer **that** to the category $<<<c, (\underline{that.s})>/<s,\underline{s}>>, \underline{that}>$, it will have exactly the properties necessary in this system to exhibit the behavior found in the paradigm with which we began. A rigorous demonstration of this fact exceeds the constraints on space imposed here, however, but will be treated in Oehrle (in preparation).

8. Concluding remarks.
As noted at the outset of our paper, there have been a number of attempts to characterize, in terms of "gaps" or "traces", the paradigm of cases with which we began. (We have made no attempt to catalogue them all.) What we have

tried to do is show that there is an algebraic family of categorial systems that includes not only **AL** and **nAL** but systems like **partial AL** between them that provide a way of characterizing this paradigm with no reference to gaps or traces. The solution that we have proposed involves prohibiting certain classes of expressions from engaging in the full range of bracketing relations allowed by the associativity axiom of **AL**. This same solution is equally applicable to reduced prepositions and the contracting forms of English aux-elements, although we cannot explore these consequences here. If the various contexts in which extraction is blocked can be shown to have common phonological properties, then we may interpret the operator (.) in **Phon** as correlating directly with these properties. In this case, our analysis provides a way of relating a class of extraction phenomena with other grammatical properties -- a step forward, we think, in comparison to theories that require ad hoc filters or constraints to characterize extractability. If these various contexts share no common phonological characterization, however, we may still construe the associative and non-associative modes of concatenation discussed here as abstract structures with properties that yield desirable consequences. The system **partial AL** allows the flexibility of **AL** to be combined judiciously with the rigidity of **nAL** in a way that provides an interesting alternative to accounts based on movement analyses, traces, and derivationally-based morphology of contracted forms.

Footnotes

1.For general background on categorial grammar, see Oehrle, Bach, and Wheeler (1988), Buszkowski, Marciszewski, and van Benthem (1988), and Moortgat (1989).

2. On the logical side, see van Benthem (1988) for an investigation of a permutation-closed variant of **AL**; on the linguistic side, note that the structural completeness of **AL** implies that in the system **AL + Permutation** which results from adding (7) to the axioms of **AL**, the GB rule "move alpha" is valid.

3. For alternative ways of treating discontinuous dependencies of this kind, see Moortgat (1989) and Pareschi (1988).

4. At least not so readily: such conjunctions are available on general grounds in the framework for conjunction of Oehrle (1987).

5. Our use of phonological variables has affinities with certain unification-based theories of grammatical composition, such as (Pollard & Sag, 1987) and Zeevat, Klein, and Calder (1987).

6. There is a failure of symmetry here: brackets do not care whether they are introduced by an element on the left of a string or by an element on the right, but axiom **P2** is asymmetrical. In a more elaborate version, this symmetry is easily restored. But in the present context, since we will only be concerned with functors which introduce bracketing around an argument to the right (for example, proclitics), we ignore the required elaboration here.

References

Ades, A., and M. Steedman. 1982. On the Order of Words. Linguistics & Philosophy 4.517-58.

van Benthem, J. 1988. The Lambek Calculus. Categorial Grammar and Natural Language Structures, ed. by R.T. Oehrle, E. Bach, and D. Wheeler, 35-68. Dordrecht: D. Reidel.

Bresnan, J. 1972. Theory of Complementation in English Syntax. MIT dissertation.

Buszkowski, W. 1988. Generative Power of Categorial Grammars. Categorial Grammar and Natural Language Structures, ed. by R.T. Oehrle, E. Bach, and D. Wheeler, 69-94. Dordrecht: D. Reidel.

Buszkowski, W.; W. Marciszewski; and J. van Benthem. 1988. Categorial Grammar. Amsterdam: John Benjamins.

Chomsky, N., and H. Lasnik. 1977. Filters and Control. Linguistic Inquiry 8.425-504.

Dowty, D. 1988. Type Raising, Functional Composition, and Non-Constituent Conjunction. Categorial Grammar and Natural Language Structures, ed. by R.T. Oehrle, E. Bach, and D. Wheeler, 153-197. Dordrecht: D. Reidel.

GKPS. 1985 = Gazdar, G.; E. Klein; G. Pullum; and I. Sag. 1985. Generalized Phrase Structure Grammar, Cambridge, Mass.: Harvard University Press.

Hoeksema, J. 1985. Categorial Morphology. New York: Garland.

Lambek, J. 1958. The Mathematics of Sentence Structure. American Mathematical Monthly 65.154-170.

Lambek, J. 1961. On the calculus of syntactic types. Symposia in Applied Mathematics XII: Structure of Language and its Mathematical Aspects, ed. by Roman Jakobson, 166-178. Providence: American Mathematical Society.

Moortgat, M. 1988. Mixed Composition and Discontinuous Dependencies. Categorial Grammar and Natural Language Structures, ed. by R.T. Oehrle, E. Bach, and D. Wheeler, 319-348. Dordrecht: D. Reidel.

Moortgat, M. 1989. Categorial Investigations: Logical and Linguistic Aspects of the Lambek Calculus. Dordrecht: Foris.

Oehrle, R.T. 1987. Boolean properties in the analysis of Gapping. Syntax and Semantics 20: Discontinuous Constitutency, ed. by G. Huck and A. Ojeda, 201-240. Orlando: Academic Press.

Oehrle, R.T. 1988. Multi-dimensional categorial grammars and linguistic analysis. Categorial Grammar, Unification Grammar, and Parsing, ed. by E. Klein and J. van Benthem, 231-260. Centre for Cognitive Science, University of Edinburgh, and Instituut voor Taal, Logica, en Informatica, Universiteit van Amsterdam, Amsterdam.

Oehrle, R.T. (in preparation). Partially-associative versions of the Lambek Calculus.

Oehrle, R.T.; E. Bach; and D. Wheeler. 1988. Categorial Grammars and Natural Language Structures, Dordrecht: D. Reidel.

Pareschi, R. 1988. A Definite Clause Version of Categorial Grammar. Proceedings of the 26th Annual Meeting of the Association for Computational Linguistics, Buffalo, N.Y., 270-277.

Pollard, C., and I. Sag. 1987. Information-Based Syntax and Semantics, Volume 1: Fundamentals, CSLI Lecture Notes 13. Chicago: University of Chicago Press.

Steedman, M. 1985. Dependency and Coördination in the Grammar of Dutch and English. Language 61.523-68.

Steedman, M. 1987. Combinatory Grammar and Parasitic Gaps. Natural Language and Linguistic Theory 5.403-439.

Zeevat, H.; E. Klein; and J. Calder. 1987. Unification Categorial Grammar. Categorial Grammar, Unification Grammar, and Parsing, ed. by N. Haddock, E. Klein, and G. Morrill, 195-222. Edinburgh: Centre for Cognitive Science, University of Edinburgh.

Binding Implicit Variables in Quantified Contexts

Barbara H. Partee
University of Massachusetts/Amherst

1. **Background and Overview.** It is well-known that English third-person pronouns can function variously as deictic or demonstrative elements, as discourse anaphors, and as bound variables, as illustrated in (1), (2), and (3) respectively.[1]

(1) Deictic or demonstrative: Who's *he*?
(2) Discourse anaphoric: A woman walked in. *She* sat down.
(3) Bound variable: *Every man* believed *he* was right.

In a typical use of (1), the pronoun gets its value from the non-linguistic context of the utterance, the context in which the speech act occurs. In a discourse anaphoric case like (2), the pronoun takes its value from the constructed discourse context. In a bound variable case like (3), the pronoun is interpreted as a variable bound by a variable-binding operator associated with the interpretation of *every man*.

Unified treatments of these uses of pronouns became available with the work of Kamp (1981) on discourse representation theory and Heim (1982, 1983) on file change semantics. Extensions to temporal and locative anaphora, where similar ranges of behavior can be found, have been made by Bäuerle (1979), von Stechow (1982), Hinrichs (1981), Partee (1984b), and Cooper (1986), among others. Some temporal examples are given in (4-6).

(4) Deictic past reference time: I didn't turn off the stove.
(5) Discourse anaphoric reference time: Mary woke up sometime in the night. She turned on the light.
(6) "Bound variable" past reference time: Whenever John wrote a letter to Mary, she answered two days *later*.

For arguments that (4) must be understood as anchored to a contextually definite past reference time rather than (as in traditional tense logic) as involving existential quantification over past times, see Partee (1972). Example (5) is parallel to example (2) in that the reference time which anchors the tense in the second sentence in (5) is introduced by an indefinite description ("sometime in the night") in the preceding sentence. And example (6) shows bound-variable-like behavior of the reference time: the dependent element *later* in the main clause is interpreted, in effect, as "later than t", with t the letter-writing time that is quantified over by the *whenever*-clause.

Against this background, the descriptive and theoretical concerns of this paper can be stated as follows. First, as the central descriptive concern, I want to argue for the need for

342

extensions of treatments of pronominal anaphora to a much broader
class of contentful context-dependent elements which can also
exhibit bound-variable-like behavior, such as *local*, *enemy*,
foreigner, *arrive*, *opposite*, *unfamiliar*. A key claim on which
this concern rests is that "anaphoric" or "dependent" elements
which exhibit the range of types of behavior illustrated in (1-3)
and (4-6) occur as commonly (proportionally) among *open-class* as
among closed-class items.

Among the demands that a descriptively adequate treatment of
such elements will place on the lexicon is the need for a way to
lexically specify constraints on the kinds of contexts that
different dependent elements may be sensitive to. For example,
although English third-person pronouns exhibit the full range of
behavior illustrated in (1-3), there are other dependent elements
that do not. The first-person pronoun *I* in English can anchor
only to the utterance context[2], as *he* does in (1), and has no
behavior analogous to that of the pronouns in (2) and (3). Thus
we cannot use *I* as a bound variable even when quantifying over
speakers[3]; (7) and (8) below have no readings where *I* ranges over
the speakers in question.

(7) Every speaker has difficulty stopping when I should.
(8) Every person in line said that I had been waiting for over
    an hour.

On the other hand, English reflexives like *himself* and *myself*
have only bound variable uses[4] and can only find their
antecedents sentence-internally. The plural first-person pronoun
we presents an interesting descriptive challenge: its
interpretation is a group which must include the *I* of the
utterance context, but whose other members may be anchored to any
of the kinds of contexts given in (1-3) or to a combination
thereof, as I will illustrate later.

I should note explicitly that there are many other
properties of anaphoric-like elements that need to be explored
within and across languages. I will be focussing here on the
variation illustrated in (1-3) and (4-6), particularly on
evidence that shows that large numbers of open-class lexical
items act as though their meaning includes something like a
bound-variable part. It is this behavior that I think argues
most strongly for a need to integrate this kind of context-
dependence more thoroughly into sentence-grammar. But I think
that this is probably just the tip of an iceberg, and that once
we start looking more systematically at the possible extension of
typological classifications of pronoun-like elements to large
parts of the open-class vocabulary, we will find a very large and
fertile field of study opening up.

The theoretical concern that naturally emerges from such
observations is how to articulate a theory which illuminates both
the commonalities and the differences between pronouns and other
dependent elements, and the kinds of parameters along which such

elements can vary both within and across languages. I do not
have such a theory to offer here, but I will suggest some
properties that I believe such a theory should have. At the very
least I am convinced that we need a more comprehensive theory of
context-dependent elements in which pronouns occupy one
relatively extreme position on a continuum and open-class
predicates with descriptive content and *no* dependence on context
are at the other. If words like *local*, *enemy*, *arrive*, etc. which
have both descriptive content and pronoun-like context-dependence
in their meanings are the norm rather than the exception, then we
can't rest with theories which divide lexical meanings into
constants (names, predicates, "R-expressions") and variables, or
into constants, variables, and demonstratives, treating these as
disjoint classes.

    In section 2 I will present some of the kinds of data that
support my basic descriptive claims about the varied kinds of
context-dependence, including bound-variable-like behavior, of
many open-class words. In section 3 I will make some brief
comparisons between pronouns and this broader class of dependent
elements with respect to syntactic constraints. Since the
similarities raise the natural suggestion that the "pronoun-like
parts" of the meanings of open-class context-dependent words
might just reflect the presence of some kind of null pronouns at
some syntactic level of representation, I will discuss this
possibility in section 4, along with my reasons for finding it
implausible and preferring to explore other approaches. Finally,
in section 5, I will offer some positive suggestions in the
direction of a unified theory of "quantified contexts", building
on Heim's view that the basic semantic values of expressions are
their context-change potentials. I think it should be possible
to extend earlier insights of Stalnaker, Kamp, Heim, and others
so as to bring context-dependence and semantic content even
closer together and to forge a more unified treatment of context-
dependence and variable-binding; but my suggestions in this
section remain speculative.

    2. **Initial Data.** The possibility of bound-variable-like
dependence of open-class predicates was first brought to my
attention by the work of Jonathan Mitchell in the early 1980's
(see Mitchell (1986)). Mitchell's observations included examples
like (9) below.

(9) (a) John visited a *local* bar.
     (b) Every sports fan in the country was at a *local* bar
        watching the playoffs.

Ignoring the sense of *local* which contrasts with *regional*,
national, *international*, etc., we can say that *local* has to be
anchored to some reference location, and means something like "in
the vicinity of [the reference location]". In example (9a), the
reference location could be the utterance location, or, if the
sentence is part of a longer narrative with John as the

protagonist, the reference location could be wherever John was at the time. These represent deictic and discourse anchors respectively. While *local* in (9b) *could* also be understood as anchored to the utterance location or some specific discourse location, the most likely interpretation and the one I am most interested in here is one with a "bound variable reference location" -- i.e., a possibly different location for every sports fan (his home or home town, for instance, or whatever it is that makes a bar "your local bar".)

A similar phenomenon, though one which looked more like a case of a null argument, had been noted by Dowty (1982), who gave examples (10a,b) below:

(10) (a) Bill was nervously biting his nails. Everyone noticed. [13]
 (b) Every secretary made a mistake in his final draft. The good secretary corrected his mistake. Every other secretary didn't even notice. [16]
 (c) Every man who shaves off his beard expects his wife to *notice*.

Intransitive *notice* is interpreted like transitive *notice* with a contextually definite object (unlike intransitive *eat*, which is interpreted as having an existentially quantified object argument). In (10a), the discourse context provides the understood value for the "missing object". Dowty offers (10b) as an example parallel to Karttunen's well-known "paycheck" sentences, where the missing object acts like a kind of "pronoun of laziness." And in (10c) we have an example that permits a bound variable interpretation, where the understood argument of *notice* is, for each man, his own newly beardless state.

The examples in (9) concerned an adjective, (10) a verb; Partee (1984a) observed that the same behavior can be found with one-place versions of some relational nouns, like *enemy* and *friend*, as in (11).

(11) (a) An *enemy* is *approaching*.
 (b) John faced an *enemy*.
 (c) Every participant had to confront and defeat an *enemy*.

Enemy in (11a) is likely to be understood as my or our enemy; note that *approaching* in (11a) is itself context-dependent, and if the context supported an understood goal argument of *approaching* other than me or us, the interpretation of *enemy* would probably shift accordingly. (This phenomenon is easier to observe if one changes the example to past tense.) In (11b), a likely interpretation of *enemy* is an enemy of John or of John's group, partly because of the choice of verb[5]. And in (11c), we have the possibility of a bound variable reading, where who counts as enemy or friend could be different for different participants.

The case of *enemy* raises interesting issues concerning the relative primacy of the two-place relation *enemy of* and the one-place property that results when the second argument is filled in -- e.g. the one-place property that Richard Nixon had in mind in compiling his "Enemies List", which might be expressed as "enemy of Richard Nixon". The two-place relation is clearly more general, but, as Mitchell (1986) argued[6], it does not follow that every instance of the one-place property is best analyzed as derived from the two-place one by filling in or quantifying over one argument place. In particular, an egocentric one-place version of *friend* or *enemy* may be ontogenetically and developmentally prior to the emergence of the two-place relation, and may remain directly accessible even for those who have fully acquired the two-place version. I could imagine (I have no empirical evidence, so I present this just as a possibility in principle) that dogs may have one-place concepts of *friend* and *enemy* -- ways of classifying people and other dogs into one category or the other -- but may lack completely the possibility of classifying some person A as a friend of B but an enemy of C. And children may well go through a stage where they similarly have a "one-place egocentric" concept of *friend* and *enemy* before developing the two-place concept that would let them acquire the adult interpretation of those words.[7] If that were the case, then we should not analyze the child's early use of the one-place *enemy* as resulting from two-place *enemy* with an argument filled in, e.g. as meaning "my enemy" (much as we have learned to analyze children's earliest uses of *bit* and *took* as unanalyzed morphemes rather than as "correct" past tense forms.) The question would then remain open whether the one-place egocentric concept is *lost* when the two-place one is acquired, or whether it remains active; the corresponding linguistic question is whether the apparently one-place common noun *enemy* is to be analyzed in all occurrences as having an implicit argument or context parameter, as it must in (11b) and (11c) on the given readings, or whether it sometimes maps directly onto the old egocentric one-place concept, as it could in (11a). It would also be interesting to look for evidence for a stage at which *enemy* takes a "point-of-view" contextual parameter but not yet an explicit argument, as a possible bridge between the purely egocentric version and a fully "objective" two-place relation; such evidence might take the form of the use of sentences like (11b) but no possibility of using *enemy* with an *of*-complement or a genitive.

Returning to our central data, it is also of interest that the famous "donkey-pronoun" sentences like (12), whose successful analysis is one of the central arguments for the theories of Kamp (1981) and Heim (1982), also have analogues with a wider class of context-dependent elements, as in (13).[8]

(12) Every man who owns a donkey beats *it*.
(13) (a) Every man who stole a car abandoned it *2 hours later*.
    (b) Every man who stole a car abandoned it $\begin{cases} \textit{within 50 miles.} \\ \textit{50 miles away.} \end{cases}$

In the standard donkey-sentence (12), the pronoun *it* in the
matrix has an indefinite NP antecedent *a donkey* embedded in a
relative clause on a quantified subject. In the examples in
(13), both the dependent and the antecedent are implicit, but
their relative locations in the sentence are just as in (12). So
in (13a), for instance, the temporal adverb *2 hours later* has an
implicit reference time parameter that must be specified for the
expression to be interpretable. Where does the reference time
come from? On the relevant reading, it's understood as 'when he
stole the car', i.e. a time indefinitely and implicitly given by
the relative clause on the quantified NP, a variable time that
will be different for different occurrences of men stealing cars.

    As a final set of initial data, to illustrate some of the
further variety of aspects of context that can be implicitly
quantified over in sentence-internal constructions, consider the
richness of spatial and perspectival structure presupposed by
systems of locative deixis and locative anaphora, as described
for instance by Fillmore (1975) for English (see Weissenborn and
Klein (1982) for a sampling of equally rich but often different
contextual factors on which the interpretation of locative deixis
and anaphora depends in other languages.) To start from examples
in simple discourse contexts, note the differences in possible
interpretations of the italicized expressions in (14b, b', b"),
taken as alternative continuations to (14a). In particular, note
the ways in which the respective interpretations of *away*, *ahead*,
and *farther away* depend upon different presupposed properties of
the context which must be supplied or inferred in order to
interpret the expressions at all.

(14) (a) John entered the store and saw a woman he knew.
    (b) Three feet *away* was a small child.
    (b') Three feet *ahead* was a small child.
    (b") Three feet *farther away* was a small child.

In the case of *away* in (14b), we need only a single reference
location, which in the given example could easily be either John
or the woman; *three feet away* is then understood as three feet
from that location in any direction. *Ahead* in (14b') requires
more: its interpretation requires both a reference location and
a direction of orientation which qualifies as 'forward'. In the
given example two likely possibilities would be (i) John's
location and his direction of travel as he entered the store, or
(ii) the woman's location and the direction of John's line of
sight when he saw her.[9] *Three feet ahead* is understood in either
case as three feet from the reference location in the reference
direction. *Farther away* in (14b") requires two reference

locations (one as for *away* and the other as an implicit argument
for the comparative) and perhaps an orientation, although it may
be only a cancellable implicature that the child is in the same
direction from John as the woman is. Be that as it may, it is
not uncommon for contextual parameters such as spatial
orientation, point of view, direction of sight or motion, etc.,
to be crucial for the interpretation of locative deictics and
locative "dependents", as Fillmore and others have richly
demonstrated. The new point I want to add to these observations
is that we find sensitivity to these same factors in sentence-
internal quantified constructions, so that the integration of
context-dependence with the sentence grammar of variable-binding
constructions has somehow got to include such aspects of context
as axis of orientation as well as more "reference-like"
parameters such as "reference time" and "reference location".

To illustrate this last claim with an example that combines
properties of the implicit "donkey anaphor" cases illustrated in
(13) with the rich locative structure illustrated in (14),
consider (15).

(15) Every traveler who stops for the night imagines that there
     is a more comfortable place to stay a few miles *farther on*.

Consider in particular the interpretation of the italicized
phrase *farther on*. Its interpretation requires, and we can
easily provide via inference from the interpretation of the
subject noun phrase, two reference locations and a path; its
meaning is paraphrasable as something like "more distant from
[source reference location] along [path from source] than
[comparison-base reference location]". (No weight should be
placed on my choice of terms for identifying the relevant
contextual parameters; there is much written in this area, and I
am not an expert in it.) What I want to draw attention to is
that we are readily able to interpret the needed parameters in
(15) in terms of the (variable) traveler's path of travel; for
each traveler, we can identify the traveler himself as the source,
his route *qua* traveler as the path, and the place where he
stopped for the night as the comparison-base reference location.
And these will in general be different for each traveler, i.e.
they act like bound variables. But much as Cresswell (1973)
argued against the analysis of contexts as discrete tuples of
contextual parameters in the early years of the study of
indexicality, I will want to suggest that the implicitness and
indirectness of all of this information in the subject NP of (15)
argues against trying to treat such cases by adding explicit
variables over locations, paths, directions of travel, etc., in
some syntactic level such as a level of deep structure or a level
of logical form. I want to suggest rather that in cases like
this we want the possibility of "quantifying over contexts" in a
rather holistic sense, although my suggestions fall far short of
providing an articulated theory. But first let's look at some of

the respects in which syntax *does* clearly play a role in the
interpretation of such constructions.

   3. **Syntactic Constraints.** To summarize the observations I
will make in this section, it appears that the constraints on the
syntactic location of dependent items like *local, enemy, notice,
later, ahead, farther on*, etc. relative to the syntactic location
of the material that provides the understood anchor or
"antecedent" for the dependent element are very similar to the
constraints on pronominal anaphora of both "coreferential" and
"bound variable" types. I cannot state the constraints with any
precision or confidence, however, for several reasons: (i) as in
the case of pronominal anaphora, judgments are often conflicting
and unclear; (ii) the history of the study of pronominal anaphora
makes it clear that far more work than I have put into this
question would have to precede any even halfway trustworthy
generalizations; (ii) and to make matters even harder in this
case, both the dependents and the "antecedents" are hard to
localize in many of the most interesting of these cases; their
very implicitness and the uncertainty of whether they exist in
the syntax at all means that questions such as whether the
"antecedent" c-commands the "dependent" in a given case run the
risk of being ill-founded and unanswerable questions. Hence what
follows is brief and approximate.
   With those caveats, I will claim that the basic (precede
and) command types of syntactic constraints on sentence-internal
"bound" context-dependence and "discourse-anchored" context-
dependence are either just like the constraints on the
corresponding uses of pronouns or slightly less restrictive
(perhaps closer to the anaphoric uses of definites[10]); in clear
cases, the judgments generally agree. So for instance (16a),
with a referential anchor, is grammatical, just as backwards
coreferential pronominal anaphora is as long as the pronoun
doesn't directly c-command the antecedent. But (16b), with a
quantified anchor, is pretty bad when we try to interpret *away* as
anchored to the variable pigeon locations, in line with the
observation that for bound-variable anaphora a quantified
antecedent must usually c-command the pronoun.

   (16) (a) From five feet *away* I tried to toss a peanut to
            the pigeon.
        (b) #?From five feet *away* I tried to toss a peanut
            to *every pigeon*.

Certainly the difference in acceptability in (17a) and (17b) is
in the expected direction: it is much harder in (17a) than in
(17b) to understand there to be possibly different local unions
involved for the different professors.

   (17) (a) #?The leader of the *local* union wrote a letter to
            every untenured professor in the state.

     (b) *Every untenured professor in the state* received a
        letter from the leader of the *local* union.

The same contrasts are illustrated in (18a-c), where on the
quantified reading we are interested in nearness to each
respective senator.[11] The relative badness of (18b) on a bound
interpretation of *nearest* seems comparable to, if perhaps
slightly less pronounced than, the relative badness of a bound
variable pronoun in the same position, as illustrated in (19a-c).

  (18) (a) Only the *nearest* photographer got a good picture
           of *Reagan*.
      (b) #?Only the *nearest* photographer got a good picture
           of *every senator*.
      (c) *Every senator* directed a smile at the *nearest*
           photographer.
  (19) (a) Only *his* top aide got a good picture of *Reagan*.
      (b) #?Only *his* top aide got a good picture of *every
           senator*.
      (c) *Every senator* directed a smile at *his* top aide.

Given these similarities in syntactic constraints between
open-class dependent elements and pronouns, and given their
similar ranges of semantic behavior as illustrated in section 2,
there are at least two ways one might proceed to try to account
for the new data. One way, the one I favor, is to try to
redesign our theories so that open-class-context-dependent
elements like *enemy*, etc., are the general case, and pure
pronouns and context-independent content words are extreme cases
at opposite poles. But another approach with considerable
plausibility would be to posit empty pronouns in the
representations at some appropriate level to make the anaphoric
or pronoun-like parts of the meanings of these various dependent
elements explicit. This is particularly plausible for examples
like *notice*, *away*, *enemy*, which can be argued to have an argument
structure that would naturally accommodate an implicit argument
(*notice x*, *away from x*, *enemy of x*.) The phenomena I have been
discussing might just be reflections of the behavior of a certain
kind of empty category, one which might or might not be identical
to some previously posited empty category.
    I have no conclusive arguments against the latter approach,
but I can and should say something about my reasons for being
skeptical about it.[12] The following section is directed to that
issue.
    4. **Why not do it all with pronouns?** The question of this
section is not an easy one. I'm familiar with a lot of the
properties of real pronouns, and I can demonstrate some clear
differences between the behavior of overt pronouns and the
behavior of the "empty" pronouns that might be posited in the
open-class cases. But I'm in the uncomfortable position of not
being at all familiar with the properties of empty pronouns and

not being sure whether that's inevitable because there aren't any or whether my resistance to acknowledging their existence has just prevented me from learning to recognize them and become acquainted with their properties. In any case, all I can do here is offer some of my own reasons for finding it implausible to try to "do it all with pronouns", reasons which might well evaporate if a suitable theory of such pronouns were developed. (It is in any case perfectly consistent with these arguments that *some* of the cited examples might use some kind of null pronouns.)

What I mean by a "do it all with pronouns" approach, or "uniform pronoun approach" for short, would be an approach which analyzes intransitive *notice* as differing minimally from the phrase *notice it*, but with a phonologically null pronominal element in place of the *it*, and which then proceeds to find ways to analyze *all* context-dependent predicates of the sort I have been discussing into a context-independent lexical predicate plus suitable pronouns or pronoun-like elements, presumably filling argument positions of the given predicate.

The problems I see for such a uniform pronoun approach are of two sorts, the first concerning the antecedents and the second concerning the decompositional analysis of the dependent elements. The first is that overt pronouns in their discourse anaphoric and bound variable uses normally require overt antecedents.[13] We will see below some examples with quantified contexts but no overt "antecedent" where a bare dependent element like *nearby* without an overt pronominal argument can be used, but a corresponding form *with* an overt pronoun cannot (*near it*, *near there*). The second problem is that not all dependent elements take complements or admit of a plausible (to me, at least) decomposition into a context-independent predicate plus pronominal arguments. We will also see examples of that below. But it is clear, as I indicated above, that these problems are not necessarily insurmountable; they can simply be taken as challenges by those who would prefer to try the uniform pronoun approach.

I gave some initial hints of my arguments against the uniform pronoun approach in my discussion of (15) in section 2. To make the arguments more explicit, let's look at some other examples.

As a first example consider the discourses in (20a-c) containing *left* and *right*. *Left* and *right* as used in these examples are context-dependent with two arguments or parameters: to the left *of what* and *from whose point of view*. The former is naturally expressed as an argument of an *of*-complement, but the latter can only be made explicit via the sort of paraphrase just given ("from the point of view of x"),[14] which looks like some sort of an adjunct more than an argument. The ungrammatical (20b) represents an attempt to make the second "argument" overt as a source or experiencer.

(20) (a) John had a black spot on the middle of his forehead.
To the left of it (from John's point of view/from an observer's point of view) was a green "A".
(b) ...*? to the left of it from/for *him*
(c) Every man had . . .   [**same data**]

For a similar set of examples, but showing the existence of idiosyncratic lexical variation among similar words in the ability to take overt pronominal arguments, consider (21a-b).

(21) (a) Citizens of every country tend to find $\left\{\begin{array}{l} foreign \text{ cars} \\ foreigners \\ strangers \end{array}\right\}$ attractive.

(b) [*foreign* to them/that country], [a *stranger* to them/that country], *[a *foreigner* to them/that country]

All the examples in (21a) are well-formed, with the context-dependence of *foreign*, *foreigner*, and *stranger* all left implicit. But (21b) shows that while *foreign* and *stranger* can also take overt pronominal arguments, *foreigner* evidently cannot. (Whatever approach one takes to these phenomena, it is already a challenge to try to imagine how to represent such apparent idiosyncratic differences between a lexical item's subcategorization for overt pronominal arguments and its semantic dependence on given (potentially covert) context parameters.)

The following examples use the dependent adjectives *opposite*, *different*, and *similar*. These adjectives can take an overt pronominal argument when there is an overt accessible NP antecedent for the pronoun, but in the examples in (22) the "antecedent" for the use of *opposite*, etc., while sentence-internal and even quantified, is indirect and inferential with respect to its introduction of a child-rearing method (22a), a strategy (22d), a sleep pattern (22e), a problem (22f), and does not support the use of a pronoun.

(22) (a) Not everyone who thinks their parents did a bad job of bringing them up actually switches to the *opposite* child-rearing method.
(b) Interpretation: for each x, the child-rearing method opposite to the method used by x's parents in bringing x up.
(c) *... the child-rearing method opposite to *it*.
(d) Every beginning general who loses his first battle switches to a *different* strategy in his second. (# a strategy *different from that/it*)
(e) Why do so many people marry people with the *opposite* sleep pattern? (# sleep pattern *opposite from that/it*)
(f) I wish that just once when I had just worked out a good solution for one client, my next client would come in with a *similar* problem. (# *similar to it/that*)

The similar but good examples (23) below contrast minimally with
(22d) above, strongly suggesting that it is not the simple lack
of an overt NP antecedent denoting a strategy that makes (22d)
bad, but the combination of that fact with the fact that the
inferred strategy in (22d) may be a different one for each
general. Neither of these factors alone is fatal: (23a) lacks
an NP antecedent for the strategy but introduces a unique
strategy in the VP "played hard-to-get"; (23b) introduces an NP
antecedent for the strategy but, as in typical donkey-pronoun
sentences, as a quantified indefinite it may be a different
strategy for each general.

> (23) (a) Few of the women who had played hard-to-get in the
> 50's switched to the *opposite* strategy after their
> first divorces in the 70's. (also OK: strategy
> *opposite to that*)
> (b) Every beginning general who loses his first battle
> using one strategy switches to a *different* strategy
> in his second. (also OK: a strategy *different from
> that*)

This last-illustrated phenomenon can also be seen with
example (13), repeated below.

> (13) (a) Every man who stole a car abandoned it *2 hours later.*
> (b) Every man who stole a car abandoned it $\begin{cases} within\ 50\ miles \\ 50\ miles\ away \end{cases}$

We cannot substitute *later than that, within 50 miles of
there, 50 miles away from there* in (13a-b) as they stand, but if
we added a simple *at some time* or *somewhere* in the respective
antecedent relative clauses then we could.
Turning back to the locative domain, it seems to me that
many of the parameters to which locative deictics and dependents
are sensitive are reflections of the richly structured
presupposed spatial/motional context in which such expressions
are used rather than "arguments" of those expressions in any
familiar sense. And even when such expressions can be used with
a pronominal argument, the way locative anchoring works when we
quantify over shifting 'points of view' or displacements of the
understood axes of orientation does not seem to be the same as
the way pronominal anchoring works (though I am far from being
able to articulate the differences in any systematic way.) The
examples in (24) illustrate these claims.

> (24) (a) In all my travels, whenever I have called for a doctor,
> one has *arrived* (*set out, *departed*) within
> an hour.
> (b) ... *arrived there, *set out for there* ...
> (c) ... *arrived here, *set out for here* ...

The contrasts in (24) are particularly interesting in suggesting differences between *here*, *there*, and an implicit contextual point-of view. I believe the anchor for *arrive* and *set out* in (24a) is the *I* in the sense that it is "my" point of view that establishes the frame of reference. The implicit reference place being quantified over is wherever I was on any given occasion of calling for a doctor; that reference place provides the needed goal parameter (or argument) for *arrive*. (The contrast between *set out* and *depart* I don't understand, but my location also apparently serves as the goal for *set out*. It may be that *depart* obligatorily requires a specified *source* and *set out* doesn't.)

Now part of what's interesting in this case is that my varying location seems to be something like a quantified-over shiftable "here". But the actual word *here*, as shown by the impossibility of (24c), does not allow such a bound-variable interpretation. Although *here* is more shiftable than *I* and can anchor to a third-person discourse protagonist's subjective point of view in a narrative, it cannot anchor to a quantified antecedent as would be required for (24c) to be well-formed. *There*, on the other hand, can function perfectly well as a bound variable, but its antecedent or anchor must be "third-person-like", a place looked at from somewhere else, so to speak, not the "here" of ego's point of view. This is apparently the source of the badness of (24b). In fact if we just changed "called for a doctor" to "called from any place for a doctor", (24b) would become fine; "any place" apparently provides a sufficiently externalized perspective on the places where I was when I called to license *there*.

Putting the examples in (24a,b,c) together, we can roughly summarize the situation by saying that *here* must be anchored to the *origo* of the utterance or discourse and disallows a bound variable use; *there* can be anchored to the non-first-person reference location of the utterance, discourse or sentence-internal context, including the possibility of acting as a bound variable; while *arrive* with its implicit goal parameter can anchor to an explicit or implicit *origo*[15] in the utterance context, the discourse context, or a sentence-internal quantified context. The behavior of the latter thus has properties which overlap those of first-person and third-person locative anaphors but is interestingly different from both.

To summarize this section, I suggest that it would be most fruitful to try to get a picture of the full range of behavior of different open-class and closed-class context-dependent and anaphoric elements, looking at all of them on their own terms, so to speak, before reaching any conclusions about the extent to which it is possible and appropriate to regiment all the cases into a narrow typology using decomposition, for instance, to bring the unfamiliar kinds of cases into line with more familiar patterns.

5. **Steps toward a unified theory of "quantified contexts".**
5.1 **Contexts, cases, and tripartite structures.** My goal in

this section is to try to suggest ways in which natural
extensions of the work of Stalnaker, Lewis, Kamp, Heim and
Kratzer might help us to unify context-dependence and variable
binding in the kinds of ways the data presented above appear to
demand. Stalnaker (1978, 1984) made the notion of *conversational
background* prominent and emphasized the two-way dynamics of the
relation between the context and the interpretation of successive
sentences, the latter both depending on and affecting the former.
Lewis (1979) posits a "conversational scoreboard" as an abstract
accompaniment to the interpretation process: the "scoreboard" is
used to record relevant aspects of the context, such as speaker,
reference time, currently most salient individuals, etc.; the
scoreboard is updated as the conversation progresses.

What the examples in the previous sections have shown is
that many elements can be sensitive "in the same way" to various
aspects of any of three different sorts of context: the external
context of the utterance, the discourse-level linguistic context,
and the sentence-internal linguistic context, which in
quantificational constructions can be a quantified context. This
last shows the necessity of integrating the relevant "scoreboard"
information into the recursive mechanisms of sentence grammar.
The parallel sensitivity to all three kinds of context is
reminiscent of the behavior of pronouns which motivated the Kamp-
Heim theory, and suggests the use of "tripartite structures" as
in the Kamp-Heim treatment of donkey-sentences. These tripartite
structures, illustrated schematically in tree form in (25a) and
in Kamp's box-like Discourse Representation Structure (DRS) in
(25b)[16], have historical antecedents in Lewis's (1975) treatment
of adverbs of quantification, in McCawley's (1981) emphasis on
the preference of natural languages for restricted rather than
unrestricted quantification, and in Kratzer's (1977) work on the
semantics of modals and conditionals.

(25) a.

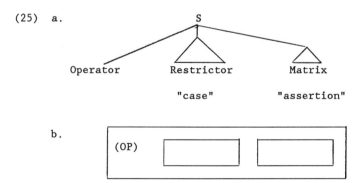

The work of Kamp, Stalnaker, Lewis, Heim, and Kratzer (and
others) has made great progress in bringing context-dependence
and semantic content closer together. Heim's theory is expressed
in terms of "context-change potential", and the manipulations of

356

context in the process of interpretation in her framework are reminiscent of the familiar manipulations of the time index, world index, and variable assignments in other theories.

Kamp's and Heim's theories incorporate a notion of *accessibility* for potential antecedents of pronominal elements; this notion, though syntactically expressible, is fundamentally semantically determined.[17] In a structure like (25a) or (25b), a pronoun in one part can anchor to an antecedent in any higher part, where *higher than* (not their term) is defined as follows: the restrictor is higher than the matrix, and the outer discourse structure is higher than either. As Heim has emphasized, the satisfaction of presuppositions in quantificational and non-quantificational structures shows a similar sensitivity to this kind of structure: the presupposition in the matrix can be satisfied via material introduced in the restrictor clause or anywhere "higher".

So it seems very natural to add the generalized context-dependence we've been discussing to this same schema: a context-dependent element of any kind in the matrix clause can anchor onto material in the restrictor or anywhere "higher". This then would seem to unify pronominal anaphora, presupposition, and the varieties of context-dependence illustrated in the previous sections. This observation does not, of course, constitute a theory; fleshing out a real theory along these lines will take much more work.

But I can give a rough sketch of the sort of treatment I imagine; (26) below represents a first approximation in extended DRS terms to a structure for (12a), repeated below.

(12a) Every man who stole a car abandoned it 2 hours *later*.

(26) DRS for (12a) (first approximation)

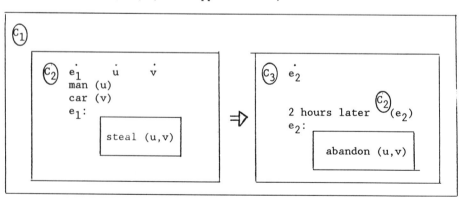

The circled C_0, C_1, etc. represent nested contexts: C_0 the
external context of utterance, C_1 the context of the discourse at
the point at which (12a) is evaluated, C_2 the (quantified)
context of the restrictor clause, and C_3 (understood as an
extension of C_2) the context of the matrix, which is thus
embedded within all three of the others. In (26), the element
later in the matrix needs an anchor: my suggestion is that rather
than introduce an explicit time variable to mediate this
dependency, we simply index *later* to some accessible **context**. It
is part of the lexical semantics of *later* that whatever context
it anchors to must have, either overtly or inferably, a reference
time to interpret *later* in terms of. For the quantified
interpretation, illustrated in (26), *later* is   marked as
anchored to the context C2, whose (variable) reference time would
be times of the stealing events that are being quantified over.

In general in such tripartite structures,the matrix is
interpreted relative to a "case" as established by the
"restrictor". The specification in the restrictor will generally
establish a partially-defined context. In (26), for instance,
each "case" (i.e. each car theft) provides an implicit time,
place, original owner, motive, method, and undoubtedly more.
Insofar as the whole construction is interpreted as quantifying
over such "cases", with the matrix interpreted in the quantified
context established by the restrictor, we may then be able to
interpret many context-dependent elements in the matrix just by
indexing them globally to the context of the restrictor, without
having to posit explicit variables for time, place, manner,
motive, etc.

5.2 **Syntactic and semantic c-command-type restrictions**. The
kinds of c-command restrictions discussed in section 3 should
probably be related to the construction and manipulation of
nested contexts, and to the hierarchy of accessibility for
pronominal anaphora as graphically articulated in file change
theory or DRS theory. It is important to realize that most
occurrences of expressions are located in many contexts at once,
including nested contexts such as were illustrated in (26). For
many dependent elements, particularly those sensitive to first-
person-like *I*, *here*, *now* parameters of the context, just indexing
them to a whole *context* may suffice, since many relevant aspects
of context seem to be of a "unique-per-context" sort (e.g. the
temporal anchor for *later* in (26)). But this is clearly not the
case for third-person pronouns, and may be similarly too strong
for other third-person-like elements such as locative *there*.

The idea of nested contexts and indexing to context can be
further illustrated with an example involving *we*, showing not
only ambiguity in nested context situations, but the possibility
of anchoring to a context which draws elements into itself from
some of the higher accessible contexts.

Consider the sample text in (27) and the DRS in (28).

(27) John often comes over for Sunday brunch.
      Whenever someone else comes over too,
      we (all) end up playing trios. (Otherwise
      we play duets.)

(28)

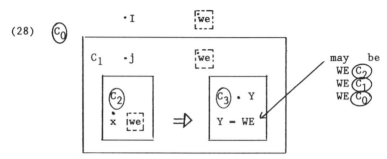

The *we* that occurs in the matrix has as its most plausible
interpretation a bound variable interpretation anchored to
(accommodated into) the restrictive clause; that *we* in turn can
be understood to denote a group including me, John, and the
somebody else being quantified over in the sentence, i.e. a
combination of individuals from the external utterance context,
the discourse context, and the context of quantification. Of
course there are other readings in principle possible for the *we*:
it could anchor to the utterance context alone (*we* being then
some particular known individuals in the speech situation, e.g.
my family) or to the discourse situation alone (where it would
likely pick up *John and me* as the salient group).

    As another example of nested contexts, consider sentence
(29) and the rough DRS (30) for it.

(29) Most Europeans speak a foreign language.

(30)

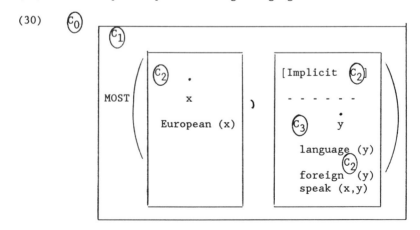

If, as in the given diagram, we anchor *foreign* to the quantified context C_2, we mean *foreign* from each European's point of view - French for Germans, English for Danes, etc. However, the sentence could also be used by the stereotypical "ugly American" to say why he doesn't like to travel in Europe: to him the Frenchman speaking French is speaking a foreign language. That would be represented by anchoring *foreign* to C_0, giving the egocentric point of view. And an anchoring to the discourse content C_1 could represent the egocentric point of view of a discourse protagonist - e.g. in a narrative about a certain ugly American and his attitudes.

The sentence (31), offered by Gregory Ward, shows the same ambiguities and more.

(31) Most foreigners speak a foreign language.

While both occurrences of *foreign* could be egocentrically anchored to C_0 (the ugly American again), a more interesting reading is one where the first occurrence of *foreigners*, which will be in the restrictor clause, is anchored to the utterance or discourse context, while the second, in the matrix, is anchored to the restrictor, i.e. to the perspective of the (variable) subject.

5.3 **Lexical information about dependent elements.** One of the principal tasks that faces the working out of a theory along the lines of these suggestions is to articulate a framework in which the relevant lexical information about dependent elements can be appropriately captured. In general, I think we can say that dependent elements, both closed-class and open-class, are interpreted as *functions from contexts to semantic values or referents*. This means that we would have to specify at least the following three kinds of information about each dependent element:

(32) (i) what *kind(s)* of context it can anchor to (utterance situation, discourse, sentence-internal);

(ii) *requirements* on the context for the element to be defined, as presuppositions or implicatures. (e.g. *farther on* requires a point of view and a reference location.);

(iii) *meaning*, generally as a function of the elements required in (ii), which is presumably why they're required. (*Farther on*: "more distant from the point-of-view location along the point-of-view directional orientation than the reference location is").

When a dependent element occurs in several nested contexts at once, the requirements of type (i) and (ii) may or may not disambiguate it; if not, plausibility factors may disambiguate it or it may remain genuinely ambiguous. The ease with which we

seem to disambiguate most such elements in natural speech may
partially account for the apparent lack of attention to their
pronoun-like properties. For the pronouns, there is essentially
no descriptive meaning beyond the identification with an
antecedent, so one can't help but notice their dependence
properties, a point which leads us to the topic of the next
section.

5.4 **Pronouns as an extreme case.** As I have tried to suggest
throughout this paper, I believe that the general case of lexical
meaning is a combination of inherent meaning and dependence on
context. As we seek a theory that adequately captures the right
amount of power, the right constraints, and the right
articulation of important properties and parameters, we have to
simultaneously try to analyze the linguistically relevant
properties of contexts and the relevant properties of the lexical
items.

One observation that seems to surface from the examples we
have looked at is that some aspects of contexts seem to be
generally unique per context, at least if we analyze contexts
into the right size chunks: e.g. reference time, reference place,
point-of-view. And there seems to be a corresponding subclass of
context-dependent elements which anchor onto such properties of
contexts, and for which indexing to a choice of context is
therefore probably sufficient and appropriate, rather than trying
to introduce an overt empty pronoun or variable to try to capture
the anchoring via explicit identity. I suspect, as I mentioned
above, that this is more generally the case for "first-person-
like" dependents which anchor to the *I-here-now* or point of
view of a context, the implicit versions of which seem to be much
more shiftable and bindable than their explicit counterparts (as
discussed above in connection with example (24)).

Other aspects of contexts, such as salient individuals, are
not generally unique per context, and for the corresponding
dependent elements which anchor onto them, there may be more than
one potential anchor per context and hence a need to structurally
indicate not only the choice of anchoring context but the choice
of a particular antecedent within it. This is probably the
general rule for third person pronouns and "third-person-like"
dependents in general, and if so, this would support something
like the familiar uses of indexing and coindexing mechanisms. I
am therefore not proposing the elimination of explicit variables
or indices altogether, but just arguing that not all context-
dependence should be so represented.

Third-person pronouns, then, appear from this perspective to
be a limiting case of a broader phenomenon. They have essentially
no descriptive content of their own, so that their interpretation
is exhausted by a description of their anchoring and binding
possibilities. They may have many potential antecedents per
context, and their antecedents must normally be overt NP's,
especially in the bound-variable case. From a broader

perspective we can see that none of these properties hold of all
dependent elements.

6. **Summary.** The fact that context-dependent phenomena of
many kinds operate even in quantified contexts argues strongly
for the integration of such kinds of context-dependence into
sentence grammar. Theories such as DRS theory and file change
semantics which emphasize the dynamics of context change have
helped to unify the treatment of presupposition and anaphora in
quantified constructions, and although much work remains to be
done, it looks possible and necessary to generalize and extend
these ideas to context-dependence of many kinds. It will be
important to look at as many languages as possible, and as many
kinds of "pronoun-like" elements as possible, and to try to
identify other linguistically relevant aspects of context that
the interpretation of such elements can be sensitive to. Several
approaches to further work in this direction suggest themselves,
and I expect that pursuing them all will be valuable. One task is
to go through studies of the properties of pronouns (in various
languages and in various theories) and see which of these
properties extend to or contrast with properties of open-class
context-dependent elements. Another important task is to start
from studies of context-dependence of many kinds and in many
languages, and see which properties need to be recognized within
sentence grammar, using the behavior of bound-variable contexts
as a diagnostic. I would expect that we will find many purely
pragmatic context-dependent phenomena that do *not* integrate into
sentence grammar, such as e.g. the use of honorific forms.

When we have a better idea of the range of the phenomena,
both in terms of the class of dependent elements and in terms of
the properties of contexts they are dependent on, we will be in a
better position to identify properties and parameters that play
an explanatory role in the overall organization of the system(s)
of dependence. The observations in this paper suggest what some
of the important properties might be, but the central questions
in this area are still open ones.

Acknowledgments

Earlier versions of this material were presented at the
Linguistics Institute in 1986, at the 6th Amsterdam Colloquium on
Formal Linguistics in 1987, and at colloquia at Cornell, the
University of Massachusetts, and at Swarthmore College. I am
grateful for useful comments received at CLS and on all those
earlier occasions, particularly from Emmon Bach, Steve Berman,
Wayles Browne, Janet Fair, Irene Heim, Jim Huang, John Kingston,
Angelika· Kratzer, Richard Larson, David Pesetsky, Luigi Rizzi,
and Jerry Sadock.

This material is based upon work supported in part by System
Foundation Development Grant #650, and in part by the National
Science Foundation, Grant #8719999, support which is hereby
gratefully acknowledged.

362

Footnotes

1. See, for instance, Partee (1984b). I am ignoring finer distinctions and controversies which are irrelevant to the main concerns of this paper
2. In Amharic, on the other hand, the first-person pronoun is also used as a logophoric pronoun coreferential with the subject of a verb of saying or believing (Emmon Bach, p.c.); I would conjecture that this would lead to bound variable possibilities in examples like (8) below, though not (7).
3. There does seem to be the possibility of a bound-variable use of *I*, not with quantified antecedents, but in the formation of relative clauses by predicate abstraction in certain cases where tension between syntactic agreement and semantic interpretation undoubtedly plays a role. Thus (i) below tends to admit a bound variable reading of the second *I*, perhaps even as its preferred reading.
   (i) I'm the only one around here who will admit that I could
       be wrong.
4. Some speakers can also apparently get external referential anchoring for the English reflexives. The difference shows up in tests for strict vs. sloppy identity in examples like (i) and (ii), where the bound variable-only "dialect" gets only sloppy identity (Bill voted for himself), and the other "dialect" can also get a strict-identity reading (Bill voted for John/me).
   (i) John voted for himself, and so did Bill.
   (ii) I won't vote for myself unless Bill does.
5. Among the important properties I am ignoring here are some that would be involved in distinguishing between reflexive-like and non-reflexive-like "implicit arguments", including issues of locality requirements on the relation between antecedent and implicit argument.
6. Mitchell discusses a variety of examples of perspectival properties including some for which various species seem to be "hard-wired" for an egocentric version. The information a bat obtains from its sonar system is an example of such a case; all the information it obtains about distance and direction and speed of motion of objects it detects are relative to the bat's own position, orientation, and direction and speed of motion.
7. Janet Fair reported to me after the oral presentation of this paper that her 3-year-old had gone through a noticeable evolution in the understanding of enemy from about 33 months to about 36 months, including passage from the question "What's an enemy?" to the questions "What's an enemy to a mouse?",
"What is an enemy to a bear?"
8. These examples were first brought to my attention by Roger Schwarzschild.
9. I'm not sure whether shuffling these pairs yields available contextual anchors as well or not; I suspect not. If John's line of sight is the same as his direction of motion, we can't tell;

if he sees the woman to his left while walking straight ahead
through the door, my intuition is that we have to be consistent
in the sense of taking both the location and the orientation from
the same conjunct of (14a). This intuition is reinforced by the
fact that if we give the second conjunct of (14a) a separate
temporal adverb, such as "and two minutes later saw...", then
(14b') must get its temporal and locative anchors all from the
same conjunct, presumably the second.
10. Irene Heim (personal communication) noted that weak crossover
effects tend to be milder in German examples with die Mutter 'the
mother' than in corresponding English examples with his mother.
The context-dependent elements I discuss may line up more with
the anaphoric definites than with the overt pronouns, where these
differ; in fact, anaphoric definites may well be an example of
the kind of context-dependence I am trying to treat here.
11. It was pointed out to me by Zi-Qiang Shi that (18b) improves
noticeably if the (episodic) got is replaced by (generic or
habitual) gets. This would seem to be the result of introducing
quantification over situations of photographing, and no longer
limiting the quantification to the senators. But I have no
explanation in detail.

The following examples, from John Kingston, are likewise
generic, and it may be that the for everybody in (i) and (iii)
is a adjunct delimiting the domain over which the generic claim
holds.
   (i)   The nearest exit isn't the best for everybody.
   (ii)   The girl next door is the best wife for every man.
   (iii) A seat in the local bar is the best place to watch the
          superbowl for everybody.

An even harder apparent class of counterexamples was
pointed out to me by Wayles Browne; these have the structure of
"MIGS and pilots" sentences.
   (iv)   The successors were better than the predecessors.
   (v)   The successors are always an improvement over the
          predecessors.
I have no account for (iv) and (v).
12. I will offer what seems to me to be rational grounds for my
skepticism, but I have to confess to sometimes wondering if I
don't have a temperamental objection to the uniform pronoun
approach. I have resolved several times in the past to try to
work out an analysis with pronouns, and have not been able to
bring myself to do it. But I hope someone will try to work out
such a theory so that results can be compared.
13. The claim that overt pronouns require overt antecedents
requires caveats. It accounts for the difference between my old
examples (i) and (ii), but (ii) is not totally ungrammatical with
a substantial pause before it, and other instances of
"accommodated" antecedents can be found in the literature.
   (i)   One of the ten balls is missing from the bag. It's under
          the couch.
   (ii)   Nine of the ten balls are in the bag. #It's under the couch.

364

14. Jerry Sadock pointed out in discussion that to his right is unambiguous in a way that to the right of him is not.
15. A term introduced by Bühler (1934); see discussion in Weissenborn and Klein (1982).
16. The double arrow in (26) and (28) is an abbreviation for a special case of the operator of (25a,b), (30), namely for the selective universal quantifier.
17. This is pointed out by Heim (1982) and discussed more fully by Chierchia and Rooth (1984).

References

Bäuerle, R. 1977. *Tempus, Temporaladverb und die temporale Frage*. Doctoral Dissertation, Konstanz.
Bäuerle, R. 1979. *Temporale Deixis, temporale Frage*. Tuebingen:Gunter Marr.
Bühler, Karl. 1934. *Sprachtheorie*. Jena:Fisher.
Chierchia, Gennaro and Mats Rooth. 1984. Configurational Notions in Discourse Representation Theory, in Charles Jones and Peter Sells (eds.) *Proceedings of NELS 14*. Amherst, MA:UMass GLSA
Cooper, Robin. 1986. Tense and discourse location in situation semantics. *Linguistics and Philosophy* 9, 17-36.
Cresswell, M.J. 1973. *Logics and Languages*. London:Methuen.
Dowty, David. 1982. Quantification and the lexicon: a reply to Fodor and Fodor. *in* T. Hoekstra, H. van der Hulst, and M. Moortgat (eds.), *The Scope of Lexical Rules*. 79-106. Dordrecht:Foris Publications.
Fillmore, Charles. 1975. Santa Cruz lectures on deixis. Bloomington:Indiana Univ. Linguistic Club.
Heim, Irene. 1982. *The Semantics of Definite and Indefinite Noun Phrases*. unpublished Ph.D. dissertation, University of Massachusetts. Amherst,MA:UMass GLSA.
Heim, Irene. 1983. File change semantics and the familarity theory of definiteness. in Bäuerle, Schwarze, and von Stechow (eds.), *Meaning, Use and Interpretation of Language*. Berlin:Walter de Gruyter.
Hinrichs, Erhard. 1981. Temporal Anaphora im Englischen. Unpublished Zulassungarbeit, University of Tübingen.
Hinrichs, E. 1985. *A Compositional Semantics for Aktionsarten and NP-reference*. Doctoral dissertation, Columbus, Ohio:The Ohio State University.
Kamp, H. 1981. A Theory of Truth and Semantic Representation in J. Groenendijk, T. Janssen and M. Stokhof, eds., *Formal Methods in the Study of Language: Proceedings of the Third Amsterdam Colloquium*. Mathematical Centre Tracts. Amsterdam; reprinted in J. Groenendijk, T.M.V. Janssen and M. Stokhof, eds. (1984) *Truth, Interpretation and Information*, GRASS 2. Foris:Dordrecht.
Kratzer, Angelika. 1977. What 'must' and 'can' must and can mean. *Linguistics and Philosophy* 1, 337-355.

Lewis, David. 1975. Adverbs of Quantification. in E. L. Keenan, ed., *Formal Semantics of Natural Language*. Cambridge: Cambridge University Press.

Lewis, David. 1979. Scorekeeping in a language game. in R. Bäuerle, et al, eds., *Semantics from Different Points of View*, Berlin:Springer.

McCawley, James. 1981. *Everything that Linguists have Always Wanted to Know about Logic* *but were ashamed to ask*. Chicago:University of Chicago Press.

Mitchell, J. 1986. *The Formal Semantics of Point of View*. Ph.D. dissertation University of Massachusetts. Amherst, MA:UMass GLSA.

Partee, Barbara. 1973. Some structural analogies between tenses and pronouns in English. *The Journal of Philosophy* 70, 601-609.

Partee, Barbara H. 1984. Compositionality. in Fred Landman and Frank Veltman, eds. *Varieties of Formal Semantics*. pp. 281-311, Dordrecht:Foris Publications.

Partee, Barbara H. 1984. Nominal and temporal anaphora. *Linguistics and Philosophy* 7.3, 243-286.

Stalnaker, Robert. 1978. Assertion. in Peter Cole, ed. *Syntax and Semantics, Vol. 9: Pragmatics*. 315-332. New York:Academic Press.

Stalnaker, Robert. 1984. *Inquiry*. Cambridge:Bradford Books.

Stechow, A. von. 1982. Three Local Deictics. in: R. Jarvella and W. Klein (eds.), *Speech, Place, and Action: Studies in Deixis and Related Topics*. 73-99. New York:John Wiley and Sons.

Weissenborn, J. and W. Klein, eds. 1982. *Here and There: Cross-Linguistics Studies on Deixis and Demonstration*. Amsterdam:John Benjamins.

On the Postverbal Position of the Direct Object
in Mandarin Chinese

Stephen R. Poteet
UC San Diego

0. Introduction

One of the main tasks of grammatical theory is generally
recognized as giving an account of how words and phrases (or
classes of words and phrases) are ordered in a sentence. It is
generally assumed by theories of autonomous syntax that semantics
is either irrelevant or only indirectly relevant in this
determination, being at best mediated by one or more levels or
modules of syntactic structure which are assumed to operate on the
basis of principles entirely independent of semantics. Below I
analyze some principles that determine whether a direct object can
follow a verb in Mandarin Chinese in sentences with a postverbal
coverb phrase (locative with zai 'at', directional with dao 'to',
and dative with gei 'to') and how these principles interact. It
will be shown: 1) that the phenomena cannot be explained if we
restrict ourselves to the vocabulary of arguments and adjuncts
and/or grammatical relations; 2) that, while a number of distinct
principles are required, they all suggest an iconic relation
between aspects of the scene being portrayed and the phonological
devices being used to represent them, word order and adjacency;
and 3) these principles do not interact in a modular fashion, but,
rather, in parallel, to determine surface word order. Finally,
despite the seeming complexity and intractability of the phenomena
from the point of view of autonomous syntax, I hope to show that
it is quite plausible given the view that meaning has to do with
the way a situation is being construed and portrayed and that
grammar is fundamentally symbolic in nature.

1. The Phenomena

Li and Thompson (1981:406,410) have suggested that
postverbal locative and directional phrases obey the following
constraint:

    (1) The postverbal locative/directional phrase must
          immediately follow the verb.

This constraint is motivated by contrasts in acceptability between
sentences like (2) and (3):

    (2) *Wo cang bao   -shi   zai xiangzi-li.
        1s hide precious-stone at   chest -inside[1]
        I hid the precious stones in the chest.
    (3) Wo ba bao   -shi   cang zai xiangzi-li.
        1s OM precious-stone hide at   chest -inside
        I hid the precious stones in the chest.

In (2), which is unacceptable, the direct object bao-shi 'precious
stone(s)' immediately follows the verb cang 'to hide, store', and
is in turn followed by the locative complement zai xiangzi-li 'in
the chest', which indicates the location of the direct object as a
result of the action profiled by the verb. (3), on the other
hand, introduces the patient bao-shi in preverbal position with
the coverb[2] ba, and the sentence is fine.

However, the fact that (4) below is also acceptable shows
that Constraint (1) is not the whole story:

(4)   Wo ganggang cang-le yi pi bao   -shi   zai
       1s just   hide-PFV one CL precious-stone at
       I just hid a bunch of precious stones in
           xiangzi-li.
           chest -inside
           the chest.

(4), like (2), has a direct object immediately following the verb
and a locative phrase following the direct object. (4) differs
from (2) in having a temporal adverb ganggang 'just now', the
perfective aspect marker -le on the verb, and an indefinite direct
object.
      In fact, the acceptability of a postverbal direct object
with a postverbal coverb phrase (including locatives with zai
'at', directionals with dao 'to', and recipients with gei 'to')
depends on a host of factors. In this paper I will be concerned
with those related to: 1) definiteness and contrastive focus of
the direct object; 2) the nature of the coverb; and 3) the nature
of the verb. It will be shown that Li and Thompson's constraint
is both too strong and too weak. It is too strong in excluding
postverbal indefinite noun phrases with locatives and it is too
weak in that it fails to account for the unacceptability of some
sentences with postverbal noun phrases and dative phrases.
      Here I will provide a unified account of the behavior of
noun phrases in sentences containing all three types of coverb
phrase, further accounting for differences between the different
coverb phrases and indeed differences between sentences with the
same coverb phrase, but different verbs.
      Consider first the verb diu 'to toss' with a resulting
location introduced with zai 'at':

(5)   Ta diu -le yi ben shu zai zhuozi-shang.
       3s toss-PFV one CL book at table -top[3]
       She tossed one/a book on the table.
(6)   ?Ta diu -le nei ben shu zai zhuozi-shang.
       3s toss-PFV that CL book at table -top
       She tossed that book on the table.[4]
(7)   ?*Ta diu -le nei ben shu zai zhuozi-shang.
       3s toss-PFV that CL book at table -top
       She tossed that book on the table.
(8)   ??Ta diu -le shu zai zhuozi-shang.
       3s toss-PFV book at table -top
       She tossed the book on the table.
(9)   *Ta diu -le shu zai zhuozi-shang.
       3s toss-PFV book at table -top
       She tossed the book on the table.

Examples (5) and (9) contrast quite distinctly in their
acceptability and the only difference is in the definiteness of
the direct object NP, indicated by the numeral+classifier phrase
yi ben in (5) and its absence in (9). Definite NPs, as in (9),
are used appropriately only when a particular book or set of books
has already been established in the universe of discourse, whereas
yi ben shu in (5) introduces a book into the universe of
discourse.
      (7), with the demonstrative nei 'that' also may introduce a
particular book into the current universe of discourse, however

the book must be more accessible than in (5), typically by being present in the immediate physical environment of the speaker and listener.[5] There is a generally accepted sense of 'definite' that includes not only the restricted cases described in the previous paragraph (presence in the established universe of discourse) but also NPs marked with demonstratives. There is a natural way of grouping demonstratives with the more restricted definites (which would be manifested by 'the' in English) in that both are appropriate when the entity designated by the NP is immediately accessible to the listener independently of the NP. In the one case, it is accessible because it is already a part of the discourse space; in the other, it is perceptually accessible to the listener. The NP with nei is not a prototypical definite, however, because, while it is present in the physical environment, it is not part of the universe of discourse before (7) is uttered, and the data above show that they must be distinguished. Like the prototypical definite NP in (9), it resists postverbal object position, but not as much.

Examples (6) and (8) differ from (7) and (9), respectively, in having contrastive stress (indicated by **boldface**), either on the demonstrative in (6) or on the noun itself in (8). Contrastive stress, as in English, is used to indicate a referent that is other than the one expected. In (6), it means that the indicated book, rather than another book that is more expected by the listener, is the intended referent. In (8), contrastive stress is appropriate when, even though the book has been introduced into discourse and is still salient, and the NP representing it is therefore definite, there are other objects equally salient in the universe of discourse and more expected as the thing the subject tossed onto the table. In either case, (6) or (8), contrastive stress, while not rendering the sentence fully acceptable, makes it distinctly preferable to the corresponding sentence without contrastive stress.

Next, consider the same verb diu with the resulting location marked with dao 'to':

   (10)   Ta diu -le yi ben shu dao zhuozi-shang.
              3s toss-PFV one CL book to table -top
              She tossed one/a book onto the table.
   (11)   Ta diu -le **nei** ben shu dao zhuozi-shang.
              3s toss-PFV that CL book to table -top
              She tossed **that** book onto the table.
  (12)??Ta diu -le nei ben shu dao zhuozi-shang.
              3s toss-PFV that CL book to table -top
              She tossed that book onto the table.
   (13)   Ta diu -le **shu** dao zhuozi-shang.
              3s toss-PFV book to table -top
              She tossed the **book** onto the table.
   (14) *Ta diu -le shu dao zhuozi-shang.
              3s toss-PFV book to table -top
              She tossed the book onto the table.

Zai 'at' and dao 'to' can both mark the resulting location of a theme, or entity profiled as moving. Unlike dao, zai can also occur with verbs which profile or designate the location of an entity without referring to any motion, such as liu 'to keep (in a position)', gua 'to be hanging (somewhere)', zhu 'to live at' etc. Zai is also the unmarked or only acceptable coverb with verbs that designate the placing of some object in some location, where there is minimal difference between the resulting location of the object and its initial location or the location of the agent (eg. fang 'to put', gua 'to hang'). With some verbs designating an action of the agent on an object and the resulting separation of the agent and patient (eg. diu 'to toss', reng 'to throw'), either zai or dao are acceptable, but with dao typically suggesting a longer more salient path. In general, sentences with dao seem to be more tolerant of postverbal direct objects than the corresponding sentence with zai.

In examples (10) through (14) we see basically the same pattern of acceptability as in examples (5) through (9), except that, with diu and dao, the sentences corresponding to those that were marginal in the previous set, (11) and (13), are here more acceptable, and (12) is distinctly better than (7).[6]

Diu can also occur with a recipient marked with gei, instead of a resulting location marked with zai or dao. With gei most of the sentences that were bad or marginal with zai are better yet:

(15) Ta diu -le yi ben shu gei Zhangsan.
      3s toss-PFV one CL book to Zhangsan
      She tossed one/a book to Zhangsan.

(16) Ta diu -le **nei** ben shu gei Zhangsan.
      3s toss-PFV that CL book to Zhangsan
      She tossed **that** book to Zhangsan.

(17) ?Ta diu -le nei ben shu gei Zhangsan.
      3s toss-PFV that CL book to Zhangsan
      She tossed that book to Zhangsan.

(18) Ta diu -le **shu** gei Zhangsan.
      3s toss-PFV book to Zhangsan
      She tossed the **book** to Zhangsan.

(19) *Ta diu -le shu gei Zhangsan.
      3s toss-PFV book to Zhangsan
      She tossed the book to Zhangsan.

Finally, consider the verb ji 'to mail', both with a destination introduced by dao 'to' and with a recipient introduced by gei 'to':[7]

(20) Ta ji -le yi ben shu dao Niuyue.
      3s mail-PFV one CL book to New York
      She mailed one/a book to New York.

(21) Ta ji -le **nei** ben shu dao Niuyue.
      3s mail-PFV that CL book to New York.
      She mailed **that** book to New York.

(22) ?Ta ji -le nei ben shu dao Niuyue.
      3s mail-PFV that CL book to New York
      She mailed that book to New York.

(23) Ta ji -le **shu** dao Niuyue.
      3s mail-PFV book to New York
      She mailed the **book** to New York.

(24) *Ta ji -le shu dao Niuyue.
      3s mail-PFV book to New York
      She mailed the book to New York.[8]

(25) Ta ji -le yi ben shu gei Zhangsan.
      3s mail-PFV one CL book to Zhangsan
      She mailed one/a book to Zhangsan.

(26) Ta ji -le **nei** ben shu gei Zhangsan.
      3s mail-PFV that CL book to Zhangsan
      She mailed **that** book to Zhangsan.

```
(27)  Ta ji  -le  nei  ben shu  gei Zhangsan.
      3s mail-le  that CL  book to  Zhangsan
      She mailed that book to Zhangsan.
(28)  Ta ji  -le  shu  gei Zhangsan.
      3s mail-PFV book to  Zhangsan
      She mailed the book to Zhangsan.
(29) *Ta ji  -le  shu  gei Zhangsan.
      3s mail-PFV book to  Zhangsan
      She mailed the book to Zhangsan.
```

Compared to diu, ji is more tolerant of postverbal NPs, but the other factors are still relevant. With either dao or gei, definite direct objects are still prohibited if they are not contrastively stressed. However, with unstressed nei, only the sentence with gei is fully acceptable, while the sentence with dao has a level of acceptability intermediate between indefinite NPs and unstressed definite NPs. All the other sentences with ji are fully acceptable.

By and large the same gradients of acceptability occur with all verbs that designate the action of an agent on an object and the resulting motion of the object (although sometimes other factors also seem to be involved and interact with these in determining the acceptability of postverbal direct objects).

In all of the unacceptable sentences above, if the NP precedes the verb, either immediately with ba, immediately without ba (a kind of topic position), or in sentence initial (topic) position, the sentence becomes acceptable. Each of these three preverbal positions is associated with slightly different semantics, but the fact that all of them yield fully acceptable sentences with NPs that render the postverbal position unacceptable (to various degrees), suggests that it is preverbal and postverbal position that is interacting with these factors and not, say, the meaning of the morpheme ba or of topic position per se. In fact, I will suggest that one factor has to do with pre- and postverbal position per se, and another has to do with the resulting adjacency of the main verb and the coverb.

The above sets of examples show that, when there is a postverbal coverb phrase, postverbal position of the direct object is more acceptable:

    i.   when the NP is indefinite than when it is definite, with demonstrative-marked NPs occupying an intermediate position;

    ii. when the NP is contrastively stressed than when it is not;

    iii. when the verb indicates a long trajectory (as with ji 'to mail') than when it portrays a short trajectory (as with diu 'to toss');

    iv. when the most salient trajectory is in a non-spatial domain (i.e. when a recipient is introduced by gei) than when it is in the domain of physical space (i.e. when a destination is introduced by dao or zai).

2. Principles Affecting the Position of the Direct Object

Two questions are raised by the above observations:

    1. Why should the properties of the NP indicated by points (i) and (ii) be relevant to the position of the NP?

2. Why should the features of the trajectory indicated in points (iii) and (iv) be relevant to the position of the direct object?

Tai (1985) has suggested that word-order in Mandarin is highly iconic with temporal aspect of the scene being portrayed. One of the most obvious and concrete examples of this phenomenon is the fact that with verbs of motion, the NP indicating the initial location of the mover, marked with the coverb cong 'from', occurs before the verb, and the NP indicating the final location of the mover, marked with zai or dao, occurs after the verb:

(30) Ta ba yizi   cong keting   ban dao wofang.
     1s OM chair from living:room move to bedroom
     She moved the chair from the living room to the
     bedroom.

In Poteet (1987) I have elaborated and refined Tai's analysis, showing that, while it is not always temporal sequencing of states, objectively construed, that determines word-order, the order of constituents nevertheless often reflects the natural flow of attention along some path, often abstract and/or subjectively construed. The notion 'natural flow of attention' was used by DeLancey (1981) in his analysis of split ergativity, and extended and elaborated in Langacker (1988) in a general analysis of case and grammatical relations. I propose to analyze the present phenomena relating to definiteness and contrastive stress along the same lines.

First, note that in all the examples, the agent-subject performs some kind of activity that results in the change of location (and possibly ownership) of the object. The action of an agent on a patient, with a subsequent change in the patient can be represented schematically as a chain of entities linked by the flow of energy (see Fig. 1). In Langacker (1988) this is termed an action chain and is proposed as the prototypical meaning of a transitive clause. The double sided arrows represent the energy transmitted from the agent to the patient (or to an intermediate object, such as an instrument, and thence to the patient). The dotted arrow inside the circle on the **right** (the patient) represents the change of state undergone by the patient. In our examples it is made explicit by the coverb. The direction involved in the action chain and the position of the agent and patient at its endpoints motivates the unmarked positions of the subject and object before and after the verb in Mandarin, but other factors can create marked orders.

Also, note that the coverb phrases in the above examples all designate the change of state of the patient, either its final location in physical space (with zai or dao) or its final state of possession (with gei).

Now consider the NP properties in (i) and (ii) above. It has long been noted that definite NPs tend to occur before the verb in Mandarin (Li and Thompson, 1975;1981:20). Why might this be? If we consider the contrast between definite and indefinite NP, we can see that position in the sentence is basically symbolic for presence in the universe of discourse before and after the uttering of the sentence. A definite NP in its most prototypical sense refers to something that has been previously established in the universe of discourse, is presently salient, and is more-or-less uniquely identifiable by the listener from the description provided by the NP. A prototypical indefinite NP is one that has not been introduced into the universe of discourse before the utterance of the sentence in which it occurs. Position in a sentence can thus be considered as symbolic of the time in discourse when an entity is present in the universe of discourse, with the main verb as a sort of pivot mapping onto the time of utterance, preverbal position mapping onto presence in the universe of discourse prior to the time of utterance, and postverbal position mapping onto presence in the universe of discourse (only) after the time of utterance. Position before or after the verb is actually temporal location in the phonological space defined by a single sentence (or clause). Since this symbolizes the point in time in the flow of discourse (before or after the utterance) when the entity exists in the universe of discourse, this is actually an iconic representation.

Another way to look at the relation between definites and indefinites, is to note that typically our attention moves from things that are already well established in a scene toward things that have just been introduced into the scene. In fact, there are even low level cognitive mechanisms that cause us to shift our attention toward novel objects that appear at the periphery of the visual field. There is thus a high correlation in experience between time of attending and the novelty of an object in the current scene (and in fact this has a high adaptive value, since new things are more likely to provide more information than things that have been around for a while). This defines one dimension of the natural flow of attention, a subjective path from old and well established components of a scene to newly established components. This directing of attention to novel entities can be expressed diagrammatically as in Fig. 2. The two large circles represent the universe of discourse at different times in a conversation. The arrows from the entities in the discourse at the time of the utterance represent the path of attention from entities that were present in the scene prior to the utterance to the newly introduced entity. The order "definite before indefinite" reflects the function of leading the listener's attention along this path.

One caveat: above I have discussed the prototypical meanings of definite and indefinite. It is not always the case that the universe of discourse or the status of objects within it is so well-defined. Conversations may be interrupted and resumed days later, and the universe of discourse may, under certain conditions, be presumed to remain in force. Objects may be introduced implicitly via culturally shared scenarios and subsequently treated as definite (e.g. "I got on a bus. The bus driver said . . .", where 'bus' introduces a scenario with a unique driver). Even when objects have not been introduced into the discourse, either directly or indirectly, they may be more accessible to the listener than the prototypical indefinite and thus may be treated as more definite. The case of NPs marked with demonstratives is just such an intermediate case.

The prototypical, though by no means the only, use of a demonstrative, is to pick out an object in the immediate shared physical environment of the speaker and listener and introduce it into the universe of discourse. Confining ourselves to this use, an NP marked with a demonstrative is clearly not definite in the prototypical sense defined above; its referent has not already been introduced into the universe of discourse. Nevertheless, it is saliently available to both speaker and listener in ways that a prototypical indefinite is not, by virtue of its presence and visibility in the immediate physical environment. In dealing with the prototypical definite and indefinite NP above, it was tacitly assumed that NPs could be unproblematically classified as either present in or absent from the universe of discourse; however, it is actually the relative salience (and uniqueness) of an object within the current, already constructed universe, as construed by the speaker, that determines whether the object will be portrayed as definite.   The relative accessibility symbolized by the prototypical demonstrative is also related to salience within a scene that is currently accessible to speaker and listener; however, the scene is not one that has been built up in discourse, but rather that exists in their shared representation of the immediate physical environment.   Nevertheless, this shared property of salience within a currently accessible scene is what accounts for the interaction of marking with a demonstrative and definiteness as symbolized by position before or after the verb.

Why should contrastive stress tend to make a definite or demonstrative-marked NP more acceptable after the verb? As noted above, contrastive stress is used when the speaker believes that the listener is expecting a different object in the given role in the scene. For example, in (8) above, <u>shu</u> 'book' would be contrastively stressed if the speaker assumed that the listener had prior expectations that some other object, say, a pen that had also been previously referred to, was what had been put on the table.   The contrastive stress serves to draw the listener's attention away from the expected referent, the pen, to the correct referent, the book. Both the book and the pen may be equally present and salient in the universe of discourse at the time of the utterance, and therefore definite, but, relative to a particular role in the scene, i.e. the object being placed on the table, the pen is more salient for the listener than the book. Postverbal position of contrastively stressed objects again symbolizes the fact that the correct referent is the endpoint of a subjective path from the expected referent to the unexpected but correct referent. Fig. 3 expresses schematically the flow of attention from competing entities toward the correct referent.

These properties of the object referred to by the direct object NP are abstract and subjective in that they pertain to the relationship between the object referred to and the speaker and listener as construers of an evolving scene. Nevertheless, it is not too difficult to imagine how properties of an NP could influence the position of that NP. It is not so obvious why the nature of the trajectory, as portrayed by the verb and the coverb, would be relevant. I will here propose a tentative explanation of this phenomenon.

As argued in Langacker (1986), the prototypical transitive clause reflects the prototypical dynamic event: the action of an agent on a patient with the resulting change of state of the patient. On the one hand, these two phases are perceived as an integrated whole; on the other, they are more or less distinguishable. In the most prototypical transitive event, the two phases have much in common: the action of the agent on the patient is physical and unfolds in time and the change of state of the patient is also typically physical and also has a temporal dimension. These similarities and the fact that the change in the patient typically occurs in close temporal contiguity with the first phase account for the perception of these events as a unified gestalt. However, when the change of state of the patient involves motion through space, there may also be a temporal distinction between the two phases, with the energy transfer over long before the resultant motion of the patient is (e.g. in the act of throwing an object).

What I wish to suggest is that, insofar as the change of state of the patient is seen as intrinsic to the action of the agent, the coverb symbolizing that change will preferably occur adjacent to the main verb. In sentences with <u>zai</u>, where the object traverses a very short path and its resulting location is virtually determined by the action of the agent, the change in the patient is naturally construed as very intrinsic to the action performed by the agent. These sentences are the least tolerant of an NP intervening between the main verb and the coverb.

In sentences with <u>diu</u> 'to toss' and <u>dao</u>, the path traversed by the patient is longer and less under the control of the agent. In fact my informant volunteered the observation that "something is more likely to interfere with the motion of the object." While there is still a path or resulting location designated schematically in the meaning of the main verb <u>diu</u>, the change in the object is portrayed as occurring over a much longer period of time than the action of the agent and the final result is less assured than with <u>zai</u>; the change is thus construed as correspondingly less intrinsic to the action of the agent and the sentences are more tolerant of a NP separating the main verb and coverb phrase.

In the sentences with <u>ji</u> 'to mail' and <u>dao</u>, the resulting location is even less under the control of the agent: a rather complicated and not always reliable institution being involved in getting the book to its final destination, and the sentences are better than with <u>diu</u> and <u>dao</u>.

Finally, in sentences indicating transfer of possession, a completely different domain is invoked: the socio-cultural domain. While in the prototypical case, change of possession involves change of location, this is not necessarily the case: when one sells a house it seldom moves. In the examples above, however, physical change of location is still implicit, and in fact mediates change of possession: the addressee does not become a recipient unless the book arrives at his address. Nevertheless, with <u>gei</u> the socio-cultural domain is made more prominent. Because <u>gei</u> is defined in the socio-cultural domain, the change it profiles is more distinct from, less intrinsic to, the action of the agent than the changes designated by <u>zai</u> and <u>dao</u>, which are purely spatial. The sentences with <u>gei</u> are thus maximally tolerant of a postverbal NP separating the main verb from the coverb phrase.

3. Supporting Evidence

There is another piece of evidence that supports the claim that verb-coverb adjacency symbolizes the intrinsicness of the change profiled by the coverb to the action of the main verb. If this were the case, we would expect sentences that designate changes of inherent properties of the object (rather than location or possession) to be the least tolerant of the direct object intervening between the verb and the morpheme expressing the change. And, in fact, this is the case:

   (31) *Ta qie-le yi kuai rou cheng pian.
         1s cut-PFV one piece meat become slice
         He cut a piece of meat into slices.
   (32) Ta ba yi kuai rou qie-cheng pian.
         1s OM one piece meat cut-become slice
         He cut a piece of meat into slices.

In examples like these, even indefinite noun phrases cannot intervene between the main verb and the morpheme expressing the change of state (usually referred to as a resultative complement).

There is one other piece of evidence suggesting that the verb and coverb are construed as a single process when they are adjacent, as would be expected if adjacency symbolizes the intrinsicness of the change to the action of the agent. The perfective particle -le always attaches to the verb, but in cases where the coverb is adjacent to the main verb, it (at least preferentially) attaches to the coverb and cannot separate the verb and the coverb:

(33) *Ta ba shu diu -le dao zhuozi-shang.
     1s OM book toss-PFV to table -top
     He tossed the book onto the table.
(34) Ta ba shu diu -dao-le zhuozi-shang.
     1s OM book toss-to -PFV table -top
     He tossed the book onto the table.
(35) ?Ta ba shu diu -le gei Zhangsan.
     1s OM book toss-PFV to Zhangsan
     He tossed the book to Zhangsan.
(36) Ta ba shu diu -gei-le Zhangsan.
     1s OM book toss-to -PFV Zhangsan
     He tossed the book to Zhangsan.

(For reasons I do not fully understand, -le is incompatible with zai.) Again, gei seems to tolerate separation from the main verb by -le somewhat more than dao does, even when there is no intervening direct object, but in both cases the coverb seems preferentially to fuse with the verb as a unit, with aspect marking applying to the whole unit.

4. Conclusion

I have by no means exhausted all the factors relevant in general to the postverbal position of a constituent, or, for that matter, even of a direct object. I have only considered one small set of transitive verbs close to the prototype, verbs that share the fact that they include in their profile the action of an agent on a discrete physical object, and the consequent motion of that object through physical space. I have not considered, for example, transitive verbs that do not result in any change of the object, or, for the most part, those whose change does not include movement through space, or verbs whose objects are abstract.
Nevertheless, I have tried to isolate a small set of parameters that are relevant. I have tried to show how definiteness, demonstrative marking and contrastive stress are systematically related to each other via the notion 'natural flow of attention' and iconically related to the phonological device used to represent them, constituent order. I have also tried to show that the notion of the intrinsicness of the change an object undergoes to the action performed by the agent is relevant for determining the preverbal position of the direct object indirectly, by motivating adjacency of the coverb phrase and the main verb, thereby pushing the object NP to the front.
I have presented evidence against the claim that a simple categorical statement like Constraint (1) can handle the facts concerning postverbal position of a direct object. While the consideration of contrasting pairs from opposite corners of a multidimensional spectrum might suggest such a constraint as an initial hypothesis, more detailed evidence argues against such a simplistic solution.
These data also show that, not only is the acceptability of a postverbal direct object influenced by more parameters than just

the existence of a locative or directional phrase, it is also not a discrete yes-or-no decision, even given more parameters, but rather a matter of degree. Nevertheless, the acceptability judgments are clearly systematically related to the parameters I have isolated.

These phenomena also show that, in Mandarin at least, while the nature of the verb is clearly relevant to the postverbal position of the direct object, the latter is not discretely determined by the verb. The phenomena is thus not amenable to an analysis in terms of discrete lexical features like ± transitive or its GB equivalent ± Case-assigner.

The analysis given here also brings in a different perspective on the long recognized fact that preverbal vs. postverbal position of an NP symbolizes definiteness vs. indefiniteness (e.g. Li and Thompson, 1981:20). While the data show that this is indeed a factor, they also show that: 1) definiteness is a matter of degree, and 2) definiteness is not the sole determinant of preverbal vs. postverbal position, even for direct objects.

Finally, the fact that acceptability varies simultaneously with aspects of the objective content (the length of the trajectory), relative salience of other aspects of the objective content (i.e. the spatial trajectory vs non-spatial trajectory, manifested by specification of the destination with dao or the recipient with gei), and subjective or epistemic aspects of the scene (definiteness and contrastive stress), suggest that acceptability judgments reflect the global and parallel assessment of the fit between all aspects of an image (broadly construed) and a phonological sequence, rather than a modular organization, where information relevant at one level of structure is unavailable to other levels.

Footnotes

1. The following is a brief translation of the abbreviations used in glossing the Mandarin examples:
   OM   the preposed object marker, a coverb
   CL   nominal classifier
   PFV   the perfective suffix -le
   1,2, first, second or third person pronoun, respectively
   3
   s   singular personal pronoun

2. Coverbs play a role in Chinese roughly analogous to English prepositions. The term coverb was originally used because most of them have homophones which are unambiguously verbs, and all of them are historically derived from verbs. Some authors (e.g. Li and Thompson, 1981) have argued that they actually are just prepositions, but in fact they have properties, in particular their influence on the aspect of the sentence, that suggest that they are more verbal than English prepositions. Hence, I will refer to them as coverbs.

3. Yi can be translated as either 'one' or the indefinite article 'a', depending on whether it is stressed or not. In either case I am considering the NP it marks as indefinite.

4. I use boldface to indicate contrastive stress.

5. I do not claim that this is the only meaning of nei or of
demonstratives in general, but here I focus on the acceptability
of these sentences with this meaning.

6. Although I use traditional grammaticality/acceptability
marking (*, ?, ??), they should not be taken as indicating any
kind of absolute acceptability or grammaticality, but rather as a
convenient but clumsy way of expressing relative acceptability
among the examples in the text.

7. Because of the distance of the trajector associated with ji
'to mail', it does not allow destinations introduced by zai,
unlike fang 'to put'. See Poteet (1988) for an in depth
comparison of the semantic effects of zai and dao marked
destinations with verbs of motion.

8. Unlike the corresponding sentence with fang 'to put', this
sentence and (24) below, with unmarked direct objects, have
acceptable readings with the direct object interpreted as
indefinite. I will not be concerned here with this interpretation
and the unacceptability refers to the definite
reading.

9. Although here I concentrate on factors influencing the
position of the object, the subject can also occur in a marked
postverbal position in existential and presentative constructions.

References

DeLancey, Scott. 1981. An Interpretation of Split Ergativity and
    Related Phenomena. Language, 57:626-57.
Langacker, Ronald W. 1988. Case and Grammatical Relations in
    Cognitive Grammar. Linguistics Notes from La Jolla, 14:57-
    94.
Li, Charles N. and Sandra A. Thompson. 1975. The Semantic Function
    of Word Order in Chinese. In Word Order and Word Order
    Change, Charles Li (ed.). Austin: University of Texas Press.
-----. 1981. Mandarin Chinese: a Functional Reference Grammar.
    Berkeley: University of California Press.
Poteet, Stephen R. 1987. Mandarin Word Order: A Refinement of
    Tai's Theory of Temporal Sequence. UCSD ms.
-----. 1988. Paths Through Different Domains: A Cognitive
    Grammar Analysis of Mandarin Dao. UCSD ms.
Tai, James H.-Y. 1985. Temporal Sequence and Chinese Word Order.
    In Iconicity in Syntax, John Haiman (ed.). Amsterdam: John
    Benjamins.

Fig. 1

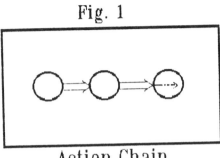

Action Chain

Fig. 2

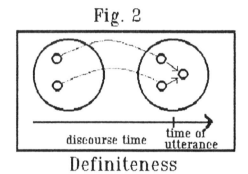

Definiteness

Fig. 3

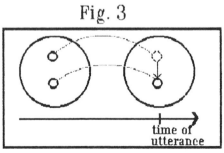

Contrastive Focus

THE ROLE OF CORONAL IN ARTICULATOR BASED FEATURES [1]

Edwin G. Pulleyblank

University of British Columbia

The joint article by Peter Ladefoged and Morris Halle (1988) offers an exciting new perspective to the problem of correctly defining the relationship between the distinctive features of vowels and consonants. They propose to base the definition of phonetic features on the contributions made by the active articulators -- 'the lips, the tongue tip and blade, the tongue body, the tongue root, the soft palate and the larynx' -- rather than in terms of the classical opposition consonant/vowel and the separate classification of consonants in terms of voicing, place and manner, and vowels in terms of height, frontness and rounding. They suggest replacing the traditional concept of 'place of articulation,' defined as the point of contact or closest approach to the upper side of the pharyngeal/oral cavity, by a Place node directly dominated by the Root which in turn dominates nodes for 'the four major active articulators,' Labial, Coronal, Dorsal and Radical, vowels being specified 'by means of the features of the Dorsal and, to a lesser extent, the Radical and Labial articulators.' This proposal incorporates ideas of feature geometry that have recently been put forward by Clements, Sagey and others.

The reference to Labial clearly reflects the proposal that has recently been advanced by a number of scholars that the feature [round] is dominated by the Labial articulator (Sagey 1986, McCarthy 1988, Yip 1988). This leaves Coronal as the only articulator that does not participate in the specification of vowels. This is the point at which I think their formulation needs to be modified. I shall argue that the relationship between front vowels and coronal consonants is similar to that between rounded vowels and labial consonants. Specifically I shall propose that the feature [back] should be detached from the Dorsal articulator, renamed [front], and placed under Coronal. The change of name is more than merely terminological. It will emerge from the discussion that so-called 'back' vowels are not even [+back] in the sense of [-front], but simply Dorsal without any specification for this Coronal feature. The feature [-front] turns out, rather, to be an appropriate specification for apical as opposed to laminal articulation and for retroflexion. This leaves only the linked features [high] and [low] as functions of the Dorsal articulator. The role, if any, of a separate Radical articulator in defining the vowel feature [advanced tongue root] is a further problem that I shall not go into.

It is, of course, an essential characteristic of all true vowels to be specified (in traditional terms) for tongue height and, in that sense, they must involve the action of the Dorsal articulator. What my proposal means is that front, rounded, and front-rounded vowels are complex in the same sense that labiovelar consonants are complex, that is, they involve the simultaneous action of two or more articulators. Labiovelar consonants and (back) rounded vowels, which are specified as [+high, +round], involve the simultaneous action of the Dorsal and Labial articulators. Similarly palatal consonants and front vowels, which are [+high, +front], involve the simultaneous action of the Dorsal and Coronal articulators. Labiopalatal consonants and front-rounded vowels involve the simultaneous action of all three articulators.

Evidence for the dominance of the feature [round] by Labial.

Various kinds of evidence have been put forward to show that the vowel feature [round] is dominated by the Labial articulator.

(1) Campbell (1974:53) refers to diachronic and synchronic processes in which labiovelar [k^W] becomes bilabial [p]. If [round] depends on Labial, [k^W] involves the action of two articulators, Dorsal and Labial, and the change to [p] is explicable as simplification of the complex articulation by removing the dorsal component.

(2) Sagey (1986: 142) notes that in some Shona dialects labiovelar /k^W/ surfaces simply as a velar stop with an accompanying [w] glide, while in others it surfaces with a doubly articulated stop [k͡p^W]. The production of a labial closure along with the velar closure of the stop is inexplicable if the features [+round, +high] of the glide [w] are independent of those of the labial

379

stop [p] but receive a natural explanation if [round] is recognized as being dependent on the participation of the Labial articulator.

(3) One may compare this with Vietnamese in which, according to Henderson (1966: 170-71), a final velar stop or nasal is pronounced with a simultaneous bilabial closure if it is preceded by a [w] glide : -oc [auk͡p], -ong [auŋ͡m], -ôc [əuk͡p], -ông [əuŋ͡m].[2] I assume that, though realized as a sequence, the glide and the stop are underlyingly simultaneous as in the case of labiovelars in the African languages analyzed by Sagey. Note that such double articulation is not found after the high vowel [u], which give -uc [uk], -ung [uŋ]. This restriction has the effect of excluding the possibility of successive occurrences of /u/ as a [+syllabic] segment and a [-syllabic] secondary articulation of the final closure, which would presumably be a violation of the Obligatory Contour Principle. In the Fuzhou dialect of Chinese a similar doubly articulated nasal [ŋ͡m] may occur facultatively in the finals /owŋ/ and /awŋ/.

(4) Rounding harmony of labial consonants in Ponapean, which distinguishes rounded /pʷ/ and /mʷ/ from unrounded /p/ and /m/ and requires that, within the same root morpheme, labial consonants must agree in rounding (McCarthy 1988). The assumption is that, since [round] depends on Labial, separate specifications for [round] would also require separate specifications for Labial on successive consonants which would be ruled out by the Obligatory Contour Principle.

(5) Constraints on the cooccurrence of rounded vowels and labial consonants in the same syllable are described for Cantonese by Yip (1988). Mandarin provides what may be even better evidence for the association of [round] with Labial. Mandarin, unlike Cantonese, allows for initial clusters of consonant + glide but rounded glides are never found after labial initials:

```
*C      G
 |      |
Labial Labial    *[pwan], *[mwei] (Compare [twan], [kwei])
```

Rounded nuclear vowels are not excluded after labial initials but occur only in the finals [-u] and [-ɔ^][3]. In both cases one can plausibly argue that the rounded vowel is not underlying but is derived by spreading of the feature [+round] from the initial. Thus syllables such as $b\bar{o}$ [pɔ^] 'wave" and $f\acute{o}$ [fɔ^] 'Buddha' correspond both to the unrounded final [ɤ^] and to the rounded final [wɔ^] which are contrastive after non-labial initials, as in $d\acute{e}$ [tɤ^] 'virtue' vs. $du\bar{o}$ [twɔ^] 'many', $g\bar{e}$ [kɤ^] 'song' vs. $gu\acute{o}$ [kwɔ^] 'country'. Both *[pɤ^] and *[pwɔ^] are excluded. This is explicable if we assume that in the case of labial initials, the feature [+round] spreads from the initial labial consonant, but without producing the overt medial glide that is found when the melody consists of two elements, a non-labial consonant and a labial glide.

The final [-u] is one of a small set of finals with no final consonant or glide which also includes the high vowels [-i] and [-y] and syllabic [-ɹ] and [-ʐ] in syllables such as $zh\bar{\imath}$ [tʂɹ] 'know' and $s\bar{\imath}$ [sʐ] 'private'. Since syllabic [ɹ] and [ʐ] are found nowhere else and are replaced by [ə] when the diminutive suffix /r/ is added, it is simplest to assume that such syllables have no underlying vowel and are syllabified by spreading of the continuant portion of the initial consonant, voicing being supplied by association with the V node.

Syllables in -i, -u, and -y can be similarly derived if one assumes that in such cases the melody consists of two elements, an initial consonant (which may be zero) and a glide. The glide spreads on to the V-node of the syllabic template, but if it is a front glide it detaches from the V-node when the retroflex suffix is added.

If we assume that a sequence of two Labial specifications on an initial consonant and a following glide/vowel is excluded underlyingly, the only way in which the syllables *bu, pu, fu, mu,* can be derived is by assuming that syllabic [u] arises from spreading the feature [+round] from the initial labial consonant. We must assume that the Dorsal feature [+high] and the Laryngeal feature [+voice] are added by default from association with the V node of the syllable template.

(6) The English prohibition against syllable initial clusters of labial or labiodental consonants and [w] is cited by McCarthy (1988:19) as a parallel to the restrictions on consonant and vowel cooccurrence in Cantonese and is obviously even more apposite as a parallel to the similar prohibition in Mandarin. It should be noted further that, while English does not exclude combinations of rounded vowels and labial or labiodental consonants in syllable final position, it does exclude such consonants after the diphthong [aw]. Historically the restriction on the cooccurrence of a [w] glide before a labial consonant in the same syllable applied to the Middle English vowel shift, so that, while Middle English *hūs* gives Modern English *house* [haws], Middle English *rūm* gives Modern English *room* [ru:m], not **room* [rawm]. Note that this was a language particular restriction. There was no similar restriction when long high vowels in German and Dutch underwent a parallel diphthongization. Hence German *Raum* and Dutch *ruim* [rœɥm].

It should be noted that in the new theory of place features based on active articulators the feature Labial is privative, that is, it is either present or it is not and a specification *[-labial] is meaningless. This does not apply, however, to the subordinate feature [round], for as we have seen in the case of Ponapean, labial consonants can be [-round] as well as [+round]. In the case of Mandarin we must suppose that labials are implicitly [+round] even when they do not give rise to an overt glide. In the case of Cantonese initial labials, however, it may be that we should distinguish [+round] labiodental [f] and labiovelar [w] from [-round] bilabial [p] [pʰ] and [m]. This will account for the fact that we have the syllables [pow] [pʰow] [mow] but no *[pu:], *[pʰu:], *[mu:], while on the other hand, we have the syllables [fu:], [wu:], but no *[wow] or *[fow]. In what must have been the fairly recent past all open high vowel finals in Cantonese have been subject to a dissimilatory process rather similar to what must have been the first stage in the diphthongization of the long high vowels in Middle English, German and Dutch: -i: > -ej, -u: > -ow, -y: > -øɥ. This process was inhibited if the preceding initial was palatalized (in the case of -i: and -y:) or rounded (in the case of -u:). The result is that -ow after unrounded initials, including p, pʰ and m, is in complementary distribution with -u: after rounded initials, including labiovelar kʷ and kʷʰ as well as f and w.

The feature [Labial, -round] can presumably be identified with 'lip compression' in Swedish [ʉ] as opposed to 'lip protrusion' in Swedish [y] (Lindau 1978, 548-49). The high back vowel *u* of Japanese is usually described as unrounded [ɯ] but is probably better regarded as [Labial, -round]. It reveals its labial character by its alternations with [w] in inflections, e.g. *tsukau* 'use', *tsukawareru* 'is used', and by the fact that in front of it /h/ is realized as a bilabial fricative: /ha/ [ha], /hi/ [çi], /hu/ [ɸɯ], /he/ [he], /ho/ [ho].

Evidence for the dominance of the feature [front] by Coronal

The kind of evidence for associating coronal consonants with front vowels is very similar to that for associating labial consonants with rounded vowels.

(1) In Cantonese non-low rounded vowels are fronted after coronals: *ty:n* 'end, tip' < Late Middle Chinese (LMC) /tuan/, Mandarin *duān* [twan]. Contrast *ku:n* < LMC /kuan/ 'official', Mandarin *guān; pu:n* 'half' < LMC /puan`/, Mandarin *bàn*.

(2) In Pekingese underlying /jan/ is realized as [jɛn]. The only source for the fronting is the coronal nasal ending. The vowel is not found in the finals /jaH/ [jɑ], /jaŋ/ [jɑŋ], /jaw/ [jɑw], and the fronting is lost when the retroflex suffix -r, which is [-front], is added to [jɛn], giving [jar].

(3) In Lhasa Tibetan non-front vowels have undergone fronting before coronals, except -*l*. These include -*n*, as well as -*d*, and -*s*, which have since dropped. Orthographic *zan* is [sɛn], *kun* is [kyn], *bon* is [bœn], *čʰad-pa* is [čʰɛpa], *dud-pa* is [dypa], *bod* is [bœ], *kʰas* is [kʰɛ], *gus* is [gy], *gos* is [gœ], etc.

(4) The deletion of the glide [j] before the vowel [uw] after coronals in some English dialects, as in *new* [nuw], *tune* [tuwn], in contrast to *pew* [pjuw], *cute* [kjuwt], can be compared to the above-mentioned English prohibition on a [w] glide after labials.

An alternative to dissimilation of /tj/ to /t/ is palatalization, as in *infatuation* [infætʃuejʃən], where /tj/ is posttonic. Using traditional place of articulation features but allowing for contour segments, we can define this as a change from two segments specified respectively as [-sonorant, -continuant, +coronal, +anterior, -high, -back] and [+sonorant, +continuant, -coronal, -anterior, +high, -back] to a single segment with successive [-continuant] and [+continuant] components which share the features [-anterior, +coronal, +high], that is, as a process of assimilation working in both directions between the place features of the two original separate segments. This will not work, however, if [high] and [back] are both assumed to be dependent on Dorsal. In this case /t/ is specified as [Coronal, +anterior], while /j/ is [Dorsal, +high, -back] and /tʃ/ is [Coronal, -anterior]. There is no way in which this can be called assimilation of /t/ to the features of /j/, since [high] and [back] are dependent on Dorsal articulation, which is assumed to be absent in the case of /tʃ/, while [anterior], the feature which changes, is solely a function of [Coronal]. If [front] is made dependent on Coronal, however, things become much clearer. Before assimilation [t] is [-continuant] with the place feature [Coronal], while [j] is [+continuant], with the place features [Coronal, +front, Dorsal, +high]. After assimilation the affricate [tʃ] has two successive [-sonorant] elements which are [-continuant] and [+continuant] but which share the place features [Dorsal, +high] and [Coronal]. (I claim that [ʃ], like [t], while Coronal, is unspecified for the subordinate feature [front].) Not only does this make explicit the sharing of features that results from the assimilation. It also shows that the stop portion and the continuant portion of the affricate can be derived respectively from the [-continuant] stop and [+continuant] glide through the addition of a Dorsal component to the place node of the stop and changing the glide from [+sonorant] to [-sonorant]. The [-continuant] portion becomes [+strident] and, if my analysis is correct, also loses its specific marking as [+front] when it becomes an obstruent. These are changes that can be attributed to universal marking conventions.[4]

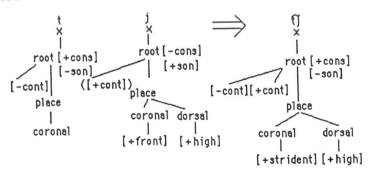

(5) The shift of a palatoalveolar affricate to an alveolar or dental affricate, as when proto-Romance [tʃ] became [ts] in Old French, later simplifying to [s], in words like *cent* [sã] 'hundred', Latin *centum* [kentum], Italian *cento* [tʃɛnto], for which there are many parallels in diachronic sound change in other languages, is a simplification of the same kind as the change of labiovelar [kʷ] to bilabial [p]. That is, it merely involves delinking of the Dorsal articulator and does not require a feature change from [-anterior] to [+anterior]. In fact, the feature [anterior] becomes totally superfluous under this analysis.

(6) Palatalization in Ancient Greek is a complicated phenomenon but it is noteworthy that in all cases the resultant forms attested in the classical period are either dental stops [t] [tʰ] [d] or dental sibilants [s] [zd]. Thus labiovelar *kʷ and *kʷʰ became [t] and [tʰ] before the front vowels [e] and [i], *gw became [d] before [e] (but not [i]),*kʷj became [t], in syllable initial position, and [tt] intervocalically, while on the other hand *tj and *tʰj became [s] in syllable initial position and [s] or [tt] between vowels and *dj and *gwj became [zd] in the same environments. Allen (1957) assumes that, in all cases, the first effect of palatalization on the consonant was the production of a palatal affricate, followed by a shift to a dental affricate and loss of either the sibilant portion or the stop or, in the case of the voiced reflexes, metathesis of stop and sibilant: *tʃ > *ts > [t] or [s]; *dʒ >*dz > [d] or [zd]. To account for the divergency in the final stages, he assumes differences in chronology: *ts > [s] and *dz > [zd] at one period but *ts > [t] and *dz > [d] at another. It may not be necessary, however, to suppose that, where the result was a stop, there was any affricate stage at all. Thus *kʷe- could have become *kʲʷe-, with simultaneous dorsal, labial and coronal articulation, and then simplified to [te] directly through loss of both the labial and the dorsal components.

An interesting further point about the palatalization of labiovelars in Greek is that plain velars underwent no such palatalization before front vowels. This has been interpreted to mean that it was the glide component of the labiovelar consonant that was first affected, which in turn implies that *kʷ consisted of distinct [+consonantal] stop and [-consonantal] glide components. This creates difficulties for a theory which treats labiovelars as unitary segments with a single root node but is easily accommodated if, as argued below, a consonant with secondary articulation has two root nodes attached to the same timing slot

Ancient Greek *pj- changed to pt-, as in the present tense of verbs like *kóptō* < *kopjō* 'smite'. This can be understood as assimilation of the [-consonantal] glide -j- to the preceding stop in the stricture feature [-continuant] and the laryngeal feature [-voice], accompanied by loss of the dorsal component of the articulatiqn. To assume, with Allen (1957: 119 n.36), that there was an intermediate stage [p(t)ʃ] in which [j] was a replaced by an affricate seems to be an unnecessary complication. Allen refers to a development of [pʃ] from [pj] in some modern Greek dialects but he also refers to evidence from Russian that palatalized [pʲ] may be realized with a transitory palatalized dental occlusion [ptʲ] and to similar phenomena in various Romance languages. From the point of view of the present discussion the important thing to note is that palatalization of labials (as well as that of velars and labiovelars) implied the acquisition of coronality.

(7) In Sino-Vietnamese the labial stops /p/ and /pɦ/ of Late Middle Chinese are sometimes represented by dental [t]. According to my reconstruction (Pulleyblank 1970-71, 1984), the conditioning factor was a following high front glide /j/, as in *ti* 'low' for LMC pji (Mandarin *bēi*), *tân* 'frequently' for LMC pɦjin (Mandarin *pín*). It is clearly a palatalization phenomenon. It cannot, however, represent simply a replacement of the labial stop by a palatal which later fronted to a dental, since Vietnamese also has palatal *ch* which is still a palatal stop in some dialects and regularly stands for Middle Chinese palatal affricates. Besides representing /pj/, Vietnamese *t* is the regular reflex of the LMC dental sibilants /ts, tsɦ, s, sɦ/, while LMC /t, tɦ/ are represented by Vietnamese *đ*, phonetically preglottalized [ɗ], with a more alveolar articulation than *t*.. The exact form in which LMC /pj/ was first borrowed into Vietnamese can only be conjectured. The likeliest scenario is that the first stage was a palatalized bilabial [pʲ] which developed either a simple coronal occlusion [pt̚ʲ] or affricated [ptsʲ] after which both the secondary

articulation and the labial component of the occlusion were lost, giving either [t] directly or [ts] which simplified to [t] as part of the regular development.

(8) In some Northeastern Czech dialects, now becoming obsolete, palatalized labial stops and nasals shifted to dentals, e.g. [tɛt] for Standard Czech [pʲɛt] 'five', [tiːvɔ] for [pʲiːvɔ] 'beer', [tɛknʲɛ] for [pʲɛknʲɛ] 'nicely', [nɛstɔ] for [mʲɛstɔ] 'town' (Ohala 1979, 358; Andersen 1973, 765). In his discussion of this phenomenon, which also refers to the palatalization of labials in Ancient Greek, Ohala provides acoustic evidence for the possibility of auditory confusion between a palatalized labial and a dental.

(9) In his general discussion of palatalization Bhat (1978) distinguishes between palatalization of velars, which involves fronting, and palatalization of dentals and alveolars which requires raising. He gives examples from various languages in which dentals/alveolars are palatalized in front of any high vowel, including back unrounded and back rounded. On the other hand velars may be undergo palatalization in front of low front vowels, as in French *chat* from Latin *cattus*, etc. This receives a natural explanation if palatals are complex segments combining [Dorsal, +high] and [Coronal, +front].

(10) In response to criticism by a number of scholars of the definition of [coronal] in Chomsky and Halle (1968), which nearly but not quite corresponds to the earlier acoustic feature [grave], Halle and Stevens (1979) have proposed to redefine palatal consonants, including the glides [j] and [ɥ], as [+coronal]. See also Halle and Mohanan (1985, 85 n.17), where this is explicit stated to include syllabic [i] and [ɭ]. This is not referred to in Sagey (1984, 1986) or other recent discussions of feature geometry as far as I am aware (including Ladefoged and Halle 1988!), though it obviously contains the germ of the proposal I am making here. If one defines high front vowels as [+coronal] as well as [+high, -back], it seems to imply the possibility of a specification [+high, -back, -coronal] for vowels, though it is not clear what this could possibly mean; nor is the situation improved if [coronal] is interpreted as a privative articulator node rather than a binary feature. The obvious inference seems to be that [-back] implies coronal, that is, that it depends on the coronal articulator rather than the dorsal articulator. The feature [+high], however, must surely remain under the Dorsal node which can only mean that, as I am proposing, high front vowels and glides are doubly articulated.[5]

The feature [-front]

The parallel with the feature [round] under the Labial articulator suggests that, while [+front] is the unmarked default setting for this feature under the Coronal articulator, there may also be the possibility of the negative value [-front]. This seems to provide exactly what is required as a specification for retroflexes in Chinese, which, both synchronically and diachronically, show a marked antagonism to high front vowels and glides. When the retroflex suffix /r/ is added to Mandarin syllables, it causes high front vowels, both unrounded and rounded, to delink from the nucleus, after which syllabicity is restored by shwa insertion: [ti + r] = [tjər], [ny +r] = [nɥər], [piŋ + r] = [pjr], etc. Diachronically the vowel [i] was deleted after retroflex sibilants between Early and Late Middle Chinese: *shēng* 'be born' EMC [ʂiajŋ] > LMC [ʂaajŋ] (note the compensatory lengthening in the case of the VV syllable); *shòu* 'emaciated' EMC [ʂuwʰ] > [ʂywʰ] > [ʂiwʰ] > LMC [ʂəwˋ]. The contrast was restored in Late Middle Chinese through the phonemic merger of palatal sibilants, which were only found before high front vowels, with the retroflexives: *shēng* 'voice' EMC [ɕiajŋ] > LMC [ʂiajŋ]; *shòu* 'animal' EMC [ɕuwʰ] > [ɕywʰ] > [ɕiwʰ] > LMC [ʂiwˋ]. This contrast was still found in Early Mandarin (EM) but it has since been eliminated once more by a repetition of the same rule, so that, EM [ʂiŋ] 'voice' has become [ʂəŋ], merging with EM [ʂəŋ] 'be born', and EM [ʂiwˋ] 'animal' has merged with EM [ʂəwˋ] 'emaciated'.

The feature [-front] can also be used to distinguish alveolars from interdentals in Australian languages, which typically have a four-way distinction between interdental, alveolar, postalveolar and palatal stops, commonly transcribed as *dh, d, rd*, and *j* respectively (Dixon 1980: 150 ff.). Palatals and interdentals, which are laminal, pattern together in contrast to the alveolars and postalveolars, which are apical. The two features [front] and [high] are all that is necessary to specify these contrasts. *Dh* and *j* are [+front], while *d* and *rd* are [-front]; *rd* and *j* are [+high], that is, they have a dorsal as well as a coronal component, while *dh* and *d* involve only the coronal articulator and therefore have no specification for [high]. Dixon notes that there are some languages which lack a phonological opposition between the two laminal series. Typically in such cases there is a single phoneme, with palatal allophones before /i/ and interdental allophones before /a/ and /u/, though there are also cases in which only a palatal or (more rarely) an interdental pronunciation is found. The situation is similar in the case of the apicals. Languages which lack two contrasting apical series may either use *d* exclusively or may have *d* before /a/ and /i/ and *rd* before /u/. This is exactly as we should expect. In the case of the laminals, which are [+front], if there is an allophonic distinction, the palatal allophone is found only before the [+front, +high] vowel [i]. In the case of the apicals, which are [-front], there may be assimilation to the [+high] vowel [u], giving retroflex *rd*, but not to the [+high] vowel [i], which is [+front].

The feature [distributed] which is used in the traditional Chomsky-Halle feature system to distinguish alveolars and retroflexes from dentals and palatoalveolars cannot account for the correlations with vowel features that we have found in the case of Chinese and Australian languages. Under the present proposal it is replaced by the feature [front].

The same correspondence between [+front] dentals and palatals and [-front] alveolars and retroflexes is found in Dravidian languages. Mohanan (1986, 64) defines alveolars and retroflexes in Malayalam as [-distributed] in contrast to dentals and palatoalveolars which are [+distributed]. Schiffman (1975) makes a similar proposal for Tamil. He notes that if dental /t/ and palatal /c/ are defined as [+distributed] in contrast to alveolar /t̲/ and retroflex /ṭ/, which are [-distributed], the feature [back] becomes redundant and points out that the palatalization of dental /t/ to /c/ before /y/ shows that these two series share a common feature.

Mohanan makes and additional distinction between he calls palatal [k'] and palatoalveolar [c] in Malayalam, though he also argues (Mohanan and Mohanan 1984) that the palatals are not underlying but are derived predictably from velars after front vowels. (Ladefoged (1982:145) does not include these palatalized velars in his table of Malayalam contrasts in place of articulation.) It seems likely that [k'] has palatalization as a secondary articulation, while the so-called palatoalveolar stop [c] is a true palatal, with simultaneous Coronal and Dorsal occlusion. The question of secondary articulations will be discussed further below.

Many languages do not distinguish phonemically between [-front] and [+front] Coronal consonants, just as many languages do not distinguish between [-round] and [+round] Labials. I assume that in such cases the consonants are unspecified for the feature [front], though under appropriate conditions they may receive the default value [+front] which may then reveal itself in phonological processes. In English the strident alveopalatal fricative [ʃ], which both historically and synchronically is the product of various processes of palatalization, may sometimes behave as [+front] as well as [+high]. There is, however, no contrasting [-front] retroflex sibilant and [ʃ] replaces [s] in front of retroflex /r/, which is [-front], presumably because both have a [Dorsal, +high] component. Acoustically English [ʃ] is closer to Mandarin retroflex [ʂ] than to palatal [ç]. On the other hand, it is also closer to Cantonese [ʃ] (for those who have this variant of what is a single phoneme varying between alveolar [s] and palatoalveolar [ʃ]), which is clearly [+front] in its phonological behaviour.

The articulatory and acoustic features of vowels

For consonants of all kinds, the unmarked case is to involve only a single articulator. Consonants which involve the action of only one articulator, such as a bilabial stop [p] or an alveolar or dental stop [t], are simpler and less marked than ones which involve the combined action of two articulators, such as labiovelar [k͡p] or palatal [c]. True vowels, however, necessarily require the action of the Dorsal articulator (Chomsky and Halle 1968: 302, quoting Sievers 1901). Syllabic [ʋ], which is purely Labial, does occur in the Bai language of South China (Dell 1981) but must be extremely rare among the world's languages. Syllabic Coronals, such as [l̩] and [r̩] are more common but still rare compared to high front vowels. Front, (back-)rounded, and front-rounded vowels are articulatorily complex, since they add coronal and labial articulations to the basic dorsal articulation. The unmarked cases for Labial and Coronal vowels are [u] and [i] respectively, with the feature [Dorsal, +high] in addition to [+rounded] or

[+front]. When the coronal and labial articulators are not involved there is still a contrast between the unmarked or default settings for consonants and vowels. For consonants the unmarked case is velar [k], which is [+high], while for vowels it is [a], which is [+low]. While [a] is virtually universal in some form or other, high central [ɨ] and back unrounded [ɯ] (which as far as I know are never found contrastively in the same language) are comparatively uncommon.

The simplest vowel of all from this point of view is the vowel /a/, which has only a Dorsal articulation with the setting [+low]. Acoustically this corresponds to raising the value of the first formant of the sound spectrum to its maximum. The vowel /i/ brings the Coronal articulator into play with the unmarked setting [+front]. At the same time it has the Dorsal setting [+high]. This lowers the value of the first formant, which is the main contribution of the Dorsal articulator, to a minimum while raising that of the second formant to a maximum. The vowel /u/ keeps the Dorsal setting [+high] while bringing the Labial articulator into play with the unmarked setting [+round], which gives a minimum value for the second formant. In this way the three articulators define the acoustic frame of the a-i-u vowel triangle.[6]. This correlation between articulation and the acoustics of vowels is probably the fundamental reason why the contribution of the tongue to place features for both consonants and vowels has just one primary division into dorsal and coronal and justifies Roman Jakobson's insight that the vowel triangle a-i-u has an acoustic counterpart in the consonantal triangle k-t-p.

Adding lip rounding to front vowels has the effect of lowering the higher formants, while removing lip rounding from back vowels has a corresponding raising effect on the second formant, so that both front-rounded and back-unrounded vowels move towards the centre of the formant chart (Ladefoged 1982: 205). This is no doubt the reason why the two types can sometimes interchange, as in the Min dialects of Chinese where Fuzhou has [y] corresponding to Chaozhou [ɯ]. It will also account for the fact that speakers of languages with mid front-rounded vowels often hear Pekingese back-unrounded [ɤ] as front-rounded [ø] or [œ]. Compare the traditional French romanization system which spells this sound as -eu [œ] and the transcription of Pekingese by the Danish linguist Egerod (1956). Nevertheless the two processes are quite distinct from an articulatory point of view, a fact that must lie behind the insight of traditional Chinese rhyme table phonology that front-rounded [y] is an additive combination of [i] and [u], while a back unrounded vowel like [ɤ] is simply 'open mouth', lacking both a fronting and a rounding component.

If as we have suggested above, Swedish central rounded [ʉ] is phonologically [Labial, -round], this points to another way in which a change in articulation can effect a shift towards the centre of the vowel diagram. It would be interesting to investigate experimentally whether the high back unrounded vowel [ɯ] of Japanese, which also seems to be phonologically [Labial, -round], may also involve lip compression in its articulation or whether the underlying labial component simply fails to surface.

If we are right in defining retroflex consonants as [Coronal, -front], we shall expect retroflex vowels also to be [Coronal, -front], with the addition of the appropriate Dorsal component. This implies that there should be no possibility of [+front] retroflex vowels. This restriction is confirmed for Mandarin Chinese in which, as we have seen above, the addition of the suffix /r/ causes front vowels to be eliminated from the nucleus (Pulleyblank 1984b). This permits retroflexion to spread back into the vowel.

This interpretation of retroflexion in vowels is also borne out by evidence from Dravidian languages. In his work on comparative Dravidian Zvelebil remarks (1970, 38): 'under the influence of the following cacuminal and retroflex consonants, the vowels usually tend to be back and receive a specific retroflex quality. In some languages the retroflex character of the vowels is preserved even if the following retroflex consonants are lost'. He writes retroflexed high and mid vowels as ï, ë̠, ü, ö̠, which he defines respectively as 'high back unrounded', 'mid-back unrounded', 'high back rounded' [sic] and 'central rounded.' According to Emeneau (1939. 44) Badaga, a Dravidian language of South India, has two degrees of retroflexion, half-retroflexed and fully retroflexed, applicable to all five vowels, a, e, i, o, u, long and short. His description of the retroflexed front vowels confirms our analysis of retroflexion as equivalent to [-front]: 'In both these [retroflexed] resonances, e and i occur in varieties very reminiscent of the more classical types of back, unrounded vowels, in the fully-retroflexed phonemes the elevation of the tongue to the mid and high position being as far back in the oral cavity as possible, in the half-retroflexed phonemes advanced almost to the mixed position.' It is evident that, as we should expect, retroflexion has the effect of removing the frontness of the underlying vowels. I have no suggestion to offer as to how one could accommodate two degrees of retroflexion in a feature system. Unfortunately Emeneau does not refer to this phenomenon in his *Dravidian Comparative Phonology* (1970), nor is it mentioned by Zvelebil, so the status of this observation on Badaga remains unclear.

With the removal of the coronal articulation, retroflex vowels in Chinese may convert to back unrounded vowels. Thus, the Hankou dialect has [Dorsal +high] [ɯ] corresponding to Pekingese [əɹ]. English dialects that drop -r before a following consonant or a pause, convert it into a [Dorsal, +low] glide (see below). French uvular [ʁ] replacing the lingual trill [r] seems to be better described as a fricative rather than a glide, but is presumably similar in getting rid of all its Coronal features.

Glides

Already in Chomsky and Halle (1968) the feature [vocalic] was replaced by [syllabic] and it is now widely agreed that this is not a segmental feature with specific phonetic content. Instead syllabicity is assigned automatically by position in the syllable. Thus the same phoneme /m/ is [+syllabic] [m̩] when it occupies a syllabic nucleus and [-syllabic] [m] when, as is more usual, it occurs in the non-syllabic margin. Similarly the vowel [i] and the glide [j] differ only in their position in the syllable. It is still, however, necessary to distinguish between true vowels, which normally function as syllabics in all languages, and other sonorants, which are normally non-syllabic and only occupy syllabic nuclei under special circumstances.

In the feature system of Chomsky and Halle (1968) such sounds are characterized as [-consonantal] (which, however, also includes the laryngeals /ʔ/ and /h/ which are never syllabic as such). Following the discussion in the previous section and excluding the laryngeals, one might define [-consonantal] sounds as dorsal sonorant continuants. The stipulation that they are [+continuant] excludes velar or uvular nasals while allowing for nasalized vowels and glides. In this case [consonantal] is fully defined in terms of other features and ceases to be distinctive.[7]

Conversely, one must recognize and, if possible, explain the fact that only a very limited number of vowels do, in fact, function both as syllabics and as non-syllabics.

The two most widely recognized glides are [j] and [w], that is, the non-syllabic variants of two of the three quasi-universal point vowels, namely the ones that combine a [Coronal, +front] or [Labial, +round] component with the Dorsal setting [+high]. To these one must add front-rounded [ɥ], which combines the features [+front, +round, +high]. Glides which develop from [-high] or [+low] front, rounded or front-rounded vowels regularly switch their dorsal feature to the default setting [+high]. One example is the change of -e and -o to -ay- and -av- before a vowel in the rules of internal sandhi in Sanskrit, in which the dorsal [+low] component remains syllabic, while the coronal or labial component is converted into a non-syllabic [+high] glide. Innumerable other examples or the same sort of thing are to be found in synchronic and diachronic processes in other languages.[8]

The feature system developed here offers the possibility of having a retroflex glide which is [Coronal, -front, Dorsal, +high]. This may, in fact, be the appropriate specification for English [ɻ], which has often been described as a glide, and also for the retroflex [ɻ] of Mandarin Chinese, which is certainly phonologically a sonorant though it is often transcribed as [ʐ] in IPA as if it were a voiced fricative. The English and Chinese sounds are by no means identical. In particular, the Chinese phoneme lacks the lip rounding that is characteristic in English, but this may be considered a matter of language particular rules of phonetic implementation. By our definition, the decision whether to call these sounds glides depends on whether they have a dorsal component or are purely coronal, which is presumably the case for alveolar trills and flaps.

The possibility of non-syllabic alternants for purely Dorsal vowels is not so widely recognized. The IPA chart has only recently introduced a special symbol [ɰ] for a velar glide as distinct from the voiced fricative [ɣ], that is, a non-syllabic alternant of high back-unrounded [ɯ].

Such a glide is, however, quite familiar to linguists who deal with Southeast Asian languages. See, for example, F. K. Li (1977), Thompson (1965), Henderson (1966, 1985). There is even less recognition for a non-syllabic form of the [+low] dorsal vowel [a]. I have argued for some time, however, that such a glide occurs both syllable initially and syllable finally in Pekingese Mandarin, transcribing it either as /ă̯/, with the IPA diacritic for a non-syllabic vowel, or as /H/. I have also shown that recognition of of the phonological role of such a glide greatly assists in understanding the diachronic changes from Middle Chinese to Mandarin. Other places where I believe that it needs to be recognized are (a) in ḥa-čḥuŋ, 'little ḥa', which contrasts with ʔa-čḥen 'big ʔa', that is glottal stop /ʔ/, in the Tibetan alphabet, (b) French h-aspiré and back unrounded [ɑ], (c) the offglide which replaces postvocalic [r] in dialects of English. See Pulleyblank (1981,1984a, b, 1986); and also Yip (1983) for a discussion of glide formation from the vowel /a/ in Axininca Campa.

Glides have the place features of vowels but function as consonants in syllable structure. The phonology of glides can therefore offer revealing insights into the relationship between the features vowels and consonants. There is an ambiguity in terms of markedness. Though labial and coronal vowels necessarily have a dorsal articulation, the involvement of more than one articulator adds complexity in the case of consonants. Hence it is not surprising that non-syllabic alternants of such vowels may lose their dorsal component. This is particularly common in the case of labiovelar [w], which may become a labiodental continuant [ʋ], as in Sanskrit and modern Indian languages as well as in Dutch and Pekingese Mandarin, or a voiced fricative [v], as in the treatment of Latin consonantal [ʋ] in French and Italian or the treatment of [u] as the second element in a diphthong in Modern Greek. Many other examples could be given. Consonantalization may also take a different direction, as when Germanic [w] was borrowed into Romance languages as [gw], later simplifying to [g] in French.

The palatal glide [j] seems to be much more stable. This is in keeping with the observation that palatal or palatoalveolar consonants are much commoner on a world-wide basis than labiovelars. Nevertheless [j] may undergo various changes that can be attributed to the different markedness of vowels and consonants. Straightforward loss of the dorsal component would be expected to give a frictionless coronal continuant, perhaps something like the flapped intervocalic [D] of American English or a lateral [l]. I do not know of clear examples of such a change. It is worth noting, however, that in the 17th century missionary romanization of Vietnamese the initial consonant derived from proto-Viet-mu'o'ng and Sino-Vietnamese *j was represented by the letter d which seems from descriptions to have been a lax dental stop with, perhaps, palatalization as a secondary articulation. It is now pronounced as a voiced alveolar fricative [z] in the Hanoi dialect, having merged both with the spelt gi, which stood for an alveopalatal [dʒ], like the corresponding spelling in Italian. In southern dialects both d and gi are now pronounced [j]. (See Thompson 1965) A consonantalization of [j] that is more familiar is the change of Latin [j] to the alveopalatal affricate [dʒ] in Romance, with various further changes in the different branches. The change from sonorant to obstruent involved the acquisition of stridency and probably also the specification of the coronal articulation as [+front]. These are changes that can be attributed to the different markedness of consonants and vowels.

Front rounded [ɥ] is doubly complex, having both coronal and labial components in addition to dorsal, and we might expect it be correspondingly unstable. The evidence for this that I have accumulated so far is quite limited but the following may be of interest. Between Late Middle Chinese and Early Mandarin [ɥ] lost its coronal component and simplified to [w] before back unrounded [ɑ]. Between Early and Modern Mandarin, the combination /ju/ in syllable initial position, in which the glide tends to be phonetically rounded to [ɥ], has been replaced by [r] in certain environments, as in rong [ruŋ] 'room, space' < Early Mandarin /juŋ/. Assuming that /j/ was phonetically [ɥ] and that /r/ is a [-front] glide, this is a change from [Coronal, +front, Labial +round, Dorsal +high] to [Coronal, -front, Dorsal, +high]. This is a simplification in terms of articulation, while the change from [+front] to [-front] has a centralizing effect acoustically which compensates for the loss of the feature [+round].

The consonantalization of the [+low] glide /H/ is an interesting problem that there is no space to go into here.

The feature geometry of secondary articulationss

Ladefoged and Halle (1988) touch only briefly on the question of secondary articulations. They suggest noncommitally that a solution may be found along the lines proposed by Sagey (1986) in her discussion of contour and complex segments. Sagey adopts the following hierarchical representation of distinctive feature structure:

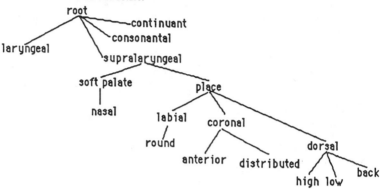

To adapt this to the proposals made in this article we shall, of course, want (a) to remove the features [anterior] and [distributed from the coronal node and add the features [front] and [strident] (perhaps also [lateral], which we have not discussed), and (b) to remove the feature [back] from dorsal. McCarthy (1988) questions the need for a supralaryngeal node and attaches soft palate and place directly to the root. This is also the formulation suggested by Ladefoged and Halle (1988). Nothing much in our discussion here seems to hinge upon this change.

Sagey discusses at length the problem of how to allow for differing degrees of closure on two articulators involved simultaneously in a complex segment in such a hierarchy, in which stricture is directly dominated by the root. Her solution is to distinguish between the major articulator, which is governed by the stricture specified at the root, and the minor articulator which either receives the universal default specification of [-consonantal] or some other fixed, but language particular, value. She distinguishes the major articulator by a pointer from the root, as in the following representations of [k^W] and [kʲ] (omitting the supralaryngeal node)(pp.216-217).

(a)   (b)

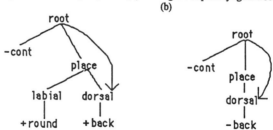

This representation of [k^W] correctly predicts that the [-continuant] portion of the articulation will be dorsal, namely [k], but does not show that the [Labial +round] articulation must also have a dorsal component in order to surface as a [w] glide. Still less satisfactory is the representation of [kʲ]. There is nothing at all to indicate that the [-back] feature is a secondary articulation which may surface as a [-consonantal] glide. This could, of course, be remedied, if [-back] is replaced by [+front] under a separate coronal articulator, specified by default as minor, but again one must add the [-consonantal] dorsal articulation for the glide as something which is understood but not shown in the diagram.

The difficulty becomes even greater if one accepts McCarthy's argument (1988:15) that the class features [sonorant] and [consonantal] are not, like [continuant] and [nasal], features which depend on the root, but the features which define the root, which seems to be equivalent to saying that what is dominated by the same root cannot be both [+consonantal] and [-consonantal] or both [+sonorant] and [-sonorant] at the same time. If this is the case, it is difficult to see how even a minor articulation designated by the place node under a root which is [+consonantal] could be [-consonantal].

This suggests that as proposed in Pulleyblank (1984b), one should assume that the consonant and the glide each has its own root node linked to the same timing slot and that both are realized simultaneously. The [-consonantal] dorsal approximation required for the glide portion of [kʷ] or [kʲ] will be overridden during the [-continuant] closure of the stop but may become overt either before this closure, as in the case of the final labiovelars and palatalized velars of Vietnamese, or after it, as in the case of the initial labiovelars of Cantonese. In Russian, which distinguishes palatalized [kʲ] alone from the combination of this phoneme plus palatal glide [kʲj], the palatalization must be kept strictly simultaneous with the stop. Nevertheless, as Halle remarked (1959, 153), 'the transitional effects [on the second and third formants] explain why foreigners often perceive Russian sharped consonants as being followed by [j].' A palatal stop [c] and a doubly articulated labialvelar stop [k͡p], on the other hand, differ from palatalized [kʲ] and labialized [kʷ] in having a single [+consonantal] root.

Conclusion

The new proposals for features of vowels and consonants (including some points that could not be discussed here for reasons of space) are summed up in the following tables. Default values of features are placed in parentheses.

Syllabic Vowels

		Dorsal high	Dorsal low	Coronal front	Labial round
Dorsal	a		+		
	ɨ	+	(-)		
	ə	-	-		
	shwa*	(-)	(-)		
Coronal	i	(+)		+	
	ɛ		+	+	
	e	-	-	+	
	əʲ	-	-	-	
	aʲ	(-)	+	-	
Labial	u	(+)			+
	ɔ		+		+
	o	-	-		+
	ʉ	+	(-)		-
Cor-Lab	y	(+)		+	+
	œ		+	+	+
	ø	-	-	+	+

*When it is epenthetic and not underlying, I asssume that shwa is completely unspecified. It may receive the default value [Dorsal, -high, -low] which gives it a neutral position *vis-à-vis* specified vowels but it may also receive other phonetic interpretations depending on language specific rules. Thus it surfaces as [œ] in French and is assimilated to a following high glide in Mandarin and Cantonese.

Non-syllabic glides

		Dorsal high	low	Coronal front	Labial round
Dorsal	H		+		
	щ	+			
Coronal	j	(+)		+	
	ل	(+)		-	
Labial	w	(+)			+
Cor-Lab	ɥ	(+)		+	+

Secondary articulations

Secondary articulations of consonants are assumed to be the result of linking a non-syllabic vowel and a consonant to the same timing slot. The five possibilities are defined by the five glides -- /щ/ for velarization, /H/ for pharyngealization, /j/ for palatalization, /w/ for labialization and /ɥ/ for palato-labialization.

Obstruents

		contin.	Dorsal high	low	Coronal front	strident	Labial round
Dorsal	k	-	+				
	x	+	+				
	q	-	-	-			
	χ	+	-	-			
	ħ	+		+			
Coronal	t	-			(+)		
	ţ	-			+		
	t*	-			-		
	s	+			(+)	+	
	θ	+			(+)	-	
Dor-Cor	c	-	+		+		
	ţ	-	+		-		
	ç	+	+		+	-	
	ç	+	+		+	+	
	ʃ	+	+		(+)	+	
	ş	+	+		-	+	
Labial:	p	-					(+)
	f	+					+
	φ	+					-
Dor-Lab	kp	-	+				(+)

t* means a contrastive apical alveolar which contrasts with dental ţ, as in Australian languages, as opposed to a neutral /t/ such as that of English which can vary between dental and alveolar.

REFERENCES

Allen, W. Sidney, 1957. "Some problems of palatalization in Greek," Lingua 7: 113-133.
Andersen, Henning, 1973. Abductive and deductive change, Lg. 49: 765-793.
Bell, Alexander, 1867. *Visible Speech*.
Bhat, D. N. S., 1978. A general study of palatalization, in J. H. Greenberg, ed., Universals of human language, v.2, Phonology. 47-92. Stanford.
Campbell, Lyle, 1974. Phonological features: problems and proposals, Lg. 50: 52-65.
Catford, J.C., 1977. Fundamental problems in phonetics. Bloomington.
Chomsky, Noam, and Morris Halle, 1968. The Sound Pattern of English. New York.

Clements, G. Nickerson., 1985. The geometry of phonological features, Phonology Yearbook 2:225-52.

Clements, George N., and Samuel Jay Keyser, 1983. CV phonology: a generative theory of the syllable. Cambridge, Mass.

Dell, François, 1981. La langue bai: phonologie et lexique. Paris.

Dixon, R. M. W.,1980. The languages of Australia. Cambridge.

Egerod, Søren, 1956. The Lungtu dialect. Copenhagen.

Emeneau, M. B., 1939. The vowels of the Badaga language, Lg. 15, 43-47.

Emeneau, M. B., 1970. Dravidian comparative phonology. Annamalainagar.

Ferguson, Charles A., and Munier Chowdury, 1960. The phonemes of Bengali, Lg. 36, 22-59.

Halle, Morris, 1959. The sound pattern of Russian: a linguistic and acoustical investigation. 's-Gravenhage.

Halle, Morris, and K. P. Mohanan, 1985. Segmental phonology of Modern English, Linguistic Inquiry 16, 57-116.

Halle, Morris, and K. Stevens, 1979. Some reflections on the theoretical bases of phonology, in B. Lindblom and S. Öhman, eds., Frontiers of speech communication research. London. 335-349.

Henderson, Eugénie J. A., 1966. Towards a prosodic statement of the Vietnamese syllable structure. In C.J. Bazell, et al., ed., In memory of J. R. Firth. 163-197. London.

Henderson, Eugénie J. A., 1985. Greenberg's 'universals' again: a note on the case of Karen. In Graham Thurgood, James A. Matisoof and David Bradley, eds., Linguistics of the Sino-Tibetan Area: the state of the art, Canberra. pp.139-140.

Keating, Patricia, 1987. A survey of phonetic features. UCLA working papers in phonetics 65, 124-150.

Ladefoged, Peter, 1982. A course in phonetics. 2nd ed. San Diego, New York.

Ladefoged, Peter, and Morris Halle, 1988. Some major features of the International Phonetic Alphabet, Lg. 64:577-82.

Li, Fang-kuei, 1977. Handbook of Comparative Tai. Honolulu.

Lindau, Mona, 1978. Vowel features, Lg.. 54: 541-63.

McCarthy, John, J., 1988. Feature geometry and dependency. To appear in O. Fujimura, ed., Articulatory Organization -- from phonology to speech signals. Basel.

Mester, R. Armin, and Junko Ito, 1989. Feature predictability and underspecification: palatal prosody in Japanese mimetics. To appear in Language.

Mohanan, K.P., 1986. The theory of Lexical phonology. Dordrecht.

Mohanan, K. P. and Tara Mohanan, 1984. Lexical phonology of the consonant system in Malayalam, Linguistic Inquiry 15: 575-602.

Ohala, John J., 1979. Acoustic phonetics and phonology. In B. Lindblom and S. Öhman, eds., Frontiers of speech communication research. London. 355-363.

Pulleyblank, Edwin G., 1970-71. Late Middle Chinese. Asia Major 15:197-239, 16:121-68.

Pulleyblank, Edwin G., 1981. Distinctive features of vowels and Pekingese phonology in historical perspective. In Proceedings of the International Conference on Sinology, August 15-17, 1980. Section on Linguistics and Paleography. Taipei. pp.75-93.

Pulleyblank, Edwin G., 1984a. Middle Chinese: a study in historical phonology. Vancouver.

Pulleyblank, Edwin G., 1984b. Vowelless Chinese? an application of the three tiered theory of syllable structure to Pekingese. In M. Chan ed., Proceedings of the XVI International Conference on Sino-Tibetan Languages and Linguistics. Seattle.

Pulleyblank, Edwin G., 1986a. Some issues in CV phonology with reference to the history of Chinese. Canadian Journal of Linguistics 31: 225-266.

Sagey (Walli), Elizabeth, 1984. On the representation of complex segments and their formation in Kinyarwanda. In Wetzels, Leo, and Engin Sezer, eds., 1986. Studies in compensatory lengthening. Dordrecht.

Sagey, Elizabeth, 1986. The representation of features and relations in non-linear phonology. Ph. D Dissertation. MIT.

Selkirk, Elizabeth, 1988. A two-root theory of length. To appear in Proceedings of NELS 19.

Schiffman, Harold F., 1975. On the ternary contrast in Dravidian coronal stops. In Harold F.
    Schiffman and Carol M. Eastman, eds., Dravidian phonological systems. Seattle.
Sievers, E., 1901. Grundzüge der Phonetik. Leipzig.
Thompson, Laurence C., 1965. A Vietnamese grammar. Seattle.
Yip, Moira, 1983. Some problems of syllable structure in Axininca Campa. Proceedings of
    NELS 13.
Yip, Moira, 1988. The Obligatory Contour Principle and phonological rules: A loss of identity.
    Linguistic Inquiry 19: 65-100.
Zvelebil, Kamil, 1970. Comparative Dravidian phonology. The Hague.

---

[1] Patricia Shaw and Moira Yip have been of great assistance in referring me to relevant literature and other ways. They are of course not responsible for any failure on my part to benefit from their advice.

[2] Henderson also records a doubly articulated labiovelar nasal after undipthongized [ɔ] in -oong [ɔŋm̂] for the northern dialect but not the southern. The status of this final, which is found only in a few recent loanwords from French, is marginal and one may suspect that its pronunciation with a doubly articulated nasal is influenced by that of the diphthongized final -ong. Henderson notes that her Southern informant kept it distinct from -on, which is pronounced [ɔŋ], without double articulation, in that dialect.

[3] Syllables such as fou and mou are an apparent exception to this statement but the mid-high rounded vowel [o] is found only in this final and is derived from underlying /ə/ by assimilation to the final glide.

[4] The representation of the affricate with successive [-cont] and [+cont] specifications attached to the same root node corresponds to that in Sagey (1986, 81). It differs from representations such as found in Clements and Keyser (1983) which imply that the stop and fricative portions are separately attached to the same timing slot.

[5] Keating (1987, 127) cites X-ray evidence that palatal consonants are simultaneously coronal and [+high, -back] but suggests that palatoalveolars are simply coronal. This differs from my proposal in that I regard palatoalveolars as also having both Coronal and Dorsal components. Mester and Ito (1989) go further and suggest that palatalization should be renamed coronalization, which 'in general... consists in the addition of a coronal component or, if such a component is already present, in its enhancement (by the addition of [-ant]).' They go on to say, 'Our proposal is that the features characterizing front vowels reside on the Coronal node, and not on the Dorsal node.' This proposal too gets quite close to mine but differs from it in not recognizing the doubly articulated character of both front vowels and palatal (including palatoalveolar) consonants, so that [-anterior] is made to serve for what, I would argue, is simply [+high].

[6] Catford (1977: 171) remarks that before the publication of Alexander Bell's Visible Speech in 1867, which established tongue height and backness as the primary parameters for vowel classification with rounding as a separate additional parameter, phoneticians classified the front vowels [i] [e] [æ] as "linguals" and the back vowels [u] [o] [ɔ] as "labials." This would not be the only time in the history of science when an advance in one direction has obscured earlier insights.

[7] In some recent literature (e.g. Selkirk 1988) glides are treated as [+consonantal]. I suspect that the phenomena which have led to this departure from the principle that syllabicity is not a phonetic feature need to be handled by revisions in the theory of syllabic templates but I am not in a position at present to show how this could be done.

[8] According to Ferguson and Chowdury (1960) Bengali has the semivowels e̯ and o̯, distinct from i̯ and u̯, yielding contrasts such as monosyllabic cae̯ versus disyllabic ca-e, and even jee̯ versus ce-e and soo̯ versus so-o. If this analysis is correct, it constitutes a rare counterexample to the claim that [-high] front and back-rounded vowels switch to [+high] when they become non-syllabic.

Structural Domains and Derivational Domains in Inflection:
The Morphophonology of Guaraní Agreement Paradigms*

William Robboy
University of California, San Diego

0.   Introduction: Two notions of morphophonological domain.

Correlations of particular groups of affixes with particular groups of phonological processes are a pervasive phenomenon in natural language, and a long-standing topic of theoretical interest. In certain current theoretical frameworks, these convergences are captured by locating a particular group of affixes and its associated phonological rules within a particular **domain**. Two very different notions of "domain" exist in recent theory.

One of these notions is the **structural domain** defined in terms of morphological constituent category types. For example, Selkirk (1982, 1984) posits word-structure rule schemata for English which generate the recursive category types **Root** and **Word**, as well as the category type **Affix**. Two different classes of affixes, distinguishable in terms of both their linear distribution and their interaction or non-interaction with particular phonological rules, are characterized by different subcategorization frames: Class I consists of those that subcategorize for roots; Class II consists of those that subcategorize for words. A phonological rule may specify a category type as its domain: e.g. the domain of English stress assignment is **Root**.

The second notion of "domain" is the **derivational domain**. For example, the framework of Lexical Phonology (LP), exemplified in the work of Mohanan (1982, 1986), Kiparsky (1982, 1985), and others, posits ordered derivational levels or **strata** as domains for both affixation processes and phonological processes. The group of English affixes corresponding to Selkirk's Class I consists of those whose domain is specified as **stratum 1**, while the group corresponding to Class II consists of those whose domain is **stratum 2**. The domain of English stress assignment is **stratum 1**.

Assuming the derivational domain is the correct option for capturing such affixation-phonology correlations, the following issue can be raised: To what extent might grammars *still* need to differentiate among word-internal category types? Or to pose the question from another angle, to what extent is word structure autonomous from morphophonology? This issue has been a neglected one within the LP framework. To the extent that it is addressed in language-particular analyses, it is assumed that no morphological constituent levels are required beyond those necessary to distinguish between stems and affixes (if even that). In such an analysis, apparent restrictions on the linear order of affixes are purely a consequence of the order in which affixes are attached in the derivation, rather than a consequence of structural subcategorization.

The question naturally arises whether the inventory of morphological category types is universally so restricted. Incorporating a claim to that effect into LP would predict that a language can have no restrictions on the linear order of affixes beyond those that can result automatically from level-ordering and rule-ordering within levels. As a result, the classlike behavior of groups of affixes in terms of their linear distribution should be quite closely yoked with the classes they fall into in terms of their morphophonology.

This claim corresponds to an unofficial assumption in LP work, if only by default. I am not aware of any proposed LP analysis inconsistent with this assumption. In fact, it is taken for granted to such an extent that explicit note is seldom taken of it, though it is not a logically necessary assumption for the framework.[1] Thus it is worthwhile to examine its content more closely. It is by no means self-evident what sort of situation would be incompatible with such a claim, while still compatible with a level-ordered morphophonology.

In this paper I describe a set of facts from Guaraní[2] verbal agreement morphology, in which subject and object prefixes diverge with respect to their morphophonological behavior, but compete for the same linear slot. I show that a version of LP which elevates the above-mentioned

Transitive verbs are marked for the argument highest on the person and relational hierarchies in (4-5).

(4) Person hierarchy: 1ST>2ND>3RD
(5) Relational hierarchy: 3RD SUBJ > 3RD OBJ

The only cases in which *both* subject and object are marked are combinations of first-person subject with second-person object, where both arguments are marked in a single portmanteau agreement prefix. The paradigms in (6-8) for *juka* 'kill' exemplify subject, object, and portmanteau agreement in transitive verbs.[4]

(6) Subject agreement.

	SG	PL	
		INCL	EXCL
1ST	a-juka	ja-juka	ro-juka
	'I kill'	'we kill'	'we kill'
2ND	re-juka	pe-juka	
	'you kill'	'you kill'	
3RD	o-juka		
	'he/she/they kill(s)'		

(7) Object agreement.

	SG	PL	
		INCL	EXCL
1ST	xe-juka	ñande-juka	ore-juka
	'kill(s) me'	'kill(s) us'	'kill(s) us'
2ND	nde-juka	pende-juka	
	'kill(s) you'	'kill(s) you'	

(8) Portmanteau agreement

	2ND SG OBJ	2ND PL OBJ
1ST SUBJ	ro-juka	po-juka
	'I/we kill you SG'	'I/we kill you PL'

1.2.0 Phonological phenomena distinguishing subject from object marking

At least three different morphophonological processes differentiate between subject and object prefixes in Guaraní. The two to be discussed in this paper[5] are a rule of Glide Insertion and a rule of Elision. In each case the rule is characteristic of subject marking and not of object marking. Portmanteau prefixes pattern morphophonologically with subject rather than object prefixes.

Glide Insertion occurs in an arbitrary but fairly large lexical class of verbs, referenced by the diacritic +G in the formulation in (9). A front unrounded glide (written orthographically as *i* in the examples) is inserted between a subject agreement prefix and the root, illustrated in (9a). The glide does not appear between an object-agreement prefix and the root, as shown by (9b).[6] [7]

default assumption to the status of a universal claim fails to provide an account of the Guaraní facts. I then propose an analysis of the data which enriches the framework by increasing the number of morphological constituent levels and by allowing affixes to subcategorize for a particular structural level as well as specify a stratal domain. This allows the necessary degree of independence between structural class and morphophonological class. It is concluded that morphophonological domains and linear affix order cannot *both* be cast in derivational terms universally. Rather, a level-ordered framework of morphophonology must countenance a richer theory of word-internal constituent structure, and thus a somewhat broader autonomy of word structure from stratal organization, than has been implicitly assumed in LP work.

1. The data.

1.1 A sketch of Guaraní agreement morphology

Guaraní verbs conform to the descriptive template shown in (1), where it can be seen that subject and object agreement alternate in the same linear position.

(1) $$\sqrt{\ }\left[\left(\begin{matrix}\text{Negation} \\ \text{Mood}\end{matrix}\right) - \left\{\begin{matrix}\text{Object prefix} \\ \text{Subject prefix} \\ \text{Imperative}\end{matrix}\right\} - \text{(other prefixes) - Root - (suffixes)}\right]\sqrt{\ }$$

The data that are of crucial interest in this paper involve transitive verbs, since it is there that direct contrasts can be seen between subject and object marking. However, in order to identify subject or object agreement as such, it is helpful to refer to agreement marking in intransitive verbs. Guaraní intransitive verbs fall into two classes, which for discursive purposes I will refer to as unergatives and unaccusatives.[3] The agreement prefixes for unergative arguments are identical to those for transitive subjects, and are shown in (2). The agreement prefixes for unaccusative arguments are identical to those for transitive direct objects, and are shown in (3).

(2) Unergative and transitive subject agreement prefixes.

	SG	PL	
		INCL	EXCL
1ST	a-	ña-/ja-	ro-
2ND	re-	pe-	
3RD	o-		

(3) Unaccusative and transitive object agreement prefixes.

	SG	PL	
		INCL	EXCL
1ST	xe-	ñan(d)e-	ore-
2ND	n(d)e-	pen(d)e-	
3RD	i-		

(9) Glide-insertion $\emptyset --> y \,/\, \_[_{+G}$

(a) a i - nupă   (b) x e - nupă
     1SG-beat   1SG-beat
     'I beat'   'beat(s) me'
     * a - nupă   *x e i - nupă

Elision, formulated in (10), affects two affixes: the mood prefix *na-* and the subjunctive mood prefix *ta-*, which comprise the morphemes filling the position at the far left of the template in (1). Since the two prefixes are completely parallel in their morphophonological behavior, I will refer henceforth only to the mood prefix. The deletion of the prefix's final vowel is conditioned by the initial vowel of a subject-marked stem, as seen in (10a), but not by that of an object-marked stem, as shown by (10b).[8]

(10) Elision $V --> \emptyset \,/\, \_[V$
(a) t - oi-nupă   (b) t a - ore-nupă
     MOOD-3-beat   MOOD-1EXCL-beat
     '(s)he/they beat'   'beat us EXCL (subjunc.)'
     * t a - oi-nupă   * t - ore-nupă

2. Stratal domain assignments.

At this point we can explore how a level-ordered morphology and phonology might capture the dichotomy between subject and object prefixes with respect to the two processes just described. I will be assuming a version of LP like that of Mohanan (1986), in which affixes are listed in morphemic entries with a subcategorization frame, stratal domain specification, category level specification, and other information; they become attached to stems by rule during their appropriate stratal domain in the course of the derivation. Furthermore, I will initially consider a version of LP that follows Mohanan's (1986) analysis of English in assuming that the only category levels available are X^0, for roots, and X^{-1}, for affixes. Thus the only information directly provided about the structural position of a prefix is the fact that it *is* a prefix. Entries for some representative morphemes will look something like those in (11-13), with their stratal domains left for the moment unspecified. Informally, (13) say essentially that *nupă* is a verb stem of the Glide-insertion class, that *a* is a prefix which subcategorizes for verb stems and bears agreement features for first-person singular subject,[9] and that *ta-* is a prefix subcategorizing for verbs.

(11) *nupă*, V^0, +G

(12) $a, X^{-1}, \_[V]^0, 1ST_{SUBJ}, SG_{SUBJ}$

(13) $ta-, X^{-1}, \_[V]$

I will assume Glide-insertion (GI) and Elision are formulated as in (9-10), with the addition of stratal domain specifications, which now remain to be determined.

Let us assume minimally two distinct strata to which subject and object prefixation are respectively assigned. Since subject but not object prefixation feeds GI, the obvious move is for subject prefixes and GI to share a stratal domain, while the domain of object prefixes lies in another stratum. There is evidence that the former domain must be the earlier one: Causative formation with the prefix *mo-* also participates in GI in verbs of the GI class, as illustrated in (14).[10] As seen in (15), the causative is input to object prefixation.

(14) mo + kove   --->   mo i-ngove
CAUS + 'survive' 'resurrect'

(15) xe-moi-ngove
1SG-CAUS-survive
'resurrect(s) me'

As already established, object prefixation does not trigger GI. Hence GI (and causative prefixation) must apply at an earlier stratum than object prefixation. We conclude that the causative and subject prefixes attach at stratum 1, and that GI applies there as well, while object prefixes attach at stratum 2.

The question then is at what stratum the mood prefix attaches. Since object prefixation is input to mood prefixation, the latter's domain must extend at least as late as the former's. Let us hypothesize initially that mood affixation is ordered after object prefixation within stratum 2.[11] If the domain of mood affixation *only* includes stratum 2, Elision must also apply there, since it is triggered by mood affixation. But if Elision applies at level 2, it will do so indiscriminately regardless of the level at which the agreement prefix attached. Thus Elision correctly applies in the subject-marked case (16), but also incorrectly applies in the object-marked case (17).

(16) **Stratum 1**
Root   [nupǎ]
Subject prefix   [o[nupǎ]]
GI   [oi[nupǎ]]
Stratum 2
Mood prefix   [ta[oinupǎ]]
Elision   [t[oinupǎ]]
surface form   toinupǎ

(17) **Stratum 1**
Root   [nupǎ]
Stratum 2
Object prefix   [ore[nupǎ]]
Mood prefix   [ta[ore[nupǎ]]]
Elision   [t[ore[nupǎ]]]
surface form   * t orenupǎ
(correct form: t a orenupǎ)

Clearly, the domain of Elision must be stratum 1 in order for it to involve subject prefixes but not object prefixes. Recall that the domain of the mood prefix, on the other hand, must at least include a later stratum. We might attempt to solve the problem by assigning the mood prefix a multistratal domain, spanning strata 1 and 2. The derivations in (18) and (19) for *toinupǎi* and *taorenupǎi*, respectively, would have the correct results.

(18) **Stratum 1**
Root   [nupǎ]
Subject prefix   [o[nupǎ]]
GI   [oi[nupǎ]]
mood prefix   [ta[oi[nupǎ]]]
Elision   [t[oi[nupǎ]]]
Stratum 2
no rule applicable   toinupǎ

(19) **Stratum 1**
      Root   [nupã]
      Stratum 2
      Object prefix   [ore[nupã]]
      mood prefix   [ta[ore[nupã]]]
      surface form   taorenupã

But once the domain of the mood prefix is allowed to span both strata, there is no longer any way to ensure the correct order of affixes. Nothing will stop the mood prefix from attaching to a bare root at level 1, with an object prefix attaching at stratum 2, deriving ungrammatical scrambled forms like the one in (20).

(20) **Stratum 1**
      Root   [nupã]
      Mood prefix   [ta[nupã]
      GI   [tai[nupã]]
      Stratum 2
      Object prefix   [ore[tainupã]]
      surface form   *oretainupã

The problem can be summarized as follows: if morphophonological affix class and linear affix order are to be captured in the same terms, i.e. in derivationally sequential terms, we are faced with a paradox. Subject prefixes have the same linear distribution as object prefixes. Yet subject must differ from object prefixes by interacting with both an "early" phonological process (Glide-insertion) and a "later" prefixation. Clearly, affixal order and morphophonological affix classes cannot both be characterized in purely derivational terms, but must be allowed some degree of mutual independence.

3. A solution.

The necessary degree of mutual autonomy between affix order and morphophonology can be afforded by enriching the theory of word-internal constituent structure. Suppose that the phrase-structure rules in (21) (loosely inspired by Selkirk (1982)), exist to generate Guaraní verbs.

(21) (a)   Word --> (Affix) Stem
      (b)   Stem --> Affix Root
      (c)   Root --> (Affix) Root

Suppose further that Guaraní has morphemic entries including information like that in (22).

(22) Morphemic entries.

      (a)   *nupã*, V_{Root}, +G

      (b)   *a*, X_{Affix}, $[\_[V]_{Root}]_{Stem}$, 1_{SUBJ}, SG_{SUBJ}, stratum 1

      (c)   *xe*, X_{Affix}, $[\_[V]_{Root}]_{Stem}$, 1_{OBJ}, SG_{OBJ}, stratum 2

      (d)   *ta*, X_{Affix}, $\_[V]_{Stem}$, strata 1-2

The entries in (22) reflect the descriptive fact that while subject prefixes like (22a) and object prefixes like (22b) belong to different morphophonological classes, corresponding to their different stratal domains, they have identical structural distributions: they attach to roots to form stems. While *ta* has a multistratal domain in the morphophonology, reflecting its variability with respect to Elision, its structural position is rigidly fixed: it attaches only to stems. Let us assume Elision and GI as formulated earlier, with their domain specified as stratum 1. (23-24) show derivations produced by this system.

(23) **Stratum 1**
Root	$[nup\check{a}]_{Root}$
Subject prefix	$[o[nup\check{a}]]_{Stem}$
GI	$[oi[nup\check{a}]]$
Mood prefix	$[ta[oi[nup\check{a}]]]_{Word}$
Elision	$[t[oi[nup\check{a}]]]$
Stratum 2	
no rule applicable	$[toinup\check{a}]$

(24) **Stratum 1**
Root	$[nup\check{a}]_{Root}$
Stratum 2	
Object prefix	$[ore[nup\check{a}]]_{Stem}$
Mood prefix	$[ta[ore[nup\check{a}]]]$

Negative affixation is now allowed to take place either at stratum 1, where it feeds Elision, or at stratum 2, where it escapes Elision. It will never attach to a bare root, however, since its subcategorization does not allow it. A problem does remain, however. When a subject prefix has attached at stratum 1, mood affixation must not be allowed to wait until stratum 2, escaping Elision, as in (25).

(25) **Stratum 1**
Root	$[nup\check{a}]$
Subject prefix	$[o[nup\check{a}]]$
GI	$[oi[nup\check{a}]]$
Stratum 2	
Mood prefix	$[ta[oinup\check{a}]]$
surface form	*$taoinup\check{a}$

We therefore posit the (possibly universal) constraint in (26), which will ensure that mood affixation applies at level 1 if it can.[12]

(26) Timeliness Constraint: If an affix attaches to to a given input, it must do so at the earliest stratum in its domain at which its subcategorization is satisfied.

4. Conclusion

The behaviors of Guaraní verbal prefixes with respect to linear order and with respect to their interaction with phonology diverge in such a way that both behaviors cannot be captured in purely derivational terms. The facts thus motivate a version of LP with a rich enough inventory of word-internal constituent levels to allow morphological structure a certain degree of autonomy from derivational process, even though the domains of interface between morphology and phonology are envisaged as derivational in nature. Such a theory explicitly abandons the default assumption pervasive in LP work, under which apparent constraints on affix order are a mere side effect of derivational history.

It seems clear that the Guaraní facts described here cannot be captured purely in terms of structural domains, either: It is hard to imagine how a mood-marked verb could constitute one domain when containing within it a subject-marked form, but another domain when containing within it an object-marked form.

The topic of derivational vs. structural characterizations of morphology has been an enduring issue since at least the days of American structuralism, as elucidated by Hockett (1953). In recent years the scope of the issue has been extended to the morphology-phonology inter-face, in the guise of derivational vs. structural domains. The Guaraní facts indicate that in the arena of morphophonological domains, both process and structure must come into play.

5.   Appendix: Additional sample paradigms.

    (27) Unergative paradigm.

	SG	PL	
		INCL	EXCL
1ST	a-puka 'I laugh'	ja-puka 'we laugh'	ro-puka 'we laugh'
2ND	re-puka 'you laugh'	pe-puka 'you laugh'	
3RD	o-puka 'he/she/they laugh(s)'		

    (28)   Unaccusative paradigm.

	SG	PL	
		INCL	EXCL
1ST	xe-mandu'a 'I remember'	ñane-mandu'a 'we remember'	ore-mandu'a 'we remember'
2ND	ne-mandu'a 'you remember'	pene-mandu'a 'you remember'	
3RD	i-mandu'a 'he/she/they remember(s)'		

Transitive subjunctive paradigms (Glide-Insertion class).[13]

    (29) Subject paradigm.

	SG	PL	
		INCL	EXCL
1ST	t-ai-nupã 'I beat'	ta-ñai-nupã 'we beat'	to-roi-nupã 'we beat'
2ND	te-rei-nupã 'you beat'	ta-pei-nupã 'you beat'	
3RD	t-oi-nupã '(s)he/they beat'		

(30) Object paradigm.

	SG	PL INCL	EXCL
1ST	ta-xe-nupã 'beat me'	ta-ñane-nupã 'beat us'	ta-ore-nupã 'beat us'
2ND	ta-ne-nupã 'beat you'	ta-pene-nupã 'beat you'	

(31) Portmanteau paradigm.

	2ND SG OBJ	2ND PL OBJ
1ST SUBJ	to-roi-nupã 'I/we beat you SG'	ta-poi-nupã 'I/we beat you PL'

Notes.

*I am grateful to the following people for their comments on earlier versions of this material: Farrell Ackerman, Matthew Chen, Sandra Chung, Katarzyna Dziwirek, Jeffrey Elman, Patrick Farrell, Jeanne Gibson, Margaret Langdon, and David Perlmutter. Thanks also Marina dos Santos and Maura Velázquez for the data. Any shortcomings or errors in the paper, however, are my own.

[1] Mohanan (1986) explicitly limits the English inventory of word-internal constituent levels to X^0 (for stems) and X^{-1} (for affixes), but stops short of suggesting that more levels are or are not needed cross-linguistically.

[2] Guaraní is a language of the Tupi-Guaraní family; the dialect represented here is Paraguayan Guaraní, spoken in eastern Paraguay and northern Argentina. Most of the positive data in this paper are not new, since the raw facts of Guaraní verbal morphology are well-documented (e.g. in Gregores and Suárez (1967) and Guasch (1976)). To my knowledge, however, the facts have not previously been organized and framed in this manner, as a systematic dichotomy between the two prefix types. All the data presented here were elicited from or checked with native speakers in San Diego: Marina dos Santos, from Pilar, Paraguay, and/or Maura Velázquez, from San Pedro, Paraguay. Data were collected by me and other UCSD linguists between 1984 and 1989.

[3] Hare (1986 and personal communication) has found evidence that these behave as syntactic (as well as morphological) classes, suggesting that they may be characterizable in Relational Grammar as taking initial unergative and unaccusative arguments, respectively.

[4] "Agreement" may be a somewhat misleading term with respect to object marking. Complementarity of object prefixes with overt independent direct object NPs (in unmarked discourse contexts) suggest that these prefixes have a pronominal function in transitive clauses (though not in the unaccusative cases). Transitive and unergative subject prefixes, as well as unaccusative prefixes, may freely cooccur with overt subject NPs. Portmanteau prefixes show complementarity with direct object NPs but may cooccur freely with subject NPs. These facts suggest that with respect to subjects, agreement prefixes fulfill a role corresponding to Bresnan and Mchombo's (1987) "grammatical agreement," while with respect to objects they function in a way corresponding to Bresnan and Mchombo's "anaphoric agreement."

[5] Another such phenomenon (a thematic consonant mutation) would belong with these others in a full description of Guaraní verbal morphology. I omit it from this paper because its bearing on the theoretical issue is less clear.

[6] Evidence that this alternation reflects an insertion rather than a deletion comes from its relationship with a rule of Morpheme-Initial Sandhi. Discussion will be found in Robboy (in

preparation).

[7] A few unergative verbs are in the Glide-Insertion class. However, no unaccusative verbs display Glide Insertion--exactly as we would expect if the phenomenon occurs with the prefixes in (2) but never with those in (3).

[8] There is in fact only one object prefix in the transitive paradigm with an initial vowel. The failure of object-marked stems to condition Elision is corroborated by the unaccusative paradigm, where there is an additional such prefix, third-person *i-*, which likewise fails to condition Elision. (No third-person object prefix ever appears in transitive verbs, since third-person object is always outranked on the person and relational hierarchies in (4-5).

[9] I assume that agreement affixes bear abstract person and number features, which they impart through percolation to the verbs created when they are attached. I assume also that verbal agreement features are tagged with indices directly corresponding to grammatical relations. (Such a position is taken by Zwicky (1986a, 1986b)). I am assuming furthermore that all affixation rules are optional, but that some language-particular filter(s) in the syntactic component will ultimately ensure that verbs bear appropriate features.

[10] The *k/ng* alternation in (14) is due to a sandhi process discussed in Robboy (1987) and Robboy (in preparation).

[11] Extrinsic ordering of morphological rules within strata is argued for by Hargus (1988).

[12] Note that the bad derivation in (25) is also generated under the last hypothesis considered in section 2, where mood affixation spans both strata, but affixal subcategorizations do not choose among different category types. Under such a theory, the Timeliness Constraint in (26) would not be coherent, since it would simply serve effectively to ban multistratal domains.

[13] A vowel copying or spreading process appears to affect the mood prefix in some forms in the subject and portmanteau paradigms. From the small number of forms involved it is not clear whether this phenomenon crucially distinguishes between comparable subject and object prefixes.

References.

Bresnan, J., and S.A. Mchombo (1987) Topic, pronoun, and agreement in Chicheŵa. *Language* 63:741-782.

Gregores, E., and J. Suárez. (1967) *A Description of Colloquial Guaraní*. The Hague: Mouton.

Guasch, A. (1976) *El idioma guaraní*, 4ᵃ ed. Asunción: Ediciones Loyola.

Hare, M. (1986) Causative constructions in Guarani. Unpublished MS., UCSD.

Hargus, S. (1988) *The Lexical Phonology of Sekani*. Revision of UCLA doctoral dissertation. New York: Garland.

Hockett, C.F. (1954) Two models of grammatical description. *Word 10*. Reprinted in M. Joos, ed., *Readings in Linguistics I*, 4th ed. Chicago: University of Chicago Press, 1966.

Kiparsky, P. (1982) From cyclic phonology to lexical phonology. In H. van der Hulst and N. Smith, eds., *The Structure of Phonological Representations*, part 1, pp. 131-175. Dordrecht: Foris.

---(1985) Some consequences of Lexical Phonology. *Phonology Yearbook* 2:85-138.

Mohanan, K.P. (1982) *Lexical Phonology*. Doctoral dissertation, MIT. Reproduced, Bloomington: Indiana University Linguistics Club, 1982.

---(1986) *The Theory of Lexical Phonology*. Dordrecht: Reidel.

Robboy, W. (1987) Rule-specific transparency and P-bearingness: evidence from Guaraní nasality processes. In M. Crowhurst, ed., *Proceedings of the West Coast Conference on Formal Linguistics* 6:265-279. Stanford: Stanford Linguistics Association.

---(in preparation) *Topics in Guaraní Morphophonology and Morphosyntax*. Doctoral dissertation, UCSD.

Selkirk, E. (1982) *The Syntax of Words*. Cambridge, Mass.: MIT Press.

---(1984) *Phonology and Syntax*. Cambridge, Mass.: MIT Press.

Zwicky, A.M. (1986a) Agreement features: layers or tags? In A.M. Zwicky, *Interfaces*, pp. 146-148. *Ohio State University Working Papers in Linguistics* 32.

---(1986b) Imposed versus inherent feature specifications, and other multiple feature markings. In *Indiana University Linguistics Club Twentieth Anniversary Volume*, pp. 85-106. Bloomington: Indiana University Linguistics Club.

On the Phrase Structure of Serial Verb Constructions

Eric Schiller
University of Chicago

The grammar of Serial Verb Constructions has been the subject of intermittent study over the years, often in work confined to a single linguistic area, with a great deal of ignorance of work done outside that area. In this paper* some of the insights of earlier work on serial verbs, such as that of Schachter (1974) and Filbeck (1975)[1], and some of the more recent observations of Sebba (1987) and Baker (1989) will be recast in the light of advances in modular views of grammar, and in particular, the framework of Autolexical Syntax. The proposals made here should, however, hold for any theory of grammar which includes an X̄-like base component.

I will begin by discussing the range of data to be considered in the paper, and then briefly sketch three treatments with the frameworks of Generalized Phrase Structure Grammar, Generative Semantics and Government and Binding. After discussing some of the problems which afflict these accounts, I will then present an account within the framework of Autolexical Syntax which, I believe, simply and elegantly accounts for the structures under consideration.

One serious problem in the discussion of Serial Verb Constructions is the lack of agreement on just what counts as an Serial Verb Construction. Some approaches, e.g. Mikami (1979) include everything from passive and causative sentence types to more typical Serial Verb Constructions, while Sebba and Baker are much more restrictive. This examination of Serial Verb Constructions will include only those constructions which show an uninterrupted sequence of verbs or verb phrases in which one verb or verb phrase bears the primary propositional meaning of the sentence (following Filbeck) and in which the others are subordinate (following Filbeck, Sebba). These will be designated Subordinating Serial Verb Constructions. Coördinate serial verb constructions which lack a surface conjunction are largely excluded from consideration. Sebba (1987) convincingly distinguishes Subordinating Serial Verb Constructions from Coördinating Serial Verb Constructions, the former showing the following characteristics:

(1)   i.   "Although two or more verbs are present, the sentence is interpreted as referring to a single action rather than a series of related actions. Although the action may involve several different motions there is no possibility of a temporal break between these and they cannot be performed, for example, with different purposes in mind..."
        ii. "There is a strict ordering relationship between the verbs..."
        iii. "Furthermore, the first verb in a series may subcategorize for a particular verb or class of verbs..."
        iv. "In some cases, each transitive verb in the series has its own object..."

With regard to the second point above, it should be noted that the strict ordering relationship must be taken as a constraint independent from the temporal sequencing principles presented by Tai (1985), which provide an explanation for the sequence of predicates in both Subordinating Serial Verb Constructions and Coördinating Serial Verb Constructions.

It can be stated, then that in order for two verb phrases to be considered a Subordinating Serial Verb Construction they must meet the Tense-Aspect Simultaneity Condition (2) and the Unsunderability Condition (3).

(2) Tense-Aspect Simultaneity Condition: The serialized constituents involved may not be marked with more than one tense or aspect.

(3) Unsunderability Condition: No conjunction[2] can appear in, or be inserted between, the serialized constituents without altering the meaning of the sentence.

These will not apply to Coördinating Serial Verb Constructions, which may have mixed tenses or aspects, and which can have conjunctions inserted. Thus English can be said to have Coördinating Serial Verb Constructions such as (4) but not Subordinating Serial Verb Constructions.

(4)   a. Go play in the yard.
        a'. Go and play in the yard.
        b. He up(ped) and died on me.

In (4a), a surface conjunction can be inserted (4a') without, as far as I can tell, any change in meaning. Notice that (4b) has the semantic properties often ascribed to Subordinating Serial Verb Constructions, even on Sebba's tests, but requires a surface conjunction (often phonologically reduced, but still there).

Sebba (1987) presents a very brief list of Serial Verb Construction, consisting of some West African languages, some Caribbean creoles, and Tok Pisin and Mandarin. No Southeast Asian languages appear, despite the fact that verb serialization is practically an areal phenomenon there[3]. Bickerton (to appear) gives further evidence that the syntactic census takers have grossly undercounted the number of languages which display this phenomenon, even so restrictively defined.

Typical Subordinating Serial Verb Constructions are presented in (5)[4]. The past tense glosses of Thai and Khmer does not reflect any overt tense markings - both languages lack deictic tense and, as I have argued elsewhere (Schiller 1988), any overt consequence of functional empty categories such as INFL.

(5) a. dèk   pay   sïï   khanŏm   (Thai)
        child   go   buy   candy
        The child went to buy candy.

      b. sùk   aw   máy   maa   bâan   (Thai)
        Sook   take   wood   come   house
        Sook brought the wood home.

      c. sùk   aw   máy   maa   sâaŋ   tó?   (Thai)
        Sook   take   wood   come   build   table
        Sook brought wood to build a table.

      d. Kofi   fringi   a   tiki   fadon   naki   Amba   (Sranan)
        Kofi   threw   the   stick   fall   hit   Amba
        Kofi threw the stick at Amba.

      e. koun   baoh   sɔm?aat   phteah   (Khmer)
        child   sweep   clean[CAUS]   house
        The child sweeps the house clean.

      f   o   ra   isu   fún   mi   (Yoruba)
        he   buy   yam   give   me
        He bought a yam for me.

g. kŏat   teñ   dɔmlooŋ-cvie   ʔaoy   khñom   (Khmer)
   he   buy   yam   give   me
   He bought a yam for me.

h. Mi   e   teki   a   nefi   koti   a   brede   (Sranan)
   I   ASP   take   the   knife   cut   the   bread
   I cut the bread with a knife.

i. prichaa   chǎy   mîit   taʿt   nǐa   (Thai)
   Prichaa   use   knife   cut   meat
   I cut the bread with a knife.

While many discussions of serialization (e.g. Filbeck 1975, Sebba 1987, Matisoff 1972) taxonomize the types of Serial Verb Constructions using such terms as "resultative", "benefactive" "purpose", "control", "factitive", etc., the Autolexical approach simply identifies each syntactic unit as a ∇, although some of the taxonomy will be captured in terms of semantic case, to be discussed below. Baker (1989 p.11) also argues convincingly for the ∇ status of the constituents. Following Filbeck and Schachter, we adopt an analysis of Subordinating Serial Verb Construction languages as having a recursive phrase structure rule which can be formulated as in (6)[5]:

(6) $S \rightarrow (\bar{X}) (\bar{N}) \nabla*$

In adopting a flat structure it will be argued that Sebba's analysis is incorrect, and that the subordination is more semantic than syntactic, as has already been suggested by Filbeck and others.

The main question we are concerned with is the structural description of the subordinating serial verb construction. Sebba (p. 115) argues for the structure presented in (7), motivated at least in part by semantic considerations. Sebba must account for the semantically subordinate nature of the material in the lower clause, and his formal mechanism - GPSG - does not allow non-isomorphism of syntactic and semantic components. The constituent dominated by VP_1 is a single syntactic unit which has, by the Rule-to-Rule hypothesis, a parallel semantic constituent. The VP_2 is dominated by VP_1 and is the complement of the head verb of that phrase. Thus configurationally VP_2 can be said to be subordinate to VP_1.

(7)

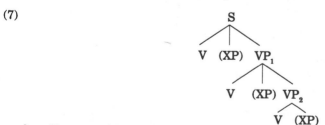

where X can stand for N or P. (The top left V was probably intended to be NP.)

In favor of his analysis, he points to the fact that it treats the whole predicative structure as a constituent and that it does not involve coordination at any level.

The drawback to this approach is that it provides no independent SYNTACTIC, as opposed to SEMANTIC, justification for the syntactic structure. In addition, it requires a different SYNTACTIC structure for Coördinating Serial Verb constructions, which he treats in the same manner as Filbeck and Schachter, to whom we now turn.

Filbeck's analysis (and Schachter's as well) is based on the syntactic rule (8a) (PDP stands for Predicate Phrase) represented by the tree structure in 8b:

(8)　a.　$S \rightarrow NP + PDP$, where $PDP \rightarrow (Aux) VP^* (S))$

　　　b.

PDP

(Aux)　VP_1　VP_2 .... VP_n　(S)

V　(NP)　V　(NP)　V　(NP)

The syntax and semantics of Subordinating Serial Verb Constructions are characterized by Filbeck (1975) as follows: "The initial verb, or V_1, of a series is propositional, i.e. this is the verb that carries the true predicate meaning of the proposition; any subsequent verb, or V_{1+n}, states a functional meaning which is related to the predicate or propositional meaning of the initial verb."

Filbeck's insights are, to my mind, very much in the right direction. One problem here, and with Schachter's analysis, is that syntax and semantics are conflated, as in Sebba's GPSG account. More serious, however, is the erroneous identification of the INITIAL verb as the one which bears the primary meaning. Return to (5.h-i) above. Clearly the primary proposition involves the cutting of bread here, as reflected by the translations provided by the author.

In Baker (1989), an analysis is proposed within the framework of Government and Binding, where a single object is shared by two verbs. He provides the following tree of a sentence of Sranan *(9 at right)* →.

The motivation for this analysis lies with the need to reconcile the data with Chomsky's Projection Principle, a problem which is entirely theory internal and need not concern us here. Thematic roles are assigned by each of the verbs, leading to double marking on the object. Baker then presents a very ingenious account of why the shared object must be situated between the two verbs. The restriction on location of the shared object posited by Baker is not universal. In fact, it doesn't even hold for the language under consideration! Consider the following example from

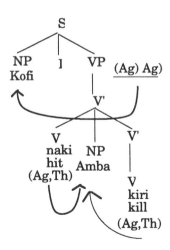

'Kofi struck Amba dead'

Sebba (p.93) (10a) and the similar (10b and 10c) from Khmer and the Oceanic language Paamese:

(10) a. Kofi   nake   kiri   Amba   (Sranan)
              Kofi   hit   kill   Amba
              Kofi struck Amba dead

      b. koun   baoh   sɔmʔaat   phteah   (Khmer)
              child   sweep   clean$_{[CAUS]}$ house
              The child sweeps the house clean

      c. Inau   namutelas   mōtain   aim   (Paamese)
              (Inau   na-mutelasi   mootaini aimo)
              1sg   1sg-real-sweep clean   house

Although one MIGHT argue that this is either a lexical compound verb (unlikely) or a complex verb created by the sort of incorporation discussed in Baker's 1988 book.

In (11) (= Baker's 18a) the ungrammaticality of the sentence is explained by the fact that the triadic verb 'give' cannot appear before the dyadic verb 'buy' due to word order principles.

(11)   *Olú fún Sadé ra aso   (Yoruba)
          Olu give Sade buy dress
          Olu bought a dress for Sade

It is possible to object that 'buy' can be viewed as a triadic verb itself. In a syntactically polysemous language (that is, a language in which a single word form may fill a variety of syntactic roles without changing its shape), where the verb 'give' has a variety of argument structures, this cannot be stated lexically, since the following Khmer example is perfectly grammatical:

(12)   Sok   ʔaoy   Kim   teñ   ʔaaw-madam   (Khmer)
          Sok   give   Kim   buy   dress
      a. Sok let Kim buy a dress (where Sok bought it).
      b. Sok let Kim buy a dress (where Kim bought it).

Leaving aside the usual difficulties of translation, we can see that the two constructions are syntactically identical and that semantically they are extremely close. Informants pointed out that the Khmer sentence can be used where the act of buying is accomplished entirely by Sok. Here the acts of buying and giving must be simultaneous. If Sok bought the dress and later gave it to Kim, then (13), which is ambiguous between readings in which the lower clause is purpose or a separate act of giving, must be used.

(13)   Sok teñ ʔaaw-madam ʔaoy Kim   (Khmer)
          Sok buy dress   give Kim
          Sok bought a dress for Kim.

But a more serious problem is that Baker, while concentrating on thematic roles, neglects to give an explicit account of case marking or (Case) in Serial Verb Constructions. Let's now consider the Autolexical approach.

The surface syntax was properly described by Filbeck and Schachter. As Bickerton (to appear) has noted, this may be an instance of a more general situation, whereby verbs can take a variety of clausal complements. Syntactically, we can consider the "importance" of one verb in the string is a result of it being marked with the feature head ([+hd]). The syntactic head can be identified by a number of (language-specific) means, including placement of negative marker, ability to take certain affixes, and position in the sentence in strict word-order languages. In general, one expects that the syntactic and semantic heads of a sentence will be associated. The proposal that each component of an autolexical representation will have headed constituents is appropriate to the principle (Sadock (to appear)) that relationships in each component should be represented in such a way as to enable connections with other components. This idea also provides support for the notion of case in each component (Schiller (to appear)), which will figure in the discussion below. We can state the following principle:

(14)   Head Correspondence Principle: *A head in one component will associate with a head in each other component.*

As with most Autolexical principles, violations may only occur if they are licensed by defined, usually parametric, language specific rules. One goal of Autolexical theory is to define the circumstances under which the general principles may be violated, and then to reduce these exceptions to principles rather than stipulations.

To account for the cross-linguistic distribution of Serial Verb Constructions, Baker (1989 p.8) suggested (15):

(15)   Generalized Serialization Parameter : *VP's (can/cannot) count as the projection of more than one distinct head.*

where languages such as Yoruba, Sranan, Thai, Khmer, Mandarin, etc., can allow VP's to count as the projection of more than one distinct head and languages such as English, French, and Russian cannot. This is one principled way of explaining why Serial Verb Constructions are allowed, but says nothing about why languages which allow them use only that mechanism and do not have optional variants. This can be explained by the interaction of a number of independent principles in Autolexical Theory:

(16)   Relative Abstractness of Levels (REAL): *Morphology is less abstract than Syntax which in turn is less abstract than Semantics.*
(17)   Relative Degree of Universality (REDU): *Cross-Linguistic Universals are more likely to be found in more abstract levels.*
(18)   General Right of Way (GROW): *In a conflict between the requirements of two levels, the demands of the less abstract level take precedence.*
(19)   Semantic Case Instantiation Principle (SCIP): *Semantic Case relations are instantiated by the most concrete possible mechanism.*

Taken together, (16-19) explain the distribution of Serial Verb Constructions in the world's languages as follows, taking the instrumental type as an example. These are constructions in which one constituent describes the manner in which an act represented by another constituent is carried out. In some languages this is encoded by a prepositional phrase, as in (20a), in others via morphological case as in (20b), while in Subordinating Serial Verb Construction languages this can be accomplished with a serial verb construction (20c,d). In some languages, both prepositional and serial constructions can be used (cf. 20 e,f), a fact pointed out in Nylander (1986), who also notes that diachronically a language can develop verb serialization even though it already has prepositions. All of the examples below can be glossed as 'He cuts the bread/meat with a knife.'

(20)   'He cuts the bread/meat with a knife.'
  a. Ya režu khleb nožom.   (Russian)
      I$_{\text{[NOM]}}$ cut bread$_{\text{[ACC]}}$ knife$_{\text{[INST]}}$
  b. I cut the bread with a knife. (English)
  c. Mi   e   teki   a   nefi   koti a   brede   (Sranan)
      I   ASP   take   the   knife cut   the   bread
  d. fu   burede   ije   sime abe   ufu   (Barai)
      3sg   bread   def   knife   take cut
      He cut the bread with a knife.
  e. prichaa   cháy   míit   ta't   nřa   (Thai)
      Prichaa   use   knife cut   meat
  f. Sokh   kac   sac   nɯɯŋ kɔmbut   (Khmer)
      Sok   cut   meat   with   knife
  g. Sokh   yɔɔk   kɔmbut təu   kac   sac   (Khmer)
      Sokh   take   knife   go   cut   meat
  h. a   tei   faka   fu   koti en   ma   an   koti en (Saramaccan)
      he   take   knife to   cut   it   but he-not cut it
  i. *a   tei   faka   koti en   ma   an   koti en
  j. i   ti   pran   kuto pu   kup   li   be   i   pa   kup li (Seselwa)
      he   TNS   take   knife to   cut   it   but he   didn't cut it
  k. i   ti   pran   kuto kup   li   be   i   pa   kup li
      he   TNS   take   knife cut   it   but he   didn't cut it

   In the Khmer case, the form presented in (20f) is the one which is parallel to the others considered here. (20g) is not a subordinating serial verb construction, as it can only be used for a situation in which Sokh has picked up the knife but has not yet cut the meat, thus violating the Tense-Aspect Simultaneity Condition (2). Compare this with (20c), which Sebba (p.171) claims that his informants confirm that it "implies that he <u>actually</u> cut the meat, i.e. There is no possibility of <u>korta e karni</u> being a "purpose clause". Additional examples of this contrast in two unrelated creole languages are presented in (20h & i and j & k), where we have judgements on the acceptability of explicitly negating the act of cutting.
   Thus Russian, with the ability to express instrumentality via morphological case, will not have verb serialization. Nor will English, which uses syntactic prepositional phrases to achieve the end. But Sranan and Thai lack (appropriate) prepositions, so the semantic relation of instrumentality can only be expressed by using concatenated verb phrases, relying on headedness and the temporal ordering principles of Tai (1985) for the correct interpretation, a matter we shall return to below. In the case of Khmer, we have a mixed system, where there are lexical prepositions available to express some semantic case relations (e.g. instrumental), but not others. Here there is a significant difference between Khmer and Thai, the former having more words which might be appropriately classed as prepositions. My explanation for the contrast between Khmer and Sranan lies in the fact that Khmer has the possiblity of (20f), and thus must employ the hierarchically superior prepositional phrase construction to the serial verb form, following Semantic Case Instantiation Principle (19)[6].
   Let us now examine an autolexical representation of the instrumental

412

type of Subordinating Serial Verb Construction (21). The upper half of the tree represents the syntactic representation and the lower half of the tree represents the semantic representation, the node labels for which will be discussed below (for now, it is enough to know that F indicates a proposition, with the number of arguments required indicated, and Q̄ represents a binder expression, or, more generally, an argument).

(21)   An autolexical representation of (20c & 20d):

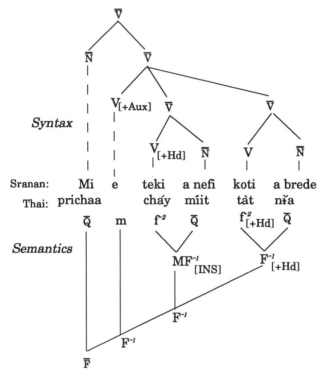

Baker (1989) criticizes Sebba and others who propose base-generated iterated V̄'s on the grounds that although this correctly accounts for the surface structure of Serial Verb Constructions, this is achieved "at the cost of relying on (largely unexplored) rules of a semantic component to determine which NP's are arguments of which verbs." In the Autolexical approach, this question can be handled by a mechanism entirely within the semantic component (Schiller to appear). We will return to this topic below.

Our autolexical representation of Serial Verb Constructions in general is given in (22), where the top tree represents the syntax, and the bottom tree, the semantics.

As seen from (22) the semantics of the Serial Verb Construction is represented by a set of propositions where one of the predicates is marked as bearing the *head* feature. This proposal greatly simplifies the analysis of Serial Verb

(22)

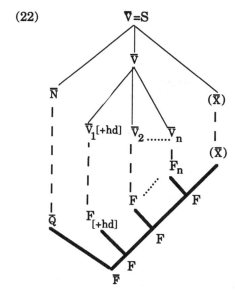

Construction languages. It does not require elaborate case systems to be applied to the syntactic component. Many Serial Verb Construction languages show no overt signs of case-marking at all. The semantic interpretation of case relations is left to the semantic component in the present Autolexical analysis.

In an Autolexical analysis, this fact is predicted from the semantic representation, where the "propositional" verb is the closest to the root node (the semantic component involving only dominance, and not precedence relations)[7].

We can thus define a semantic head as follows:

(23)   *The head of a constituent in the semantic component is the predicate (f) closest to the root node.*

Semantic factors must be called into play in order to account for the following Sranan example, which, peripheral as it seems, is the major justification in Sebba and Baker for opposing the flat syntactic structure:

(24) a. *Kofi   sutu   Amba kiri   Kwaku   (Sranan)
          Kofi   shoot   Amba kill   Kwaku
          Kofi shot Amba and killed Kwaku.
      b. *Kofi   tyari   nyan go   gi   Amba ptata
          Kofi   carry   food go   give   Amba potatoes
          Kofi carried food and gave Amba the potatoes.

Baker's explanation for the ungrammaticality of the string is based on θ-role assignment: 'kill' heads both the V' and the VP, with two NP's present, but 'kill' can only assign a single internal θ-role by virtue of its lexical specification.

But suppose one were to replace 'Kwaku' with an NP co-referent with Amba. Compare the English examples in (25):

(25) a. ?The Ayatollah shot at Rushdie to kill Reagan.
      b. The Ayatollah shot at Rushdie to kill the heretic.
      c. The Ayatollah shot at Rushdie to kill the one who had brought shame to the true believers.

(24b) presents a more interesting problem, since there does not seem to be any semantic flaw under the given translation. But no translation at all appears in Sebba, only in Baker, and the translation may be misleading. If this is a subordinating serial construction, and it is by no means clear to me that it is not in fact a coördinating one, the oddity might be purely semantic or pragmatic:

(26) 'Kofi carried the food in order to give Amba the potatoes'.

Even in English this is more than a little bit odd, especially when compared with the construction in which the object NP's are reversed:

(27) 'Kofi carried the potatoes in order to give Amba food/'the food'.

In any event, I have no command of Sranan and cannot elaborate further. Nevertheless, the objections to the flat ∇ structure seem very poorly motivated. Why should the comparable (in the sense of being paraphaseable in similar ways, used in similar situations, etc.) English constructions be marked, even though English is not a serializing language? Clearly, Baker and Sebba have an obligation to present much more data than the two sample sentences if their objection to the flat structure is to be taken seriously.

The semantically subordinate nature of the lower clauses of Subordinating Serial Verb Constructions have already been mentioned. There are many types of semantic relationships, as noted by numerous authorities. Let us consider a few of these sub-types, which we classify semantically, rather than syntactically.

Both directional and resultative sub-propositions can be subsumed under a general rubric of goal.

(28) a. Kofi   fringi   a   buku   fadon   (Sranan)
          Kofi   throw   the   book   fall
          Kofi threw the book down.
      b. Sokh   boh   siewphew   təu   dai
          Sok   throw   book   go   ground
      c. Sokh   boh   siewphəu   caol
          Sok   throw   book   abandon

Of this type of construction Baker observes:

"This structure has two implications for the intransitive V2: (i) V2 must be lexically capable of assigning an internal θ-role, and (ii) its θ-role must be assigned to the object of V1, rather than to the subject of V1."

It is not clear however, that transitivity is the appropriate notion here. For example, in (28b) the verb təu takes an object, while in (28c), where the result is that the book is abandoned, the verb caol is generally transitive.

In Autolexical terms nothing need be stipulated in the syntax, since the language in question has the appropriate recursive phrase structure rules given above. Semantically, verbs involving motion are marked to permit directional complements of a goal. Our lexical entries for fringi and fadon is therefore:

(29) a. /fringi/ 'throw' (also Khmer /boh/)
          Syntax: V
          Semantics: $f^2/\pm$[GOAL]

      b. /fadon/ 'fall'
          Syntax: V
          Semantics: f^1[+GOAL]

Thus _fringi_ is a verb which acts as a two place predicate which may optionally include a goal phrase in its complement. This allows the acceptability of any sort of goal phrase (i.e., any semantic constituent whose head is marked [+GOAL] (e.g. 22b) to be associated with the word _fringi_. That the predication applies to the object of the matrix verb rather than its subject is supplied by the semantic representation in which the goal-marked constituent is internal to the predicate. (30) represents the structure common to both the Sranan and Khmer examples.

(30)

Kofi					
Sokh		$f^2_{[+hd]}$	$\bar{Q}$	$f_{[+GOAL]}$	
		fringi	a buku	fadon	{caol/təu dəi}
		boh	siewphəu		

The semantic structure of the two sentences is roughly the same, the only difference being that the goal phrase is instantiated in the Khmer examples by either a simple predicate _caol_ or a phrasal predicate _təu dəi_. In either case he argument sharing is licensed by the language specific parameter which permits Subordinating Serial Verb Constructions in the first place. It would be reasonable to ask at this point how _fadon_ fills its missing argument with the entity 'book' rather than the matrix subject 'Kofi'. This will be discussed below.

We have already considered the instrumental type of Subordinating Serial Verb Construction. Baker (p.28) suggests that constructions of the type of (20c) involve triadic verbs, subcategorized for instrumental rather than dative tertiary objects. The problem here is that so many verbs can take instrumental oblique objects that it would seem that most transitive verbs should be treated as triadic. A better strategy is to freely permit instrumental complements while requiring lexical licensing for directional and goal complements.

Another common use of verb serialization involves a subordinate notion of purpose.

(31=1a)　deˀk　pay　sɯ̃　khanŏm　　　　　　　(Thai)
　　　　child　go　buy　candy
　　　　The child went to buy candy.

(32)　a.　bɔɑŋ　　　khñom　yɔ̀ɔk　kasaet　ʔaan　　(Khmer)
　　　　old. brother　my　　　take　newspaper　read
　　　　My older brother took the newspaper to read it.

　　　b.　bɔɑŋ　　　khñom　yɔ̀ɔk　kasaet　daəmbəi　　ʔaan
　　　　old. brother　my　　　take　newspaper　in order to　read
　　　　My older brother took the newspaper to read it.

　　　c.　*bɔɑŋ　　khñom　yɔ̀ɔk　kasaet　ʔaan　viə
　　　　old. brother　my　　　take　newspaper　read　it
　　　　My older brother took the newspaper to read it.

In this (32a) there is no explicit marker of the purpose clause, although one can be inserted, as in (32b).

I have thus far failed to present a mechanism for the incorporation of thematic roles into the semantic component. One approach to this question was presented at the 4/26/89 Autolexical Workshop by Jan Terje Faarlund. This requires a separate component to deal with the question of thematic roles.

An alternative strategy, discussed in my talk on 4/26/89 , is to treat thematic relations as semantic case. If we assume that thematic roles are appropriately specified in the lexicon (whether for a separate component or as part of a semantic specification), we can establish a three-way default specification as follows:

(33)	a.	(example)	Syntax	Semantics	Thematic Roles
		give	V	f^3	Ag, Th, Go
		kill	V	f^2	Ag, Th
		die	V	f^1	Th

In a non-ergative SVO language, we can say that in the default case the Agent precedes the Theme (Patient), i.e. Ag > Th. Many details remain to be worked out with regard to thematic roles, but they do not seem to involve any potentially major problems.

Another seemingly impressive point of Baker's analysis is the explanation, with regard to SOV languages, of the order of the Serial Verb Construction Here the sequence of the verb phrases is determined by the order in which the actions take place. The knife must be in the hand before the bread can be cut, and this will be reflected in the word order.

But of more interest is the Ijo example quoted by Baker:

(36)	dúma	tun-nì	a-píṛi	(Ijo)
	song	sing-Ø	her-give	
	sing a song for her			

Ijo is a head-final serializing language described in Williamson (1965). Here Tai's explanation is not exactly rejected by Baker, who seems to object because it is possible to construct a semantic analysis in which the actions would not be temporally sequenced: "One might say that the singing causes 'her' to be pleased, but one could just as well say that the will to please 'her' causes the subject to sing." I think that Baker is grasping at straws here. The fact that the VP's appear in the order that they do makes perfect sense, and Tai's word-order independent principle of temporal ordering can, indeed, account for these cases. Baker, of course, provides a GB internal explanation involving θ-role assignment, but as we have seen, his θ-role assignment explanation fails to account for some relevant data (cf. 5e above.)

Tai's approach is justified by the following example from the Barai example cited in (20d), repeated here as (37), where the I do not see how Baker's approach will work, unless perhaps he incorporates V̄1 into the main verb ufu. An autolexical description is provided.

(37)	fu	burede	ije	sime	abe	ufu	(Barai)
	3sg	bread	def	knife	take	cut	
	He cut the bread with a knife.						

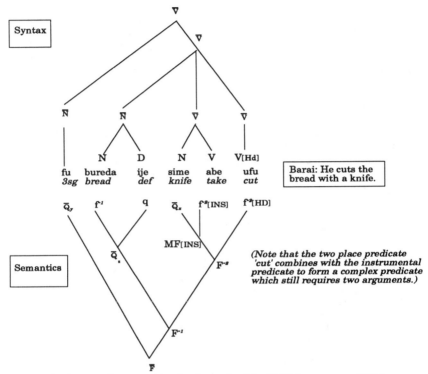

Syntax

fu	bureda	ije	sime	abe	ufu
3sg	bread	def	knife	take	cut

Barai: He cuts the
bread with a knife.

Semantics

MF[INS]

(Note that the two place predicate
'cut' combines with the instrumental
predicate to form a complex predicate
which still requires two arguments.)

An interesting question is also raised by VSO languages. (38) is an example from Ravüa, the Wa language presented in Drage (1907) and discussed in (Schiller 1985a).

(38)   ti   me   ho   taw   lik   me   pin   ke-en
       take you   go   send letter you accompany to here
       Go, take the letter, and come back.

Notice the strict temporal ordering (not reflected by Drage's translation) of the verb phrases. The direct object of the initial verb is found in the subordinate clause.

There is insufficient space to discuss this or the preceding tree in detail. For the Wa example, the crucial observations are these. The Syntax must represent the entire string as a single entity, in order to conform to the rule that all sentences must be verb initial, though subordinate and coordinate structures may involve SVO order in the second and subsequent clauses. Semantically, there are two sets of propositions, one of which contains subpropositions. There is a coordinate structure involving the predicate structures 'take the letter' and 'go send the letter', the latter involving a subordinate relationship between 'go' and 'send the letter'. Both semantically and syntactically the structures are well-formed, with the NP 'you' joined to a recursive VP structure in the syntax. The external semantic argument 'you' combining with the three separate predicates phrases, while the argument letter acts as the internal argument for both 'take' and 'send'. There is no need to conjoin the semantic structures though one might want to do so in some discourse module. Though the semantic representation seems complex, involving line crossings, this is not in fact the case when one keeps firmly in mind the fact that the semantic component includes no linear precedence relations.

We have considered two objections to the recursive ∇ account of Subordinating Serial Verb Constructions. Sebba's objections only apply to theories in which syntax and semantics are isomorphic, a restriction which does not apply in Autolexical Syntax. Baker's analysis is motivated by a need to conform to GB's projection principle and θ-criterion, matters which are theory internal. Within the Autolexical framework all of the data can be accounted for without difficulty, and without any stipulations. The analysis presented here makes use of two devices ([hd] and semantic case) which are already in use for the explanation of other phenomena.

Endnotes

*A number of people deserve mention for their contributions to this paper. Alexander Caskey, Jerry Sadock, Jan-Terje Faarlund, James Yoon, Bill Eilfort, Zixin Jiang, Li Ligang, Elisa Steinberg and Jeff Lear have all critiqued or commented on the material covered here. I have sometimes adopted their suggestions, and sometimes not, so all of them are to be absolved of any responsibility for errors of omission or commission. Prof. Caskey was especially helpful in bringing to my attention important literature regarding Creole and African languages. Francis Byrne provided much food for thought during his brief 1989 visit to the University of Chicago. I regret that time did not permit me to include more on the fascinating Saramaccan language. Jean Longmire checked some of the Khmer data with the Cambodian population in Stockton CA, for which I am most grateful.

[1] It is by no means clear who was the first to articulate the ideas expressed in works by Filbeck and Schachter. It is indeed regrettable that there has been such a small amount of information exchanged between Africanists and Creolists, on the one hand, Southeast Asianists on another hand, and Oceanic scholars on yet a third hand.

[2] If one views conjunctions as a subclass of a syntactic category of preposition, one might even be able to generalize this to a restriction on P.

[3] This major gap in the data afflicts a number of writers on the subject.

[4] Sources of the examples are as follows (unless otherwise indicated): Thai: Filbeck (1975); Khmer: all checked with informants, some examples taken from Huffman (1970), Huffman & Proum (ms.) and Ehrman (various); Sranan: Sebba (1987); Yoruba: various, including: Ekundayo and Akinnaso (1983) as cited in Baker (1989) and Sebba (1987); Paamese and Barai from Crowley (1987); Saramaccan from Byrne (1987).

[5] For many of the languages under consideration I take S as a projection of V, i.e. ∇, but this is not particularly relevant to our discussion.

[6] One might expect to find a language in which none of the strategies are available. Jerry Sadock (pc) suggests that this is a case with the Papuan language Kalam described in Pawley 1980.

[7] The semantic [hd] feature also proves useful in sorting out some facts concerning negation. In at least some languages the negative marker is always attached to the verb which bears this feature (see Matisoff 1973:267 for relevant data and discussion), as one might expect from Filbeck's analysis which has one verb only acting propositionally. The most obvious application of this analysis is for what has gone under the name of 'Negative Raising' or 'Negative Transportation'.

References

Baker, Mark. 1988. Incorporation: A Theory of Grammatical Function Changing. Chicago: University of Chicago Press.
Baker, Mark C. 1989. Object Sharing and Projection in Serial Verb Constructions. LI to appear
Bickerton, Derek. to appear. Seselwa Serialization and its Significance. JPCL
Byrne, Francis. 1987. Grammatical relations in a radical creole: Verb complementation in Saramaccan. Amsterdam: John Benjamins.
Crowley, Terry. 1987. Serial Verbs in Paamese. St. in Lang. 11 (1) : 35-84.
Drage, Godfrey. 1907. A Few Notes on Wa. Rangoon: Superintendent's Office.
Ekundayo, S.A., and F.N. Akinnaso. 1983. Yoruba Serial Verb String Commutability Constraints. Lingua 60 : 115-133.
Faarlund, Jan Terje. 1989. Autostructural Analysis of Semantic Roles: Causative Constructions. Paper presented at the Workshop on Autolexical Syntax, University of Chicago. 4/26/89.
Filbeck, David. 1975. A Grammar of Verb Serialization in Thai. In Studies in Thai linguistics in honor of William J. Gedney. Edited by J. G. Harris and J. R. Chamberlain. 112-29. Bangkok: Central Institute of English Language.
Holm, John. 1988. Pidgins and Creoles. Edited by B. C. e. al. Cambridge Language Surveys. Cambridge: Cambridge University Press.
McCawley, James D. 1988. The Syntactic Phenomena of English. Chicago: University of Chicago Press.
Mikami, N. 1979. Serial Verb Construction in Vietnamese and Cambodian. 79: 95-117.
Nylander, Dudley. 1986. Short Note. JPCL 1 (1) : 153-58.
Pawley, Andrew. 1980. On Meeting A Language That Defies Description by Ordinary Means. Paper presented at the Kivung Congress of the Linguistic Society of Papua New Guinea. Subsequently published (ref. unavailable.)
Sadock, Jerrold M. 1985. Autolexical Syntax: A Proposal for the Treatment of Noun Incorporation and Similar Phenomena. NLLT 3 : 379-439.
Sadock, Jerrold M. to appear. Autolexical Syntax.
Schachter, Paul. 1974. A Non-Transformational Account of Serial Verbs. SAL 1 : 60-99.
Schiller, Eric. 1985a. An (initially) surprising Wa language and Mon-Khmer word order. CWIPL 1 : 104-119.
Schiller, Eric. 1985b. Aspects of Khmer. University of Chicago ms.
Schiller, Eric. 1988. The Parametrics of INFL. to appear in ESCOL 5
Schiller, Eric. to appear. The Case for Autolexical Case. Paper presented at the Workshop on Autolexical Syntax, University of Chicago. 4/26/89.
Sebba, Mark. 1987. The Syntax of Serial Verbs. Edited by P. Muysken. Creole Language Library. Amsterdam: Benjamins.
Tai, James H.-Y. 1985. Temporal sequence and Chinese word order. In Iconicity in Syntax. Edited by J. Haiman. 49-72. Amsterdam: Benjamins.
Travis, L. 1984. Parameters and Effects of Word Order Variation. Ph.D. dissertation, M.I.T.
Williamson, K. 1965. A Grammar of the Kolokuma Dialect of Ijo. Cambridge: Cambridge University Press.

The Absence of ṼC[+voi] Sequences in Hindi: The Interaction of Global Constraints and Rule Application

Veneeta Srivastav
Cornell University

Introduction: In this paper I will present evidence from Hindi to argue for the possibility of negative constraints on rule application. The phenomenon I will be considering has to do with permissible sequences in the language, involving nasal vowels and following obstruents. In particular, if a nasal vowel is followed by a voiced stop a nasal always intervenes but it may or may not be present when the vowel is followed by a voiceless stop. Thus there are no forms like 1(b) in Hindi:[1]

(1)   a. čãndi   *b čãdi   c. šãnti   d. sãp
         silver   silver   peace   snake
         ṼNC[+voi] ṼC[+voi] ṼNC[-voi] ṼC[-voi]

In Kelkar (1968) this is recognised as a significant problem but is not dealt with in detail. In Ohala (1983) the absence of 1(b) is explained by positing a sequential constraint against ṼC[+voi] in Hindi. This paper draws heavily upon Ohala (1983) for the data but differs in the analysis. It argues that the absence of 1(b) is due to a rule which spreads nasality from a vowel to a following stop, resulting in the creation of prenasalized stops. There are no forms like 1(b) since the application of this rule results in forms like 1(a). It further proposes that there is a global constraint in Hindi against [-voice, +nasal] segments which blocks the application of the rule to 1(d). If the rule were to apply to forms like 1(d) voiceless prenasalized stops would be created, in violation of this constraint.

While both approaches account for the facts in (1), they make different claims about the phonological representation of the nasal-consonant sequences in 1(a) and (c). While Ohala's sequential constraint does not distinguish between the two, in the approach being pursued here the NC sequence in 1(a) is a prenasalized stop while the sequence in 1(c) is a cluster. I will show that such a distinction needs to be made in order to account for the full range of facts.

The paper is organized as follows. In section 1 I discuss some facts relevant to the issue of nasalization in Hindi. In section 2 I analyse the absence of ṼC[+voi] sequences, arguing for an approach based on negative constraints. I focus primarily on long vowels, showing only that short vowels do not require any modification of the analysis proposed. In section 3 I compare it to Ohala's approach, noting the points at which the two diverge. An analysis based on negative constraints is shown to be preferable on empirical as well as theoretical grounds to one based on sequential constraints. In section 4 I take up the issue of learnability, suggesting that negative constraints, if global, do not pose a problem for acquisition.

Section 1: There have been many studies of nasals and nasalization in Hindi and there is considerable disagreement with regard to the analysis and the data. I will therefore go over some of the basic facts and justify the assumptions I am making in this paper.

Nasality is disinctive in the vowel system of the language, as can be seen in (2). There are minimal pairs which are distinguished only by the nasality on the vowels:

(2) a. bas "smell" bãs "bamboo"
    b. sas "mother-in-law" sãs "breath"

Since nasal vowels are marked with respect to oral vowels it is pertinent to ask whether nasal vowels should be recognised as part of the phonemic inventory of the language, or whether they are phonologically or phonetically conditioned.

Historically, nasal vowels derived from underlying sequences of vowels followed by nasal consonants (See Misra 1967, Kelkar 1968 and Ohala 1983 for discussion). As Old Hindi developed from Modern Indo Aryan (MIA), nasal vowels came into existence. Vowels became nasalized before a following nasal. When the nasal was followed by a consonant it was deleted and the preceding vowel lengthened. This can be represented as in (3) and illustrated with examples such as (4):

(3) V N C --> V[+long, +nasal] C
(4) <u>MIA</u>   <u>Old Hindi</u>
     čəndə   čãd   "moon"

The question to be answered, however, is whether nasal vowels can be similarly derived in a synchronic grammar of Hindi. Narang and Becker (1971), among others, argue that nasal vowels need not be recognised at the level of underlying representation. They propose a rule very similar to (3) above, in which the vowel assimilates nasality from a following nasal and the nasal is subsequently deleted. A rule such as (5) would yield the the following derivations for the forms in (2):

(5) V N C --> V[+nasal] C
(6) <u>UR</u>   <u>Nasalization</u>   <u>SR</u>
     /bas/   --   [bas]   "smell"
     /bans/   /bãs/   [bãs]   "bamboo"
     /sas/   --   [sas]   "mother-in-law"
     /sans/   /sãs/   [sãs]   "breath"

While the analysis seems to work in cases like (2), it has come in for heavy criticism (Bhatia and Kenstowicz 1972 and Ohala 1983). Consider, for example, the forms in (7):

(7). a. bã̄ "bellowing of a cow" bã̄n "arrow"
     b. jũ̄ "louse"   jũ̄n "season"

Under the Narang and Becker analysis the two members of the pair would be identical at UR -- that is, /ban/ and /jun/.[2] There is then no way of predicting which nasal should be deleted and which one retained. Alternatively, the forms in (7) can be easily derived by positing underlyingly nasal vowels in the first members of the pairs: /bã̄/ and /jũ̄/. The second members of the pairs would have the consonant in their base forms: /ban/ and /jun/. The vowels may be underlyingly nasal or phonetically nasalized.

To sum up this part of the argument I agree with Bhatia and Kenstowicz and Ohala that nasal vowels in Hindi are not phonologically conditioned and must be recognised at UR. I am also assuming that vowels may be underlyingly nasal or they may be nasalized in the environment of a nasal. It may even be possible to distinguish between the two types of nasality. Ohala claims that there are minimal pairs in which vowels differ in the quality of nasality:

(8) a. /mas/ [mãs] "month"   /mãs/ [mãs] "meat"
    b. /mɛ/ [mɛ̃] "wine"   /mɛ/ [mɛ̃] "I"

Nasographic data shows that the degree of nasality is the same at the beginning of the vowel in both members but tapers off towards the end in the case of "month" and "wine" (p.104). In ordinary speech, however, it is difficult to distinguish between the two. I note this here merely to point out that what may appear on the surface as a nasal vowel may be an oral vowel at UR if it occurs in the environment of a nasal. Sometimes, the analysis may remain underdetermined as in the case of [bã̄n] and [jũ̄n] in (7) above. In the rest of the paper the choice between the two will be made without the support of experimental data.

Based on the discussion so far, I give a chart of the vowel system of Hindi, for reference:

	Front	Central	Back	
High	i ĩ		ũ u	Long
	ɪ ɪ̃		ʊ̃ ʊ	Short
Mid	e ẽ		õ o	Long
	ɛ ɛ̃	ə ə̃	ɔ̃ ɔ	Short
Low		a ã		Long

TABLE 1: THE VOWELS OF HINDI

Section 2: In this section I will address the problem posed by the paradigm in (1) which can be fleshed out with the following examples:

(1) a. čãndi "silver"   c. šãnti "peace"   d. sãp "snake"
        tãmba "copper"   prãnt "province"   pũčh "tail"
        pũñji "wealth"   dãnt "suppressed"   bãṭ "divide"
        bhãñja "brandished"   khəzãñči "treasurer"   ghũṭ "gulp"
        ḍhoŋgi "hypocrite"   jãč "investigate"

I am assuming the following stages of development for Hindi, based on Misra (1967), Kelkar (1968) and Ohala (1983):

(9)   MIA   Old Hindi   Modern Hindi
      VNC   ṼC   (a) ṼNC[+voi]
                           (c) Ṽ̇NC[-voi]
                           (d) Ṽ̃C[-voi]

(1) and (9) raise two interesting questions:
(i) Why are there no ṼC[+voi] sequences corresponding to ṼC[-voi] in Modern Hindi ?
(ii) What is the phonological representation of the NC sequences in Modern Hindi ?
    In answer to the first question I propose that in the development from Old Hindi to Modern Hindi, a rule of Nasal Spread (NS) entered the language. This rule may be represented as (10):

(10)   Nasal Spread   (NS)   V   X

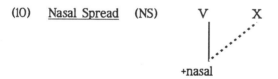

                                       +nasal

The effect of NS is to spread nasality from vowels on to following segments. When the following segment is a stop, a prenasalized stop is created, thereby converting ṼC (1b) to ṼNC (1a).[3] It can be shown that this rule is operative in the language today. In 11(b) we see it working across morpheme boundaries:

(11) a. /ho + ge/   [hoge]   "you (familiar) will be"
       b. /hõ + ge/   [hõnge]   "you (formal) will be"
       c. /jũ + ke/   [jũke]   "louse's"

(11) also shows that the rule is sensitive to the feature voicing on the target. The future tense suffix -ge triggers its application (11b). In contrast, the genitive suffix -ke does not (11c).

It is worth considering how this should be incorporated into the rule. One simple solution would be to write [+voice] into the structural description of the rule:

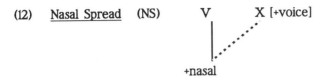

(12)   Nasal Spread   (NS)   V   X [+voice]

                                    |
                                    |
                                +nasal

Notice, however, that (10) could as easily be modified to incorporate [-voi] instead of [+voi]. In current theoretical work the attempt is to eliminate specification in the writing of rules and to derive the effect through general principles of grammar. It would therefore be desirable if the effect of (12) could be obtained without specifying the value for voicing on the target. This can be done if the rule is kept general, as in (10), but is blocked from applying if the target is voiceless.

Let us assume that Hindi has a negative constraint against [-voice, +nasal] segments that is operative at all levels of the grammar:

(13) Global Constraint: * [-voice,+nasal]

The application of (10) will interact with (13) and will be blocked just in case the following stop is voiceless. Let us consider the effect of (10) on the forms in 11(b) and (c):

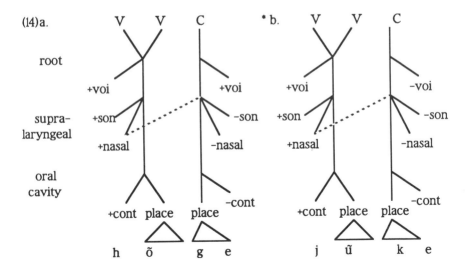

I am assuming here the feature geometry argued for in Clements (1987) and the representation of prenasalized stops given in Sagey (1986).[4] The two representations are identical except for the feature voicing on the target. Yet 14(a) is well formed while 14(b) is not. In 14(a) NS creates a voiced prenasalized stop; in 14(b) it creates a voiceless prenasalized stop, in violation of (13). It is therefore prevented from applying in this environment. (10) in conjunction with (13), we see, achieves the same effect as (12).

This approach, I believe, is to be preferred on theoretical grounds to an approach which uses a rule like (12) to acount for the data. Let us consider a hypothetical situation in which the following pattern holds in Hindi: $\tilde{V}$NC[+voi], $\tilde{V}$C[+voi], $\tilde{V}$NC[-voi] and * $\tilde{V}$C[-voi]. There is nothing to prevent us from writing a rule like (12), say (12'), except that it specified the value [-voi] on the target to explain this data. The only motivation for the modification in (12) or (12'), then, is the data under consideration. An approach that uses negative constraints, on the other hand, is limited in its power. For example, it cannot be used to explain the situation described above since it is not possible to propose a constraint against [+voice, +nasal] , given that Hindi nasal consonants and vowels are voiced. In this sense, the two approaches are not equivalent though they provide the same empirical coverage for (1). (12) is a descriptive statement of the facts, and could have been modified to describe an opposite set of facts; (10) + (13) has explanatory force, (13) being independently verifiable.

The account developed above correctly predicts that in the development from Old Hindi to Modern Hindi $\tilde{V}$C sequences were converted to $\tilde{V}$NC in the case of voiced consonants (1a), but remained $\tilde{V}$C in the case of voiceless consonants (1d). This, however, does not explain the presence of sequences like $\tilde{V}$NC[-voi] (1c). Forms like (1c) have sometimes been considered exceptional (Narang and Becker 1971, for example) but as pointed out by Bhatia and Kenstowicz (1972) such forms constitute a sizable though limited set. There is, however, a simple historical explanation for their apparent deviation. All the items that belong in this set constitute late borrowings into the language (Ohala 1983, p.87). As such, they never underwent the historical process of being converted from VNC to $\tilde{V}$C. Under my analysis the nasals in 1(c) are not the result of NS at all but are present in the base forms. There is no violation of the negative constraint since there is no single segment that is [-voice, +nasal]. These forms contain a nasal-stop cluster. The nasalization on the vowel may very well be phonetically conditioned.

The explanation I have outlined for the absence of $\tilde{V}$C[+voi] thus yields an answer to the question of the phonological representation of NC sequences in Hindi. While $\tilde{V}$NC[+voi] have the representation in 15(a), $\tilde{V}$NC[-voi] must necessarily be like 15(b):[5]

(15)a.

Given this analysis we would expect prenasalized stops (15a) to behave differently from clusters (15b). And indeed they do. Consider that Hindi has NC sequences with non-homorganic nasals. These can only be analysed as clusters. In certain speech styles these clusters may be broken up by an epenthetic vowel as shown in (16):

(16) a. /kimti/   [kĩmə̃ti]   "expensive"
     b. /janki/   [jãnə̃ki]   "proper noun"
     c. /umda/   [ũmə̃da]   "good"

While epenthesis is generally harder with homorganic nasal-stop clusters, it is possible to find near minimal pairs like /šanti/ and /čadi/ which behave differently in this respect. Native speakers accept [šãnə̃ti] but not [čãnə̃di]. This is to be expected if the first has a cluster and the second contains a prenasalized stop.

My analysis of Hindi has so far concentrated on sequential patterns involving long vowels. In Table 1, however, short vowels are also claimed to display an oral/nasal constrast. I will consider next how my analysis extends to sequences involving short vowels. We will see that they do not require any weakening of the analysis.

The status of short nasal vowels in Hindi is controversial. Misra (1967) claims that in Old Hindi there were no short nasal vowels (p.203). This is perhaps due to the fact that vowel nasalization was historically accompanied by vowel lengthening, as seen in (3). It is also accepted that in Modern Hindi short nasal vowels are far fewer than long ones. However, Ohala (1983) points out cases of so-called "spontaneous nasalization", usually in the environment of a voiceless fricative (p.78). Other instances of short nasal vowels involve forms which are lexically derived from forms with long vowels. For these reasons, short nasal vowels have to be accepted in the language. In (17) we have some examples:

(17) a. pahũč   "reach"
     b. hãsi   "laughter"
     c. sĩčai   "irrigation"   from sĩčna   "to irrigate"
     d. ũčai   "height"   from ũča   "high"

In connection with short nasal vowels Ohala notes that a nasal tends to intervene between such vowels and a following stop, regardless of voicing. If this were indeed the case, it would pose a problem for my analysis. Following Misra, and others, however, I take most short ṼNC sequences to have oral vowels at UR. The voicing on the consonant is not relevant since they are clusters. What needs to be considered are those short vowels that are underlyingly nasal. As Ohala herself notes, the tendency for nasals to intervene between short nasal vowels and stops is not invariant. Some of the relevant examples are given in (17). There are no instances of NC sequences here. In 17(a), (c), and (d) the following stops are voiceless and the surface forms behave as expected with respect to prenasalization. Jim Gair points out that parallel to 17(c)-(d) would be forms derived from long vowels followed by voiced stops. These should always have a nasal consonant as shown in (18):

(18) a. mə̃ñjna "to be cleansed" from mãñjna "to cleanse"
     b. bə̃ndhna "to be tied" from bãndhna "to tie"

I believe that these NC sequences are prenasalized stops but I leave it for further research to determine which short ṼNC[+voi] have prenasalized stops and which have clusters.

The forms in (17) often have a familiar variant with an oral vowel as shown in (19):

(19) a. hə̃si   həsi
     b. sĩčai   sɪčai
     c. ũčai   učai

While this does not directly bear upon my analysis some explanation is needed. Let us assume that short nasal vowels are marked in Hindi. If we posit a rule that optionally delinks a [+nasal] linked to only one slot on the timing tier, the variation in (19) can be explained as a kind of regularization process. Ohala, too, allows for this regularization. Given that she considers ṼNC the norm for short vowels, it is not clear why regularization would not involve converting (17) to ṼNC rather than VC. Her regularization process for short vowel sequences involves denasalization while the regularization process for long vowels involves insertion. This seems to me an unsatisfactory aspect of the account.

Before comparing my analysis to the one in Ohala (1983) a few points need to be clarified. The first has to do with the representation of prenasalized stops though the issue is controversial and beyond the scope of this paper. I have adopted in (14) the feature representation argued for in Clements (1987). The representation for the prenasalized stop, however, follows Sagey (1986) in that the contour segment created by NS branches at the terminal node. The nasal part of the consonant depends for all its features on the host segment, except for [+sonorant]. Clements (1987) comments that [sonorant] is relatively inert and changes its value largely as an effect of other feature changes. Since any representation of prenasalized stop has to account for this feature, I do not consider this a problem specific to my analysis.

I will use the representation in (14) without argumentation to discuss the effect of NS on to segments that are not stops. We have seen in (2) that nasal vowels do not trigger prenasalization before fricatives: [sãs] and [bãs]. These are voiceless so the negative constraint may be invoked to rule it out. I do not have examples to show whether NS applies before voiced fricatives.[6] In the case of nasals, the effect of NS cannot be detected, but prenasalization does not occur before liquids and glides. Since these segments are voiced the negative constraint cannot be invoked here. Ohala points out that [l] and [l̃] are phonetically distinct in Hindi (p.c.). While this may be so, the contrast is non-distinctive. This suggests that even though [+nasal] may spread, in such cases, it cannot be realised as a stop. This may have to do with the oral cavity features of the host segment.

The account I have outlined above uses fully specified segments but most current theories assume some degree of underspecification (Archangeli and Pulleyblank 1986 and Steriade 1987). It is not possible for me to argue for any version of underspecification here. I will merely mention some possiblities based on the analysis developed above.

The two features that play a critical role in the analysis are [voice] and [nasal]. Given that all sonorants are voiced, and voiceless obstruents are generally considered unmarked, the only segments specified for the feature would be voiced obstruents. Presumably, redundancy rules would fill in the value [-] for unspecified obstruents and [+] for sonorants. In order for the negative constraint to take effect [-voi] has to be filled in before the application of (10), explaining the absence of a nasal consonant in 1(d). Another possibility is that (10) applies but the output is filtered out at the point where [-voi] is filled in.

In the case of [nasal], all obstruents are [-nasal] and the unmarked value for sonorants is [-nasal]. Thus only nasal consonants and vowels are expected to carry the specification [+nasal] at UR. For (10) to create a contour segment in (14a) it would seem that [-nasal] must be present on the target. Another possibility would be to fill in the value later, on the basis of the redundancy rule: [-sonorant] --> [-nasal]. I will not pursue these issues any further in this paper though they are obviously important.

To sum up this section, I propose that there are no instances of ṼC[+voi] because nasality spreads rightwards creating prenasalized stops. There are instances of ṼC[-voi] since the creation of prenasalized stops is blocked by the proposed negative constraint. All sequences of ṼNC[-voi] are necessarily clusters; ṼNC[+voi] may be clusters or prenasalized stops. Short vowel sequences provide no evidence against this account of the facts in (1).

Section 3: Since Ohala (1983) focuses on the specific paradigm in (1), it is appropriate that my proposal be evaluated against hers.

In her account the absence of ṼC[+voi] (1b) is explained by a sequential constraint like (20):

(20) * ṼC[+voi]

As far as the problem under discussion is concerned the two analyses seem to be equivalent. I believe, however, that they make different theoretical claims. I would therefore like to interpret the constraint in (20) with a view to isolating those points on which the two analyses diverge.

In analysing ṼNC[+voi] sequences given in 1(a) Ohala tentatively proposes that the vowels may be underlyingly oral (p.103). This is plausible for later borrowings into the language. In that case, however, the inventory of ṼNC[+voi] would be equivalent to the inventory of ṼNC[-voi]. This is clearly not so, since these sequences involve many items such as [čãnd] which is a <u>tadbhava</u> form deriving from Old Hindi. I therefore take it that they have nasal vowels in their base forms.

Ohala suggests that this sequential constraint could be an "anywhere" constraint and therefore equivalent to a global rule. Thus the operation of (20) across morpheme boundaries, as in example 11(b), would be expected. Consider, however, the mode in which the constraint takes effect. When there is the possibility of an impermissible sequence, a nasal is inserted. A sort of clean-up rule inserting nasals has to be posited for Hindi. It does not seem that this clean-up operation can be effected purely in the phonetics, as suggested by Ohala (p.c.). Consider example (21):

(21) a. nãd   * nãnd   "trough"
      b. jə̃mãdar   * jə̃mãndar "janitor"
      c. pãĩbag   * pãĩmbag   "garden"

At the phonetic level the examples in (21) have nasalized vowels but there is no nasal consonant before the following voiced stop. As such, these are potential counterexamples to (20), if it is interpreted as an anywhere constraint. I take (21) to argue instead for a phonological rule of nasal insertion (such as I have given under 10 in section 2) distinct from a phonetic rule of nasalization. This rule applies prior to the phonetic level so that the nasals are already present in the. representation at the point where phonology feeds into phonetics. [pãĩbag] is not an exception if we take only the first vowel to be underlyingly nasal. Similarly, [nãd] and [jə̃mãdar] contain oral vowels at UR and are not expected to trigger nasal insertion.

There are other reasons for distinguishing the rule inserting nasals from a phonetic rule of nasalization. In (22) we see that vowels to the left and right of a nasal can be nasalized. In contrast, nasal insertion is only to the right:

(22) a. kãn "ear" b. nãk "nose"

In (23) we see that nasalization operates across glides but as shown by 21(c) nasal insertion is purely local:

(23) a. /jhãwa/   [jhãw̃ã]   "pumice"
     b. /kũwər/   [kũw̃ər]   "prince"

These facts are not a priori incompatible with an analysis using sequential constraints but they do require a phonological rule of nasal insertion. Such a rule is not explicitly given by Ohala.

A significant point of difference between Ohala's approach and mine, then, is the phonological status of the nasal in VNC sequences in Hindi. In her account there is no formal rule introducing the nasal before voiced consonants. By implication there is no distinction between the nasal in 1(a) and 1(c). In my analysis 1(a) contains a prenasalized stop while 1(c) contains a cluster. It was shown in section 2 that the two behave differently with respect to epenthesis (16). The epenthesis facts are left unexplained in Ohala's account.

A consequence of my analysis, however, is that the NC[+voi] sequence in 1(a) occupies only a single slot on the timing tier (15a) and it is expected that this would have a phonetic reflex. The spectogram in Ohala (1983, p.95) shows a full nasal consonant and seems to contradict this. However, there is some support for my position in the literature. Kelkar(1968) notes "all voiced stops are prenasalized after Ṽ . . . that is, they have a short nasal consonant as an on-glide" (p.24). Narang and Becker(1971) say that a "homorganic nasal consonant of very short duration before voiced stops" is inserted (p.665) -- emphases mine. Dasgupta (1983) in a review of Ohala (1983) comments on the significance of the durational status of the nasal in these sequences, noting that more instrumental data are required to settle the issue.

While Ohala's spectorgram does show a nasal consonant, in order to determine its durational status, I believe, it is important to compare not only the nasal in forms like [čãndi] and [šãnti], but minimal pairs like the following:

(24) a. /bhãja/   [bhãñja]   "brandished" /bhanja/   [bhãnja]   "nephew"
     b. /pũji/   [pũñji]   "wealth"   /pun + ji/ [pũnji]   "name (hon)"

I have included the underlying forms for clarity. In 24(a), the orthography suggests that /bhanja/ entered the language later while /bhãja/ is a tadbhava form. In (24b) the second member derives from /pun + ji/ while the first is a regular tadbhava form. Under the present analysis the first members have prenasalized stops, the second have clusters. In a preliminary experiment I conducted, spectograms showed the nasal in the first member to be durationally shorter than in the second.[7] The recording was then played to a native speaker who was asked to choose the appropriate meanings for the tokens he heard. He was allowed to choose more than one meaning per token but he consistently chose the meanings "brandished" and "wealth" when given the token with the shorter nasal and "nephew" and "name" when given the one with the longer nasal. While this sample is too small to make definitive claims, it does show that there may be a distinction in length between prenasalized stops and clusters to which native speakers are sensitive. The instrumental data provided in Ohala therefore do not settle the issue of length.

The present analysis, we see, makes predictions and raises questions that are left unaddressed in Ohala's account. It therefore provides an alternative account of the data. I have claimed that there are empirical and theoretical considerations that favor it.

Section 4: Finally, I would like to speculate on how the negative constraint in (13) would be acquired by the child learning Hindi. A basic consideration in evaluating the learnability of a proposed analysis is the kind of evidence required by the acquisition process. Negative evidence is generally considered harder to obtain while positive evidence is always available.

It seems reasonable to think that the absence of a marked phenomenon would be assumed in the process of language acquisition, unless there was evidence to the contrary. Voiceless nasals are generally considered marked in the world's languages so that a constraint against them may be acquired as part of the redundancy rules of a language. A child would not need negative evidence in order to find out that her language did not contain voiceless nasals. On the other hand, if she had evidence of the existence of voiceless nasals, she would infer that the constraint did not hold in her language. If there were a rule like NS in that language which created prenasalized stops, it would be predicted to apply to voiced as well as voiceless stops.

The negative constraint in (13) has been construed as a global constraint, holding at all levels in the grammar of Hindi. It functions like a well-formedness condition that filters out derivations violating it at any level. It is also possible, however, to conceive of a negative constraint that may hold at some levels and not at others. Consider a language in which a constraint like (13) holds at UR, but voiceless nasals appear at SR due to the operation of phonological rules. I believe it would be harder for children to acquire this constraint since surface voiceless nasals would provide some evidence against the existence of such a constraint. The use of this constraint in linguistic analysis may be problematic from the point of view of learnability. On the other hand, a global constraint, such as the one proposed for Hindi, does not present this problem.

I would therefore conclude that global constraints may exist in languages, blocking rule application and that such constraints are compatible with what we know of the acquisition process. The pattern of possible sequences in Hindi that I have analysed, that is the pattern in (1), is one evidence of it.

Footnotes

* This paper has benefitted greatly from discussions with Nick Clements, John Kingston, Chilin Shih, Jim Gair, Susana Sainz, Kate Davis and Beverley Goodman. I would also like to thank Manjari Ohala, Manindra Verma, Curt Rice and John Goldsmith for comments on an earlier version of the paper. As always, I am indebted to Bill McClure for the formatting. All remaining errors and omissions are my own.

1. The forms in 1(a) are often transcribed without a nasal consonant (Bhatia and Kenstowicz 1972, for example). This is probably influenced by the orthography which reflects a stage in the history of the language when this was the case. In modern Hindi, however, all such forms are pronounced with a nasal, as argued by Ohala (1983).
2. There are a limited number of items in which word final nasal vowels may be said to derive from nasal consonants. They usually have a variant in which the nasal is retained [asman] vs. [asmã] and [jãn] vs. [jã]. However, this is not a productive rule and may be said to be stylistically motivated. In any case the examples in (7) are different in that [jũ] can never be realised as [jũn] and vice versa.
3. I leave aside for the moment the question of what happens when the following segment is not a stop.
4. These issues are not uncontroversial but I leave that aside for the moment.
5. As pointed out by Manindra Verma (p.c) there are later borrowings like [bãind] "band" from English which may very well have a representation similar to the later borrowings involving voiceless stops. The claim of prenasalized stops presented here is for the tadbhava forms, those that have developed from Old Hindi.
6. The status of the voiced fricative in Hindi [z] is not very clear. Speakers often change it to [j]. Prenasalization does occur before [j]. The significant difference between the two would be in the feature [continuant]. The representation in (14) suggests that prenasalization will not occur before [z] if [-continuant] is required in the host segment.
7. I thank Chilin Shih for help with the measurements.

References

Archangeli, D. and D. Pulleyblank. 1986. The content and structure of phonological representations. Univ. of Arizona and USC ms.

Bhatia, T.K. and M.J. Kenstowicz. 1972. Nasalization in Hindi: a reconsideration. Papers in Linguistics 25.206-12.

Calabrese, A. 1988. Towards a theory of phonological alphabets. Ph.D. thesis, MIT.

Clements, G.N. 1987. Phonological feature representations and the description of intrusive stops. CLS 23.

Dasgupta, P. 1983. Review of M.Ohala 1983. Indian Linguistics. 44.103-126.

Kelkar, A.R. 1968. Studies in Hindi-Urdu, I: introduction and word phonology. Building Centenary and Silver Jubilee Series, 35. Poona: Deccan College.

Misra, B.G. 1967. Historical phonology of Modern Standard Hindi: Proto-Indo-European to the present. Ph.D. thesis, Cornell University.

Narang, G.C. and D.A. Becker. 1971. Aspiration and nasalization in the generative phonology of Hindi-Urdu. Language 47.646-67.

Ohala, M. 1983. Aspects of Hindi phonology. Delhi: Motilal Banarsidass.

Sagey, E. 1986. The representation of features and relations in non-linear phonology. Ph.D. thesis, MIT.

Steriade, D. 1987. Redundant values. CLS 23 Parasession on Autosegmental and Metrical Phonology. 339-363.

ON METATHESIS IN DIACHRONY

Dieter Wanner
The Ohio State University

Metathesis designates a number of heterogeneous phenomena united by the observed transposition of two integral segments, /... a ... b .../ -> /... b ... a .../.* While the synchronic cases frequently cannot assess the ultimate validity of metathesis as a prime phonological process, the diachronic instances reveal the phenomenon's heterogeneity and derived status. The present non-linear reinterpretation of various subcases of metathesis, concentrating on the rich history of Spanish, recognizes the relevance of various contributing principles, from multiple manner speci-fication and coarticulation (e.g. palatalization, nasalization, lateralization, labiovelarization) to timing control and adjustment to canonical syllable patterns. The performance-bound domain of speech production, including speech errors, will offer some valuable insight into the characteristics of metathesis as an illusory formal property of grammars. The discussion must necessarily be more exploratory and tentative than formal and definitive given the data situation and the state of comprehension of the problems involved.

The paper is organized in the following way: Section 1 gives an overview of metathesis in its different manifestations. The following sections will provide a closer examination of metathesis between contiguous elements yielding complex segments (section 2) as opposed to those resulting in coarticulations (section 3). Section 4 discusses distance metathesis based on syl-lable structure, followed by brief conclusions (section 5).

1. An overview of metathesis

1.1 Metathesis in synchronic phonological systems requires the descriptive power of transformational rules, a status which it shares only with coalescence rules (Kenstowicz and Kisseberth 1979:370-1). While this may be too much power for the demonstrable descriptive needs (Chomsky and Halle 1968:427), other synchronic alternatives have always proved to be round-about escape routes forbidden by the logic of descriptive parsimony (Occam's razor). Metathetic data situations are well known. Examples like Central Sierra Miwok /VC/ to /CV/ metathesis (Callaghan 1986), the celebrated Kasem nominals (e.g. Chomsky and Halle 1968:358-64, Greenberg 1981, Haas 1987), or the Rotuman /-CV#/ to /-VC#/ alternations (e.g. Ultan 1978, Janda 1984, Besnier 1987) all involve non-phonological dimensions. Metathesis here is a conse-quence or overt marking of a morphological category under certain phonological conditions. In Miwok a morphosyntactically meaningful verb stem alternation is expressed by the metathesis of the stem final /-VC/ to /-CV/ (1a,b), especially before certain suffixes, extending even to relatively recent loan words (1c).

(1) a. Central Sierra Miwok
         V stem 2: [C_1 V C_2 V C_3] "past"   V stem 4: [C_1 V C_2 C_3 V] "nom., infin."
         ṭujaŋ-:e-t   "I recently jumped"   ṭujṇa   "to jump"
         hɨwat-:e-t   "I ran"   hɨwta-ʔ   "a race (nom.)"
     b. Lake Miwok
         letój-pa   "to lick (iterat.)"   létjo-pa   "to lick once"
     c. Bodega Miwok
         'tawhal-   "(to) work"   'tawhla-ṭi "to work (perfective)"
                                                            (< Sp. trabajar)

On the spur of the multi-tier analysis of Arabic (McCarthy 1981) the stem pattern regularity in Miwok (and in the other cases mentioned) corresponds to different prosodic templates to which the root nodes are attached by normal association conventions. The only essential stipulation is the independence of the vocalic from the consonantal tier, so that the no-crossing constraint can be maintained; cf. (2).[1]

(2)

1.2. Metathesis is not involved in such alternations if described in non-linear terms, and no good instances of non-morphological metathesis are known in synchrony (Ultan 1978). In diachronic perspective there are, however, countless cases of clearly documented segment inversions which are a-functional, guided by purely phonetic/phonological constraints, typically quite irregular in their distribution (Hock 1985, 1986:110), heterogeneous in their nature, and highly likely to involve liquids.[2] Metathesis as a historical process has been claimed to defy the erroneous perspective of gradualness in the implementation of change: either /a > b/ or /b > a/, but no intermediate forms (Chomsky and Halle 1968:250). Yet the salient field of Old Spanish metathesis yields evidence for the contrary view that the visible transposition of segments may be no more than the final result of a series of intermediate steps, where different phenotypes of segment or feature transpositions can be recognized. Some of the instances involving contiguous segments depend on general principles regulating complex articulations, others represent characteristic coarticulations. The remaining cases of distance metathesis are the sporadic product of timing vacillations in performance within the context of a detailed hierarchical execution plan for the syllable (the liquid metatheses in particular). As a consequence, metathesis turns out to be a phenomenon which cannot be described insightfully in its immediate appearance. Metathesis thus need not constitute a difficulty in restricting the power of the phonological rule apparatus to non-transformational format. In multi-tier representation with prosodic templates and independently needed provisions for complex and coarticulated segments, supplemented by the required articulation of syllable structure, metathesis ceases to exist as a process, a welcome result in view of the excessive predictions implied for hypothetical metathesis rules in individual languages. The historical considerations are a valuable input permitting to constrain the theoretical framework.

1.3. Three characteristic cases of pseudo-metathesis (involving the linear reordering of two contiguous and similar segments) are given in (3), while rather indisputable metatheses (interchange of segments at a distance) are illustrated in (4).[3]

(3) a. Lt. CATE:'NA:TU "chained" > OSp. *cadnado, candado, cañado* (spelled *cannado*), *calnado* . dial. *cadenado, ca(l)nadillo*, MSp. *candado* "padlock"

     b. /poner+á/ = inf. + aux. fut. > OSp. *ponerá, ponRá, porná, pondrá, poRá*, MSp. *pondrá* "s/he will put"

     c. *decid#lo* "say (pl imper)# it" > OSp. *decidlo, decildo*, MSp. *decidlo*

     d. Lt. PRI'MA:RIU > *primáyro > Sp. *priméro* "first" (cf. Leonese, Port. *priméiro*)

(4) a. OSp. *hatˢerir, façerir* (< Lt. 'FACIE FE'RI:RE "to hit one's face", cf. OLeon. *fazfirir*), *tˢaherir*, MSp. *zaherir* "to scold"

     b. Lt. CRE'PA:RE "to creak, burst" > OSp. *crebar, quebrar* (also: *crepantar, crebantar, quebrantar* "id."), MSp. *quebr(ant)ar* "to break"

     c. Lt. ANI'MALIA "animal (pl)" > OSp. *alimaña, alemaña, alimánia, alimária* (also OGal., OCat.), *animalla*, MSp. *alimaña* "beast" (alongside learned *animal* "animal"); cf. mod. dial. *almallo, armallo* "(young) bull"

The major difference between the two groups (3) and (4) is the frequent presence of some significant intermediate forms in (3), while this is absent in (4). The nature of the reordering of segments in (3a-c) is visibly phonetic within the constraints of Late Latin and Old/Modern Spanish sound systems: /dn/, /dl/, /nr/ do not form highly favored groupings either word internally or across word boundaries. Metathesis appears to be one of the options for solving the phonotactic distress. On the other hand, the rearrangement of segments in (4) lacks any visible motivation on

436

the phonetic or morphological levels; /ḥ - dᶻ/ vs. /dᶻ - ḥ/ does not have differential preference status. The alternations present themselves as mutations of the etymological form, possibly alternating with the original sequencing (e.g. *crebar*/*quebrar*). Predictably then, the phonetically motivated cases have a class-like constitution in that all such clusters, e.g. /dn/, are similarly affected, even though with the typical alternations noted in (3a); cf. more examples of the sequence /dn/ in (5) word internally and (6) across word boundaries.

(5)   a.   Lt. ANTE'NA:TU > OSp. *adnado, andado, andrado, alnado, annado, anado* (*antenado, entenado* = learned) "forebear"
        b.   Lt. LE'GITIMU "legitimate" > **lidmo* > OSp. *le'idimo, lindo* "genuine, beautiful", MSp. *lindo* "pretty, fair"
        c.   Lt. 'RETINA > **riedna* > Sp. *rienda* "reins"
        d.   Lt. *RETUNDU > OSp., dial. *redondo, rodendo, rodedno, torrendo, torredno*, MSp. *redondo* "round" (all from García de Diego 1971:178)
        e.   Lt. SERO:'TI:NU "of late appearance" > OSp., dial. *serondo, seruendo, seruando, cerondo, cerando, zarando, seroño* "late (of fruit)"
(6)   a.   OSp. *dad # nos* "give (imper. pl) + to us (clitic)" > OSp. (to 17th c.) *dadnos, dandos*, MSp. *dadnos* "id."
        b.   OSp. *hazed # nos* "do (imper. pl) + to us" > OSp. *hazednos, hazendos*, MSp. *hacednos* "id."

There are no natively developed items with a primary or secondary cluster /dn/ which would not show at least some alternations between /dn/ and /nd/, perhaps with additional /ñ/ appearing. The same situation holds for the parallel cluster /dl/, being realized as [dl], [ld] or [λ]; cf. (7) and (8).

(7)   a.   Lt. 'SPATULA > OSp. *espadla, espalda, espaλa*, MSp. *espalda* "shoulder, back"
        b.   Lt. CA'PI:TULU > OSp. *cabidlo*, (Astur. *cabidro, cabildro*) *cabildo, cabiλo*, MSp. *cabildo* "monastic chapter"
        c.   Lt. FOLI'A:TILE > OSp. *ḥožalde, hožaldre*, MSp. *hojaldre* "puff pastry"
        d.   Lt. TI:TULU > OSp. *tidle, tilde*, MSp. *tilde* "tilde, accent mark" (Port. *til*, Old Catalan *title*, Mallorca *ti* [λ]*a*, Occitan *ti* [λ]*e* "id.")
        e.   Late Lt. *rotu'lare* > Astur., Arag. *roldar*, dial. *roλar, rondar* "to roll", OSp. *arrožar*, MSp. *arrojar* "to throw away", Sp. *arroλar* "to roll up"
        f.   Lt. A'NE:THULU > Sp. *aneldo, eneldo* "dill"
        g.   Ar. *al-'qa:ḍi:* > OSp. *alcaide, alcalde, alca* [λ]*e* "(judge), mayor"
(8)   a.   OSp. *dad # lo* "give (imper pl) + it (clitic)" > OSp. (to 17th c.) *dadlo, daldo*, MSp. *dadlo* "id."
        b.   OSp. *embiad # lo* "send (pl) + him (clitic)" > OSp. (to 17th c.) *embiadlo, embialdo*, MSp. *enviadlo* "id."

      The regularity of such treatments consists in the fact that most of the forms which produce in their diachronic derivation the clusters /dl/, /dn/ participate in this multiple reflex syndrome. On the other hand, the inclusion of an item under the grouping with interchanged segment sequence as in (4) is totally unpredictable. There is no way that the phonologically comparable forms OSp. *haziere* "s/he scolds" and *hiziere* "that s/he will be making" form a phonological class on this basis; the verb *hazer* "to make, do" does not show any changed consonant sequences **zaher* as does *haziere*/*zahiere*. The cases under (4) represent a truly accidental grouping with regard to their lexical identity, phonological class constitution, and metathetic realization. These phenomena can be regarded as phonetic mutations with the accident of survival beyond a nonce formation. Consider a few additional items in (9) and the liquid display in (10a-f) for simple metathesis, and (10g-i) for reciprocal cases.

(9)   a.   Lt. INTE'STI:NU > OSp. *estentinos, estantinos, entestinos*, MSp. *intestino* "bowels" (vulg. *istentino*)

b. Lt. ME'NTASTRU > Osp. *mastranto, mestranto*, Mozarabic *mentraš(r)o, mastranzo* (= changed suffix), *mandrasto* "a type of mint"

c. North Cast. *šustar* (OSp. normally *žustar*) > Old Judeo Spanish *suštar* "go to trial"

d. Lt. SI'NA:PI > OSp. *šenaba, šebana, šeneba, šebena* "mustard"

e. Lt. PA'LU:DE > Late Lt. *padule > OSp.ˌ*padul, pa'ul* "swamp"

f. Lt. 'MU:RE 'CAECU(LU) > OSp. *murciégalo, murciélago*, MSp. *murciélago* "bat"

(10) a. Lt. PECTO'RA:LE > OSp. *petral, pretal* (dial. *peitoral*) "chest piece (of harness)"

b. Lt. INTE'GRA:RE "to repair" > Sp. *entregar* (OSp. also *entergar*) "to hand in" (cf. Leon., Port. *enteiro* < Vlg. Lt. *en'tegro* "entire")

c. Lt. PRAE'SE:PE > OSp. *presebe, pesebre*, MSp. *pesebre* "manger" (Port., Gal. *preseve, perseve*)

d. Lt. PETRI'NA:LE > Sp. *pedernal* (OSp. also *pedrenal*) "gravel"

e. Lt. 'QUAT(U)OR > Sp. *cuatro* "four"

f. Lt. FABRI'CA:RE]ᵥ, 'FABRICA]ₙ > Asturian. *forgar* "to plane", OSp. *frogar, forgar* "to build with bricks", OSp. *'fragua, 'frauga, 'fraugua, 'frauca, 'froga*, MSp. *'fragua* "smithy"

g. Lt. PARA:BOLA > OSp. *parabla, palabra*, MSp. *palabra* "word"

h. Lt. PERI:CULU > OSp. *periglo, perigro, peligro*, MSp. *peligro* "danger"

i. Sp. *flor* ≈ vulg., dial. *frol* "flower"

The two types of metatheses can be subsumed under the labels of contiguity metathesis (for the data in (3) and (5) to (8)), and of distance metathesis (for the cases in (4) and (8) to (10)). They respond to distinct triggering conditions and phonological motivation in general. The contiguous metatheses are actually superimpositions of similar segments with ensuing resequencing, possibly producing an apparent segment transposition /a > b/ -> {a,b} -> /b > a/. Distance metatheses depend on a complex hierarchically organized syllable structure, allowing corresponding slots to be filled with available segments (chiefly liquids). The two types will be taken up separately in the next sections.

2. Contiguity Metatheses

2.1. So far, these metatheses have been characterized as being phonetically or phonotactically motivated (difficult clusters, e.g. /dn/); they affect natural classes of segmental chains (all /dn/, /d+n/, /d#n/ sequences are involved to varying degrees); they show typical variability in their results, including non-identical intermediate segments of unitary (even though long) status (besides [dn] and transposed [nd] also the heavy segment [ñ]). The phonetic chains proving difficult for (Old) Spanish phonology include the combinations /dn/, /dl/, /nr/, as already illustrated in (5-6), (7-8), and (3b) respectively. To complete the data exposition, (11) brings more cases of /nr/, especially in morpheme internal position; (12) and (13) refer to the dental affricate plus stop clusters /tˢt/, /dᶻd/, while (14) shows the inverse grouping of dental fricative plus affricate /stˢ/. (15) refers to the dental affricate plus /r/ cluster /dᶻr/.

(11) a. Lt. 'GENERU > OSp. *yenro, yerno*, MSp. *yerno* "son in law"

b. Lt. (DIES) 'VENERIS > OSp. *vienres, viernes*, MSp. *viernes* "Friday" cf. Cat. *divendres* "id."

c. OSp. /venir + á/ > /venØr + á/ "inf. + aux. fut." > *venrá, verná, verrá, vendrá*, MSp. *vendrá* "s/he will come"

(12) a. Lt. ACCE'PTO:RE > OSp. *atˢtor* (azttor 941, adtor *Cid*), *atˢor*, MSp. *azor* "hawk"

b. Ar. *mu'staʕrab* "arabicized" > OSp. *mo'tˢtarabe, mo'tˢarabe*, MSp. *moθárabe* "Mozarabic (Romance speaking and/or Christian inhabitant of Muslim Spain)"

(13) a. Lt. 'PLACITU > OSp. *pladᶻdo, pladᶻo, pladᶻto*, MSp. *plaθo* "term, deadline"

b. Lt. RECI'TA:RE > OSp. *redᶻar*, MSp. *reθar* "to pray"

c. Lt. AMICI'TA:TE > OSp. *amidᶻdad, amidᶻad* "friendship"[4]

(14) a. Lt. MI'SCE:RE "to mix" > OSp. *metˢer*, MSp. *meθer* "to rock"

b. Lt. 'NASCO:, 'NASCIS > OSp. *nasco, nat^{s}es* "I am born, you are born"
b. Lt. 'PISCE > OSp. *pet^s(e)*, MSp. *peθ* "fish"
c. Lt. FLO'RE:SCIT > Osp. *floret^{s}e*, MSp. *floreθe* "it blooms"
d. Lt. 'U:STIU > OSp. *ut^{s}o* "exit, door" (cf. toponym Ujo = [uxo] for OSp. *ušo*, near Oviedo in Asturian dialect area with typical result [š] for Lt. -SKY-, -STY-)

(15)   Lt. 'ACERE > OSp. *ad^{z}re, 'ad^{z}ere, ard^{z}e*, MSp. *arθe* "maple"[5]

The consonants which come together in all of these clusters are clearly similar for what concerns their place of articulation: dento-alveolar, either as obstruent (/t^{s}t/, /d^{z}d, /st^s/) or obstruent plus sonorant clusters (/dn/, /dl/, /d^{z}r/), or as a cluster of two sonorants (/nr/). Overt metathesis is the solution to these highly marked or outright prohibited clusters only in some cases; alternatively apparent segment deletions seem to be regular for the clusters involving dental affricate plus stop, and other third solutions for the lateral and nasal groupings. To capture the class nature of the developmental range of these clusters it is necessary to abandon the narrow focus on metathesis. The characteristic aspect of the results is that they combine the articulatory and acoustic information of the component segments in these groups to produce a modified cluster or a heavy segment. This procedure leads either to complete conservation of the constituent articulatory gestures in an improved sequence (/nd/ from /dn/ by inversion of segments), or a preservation of all but one of their characteristics (/R/ from /nr/ dropping nasality, /d^z/ from /dd^z/ from /d^{z}d/ dropping length and/or non-affrication of one segment), or a language particular unitary segment (/ñ/ from /nn/ from /nd/, reinterpreting long /n/ as a palatal consonant, as is standard in diachronic Castilian evolution).[6] The common denominator is the contiguity induced phase of a type of complex segment with multiple articulations acting as a single rooted segment with internally arranged autosegmental "diphthongization" (in the sense of Andersen 1972), i.e. sequences of polar specifications for a given feature (e.g. nasality for /dn/, /nd/, continuity for /t^{s}t/, /(t)t^s/). The inherently unstable nature of these segments in a language like Spanish (which does not have canonical complex articulation) will lead to the inevitable break-up of the complexity into resegmentalized segment sequences or stable complex or coarticulated segments, thus accounting for the typical variability of the outcomes of "metathesis" between contiguous segments.

2.2. How feasible is this proposal of reinterpretation? The complex segment cannot combine just any two components, but in order for the superimposition to be possible, the two constituents should be combinable in specific and narrow ways. Complex articulations, e.g. with multiple place of articulation or manner specifications are well known, from common affricates to clicks and similar phenomena. As the treatment in Sagey (1986:ch. 1,2) shows, an adjusted model of feature geometry (from that of Clements 1985) is adequate to describe the observable data, e.g. in some African languages. According to her definition, complex segments combine different place nodes under a single x slot on the CV tier; they may consist of two or more differentiable articulatory phenomena, which are crucially unordered, since directional phonological rules have access to any of the specifications contained in a complex segment regardless of the rule's orientation. In this sense a complex segment contrasts with a contour segment: one x slot, two articulations corresponding to a bifurcation for a terminal feature [αF$_i$] / [-αF$_i$], crucially ordered, e. g. an affricate; directional rules accessing the polar specifications only from the appropriate side of the phonological chain (cf. Sagey 1986:ch. 2:58-93).

The OSp. products tentatively labelled as "complex segments" in the above might better be termed supersegments, symbolized by braces enclosing the component segments, e.g. {d,l}. Their internal complexity is not due to combinations of more than one place of articulation; rather they diverge in terms of manner of articulation in the sense of traditional contour segments. While a typical contour segment (affricate) depends on internal sequencing of the constituent phases ([-cont] > [+cont]) by stipulation, the novel supersegments function by rearranging their discrepant phases in an unmarked pattern. The sequence of, e.g., /[αcont] > [-αcont]/ depends on the inherent specification of a component articulation, e.g. an affricate; cf. the discussion of the /t^{s}t/ clusters immediately following. Alternatively, the sequencing of the crucial variant feature may depend on segment external aspects, e.g. of phonotactic nature, as in the preferred prenasalization of the supersegment {d,n}, yielding a new /nd/ cluster from original /dn/.

The feature distance between the components of /d^{z}d/, /t^{s}t/, /st^s/ and /d^{z}r/ is small. For /d^{z}d/, /t^{s}t/ and /st^s/ it is confined to the essential [contin] specification. Each one of the three phonetic events contains three components in the input form, oscillating on the continuancy specification as /[+cont] [-cont] [+cont]/ for /st^s/, and /[-cont] [+cont] [-cont]/ for /d^{z}d/ and /t^{s}t/. Their results show a clear simplification of the chronological development of continuancy, reducing them to two phases, in the unmarked single segment order of /[-cont] [+cont]/ specifying an affricate, /t^s/ and /d^z/.[7] Notice that the originally opposite ordering between continuant and affricate in the two types of obstruent clusters, /t^{s}t/, /d^{z}d/ vs. /st^s/ does not make a difference in the outcome. This suggests that a linear segmental cluster simplification approach is inadequate, since two distinct rules are needed to accomplish the task, without any visible motivation for the complexity. The rearrangement of continuancy internal to the supersegment according to more general standards appears more convincing. The question as to whether the continuancy respecification process did yield as an intermediate step a long segment for the [-cont] vs. [+cont] portion in /t^{s}t/, /d^{z}d/ vs. /st^s/ cannot be settled on external grounds due to the insufficiency of the phonetic records. The required simplification process anyway forms an integral part of Old and Modern Spanish phonology on the level of the basic lexical forms.[8]

2.3. Mechanically, the development of the clusters in question may presuppose a previous change in syllable form due to syncope, bringing in contact the two (near) incompatible segments (16a,b); alternatively, assibilation of one member of an original cluster may also produce a difficulty (16c). The phonotactic distress factor produces as a marked solution the supersegment equivalent to two x slots (or alternatively a single x slot with double segment weight) and shared feature content, with the exception of the manner specification of continuancy (17). Since for a contour segment (affricate) the internal sequencing of the differential feature specification is crucial ([-cont] before [+cont]), the automatic sequencing of a varying feature specification for the complex overall segment will be adjusted accordingly, i.e. the additional stop or fricative specification of [-cont] or [+cont] will become a simple extension of the affricate values, producing the required unmarked sequences /t^s/, /d^z/ (18). The reduction from two to one x slots depends on the generalized geminate reduction (19).

(16)   a. *acce'pto:re* (assibilation and assimilation)> *at:^{s}e't:ore* (geminate simplification) >
           at^{s}e'tore (late syncope) > *a't^{s}tore* (loss of final vowel) > *a't^{s}tor*
       b. *a . t^{s}e . 'to . re > at^s . 'to . re, at^s . 'tor*
       c. *mi'ske:re > me'sk^{y}e:re > me'st^{y}e:re > me'st^{s}ere > me'st^{s}er > met^{s}ser*

(17)
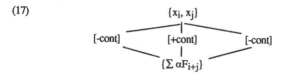

(18)   Continuancy tier:
       unmarked ordering given for contour segment: [-cont] > [+cont]
       [αcont] extending /[-cont] > [+cont]/:   [-cont] > [+cont] - [+cont]
                                      or   [-cont] - [-cont] > [+cont]
(19)   Geminate reduction:

$$\begin{array}{ccc} x & \diagdown \ \ \diagup & x \\ & \{\Sigma\,\alpha F_{i+j}\} & \end{array} \quad \Rightarrow \quad \begin{array}{c} x \\ | \\ \{\Sigma\,\alpha F_{i+j}\} \end{array}$$

The crucial step is the streamlining on the continuancy tier (18), and its essential precondition is the marked supersegment creation (17). A certain amount of justification for this exceptional treatment can be derived from the consideration that this response to phonotactic distress preserves the phonetic information present in the input structure, at the price of its sequential restructuring.

Another exceptional path is employed in those instances where the incriminated cluster does actually surface unaltered against the prevailing phonotactic constraint (e.g. in the first attestation <u>aztore</u> in a document from 941 AD, or later with another adjustment <u>adtor</u> [aδ'tor] or [ad'tor] *Cantar de Mio Cid*, but also <u>açor</u> in 13th c. *Alexandre* ; cf. Corominas and Pascual 1980.1:436).

The situation of the /dn/ and /dl/ clusters is quite similar. The crucial feature difference in the supersegment is nasality for /dn/, and laterality for /dl/. These two features occur frequently as coarticulations modifying a basic articulatory configuration, thus lending credence to the contracted state (17) mutatis mutandis. The natural sequencing of nasality (at least for Romance languages, in the context of an obstruent and across syllable boundary) is [+nas] > [-nas]. The resulting complex segment is thus a prenasalized voiced stop. Similarly, the chain of articulatory gestures requires prelateralization for {d,l} on the basis of the segmental sequence pattern tolerating /ld/ but only marginally /dl/. Supersegments of this type are predicted not to be common for languages, since they arise only as a response to phonotactic distress; thus they will also tend to decay into more stable segmental chains or unit articulations of less complexity. For OSp. this is underscored by the treatment of Arabic loans with emphatic [ḍ], which contains (acoustically?) a lateral overtone, thus coming close to a unit realization of the supersegment {d,l}. The typical Spanish result for this consonant is [ld] as in *alcalde* above (7f). The resegmentalization of {d,n} and {d,l} to /nd/ and /ld/ is an unmarked option. The complex segment may also end up in a simplified phonetic specification closer to canonical segment types of the language; this is the origin of the conversion of {d,n}, {d,l} into corresponding palatal sonorants /ñ/ and /λ/, where the obstruent has become recessive. Consider again the data adduced in (3a), (5), (6) for /dn/, and (3c), (7), (8) for /dl/.

2.4. The intermediate supersegment stage is crucial in this view. It is not there just to avoid the mechanical problem of linearizing metathesis; this is one of its consequences, but not its motivation. The treatment of the palatal sonorants is a strong indication that the holistic segment transposition is not the answer to the problem. The palatal sonorants are actually also realizations of the phonetic content preserved in the complex segment, but instead of sacrificing the unit nature of the segment, the palatal solution jetisons the obstruent's integrity, retaining of it only the heavy weight to produce the long palatal segment.[9] The third alternative is the reconstruction of the original sequence with the marked order, as manifested in the many cases with significant alternation between /nd/ and /dn/. They do not depend on a synchronically active metathesis process, rather they correspond to differential dissolutions of the highly marked situation, tentative options, of which linguistic usage will sanction one or the other, without necessarily systematic behavior.[10] The phonetically highly marked cases of /dn/, /dl/, and the affricate clusters show best group consistency in choosing the metathetic solution; but the morphosyntactically determined cases (imperative plus clitic pronoun *dad#lo -> daldo, dadlo*) all turned out to be reconstituted to the original sequence in the eventual standardization of the language (16th/17th c.). This is a functional choice, marking the intramorphemic vs. post-lexical chain characteristics as phonologically distinct.

The rather rare cluster /dᶻr/ in (15) follows a less dramatically evident pattern of rearrangement. The articulatory difficulty of the tap /r/ after the affricated sibilant is visible from inspection of the chain of events involved (especially /z/ > /r/, which would lead to the vibrant strengthening of /r/ to /R/, as in more recent examples, MSp. *lo*[zR]*íos* "the rivers"). The attempt to deal with the entire articulatory program in a holistic manner (the supersegment) cannot be successful, so resegmentalization along the continuancy tier must yield the /[-cont] [-cont] [+cont]/ pattern for /rdᶻ/. The ensuing cluster /sonorant . obstruent/ is obviously better integrated into unmarked Spanish options. No intermediate forms are known for this class, due to the small sample and the unlikely phonetic realization of the supersegment.[11]

2.5. Two further sonorant groupings show somewhat different properties due to their phonetic/articulatory content. The metathetic solution is only one option out of a larger array: for /n.r/ these include /r.n/ metathesis, /n.R/ strengthening of the vibrant articulation, /n.dr/ insertion of a transition segment (only in future/conditional forms, cf. n.11 on the chronological stratum distinction for /dᶻr/ clusters), and /R/ absorption of the nasal into the vibrant; for /l.r/ also /r.l/ metathesis, /l.R/ vibrant strengthening, /l.dr/ insertion of a transition segment (only for the most recent /lr/ clusters, i.e. future/conditional forms).[12] The parallel /λ/, absorption of the vibrant into the lateral with length-compensatory palatalization, is not recorded as an option for the instances of metathesis, but it is a characteristic solution for the postlexical cluster /r#l/ found in the combinations of infinitive plus clitic pronoun (*tomar # lo -> tomallo*, "to take it", ll = [λ], down to the 17th century).

In both clusters the second segment is dominant and will determine the outcome of the clash/superposition. An interesting link may be /R/, since it indicates that the phonetic content of the two segments is combined under complete preservation of the cluster length, and partial maintenance of their combined ingredients. The loss of nasality from {n,r} is not surprising for Castilian phonology with its absence of nasalized vowels, much less consonants with nasal coarticulation. The favored resolution of the problem cluster appears to be metathesis to /rn/, however, while the other options have a somewhat secondary, learnèd character; the same observation pertains also to /lr/ - /rl/. Even the apparently combined outcome /R/ may be the product of the independently functioning principle of vibrant onset strengthening (as for parallel /n.R/) with subsequent loss of the nasal consonant.

2.6. The remaining clusters with metathetic results constitute a disparate collection, without much documentation and only single instances, frequently based on questionable etymologies. They do not add much to the discussion (except for difficulties), and they have multiple interpretations. The cluster /ml/ is known in principle from two parallel items with distinct outcome: Lt. 'TUMULU > *'tomØlo by syncope, > *'tolmo by metathesis and documented after rhotic conversion as Sp., dial. 'tormo "glob of dirt, isolated rock", and Lt. 'CUMULU > *'comØlo > Sp. colmo "peak". The facts of the specific lexical items and of the phonetic constellation of the /ml/ cluster are such that there is no supersegment attested, and metathesis is the only recorded solution.[13]

3. Metathesis resulting in coarticulations

3.1. Another larger class of segment combinations with metathetic resolution is found in the case of contiguous consonant plus glide sequences, /Cy/ and /Cw/.[14] Here the non-metathetic nature of the development is marked by the rather clear complementarity of results. Where phonologically possible in proto-Castilian, the palatal glide ended up as a coarticulation, producing assibilated affricates from coronals (20), while it "passed through" the other consonants in apparent metathesis and subsequent metaphonic effect on the stressed vowel (21), as was the case for any of the sporadically affected labiovelar glides in morphological function, i.e. irregular perfective past formation (22a,b) and occasional metatheses around velar consonants (22c,d).

(20)   a. Lt. 'FORTIA > *"fort^{y}a > Sp. fuert^{s}a "strength, force" (no metaphony)[15]

       b. Lt. 'PALEA > *'pal^{y}a > OArag. 'paλa, OSp. 'paža, MSp. pa[x]a "straw"

(21)   a. Lt. VE:RE:'CUNDIA > *vere'go^{y}nd^{y}a > OCast. ver'goy ña, ver'gwe ña, OLeon. ver'goynd^{z}a, ver'gwend^{z}a, MSp. vergüenza "shame" [16]

       b. Lt. 'CUNEA > *'con^{y}a > *'co^{y}n^{y}a > Sp. cuña (with metaphony) "wedge"

       c. Lt. 'BASIU > *bas^{y}o > *ba^{y}s^{y}o > Sp. beso "kiss" (cf. Leon., Port. bei žu, beijo) (cf. also (3d))

(22)   a. Lt. 'SAPUI: > *'sapwi > *'sawpi > OLeon. 'soubi, OSp. 'sope, MSp. supe "I knew"

       b. Lt. 'POTUI: > *'potwi > *'powdi > OLeon. 'poudi, OSp. 'pude, MSp. pude "I was able"

       c. Lt. -IFI'CA:RE]$_V$ > -eve'gar, -ew'gar > -i'gwar (e.g. santiguar < SANCTIFI'CA:RE "to cross oneself")

       d. Lt. EXA'QUA:RE > OSp. e(n)ša'gwar, en šwa'gar, MSp. en[x]uagar "to rinse"

The labiovelar glide was never absorbed into the consonant; the segment with coarticulation passed into resegmentalization without leaving clear traces of its intermediate form (22).[17] But the palatal series shows that the coarticulated palatality could only affect some coronals: /t, d, n , l/ plus velar /k/ developing from /t^y, d^y, n^y, l^y, k^y/ to /t^s ≈ d^z, d^z, ñ, λ, t^s ≈ d^z/ respectively in Old Spanish; cf. (20), (21a,b). The labials /p, b, f, m/ and /r/ are not affected by palatality in Spanish other than that they are transparent for the feature (/s/ follows both trends in lexicalized distribution); as a consequence, it shows up in the preceding stressed syllable (21c). Castilian does not offer good evidence of the metathesis as an identifiable state of development, but neighboring dialects, especially to the West, Leonese and Galician (-Portuguese) frequently preserve such glides in the metathesized position in the stressed syllable, in addition to the palatalization effect.

3.2. A linearly conceived process of metathesis cannot explain the data found in this section, since a further pattern exists where the palatality of such an originally segmental glide has parallel effects on the preceding stressed vowel in an inverse environment, i.e. /[V, n high] y [C, -high]/ becomes /[V, [n+1 high] y [C, [+high]/ through a /y/ derived from a consonant in situ; cf. (23).

(23) a. Lt. 'FACTU: > *'fayto > *fa^{y}t^{y}o > OSp. fe čo/ he čo, MSp. hecho "done" (cf. OLeon., Port. feito without palatalization of the consonant, from *fa^{y}to)

  b. Lt. 'NOCTE > Vlg. Lt. 'nokte > *'nɔyte > *'nɔ^{y}t^{y}e > OSp. 'no če, MSp. noche "night" (cf. Arag. 'nweyte, 'nwe če, OLeon, Port. 'noyte, noite from nɔ^{y}te as in (23a))

  c. Lt. TRUCTA > Vlg. Lt. 'trokta > *'troyta > *'tro^{y}t^{y}a > OSp. 'tru ča, MSp. trucha "trout" (cf. Leon. 'truita, Port. tru(i)ta from truy^{y}ta as in (23a))

  d. Lt. 'AXE > *'ayse > *'a^{y}s^{y}e > OSp. 'e še, MSp. exe "axle" (cf. Port. ei šo also with palatalization of the consonant)

The data indicate the independence of the highness tier with regard to segmental barriers: Castilian (OSp.) spread [+high] left and right, raising a preceding stressed vowel and palatalizing a following consonant all by the one source feature of [+high] stemming from the deconsonantalization of /k/ in syllable coda position. This same strong palatalizing effect is observed in Castilian mucho ['muǒo] "much, many" from Lt. 'MULTU, Vlg. Lt. *'molto, presumably through */'mo^{y}t^{y}o/ with double action of [+high] (cf. once again Port. muito); and other such developments. Here metathesis, if at all a viable concept, concerns the inverse direction from GC -> CG, /V^{y}t/ to /V^{y}t^y/, as opposed to the direction CG -> GC (/C^y/ to /V^{y}C/) of (20) to (22). The notion of an extended prosodic domain of highness embracing consonantal as well as vocalic articulations (with language particular domain specification to account for Castilian vs. Portuguese) is more appropriate. The difference in the vocalic treatment between Castilian and its Western neighboring dialects of Leonese and (Galician-) Portuguese concerns the absorption of the high autosegment into the vowel(s) and consonant(s) within its domain, or its residual segmentalization after some metaphonic effect. The high autosegment is a dominant feature, to judge from the observable effects in (20) to (23), especially for Castilian.

The labiovelar glide did not produce a similar pattern of metaphonic influence as did yod; its only effect is visible in the formation of the strong perfect stem (22a,b), with a phonological origin, and secondary analogical extension to some other verbs. As such, the backing and raising of the stem vowel due to /w/ in the preterit is a clear mark of irregularity of the verb; the process never had a phonologically guided consistency according to the documentation. The mechanism of labiovelarization of the consonant by coarticulation, followed by its influence on the stressed preceding vowel can be assumed as plausible; the insistent variants of /gw/ and /wg/ of (22c,d) may support this view. A noteworthy aspect is the reluctance of the ensuing /Vw/ diphthongs to turn into monophthongs outside the verbal tense morphology. The absence of stable labiovelarized consonants in the development of OSp., quite in contrast with the development of many palatalized consonants, is evidently connected to the extensive absence of effect for /w/, outside the one secondarily functionalized context of irregular preterit stem formation.

3.3. In sum so far, the simple appearance of a surface pattern corresponding to a broad concept of metathesis, i.e. /a > b/ ≈ /b > a/, does not describe the more complex data situation of Castilian, where a transition of the relevant phonetic material appearing in transposed arrangement needs to interact with the interposed consonant. The evidence of intermediate forms which show this intervening consonantal "barrier" to be crucially affected by the phonetic material in transition is necessary to negate the validity of metathesis in such instances. With two consonantal articulations involved, the intermediate stage of a supersegment finds some justification in the similar phenomenon of the complex segment (multiple points of articulation with automatic sequencing) and of the contour segment (with diphthongal specification of one terminal feature in crucial ordering). The cluster nature of the two consonants in the cases discussed here is preserved by the possible outcome of a renewed, inverted consonantal sequence, or a typically long consonant (palatal sonorant, long vibrant). The two-headed properties of unit segment and long articulation characterize the pivotal supersegment. Castilian is particularly marked by this development, much more so than any of its surrounding dialects or others in the Romania. Metatheses involving two contiguous consonants correspond to phonotactic distress situations, mostly brought about by syncope. What differentiates Castilian from other Romance dialects is its extensive application of posttonic syncope, regardless of the resulting consonantal groupings (which distinguishes it e.g. from Portuguese and Italian), and a rather strong degree of retention for consonantal articulations (which sets Castilian off e.g. from Portuguese and French). The resulting clash of preserved consonantal phenomena in direct contact may be an essential cause for the high rate of Castilian supersegment creation to preserve the phonetic input as best possible. The much stricter absorption of palatal/labiovelar coarticulations into susceptible segments in Castilian (compared to Portuguese and Catalan) documents a comparable tendency to operate with unitary segments.[18]

4. Distance metathesis

4.1. If the arguments of sections 2 and 3 tried to eliminate metathesis from the range of viable explanatory options for contiguous segments of similar phonetic content, there remains the much larger data range of the holistic segment transpositions at a distance, briefly illustrated in (4). The most prominent group is comprised by liquid metatheses. Their striking aspect is that the liquid seems to jump around in the word (*fabrica - fragua - forga* , cf. (10f) above), from one position to another, from coda to onset to another syllable, or vice-versa. The non-liquid cases of reciprocal metathesis may show rather wild patterns, such as the one for *redondo* (cf. (5d)) or *mastranto* (cf. (9b)). Here entire segments are rearranged, without the benefit of possible intermediate forms.[19] The basic aspect of metathesis is indisputable. After the prosodic template group (e.g. of the Eastern Miwok languages in (1) above) and the phonotactic distress phenomena of Castilian, the essentially gratuitous transpositions of a type illustrated in (4) and (9), (10) above acquire a somewhat higher profile. They do not express morphological alternation, and they do not improve phonotactic problems, but they create equally possible structures, parallel to the etymological ones, in a pattern which is totally unpredictable. Such metatheses constitute always a minority of forms in a language. They can be viewed as deviations from motivated, canonical form, with the property of having been preserved in the standard language over their etymological counterparts (Malkiel 1962 for relevant discussion of such weak changes). These forms are spontaneous mutations, indicating in their special concentration on liquids a crucial weakness of liquid sequencing within and across syllables, not envisaged in a purely linear conception of the segmental domain, or even the syllable. In particular, these metatheses might argue for a complex syllable structure, reduced from the total options of the model proposed in Cairns and Feinstein (1982); cf. (24).

(24)

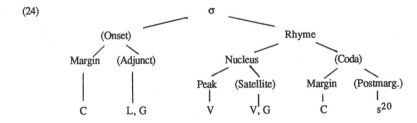

This schema contains the maximal possibilities for Spanish (not all realizable at the same time, however). The slots of interest for the metathesis discussion are Onset-Margin, Onset-Adjunct, and Coda-Margin.

4.2. For the reciprocal exchanges not involving liquids, the positions affected are corresponding Onset slots, either a single segment (*hazerir - zaherir, murciégalo - murciélago, animalia - alimaña, pared - pader, jenaba - jebena*, Vlg. Lt. *palude - padule*) or a group of segments (*intestino - estentina, mentastra - mastranto*). These cases thus show that the Onset is a relevant category for the delimitation of the metathetic target sites.[21]

4.3. The liquid metatheses require more structure. The simple metatheses, mainly of /r/, but also of some /l/, engage normally a Coda position (single segment Coda) and a margin adjunct slot in the Onset (*entergar - entregar, forgar - frogar, semper - siempre* ; and inverse direction *madrugar - madurgar, pedrenal - pedernal*). The liquid may also simply exchange its narrowly delimited position in one syllable with the corresponding one in a neighboring syllable (*petral - pretal, crebar - quebrar*; even at a distance *praesepe - pesebre*). The condition of Coda location is the simpler of the two sites, since a Spanish coda involving a liquid is no more than a single segment; the [-vocal] or [+cons] member of the Rhyme will be assigned final position by universal convention. However, it is essential that the other preferred liquid site be specified as distinct from Onset margin. Such metatheses seem to involve regularly a chain type /CVR.CV/ with some consonant (group) in true Onset position. The liquid will never become the sole Onset element (/#VR.CV/ > /*RV.CV/, e.g. *ar'cano > *ra'cano*). This is assured in word internal syllables by the resyllabification of most CR sequence as /.CR/ (excepting only sonorant C's and /s/). The absence of the word initial metatheses (type **ra'cano*), even where the preceding item might supply the final C for post-lexical resyllabification as /V# .CR/, indicates that there is an inherent affinity of /r/ (liquids?) within Onsets for Adjunct position. It is not sufficient to cite the language particular trait of syllable initial reinforcement of Spanish/Iberoromance /r/ to /R/, which could indicate the non-identity between the syllable initial and non-syllable initial realizations of /r/, hence the non-substitutability for purposes of metathesis. The same absolute preference for /.CR/ exists in other Romance dialects (e.g. Central and Southern Italian dialects) where the two allophonic articulations /. rV/ and /Vr . / are not nearly as distinct.

The required specification of privileged slot correlations, Onset to Onset for C's, Coda to Onset-Adjunct for L's, intersyllabic and intrasyllabic, do not fall out naturally from the hierarchical model; they need to be stipulated. A more immediate account in terms of sonority will be preferable. The universal sonority scale places /r/ close to the prototypical V nuclei, so that the preferred arrangements / .CRV/ and /VR. / yield good sonority slopes in both directions, regardless of structural attachment in Onset or Coda/Rhyme. This perspective captures the canonical landing site restrictions for liquid metathesis more simply. But both versions, rich hierarchical syllable structure and universal sonority tendencies, remain largely hypothetical, and subject to language particular modifications, thus being circular to a certain extent.

4.4. The parade examples of reciprocal liquid metathesis, *parabola - palabra, miraclo - milagro, periglo - peligro*) reveal themselves as non-metatheses in the present perspective. Rather they belong in the context of the extensive Iberoromance tendency to favor / . CR/ clusters over parallel / . CL/ forms. Castilian eliminates the CL clusters in a variety of ways (reduction of C, e.g. *glandula > land(r)e* "fruit of oak tree", systematic palatalization of L, e.g. *clave > llave* "key", radical palatalization of the entire group, e.g. *oc(u)lu > ojo* , OSp. [ožo], MSp. [oxo] "eye", or metathesis as in Vlg. Lat. **obli'tare* (for Lt. OBLI'VISCI:) > Sp. *olvidar* "to forget"). Remaining CL groupings are normally Latinisms, of little impact in early Spanish phases, so that the CL cluster turns out to be recessive for the native vocabulary. In Western dialects, Leonese, Galician and Portuguese, the rhotic conversion of remaining CL clusters is a typical feature (e.g. *plaᵗˢa > prasa* , MPg. *praça* "square"). The reciprocal exchange /r/ - /l/ in *miraglo - milagro* is not a straight metathesis, rather it depends on the elimination of the disfavored cluster /gl/ through its conversion to /gr/. The second step is the highly likely liquid dissimilation /r ... r/ to /l ... r/ (the inverse /r ... l/ here not being available due to the CR/CL asymmetry which gave rise to the need for dissimilation); thus *miraclo > miragro > milagro*. This dissimilation may operate in both directions, or may not be triggered at all, as the three Romance outcomes of Lat. 'ARBORE > Sp. *árbol* , It. *'albero* and Fr. *'arbre* indicate. A direct reciprocal metathesis in the cases akin to *periglo*

- *peligro* has the disadvantage of interchanging segments from sole Onset position and from the adjunct to Onset slot, which would be unique to this class of reciprocal metathesis: /pe . ri . glo/ > /pe . li . gro/. On the other hand, the phonetic argument of the high degree of dissimilarity between the two allophones involved does not apply here, since the position /V . R V/ does not trigger the articulatory reinforcement of /r/ (only after a consonantal segment in syllable final position, or after word boundary, /C . R C/ or /#R V/). Depending on the further investigation of the liquid exchanges in Spanish, and of universal syllable structure, one can envisage at least two solutions for these instances of seemingly reciprocal metathesis.

4.5. Segment metathesis across a distance may be construed as arguing for some structure of the syllable such that the canonical target sites of Onset across syllables for any segment type, and Adjunct to Onset plus Coda for liquids can be addressed at a coherent level, excluding other, arbitrary, non-observed pairings for segment displacement. These metatheses are caused by some accidental, spontaneous, and essentially unpredictable distortion in the sequential execution of syllable constituents. The syllable thus becomes the relevant speech production unit for timing, effectively connected to the Sonority Hierarchy. Whatever the precise formalization of such conditions, they will be responsible for allowing liquid and other distance metatheses, and for restricting them to comparable and commensurate exchange positions. Note that there is no good argument for claiming that the rich syllable structure sketched in (24) necessarily forms part of phonological theory. Due to the particular interpretation envisaged for distance metathesis in this paper, i.e. as a manifestation of the same dimension leading to speech errors, the locus for the constraint on syllabic structure on distance metathesis is in the performance domain, not in the range of competence, which is the domain for formal phonological properties.[22] The resolution of distance metathesis into a timing error in the execution of the syllable being articulated cannot enrich the phonological domain in any way. The excess power of the transformational rule to accommodate metathesis (cf. section 1 above) is effectively removed from phonology and transferred to the performance domain. The production mechanisms responsible for complex sequentialization of articulatory gestures execute the feature, segment, and chain patterns specified by the phonological component. Distance metathesis thus represents a generalized imprecision in the timing relation between various articulatory gestures, accidentally leading to segment transpositions by imprecisions in the firing sequence of component articulations. Since the execution timing pattern of articulations does not necessarily correspond to the perception sequence of segmental articulations, the potential for apparent crossing of association lines between abstract sequence statements and surface-bound overlap between neighboring gestures is given. Language specific rules and/or conditions need to provide the parameters of mapping from abstract phonotactic properties to the specific data characteristic of the surface level of a given language. This is largely speculative as an account for the phenomenon of distance metathesis; the well foundedness of this move will depend on the outcome of studies linking the phonological and physiological aspects of phonation.

Distance metatheses have the peculiar flavor of accidents of pronunciation, slips of the tongue, hence sporadic events.[23] In principle these are nonce forms; any other item could have been realized with such distortions, and this probably has happened repeatedly for many, even a majority of items, but in unpredictable ways and without sufficient saliency to be carried on in the communal speech. The metatheses which we observe may have been recorded in certain documents by accident, others might have entered wider linguistic circles, or even the common language, from the context of a narrow speech community, starting from a repeatable performance error, through many and varied paths of social diffusion. Distance metathesis in this view thus is a phenomenon, but it is certainly not an active phonological process at work to alter the shape of lexical items, as is e.g. a vowel harmony rule. The phonological motivation in the shape of formalized conditions for this kind of metathesis is lacking, much more so than for the previous type combining two contiguous segments into one due to a difficult phonotactic situation. But in all these cases, distance as well as contiguous metatheses, execution of articulatory movements and abstract template stand in contrast, an observation which binds the phenomenon of metathesis closely to the performance domain where errors are possible and can be captured in their essence.

5. *Conclusions*

The attempt of this paper has been to explain metathesis for diachronic purposes. Of three typical patterns it can be maintained that they correspond to three different causes: (1) morphological marking for wholesale CV/VC transpositions with morphological significance, attributable to prosodic template matching and its implications for linear sequence (no Spanish or Romance examples in general), (2) phonotactic distress situations yielding multiple attempts at preserving the phonetic content and improving the phonetic chain, attributable to an intermediate step of segment combination (numerous Spanish examples, e.g. /dn/, /dl/, /Cy/, and (3) spontaneous mutations across or within syllables in accordance with universal syllable production and sonority patterns, due to typologically constrained timing errors in the execution of set syllables.[24] The common denominator of these three categories is the question of timing of sequential events, hence the erroneous perception of metathesis as a coherent and phonological category. According to the present view, the only category of phonological significance is the morphologically functional prosodic template variety of section 1. The other two major categories, contiguous metathesis (leading to a supersegment or to coarticulation) and distance metathesis (governed by the internal hierarchical structure of the syllable) concern the foreign domain of performance. The essential role of timing in execution of articulatory gestures is evident in both categories. The supersegment depends on the often observed phenomenon of anticipation in articulation, possibly due to dominant processing demands on temporal structure in contradiction with the phonological sequencing. However, the distinction between truly phonological vs. performance oriented phenomena is not sharp: vowel harmony and metaphony function as phonological processes (formal constraints on rule operation, domain, lexical exceptions, etc.), consonant palatalization as coarticulation may be subject to phonetic or phonological restrictions, while the constitution of supersegments breaks the phonological mould in a performance oriented attempt at maintaining the phonologically circumscribed framework of phonotactics. Only the mutation-like distance metathesis is impervious to phonological principles operative in a language at the crucial time. The anchoring of this type of metathesis can only be lexical, for which it depends on sociolinguistic factors of diffusion beyond formal control.

The surface perception of static unity in metathesis is illusory, since the significance of the diverse phenomena in their dynamic dimension is quite distinct, and thus needs to be treated by distinct properties. The performance dimension may have remarkable impact on the competence level of phonology proper, and the diachronic dimension is strategically located to reveal the complex interplay of execution and linguistic codification, a concern of paramount importance not only to diachronic, but also to synchronic conceptualizations.

NOTES

* I would like to thank Catherine A. Callaghan, David Odden and Uthaiwan Wong-opasi for their help and suggestions concerning various aspects of this paper. Roberto Perry provided valuable assistance in the data collection. All responsibility for the contents rests with the author.

[1] It should be pointed out that the question of motivating the multi-tier analysis for consonantal and vocalic melodies in these languages remains open, in contrast to the massive motivation for this move in Semitic languages; cf. for some discussion Kang 1989 (in this volume). The analysis in (2) is only meant as suggestive.

[2] Some synchronic cases in the Romance languages have attracted sporadic theoretical attention (e.g. Montreuil 1981 for a minor Romansh alternation /Vr/ ≈ /rV̵/ in the verb conjugation, Dumenil 1983 for Gascon). The normal concern is with historical developments and dialect alternations, for which every Romance dialect offers unsystematic, but abundant examples (e.g. Rohlfs 1966:§322-7 and Tekavčić 1980:147-9 for Italian, Pope 1952:§124,142 for French, in addition to the Spanish data presented below). The imbalance in favor of liquid metathesis is overwhelming in all these materials.

³ The data come from a variety of sources; chief among them are Corominas and Pascual 1980: sub verbo, Menéndez Pidal 1941:175-177, 184-185, 323-324, García de Diego 1970:175-180, Lloyd 1987:7-8, 28-29, 189, 205, 311-312, 360. The range of data for an item given in the text is a composite of the various sources; the most authoritative treatment of late is the etymological dictionary by Corominas and Pascual, which yields the basic weight to the item (accuracy, documentation, etymological identification, etc.). The items given are in no way exhaustive, but only suggestive of the types identified. The label OSp. refers to Old Castilian in the first place as the standard dialect of many documents; it extends also to other dialects when they are non-distinct from Castilian in the given item. The major dialects considered in some entries are Aragonese to the east, and Leonese (with Asturian as a characteristic subtype) to the west of Castilian. The Galician-Portuguese and Catalan areas represent still more peripheral dialect types. The Latin forms are quoted in a normalized version (acc. sg. without final -M if a nominal form), indicated by small capitals; if preceded by an asterisk, the form is not attested as such. Accent in Latin is indicated by /'/, in Spanish only if different from the etymon, or if different from the basic cases (penultimate accent if the word ends in a vowel, /n/ or /s/, or final accent if the word ends in a consonant other than /n/ or /s/). The representation for OSp. is frequently a mixture of essential phonetic and unimportant graphic mode. /R/ designates the long coronal trill.

⁴ MSp. *amistad* is a partial Latinism restored for expected *$am\theta ad$ (Lloyd 1987:205).

⁵ The sequence /bd^z/, /bt^s/ is very unstable in its semipopular development: Lt. AURIFICE > OSp. *ore$\beta d^z e$* "goldsmith". The forms attested vary widely: *orebçe, orençe, orez, orese, orece, orebs, orepse* ; this latter form shows a metathetic variant *orespe* (these two forms being closely connected to the corresponding forms with affricates).

⁶ The development of the group /dd^z/ can be confirmed with non-metathetic cases where the shortening works in the manner detailed above: Lt. 'D(U)O:DECIM, 'TRE:DECIM > OSp. *dod$^z e$*, *tred$^z e$* "twelve, thirteen" through syncope of /DEC^y -/ and normal assibilation of /k/ before front vowel (Lloyd 1987:205).

⁷ The further development of the affricates to a voiceless sibilant /θ/ is independent of the metathesis discussion. Deaffrication as a common process, and devoicing of all sibilants as a particular Northern Iberic development, took place across the board (13th to 16th centuries), with the exception of peripheral Iberic dialects/languages (Catalan and Portuguese, while Judeo-Spanish reflects an archaic state of affairs of the end of the 15th century, date of the expulsion of the Jews from the Iberic peninsula).

⁸ In prefixal composition an occasional long sonorant may surface, e.g. *innato* "innate", *innatural* "unnatural", and the tense vibrant /R/ has phonological properties of a geminate (Harris 1983), but otherwise geminates are not available in the lexical cycles.

⁹ Long /n:/, /l:/ are inherently palatalizing in early Castilian. Regular sound change from Latin yields [λ] for Lt. /ll/ and [ñ] for Lt. /nn/, /mn/. If the palatal /ñ/ and /λ/ come from a long segment (with double x slot), then their development is a natural consequence of the dissolution of the difficult phonotactic situation under the heading of a single segment, preserving in addition also the cluster character of the etymological base (palatal /λ/ cannot occur in monomorphemic clusters, and palatal /ñ/ does not cluster at all).

¹⁰ A further solution consists in the (pre-)lateralization of the supersegment, yielding the rather frequent "aberrations" of *calnado* for *cadnado/candado/cañado* (cf. above (3a), and also (4c) ANIMALIA).

¹¹ The best source for additional clusters /d^{z}r/ would be the future/conditional forms of *ded$^z ir$, fad$^z er$, plad$^z er$* "to say, to do, to please", resulting from syncope of the unstressed theme vowel in the template /infinitive + áux. fut./: *did$^z ré$, fad$^z ré$, plad$^z rá$* are attested, but more common are forms with loss of the affricate, blockage of syncope or a transition consonant (depending on lexical specification): *diré, ded$^z iré; faré, feré; plad$^z drá$*, but never with metathesis *$dird^z é$, *$fard^z é$, *$plard^z á$* . The reasons for this lack of metathesis are most likely paradigmatic pressure and

the independently motivated existence of "short" stem forms for ded^zir, fad^zer < 'DI:CERE, 'FACERE with early syncope and loss of the as yet unassibilated velar: the phonotactic distress did not arise with sufficient force to lead to the extreme solution of segment transposition.

12   An interesting development is the emergence of metathesis in the inverse direction, from a preferred /rl/ to the marked /l.R/ in Lt. 'MERULU > Sp. *merlo, mirlo* , vulg. *milro* (also Port. *mélroa* with gender switch to fem in -*a* (García de Diego 1970:179; Corominas and Pascual 1980: s.v.). Such contrary developments to expected naturalness of segment chains underline in their precarious existence the relevance of the postulated transition stage of the supersegment, accessible not only from the difficult end, but also from the presumably stable result phase. The two articulations, e.g. /r/ and /l/, are effectively connected in production.

13   These cases could as well be studied under the syllable bound liquid metatheses of section 4. -- The data adduced so far are in no way exhaustive, since there do not exist previous studies collecting all instances of potential metathesis. The lists are only suggestive of the range of phenomena encountered, awaiting later completion.

14   Cf. Wong-opasi 1989 for a detailed treatment of the properties of [+high] spreading due to the /y/ in various contexts of development. The traditional approach is known as the problem of the *yod* (cf. Menéndez Pidal 1941:§8bis).

15   The metaphonic effect of /y/ on the preceding vowel is differentiated according to Latin source of yod, the preceding consonant, the quality of the stressed vowel, and the relative age of the process. The younger the yod formation, the heavier the metaphonic effect on a wider class of yod, ceteris paribus (Menéndez Pidal 1941:§8bis). Thus (20a) is the oldest formation, usually attributed to the 2nd/3rd c. AD.

16   With metaphony of /o^y/ to /u/, and the conversion of /u^y/ to the canonical diphthong form /we/ from Vlg. Lt. /'ɔ/, or else later /o+y/, presupposing an intermediate stage of resegmentalized [+hi] of /o^y/ as /oy, uy/.

17   Even the natural combination of velar obstruent plus labiovelar glide did not produce stable labiovelarized segments, as seen e.g. in the interchange between *igual* ≈ *iugal* (dialectal), i. e., [gw] vs. [wg]. The alternation *fragua/frauga* may be due to a certain level of coherence o the labiovelar /CG/ ≈ /GC/ pattern; even more clearly this holds for *enjaguar/enjuagar* (cf. (22d)).

18   In spite of the appeal to phonotactic distress as a cause for the complex development leading to apparent metatheses, the arguments based on presumably universal naturalness (e.g. Sonority Hierarchy) should not be elevated to absolute heights as triggering and motivating factors for segment realignments. A smaller number of (highly marked?) situations are on record where languages produce disfavored sequences without stringent necessity, be that through normal phonological rules or metathesis. For Spanish the inverse metathesis of *milro* from *mirlo* is relevant (cf. n. 12), as well as *god^{z}ne* "door hinges" from *gond^{z}e* , and the double evolution of Lt. 'CI:MICE > Sp. *čin če* "bug", *čizme* "gossip". To this may be added the many cases where metathesis fails to apply, from the restituted morphosyntactic cases of older *daldo* to modern standard *dadlo* (cf. (6a)) to the persistent alternate forms such as *cadnado* (cf. (3a)). Other languages present similar aspects, e.g. a Southern Italian dialect of Apulia with *'sokra* > *'sroka* "sister in law", *urmu* > *umru* (but then also *umbru*) "elm tree", and other rather improbable developments (Rohlfs 1966:455). A language such as Pashto contains a systematic phonotactic component which contradicts universal syllabic sonority expectations (Bell and Saka's 1983 reversed sonority clusters). These perhaps marginal reminders of the ultimate unpredictability of the data are an indication of the fact that the cases treated here are the result of a non-canonical development, i.e. superimposition of segments. The broadly undefined nature of the ensuing supersegments, implying their demise and reinterpretation as normative segments and resequenced clusters, predicts the possible emergence of generally disfavored clusters as marginal developments. The unorthodox status of the input cluster and its treatment bring about the option of unorthodox results.

19   The transition of contiguous sequences between /Vr/ and /rV/ could involve plausible transition phases in the form of /r/-colored vowels, as e.g. in English. Cf. some discussion of this

option for actual developments in English in Alexander 1985, Stemberger 1983; for Upper Sorbian, a similar analysis in Timberlake 1985. At any rate, this kind of explanation is not available for Spanish dialects which are not documented to contain such /r/-colored vowels, and where no circumstantial evidence can be mustered in favor of such a hypothesis. The availability of a type of explanation is clearly a function of the phonetic realities of the language in question.

20 The attribution of Spanish segment types to the various positions of syllabic structure is only tentative; not all options are simultaneously operative, and the schematic approach of (24) clashes with the finer restrictions on Spanish syllable pattern options.

21 It should be pointed out that other Romance languages are also quite rich in relevant metatheses, in particular Italian and its dialects (cf. Rohlfs 1966:454-457) and also Old French (cf. Pope 1952:§124). Two telling examples of liquid problems with longer lexical items are *crocodilus* for Late Latin, and **vespertiliu* for Italian:

    (i) Lt. CROCO'DI:LUS > Late Lt. *corco'dil(l)us, corco'drilus, croco'dil(l)us, coco'dillus, concor'dillus* "crocodile" (Väänänen 1974:113)

    (ii) Lt. VESPER'TILIU > It. dial. *vespertello, vepestrello, vipistrello, pipistrello*, MIt. *pipistrello* "bat" (Tekavčić 1980.1:149)

22 According to the detailed discussions in Laubstein 1988, the locus of such constraints is the production syllable, requiring distinction between Onset, Nucleus and Coda constituents.

23 Some relevant discussion of phonological implications of speech errors are found in Fromkin 1971, 1973, Stemberger 1984; cf. a very useful survey of existing treatments plus formulation of relevant questions in Berg 1987. With the exception of one case of distance metathesis reported in the present paper (cf. *žustar - sulštar* of (9c)), the sequential switching concerns entire segments or dominant feature complexes. This may be accidental in the data used, but it coincides with the trends noted in Berg 1987 on a cross-linguistic (but still IE) base.

24 The literature contains additional motivations for metathesis, e.g. as a device to feed the palatalization rule (Semiloff-Zelasko 1973), or as a synchronic reanalysis of difficult historical constellations (non-metathetic; cf. Janda 1984), or in response to distorted allophonic coding of the cluster components Silva (1973), or to express some specific, but open-ended structural purpose (Hock 1985). Above all, Ultan (1978) offers a broad range of presumable metatheses, most of which need closer scrutiny for safe categorization and explanation (as the extended discussion of the Kasem and Rotuman cases illustrates).

REFERENCES

Alexander, James D. 1985. *R-* metathesis in English: A diachronic account. *Journal of English Linguistics* 18.33-40

Andersen, Henning, 1972. Diphthongization. *Lg.* 48.11-50

Bell, Alan and Mohammad M. Saka. 1983. Reversed sonority in Pashto initial clusters. *Journal of Phonetics* 11.259-275

Berg, Thomas. 1987. A cross-linguistic comparison of slips of the tongue. Bloomington: IULC

Besnier, Niko. 1987. An autosegmental approach to metathesis in Rotuman. *Lingua* 73.201-223

Cairns, Charles E. and Mark H. Feinstein. 1982. Markedness and the theory of syllable structure. *LI* 13.193-225

Callaghan, Cathrine A. 1986. Miwok ablaut grades. *Papers from the 1983, 1984, and 1985 Hokan-Penutian Languages Conference*, 105-114. (*Occasional Papers in Linguistics*, 13). Carbondale: Dept. of Linguistics, Southern Illinois University

Chomsky, Noam and Morris Halle. 1968. *The Sound Pattern of English*. New York: Harper and Row

Clements, G. N. 1985. The geometry of phonological features. *Phonology Yearbook* 2.225-252

Dumenil, Annie P. 1983. *A Rule Account of Metathesis in Gascon*. Unpubl. Ph.D. diss., Univ. of South Carolina

450

Fromkin, Victoria A. 1971. The non-anomalous nature of anomalous utterances. *Lg.* 47.27-52
Fromkin, Victoria A. 1973. Introduction. *Speech Errors as Linguistic Evidence*, ed. by V. A. Fromkin, 11-45. The Hague: Mouton
García de Diego, Vicente. 1970. *Gramática histórica española.* Madrid: Gredos (3rd ed.)
Greenberg, W. J. 1981. Metathesis in Kasem. *Phonology in the 1980's*, ed. D. L. Goyvaerts, 101-118. Ghent: Story-Scientia
Haas, Wim de. 1987. An autosegmental approach to vowel coalescence. *Lingua* 73.167-199
Harris, James W. 1983. *Spanish Stress and Syllable Structure.* Cambridge: MIT Press
Hock, Hans H. 1985. Regular metathesis. *Linguistics* 23:4[278].529-546
Hock, Hans H. 1986. *Principles of Historical Linguistics.* Berlin: Mouton de Gruyter (*Trends in Linguistics, Studies and Monographs,* 34)
Janda, Richard D. 1984. Why morphological metathesis rules are rare: On the possibility of historical explanations in linguistics. *Proceedings of the 10th Annual Meeting of the Berkeley Linguistics Society*, ed. C. Brugmann and M. Macaulay, 87-103. Berkeley: Department of Linguistics, Univ. of California
Kenstowicz, Michael A. and Charles W. Kisseberth. 1979. *Generative Phonology. Description and Theory.* New York: Academic Press
Laubstein, Ann S. 1988. *The Nature of the "Production Grammar" Syllable.* Bloomington, IN: IULC
Lloyd, Paul M. 1987. *From Latin to Spanish.* Philadelphia: American Philosophical Society. (*Memoirs*, 173)
Malkiel, Yakov. 1962. Weak phonetic change, spontaneous sound shift, lexical contamination. *Lingua* 11.263-275
McCarthy, John J. 1981. A prosodic theory of nonconcatenative morphology. *LI* 12:3.373-418
McCarthy, John J. 1984. Theoretical consequences of Montañés vowel harmony. *LI* 15:2.291-318
Menéndez Pidal, Ramón. 1941. *Manual de gramática histórica española.* Madrid: Espasa-Calpe (6th ed.)
Montreuil, Jean-Pierre. 1981. The Romansch 'brat'. *Papers in Romance* 3:1.67-76
Pope, Mildred K. 1952. *From Latin to Modern French With Especial Consideration of Anglo-Norman. Phonology and Morphology.* Manchester: Manchester Univ. Press (2nd ed.)
Rohlfs, Gerhard. 1966. *Grammatica storica della lingua italiana e dei suoi dialetti.* Vol. 1: Fonetica. Turin: Einaudi
Sagey, Elizabeth C. 1986. *The Representation of Features and Relations in Non-linear Phonology.* Unpubl. Ph. D. dissertation, MIT
Semiloff-Zelasko, Holly. 1973. Glide metatheses. *Working Papers in Linguistics, Ohio State University* 14.66-76
Silva, Claire M. 1973. Metathesis of obstruent clusters. *Working Papers in Linguistics, Ohio State University* 14.77-84
Stemberger, Joseph Paul. 1983. The nature of /r/ and /l/ in English: Evidence from speech errors. *Journal of Phonetics* 11.139-147
Stemberger, Joseph Paul. 1984. Length as a suprasegmental: Evidence from speech errors. *Lg.* 60.895-913
Tekavčić, Pavao. 1980. *Grammatica storica italiana.* Vol. 1. Bologna: il Mulino (2nd ed.)
Timberlake, Alan. 1985. The metathesis of liquid diphthongs in Upper Sorbian. *International Journal of Slavic Linguistics and Poetics* 31-32.417-430
Ultan, Russell. 1978. A typological view of metathesis. *Universals of Human Language*, ed. Joseph H. Greenberg, 2:367-402. Stanford: Stanford Univ. Press
Väänänen, Veikko. 1974. *Introduzione al latino volgare.* Bologna: Pàtron
Wong-opasi, Uthaiwan. 1989. The effects of yod on the vocalic and consonantal systems: From Latin to Spanish. Paper to be delivered at ICHL IX, August 1989, Rutgers Univ.

Scope Ambiguity and Disambiguity in Chinese*

Xu Lie-jiong   Thomas Hun-tak Lee
Fudan University   Chinese University of Hong Kong

0. Introduction

Most studies on quantifiers in Chinese begin with the observation that sentences such as (1) do not display scope ambiguity, whereas its English counterpart is generally considered ambiguous (cf. May 1977, 1985).[1]

(1) Mei   ge xuesheng (dou) mai le   yi   ben shu[2]
    every CL student all   buy ASP one CL book
    "Every student bought a book."

To characterize this property which distinguishes Chinese from English, various proposals assuming an isomorphic relationship between surface properties and logical scope have been made. S.F.Huang (1981) proposes that quantifier scope is determined entirely by precedence relations: if a quantificational expression (QE) A precedes another QE B, then A has scope over B. J.Huang (1982) argues, however, that the crucial factor is c-command and not linear precedence. He suggests that if a QE A c-commands another QE B at S-structure, then A c-commands B at LF. Lee (1986) argues further that both command and precedence are involved in determining quantifier scope: if A and B command each other, the QE that precedes will take wide scope.

Attempts have also been made to account for this apparent isomorphism between surface properties and quantifier scope in terms of other syntactic/semantic differences between Chinese and English. J.Huang (1982:144-7) attributes the apparent lack of scope ambiguity in Chinese to the V' phrase structure constraint in the language, i.e. the inability of complex predicates to take complements. Aoun and Li (1987) put forward the hypothesis that verb raising is not permitted in Chinese. They then derive quantifier scope phenomena in Chinese from this as well as other principles such as the Minimal Binding Requirement and a scope interpretation principle that refers to NP traces. They further observe that contrary to what was previously thought, scope ambiguity does exist in Chinese, in passive sentences and sentences containing [V NP [P NP]pp] verb phrases. This new observation cannot be accounted for by earlier studies but follows naturally from Aoun and Li's assumptions and principles. Duanmu (1988) relates the scope disambiguity to the tendency for preverbal NPs to be definite in the language.

In this paper, we consider some of the factors that may underlie the lack of agreement on the ambiguity status of quantificational sentences in Chinese. To develop a clearer picture of quantifier scope, we examine the relative scope of numerically quantified phrases (NQP) before we look at scope phenomena involving universal quantifiers. Essentially, we argue that scope ambiguity is restricted to cases where both quantifier phrases (QNP) occur within the same verb phrase.

451

Within a clause, scope relations depend on the thematic relations borne by the QNPs as well as their linear position.

1.*Peculiar problem in the study of quantifier scope in Chinese*

An effective way to test whether a QNP in a particular position can have wide scope is to see whether a universal quantifier placed in that position can have scope over another QNP. For example, in (1), the subject QNP can have scope over the object QNP, since each of the students could have bought a different book. Some informants, however, insist that the object QNP can also have wide scope, since (1) could be used to describe situations in which all the students bought the same book, for instance, a textbook for the course they were all taking. The book they bought might happen to be tokens of the same type. This alleged scope ambiguity, however, may be spurious, since in such a case, the reading with yi ben shu 'a book' taking wide scope entails the reading with meige xuesheng 'every student' taking wide scope (cf. Reinhart 1983:195).

A better way to test whether scope ambiguity genuinely exists would be reversing the order of the two quantifiers. Unfortunately, equivalents of sentences such as (2) are not available in Chinese for several reasons.

(2) Some student bought every book.

First, the Chinese expression corresponding to the existential quantifier phrase some plus a singular noun is in fact a numeral phrase- yi+ CL+ N "one-classifier-noun". But occurrences of NQPs in the subject position are highly constrained. For example, (3) is hardly acceptable.

(3) ? Yi ge ren   si le
     one CL person   die ASP
     "A person has died."

There are various ways to relax the restriction on the use of NQPs as subjects, e.g. placing the verb you 'exist/have' in front of the NQP, adding a modifier to it, or including a topic in the sentence containing it, making the sentence a conditional clause or a sentential subject, etc. (see Lee 1986 for details). Secondly, the universal quantifier shows certain lexical idiosyncracies. A sentence containing the quantifier mei 'every' in a noun phrase in object position also seems unnatural, as (4) illustrates. As a result of these language-particular factors, the Chinese counterpart of (2), given as (5), is not acceptable, thus hindering our understanding of scope ambiguity in sentences involving existential and universal quantifiers.

(4) ? Ta   mai le   mei ben shu
     S/he buy ASP every CL book
     "S/he bought every book."
(5) ? Yi ge xuesheng   mai le   mei ben shu[3]
     one CL student   buy ASP   every CL book

"A student bought every book."

The difficulty researchers are confronted with in cross-linguistic studies on quantification is that the classic English examples that display scope ambiguity and therefore motivate the proposal of Quantifier Raising have no real counterparts in Chinese. This problem, which stems from peculiar constraints on the distribution of quantifiers in the language, cannot be ignored or bypassed. To ascertain whether scope ambiguity does exist in the language, and to what extent and in what ways it is manifested, we will first study the scope interpretations of numeral phrases (NQPs), which have less lexical idiosyncracy.

2. Relative Scope of Numerically Quantified Phrases

In this section, we consider systematically various cases where two numeral phrases occur in one sentence. The purpose is to see how many factors are involved in scope interpretation and what they are.

The interpretations more easily available are usually the group readings, either complete group readings or incomplete group readings as they are called in Kempson and Cormack (1982). A scope-differentiated reading may be preferable when group readings are ruled out for pragmatic reasons. For example, the most natural reading for (6) is the one with the subject NP taking wide scope.

(6) Genju   renkou   diaocha,   qu   li   500 ge
    According-to demographic survey   district in   CL
    ren   you guo liang ge peiou
    person have ASP two CL spouse
    "According to the demographic survey, 500 people in
    the district have had two spouses"

It is impossible to obtain a reading in which the object NP has scope over the subject NP in whatever sentence of the canonical order and in whatever context the sentence occurs. Chinese speakers can isolate at most three interpretations from the following sentence.

(7) Zhege xuexiao, liang ge zukaojiaoshi   pi le   liu fen kaojuan
    this school   two CL examiner   mark ASP six CL script
    "(In) this school, two examiners marked six scripts."

The three readings are: (a) two examiners as a group marked a group of six scripts between them; (b) two examiners marked the same set of six scripts; (c) two examiners each marked six scripts. English speakers (at least some of them) claim to be able to get the fourth interpretation for the English sentence corresponding to (7), i.e. six scripts were each marked by two examiners. Such a reading is not available in Chinese.

An apparent counterexample to the above observation is that (8) can mean that ten people sit around each table, the general practice at a Chinese banquet.

(8) Shi ge ren   zuo yi zhuo
    ten CL person   sit   one table
    "Ten people sit around one table."

On closer inspection, we find that this reading is due to the special use of yi 'one' in the sense of 'each'. This phenomenon of universal generalization of unit NQPs does not extend to other numerals. The following sentence (9) cannot be taken as a description of the situation in which ten people sit around one table and another ten around another table.

(10) Shi ge ren   zuo liang zhuo
    ten CL person   sit   two   table
    "Ten people sit around two tables."

In many examples used below, group readings may be more easily available or preferable in neutral contexts. The reader is asked to consider scope-differentiated interpretations, which are our main concern. In sub-section 2.1 we show cases in which one NQP necessarily takes scope over another, where interpretations other than group readings are possible. In sub-section 2.2 we discuss cases where scope ambiguity is possible.

2.1 Numerically Quantified Phrases in Preverbal Positions

A preverbal quantified expression necessarily has scope over a postverbal one, according to Duanmu (1988). The reason, he argues, is that in Chinese all preverbal NPs are definite. Duanmu's distinction between preverbal and postverbal positions is useful. It echoes the long-standing obervation by Chinese linguists that there is a very strong tendency in the language for the subject to be definite and the object to be indefinite (cf. Chao 1968:76), and is by and large descriptively correct. As has been demonstrated in preceding examples, in a sentence of the canonical SVO order, the quantified subject takes wide scope. A topicalized object occurring in preverbal position likewise takes wide scope. In (10) liang pian zhongdian wenzhang 'two important articles' has scope over san ge shengaoren 'three reviewers'.[4]

(10) Mei yi qi,   liang pian zhongdian wenzhang
    every one issue   two   CL   important article
    zhubian   ji gei   san   ge shengaoren
    editor-in-chief   send to   three CL reviewer
    "(In) every issue, (there are) two important articles,
    (such that) the editor-in-chief sends to three reviewers."

However, it should be noted that not all preverbal quantified NPs take wide scope. Duanmu does not discuss sentences with two or more preverbal quantified NPs, such as the following.

(11) Mei yi qi,   lian pian zhongdian wenzhang,
    every one issue   two   CL   important article,
    san   ge shengaoren   fouding le[5]

three CL reviewer reject ASP
"(In) every issue, (there are) two important articles (such that) three reviewers rejected (them)."

(12) Mei yi qi, san ge shengaoren, lian pian
   every one issue three CL reviewer two CL
   zhongdian wenzhang fouding le
   important article reject ASP
   "(In) every issue, (there are) three reviewers (such that they) rejected two articles."

(13) Mei yi qi, lian pian zhongdian wenzhang bei
   every one issue two CL important article by
   san ge shengaoren fouding le[6]
   three CL reviewer reject ASP
   "(In) every issue, (there are) two important articles (such that they) are rejected by three reviewers."

(14) Mei yi qi, san ge shengaoren ba
   every one issue three CL reviewer BA
   liang pian zhongdian wenzhang fouding le
   two CL important article reject ASP
   "(In) every issue, (there are) three reviewers (such that they) rejected two important articles."

Each of the sentences (11-14) has a base-generated topic, as well as two NQPs in preverbal position. In (11), the topicalized object liang pian wenzhang 'two important articles' precedes the subject san ge shengaoren 'three reviewers.' These two NQPs occur in reverse order in (12). (13) is an instance of the passive construction, with the agent phrase introduced by bei 'by.' In the *Ba*-construction (14), the object NQP is preposed to a position following the subject NQP but preceding the verb and is governed by the preposition *ba*. In all four sentences, the first NQP can take wide scope, while the second one cannot. The data suggest that either linear order or configuration is involved in the determination of scope.

   Second, not all preverbal NPs are definite in Chinese. It is true that the topic is usually definite or specific. It is also generally acknowledged that the subject is also definite or specific. But neither is necessarily so. Unlike English, where definiteness may be marked by articles, the definiteness of NPs in Chinese is largely contextually determined rather than morphologically marked. Thus, under the influence of the initial universal quantifier topic, the first NQP in (11-14) clearly does not necessarily refer to specific articles or reviewers. We conclude from the above discussion that when two NQPs are in subject and object positions respectively, or when both occupy preverbal positions, the first NQP always has scope over the second. This scope phenomenon cannot be satisfactorily explained by assuming (as Duanmu does) that all preverbal QNPs are definite. Rather, the relevant factor seems to be linear order.

2.2 Numerically Quantified Phrases in Postverbal Positions

   Aoun and Li (1987a,b) are the first to discuss scope ambiguity within the VP. They observe that ambiguity exists in the construction of V-NP-PP, but not in those of V-NP-NP or PP-V-NP, using the universal quantifier <u>mei</u> 'every' in their examples. Is there scope ambiguity in these constructions if NQPs are used instead? Of the following sentences, (16) is ambiguous while (15) and (17) are not.[7]

(15) Ta   gei   liang ge ren   san ben shu (unambiguous)
     s/he give two CL person   three CL book
     "S/he gave two people three books."
(16) Ta   song le   san ben shu gei   liang ge ren (ambiguous)
     s/he give ASP three CL book to   two   CL person
     "S/he gave three books to two people."
(17) Wo dui liang ge nanren   baoyuan san ge nuren (unambiguous)
     I to   two CL man   complain three CL woman
     "I complained to two men about three women."

2.2.1 Configurational Approach

The above facts can be analysed purely in terms of configuration, as in the approach adopted by Aoun and Li, who handle the data in terms of c-command. If one QNP c-commands another at LF, the former may have scope over the latter. They analyze the double object construction exemplified in (15) as containing a small clause, represented as follows.[8]

(18)

$$
\begin{array}{c}
\text{VP} \\
\diagup\qquad\diagdown \\
\text{V}\qquad\text{SC} \\
\diagup\quad\diagdown \\
\text{NP}_1\quad\text{Pred.} \\
| \\
\text{NP}_2
\end{array}
$$

After Quantifier Raising, NP_1 adjoins to VP at LF, c-commanding NP_2, which adjoins to the predicate phrase of the small clause (SC). For NP_2 to go beyond the lower clause would violate the Minimal Binding Requirement (MBR), which limits variables to local A'-binding. Hence the asymmetrical c-command.[9]

In the case of (16), they propose the constituent structure (19) in addition to (20) containing a small clause, similar to (18).

(19)

$$
\begin{array}{c}
\text{VP}_1 \\
\diagup\qquad\qquad\diagdown \\
\text{VP}_2\qquad\quad\text{PP} \\
\diagup\quad\diagdown\qquad\diagup\quad\diagdown \\
\text{V}\quad\text{NP}_1\quad\text{P}\quad\text{NP}_2
\end{array}
$$

(20)

$$
\begin{array}{c}
\text{VP} \\
\diagup\qquad\diagdown \\
\text{V}\qquad\text{SC} \\
\diagup\quad\diagdown \\
\text{NP}_1\quad\text{PP} \\
\diagup\quad\diagdown \\
\text{P}\quad\text{NP}_2
\end{array}
$$

While (20) yields the reading where <u>san ben shu</u> 'three books' has wide scope, (19) yields the reading where <u>liang ge ren</u> has wide scope. The delicate point is the adjunction site of NP_2 at LF. Aoun and Li argue that a PP is an adjunction site only if it is not an argument. In (20), the PP is a predicate of the small clause. NP_2 adjoins to the PP and is c-commanded by NP_1, which adjoins to VP. In (19) the PP is not an adjunction site, and NP_2 has to adjoin to VP_1, thus c-commanding NP_1, which has to adjoin to VP_2 according to MBR. The sentence (17) has the following constituent structure in Aoun and Li's analysis:

(21)

$$\begin{array}{c} \overset{VP_1}{PP} \overset{VP_1}{\underbrace{\hspace{2cm}}} VP_2 \\ P \quad NP_1 \quad V \quad NP_2 \end{array}$$

At LF, NP_1 is adjoined to VP_1, c-commanding NP_2, which is adjoined to VP_2.

Their approach is quite flexible. First, in structures like (19), in order for NP_2 to asymmetrically c-command NP_1, one has to assume that VP_2 is a maximal projection and not a V'. This is necessary because generally it is assumed that adjunction sites must be maximal projections (cf. May 1985). However, no limit is imposed on the number of VP's in a clause in Aoun and Li's analysis. More VP's yield more adjunction sites, so that an NP can adjoin to a higher VP in order to c-command the other NP or choose a lower VP in order to be c-commanded by it. A more restricted version of X' structure would make it difficult to obtain the desired interpretations. Second, they do not provide independent reasons for the choice of constituent structures. They refer to Larson (1986)'s arguments for asymmetrical c-command in the double object construction (as in (18)). On the basis of sentences such as (22-24), Larson argues that NP_1 asymmetrically c-commands NP_2. But the sentences Larson uses as supporting evidence have no exact parallels in Chinese.

(22) I showed Mary herself./*I showed herself Mary.
(23) I gave every worker his paycheck.
    *I gave its owner every paycheck.
(24) I showed each man the other's socks.
    *I showed the other's friend each man.

For example, (22) cannot be translated into a well-formed Chinese sentence in a single clause. A Chinese sentence corresponding to (23) with a pronoun referring to an inanimate object will sound very odd, since generally pronouns refer to humans. In addition, the possibilities of backward pronominal anaphora in Chinese are not the same as in English, since except in the case of resumptive pronouns in relative clauses, it is generally the case that a pronoun cannot be anaphoric to a following antecedent. Similarly, one will not get a grammatical rendition of (24) in Chinese, because it is a well-known fact about the language that the reciprocal construction involving the adverb huxiang 'each other' is highly restricted in occurrence (cf. Wang 1959:27-29). It seems to us that without adducing additional language-internal evidence, the validity of the particular constituent structures proposed is questionable.

Consider the following sentence, which is not the case of an oblique dative. But like (16), it is in V-NP-PP order.

(25) Ta   fang le   liang shao tang   zai san ge beizi li
     s/he put ASP   two   spoonful sugar   at three CL cup in
     "S/he put two spoonfuls of sugar into three cups."

No matter how Chinese speakers interpret the sentence, it seems that we can derive the interpretations following Aoun and Li's analysis. If lian shao tang takes wide scope, we assign (20) as its constituent structure. If san ge beizi takes wide scope, we can assign (19) to it. If it is ambiguous like (16), then it can have either. But we do not see why (26) should be less favorable as a representation, except that the MBR could not be maintained in this analysis.[10]

(26)

```
        ┌──VP───────┐
    V──┘  NP  ┌PP─┐
              P    NP
```

If, on the other hand, the reverse were empirically true, for instance, if (15) and (17) were ambiguous and (16) were not, we could simply propose an additional structure or take one away. This kind of arbitrariness stems from the lack of a minimal amount of language-internal support for constituent structures.

2.2.2 Thematic Approach

We propose an alternative analysis of the ambiguity and disambiguity of quantifier scope in Chinese which refers to the thematic roles borne by the QNPs. First of all, in view of the ambiguity of sentences such as (16), it is evident that linear order alone cannot be adequate. However, one significant fact is that we find no cases of simple clauses in which QNP_1 precedes QNP_2 but only QNP_2 may have wide scope.[11] This observation leads us to think that linear order is involved in scope interpretation.

Ambiguity arises as the result of interaction between linear order and another factor, which we call the thematic hierarchy. In Jackendoff (1972:43), it is found that the following thematic hierarchy constrains grammatical processes such as passsivization.

I. Agent
II. Location, source, goal
III. Theme

We argue that QNPs in Chinese fall into two groups according to a hierarchy akin to Jackendoff's, so that a QNP having a thematic role from group A may have scope over another QNP bearing a thematic role from group B:

(Group A) Agent, location, source, goal
(Group B) Theme, patient, factitive

Another way of looking at this is to say that the QNPs carrying group B thematic roles inherently take narrow scope as compared with those carrying group A thematic roles. Using the term Narrow Scope Thematic Role (NSTR) for ease of exposition, the generalization is that when a QNP in NSTR precedes another QNP, scope ambiguity arises. Since Theme, Goal, Location, Factitive can assume postverbal positions, the following sentences can be used to test the thematic hierarchy hypothesis.

Goal-theme: unambiguous
(27) Jihua weiyuanhui   mei nian   fenpei gei   si ge
     plan committee   every year   assign to   four CL
     yanjiusuo   liang ge zhongdian xiangmu
     institute   two   CL important project
     "The planning committee assigns four institutes two
     important projects every year."

Theme-goal: ambiguous
(28) Jihua weijyanhui   mei nian   fenpei
     plan committee   every year   assign
     liang ge zhongdian xiangmu gei   si ge yanjiusuo
     two   CL important project to   four CL institute
     "The planning committee assigns two important
     projects to four institutes every year."

Location-theme: unambiguous
(29) Qing ni   meitian zai   si ge shiguan li
     please you   everyday at   four CL testtube in
     fang   liang zhong shiji
     put   two   kind agent
     "Please put two kinds of agents in four testtubes everyday."

Theme-location: ambiguous
(30) Qing ni   meitian   fang   liang zhong shiji
     please you   everyday put   two   kind agent
     zai si ge shiguan li
     at   four CL testtube in
     "Please put two kinds of agents in four testtubes everyday."

Location-factitive: unambiguous
(31) Meitian   zai liang zhang zhi shang   hua   wu ge tuxing
     everyday at   two   sheet paper on   draw five CL diagram
     "Draw five diagrams on two sheets of paper everyday."

Factitive-location: ambiguous
(32) Meitian hua   liang ge tuxing zai   wu zhang zhi shang
     everyday draw two   CL diagram at   five sheet paper on
     "Draw two diagrams on five sheets of paper everyday."

When a QNP with NSTR is topicalized, taking a preverbal position, it has scope over QNPs following it. Compare (33-34) and (35-36).

(33) Wo song le   liang ben shu gei   san ge xuesheng
     I   give ASP two   CL book to   three CL student
     "I gave two books to three students."

(34) Liang ben shu,   wo song le gei   san ge xuesheng
     two   CL book   I   give ASP to   three CL student
     "Two books, I gave to three students."

(35) San ge xuesheng   zuo-chu le   liang dao nan   timu
     three CL student   solve ASP   two   CL difficult problem
     "Three students solved two problems."

(36) Liang dao nan   timu,   san ge xuesheng   zuo-chu le
     two   CL difficult problem   three CL student   solve ASP

"Two difficult problems, three students solved."

While (33) is ambiguous, (34) is not. In the latter case, liang ben shu 'two books' as the topic necessarily takes wide scope. In (35), san ge xuesheng 'three students' takes wide scope, but in (36) liang dao nan timu 'two difficult problems' does.

To summarize, we find that (a) when two NQPs occur in a clause, either both in preverbal position, or with one in topic/subject position and the other in postverbal position, the one on the left takes wide scope. (b) When both NQPs are postverbal and the one that bears a NSTR precedes the other, either of them can take wide scope. This suggests that two separate principles are involved in determining whether a QNP can have wide scope over another: linear order and the thematic hierarchy.

3. Relative scope of universal quantifier and numeral phrases

In the study of quantifier scope in English, linguists typically use sentences containing one universal quantifier and one existential quantifier, that is, every and some. For reasons mentioned above, one needs to use sentences with one universal quantifier mei and one numeral phrase in Chinese. We now examine sentences in which the first QNP (QNP_1) contains a numeral and the second a universal quantifier (QNP_2).

3.1 Universal quantifier in preverbal position

When a numeral phrase precedes a universal quantifier, both in preverbal position, the former invariably has scope over the latter.

(37) Liang dao nan   timu,   mei ge xuesheng   zuo le
     two CL difficult problem   every CL student   do ASP
     hao ji ci
     quite few time
     "Two difficult problems, every student did quite a few times."

(38) Liang ge xuesheng, mei dao nan   timu   zuo le
     two CL student   every CL difficult problem do ASP
     hao ji ci
     quite few time
     "Two students, (they) did every difficult problem quite a few times."

(39) Liang ge xuesheng   bei mei ge laoshi   piping le yi dun
     two CL student   by every CL teacher criticize ASP one time
     "Two students are criticized by every teacher once"

(40) Liang ge laoshi   ba mei ge xuesheng dou   piping le yi dun
     two CL teacher   BA every CL student all criticize ASP one time
     "Two teachers criticized every student once."

As far as scope is concerned, these sentences are not different from (11-14), in which both QPs are NQPs.

In Aoun and Li (1987a,b) the passive construction is said to allow ambiguous interpretations. An example they cite is (41).

(41) Liang ge xuesheng bei mei ge laoshi   jiaodao
     two CL student   by every CL teacher teach

"Two students are taught by every teacher."

The sentence sounds unnatural for an irrelevant reason. The verb jiaodao is not normally passivized. Leaving aside this point, we still cannot obtain the reading with liang ge xuesheng 'two students' having narrow scope. The sentence cannot describe the situation in which every teacher teaches different students. Some of our informants take another example of theirs to be ambiguous.

(42) Mei ge nanren bei yi ge nuren zhuazou
     every CL man   by one CL woman arrest
     "Every man was arrested by a woman."

But this sentence has the same status as (1), with the universal quantifier preceding the numeral phrase. Speakers who find (42) ambiguous should also find (1) ambiguous. As explained earlier, this is not a good test of whether QNP_2 can have wide scope. It may happen that all men were arrested by the same strong woman. Aoun and Li argue that ambiguity is possible in the passive construction because the trace of QNP_1 is c-commanded by QNP_2, though QNP_1 itself is not.[12] If their observation is empirically incorrect, then it is gratuitous to invoke the trace.

3.2 Universal quantifier in postverbal position

When we consider cases where the universal quantifier is postverbal, we are confronted with the difficulty mentioned previously: occurrences of the universal quantifier mei 'every' are restricted. S-V-O sentences with mei in object position do not lend themselves to testing scope ambiguity, since they are hardly acceptable.[13] How should the restriction on mei be stated? Let us look at more examples.

(43) Mei ge zhongguo duiyuan   dabai le   yi ge riben duiyuan
     every CL Chinese player   defeat ASP one CL Japanese player
     "Every Chinese player defeated a Japanese player."
(44) ? Yi ge zhongguo duiyuan   dabai le   mei ge riben duiyuan
     one CL Chinese player   defeat ASP every CL Japanese player
     "A Chinese player defeated every Japanese player."
(45) Ta song le   mei ge ren   liang ben shu
     s/he give ASP every CL person two CL book
     "S/he gave everybody two books."
(46) ? Ta   song le   liang ge ren   mei ben shu
     s/he give ASP two CL person   every CL book
     "S/he gave two people every book."

Based on the difference in acceptability between (43) and (44) on the one hand and (45) and (46) on the other, one may hypothesize that mei 'every' can hardly be the direct object or that it cannot be used to quantify an NP which is the theme or patient. It will be difficult to state the restriction in terms of asymmetrical c-command at LF, as the following examples show:

(47) Ta   song le   liang ben shu gei   mei ge ren
     s/he give ASP   two   CL book to   every CL person
     "S/he gave two books to everybody."
(48) ? Ta song le   mei ben shu gei   liang ge ren
     s/he give ASP   every CL book to   two   CL person
     "S/he gave every book to two people."

The two sentences are exactly the same with respect to the
configurational relationship of the two QNPs, which can c-
command each other at LF. Yet (48) is less acceptable than
(47).
    We have now arrived at an understanding of how scope
ambiguity can be tested in Chinese. Sentences with no
postverbal theme, patient, or factitive NPs quantified by mei
should be used. (47) and the sentences below are relevant
examples.

(49) Ta ji le   liang ben shu gei   mei ge xuesheng
     s/he send ASP two   CL book to   every CL student
     "S/he sent two books to every student."
(50) Liang ben shu, ta   ji gei le   mei ge xuesheng
     two   CL book s/he send to ASP   every CL student
     "Two books, s/he sent to every student."
(51) Ta fang le   liang zhong shiji zai   mei ge shiguan li
     s/he put ASP   two   kind agent at   every CL testtube in
     "S/he put two kinds of agents into every testtube."
(52) Ta   ba liang zhong shiji   fang zai mei ge shiguan li
     s/he BA two   kind agent   put in   every CL testtube in
     "S/he put two kinds of agents into every testtube."

(49-50) form a minimal pair. (50) represents sentences of QNP_1
[V -QNP_2]$_{VP}$ order and is unambiguous: only the topicalized QNP
liang ben shu 'two books' takes wide scope. In (49), however,
both QNPs are inside the VP. Thus, QNP_1 liang ben shu 'two
books' may have wide scope since it precedes the other QNP.
QNP_2 (meige xuesheng 'every student') may also have wide scope,
because it is a goal NP which occupies a higher position on the
thematic hierarchy than QNP_1, the latter being a theme NP. The
ambiguity of (49) is thus predicted. (51), which has the same
structure as (49), involves a QNP_2 which is a location or goal
NP and is therefore also ambiguous. The Ba-sentence (52)
represents a structure where QNP_1 is preverbal and QNP_2
postverbal but both fall within the verb phrase. In other words
(52) has the structure:

  [[P QNP_1]$_{PP}$ V [P QNP_2]$_{PP}$]$_{VP}$

It is reasonable to include the Ba prepositional phrase as part
of VP, since verbs have to subcategorize for Ba-PPs, i.e. not
all verbs allow the preposing of an object to the prepositional
object position of Ba. Since the Ba object liang zhong shiji
'two kinds of agent' is a theme NP and precedes QNP_2 meige
shiguan 'every testtube', our linear order and thematic
hierarchy principles will predict ambiguity. In fact, sentences

such as (52) containing *Ba*-phrases are found to be ambiguous.[14] This suggests to us that the thematic hierarchy applies as long as the two relevant QNPs both occur within the VP. (46) is most likely unambiguous, though we cannot say for certain as it is not a fully acceptable sentence. If it is unambiguous, then the universal quantifier <u>mei</u> and numerical quantifiers have the same scope pattern as follows.

(53) (the following structures do not show scope
        ambiguity; QNP_1 has scope over QNP_2)
      $QNP_1...QNP_2..V$
      $QNP_1..[V..QNP_2]_{VP}$

      (the following structures will exhibit ambiguity
       only if QNP_1 = theme, patient, factitive)
      $[..QNP_1 V..QNP_2]_{VP}$
      $[..V QNP_1..QNP_2]_{VP}$

4. Conclusion

We have examined a range of data involving numeral phrases and universal quantifiers, demonstrating that quantifier scope within the clause in Chinese can be adequately handled by means of linear order and the thematic hierarchy. The advantage of our analysis over Aoun and Li's is that (a) our empirical coverage is wider than theirs, and (b) since thematic roles are clearly relevant to scope phenomenon, reference to the thematic hierarchy eliminates the need to adopt ad-hoc constitutent structures which are not independently justified for Chinese.

Notes

*We would like to thank Shen Shiguo for comments on some of our arguments.
1. It should be noted that some English speakers find sentences such as "Every student bought a book." unambiguous and that even if it is ambiguous, the wide scope reading of <u>a</u> <u>book</u> is highly marked to them (cf. Reinhart 1983:193,197).
2. CL= classifier; ASP=aspect marker;NOM=nominalizer.
3. The sentence can be improved by replacing <u>mei</u> by another universal quantifier <u>suoyou</u>. But then the sentence is close to "A student bought all the books."
4. The universal quantifier <u>mei</u> in topic position serves to faciliate the scope-differentiated readings of the numeral phrases in the sentence. Discussion of relative scope at this point is restricted to the numeral phrases.
5. It is easier to get scope-differentiated readings when the subject is read with contrastive stress.
6. Aoun and Li (1987a,b) take passive sentences to be ambiguous and argue that it is because the NP following <u>bei</u> 'by' c-commands the trace of the surface subject. We disagree with them on empirical grounds. None of our informants can have an interpretation with <u>sange</u> <u>shengaoren</u> 'three reviewers' taking wide scope. But since Aoun and Li use examples with a numeral

phrase and a universal quantifier, we defer our comment on their example until section 3.1.

7. The pragmatic situation described by (16) favors the wide scope reading of <u>liang ge ren</u> 'two people'. Adding a universal quantifier topic at the beginning of the sentence should make the scope-differentiated readings of the NQPs clear. e.g.

Mei ge yue,   ta song   san ben shu gei   liang ge ren
every CL month,   s/he give   three CL book to   two   CL person
"(In) every month, s/he gives three books to two people."

8. This is the structure adopted from Kayne (1983). Aoun and Li give an alternative small clause structure, following Larson (1986). The latter will not be discussed here because of space considerations.

9. The Minimal Binding Requirement as stated by Aoun and Li (1987): "Variables must be bound by the most local potential A'antecedent." "A qualifies as a potential A' binder for B iff A c-commands B, A is in an A'-position and coindexing of (A,B) would not violate any grammatical principle."

10. A strict adherence to binary branching will lead one to reject a structure such as (26). However, we believe whether a V NP PP sequence must be analyzed as [V NP]$_V$, PP should rest on evidence from the relevant Chinese data (cf. Kayne (1981)'s elaborate argument for positing the above structure for some English V NP PP sequences and not others). Otherwise, the alternative (26) is just as plausible as a [V NP] PP analysis.

11. We are putting aside cases of NP-internal quantification where the QNPs concerned may themselves contain QNPs, e.g.

Wo gei le   [[qi ge ren]   de zuqiudui]   san   zhong qiuyi
I give ASP   seven person   NOM soccer-team three kind shirt
"I gave three kinds of shirts to seven-member soccer teams."
"For each of seven people, I gave (his/her) soccer team
     three kinds of shirts."

Even in these cases, one will not have a situation where only QNP$_2$ may have scope over QNP$_1$.

12. Aoun and Li's Scope Principle is stated as follows: "A quantifier A may have scope over a quantifier B in case A c-commands a member of the chain containing B or the container of B."

13. These sentences are described as 'hardly acceptable' because some sentences with <u>mei</u> quantifying the verbal object such as the one below are acceptable. Note, however, the object NP in this case is location rather than theme.

Liang ge ren   zhao   pian le   mei ge jiaoluo
two CL person   look-for   complete ASP every CL corner
"Two people looked for every corner without exception."

14. In a survey carried out in Beijing, China on two groups of college graduates who were native speakers of Mandarin, one consisting of linguists (N=9) and the other non-linguists

(N = 11), subjects were asked to assign a reading to the test sentences (i) and (ii). The results are as follows:

(i) qing   ba yi tiao maojin   gai zai   mei ge xiaohai sheng shang
     please BA one CL towel   cover at   every CL child body on
     "Please lay a towel on every child."

	wide scope of 'a towel'	wide scope of 'every child'
nonlinguists	9	2
linguists	4	4
total	13	6

(ii) qing   ba yi gen shengzi   fang zai   mei ge zhuo shang
      please BA one CL string   put at   every CL table on
      "Please put a string on every table"

	wide scope of 'a string'	wide scope of 'every table'
nonlinguists	7	4
linguists	4	4
total	11	8

We conclude from this that sentences involving a QNP which is object of *Ba* and another postverbal QNP are ambiguous (see Lee 1989 for details).

References

Aoun, J. and Li, A. (1987a) "The Syntax of Quantifier Scope" University of Southern California ms.

Aoun, J. and Li, A. (1987b) "The Syntax of Scope" University of Southern California ms.

Chao, Y.R. (1968) A Grammar of Spoken Chinese Berkeley, University of California Press.

Duanmu, S. (1988) "The Lack of Scope Ambiguity in Chinese" MIT ms.

Huang, J. C.-T. (1982) Logical Relations in Chinese and the Theory of Grammar Doctoral dissertation, MIT.

Huang, J. C.-T. (1983) "On the Representation of Scope in Chinese" Journal of Chinese Linguistics 11.1

Huang, S. F. (1981) "On the Scope Phenomenon of Chinese Quantifiers" Journal of Chinese Linguistics 9.2

Jackendoff, R. (1972) Semantic Interpretation and Generative Grammar Cambridge, MIT Press.

Kayne, R. (1981) "Unambiguous Paths" in R. May and J. Koster (eds) Levels of Syntactic Representation Dordrecht, Foris, reprinted in Kayne (1983).

Kayne, R. (1983) Connectedness and Binary Branching Dordrecht, Foris.

Kempson, R. and Cormack, A. (1981) "Ambiguity and Quantification" Linguistics and Philosophy 4:259-309

Larson, R. (1986) "On the Double Object Construction" MIT ms. later published in (1988) Linguistic Inquiry 19.3

Lee, T. (1986) Studies in Quantification in Chinese Doctoral dissertation, UCLA.

Lee, T. (1989) "The relevance of linear order and thematic relations to the acquisition of quantifier scope in Chinese", Chinese University of Hong Kong, ms.

May, R. (1977) The Grammar of Quantification Doctoral dissertation, MIT.

May, R. (1985) Logical Form:its structure and derivation Cambridge, MIT Press.

Reinhart, T. (1983) Anaphora and Semantic Interpretation, London, Croom Helm.

Wang, Li (1957) Zhongguo Xiandai Yufa (A Grammar of Modern Chinese) vol. 2, Beijing, Zhonghua Publishers.

EMPTY CATEGORIES AND COMPLEX NPs IN CHINESE[1]

Ping Xue
University of Victoria

1. Introduction: Complex NPs and Subjacency

One of the most interesting topics in Chinese syntax involves the question of formal properties of Chinese empty categories. The central issue of this question concerns complex noun phrases. Consider the structures in the following:

(1)   * Zhangsan$_i$, wo mai-le xie [NP [S t$_i$ xihuan] de] shu].
              I   buy ASP some   like   MOD book
       *'Zhangsan, I bought some books that ____ likes.'

(2)   * Heping$_i$, zhe shi [NP [S renmin xunqiu t$_i$] de] fang'an].
       peace   this is   people seek   MOD   plan
       *'The peace, this is the plan that people seek ____ .'

In (1), a NP is extracted from the relative clause, and in (2) a NP is extracted from the NP complement clause. Neither of the structures is well-formed. These examples seem to suggest that Chinese exhibits the Complex NP island effects, and therefore must obey the Subjacency Condition (see Huang 1982,1984,1987 and Liu 1987 for discussion).

However, as Xu and Langendoen (1985) show, sentences like that in (3) are perfectly well-formed:

(3)   Zheben shu$_i$, wo renwei [NP [S du-guo t$_i$] de] ren] buduo.
       this book I   think   read ASP   MOD man not many
       *'This book, I think there are not many people who read ____ .'

In this sentence, the NP 'this book' is also extracted from the relative clause. Xu and Langendoen (1985) and Xu (1986) argue that if the Subjacency Condition is relevant to Chinese, extraction in sentences like (3) would be impossible no matter whether NP and S or S' are assumed as bounding nodes (see Tang 1976, Lu 1987 for related discussion).[2]

As we can see, the difference between (1) and (3) is that (1) involves extraction from the subject position of the relative clause, while (3) involves extraction from the object position. Further, the ill-formedness of (2) indicates that extraction, even an object extraction, is impossible from a NP complement clause. This situation indeed makes it difficult to determine the relevancy of the Complex NP Constraint, and in fact has evoked a long-standing controversy in the literature on the relevancy of the Subjacency Condition to the study of Chinese syntax (see Huang 1982,1984,1987; Liu 1987; Lu 1987; Xu 1986; and Xu and Langendoen 1985).[3]

In the framework of Generalized Phrase Structure Grammar (GPSG), here I will pursue a phrase structure (PS) treatment of antecedent-gap relations in Chinese complex NPs. I will show that antecedent-gap relations in Chinese complex NPs follow from the Foot Feature Principle and the Slash termination operation proposed in Gazdar, et al. (1985).[4] I argue that the impossibility of extraction from NP complement clauses is due to a universal principle, i.e. the Proper Inclusion Principle (cf. Sanders 1974, Pullum 1979). As a result, I suggest that the relevant condition on Chinese empty categories is something like the Empty Category Principle rather than the Subjacency Condition.[5]

2.   Phrase Structure Rules for Complex NPs.[6]

GKPS proposes a general rule to introduce unbounded dependency constructions, which reads as follows:

(4)   S ---> XP, S/XP

This rule simply says that a sentence dominates a constituent XP and a sentence which contains a phonologically null constituent of category XP. I assume that this is the relevant rule responsible for introducing Chinese topicalization constructions. Parallel to the rules proposed in GKPS for English relative clauses, the following rule will serve to introduce Chinese relative clauses and NP complement clauses:[7]

(5)   NP ---> S[+DE], H

In the rule, the symbol H stands for a unspecified category which has the status of head. This rule then is expanded by three rules roughly like those in (6).[8]

(6)   a.   S[+DE] ---> VP, DE
       b.   S[+DE] ---> S/NP, DE
       c.   S[+DE] ---> S, DE

These three rules will be responsible for introducing complex noun phrases like those as shown roughly in (7).

(7) a.

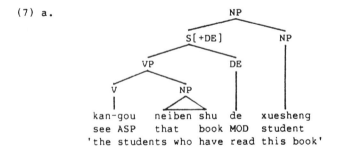

b.

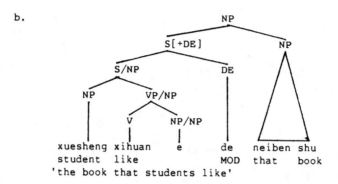

```
                                NP
                    S[+DE]              NP
            S/NP              DE
        NP      VP/NP
               V      NP/NP
    xuesheng xihuan    e       de    neiben shu
    student  like              MOD   that   book
    'the book that students like'
```

c.

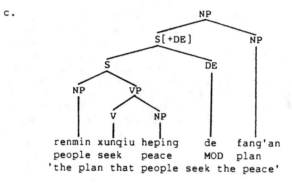

```
                                NP
                    S[+DE]              NP
            S              DE
        NP      VP
               V      NP
    renmin xunqiu heping      de     fang'an
    people seek   peace       MOD    plan
    'the plan that people seek the peace'
```

(6a) is responsible for introducing subject-gapped relative clauses like that in (7a); (6b) is for nonsubject-gapped relative clauses like that in (7b); (6c) is for NP complement clauses like that in (7c).[9]

3. The Foot Feature Principle and the Slash Termination Metarules.

GKPS introduces a universal feature instantiation principle, the Foot Feature Principle (FFP), which plays a crucial role in the GPSG analysis of unbounded dependency constructions. The FFP says roughly:

The FOOT feature specifications which are instantiated on a daughter node in a local tree must also be instantiated on the mother node in that local tree.

Instantiated feature specifications are distinguished from inherited feature specifications. Instantiated feature specifications are those which are not specified in a phrase structure rule and can occur freely in the projection of a local tree, while inherited feature specifications are directly mentioned in a phrase structure rule. Consider a tree, with relevant PS rules in (8).

(8)   a. S ---> XP, S/XP
          b. S ---> NP, VP
          c. VP ---> V, NP

```
                     S
             _____|_____
            NP              S/NP
            |          _____|_____
            |         NP            VP/NP
            |         |         _____|_____
            |         |         V           NP/NP
            |         |         |             |
        Zhangsan,    wo      rensi            t
                      I       know
            'Zhangsan, I know ____ .'
```

SLASH is a category-valued FOOT feature. Intuitively, a category C/C' is a constituent C which contains a phonologically null subconstituent C', usually known as "trace". The tree in (8) is generated from the relevant PS rules a, b, c. In the topmost local tree, SLASH is introduced by the PS rule, therefore inherited, while in other two local trees, SLASH is not mentioned in the relevant PS rules, therefore instantiated. The FFP must be satisfied in terms of each local tree. As we can see, the structure in (8) satisfies the FFP.

Slash termination is accomplished in GKPS by metarules, Slash Termination Metarule 1 (STM1) and Slash Termination Metarule 2 (STM2). STM1 reads as follows:

(9)   STM1
$$X ---> W, X^2$$
$$\Downarrow$$
$$X ---> W, X^2 \; [+NULL]$$

STM1 says roughly that any PS rule which introduces a BAR-2 category has a corresponding rule where that category carries the feature [+NULL]. Further, a Feature Co-occurence Restriction (FCR) [+NULL] --> [SLASH], and other principles interact to guarantee that every [+NULL] category contains a SLASH specification and is a terminal category. Note that being a metarule, STM1 applies only to lexical PS rules, i.e. those introducing lexical heads. This restriction is essential to the present analysis. Thus, in effect, only the sister of a BAR-0 category will be assigned the feature [+NULL] and therefore be successfully terminated.[10]

4. The FFP, the STM Operation, and Empty Categories in Complex NPs

In terms of a GPSG framework, I claim that extraction from a complex NP is possible if the structure satisfies the Foot Feature Principle and the requirement for Slash termination. As shown above, relative clauses and NP complement clauses in this analysis are generated directly from PS rules. Concerning topicalization, relevant examples are repeated below in (10).

(10)a. Zheben shu$_i$, wo renwei [NP [S du guo t$_i$] de ren] bu duo.
　　　　this book　I think　　　read ASP　MOD man not many
　　　　*'This book, I think there are not many people who read ＿＿ .'

　b. *Zhangsan$_i$, wo mai-le　xie [NP [S t$_i$ xihuan] de　shu]
　　　　　　　　I　buy ASP some　　　　　like　MOD book
　　　*'Zhangsan, I bought some books that ＿＿ likes.'

　c. *Heping$_i$, zhe shi [NP [S renmin xunqiu t$_i$] de fang'an].
　　　peace　this is　　　people seek　　MOD plan
　　　*'The peace, this is the plan that people seek ＿＿ .'

Given the PS rules stated in (5) and (6) above, the grammar will assign trees (11a), (11b) and (11c) for (10a), (10b) and (10c) respectively.

(11) a.

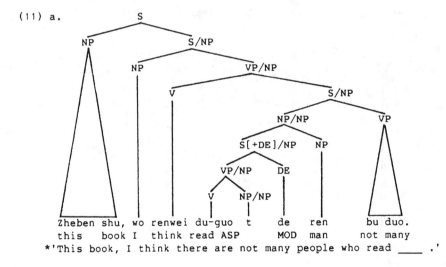

Zheben shu, wo renwei du-guo t de ren bu duo.
this　book I think read ASP　MOD man　not many
*'This book, I think there are not many people who read ＿＿ .'

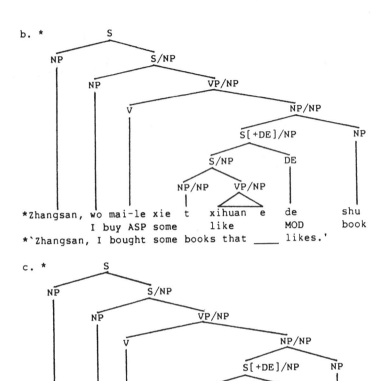

b. *

```
                    S
        ┌───────────┴───────────┐
       NP                      S/NP
                     ┌───────────┴───────────┐
                    NP                      VP/NP
                              ┌──────────────┴──────────────┐
                              V                            NP/NP
                                                   ┌──────────┴──────────┐
                                              S[+DE]/NP                  NP
                                          ┌───────┴───────┐
                                        S/NP              DE
                                   ┌──────┴──────┐
                                 NP/NP         VP/NP
                                              /    \
  *Zhangsan,  wo  mai-le  xie    t         xihuan  e    de      shu
              I   buy ASP  some             like        MOD     book
  *'Zhangsan, I bought some books that ____ likes.'
```

c. *

```
                    S
        ┌───────────┴───────────┐
       NP                      S/NP
                     ┌───────────┴───────────┐
                    NP                      VP/NP
                              ┌──────────────┴──────────────┐
                              V                            NP/NP
                                                   ┌──────────┴──────────┐
                                              S[+DE]/NP                  NP
                                          ┌───────┴───────┐
                                        S/NP              DE
                                   ┌──────┴──────┐
                                  NP           VP/NP
                                             /      \
                                            V       NP/NP
  *Heping,  zhe  shi   renmin  xunqiu  t        de    fang'an.
   peace    this is    people  seek               MOD   plan
  *'The peace, this is the plan that people seek ____ .'
```

In the light of the PS rules in (6), we can see that object extraction in (11a) is possible in a GPSG analysis in that the relative clause here involves simply a VP. In each of the local trees in the structure, the Slash category which is instantiated on a daughter node is also instantiated on the mother node. Further, the relevant local tree, i.e. the bottommost VP, is generated from a lexical PS rule and the Slash category is the sister to a lexical head. Thus, the structure satisfies both the FFP and the requirement for the application of the STM.

The problems with (11b) can be accounted for in two ways. First, the Slash category in the subject position can not be terminated simply because it is not the sister to a lexical category. Second, note that the relevant PS rule for the relative clause is: S[+DE] ---> S/NP, DE (see (6b) above). The SLASH on the daughter S node in the corresponding local tree is inherited from the rule, not instantiated. Thus, on one hand, the SLASH will not go up further in this local tree since the FFP does not require the SLASH to occur on the mother node S[+DE]. On the other hand, although the SLASH in the topmost local tree is inherited, it is instantiated in other local trees. The FFP will require SLASH to percolate all the way down to the bottom of the tree. The problem is that with respect to the PS rule of (6b) (i.e. S[+DE] ---> S/NP, DE), SLASH on the daughter S node in the relevant local tree is inherited; if instantiated SLASH on the mother S[+DE] node, as the FFP requires, is also instantiated on the daughter S/NP node, it would create a multiple Slash category like S/NP/NP, which is impossible because multiple Slash categories are prohibited by the grammar.[11] Adopting this restriction in the tree construction, (11b) has an apparent violation of the FFP since SLASH on the S[+DE] node is instantiated while SLASH on its daughter S node is inherited.

(11c) seems to be a counterexample to the analysis, since the structure appears to satisfy both the FFP and the requirement for the application of the STM. Then what should account for the ill-formedness apparently caused by the extraction from the NP complement clause? Note that the relevant intuition is: when a NP is extracted from a NP complement clause, the natural interpretation is one in which the empty category left behind, i.e. the "trace", would be associated with the head NP of the complex NP rather than with the extracted NP (i.e. the topic). In other words, if the object or the subject of a NP complement clause is "missing", the clause will be automatically interpreted as a relative clause, with the extracted NP stranded. This implies that extraction from a NP complement clause would bring about a "reconstruction". The structural relations after the "reconstruction" could be expressed as in (12).

(12) Heping, zhe shi [NP [S renmin xunqiu t_i] de fang'an$_i$.
    peace this is   people seek   MOD plan

The reason for this "reconstruction" is apparently attributable to the effect of the parallel PS rule for relative clauses. This effect disturbs the proper identification of the "gap" with its antecedent, i.e. the topic. Structurally, although the relevant PS rule for NP complement clauses is: S[+DE] ---> S, DE, when a SLASH[NP] occurs on the daughter S node, the grammar will treat it as inherited, not instantiated, since there is a PS rule: S[+DE] ---> S/NP, DE (see (6) above) in the grammar. Thus, for (11c), since the grammar treats the SLASH on the bottommost S node as inherited in that local tree, the structure violates the FFP in the same way as (11b) does: SLASH on the S[+DE] node is instantiated but SLASH on the daughter S node is inherited (although (11c) has no problem with Slash termination).

In fact, the analysis of extraction from a NP complement clause like (11c) can be accommodated by a universal principle, namely, the Proper Inclusion Principle. It can be stated roughly as follows (cf. Sanders 1974, Pullum 1979):

> For any representation, that satisfies the structural descriptions of both rule A and rule B, A applies instead of the application of B if and only if the structural description of A properly includes the structural description of B.

Referring to the present analysis, this principle has the effect that when two rules A and B seem to license a local tree, rule A applies instead of B if the structural description of A properly includes that of B. Thus, when SLASH occurs in a local tree, the PS rule for relative clauses, i.e. (6b) applies instead of the corresponding rule for NP complement clauses, i.e. (6c), since the structural description of (6b) properly includes that of (6c) plus an additional Slash feature specification. As a result, the relevant local tree in structures like (11c) can never meet the FFP.[12]

Consider another case which seems to be in favor of invoking the Proper Inclusion Principle in the grammar. The following sentence is cited from Huang (1982):

(13)   Shuiguo, wo zui xihuan xiangjiao.
         fruit   I most like banana
         'As for fruit, I like banana most.'

This is a typical example of what Xu and Langendoen (1985) call "Chinese style" topic structures. Obviously, there is a PS rule: S ---> NP, S in the grammar, responsible for generating sentences like (13). The interesting thing is that it is possible to topicalize a NP as shown in (14a), but not (14b).

(14) a. Shuiguo, xiangjiao$_i$, wo zui xihuan t$_i$.
         fruit   banana   I most like
         'As for fruit, bananas, I like ____ most.'

     b. *Xiangjiao$_i$, shuiguo, wo zui xihuan t$_i$.
         banana   fruit   I most like
        *'Bananas, as for fruit, I like ____ most.'

If the claim that topics, unlike Wh-phrases, are not island-creating is generally correct (see Liu,1987), then, why is this not true of the present case and what should account for the difference between (14a) and (14b)? As mentioned above, the following two PS rules exist side by side in the grammar:

(15) a.   S ---> NP, S
     b.   S ---> NP, S/NP

Given these two rules, (14a) and (14b) will be assigned structures respectively as in (16a) and (16b).

(16) a.

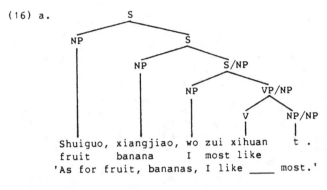

```
Shuiguo, xiangjiao, wo zui xihuan    t .
fruit    banana     I  most like
'As for fruit, bananas, I like ____ most.'
```

b. *

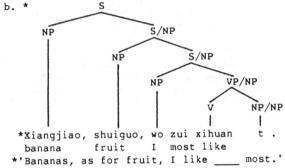

```
*Xiangjiao, shuiguo, wo zui xihuan    t .
 banana    fruit     I  most like
*'Bananas, as for fruit, I like ____ most.'
```

Note that (16b) is ill-formed only when the gap is associated with the first topic. If the gap is associated with second topic, the sentence would be perfectly well-formed (leaving lexical or pragmatical meaning aside). Intuitively, for a sentence like (16b), native speakers would associate the null category with the second topic, not the first one. This amounts to saying that the grammar does not allow SLASH to be instantiated on the second S node in the present case.[13] In terms of structure, (16b) is impossible since the grammar will treat SLASH on the lowest S node as inherited in the relevant local tree. Thus, with respect to the second local tree in (16b), the structure violates the FFP, since SLASH on the mother node is instantiated but SLASH on the daughter node is inherited.

As Pullum (1979) notes, '...when a special case and a more general case are tested for applicability, the general case should be considered to be applicable only if the special case is not. This merely guarantees that the special case will be relevant in some instance. If the general case always took precedence, there would be no instances at all in which the special case was applicable.' In Chinese, the case of relative clauses is a special case. If extraction from a NP complement clause is allowed, there would be no place for relative clauses because the interpretation for a relative clause would hardly be identified. It seems to me that this is a correct generalization for Chinese.

5. Conclusion

This analysis shows that extraction is possible in Chinese complex NPs if the relevant structure satisfies both the FFP and the requirement for Slash termination. The FFP actually ensures that an empty category is properly identified (properly linked with its antecedent through local dependencies), and Slash termination operation in effect insists that an empty category must be licenced by a lexical head. These facts indicate that a Chinese empty category must be not only properly associated with its antecedent, but also must be, in some sense, in the domain of a lexical head. This, though not stated here in terms of the Government Binding theory, suggests that the relevant condition on Chinese empty categories, at least with complex NPs, is something like a version of the Empty Category Principle, consistent with Stowell's (1985) proposal that 'an empty category requires both a head governor and an identifying element.'

The Proper Inclusion Principle, though quite plausible, has been tested largely from phonological cases. This analysis, if it is correct, provides a new case from syntax for this principle. Various fundamental principles of grammar interact to determine the status of a particular structure. As shown above, whether a structure is well-formed may involve not only the principle about empty categories but also the principle about rule interaction. Though this analysis assumes that the Proper Inclusion Principle is relevant to Chinese syntax, to what extent and under what circumstance it actually applies is a topic for further research. It is hoped that this analysis may serve as a useful stimulus to further research on relevant issues in Chinese syntax and offer direct or indirect implications for the theory of grammar.

NOTES

1 I wish to thank Thomas E. Hukari for helpful discussions and comments.

2 Huang (1987) notes that Subjacency violation is possible in Chinese, as in other languages, just in case a given gap is base-generated. However, base-generated empty categories in Chinese have never been systematically sorted out.

3 The Wh-island Constraint does not have effects in Chinese syntax, though it may hold at LF as Huang assumes. Besides, Chinese appears to lack the effects of the Sentential Subject Constraint.

4 I will refer to Gazdar, Klein, Pullum, and Sag (1985) as GKPS.

5 Xu and Langendoen (1985) argue that the "gap" in a topic structure is simply related to the topic not as a variable bound by the topic. But what Xu and Langendoen's proposal achieves, as Huang (1987) points out, is no more than a restatement of a familiar phenomenon: the comment clause must say something about the topic. A proposal like this has neither achieved anything in the sense of generative grammar, nor has said something specific about Chinese topic structures.

6 I leave open the proper analysis of linear order of categories. Thus, in this

paper, I use the term PS rules instead of ID rules.

7   I leave open the proper analysis of the modifier marker "de". In this paper, I use DE as a feature as well as an independent category. Perhaps, "de" could be treated as some special case of NP. If it is correct, the expansion rules in (6) would naturally follow with the assumption: VP > DE, since these PS rules are already in the grammar.

8   Traditionally, Chinese relative clauses are analyzed as a result of head-raising movement (see Huang 1982). In Chinese, a NP head can be modified by two or more relative clauses. In fact, there is no upper limit to the potential number of such clauses. For this situation, the derivation of head raising processes will be quite cumbersome though it is not totally impossible. By contrast, a recursive application of the general rule in (5) directly predicts the possibility of multiple relative clauses. This seems to be an empirical case in favour of a PS treatment of Chinese relative clauses.

9   For NP complement clauses, there is a variation. The modifier marker "de" sometimes doesn't occur between the head and the complement clause, but in general it does occur. Further, for the NP complement clauses without "de", it is almost always possible to insert "de"; but it is impossible to omit "de" for those which usually have it. From these facts, I assume that (6c) is the basic relevant PS rule for NP complement clauses.

10   The subject of a sentential complement which is the sister of a BAR-0 category will be assigned the feature [+NULL] and terminated by the STM2.

11   Since a category is defined as a partial function, it doesn't allow the unification of two categories which carry different values with respect to a particular feature. Two SLASH specifications of a multiple Slash category could in principle have different values, and therefore would violate the definition.

12   As Sanders (1974) notes, all explanations of proper inclusion relations between particular rules are dependent on the particular assumptions about the representations of given constituents and on the general assumption that linguistic objects are represented in terms of simplex-features. Thus, there will be considerable grounds for interpretation as to whether the principle applies in a given case.

13   Gazdar (1981) suggests that SLASH can refer to resumptive pronouns as well as empty categories. It seems to me that in this regard Chinese resumptive pronouns and empty categories behave differently. The involvement of resumptive pronouns in a structure may complicate the situation. How to treat them is a topic for further research.

478

REFERENCES

Gazdar, G. 1981. Unbounded dependencies and coordination structure. Linguistic Inquiry 12, 155-184.

Gazdar, G., E. Klein, G. Pullum, and I. Sag. 1985. Generalized Phrase Structure Grammar. Cambridge: Harvard University Press.

Huang, C.-T. J. 1982. Logical Relations in Chinese and the Theory of Grammar. Doctoral dissertation. MIT, Cambridge, Massachusetts.

Huang, C.-T. J. 1984. On the distribution and reference of empty pronouns. Linguistic Inquiry 15, 531-574.

Huang, C.-T. J. 1987. Remarks on empty categories in Chinese. Linguistic Inquiry 18, 321-337.

Liu, F.-H. 1987. On topic-traces in chinese. Proceedings of the West Coast Conference on Formal Linguistics. 142-152.

Lu, J. H.-T. 1987. Constraints on NP-movement in Mandarin Chinese. Journal of Chinese Linguistics 16, 1-29.

Pullum, G. 1979. Rule Interaction and the Organization of a Grammar. New York: Garland.

Sanders, G. 1974. Precedence relations in language. Foundations of Language 11, 361-400.

Stowell, T. 1985. Null operator and the theroy of grammar. Unpublished ms. University of California, Los Angeles.

Tang, T.-C. 1976. Studies in Transformational Grammar of Chinese. Volume 1: Movement Transformations. Taipei: Student Book Co. Ltd.

Xu, L. 1986. Free empty categories. Linguistic Inquiry 17, 75-93.

Xu, L and D. T. Langendoen. 1985. Topic structures in Chinese. Language 61, 1-27.

Long-Distance Anaphors in Korean and their Cross-linguistic Implications[*]

Jeong-Me Yoon
Cornell University

0. Introduction

Korean has several different reflexives, <u>caki</u>, <u>casin</u>, <u>caki-casin</u>, <u>pronoun-casin</u>, each of which has different binding properties. These reflexives can be divided into two distinct categories, one which is locally bound (<u>caki-casin</u>, <u>pronoun-casin</u>), and the other which can be long-distance bound (<u>caki</u>, <u>casin</u>). It is well-known that long-distance binding (LDB, henceforth) in general, which is also found in languages like Japanese, Chinese, Icelandic, Classical Latin, etc., is not readily explained with Principle A of Binding Theory (Chomsky 1981), and there have been various attempts to give an adequate account of long-distance binding in these languages. These diverse approaches to the problem can be divided into two groups. One approach treats both local and long-distance anaphors (LDAs) uniformly under Principle A of Binding Theory either by parameterizing the Binding Domain for anaphors (Yang 1983; Manzini & Wexler 1987) or by proposing LF movement for LDAs (Chomsky 1986, Pica 1987, Battistella 1986, Huang & Tang 1988). The other approach treats only locally bound anaphors under BT-A while LDAs are treated separately, usually by invoking the notion of logophoricity (Clements 1975, Thrainsson 1976, 1987, Kameyama 1984, Kuno 1987, Sells 1987, etc.).

In this paper, we will propose an account of long-distance binding in Korean which is in line with the second approach. We claim that Principle A of BT should be reserved only for local anaphor binding whereas all apparent long-distance anaphor binding should be treated differently, by appealing to the notion of logophoricity. We will first examine and compare the binding properties of differnt anaphors in Korean, particularly the logophoric properties of long-distance binding and clarify the nature of logophoric binding which has not been given an explicit account. We will also show how this idea of logophoricity can be employed to account for some cross-linguistic facts about long-distance anaphors.

1. Long-distance vs local Anaphors in Korean

The following anaphors are found in Korean.

Reflexive: <u>caki</u>, <u>casin</u>, <u>caki-casin</u>, <u>pronoun-casin</u>
Reciprocal: <u>selo</u>

Some of these anaphors can be long-distance bound, while others must be locally bound. Reciprocal selo and reflexives caki-casin and ku-casin 'he-self' are always locally bound within their minimal S as in (1) and (2) except in the subject position of an embedded clause ((3), (4)). However, caki and casin can be long-distance bound as in (5) and (6).

(1) kutul$_i$-i [John-kwa Mary$_j$-ka selo$_{*i/j}$-lul salangha-n-
    they-Nom   and   Nom each other-Acc love-Prs-
    ta]-ko sayngkakha-n-ta.
    Dec-Comp think-Prs-Dec
    'They$_i$ think that John and Mary$_j$ love each other$_{*i/j}$.'
(2) John$_i$-i [Mary$_j$-ka caki-casin$_{*i/j}$/ku-casin$_{*i/j}$
            Nom   Nom self   he-self
    -ul salangha-n-ta]-ko sayngkakha-n-ta.
    Acc love-Prs-Dec-Comp   think-Prs-Dec
    'John$_i$ thinks that Mary$_j$ loves self$_{*i/j}$.'
(3) John$_i$-i [cakicasin$_i$/ku-casin$_i$-i ttokttokha-ta]-ko
            Nom self   Nom be smart-Dec-Comp
    sayngkakha-n-ta
    think-Prs-Dec
    'John$_i$ thinks that self$_i$ is smart.'
(4) Kutul$_i$-i [selo$_i$-ka ttokttokha-ta]-ko
            Nom self-Nom be smart-Dec-Comp
    sayngkakha-n-ta
    think-Prs-Dec
    'They$_i$ think that each other$_i$ are smart.'
(5) John$_i$-i [Mary$_j$-ka caki$_{i/j}$-lul salangha-n-ta]-ko
            Nom   Nom self-Acc love-Prs-Dec-Comp
    sayngkakha-n-ta.
    think-Prs-Dec
    'John$_i$ thinks that Mary$_j$ loves self$_{i/j}$.'
(6) John$_i$-i [Mary$_j$-ka casin$_{i/j}$-ul salangha-n-ta]-ko
            Nom   Nom self-Acc love-Prs-Dec-Comp
    sayngkakha-n-ta.
    think-Prs-Dec
    'John$_i$ thinks that Mary$_j$ loves self$_{i/j}$.'

The apparent long-distance binding of local anaphors like selo, caki-casin, and ku-casin in the subject position of embedded clauses as in (3) and (4) can be given an independent explanation, and crucially, we would like to argue that it is different from the long-distance binding of anaphors like caki and casin as in (5) and (6). It is because these anaphors do show SSC effects, although they do not show NIC effects as in (7). Truly long-distance anaphors disobey SSC as well as NIC (8).

(7) John$_i$-un [$_{S2}$ Mary$_j$-ka [$_{S1}$ caki-casin$_{*i/j}$-i ttokttokha-ta]-
            Top   Nom   self-Nom be smart-Dec
    ko sayngkakha-n-ta]-ko malha-ess-ta.
    Comp think-Prs-Dec-Comp tell-Pst-Dec
    'John$_i$ told that Mary$_j$ thinks that self$_{*i/j}$ is smart.'
(8) John$_i$-un [$_{S2}$ Mary$_j$-ka [$_{S1}$ caki$_{i/j}$-ka ttokttokha-ta]-

```
        Top        Nom        self-Nom      be smart-Dec-
ko sayngkakha-n-ta]-ko malha-ess-ta.
Comp  think-Prs-Dec-Comp  tell-Pst-Dec
'John_i told that Mary_j thinks that self_{i/j} is smart.'
```

We claim that the apparent long-distance binding of local anaphors as in (3) and (4) is another reflex of the lack of NIC effects in Korean syntax. We can readily account for this non-local binding by Principle A of Binding Theory (Chomsky 1981). In the Binding Theory of Chomsky (1981), the governing category where an anaphor must be bound must contain an accessible SUBJECT, which is AGR or a subject NP. If we assume that Korean lacks AGR, there is no accessible SUBJECT in the embedded clause (the anaphor itself does not count as an accessible SUBJECT to itself), and thus, the governing category for anaphors in (3) and (4) is extended to the whole sentence, and they are bound by John and kutul 'they' respectively within the governing category. Therefore, cases of apparent long-distance binding like this, which result from the lack of NIC effects in languages like Korean, pose no real problem in the present framework of the BT, and thus must be distinguished from real long-distance binding.[1]

2. Properties of Long-distance Anaphors in Korean

Here, we examine semantic and syntactic properties of long-distance anaphors in Korean that distinguish long-distance anaphors from local anaphors. We show how the notion of **logophoricity** is relevant for long-distance anaphors, and that a unified account of local and long-distance anaphors cannot be maintained.

The following are the properties of long-distance binding which are contrasted with local binding. First of all, the possibility of long-distance binding of caki and casin varies a great deal depending on the semantic and/or pragmatic properties of predicates or contexts in the sentence they are used.

```
(9) a. John_i-i Mary_j-eykey [caki_{i/*j}-ka am-i-la]-ko
        Nom         Dat    self   Nom cancer-be-Dec-Comp
       malha-ess-ta.
       tell-Pst-Dec
       'John_i told Mary_j that self_{i/*j} has cancer.'
    b. John_i-i Mary_j-lopwute [caki_{i/j}-ka am-i-la]-ko
        Nom         from     self   Nom cancer-be-comp
       tul-ess-ta.
       hear-Pst-Dec
       'John_i heard from Mary_j that self_{i/j} has cancer.'
(10) a. [John_i-i caki_j-lul miweha-n-ta-nun] sasil-i Mary_j-
            Nom      Acc hate-Prs-Dec-Comp fact-Nom
       lul  kwelop-hi-ess-ta.
       Acc  bother-Cause-Pst-Dec
       'The fact that John_i hates self_j bothered Mary_j.'
```

b. *[caki$_i$-lul miweha]-nun salam-i Mary$_i$-lul ttaylye-
    self-Acc hate-Comp man-Nom   Acc hit-Pst-Dec
ess-ta.
'*The man who hates self$_i$ hit Mary$_i$.'

(11) a. John$_i$-i Mary-eykey [Tom$_j$-i caki$_i$-lul po-le-o-ass-
         Nom   Dat   Nom   self Acc   see-come-Pst
ta]-ko mal-ha-ess-ta.
Dec-Comp tell-Pst-Dec
'John$_i$ told Mary that Tom$_j$ came to see self$_i$.'
  b. *John$_i$-i Mary-eykey [Tom$_j$-i caki$_i$-lul po-le-ka-ass-
         Nom   Dat   Nom   self Acc see-to-go-PST
ta]-ko mal-ha-ess-ta.
Dec-Comp tell-Pst-Dec
'*John$_i$ told Mary that Tom$_j$ went to see self$_j$.'

In (9)a with the verb tell, caki can be bound only by John
and Mary cannot be antecedents for caki, however, in (9)b
with the verb hear, both John and Mary can be an antecedent
for caki. In (10)a with the verb kwelophita, 'bother', the
long-distance binding of caki with Mary is grammatical,
whereas in (10)b with the verb ttaylita 'hit' it is not
possible. Similarly in (11), long-distance binding of caki
is acceptable with the verb come (a), but not possible with
the verb go (b).
    Secondly, when long-distance bound, caki and casin
cannot take a first or second person antecedent.[2]

(12) a. ku$_i$-nun [John$_j$-i caki$_i$-lul silheha-n-ta]-ko
       he-Top   Nom   Acc hate-Prs-Dec-Comp
mit-nun-ta.
believe-Prs-Dec
'He$_i$ believes that John$_j$ hates self$_i$.'
  b. Na/ne$_i$-nun [John$_j$-i caki$_{*i/j}$-lul silheha-n-ta]-ko
     I/you Top   Nom   Acc   hate-Prs-Dec -Comp
mit-nun-ta.
believe-Prs-Dec
'I/you$_i$ think that John$_j$ hates self$_{*i/j}$.'

The incompatibility of long-distance binding with a first or
second person antecedent is contrasted with the fact that
the local reflexive like pronoun-casin[3] shows no such
restriction.

(13) Na/ne-nun na/ne-casin-ul silheha-n-ta.
    I/you-Top I/you-self-Acc. hate-Prs-Dec
    'I/you hate myself/yourself.'

    Thirdly, long-distance binders of caki and casin do not
need to c-command the anaphor, while strict c-command
condition is required in the case of local anaphors.

(14) John$_i$-un Mary$_j$-lopwute [caki$_{i/j}$-ka am-i-la]-ko
         Top   from   self-Nom cancer-be-Dec-Comp
tul-ess-ta.

hear-Pst-Dec
'John$_i$ heard from Mary$_j$ that self$_{i/j}$ has cancer.
(14')

```
                        IP
         NP  _____/_____ I'
         /\                      /\
     John-un        VP          I
                   /|          /\
                 PP  CP       V    ess-ta
                /\   /|\      |
               NP P /  \     tul
               |  | /____\
```

Mary lopwute caki-ka am-i-la-ko
(15) [John$_i$-i caki$_j$-lul miweha-n-ta-nun] sasil-i Mary$_j$-
       Nom   Acc hate-Prs-Dec-Comp fact-Nom
    lul kwelop-hi-ess-ta.
    Acc bother-Cause-Pst-Dec
'The fact that John$_i$ hates self$_j$ bothered Mary$_j$.'
(16) [caki$_i$-ka i seysang-ese ceyil yeppu-ke toy]-nun-kes-i
self Nom this world-in the most pretty become Comp-Nom
Mary$_i$-uy kkwum-i-tyo-ess-ta.
        Gen dream-Nom-become-Pst-Dec
'It became Mary's dream that self becomes the prettiest
in the world.'

In the examples (14)-(16), the antecedents do not c-command
the anaphor caki, but the sentences are all grammatical.[4]
    Fourth, LDAs, caki and casin do not require an
antecedent within the sentence but can be discourse-bound.

    (17) A: nwu-ka John$_i$-ul telye-o-ass-ni?
         who-Nom   ACC bring-Pst-Q
         'Who brought John?'
       B: caki$_i$-ka cikcep o-ass-eyo.
         self-NOM in person come-Pst-Dec
         'self in person came.'

This shows that there is no strict binding domain where
these long-distance anaphors have to be bound.
    Fifth, LDAs, caki and casin can have split antecedents
unlike local anaphors.

    (18) John$_i$-un Mary$_j$-eykey [caki-tul$_{i+j/i+x}$-i iki-lke-la]-ko
           Top   Dat   self-Plu-Nom win-Fut-Dec-Comp
      malha-ess-ta.
      tell-Pst-Dec
      'John$_i$ told Mary$_j$ that selfs$_{i+j/i+x}$ will win.'

    Sixth, in complex sentences, the preferred reading for
the LDA caki and casin is always the long-distance
antecedent, and binding of caki by a local antecedent is
very weak, although not impossible.

    (19) ku$_i$-nun [John$_j$-i caki$_{(i)j}$-lul silheha-n-ta]-ko

```
he-Top        Nom   self-Acc      hate-Prs-Dec-Comp
mit-nun-ta.
believe-Prs-Dec
'He$_i$ believes that John$_j$ hates self$_{i\rangle j}$.'
```

The preceding facts about LDAs show that for LDB, semantic conditions, which we will shortly identify as logophoricity, play a significant role, and that in their syntactic properties, they are clearly different from those of local anaphors. Namely, they do not observe the c-command antecedent condition and allow split antecedents and discourse binding. Therefore, any purely syntactic analysis of LDAs which treats them uniformly with local anaphors under the Pr. A of BT seems to face immediate problems. Although LDAs lack independent reference (therefore, [-R] expressions), since there isn't any strict domain within which LDAs must be bound, as is most convincingly shown by discourse anaphora, in terms of locality condition of standard BT, LDAs cannot be categorized as anaphors. Furthermore, those analyses fail to capture a significant aspect of LDAs, namely logophoric properties, which are basically non-syntactic.

Now let's consider how the analyses based on the notion of logophoricity can explain the properties of LDAs we have observed. The notion of logophoricity was first introduced to explain a paradigm of morphologically distinct pronouns in African languages like Ewe and Mundang. Logophoric pronouns are used to report the events under discussion subjectively, according to referent's own perception of them. Therefore, the antecedent of logophoric pronoun must be the "individual whose speech, thoughts, or feelings are reported or reflected in a given linguistic context" (Clements, 1975). Thus, logophoric pronouns are most often found in complement clauses to verbs of saying and thinking. The view of long-distance anaphors as a case parallel to logophoric pronouns found in some African languages is not new at all, but has been claimed by Clements (1975), Kuno (1986) and Sells (1987) among others, for languages like Japanese, Icelandic and Latin, etc. In the analysis of long-distance anaphors in Korean, we propose to separate two kinds of conditions on logophoric pronouns, i.e., semantic and/or pragmatic conditions which we call logophoricity on the one hand and locality condition which is purely syntactic on the other. We argue that these are two independent dimensions and that both are necessary to distinguish anaphors and pronouns in Korean. We will use the general term **logophor** for non-referential NPs which have logophoricity condition on their antecedents, and **logophoric binding** to refer to the binding of logophors to their antecedents.

Before we try to give any analysis of LDB in Korean in terms of logophoricity, the problem we have to solve, however, seems to clarify what exactly we mean by "logophoricity", since there hasn't yet been proposed a well-defined notion of logophoricity. For the purpose of this paper, it suffices to show that LDB in Korean has the logophoric properties different from local binding, and we base our analysis on a more precise notion of logophoricity of Sells (1987), although we do not think that it covers every aspect of logophoric binding in Korean.

To define logophoricity more precisely, Sells (1987) distinguishes three primitive notions underlying logophoricity, i.e., source, self, and pivot (third person point of view), and illustrates various aspects of logophoricity in terms of the interaction of these three primitives. Below, we briefly present these notions and their relevance to the analysis of the Korean data.

(1) **Source:** A logophor can corefer to the source of the report (speaker).

This is the most frequent case in logophoric binding since most of the logophoric predicates are the verbs of saying and thinking. Now if <u>caki</u> and <u>casin</u> are logophors, the contrast between sentence (9)a and b (repeated as (20)) with respect to the binding possibility of <u>caki</u> is readily explained.

(20) a. $John_i$-i $Mary_j$-eykey [$caki_{i/*j}$-ka am-i-la]-ko
          Nom   Dat self-Nom cancer-be-Dec-Comp
     malha-ess-ta.
     tell-Pst-Dec
     'John told Mary that self has cancer.'
   b. $John_i$-i $Mary_j$-lopwute [$caki_{i/j}$-ka am-i-la]-ko
          Nom   -from   self-Nom cancer-be-Dec-Comp
     tul-ess-ta.
     hear-Pst-Dec
     '$John_i$ heard from $Mary_j$ that $self_{i/j}$ has cancer.'

In (20)a, <u>John</u> is the source of what is said in the embedded clause, and therefore, only <u>John</u> can be the antecedent for <u>caki</u>, however, in (20)b, <u>Mary</u> can be the source, and thus coreference of <u>caki</u> with <u>Mary</u> is possible.[5]

(2) **Self:** A logophor can refer to the one whose mental state or attitude the content of the proposition describes. This notion is relevant in order to explain the pattern of LDB with psychological predicates.

(21) [$John_i$-i $caki_j$-lul miweha-n-ta-nun] sasil-i $Mary_j$-
        Nom   Acc hate-Prs-Dec-Comp fact-Nom
   lul kwelop-hi-ess-ta.
   Acc bother-Cause-Pst-Dec
   'The fact that $John_i$ hates $self_j$ bothered $Mary_j$.'

Here, <u>Mary</u> is the one whose mental state is being reported, and thus <u>caki</u> can be bound by <u>Mary</u>.

(3) **Pivot**: A logophor can refer to one with respect to whose (space-time) location the content of the proposition is evaluated.

Pivot is understood as the "center of deixis" , and thus, if a report is made with a specific person as the pivot, then the reporter is understood as literally standing in that person's place. This corresponds to empathy-orientation in Kuno (1987). The notion of pivot provides an explanation for the contrast in the binding possibilities of caki between the sentences like (11)a and b (repeated as (22)) below.[6]

(22) a. John$_i$-i Mary-eykey [Tom$_j$-i caki$_i$-lul po-le-o-ass
       Nom   Dat   Nom   Acc see-to-come-Pst
       -ta]-ko malha-ess-ta.
       Dec-Comp tell-Pst-Dec
       'John$_i$ told Mary that Tom$_j$ came to see self$_i$.'
    b. *John$_i$-i Mary-eykey [Tom$_j$-i caki$_i$-lul po-le-ka-ass-
       Nom   Dat   Nom   Acc see-to-go-Pst
       ta]-ko malha-ess-ta.
       Dec-Comp tell-Pst-Dec
       '*John$_i$ told Mary that Tom$_j$ went to see self$_i$.'

In the sentence (22)a, John is the pivot and the person who is reporting the sentence is standing in John's shoes. Since the verb o-ta 'come' requires the speaker's empathy with the goal, i.e., John, coreference of caki with the goal John is acceptable. (22)b with the verb ka-ta 'go', however, is not acceptable since the verb kata requires the empathy with the agent and thus John cannot be the pivot. The nature of deictic property of pivot is also evidenced by the fact that (22)b can be acceptable, if we imagine that John is not in his usual place, and Tom went to see him at the place where he is normally supposed to be.

   Until now we have seen the relevance of logophoric predicates and contexts related to the long-distance binding of caki and casin. Now, we would like to show how the analysis of caki and casin as logophors naturally accounts for the incompatibility of them with first or second person antecedents. The essential function of logophoric pronouns is to indirectly report somebody else's thought or feeling. This basic property of logophoric pronouns is well observed in the description of many African languages: "...logophoric pronouns are always coreferential with the real or imagined author of a secondary discourse" (Sells 88, p. 446). Therefore, the use of a logophor to indirectly report the thoughts or feelings of one's own (first person pronoun as an antecedent) or somebody who is present at the time of speaking (second person pronoun as an antecedent) seems to be highly unnatural.[7] A piece of evidence for this comes from the observation about logophoric pronouns in African languages (Clements (1975)). Clements reports that logophoric pronouns in African languages are not used to corefer to first person antecedents. Therefore, the fact that <u>caki</u> and <u>casin</u> are incompatible with first or second person antecedents gives another piece of evidence that notion of logophoricity is relevant for them, and that they are different from other pure reflexives which do not show this property. Other locally-bound anaphors in Korean such as <u>selo</u>, pronoun-<u>casin</u> have no such restriction

Viewing LDAs as logophors also explain the semantic contrast between the use of LDAs and pronouns. Pronouns and LDAs in Korean largely overlap in distribution. However there are interesting semantic distinctions between the use of LDAs and pronouns. In a context where both can be used as in (23), the use of LDAs implies that the external speaker is somehow identifying himself with an "internal protagonist" in the sentence, which is John in (23), whereas when pronoun is used, there is no such implication and the whole situation is described objectively in speaker's point of view.

(23) John$_i$-un [Mary$_j$-ka caki$_i$ / ku$_i$-lul sileha-n-ta]-ko
       Top   Nom self/he-Acc hate-Prs-Dec-Comp
    mit-nun-ta.
    believe-Prs-Dec
    'John$_i$ believes that Mary hates self$_i$/ him$_i$.'

This semantic contrast is explained if LDAs, <u>caki</u> and <u>casin</u> in Korean are logophoric whereas pronouns are not logophoric.

3. More facts about anaphors in Korean: caki vs casin

Until now, we have divided the anaphors in Korean into two distinct categories, namely LDAs which are logophors in our analysis, and local anaphors, which are not logophoric. For the sake of presentation, we have simplified the facts somewhat and treated <u>caki</u> and <u>casin</u> uniformly. However, there are differences between the two LDAs, <u>caki</u> and <u>casin</u>. A closer examination of <u>caki</u> and <u>casin</u> shows that although they two pattern together in terms of their locality condition, they differ from each other in other properties. First of all, <u>casin</u> is incompatible with first or second person antecedents only when it is long-distance bound. When it is locally bound, it has no such restriction. Compared to this, the incompatibility of <u>caki</u> with first or second person antecedents holds not only in long-distance but also in local binding.

(24) Na$_i$-nun casin/*caki$_i$-lul mit-nun-ta.
     I-Top   Acc believe-Prs-Dec
    'I believe self.'

Secondly, the acceptability of the sentences with <u>caki</u> bound by a local antecedent varies a lot depending on the nature of predicates, whereas it is not so for <u>casin</u>.

(25) a. John-un caki/casin-ul <u>salangha-n-ta</u>.
      Top   Acc   love-Prs-Dec
      'John loves self.'
    b. John-un ^{??}caki/ casin-ul <u>ttayli-ess-ta</u>.
        Top   Acc hit-Pst-Dec
      'John hit self.'

In general, local binding of <u>caki</u> is better with mental activity verbs than with physical activity verbs.

The above facts suggest that the long-distance and local binding of what we have termed as LDAs may show distinct properties. It seems that <u>casin</u> in local binding must be distinguished from that in long-distance binding, since it seems that <u>casin</u> is logophoric only when it is long-distance bound. As Kuno (1987) suggests, this might be due to the fact that languages use already-existing reflexives whose main function is clause-mate binding as logophoric pronouns, and thus they serve double functions. In contrast with <u>casin</u>, <u>caki</u> seems to keep its logophoricity even in local binding as the preceding facts suggest. The observed differences between <u>caki</u> and <u>casin</u> in Korean might be accounted for if we consider <u>caki</u> as inherently logophoric, whereas <u>casin</u> derives its logophoricity as a function of logophoric predicates and contexts in long-distance binding.[8]

4. Typology of anaphors in Korean

The various facts about anaphors and pronouns in Korean we have observed so far show that locality alone is not sufficient to distinguish anaphors and pronouns, and that we need another dimension of logophoricity. We propose the following classification of anaphors and pronouns using [+/-/@local] and [+/-/@logo], understanding the features like the following.

    [+local] implies that an element in question is
          [+anaphoric] and [-pronominal].
    [-local] implies that an element is [-anaphoric]
          and [+pronominal].
    [@local] implies that an element is lexically
          underspecified for locality condition

    [+logo] implies that an element in question is
          inherently logophoric.
    [-logo] implies that an element is inherently
          non-logophoric.
    [@logo] implies that an element is lexically
          underspecified for logophoricity, but
          its logophoricity is determined by the
          presence of logophoric predicates or contexts.

```
(26)            locality        logophoriciy
caki              @               +
casin             @               @
pronoun-casin     +               -
caki-casin        +               +
pronoun           -               -
```

In this classification, we allow some anaphors to be lexically underspecified for some features. Since for caki and casin, there isn't any syntactically determined domain within which they must be bound or free, they are not specified for a locality condition, and are thus [@local] in our classification. Rather their distribution is determined by semantic and discourse-oriented conditions of logophoricity. We also note that there are anaphors like casin, which is logophoric only when it is long-distance bound, therefore [@logo] in our classification. It is because for [@logo] anaphors, logophoricity is not an inherent property but is derived from the presence of logophoric predicates or contexts in LDB. Thus, for [@logo] anaphors like casin, there is a correlation between the logophoricity condition and locality condition, i.e., a [@logo] anaphor is [+logo] only when it is long-distance bound, and [-logo] when it is locally bound. However, we claim that locality and logophoricity are two independent dimensions, as is evidenced by the fact that caki is [+logo] even when it is locally bound. It seems that anaphors and pronouns in Korean manifest diverse possibilities for the combination of these two dimensions of [local] and [logo] features. The same idea is well expressed in Keenan (1988, P.228).

> To some extent distinct lexical anaphors in a given language just divide up the pie of universal possibilities differently (usually with some overlap).

5. Cross-linguistic facts about LDAs

In this section, we examine some cross-linguistic facts about LDAs and speculate how our analysis of LDAs in Korean can shed light on them. Below are the facts about LDAs that have generally not been given a principled explanation.

1. When a language has several reflexive forms, only some can be long-distance bound and others are strictly local.
2. Reciprocals are never long-distance bound.
3. In general, LDB is possible only with third person antecedents while local binding has no such restriction.
4. Languages that have LDAs, in general, allow discourse anaphora.
5. When the same anaphor is used for both local and LDB, only the latter is subject to conditions of logophoricity.

6. For languages with LDAs, there is a great discrepancy between the binding domain for anaphors and pronouns. For example, even for a language like Korean which has a very extended binding domain for anaphors, the domain within which pronouns must be free is local, namely the minimal S.

The first observation would simply be a consequence of the fact that logophoricity as well as locality classfies anaphors, and it is a lexical property whether an anaphor is [+/-/@logo]. Observation (2) will be explained since in our analysis, the so-called LDAs are logophors, but by their semantics, reciprocals are [-logo]. Logophors are used when the speaker identifies himself with somebody within the sentence. For reciprocals, however, it is difficult to imagine that the speaker identifies himself respectively with each of the antecedents at the same time. (3) is explained in the same way we have explained the Korean data, namely, you do not indirectly report your own thought or feelings (first person) or somebody who is present at the time of speaking (second person). (4) is explained since LDAs are not anaphors in our analysis, but just referentially-dependent NPs which are underspecified for their locality condition. Therefore, they do not need to be bound within the sentence. (5) is explained since we claim that most of the LDAs in languages are [@logo] anaphors like casin in Korean, and for [@logo] anaphors, logophoricity is the result of long-distance binding. (6) is explained since in our analysis binding domains for anaphors are not parameterized[7] (or minimally parameterized) and the extended BDs of Manzini & Wexler (1987), i.e., root tense for Korean, are in fact domains where logophoric anaphors are found. We think that the size of Logophoric Domain cannot be mechanically computed purely in terms of syntax, although we do not ignore the fact that some aspects of logophoricity in languages can be grammaticized, mood being one of them. As an example, a language like Icelandic requires subjunctive mood for long-distance binding. The fact that mood is closely involved as a syntactic condition on long-distance binding in languages (Latin, Greek, also) might follow from the nature of logophoric binding. As Maling (1984) suggests, the use of subjunctive mood can be understood as a sort of means to define a "transparent" domain with respect to which logophoric predicates are used in Icelandic (logophoric marking). Therefore, in this approach to long-distance binding, the apparent size of BD, or logophoric domain, should be understood in terms of how languages mark logophoric domain, and the extent of logophoricity in the language. As an example, Sells (1987) accounts for the differences in binding properties between sig in Icelandic and zibun in Japanese in terms of three primitives of logophoricity: sig in Icelandic has self orientation, whereas zibun in Japanese has pivot orientation which is more extensive.

6. Blocking effects and logophoricity

In this section, we would like to show how our analysis of long-distance binding in terms of logophoricity can naturally account for a significant part of the "blocking effects" of long-distance binding in Chinese discussed in Huang & Tang (88), which restricts all the potential antecedents of LDAs to agree in φ-features like person and number. Although they claim that number also causes blocking effects for LDB,[10] it seems that it is **person** which shows the strongest blocking effects, and as far as person is concerned, most of the blocking effects can be explained in terms of logophoricity.

Of the nine possible cases of long-distance binding as in (27), only three cases, i.e., (1), (5) and (9), will be grammatical due to blocking effects.

(27) (1) $[_{S2}\ 1_i\quad [_{S1}\ 1_i\quad LDA_i]$
    (2) $[_{S2}\ {}^{*}1_i\quad [_{S1}\ 2\quad LDA_i]$
    (3) $[_{S2}\ {}^{*}1_i\quad [_{S1}\ 3\quad LDA_i]$
    (4) $[_{S2}\ {}^{*}2_i\quad [_{S1}\ 1\quad LDA_i]$
    (5) $[_{S2}\ 2_i\quad [_{S1}\ 2_i\quad LDA_i]$
    (6) $[_{S2}\ {}^{*}2_i\quad [_{S1}\ 3\quad LDA_i]$
    (7) $[_{S2}\ {}^{*}3_i\quad [_{S1}\ 1\quad LDA_i]$
    (8) $[_{S2}\ {}^{*}3_i\quad [_{S1}\ 2\quad LDA_i]$
    (9) $[_{S2}\ 3_i\quad [_{S1}\ 3\quad LDA_i]$

In our analysis, logophoricity of long-distance binding, more specifically, the restriction on first or second person antecedents in LDB will exclude all the cases where the long-distance antecedent is first or second person. However, of the six possible cases where the long-distance antecedent is first or second person ((1)-(6)), our analysis predicts that (1) and (5) are good, since in these cases, there is no difference between local binding and LDB because the reference of I or you is the same in a single utterance. Of the other three cases where the long-distance antecedent is third person, logophoricity of LDB will correctly exclude (7) and (8), the cases where there is an intermediate first or second person antecedent. When there is a first person I in the sentence, the external speaker cannot pretend to identify with somebody other than I in the sentence, since I itself is the external speaker of the sentence. To see this more clearly, let us recall the notion of pivot for logophoric binding. If a report is made with a specific person as the pivot, then the reporter is understood as literally standing in that person's place. Therefore, if the LDA corefers with an antecedent other than I as in (7), the result will be very awkward, since in that case it is like a person is standing in two different places at the same time. The case of second person intermediate antecedents as in (8) will be excluded for a similar reason, although it will be better than the case of first person intermediate antecedents.

Thus, our analysis gives a natural account of the so-called blocking effects of LDB in Chinese, and it is very plausible that the blocking effects of LDB itself is a phenomenon which shows that the nature of LDB is logophoric.

7. Conclusion

In this paper, we gave an analysis of long-distance binding in Korean based on the notion of logophoricity and considered its implication for some cross-linguistic facts about long-distance binding. We showed that only some of the reflexives in Korean can be truly long-distance bound, and that the semantic and syntactic properties of long-distance binding are different from those of local binding. Therefore, we claim that long-distance binding of these anaphors cannot be subject to Principle A of Binding Theory, and any attempt to capture the properties of long-distance binding by an extension of Principle A of BT is misguided.

This paper was by no means a place to review all the detailed and complicated cross-linguistic facts about long-distance binding, and thus we have limited the discussion largely to the long-distance binding in Korean and gave a very sketchy explanation for the cross-linguistic facts. However, if this line of analysis is right, then the so-called long-distance binding in languages can have a more coherent analysis without any extension of BT-A. First, the trivial case of long-distance binding in the subject position of embedded clauses in languages like Korean, Japanese, and Chinese is accounted for by the fact that these languages lack AGR as an opacity-inducing element for binding domain. The other real cases of long-distance binding are not subject to BT-A at all, but are accounted for under the notion of logophoricity and logophoric binding.

Footnotes

* I would like to thank James Yoon, W. Harbert, J. Whitman, and B. Lust for their helpful comments. I also have benefited from the discussion in the Research Workshop in Cornell (1989 Spring).

[1] The same explanation holds for similar cases of long-distance binding in Japanese and Chinese, which also are claimed to lack AGR. A different way of explaining the lack of NIC effects in Korean within the framework of the revised BT (Chomsky 86) will be to assume that INFL in Korean is a proper governor.

[2] There is some difference between _caki_ and _casin_ in this aspect of binding property. When these anaphors are long-distance bound, both of them are not compatible with first or second person antecedents, however, in local binding, _casin_ can be bound by a first or second person pronoun,

whereas _caki_ cannot be. I will come back to this point later in the paper.

[3] _cakicasin_ also cannot be used with first and second person pronoun antecedents, though it is always locally-bound. This is because it is a complex form which has _caki_ as a part. It seems that we have to consider _caki_ as inherently third person.

[4] For psych predicate structures like (15), we might adopt Belletti & Rizzi (88) type analysis, and satisfy the c-command condition at D-structure. Even so, however, sentences like (14) and (16) still pose the problem for the c-command condition of anaphors.

[5] In (20)b, the subject _John_ can also be the antecedent of _caki_, and it seems to be most plausible that _John_ in this case is considered as a pivot. Although it is true that subjects qualify as the antecedents of LDAs in most of the cases, however, there are cases where even subjects cannot be the antecedent of LDAs when some semantic condition of logophoricity is not satisfied. Therefore, being a subject itself is not a sufficient antecedent condition for LDB. In general, _caki_ in when-clause is not bound by the subject antecedent in the matrix clause.

(1) a. John$_i$-un [Mary$_j$-ka caki$_{i/j}$-eykey mwul-ul epsil-ess]-
         Top   Nom   Dat water-Acc spill-Pst
    ki-ttaymun-e sec-ess-ta.
    because   got wet
   'John$_i$ got wet because Mary$_j$ spilt water to self$_{i/j}$.'
  b. John$_i$-un [Mary$_j$-ka caki$_{*i/j}$-eykey mwul-ul epsil-ess]-
         Top   Nom   Dat water-Acc spill-Pst
    ul-ttay sec-ess-ta.
    when   got wet
   'John$_i$ got wet when Mary$_j$ spilt water to self$_{*i/j}$.'

[6] See Sells(1987) for the Japanese example corresponding to this borrowed basically from Kuno.

[7] It seems that second person antecedents are better than first person antecedents in long-distance binding, and this is quite understandable since it is easier to indirectly report the listener's thoughts or feelings (or to identify with the listener) than to indirectly report our own thoughts or feelings.

[8] A more functional explanation might be that, in the case of _caki_, its function as a logophoric pronoun outweighs its original function as a clause-bound reflexive, and thus, even in the local binding, it keeps some of its property as a logophoric pronoun.

[9] This, however, does not mean that we do not need any parameterization of BD at all. According to the hierarchical definition of SUBJECT (Alec Marantz), languages can vary only with respect to the nature of SUBJECTHOOD in the language. As an example, there are languages (Gothic, e.g.) which show PIC effects but not SSC effects (See Harbert (1986)). In these languages, only the cardinal element of SUBJECT, i.e., AGR constitutes a potential

494

SUBJECT, unlike English (hierarchical definition of SUBJECT).
[10] In their analysis, gender was excluded from the φ-features since there is no gender distinction for pronouns in Chinese.

REFERENCES

Battistella, E. (1987) "Chinese Reflexivization," paper presented at the 2nd Harbin Conference on Generative Grammar, Heilongjiang University, Harbin.
Belletti, A. & L. Rizzi (1988) "Psych-Verbs and θ-Theory," Natural Language & Linguistic Theory 6, 291-352.
Chomsky, N. (1981) Lectures on Government and Binding, Foris, Dordrecht.
Chomsky, N. (1986a) Knowledge of Language; Its Nature, Origins and Use, MIT Press, Cambridge, Massachusetts
Chomsky, N. (1986b) Barriers, MIT Press, Cambridge, Massachusetts.
Clements, G. N. (1975) "The Logophoric Pronoun in Ewe: Its Roles in Discourse," Journal of West African Languages 3, 141-177.
Grimshaw, J. & S.T. Rosen (1988) "The Developmental Status of the Binding Theory, ms, Brandeis University.
Harbert, W. (1986) "Binding, SUBJECT and Accessibility," paper presented at the 1986 Syracuse Conference in Language & Linguistics.
Huang, J. & J. Tang (1987) "On the Local Nature of the Long-Distance Reflexive in Chinese," ms. Cornell University.
Kameyama, M. (1984) "Subjective/Logophoric Bound Anaphor Zibun," in CLS 20
Keenan, E (1988) "Complex Anaphors and Bind @," CLS 24
Kitagawa, Y. (1986) Subjects in Japanese and English, Doctoral dissertation, University of Massachusetts, Amherst.
Kuno, S. (1987) Functional Syntax: Anaphora, Discourse and Empathy, University of Chicago Press, Chicago.
Lebeaux, D. (1983) "A Distributional Difference between Reciprocals and Reflexives," Linguistic Inquiry 14, 723-730.
Lee, C. (1988) "Issues in Korean Anaphora," paper presented at the 6TH International Conference on Korean Linguistics, Toronto.
Lust, B. (1986) "Remarks on the Psychological Reality of Subset Principle: Its Relation to Universal Grammar as a Model of the Initial State," in C. Clifton (ed.), Proceedings of University of Mass. Cognitive Science Conference, August, 1986.
Lust, B & G. Martohardijono (1987) "On the Contribution of the Binding Theory Module to a Theory of the Acquisition of Anaphora," paper presented at the 12TH Annual Boston University Conference on Language Development.

Lust, B et al. (1986) "When is an Anaphor not an Anaphor,"
    paper presented at LSA.
Maling, J (1984) "Non-clause-Bounded Reflexives in Modern
    Icelandic," <u>Linguistics and Philosophy</u> 7, 211-241.
Pica, P (1986) "On the Nature of the Reflexivization Cycle,"
    in J. Mcdonough & B.Plunkett(eds.), Proceedings of 17TH
    Annual Meeting of NELS.
Sells, P. (1987) "Aspects of Logophoricity," <u>Linguistic</u>
    <u>Inquiry</u> 18 (3), 445-479.
Thrainsson,, H (1987) "Long-Distance Reflexives and the
    Typology of NPs," ms.
Wexler. K & R. Manzini (1987) "Parameters and Learnability
    in Binding Theory," in T. Roeper & E. Williams (eds.),
    <u>Parameter Setting</u>, D. Reidel, Dordrecht.

Language Index